MW01038557

JERUSALEM IN BIBLE
AND ARCHAEOLOGY

Society of Biblical Literature

Symposium Series

Christopher R. Matthews,
Editor

Number 18

JERUSALEM IN BIBLE
AND ARCHAEOLOGY
The First Temple Period

JERUSALEM IN BIBLE
AND ARCHAEOLOGY

The First Temple Period

Edited by
Andrew G. Vaughn and Ann E. Killebrew

Society of Biblical Literature
Atlanta

JERUSALEM IN BIBLE
AND ARCHAEOLOGY
The First Temple Period

Copyright © 2003 by the Society of Biblical Literature

All rights reserved. No part of this work may be reproduced or transmitted in any form or by any means, electronic or mechanical, including photocopying and recording, or by means of any information storage or retrieval system, except as may be expressly permitted by the 1976 Copyright Act or in writing from the publisher. Requests for permission should be addressed in writing to the Rights and Permissions Office, Society of Biblical Literature, 825 Houston Mill Road, Atlanta, GA 30329 USA.

Library of Congress Cataloging-in-Publication Data

Jerusalem in Bible and archaeology : the First Temple period / edited by Andrew G. Vaughn and Ann E. Killebrew.
     p. cm. — (Society of Biblical Literature symposium series ; no. 18)
     Includes bibliographical references and index.
   ISBN 1-58983-066-0 (alk. paper)
     1. Jerusalem in the Bible. 2. Jerusalem—History. 3. Jerusalem—Antiquities.
4. Bible. O.T.—Antiquities. I. Vaughn, Andrew G. II. Killebrew, Ann E. III. Series:
Symposium series (Society of Biblical Literature) ; no. 18.
   BS1199.J38J38 2003
   221.9'5—dc21   2003007005

11 10 09 08 07 06 05 04 03   5 4 3 2 1

Printed in the United States of America
on acid-free paper

Contents

Preface

Most of the essays in the present volume had their genesis as papers that were presented in the "Consultation on Jerusalem in Bible and Archaeology" at the Annual Meeting of the Society of Biblical Literature. The papers were presented over a period of four years (1998–2001). The Consultation was co-chaired by Ann E. Killebrew and Andrew G. Vaughn, the editors of the volume. The steering committee for the Consultation (Melody Knowles, Gunnar Lehmann, William Schniedewind, and Tammi Schneider) also contributed to the selection of the components of the Consultation and subsequently of the present volume.

Support for the present volume was provided by Gustavus Adolphus College through the funding of the following research assistants for Vaughn: Susan Schumacher helped edit all of the articles; Dan Pioske did proofreading and compiled the indexes; and Rachel Schwingler proofread the articles and the index. Vaughn's work was supported in part by a Research Scholarship and Creativity Grant from Gustavus Adolphus College. Killebrew would like to express her thanks to The Pennsylvania State University for providing her with a research semester in 2003, during which much of the final editorial work on this volume was completed. The editors are also indebted to the excellent editorial staff at the Society of Biblical Literature: Leigh Andersen, Kathie Klein, and Rex Matthews. Bob Buller served as copy editor and typesetter and went far beyond what was expected to make sure the volume looked as professional as possible. Finally, but certainly not least, appreciation is due to the series editor, Chris Matthews, for both his patience and guidance.

Abbreviations

BAIAS	*Bulletin of the Anglo-Israel Archeological Society*
*BAL*²	*Babylonisch-assyrische Lesestücke*. R. Borger. 2d ed. AnOr 54. Rome: Pontifical Biblical Institute, 1979.
BAR	*Biblical Archaeology Review*
BASOR	*Bulletin of the American Schools of Oriental Research*
BBB	Bonner biblische Beiträge
BBVO	Berliner Beiträge zum Vorderen Orient
BEATAJ	Beiträge zur Erforschung des Alten Testaments und des antiken Judentum
BETL	Bibliotheca ephemeridum theologicarum lovaniensium
Bib	*Biblica*
BN	*Biblische Notizen*
BO	*Bibliotheca orientalis*
BRL	*Biblisches Reallexikon*. 2d ed. Edited by K. Galling. HAT 1/1. Tübingen: Mohr Siebeck, 1977.
BWANT	Beiträge zur Wissenschaft vom Alten und Neuen Testament
BZAW	Beihefte zur Zeitschrift für die alttestamentliche Wissenschaft
CAD	*The Assyrian Dictionary of the Oriental Institute of the University of Chicago*. Chicago: University of Chicago Press, 1956–.
CAH	Cambridge Ancient History
CahRB	Cahiers de la Revue biblique
CANE	*Civilizations of the Ancient Near East*. Edited by J. Sasson. 4 vols. New York: Scribner, 1995.
CAT	Commentaire de l'Ancien Testament
CBQ	*Catholic Biblical Quarterly*
CBQMS	Catholic Biblical Quarterly Monograph Series
CBET	Contributions to Biblical Exegesis and Theology
CdÉ	*Chronique d'Égypte*
CHJ	Cambridge History of Judaism
ChrCent	*Christian Century*
CTN	Cuneiform Texts from Nimrud
CurBS	*Currents in Research: Biblical Studies*
Ebib	Etudes bibliques
EgT	*Eglise et théologie*
ErIsr	*Eretz-Israel*
ESI	*Excavations and Surveys in Israel*
FAT	Forschungen zum Alten Testament
FO	*Folia orientalia*
FOTL	Forms of the Old Testament Literature
FRLANT	Forschungen zur Religion und Literatur des Alten und Neuen Testaments

HANEM	History of the Ancient Near East Monographs
HAT	Handbuch zum Alten Testament
HBT	*Horizons in Biblical Theology*
HO	Handbuch der Orientalistik
HS	*Hebrew Studies*
HSM	Harvard Semitic Monographs
HTR	*Harvard Theological Review*
HUCA	*Hebrew Union College Annual*
ICC	International Critical Commentary
IDB	*The Interpreter's Dictionary of the Bible*. Edited by G. A. Buttrick. 4 vols. Nashville: Abingdon, 1962.
IDBSup	*Interpreter's Dictionary of the Bible: Supplementary Volume*. Edited by K. Crim. Nashville: Abingdon, 1976.
IEJ	*Israel Exploration Journal*
Int	*Interpretation*
IOS	*Israel Oriental Studies*
JANESCU	*Journal of the Ancient Near Eastern Society of Columbia University*
JAOS	*Journal of the American Oriental Society*
JARCE	*Journal of the American Research Center in Egypt*
JBL	*Journal of Biblical Literature*
JCS	*Journal of Cuneiform Studies*
JBL	*Journal of Biblical Literature*
JEA	*Journal of Egyptian Archaeology*
JNES	*Journal of Near Eastern Studies*
JNSL	*Journal of Northwest Semitic Languages*
JPOS	*Journal of the Palestine Oriental Society*
JQR	*Jewish Quarterly Review*
JSJSup	Supplements to the Journal for the Study of Judaism
JSNTSup	Journal for the Study of the New Testament Supplement Series
JSOT	*Journal for the Study of the Old Testament*
JSOTSup	Journal for the Study of the Old Testament Supplement Series
JSPSup	Journal for the Study of the Pseudepigrapha Supplement Series
JTS	*Journal of Theological Studies*
KAI	*Kanaanäische und aramäische Inschriften*. H. Donner and W. Röllig. 2d ed. Wiesbaden: Harrassowitz, 1966–69.
LA	*Liber Annuus*
MDOG	*Mitteilungen der Deutschen Orient-Gesellschaft*
NCB	New Century Bible
NBD²	*New Bible Dictionary*. Edited by J. D. Douglas and N. Hillyer. 2d ed. Downers Grove: InterVarsity, 1982.
NEA	*Near Eastern Archaeology*

NEASB	*Near Eastern Archaeology Society Bulletin*
NEAEHL	*The New Encyclopedia of Archaeological Excavations in the Holy Land.* Edited by E. Stern. 4 vols. Jerusalem: Israel Exploration Society, 1993.
OBO	Orbis biblicus et orientalis
OBT	Overtures to Biblical Theology
OEANE	*The Oxford Encyclopedia of Archaeology in the Near East.* Edited by E. M. Meyers. New York: Oxford University Press, 1997.
OLA	Orientalia lovaniensia analecta
OJA	*Oxford Journal of Archaeology*
Or	*Orientalia* (NS)
OTL	Old Testament Library
PEFQS	*Palestine Exploration Fund Quarterly*
PEQ	*Palestine Exploration Quarterly*
PJ	*Palästina-Jahrbuch*
PNA	*Prosography of the Neo-Assyrian Empire.* Edited by Karen Radner and Heather D. Baker. 3 vols. Helsinki: Neo-Assyrian Text Corpus Project, 1998–.
PSB	*Princeton Seminary Bulletin*
Qad	*Qadmoniot*
QDAP	*Quarterly of the Department of Antiquities in Palestine*
RAI	Rencontre assyriologique internationale
RB	*Revue biblique*
RelSRev	*Religious Studies Review*
SAA	State Archives of Assyria
SAAB	*State Archives of Assyria Bulletin*
SAAS	State Archives of Assyria Studies
SBLABS	Society of Biblical Literature Archaeology and Biblical Studies
SBLDS	Society of Biblical Literature Dissertation Series
SBLEJL	Society of Biblical Literature Early Judaism and Its Literature
SBLMS	Society of Biblical Literature Monograph Studies
SBLSP	Society of Biblical Literature Seminar Papers
SBS	Stuttgarter Bibelstudien
SBT	Studies in Biblical Theology
SBTS	Sources for Biblical and Theological Study
ScrHier	Scripta hierosolymitana
SEL	*Studi epigrafici e linguistici*
SHANE	Studies in the History of the Ancient Near East
SHCANE	Studies in the History and Culture of the Ancient Near East
SJOT	*Scandinavian Journal of the Old Testament*

SOTSMS	Society for Old Testament Studies Monograph Series
SSEAJ	*Society for the Study of Egyptian Antiquities Journal*
SWBA	Social World of Biblical Antiquity
TA	*Tel Aviv*
Them	*Themelios*
Transeu	*Transeuphratene*
TynBul	*Tyndale Bulletin*
UF	*Ugarit-Forschungen*
USQR	*Union Seminary Quarterly Review*
VT	*Vetus Testamentum*
VTSup	Supplements to Vetus Testamentum
WBC	Word Biblical Commentary
WMANT	Wissenschaftliche Monographien zum Alten und Neuen Testament
WTJ	*Westminster Theological Journal*
WUNT	Wissenschaftliche Untersuchungen zum Neuen Testament
ZAW	*Zeitschrift für die alttestamentliche Wissenschaft*
ZDPV	*Zeitschrift des Deutschen Palästina-Vereins*

Jerusalem in Bible and Archaeology:
Dialogues and Discussions

Ann E. Killebrew and Andrew G. Vaughn

For several centuries scholars have used the Bible as a primary historical source for understanding both the material and spiritual biblical worlds. Of course, their assumptions, goals, and methods have varied and developed over the years. Early critical analysis of the Bible during the eighteenth and nineteenth centuries focused on the task of determining whether certain narratives in the Bible were factual or not. This focus led, by the end of the nineteenth century, to an optimism that, through critical analysis of the texts, "factual" questions could be resolved that would illuminate the way the biblical narratives must be understood. For much of the twentieth century this optimism grew into a positive attitude among scholars who believed that, by critically examining the Bible in light of historical texts, considered together with new discoveries being uncovered by archaeology in biblical lands, it would be possible to write a secular history of the Bible. Consequently, funding for large-scale excavations in biblical lands reached an apex during the first half of the twentieth century, especially between the two world wars. After World War II, renewed excavations in the 1950s through the mid-1970s reflected the optimism and promise of a "biblical archaeology" and the close cooperation between researchers, theologians, philanthropists, private and government funding agencies, and broad-based interest on the part of the general public.

This situation changed dramatically, however, during the last three decades of the twentieth century. Scholars trained specifically as archaeologists dominated archaeological fieldwork in the modern nation-states of the ancient biblical world, and many of their discoveries, the result of a more systematic approach to archaeological fieldwork, raised difficult questions regarding the historicity of biblical texts. At times the results even seemed to contradict events described in the Bible. Whereas the early generation saw some hope in finding an "essential continuity" between the events that were deemed factual and the biblical narratives, the results of recent research have tended to conclude that such continuity is unlikely to emerge.

1

The rise of a more specialized discipline (dubbed Syro-Palestinian archaeology) during the later 1970s and 1980s coincided with new methodological and science-based approaches to archaeology, sometimes referred to as "new archaeology" or "processual archaeology." The rise of processual archaeology intensified the split between biblical studies and field archaeology that had begun even before the 1970s, with the separation becoming greater still as new scientific investigations failed to "prove" biblical events. This parting of the ways was particularly evident in North America and Europe, where archaeology generally was traditionally taught in anthropology departments in a university setting but archaeology of the land of the Bible was still considered to be part of biblical studies. These developments, combined with the exponential increase in scholarly publications and archaeological data and the required level of expertise in each of these fields, has led to a tendency for a more specialized and fragmented approach to the related fields of Bible, history, and archaeology. The optimistic days when scholars such as William F. Albright and G. Ernest Wright could proclaim that archaeology would resolve many biblical debates were over.

As we assess the situation at the beginning of the twenty-first century, we recognize that archaeologists of the lands of the Bible and biblical scholars have long since departed from a common path of shared goals. Such a separation is in many ways the natural conclusion to the larger academic trend of specialization. It is rare to find well-trained generalists even in liberal arts colleges, much less in research universities or seminaries. Given the explosion of data during the second half of the twentieth century and the vast increase in the number of publications, scholars must specialize out of necessity. Thus, it is becoming increasingly difficult to find scholars with broad expertise in theology, biblical history, philology, form criticism, literary analysis, comparative religions, and archaeology, though such expertise was deemed to be requisite for any biblical scholar during the first half of the twentieth century.

Field archaeologists by necessity concentrate more on anthropological and archaeological theory or material culture studies than on the literary history of the Bible. Likewise, biblical scholars today tend to focus their research within the subfields listed above; they have little time to work in any depth in areas closely related to their specialty and at best only "dabble" in archaeology. Many biblical scholars seem to think that participation in a few field excavations is enough to make one a proficient archaeologist, while many field archaeologists believe that knowledge of Hebrew is enough to master the biblical texts or to reconstruct a history of the biblical world. In reality, however, both disciplines require years of intensive study to attain a fluency in the languages of material culture or the related subspecialties of biblical studies. The result is that archaeologists and biblical scholars spend less and less time communicating with each other, which fosters the perception that the related fields of material culture and text have very little to contribute to each other. Even when the conversations take place, the two groups often find themselves speaking different languages.

The present volume began quite literally through an archaeologist and a biblical scholar's attempt to talk with each other. The editors of this volume, Ann E. Killebrew and Andrew G. Vaughn, were both fellows at the Albright Institute of Archaeological Research during the 1993–94 academic year. During the course of our conversations, we began to discuss the need for better communication between archaeologists and biblical scholars. We recognized that we all have a great deal to learn from the related fields of Bible, history, and archaeology. In addition, as in any good conversation, dialogue needs to be based on understanding, not merely argumentation, or the conversation will quickly turn into a polemical chess match.

Our conversations continued over the years. In 1997, when the Society of Biblical Literature and the American Schools of Oriental Research finally split their respective annual meetings, we felt that this parting of the ways was somehow symbolic of a deepening chasm between the fields of text and archaeology. We thus realized that there was a real need proactively to broaden the conversation. Our consultation on "Jerusalem in Bible and Archaeology" was an attempt to provide a venue for this conversation to take place.

Jerusalem was the logical choice for both archaeologists and biblical scholars. Indeed, Jerusalem is the most widely excavated city in all of Palestine and Israel, yet even with the increased archaeological data and textual analyses, there is no clear consensus regarding much of Jerusalem's history and ancient significance. Jerusalem is also central to any theological interpretation of the Hebrew Scriptures, though the polemical nature of Jerusalem in the Hebrew Bible is equally problematic. It is often difficult to separate Jerusalem's material world from the descriptions of a heavenly and glorious Jerusalem. This dilemma is especially true for the period of the united monarchy (the reigns of David and Solomon). The archaeological evidence is at best scant, while the Bible describes a city with magnificent palaces, public buildings, and a temple.

In sum, because of Jerusalem's significance for biblical scholars, historians, theologians, and archaeologists, this city should be the place where biblical archaeologists and biblical scholars can find a common language— or at least an interest in promoting dialogue. The present volume contains most of the essays presented over a three-year period in the consultation on "Jerusalem in Bible and Archaeology." The volume is not a "case study" but rather a focused example of how the integration of archaeology and biblical studies can take place with reference to the central site of

Jerusalem. We are able to see that biblical interpretation, historical investigations, and archaeological research can successfully dialogue even in the absence of consensus about the "facts."

The Layout and Approach of the Book

The volume is divided into three sections: (1) the period of David and Solomon (the tenth century B.C.E.); (2) the last century and a half of the Judahite monarchy (the end of the eighth century B.C.E. to the early sixth century B.C.E.); and (3) synthetic essays that attempt to integrate all of the material. Each section contains studies by both biblical scholars and archaeologists. Some of the articles in each section provide historical and archaeological summaries of Jerusalem during the respective periods, several present competing theories about the archaeological data, and others focus on the biblical interpretation of Jerusalem in the period being discussed.

Part 1: Jerusalem during the Reigns of David and Solomon

The period of the united monarchy was once held to be the anchor for historical discussions of Israel,[1] but the consensus on Jerusalem from a half a century ago has degenerated into heated debates about whether the city was a mere hamlet or a strong capital city. Jane M. Cahill's exhaustive treatment of "Jerusalem at the Time of the United Monarchy: The Archaeological Evidence" sets the stage for the debate in this volume. Cahill thoroughly reviews the vast history of archaeological research conducted in Jerusalem over the past century. The first half of Cahill's essay is thus indispensable for anyone seeking to understand the background of the current debates. The second part presents the most up-to-date data from Yigal Shiloh's excavations in the City of David.[2] Cahill's essay presents for the first time pottery plates and photos suggesting that the City of David was indeed an important town during the tenth century B.C.E. and supporting the claim that Jerusalem was the capital of a united monarchy during the reigns of David and Solomon. As seen in the contributions that follow, not all scholars agree with Cahill's conclusions, but they must surely take into account the data she presents in this essay.

The next three articles, also by archaeologists, present alternative interpretations of Jerusalem during the tenth century. The papers by Israel

---

[1] See the bibliography and discussion in Gary N. Knoppers, "The Vanishing Solomon: The Disappearance of the United Monarchy from Recent Histories of Ancient Israel," *JBL* 116 (1997): 19–44.

[2] Following Shiloh's untimely death, the publication of the excavations in Area G has been assigned to Cahill, who is thus the leading authority on the data from these excavations.

Finkelstein and David Ussishkin approach the issue through a focused reexamination of the archaeological data from Jerusalem, while Gunnar Lehmann investigates the likely role of Jerusalem in the tenth century by incorporating survey data from the Judean hill country and Shephelah regions during this time period. Like Cahill, both Finkelstein and Ussishkin offer their own reviews of the history of research (albeit in much briefer form), and one should note the differences in each of the summaries. These differences highlight the fact that the data from all the excavations can be interpreted legitimately in a number of ways. No one doubts that Jerusalem was a settlement from the Middle Bronze Age (early second millennium) through the end of the Iron Age (sixth century). However, based on various interpretations of the archaeological data, different scholars reach opposite conclusions regarding the magnitude of the settlement and Jerusalem's existence either as a fortified city or an unwalled village.

Finkelstein's essay ("The Rise of Jerusalem and Judah: The Missing Link") departs from Cahill's interpretation in at least three ways: (1) he concludes that Jerusalem did not undergo expansion beyond a village until well into the ninth century; (2) he follows the low chronology that systematically dates twelfth- to ninth-century remains a century later; and (3) he suggests a ninth-century or later date for the construction of the stepped stone structure, the only monumental feature that may have been in use during the tenth century or earlier and the centerpiece of the Jerusalem debate. Finkelstein concludes that the Omrides, not David and Solomon, were responsible for the development of Jerusalem and Judah.

Ussishkin's contribution ("Solomon's Jerusalem: The Text and the Facts on the Ground") represents another attempt to present the "objective facts" known from archaeology. His review of the data, however, proves that there are few objective facts when it comes to interpreting the history of Jerusalem. With Finkelstein and against Cahill, he concludes that there is no evidence for significant fortifications or for the reuse of the Middle Bronze II fortification wall during the Late Bronze to the Iron IIB periods. According to Ussishkin, Jerusalem during the reigns of David and Solomon was a small town or village that probably included a modest temple and palace on Mount Moriah.

Lehmann approaches the same question from a different angle in "The United Monarchy in the Countryside: Jerusalem, Judah, and the Shephelah during the Tenth Century B.C.E." He utilizes the archaeological data in Jerusalem but focuses his discussion on survey data that permit him to gain a better understanding of the entire region of Judah during the tenth century. Building on anthropological and sociological models, Lehmann concludes that the evidence from the larger countryside during the tenth century suggests that Jerusalem was a settlement limited in size.

The last two essays in this section are written by biblical scholars who incorporate historical and archaeological data into their interpretive essays. J. J. M. Roberts presents an updated version of his theories on the Zion tradition in "Solomon's Jerusalem and the Zion Tradition." Roberts forcefully argues on historical and biblical grounds that the Zion tradition dates back to the reigns of David and Solomon. He admits that the tradition was developed during later periods, but he contends that the roots of the tradition can be authentically traced to David and Solomon. Roberts further concludes that the archaeological evidence supports only his historical findings that in fact Jerusalem was the capital of a united monarchy during the tenth century B.C.E.

In "Solomon and the Great Histories," Richard E. Friedman presents literary evidence to support the view that much of the Deuteronomistic History had its genesis during Solomon's reign. Friedman argues that, if this material can be dated to Solomon's reign, the monarch must be viewed as an important historical figure who would be expected to have undertaken the expansion of the kingdom that is described in the Bible. Friedman does not directly address the archaeological data, but his conclusions suggest that an interpretation of Jerusalem similar to Cahill's should be preferred over the alternative views.[3]

PART 2: THE FINAL TWO CENTURIES OF FIRST TEMPLE JERUSALEM

Whereas the period of David and Solomon is characterized by difficulties interpreting both the biblical text and archaeological evidence, the eighth, seventh, and early sixth centuries B.C.E. represent periods for which reliable data abounds. There are numerous references to Judah in Egyptian, Assyrian, and Babylonian texts, and the archaeological data are clearer and more numerous. The increase in material cultural remains allows for more consensus conclusions, yet more detailed questions remain unsolved. In addition, every new solution presents a deeper level of problems that require even more data to resolve specific problems or questions. The possibilities to incorporate historical, archaeological, and biblical interpretations are still more numerous and far more reliable, both on historical and archaeological grounds.

In "Western Jerusalem at the End of the First Temple Period in Light of the Excavations in the Jewish Quarter," Hillel Geva sets the stage for the discussion in this section by thoroughly reviewing the history of archaeological research that has a bearing on Jerusalem during the eighth and ninth centuries. Geva then proceeds to summarize the newest finds and

---

[3] See Vaughn's synthetic overview essay for one way that Friedman's position can be modified.

results from the late Nahman Avigad's excavations in the Jewish Quarter, concluding that earlier "maximalist" views of late eighth and seventh century B.C.E. Jerusalem have been justified. Ronny Reich and Eli Shukron's "The Urban Development of Jerusalem in the Late Eighth Century B.C.E." incorporates the latest data from outside the Jewish Quarter in a discussion of the development of Jerusalem during the latter part of the eighth century (i.e., the reigns of Hezekiah and his predecessors). Their recent excavations around the Gihon Spring and along the lower slopes of the City of David have revealed important evidence and new perspectives on the fortification system of the later Iron II period. Noteworthy is the lack of any evidence that would point to the existence of significant fortifications from the Late Bronze Age through the ninth century B.C.E.

The next three essays put the archaeological material in context by means of a discussion of extrabiblical texts. James K. Hoffmeier begins this discussion with an extensive overview of the Egyptian epigraphic finds, so often neglected in a discussion of Jerusalem and Judah. Hoffmeier reviews the debates, translates many key passages, provides a useful bibliography, and presents his own interpretation about how these data should be understood in relation to Jerusalem. In particular, readers will find his detailed and thorough summary of all the Egyptian kings from the last quarter of the eighth century (Pi[ankh]y to Shabataka) extremely useful as a tool for understanding the major debates concerning the use of Egyptian texts relating to the biblical narratives. His survey of the Egyptian material allows Hoffmeier to comment on the historical setting of several chapters of Isaiah and Hosea as well as on the Egyptian involvement in the rebellion at Ekron and the coalition against Sennacherib in 701. As is seen in the later essay by J. J. M. Roberts, the Egyptian texts are certainly important in order to understand the historical events, but their interpretation is open to debate.

The essay by K. Lawson Younger Jr. takes up a similar task with regard to the Assyriological material. He rehearses the most important theories and debates about the relevant Assyrian textual evidence, provides many translations and even more citations, and presents an extremely important bibliography for anyone wishing to delve deeper into the question. Like Hoffmeier, he then proceeds to offer his own interpretations about how these Assyrian texts should influence our understanding of Jerusalem. Perhaps most important, Younger shows how the Assyrian sources are ideological texts that must be interpreted just as one must interpret the biblical narratives. Younger moves beyond reading descriptions and epithets at face value to an attempt to understand how descriptions, titles, and lists are used by the different Assyrian kings. The result is that he lays out a useful approach for correlating the significance of the Assyrian texts for understanding the Bible.

J. J. M. Roberts presents a thorough and critical response reexamining the Egyptian and Assyrian texts discussed by Hoffmeier and Younger. Roberts revisits some of Hoffmeier's conclusions by discussing places where Egypt is mentioned in the Assyrian material. Although Roberts departs at several key points from Hoffmeier, he concurs with most of Younger's conclusions. However, there is one notable disagreement: their interpretation of the historical setting of Isa 10:27–32. Roberts's discussion shows that, although there is much that can be agreed upon because of the exhaustive extrabiblical material, these historical documents also require interpretation and are open to biases. The fact that Roberts can arrive at different conclusions from Hoffmeier and Younger should make clear that, even with the presence of extrabiblical texts, not all of our questions will be resolved.

The final two essays in this section bring the discussion into the Persian period and past the fall of Jerusalem at the hands of the Babylonians. Lynn Tatum's "Jerusalem in Conflict: The Evidence for the Seventh-Century B.C.E. Religious Struggle over Jerusalem" examines late eighth- and seventh-century Judah within a more theoretical framework. That is, Jerusalem's rise in importance during this period should be understood from the perspective of a segmentary/centralizing conflict that took place within Judah rather than solely as a result of outside political events. Thus Tatum analyzes the eventual downfall of the southern kingdom in light of Colin Renfrew's model of "secondary state collapse" and does not attribute its demise simply to foreign invasions.

In "'The City Yhwh Has Chosen': The Chronicler's Promotion of Jerusalem in Light of Recent Archaeology," Gary N. Knoppers explores why Chronicles, a postexilic text that he dates to the fifth or fourth century B.C.E., depicts Jerusalem as so significant. In light of the archaeological and textual evidence, it is clear that the Achaemenid-era Jerusalem sanctuary had several rivals. This, Knoppers suggests, was one of the major reasons the Chronicler stressed Jerusalem's value and promoted the authority of the Jerusalem temple. Knoppers discusses in detail how the author advanced Jerusalem's importance through his genealogical introduction, his portrayal of Jerusalem during the united kingdom, and his strong emphasis on the historical centrality of the Jerusalem cult. However, the Chronicler's portrayal of the historic importance of the Jerusalem temple in earlier periods should be seen first and foremost as being directed toward strengthening the position of Jerusalem within the international context of Yehud during the Achaemenid period.

PART 3: SYNTHETIC APPROACHES THAT INTEGRATE THE DISPARATE DATA

The third section begins to bring the various data together in an effort to see if there is some common ground that can serve as a foundation for future discussions between archaeologists and biblical scholars. Ann E.

Killebrew's essay ("Biblical Jerusalem: An Archaeological Assessment") reviews the archaeological material presented in the previous two sections. She stresses the need to evaluate biblical Jerusalem based on the evidence excavated and discourages speculation on what might have been. Killebrew ends her essay with a summary of what we can conclude with some degree of certainty, what interpretations are likely but cannot be proven, and where a consensus now exists. Her essay shows that, although there is much that archaeologists cannot agree upon, there is also much that can be discerned, and these data can serve as a basis for further discussion, even if all of the questions are not resolved.

Although Killebrew's synthesis can be seen as a "middle ground" in an effort to determine what can be known with some degree of certainty, the reader will discover that some degree of certainty is never a matter for consensus with Jerusalem. The editors thus invited Margreet Steiner, an archaeologist who is publishing Kathleen Kenyon's excavations in Jerusalem, to offer her critique of Killebrew's synthesis. Whereas Killebrew argues that Jerusalem was limited in size during the Late Bronze Age, Steiner presents arguments for the absence of any significant occupation during this period. In response to the possibility of the stepped stone structure and its mantle being constructed simultaneously, Steiner presents evidence from the broader excavations of Kenyon as part of an argument that they were constructed separately and at different times. Finally, Steiner develops her theory about the absence of settlement during the Late Bronze Age to present arguments that Jerusalem began as a *new* settlement during the tenth and ninth centuries B.C.E. that served as a significant administrative center of Judah. It did not, however, develop into a real city until the eighth century.

The next two essays offer reflections based on the archaeological data about the role Jerusalem plays in the biblical literature. Yairah Amit's "Jerusalem in Bible and Archaeology: When Did Jerusalem Become a Subject of Polemic?" uses a literary investigation to explore why Jerusalem can be used in a polemical way in the biblical texts. Her essay is important in the effort to understand how and why biblical writers can choose to use or omit particular historical data. Amit emphasizes that the biblical writers had agendas that were not limited to presenting an essential continuity between the historical data and their written narratives.

In "Jerusalem, the Late Judahite Monarchy, and the Composition of Biblical Texts," William M. Schniedewind continues the discussion begun by Amit with a focused treatment of the role of Jerusalem in the biblical prophetic material. Schniedewind begins by reviewing the relevant archaeological and historical conclusions that illuminate the prophets. He then explores how these archaeological and historical data can illuminate the composition of the biblical narratives, especially the prophetic material. Schniedewind's essay thus not only presents a synthesis of the material but also provides a helpful summary on the role of Jerusalem in the works of the prophets.

The final two essays are more philosophical in nature. In spite of much agreement, in the end many of the essays present opposite conclusions. In light of this reality, Neil Asher Silberman ("Archaeology, Ideology, and the Search for David and Solomon") reviews the various ways that archaeological material has been interpreted and used throughout the last century and concludes that there is no such thing as an objective conclusion. Silberman shows how all the interpreters, even the archaeologists, have been influenced by philosophical or political presuppositions and concerns.

The synthetic essay by Andrew G. Vaughn ("Is Biblical Archaeology Theologically Useful Today? Yes, A Programmatic Proposal") agrees that philosophical and political presuppositions pose a major obstacle in the effort to draw firm conclusions. However, Vaughn argues that the situation is not hopeless but that biblical theologians *and* archaeologists are most prone to the trap that Silberman illustrates when they are not intentional about putting their conclusions in conversation with external, historical data. When the conversation with external data does not take place, archaeologists and biblical theologians alike are prone to the trap of super-dogmaticism. However, Vaughn illustrates that an overreliance on historical data leads to another trap: a tendency toward essentialism. Vaughn concludes that the archaeologist and biblical theologian can and must move forward and that the best method for moving forward is somehow to strive to find a middle ground between the tendency to let one's dogma control one's conclusions and the desire to seek an essentialist resolution. His essay concludes by using the material from Jerusalem as an example of what such a proposal for biblical interpretation might look like.

In conclusion, the essays contained in this volume are representative of the current state of scholarship in the twenty-first century on biblical Jerusalem after well over a century of research and exploration. As these chapters demonstrate, there are several areas in which a consensus can be reached between Bible and archaeology, and we have no doubt that productive dialogue between the various disciplines is possible. We hope that this volume can serve as a foundation for future discourses between text and material culture and will encourage further fruitful cross-disciplinary discussions in our attempts to reconstruct a spiritual and physical biblical Jerusalem.

PART 1

JERUSALEM DURING THE REIGNS OF DAVID AND SOLOMON

Jerusalem at the Time of the United Monarchy: The Archaeological Evidence

© 2003 *Jane M. Cahill*
The Hebrew University of Jerusalem

Jerusalem has been occupied for at least six thousand years, has played a prominent role in world history, and is one of the most extensively excavated sites in the Middle East. Nevertheless, the historical record is scant, and Jerusalem's archaeological remains are fragmentary, difficult to excavate, and mostly unpublished. Consequently, many unresolved questions about Jerusalem's historical development have generated and continue to generate (often bitter) debate among scholars trying to draw factual conclusions from bodies of evidence that will always be incomplete and subject to change. Although a definitive picture of the city's historical development cannot yet—and may never—be presented, many of the topographical and archaeological features from which the city's historical development must be reconstructed are known, and interpretation of what those features reflect about the period of the united monarchy can be offered. Because many of these features existed long before the period of the united monarchy, any attempt to reconstruct the city's appearance at that time must start at the very beginning.

NATURAL FEATURES

Topographically, Jerusalem is located in the Judean Hills that comprise roughly the middle section of a low mountain range that transects the region on a north-south axis. Bounded on the west by the Shephelah (foothills) and on the east by the Judean Desert, the Judean Hills consist of isolated mountain blocks delineated by steep valleys. The Judean Hills are commonly divided into three subregions: the Hebron Hills, where the highest peak is Mount Halhul (1,020 m); the Jerusalem Saddle; and the Bethel Hills, where the highest peak is Baal Hazor (1,016 m).[1] Although

---

[1] David Charles Hopkins, *The Highlands of Canaan: Agricultural Life in the Early Iron Age* (SWBA 3; Sheffield: JSOT Press, 1985), 58–62.

the Jerusalem Saddle forms the plateau-like core of the Judean Hills, it is nonetheless dissected by steep valleys: draining to the east is the Kidron Valley; draining to the west are the Sorek and Ayalon Valleys. Formed by streams that once transected the area, each of these valleys is "predominantly v-shaped with no accompanying flood plain."[2] The mountainous spurs (interfluves) standing between these valleys are capped by flat or gently rounded blocks of bedrock. Jerusalem of the Chalcolithic, Bronze, and early Iron Ages was located on one of these mountainous spurs—a narrow, triangle-shaped ridge known today as the City of David.

The City of David is bounded on the east by the Kidron Valley and on the west and south by the valley known to the Roman author Josephus as the Tyropoeon, or Cheesemakers', Valley (*War* 5.4.1 §140). On the north the City of David rests against the Temple Mount (known also as Mount Moriah and the Haram es-Sharif). At its northern base, the City of David is approximately 220 m wide; its length from there to its southern apex is roughly 630 m; the level area along its crest is approximately 49 dunams or about 12 acres.[3] The Temple Mount is approximately 740 m above sea level; the southern tip of the City of David is roughly 640 m above sea level, making the decrease in elevation close to 100 m.[4] Of the hills in its immediate vicinity, the City of David is the lowest (Ps 125:2). In antiquity, the natural features of the land virtually predetermined the placement of ancient roads.[5] Jerusalem's prominence during the Iron Age may have been due, at least in part, to its position guarding the northern end of a bottleneck on the north-south route that followed the watershed through the center of the region, "for Jerusalem is situated at the point where this highway reached the end of the confining ridge from Bethlehem and arrived at the southern end of the broad, fertile plateau of Benjamin, from which important roads fanned out in various directions to the east, north, and west."[6]

---

[2] Ibid., 60.

[3] Yigal Shiloh, *Excavations at the City of David, vol. I, 1978–1982: Interim Report of the First Five Seasons* (Qedem 19; Jerusalem: Institute of Archaeology, Hebrew University of Jerusalem, 1984), 3; idem, "Excavating Jerusalem: The City of David," *Arch* 33/6 (1980): 8–17, esp. 11.

[4] Shmuel Ahituv and Amihai Mazar, eds., *The History of Jerusalem: The Biblical Period* [Hebrew] (Jerusalem: Yad Izhak Ben-Zvi, 2000), map of Jerusalem attached to back cover.

[5] David Alden Dorsey, *The Roads and Highways of Ancient Israel* (Baltimore: Johns Hopkins University Press, 1991), 40–41.

[6] Ibid., 124.

Structurally, the City of David is a step-faulted block with inclinations of 10 to 15 degrees.[7] The surface consists of hard, nonporous dolomite—known locally as *Mizzi Ahmar*—exposed along the lower eastern slope of the spur, and of porous, white limestone—known locally as *Meleke*—exposed along the spur's upper eastern slope and crest. Two groups of small faults, with vertical displacements of 20 to 30 meters, pass through the area: one down faults primarily to the east; the other down faults primarily to the south.[8] Although the bedrock along the City of David's eastern slope rises at an angle of 25 to 30 degrees, its ascent is punctuated by steep escarpments.[9] In antiquity these escarpments were largely exposed, but today they are covered by deep deposits of archaeological debris that have created a steeply sloped surface reaching angles as sharp as approximately 45 and 58 degrees.[10]

Both the dolomite (*Mizzi Ahmar*) and the limestone (*Meleke*) strata found in the City of David are carbonate formations whose susceptibility to dissolution by circulating groundwater (karst) has been increased by several phases of tectonic stress.[11] Jerusalem's only perennial source of water, the Gihon Spring, is "one of the most indicative manifestations of the prevalence of karstic features in the strata underlying the City of David."[12] Located on the western edge of the Kidron Valley, the Gihon Spring issues into a cave that lies approximately 10 m below the modern ground surface at an elevation of 635.26 m above sea level.[13] Although no

---

[7] Dan Gill, "The Geology of the City of David and Its Ancient Subterranean Waterworks," in *Excavations at the City of David 1978–1985 Directed by Yigal Shiloh, vol. IV, Various Reports* (ed. D. T. Ariel and A. De Groot; Qedem 35; Jerusalem: Institute of Archaeology, Hebrew University of Jerusalem, 1996), 1–28, esp. 4.

[8] Ibid., 4.

[9] Ibid., 6; Kathleen M. Kenyon, *Jerusalem: Excavating Three Thousand Years of History* (London: Thames & Hudson, 1967) 31; idem, *Digging Up Jerusalem* (London: Benn, 1974), 94. See also Shiloh, *Excavations at the City of David I,* pl. 14:2 (example of steep escarpment); and Margreet L. Steiner, *Excavations by Kathleen M. Kenyon in Jerusalem 1961–1967, vol. III, The Settlement in the Bronze and Iron Ages* (Copenhagen International Series 9; London: Sheffield Academic Press, 2001), 37 (composite map depicting levels of bedrock measured during excavations directed by Macalister and Duncan and Kenyon).

[10] Kenyon, *Digging Up Jerusalem,* 77; Donald T. Ariel and Yeshayahu Lender, "Area B Stratigraphic Report," in *Excavations at the City of David 1978–1985 Directed by Yigal Shiloh, vol. V, Extramural Areas* (ed. D. T. Ariel; Qedem 40; Jerusalem: Institute of Archaeology, Hebrew University of Jerusalem, 2000), 1–32, esp. 2.

[11] Gill, "Geology of the City of David," 11.

[12] Ibid., 17.

[13] Ibid., 19.

hydrological study of the Gihon Spring has ever been undertaken, it is commonly believed to be a syphon-type karstic spring because its flow has been described as pulsating rather than constant. The spring's pulsating flow appears to be reflected in its name, which derives from the Hebrew root גיח or גוח, meaning "to gush."[14] Syphon-type karstic springs typically consist of a subterranean hollow connected to a spring cave by an arch-shaped fissure that, when filled with water, creates a natural siphon that empties water from the hollow into the spring cave.[15] Although no systematic measurement of the Gihon Spring's flow has ever been reported, Hecker estimated its flow to vary from 200 to 1,100 m³ per day, depending both on the season of the year and the annual amount of rainfall.[16] Measurements made intermittently between 1978 and 1985 yielded a low of 700 m³ per day during September of 1979 at the end of a warm, dry summer, and a high of 4,750 m³ per day during February of 1983 in the midst of a cool, rainy winter.[17]

Climatically, Jerusalem and the hills surrounding it are located in the Mediterranean zone, though the City of David lies very close to the border with the Judean Desert zone. Meteorological data for Jerusalem has been recorded systematically for well over one hundred years. These data demonstrate that the rainy season usually begins in late October or early November and lasts until May, that the average annual rainfall is 556.4 mm, with actual recorded figures ranging from an annual low of 206.4 mm in 1959/60 to an annual high of 1,134 mm in 1991/92.[18] Between the dry, warm summers and the wet, cool winters are "two short, irregular transitional periods that ... do not deserve full designation as seasons."[19] These transitional periods usually last only a few weeks and are characterized by sporadically occurring *sharav* and *hamsin* conditions. Although the

---

[14] Ibid., 17, citing references dating from as early as 1884.

[15] Avner Goren, "The Gihon and the Installations Built by It" [Hebrew], *Teva Vaaretz* 11 (1968–69): 22–26, esp. 22.

[16] Mordechai Hecker, "Water Supply of Jerusalem in Ancient Times" [Hebrew], in *Sefer Yerushalayim* (*The Book of Jerusalem*) (ed. M. Avi-Yonah; 2 vols.; Jerusalem: Bialik Institute and Dvir, 1956–87), 1:191–218, esp. 193.

[17] Alon De Groot, "Jerusalem's First Temple Period Water Systems" [Hebrew], in *Jerusalem during the First Temple Period* (ed. D. Amit and R. Gonen; Jerusalem: Yad Izhak Ben-Zvi, 1990), 124–34, esp. 124.

[18] Rehav Rubin, "Jerusalem and Its Environs: The Impact of Geographical and Physical Conditions on the Development of Jerusalem" [Hebrew], in Ahituv and Mazar, *History of Jerusalem,* 1–12, esp. 2–3, nn. 5–7. See also Frank S. Frick, "Palestine, Climate of," *ABD* 5:119–26, esp. 123.

[19] Hopkins, *Highlands of Canaan,* 80.

Hebrew term *sharav* and the Arabic term *hamsin* are often used interchangeably, they "do not refer to precisely the same conditions."[20] *Sharav* conditions occur when ridges of high pressure that compress, heat, and desiccate stagnant air create thermal inversions; *hamsin* conditions occur when centers of low pressure attract dust-carrying east winds from the Arabian Desert. While *sharav* conditions occur more frequently than *hamsin* conditions, both can raise temperatures by 15 degrees Celsius and cause the relative humidity to fall by 40 percent.[21]

HISTORY OF ARCHAEOLOGICAL RESEARCH

Modern archaeological investigation of the City of David began in 1838 when Edward Robinson traversed the subterranean water supply system known today as Hezekiah's Tunnel.[22] Since then archaeologists too numerous to name have conducted expeditions to the City of David in search of remains from the biblical period, and virtually all of them claim to have found evidence from the period of the united monarchy. The most significant excavations were directed by Charles Warren, 1867–70; Montague B. Parker, 1909–11; Raymond Weill, 1913–14, 1923–24; Robert Alexander Stewart Macalister and J. Garrow Duncan, 1923–25; Kathleen M. Kenyon, 1961–67; and Yigal Shiloh, 1978–85.[23] Current excavations are being conducted by Ronny Reich and Eli Shukron.[24]

---

[20] Frick, "Palestine, Climate of," 5:125, citing Denis Baly, *The Geography of the Bible: A Study in Historical Geography* (2d ed.; New York: Harper & Row, 1974), 52.

[21] Hopkins, *Highlands of Canaan,* 80–81. See also Frick, "Palestine, Climate of," 5:125.

[22] Edward Robinson, *Biblical Researches in Palestine, Mount Sinai and Arabia Petraea: A Journal of Travels in the Year 1838 Undertaken in the Reference to Biblical Geography* (3 vols.; London: Murray, 1841), 1:342.

[23] For chronological tables listing the various excavations, see Hillel Geva, "History of Archaeological Research in Jerusalem," *NEAEHL* 2:801–4; idem, "List of Major Archaeological Excavations in Jerusalem, 1967–1992," in *Ancient Jerusalem Revealed* (ed. H. Geva; Jerusalem: Israel Exploration Society, 1994), 325–30. For a comprehensive bibliography of the resulting reports, see Klaus Bieberstein and Hanswulf Bloedhorn, *Jerusalem: Grundzüge der Baugeschichte vom Chalkolithikum bis zur Frühzeit der osmanischen Herrschaft I–III* (Wiesbaden: Reichert, 1994).

[24] For preliminary reports of the recent excavations, see Ronny Reich and Eli Shukron, "Channel II in the City of David, Jerusalem, Some Technical Features and their Chronology" [Hebrew], in *Eleventh International Conference on Water in Antiquity* (Jerusalem: Israel Nature and Parks Authority, 2001), 3; idem, "Jerusalem, Gihon Spring," *ESI* 20 (2000): 99*–100*; idem, "Jerusalem, City of David," *ESI* 18 (1998): 91–92; idem, "The System of Rock-Cut Tunnels Near Gihon in Jerusalem

These and other excavations in the City of David have demonstrated that Jerusalem's archaeological composition conforms to a pattern common in the central hill country, where stone was and is the most commonly available building material.[25] Because buildings in Jerusalem have traditionally been constructed of stone rather than brick, Jerusalem's builders have traditionally excavated to bedrock to secure both firm foundations and building stones. As observed by Shiloh, these building practices have prevented the accumulation of superimposed archaeological strata characteristic of tells:

> The continuity of accumulation of the strata in the various excavational [*sic*] areas was not uniform. The builders in each stratum sought to found their structures directly on bedrock, and thus often they damaged earlier strata, which occasionally were even destroyed altogether. For this reason, Strata 12–10 were especially preserved, for they are the last major construction strata on the eastern slope.[26]

Moreover, as lamented by Kenyon, these building practices have also caused irreparable damage both to the archaeological record and to the City of David ridge:

> Evidence of early occupation on the summit area [of the City of David] does not exist. This lacuna is mainly because Roman quarrying and Byzantine buildings have destroyed all earlier structures and earlier occupation. For all we know, the original height of the eastern [i.e., City of David] ridge may have been appreciably above that of the surviving rock.[27]

Reconsidered," *RB* 107 (2000): 5–17; idem, "Light at the End of the Tunnel," *BAR* 25/1 (1999): 22–33, 72; idem, "A Wall from the End of the First Temple Period in the Eastern Part of the City of David" [Hebrew], in *New Studies on Jerusalem: Proceedings of the Fourth Conference* (ed. A. Faust and E. Baruch; Ramat Gan: Bar-Ilan University, 1998), 14–16; idem, "New Excavations in the City of David" [Hebrew], in *New Studies on Jerusalem, Proceedings of the Third Conference* (ed. A. Faust and E. Baruch; Ramat Gan: Bar-Ilan University, 1997), 3–8; Eli Shukron, "A New Look at the Overflow Channel (IVA) and the Siloam Channel (II) in the Light of the New Excavations in the City of David—1995" [Hebrew], in *Twenty-Second Archaeological Conference in Israel: Synopses of Lectures* (Jerusalem: Israel Exploration Society and Israel Antiquities Authority, 1996), 5.

[25] See Asher Shadmon, *Stone in Israel* (Jerusalem: Ministry of Development, 1972).

[26] Shiloh, *Excavations at the City of David I,* 25.

[27] Kenyon, *Digging Up Jerusalem,* 94.

Thus, the best-preserved structures in Jerusalem are those most recently constructed, with earlier remains preserved only when exploited or avoided by later builders.[28]

DEVELOPMENT PRECEDING THE PERIOD OF THE UNITED MONARCHY

CHALCOLITHIC AND EARLY BRONZE AGES

Evidence for Jerusalem's earliest settlement comes from natural pits (karstic sinkholes) in the bedrock. Although exposed to the air when the site was initially settled, natural pits excavated during Shiloh's excavations were found filled with debris, including pottery ascribed to the Chalcolithic Age and dated by form and fabric to the fourth millennium B.C.E.[29] Jerusalem's earliest architectural remains are similarly preserved because they were sheltered by natural depressions in the bedrock. These remains, found during Shiloh's excavations, consist of two rectangular, broad-room buildings ascribed to the Early Bronze Age and dated on the basis of form and content to the third millennium B.C.E.[30] Before Shiloh found the remains preserved in these sinkholes and depressions, evidence for the city's earliest period of occupation consisted solely of a few tombs, a "rough stone structure" ascribed to the Early Bronze Age unearthed in the vicinity of the Gihon Spring, and pottery attributed to the Early Bronze Age found scattered along the City of David's east slope.[31] Articulated

---

[28] See Kenyon, *Jerusalem,* 51–53, describing the difference between tell sites in which structures were built of brick and hill-country sites in which structures were built of stone.

[29] Shiloh, *Excavations at the City of David I,* 25; idem, "Jerusalem, City of David, 1985," *IEJ* 35 (1985): 301–3, esp. 302. For a comprehensive account of all archaeological material found in Jerusalem from the premonarchic period, including possibly prehistoric materials found in the surrounding hills, see Aren Maeir, "Jerusalem before King David: An Archaeological Survey from Protohistoric Times to the End of the Iron Age I" [Hebrew], in Ahituv and Mazar, *History of Jerusalem,* 33–65.

[30] Alon De Groot, "City of David Excavations" [Hebrew], in *Jerusalem during the First Temple Period* (ed. D. Amit and R. Gonen; Jerusalem: Yad Izhak Ben-Zvi, 1990), 40–50, esp. 42–43; Yigal Shiloh, "Jerusalem, City of David, 1982," *IEJ* 33 (1983): 129–31, esp. 130; Shiloh, "Jerusalem, City of David, 1985," 303.

[31] For the tombs, see Louis-Hugues Vincent, *Underground Jerusalem: Discoveries on the Hill of Ophel (1909–1911)* (London: Cox, 1911), 24–29, pls. VIII–XII; and Robert Alexander Stewart Macalister and J. Garrow Duncan, *Excavations on the Hill of Ophel, Jerusalem, 1923–1925* (Palestine Exploration Fund Annual 4; London: Palestine Exploration Fund, 1926), 22–25. For the "rough stone structure," see Kathleen M. Kenyon, "Excavations in Jerusalem, 1962," *PEQ* 95 (1963): 7–21, esp. 11,

structures ascribable to the Early Bronze Age were not found until the final
seasons of Shiloh's excavations when part of the city's Middle Bronze Age
fortification wall was removed and the two broad-room structures were
discovered underneath.[32] In light of these remains, Shiloh concluded "the
first settlement on the hill of the City of David was built on the rock of the
eastern slope, above the Gichon [*sic*] Spring and near cultivated plots in
the Kidron Valley. From the point of view of its urban character, the [Early
Bronze Age] settlement … was a pre-urban, unfortified settlement."[33]
Although Shiloh surmised that cultivated plots were restricted to the floor
of the Kidron Valley, the valleys transecting the Jerusalem Saddle are characteristically v-shaped, meaning that they lack level floors and flood plains
offering broad expanses of fertile land suitable for cultivation.[34] The discovery of agricultural terraces dating to the Early Bronze Age at Sataf on
the slopes of the Sorek Valley west of Jerusalem and the presence of agricultural terraces in the vicinity of the spring at ʿEin Farah east of Jerusalem,
where recent surveys have revealed evidence of settlement solely during
the Early Bronze Age, suggest that the Early Bronze Age settlement on the
City of David ridge may also have included agricultural terraces located on
the slopes above the floor of the Kidron Valley.[35]

---

but note that Kenyon did not mention this structure in subsequent publications.
The recently published report of Kenyon's excavations describes these remains
under the heading "Cave V" as follows: "behind a small wall A (=W95) material
from the EBA appeared. These were possibly occupational layers, although in the
field notebook, they were described as 'silt and clay with stones.' The pottery can
be ascribed to EB I or the beginning of EB II" (Steiner, *Excavations in Jerusalem
III,* 7). For isolated discoveries of Early Bronze Age pottery, see Macalister and
Duncan, *Excavations on the Hill of Ophel,* 32, 175–77; John Winter Crowfoot and
Gerald M. Fitzgerald, *Excavations in the Tyropoeon Valley, Jerusalem, 1927* (Palestine Exploration Fund Annual 5; London: Palestine Exploration Fund, 1929), 20–22,
65–66, pl. 11:1; Kathleen M. Kenyon, "Excavations in Jerusalem, 1967," *PEQ* 100
(1968): 97–111, esp. 106; idem, "Excavations in Jerusalem, 1962," 11–12; Shiloh,
Excavations at the City of David I, 25; Eilat Mazar, "Jerusalem, The Ophel—1986,"
ESI 5 (1986): 56–58, esp. 57.

[32] Shiloh, "Jerusalem, City of David, 1982," 130; idem, *Excavations at the City
of David I,* 25; idem, "Jerusalem, City of David, 1985," 302–3.

[33] Shiloh, "Jerusalem, City of David, 1985," 303. For a similar conclusion, see
Maeir, "Jerusalem before King David," 38.

[34] Hopkins, *Highlands of Canaan,* 60.

[35] For a general discussion concerning the introduction of agricultural terracing
to the region, see Shimon Gibson, "Agricultural Terraces and Settlement Expansion
in the Highlands of Early Iron Age Palestine: Is There Any Correlation between the
Two?" in *Studies in the Archaeology of the Iron Age in Israel and Jordan* (ed.

MIDDLE BRONZE AGE

During the Middle Bronze Age, a fortification wall constructed of "especially large cyclopean stones" was built above a steep scarp in the bedrock located close to the center of the City of David's eastern slope.[36] Sections of this wall have been revealed by both Kenyon and Shiloh, each of whom dated its construction to approximately 1800 B.C.E.,[37] a date that corresponds roughly to that of the Execration Texts, which are commonly thought to contain the earliest historical references to Jerusalem.[38] Kenyon found this fortification wall to have been approximately 2 m thick and built on top of "a horizontal rock ledge."[39] Shiloh found it to have been constructed in phases. Shiloh found that during its initial phase the Mid-

---

A. Mazar; JSOTSup 331; Sheffield: Sheffield Academic Press, 2001), 113–46. For preliminary results of the excavations at Sataf, see Shimon Gibson et al., "The Sataf Project of Landscape Archaeology in the Judaean Hills: A Preliminary Report on Four Seasons of Survey and Excavation (1987–1989)," *Levant* 23 (1991): 29–54. For results of the surveys at Khirbet ʿEin Farah, see Zeharia Kallai, "The Land of Benjamin and Mt. Ephraim" [Hebrew], in *Judaea, Samaria and the Golan: Archaeological Survey 1967–1968* (ed. M. Kochavi; Jerusalem: Archaeological Survey of Israel, 1972), 185, site 137; Uri Dinur and Nurit Feig, "Eastern Part of the Map of Jerusalem (Sheet 17–13: Sites 429–544)" [Hebrew], in *Archaeological Survey of the Hill Country of Benjamin* (ed. I. Finkelstein and Y. Magen; Jerusalem: Israel Antiquities Authority, 1993), 414–15, site 541, 70* (English summary).

[36] Shiloh, *Excavations at the City of David I,* 12.

[37] Ibid., 26; Kenyon, *Digging Up Jerusalem,* 78. See also Steiner, *Excavations in Jerusalem III,* 12. Parker, too, appears to have uncovered a segment of this fortification wall (see Vincent, *Underground Jerusalem,* 29; pl. VI:17). The segment discovered by Parker was not recognized as part of the Middle Bronze Age wall at the time of its discovery. For the wall's ascription to the Middle Bronze Age, see Ronny Reich, "Four Notes on Jerusalem," *IEJ* 37 (1987): 158–67, esp. 163–64. See also Margreet Steiner, "Letter to the Editor," *IEJ* 38 (1988): 203–4.

[38] The name Rušalimum appearing on a ceramic bowl dated roughly to the nineteenth century B.C.E. and on a terra cotta figure dated roughly to the eighteenth century B.C.E. are often cited as the earliest historical references to Jerusalem. See, e.g., Philip J. King, "Jerusalem," *ABD* 3:747–66, esp. 751. For the early group of texts, see Kurt Sethe, *Die Ächtung feindlicher Fürsten Völker und Dinge auf altägyptischen Tongefässcherben des Mittleren Reiches* (Berlin: Akademie der Wissenschaften, 1926). For the late group of texts, see Georges Posener, *Princes et pays d'Asie et de Nubie* (Brussels: Fondation Egyptologique Reine Elisabeth, 1940). But see Nadav Naʾaman, "Canaanite Jerusalem and Its Central Hill Country Neighbours in the Second Millennium B.C.E.," *UF* 24 (1992): 275–91, esp. 278–79, challenging the identification of Rušalimum as Jerusalem.

[39] Steiner, *Excavations in Jerusalem III,* 10.

dle Bronze Age fortification wall was approximately 3 m thick but that over the course of time buttressing added to its inner face made it even thicker.[40] More importantly, however, Shiloh found that buttressing added to the wall during the course of the Middle Bronze Age covered remains of contemporary structures that have been preserved in the archaeological record because both the fortification wall and the buttressing added to it continued in use until the Iron Age II.[41] Evidence that this fortification wall remained in use from the Middle Bronze Age II until the Iron Age II was also found by Kenyon at the northeastern edge of her Trench I where the wall turned west, and Kenyon speculated that a tower or city gate once guarded access to the Gihon Spring.[42] Although Kenyon was not

------

[40] Shiloh, *Excavations at the City of David I,* 12, 52, fig. 14. Although Kenyon did not report the discovery of buttressing added to the section of the Middle Bronze Age wall that she excavated, a recently published drawing of it made during the excavation suggests buttressing may have been added to a wall that was originally little more than 1 m thick. See Steiner, *Excavations in Jerusalem III,* 12, fig. 3.3.

[41] See, e.g., the conclusion published by Shiloh, *Excavations at the City of David I,* 26: "The line of the solid, massive city wall of this period [i.e., the Middle Bronze Age] midway down the eastern slope, as found by Kenyon and the present expedition, determined the line of fortifications of the City of David on this flank down to its total destruction in Stratum 10, in the 6th century B.C.E. The major difficulty in identifying the early phase of the city wall, in Strata 18–17, stems primarily from the repeated utilization of this selfsame line, and in the early nucleus of the wall itself, which continued in use in the successive phases." Shiloh expressed the same conclusion again in the preliminary report published after the 1985 season of excavation: "[I]n this area situated at the peak of the rock outcrop, ... the city-wall, built at the beginning of the MB II, continued in use until the destruction of the Iron Age city in 586 B.C.E." (idem, "Jerusalem, City of David, 1985," 303).

[42] Kenyon published several different statements asserting that the fortification wall built during the Middle Bronze Age remained in use until the second half of the Iron Age. See, e.g., Kenyon, "Excavations in Jerusalem, 1962," 9–10, where she states: "[C]learance on the inner side confirmed emphatically that the date of the original construction was early in Middle Bronze Age II, c. 1800 B.C. ... But immediately against the outer face of the wall, there were Iron Age levels down to bedrock, probably going down as late as the 7th century B.C. ... The life of the wall therefore spans the periods of Canaanite-Jebusite Jerusalem and the greater part of the Jewish monarchy. Its existence is proved only for the earliest and latest periods, but it is reasonable to conclude that it was in use throughout the intervening period. ... The reason that no deposits of these periods are found associated with it is accounted for by the effect of erosion on this terrific slope"; idem, "Excavations in Jerusalem, 1963," *PEQ* 96 (1964): 7–18, esp. 8, where she states: "In the 1962 season, it was proved that this wall continued in existence as the town wall

able to establish conclusively the location of the wall's northern line, her scholarly heir, Margreet Steiner, maintains that it is evidenced by two wall segments built of exceptionally large boulders that Kenyon found on the hill crest in her Squares H/II-III and Area P.[43] Because pottery ascribable to both the Early and Middle Bronze Ages was found near the base of one of these wall segments, and because they were both "built on the bedrock, using the same building technique" as the Middle Bronze Age fortification wall located downslope, Steiner cautiously identifies both wall segments as having belonged to the Middle Bronze Age fortification wall.[44]

---

from c. 1800 B.C. to the 7th century B.C., when it was succeeded by another [wall] slightly to the west"; idem, "Excavations in Jerusalem, 1967," 105–6, where she states: "The excavations in Area A were confined to the sites at the lower end of Trench I. There, the line of the original Jebusite wall, reused by David and continuing in use perhaps till the seventh century B.C., was found in 1961 and further exposed in 1962.... A[n] ... interesting development was some substantial walls running on an irregularly curved line north-east from the salient of the original wall. Associated with them was a succession of structures and floors. The original Middle Bronze Age town wall was upstanding above their level, and the assumption is that it was still in use as a town wall at the time of these structures, which certainly date to the Iron Age II." For additional comments about the continued existence of the fortification wall built during the Middle Bronze Age, see idem, *Digging Up Jerusalem,* 78, 81–83, 89–91. Although Steiner rejects Kenyon's conclusion that the Middle Bronze Age fortification wall remained in use until the Iron Age II, she does not reject the eighth–seventh century B.C.E. date that Kenyon proposed for occupational remains found outside the wall's eastern face. See Steiner, *Excavations in Jerusalem III,* 10, which states: "Occupational remains east of the [MBA] wall may date from the 8th–7th centuries BC." For Kenyon's comments regarding the tower or city gate in Trench I, see Kenyon, "Excavations in Jerusalem, 1967," 106; idem, "Excavations in Jerusalem, 1965," *PEQ* 98 (1966): 73–88, esp. 76. For a suggested reconstruction of a city gate at this location, see Dan Bahat, with Chaim T. Rubinstein, *The Illustrated Atlas of Jerusalem* (trans. S. Ketko; New York: Simon & Schuster, 1990), 22. Regarding the possible tower or city gate, Steiner states only: "In Square A/XIV, the town wall turned west. Next to the corner a stone structure was found, which is called 'tower' on the field drawings; there is no evidence for its dating. The question of whether Kenyon had found the northern boundary of the town or whether the town wall ran further north cannot be answered with certainty" (Steiner, *Excavations in Jerusalem III,* 10–11).

[43] Steiner, *Excavations in Jerusalem III,* 12–14, 16 (Walls 50 and 51).

[44] Ibid., 14, 16. None of the pottery associated with these walls has been published. See also Kenyon, *Digging Up Jerusalem,* 92, where Kenyon states: "Some element in the complex of walls along the south side of Site H must have constituted the boundary of the earliest Jerusalem."

During salvage excavations recently conducted in the vicinity of the Gihon Spring, Reich and Shukron uncovered remains that they interpret as having belonged to two (possibly free-standing) towers built during the Middle Bronze Age from cyclopean stones, some of which are over 2 m long. Reich and Shukron ascribe the construction of these towers to the first of two phases that they have identified for the Warren's Shaft water system. According to Reich and Shukron, these towers guarded both the entrance to the Gihon Spring and a pool from which its water could be drawn. Stratigraphic evidence adduced by Reich and Shukron during excavation of these towers also indicates that construction of the water supply system known as Channel II or the Siloam Channel preceded construction of the towers.[45] A composite system, consisting partly of a rock-hewn channel capped by cyclopean boulders and partly of a rock-hewn tunnel punctuated by side openings presumed to have released water for irrigating the Kidron Valley, Channel II is thought to have carried water from the Gihon Spring along the City of David's eastern slope to a pool located at the confluence of the Kidron and Tyropoeon Valleys.[46] Often identified with "the waters of Shiloah that go softly" mentioned in Isa 8:6, Channel II appears to have remained in use at least until Hezekiah's Tunnel was cut in roughly the eighth century B.C.E.[47]

Although Shiloh and his staff have identified several openings in the eastern side of Channel II as "windows" intended to release water onto agricultural plots located in the Kidron Valley, no serious study of how this irrigation system actually operated has ever been undertaken.[48]

---

[45] Reich and Shukron, "Light at the End of the Tunnel," 30–32.

[46] Ariel and Lender, "Area B," 13–18; Alon De Groot et al., "Area A1," in *Excavations at the City of David 1978–1985 Directed by Yigal Shiloh, vol. III, Stratigraphical, Environmental, and Other Reports* (ed. A. De Groot and D. T. Ariel; Qedem 33; Jerusalem: Institute of Archaeology, Hebrew University of Jerusalem, 1992), 1–29, esp. 19–22; Shiloh, *Excavations at the City of David I,* 22–24; Vincent, *Underground Jerusalem,* 6–8.

[47] Reich and Shukron, "Light at the End of the Tunnel," 32. See also Vincent, *Underground Jerusalem,* 32, who reasons that the lower water level created by operation of Hezekiah's Tunnel put Channel II out of use; contra Ariel and Lender, "Area B," 18, who reason that Channel II "could have been reactivated intermittently by damming and restoring the original water level," and Shiloh, *Excavations at the City of David I,* 24, who reasoned that Channel II could nevertheless have remained in use "as an aqueduct for the fields along the Kedron Valley."

[48] Neither the exact height of the Kidron Valley's floor above sea level nor the height of the Gihon Spring above the valley floor has been established. See Shiloh, *Excavations at the City of David I,* 22–24; De Groot et al., "Area A1," 19–22; Ariel and Lender, "Area B," 15–18. But see Reich and Shukron, "Channel

Nevertheless, because the Gihon Spring is itself located above the valley floor, and because the beginning of Channel II is located appproximately 2.5 m above the level of the Gihon Spring, Channel II appears to have been located well above the valley floor.[49] Consequently, water released directly from Channel II would have been wasted if it had to travel from there to the valley floor before reaching an agricultural plot that needed to be irrigated. Thus, although evidence for the existence of agricultural terracing below the line of Channel II has not yet been identified in the archaeological record, the mere existence of Channel II suggests that such terracing must have been in place at the time Channel II was cut, if not before. Because stratigraphic evidence adduced by Reich and Shukron indicates that Channel II preceded the towers that they ascribe to the Middle Bronze Age II, both Channel II and the agricultural terraces it was intended to irrigate appear to have been in use at least as early as the Middle Bronze Age II, perhaps even earlier.[50] While expansion of cultivatable land in the v-shaped valleys surrounding Jerusalem by means of agricultural terracing is attested at Sataf and perhaps at ʿEin Farah from the preceding Early Bronze Age, development of Channel II in Jerusalem appears to represent the earliest known attempt to irrigate hillside terraces and thereby mitigate the negative impact the region's long, dry summers and erratic annual rainfall imposed on local agriculture.[51]

II," 3, challenging both Channel II's use as an irrigation system and the Middle Bronze Age date of its southern end.

[49] Although neither the exact height of the Kidron Valley's floor above sea level nor the height of the Gihon Spring above the valley floor has been established, the towers unearthed by Reich and Shukrun outside the spring are founded on bedrock at levels below that reported for the spring (oral communication, Ronny Reich). For the difference in level between the Gihon Spring and the beginning of Channel II, and for the need of a damming device to raise the water to the level of Channel II, see Gill, "Geology of the City of David," 25, citing previous literature.

[50] Reich and Shukron, "Light at the End of the Tunnel," 32. For a recent survey of archaeological evidence for the earliest use of agricultural terracing in the region, see Gibson, "Agricultural Terraces and Settlement Expansion," 128–33. For a reconstruction of agricultural terraces on the slopes below the Siloam Channel during the Iron Age, see Lawrence E. Stager, "Jerusalem and the Garden of Eden," *ErIsr* 26 (1999): 183*–94*.

[51] An even earlier attempt to irrigate hillside terraces may be evidenced by a partly built, partly rock-cut passage known as Channel I, which starts approximately 0.8 m below the level of the Gihon Spring and over 3 m below the beginning level of Channel II. Because water from the Gihon Spring could not rise high enough to enter Channel II unless access to Channel I was blocked, Channel I appears to have predated Channel II. Alternatively, the wall blocking Channel I

Although surveys and excavations conducted in the hills surrounding Jerusalem have revealed a fairly dense concentration of settlement and burial sites ascribable to the Middle Bronze Age II throughout the region,[52] additional evidence for occupation of Jerusalem during this period consists of no more than a few poorly preserved walls and floors found in proximity to the fortification wall, isolated occurrences of pottery found as far north as the slopes of the Temple Mount, and a few burials in the City of David.[53] Nevertheless, archaeological remains from the Middle Bronze Age II recovered both in Jerusalem and in the surrounding countryside are commonly cited as evidence that during this period Jerusalem served as capital of an urbanized city-state that dominated the southern part of the central hill country.[54] Although the end of the Middle Bronze Age is marked by the violent destruction of virtually every fortified site in the region, no evidence has yet been found that Jerusalem was destroyed at this time.[55]

---

could have had a sluice gate located at its base, which would have allowed Channel I to be used together with Channel II. See Vincent, *Underground Jerusalem,* 6 and pl. II. See also Donald T. Ariel and Alon De Groot, "The Iron Age Extramural Occupation at the City of David and Additional Observations on the Siloam Channel," in Ariel, *Excavations at the City of David V,* 155–69, esp. 166–67 (discussing Iron Age irrigation systems).

[52] See, e.g., Emanuel Eisenberg and Alon De Groot, "Jerusalem and Its Environs in the Middle Bronze II Period" [Hebrew], in *New Studies on Jerusalem: Proceedings of the Seventh Conference* (ed. A. Faust and E. Baruch; Ramat Gan: Bar-Ilan University, 2001), 7–12, 5* (English summary); Zvi Greenhut, "The Periphery of Jerusalem in the Bronze and Iron Ages—New Discoveries" [Hebrew], in *New Studies on Jerusalem: Proceedings of the Second Conference* (ed. A. Faust; Ramat Gan: Bar-Ilan University, 1996), 3–8; and Maeir, "Jerusalem before King David," 46–48.

[53] For structural remains, see Steiner, *Excavations in Jerusalem III,* 16–20; Kenyon, "Excavations in Jerusalem, 1962," 12; and Shiloh, *Excavations at the City of David I,* 12, 26. For isolated occurrences of Middle Bronze Age II pottery, see Steiner, *Excavations in Jerusalem III,* 24, 36–37; Macalister and Duncan, *Excavations on the Hill of Ophel,* 177–78; Shiloh, *Excavations at the City of David I,* 26; and Dan Bahat, "City of David Excavations 1998" [Hebrew], in Faust and Baruch, *New Studies on Jerusalem: Proceedings of the Fourth Conference,* 22–26, esp. 23–24. For the Middle Bronze Age burials, see Maeir, "Jerusalem before King David," 42 and 44 n. 54.

[54] See, e.g., Maeir, "Jerusalem before King David," 49–50. For an alternative view, see Naʾaman, "Canaanite Jerusalem," 278–79.

[55] See, e.g., James M. Weinstein, "The Egyptian Empire in Palestine: A Reassessment," *BASOR* 241 (1981): 1–28; idem, "Egypt and the Middle Bronze IIC/Late Bronze IA Transition in Palestine," *Levant* 23 (1991): 105–15; William G. Dever, "Hyksos, Egyptian Destructions, and the End of the Palestinian Middle Bronze

LATE BRONZE AGE

The Late Bronze Age was a period during which settlements were smaller in both number and size than during the previous Middle Bronze Age and during which virtually all settlements, regardless of strategic location and/or importance, remained either unfortified or fortified solely by defense systems built during the Middle Bronze Age.[56] Although stratified remains attributable to the first half of the Late Bronze Age (ca. sixteenth–fifteenth centuries B.C.E.) have yet to be identified in Jerusalem, ceramic remains characteristic of the transitional period spanning the end of the Middle and the beginning of the Late Bronze Age have been recovered both from fills attributed to later periods of occupation in the City of David and from tombs excavated in the surrounding hills. Examples of ceramic remains found in fills attributed to later periods of occupation include sherds of a ledge-rim cooking pot, a Bichrome vessel, and a Chocolate-on-White vessel found during Shiloh's excavation of Area G.[57] Tombs containing ceramic assemblages spanning the period from the Middle Bronze Age II through the beginning of the Late Bronze Age include those investigated by Saller in Bethany and on the western slope of the Mount of Olives.[58]

Age," *Levant* 22 (1990): 75–81; James Karl Hoffmeier, "Reconsidering Egypt's Part in the Termination of the Middle Bronze Age in Palestine," *Levant* 21 (1989): 181–93.

[56] Rivka Gonen, "Urban Canaan in the Late Bronze Age Period," *BASOR* 253 (1984): 61–73; Aharon Kempinski, "Middle and Late Bronze Age Fortifications," in *The Architecture of Ancient Israel* (ed. A. Kempinski and R. Reich; Jerusalem: Israel Exploration Society, 1992), 127–42, esp. 136–40.

[57] Although Kenyon reported the discovery of "one substantial wall and a slender cross wall" with which she associated "a number of large storage jars, ... Middle or early Late Bronze Age in date" (Kathleen M. Kenyon, "Excavations in Jerusalem, 1964," *PEQ* 97 [1965]: 9–20, esp. 13), analysis of these storage jars has led Steiner to redate them and the associated architecture to the Iron Age I (Margreet L. Steiner, "Re-dating the Terraces of Jerusalem," *IEJ* 44 [1994]: 13–20). Detailed analysis of the pottery from Shiloh's Area G will be published by the author in Jane M. Cahill, *Excavations at the City of David 1978–1985 Directed by Yigal Shiloh, vol. VII, Area G* (in preparation).

[58] Sylvester John Saller, *Excavations at Bethany (1949–1953)* (Jerusalem: Franciscan Press, 1957); idem, "Jerusalem and Its Surroundings in the Bronze Age," *LA* 12 (1962): 147–76; idem, *The Excavations at Dominus Flevit (Mount Olivet, Jerusalem) Part II: The Jebusite Burial Place* (Publications of the Studium Biblicum Franciscanum 13; Jerusalem: Franciscan Press, 1964). For a discussion of additional tombs containing Late Bronze Age pottery and artifacts, see Maeir, "Jerusalem before King David," 46–47 nn. 56 and 60, 51 n. 76.

The second half of the Late Bronze Age (ca. fourteenth–thirteenth centuries B.C.E.) is well attested both by stratified remains excavated in the City of David and by tombs excavated in the hills surrounding Jerusalem.[59] Although stratified remains within the City of David consist solely of fragmentary structures found on or near the bedrock, these remains have been found in at least six different locations: Kenyon's Area A, Trench I, and Area P, and Shiloh's Areas D, E, and G.[60] The fragmentary nature of the stratified evidence for this period is exemplified by the remains of two walls (W55 and W56), a plastered floor, and pottery recovered in Kenyon's Square A/I, and the remains of two walls (W770 and W787), two floor surfaces, and the threshold linking them together recovered in Square E4 of Shiloh's Area G, located approximately 30 m north of Kenyon's Square A/I[61] (see fig. 1.1). The building remains recovered by Kenyon in Square A/I and those recovered by Shiloh in Square E4 can all be dated to the Late Bronze Age by ceramic assemblages recovered both from their floors and from their underlying fills (see fig. 1.2).[62] Moreover, imported Mycenaean

---

[59] For concise summaries of evidence from the tombs, see Maeir, "Jerusalem before King David," 54–56; and Rivka Gonen, *Burial Patterns and Cultural Diversity in Late Bronze Age Canaan* (ASOR Dissertations 7; Winona Lake, Ind.: Eisenbrauns, 1992), 63–64, 134–35.

[60] For Kenyon's Area A, see Steiner, *Excavations in Jerusalem III*, 24. For Kenyon's Trench I, see Steiner, *Excavations in Jerusalem III*, 36; Hendricus Jacobus Franken and Margreet L. Steiner, *Excavations by Kathleen M. Kenyon in Jerusalem 1961–1967, vol. II, The Iron Age Extramural Quarter on the South-East Hill* (British Academy Monographs: Oxford: Oxford University Press, 1990), 6–7, fig. 2–2. For Kenyon's Square P, see Steiner, *Excavations in Jerusalem III*, 36; Kathleen M. Kenyon, "Excavations in Jerusalem, 1964," 12; idem, "Excavations in Jerusalem, 1965," 76; idem, *Digging Up Jerusalem*, 92. For Shiloh's Area D, see Donald T. Ariel et al., "Area D1: Stratigraphic Report," in Ariel, *Excavations at the City of David V*, 33–89, esp. 77, where fill Locus 377 is described as having contained ceramic material ranging in date from Stratum 16 of the Late Bronze Age to Stratum 12 of the eighth century B.C.E. For Shiloh's Area E, see Shiloh, "Jerusalem, City of David, 1982," 130; idem, *Excavations at the City of David I*, 12, 26. For Shiloh's Area G, see David Tarler and Jane M. Cahill, "David, City of," *ABD* 2:52–67, esp. 55.

[61] Steiner, *Excavations in Jerusalem III*, 24.

[62] Ceramic assemblages recovered from the floors of both structures can be dated typologically to the Late Bronze Age II; ceramic assemblages recovered from shallow fills found beneath the floors in both structures contained pottery ascribable to the Middle Bronze Age II. For Kenyon's evidence, see ibid., 28, figs. 4.5 and 4.6. Without discussing the significance of the ceramic assemblage found on the plaster floor recovered by Kenyon, Steiner dates the structure in which it was found to the transitional period spanning the Late Bronze Age II and the Iron Age I. Her

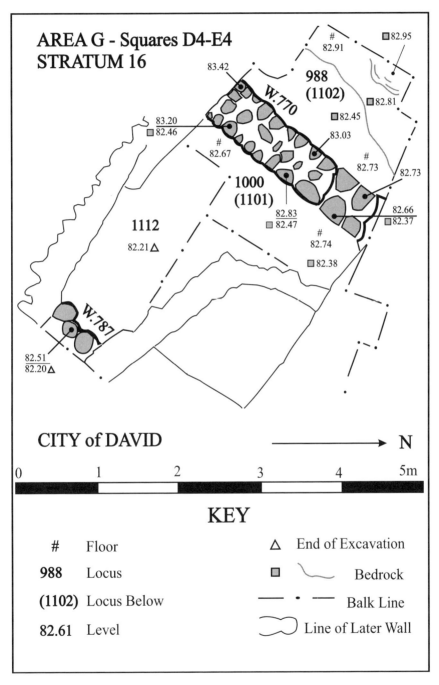

Fig. 1.1. Top plan of Late Bronze Age architecture in Shiloh's Square E4

Jane M. Cahill

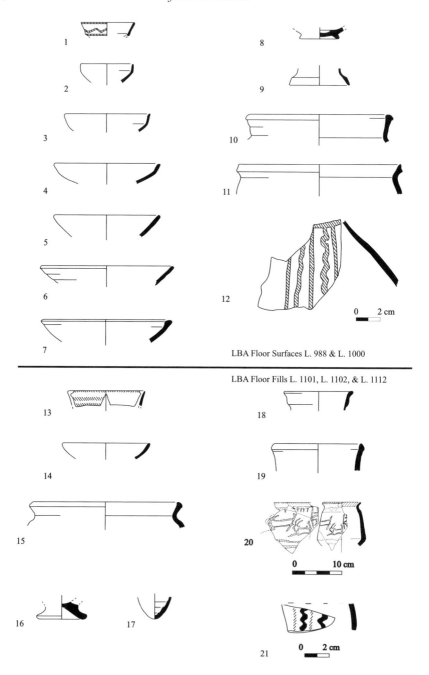

LBA Floor Surfaces L. 988 & L. 1000

LBA Floor Fills L. 1101, L. 1102, & L. 1112

Fig. 1.2a. Pottery associated with Late Bronze Age Architecture in Shiloh's Square E4

Fig. 1.2b. Pottery associated with Late Bronze Age Architecture in Shiloh's Square E4

#	NUMBER	LOCUS	IDENTITY	DESCRIPTION	
				WARE	SURFACE TREATMENT
1	G11958-4	988	Floor	Pink 7.5 YR 7/4	Exterior hand burnished; Paint: Dark Reddish Brown 5 YR 3/4
2	G15213-2	1000	Floor	Pink 7.5 YR 7/4	Interior and upper half of exterior slipped Pinkish White 7.5 YR 8/2
3	G15213-1	1000	Floor	Pale Red 10 R 6/4	None
4	G11930-1	988	Floor	Not Available	Not Available
5	G15213-3	1000	Floor	Pinkish Gray 7.5 YR 7/2	Exterior slipped Pinkish White 7.5 YR 8/2
6	G11957-2	988	Floor	Pinkish White 7.5 YR 8/2	Interior hand burnished
7	G11905-2	988	Floor	Light Brown 7.5 YR 6/4	None
8	G15213-5	1000	Floor	Reddish Yellow 7.5 YR 6/6	None
9	G11958-1	988	Floor	Pink 7.5 YR 7/4	Exterior self slipped
10	G11958-3	988	Floor	Pale Red 10 R 6/4	Interior and exterior slipped Pinkish White 7.5 YR 8/2
11	G11958-2	988	Floor	Red 2.5 YR 5/6	None
12	G11905-1	988	Floor	Light Reddish Brown 5 YR 6/3	Exterior slipped White 10 YR 8/2; Paint: Reddish Brown 5 YR 5/3
13	G15229-1	1101	Fill	Pink 7.5 YR 7/4	Interior hand burnished; Paint Dark Reddish Brown 5 YR 3/4
14	G15229-4	1101	Fill	Pinkish Gray 7.5 YR 6/2	None
15	G15356-1	1112	Fill	Light Red 2.5 YR 6/6	None
16	G15215-1	1101	Fill	Pink 7.5 YR 7/4	Interior and underside hand burnished
17	G15229-2	1101	Fill	Pink 7.5 YR 7/3	Exterior self slipped
18	G15229-3	1112	Fill	Pink 7.5 YR 8/3	Exterior self slipped
19	G15356-2	1112	Fill	Pink 5 YR 7/3	Exterior slipped White 10 YR 8/2
20	G15276-1	1101	Fill	Pink 5 YR 7/3	Exterior slipped Pinkish White 5 YR 8/2
21	G15272-1	1101	Fill	White 10 YR 8/2	Exterior painted Red and Black

and Cypriot pottery characteristic of the Late Bronze Age II has been discovered in the City of David by Macalister and Duncan, Kenyon, and
Shiloh.[63] Although the fragmentary nature of these remains and their publication has led some authors to conclude that during the Late Bronze Age
Jerusalem was either uninhabited or, at most, the location of a fortified
baronial estate,[64] Jerusalem's true status is attested by six cuneiform letters written by Abdi-heba, king of Jerusalem discovered at Tell el-Amarna
in Egypt.[65]

---

date is based primarily on the presence of a complete rim of a collar-neck pithos
decorated with reed impressions. Another complete pithos rim decorated with reed
impressions like that published by Steiner has been found at Manahat in a building ascribed to the Late Bronze Age II on the basis of an accompanying assemblage
of pottery and artifacts that includes everted-rim cooking pots and Nineteenth
Dynasty Egyptian scarabs. See Gershon Edelstein et al., *Villages, Terraces and Stone
Mounds: Excavations at Manaht, Jerusalem, 1987–1989* (IAA Reports 3; Jerusalem:
Israel Antiquities Authority, 1998) 47, 52–53, fig. 4.10:6. Detailed analysis of the pottery from Shiloh's Area G will be published by the author in Cahill, *Excavations at
the City of David VII.*

[63] Macalister and Duncan, *Excavations on the Hill of Ophel,* 33, 74; Steiner, *Excavations in Jerusalem III,* 29, 36; Kenyon, "Excavations in Jerusalem, 1962," 13. The
Mycenaean and Cypriot pottery from Shiloh's Area G will be published by the
author in Cahill, *Excavations at the City of David VII.* Imported pottery may also
have been found by other excavators but remains unknown because no attempt
has been made to catalogue unpublished material from earlier excavations.

[64] For assertions that the City of David ridge was wholly unoccupied or at most
the site of a baronial estate during the Late Bronze Age, see, e.g., Steiner, *Excavations in Jerusalem III,* 39–41; idem, "Jerusalem in the Tenth and Seventh
Centuries BCE: From Administrative Town to Commercial City," in Mazar, *Studies
in the Archaeology of the Iron Age,* 280–88, esp. 283; idem, "Jerusalem in the Late
Bronze and Early Iron Ages: Archaeological versus Literary Sources?" in Faust,
New Studies on Jerusalem: Proceedings of the Second Conference, 3*–8*; Ernst
Axel Knauf, "Jerusalem in the Late Bronze and Early Iron Ages: A Proposal," *TA*
27 (2000): 75–90. For assertions that Late Bronze Age Jerusalem was occupied but
only sparsely, see David Ussishkin, "Jerusalem during the Period of David and
Solomon—The Archaeological Evidence" [Hebrew], in Faust and Baruch, *New
Studies on Jerusalem: Proceedings of the Third Conference,* 57–58; and Hendricus
Jacobus Franken and Margreet L. Steiner, "Urusalim and Jebus," *ZAW* 104 (1992):
110–11. [Editors' note: See also the essays by Finkelstein, Lehman, and Ussishkin
in this volume.]

[65] See Nadav Na'aman, "The Contribution of the Amarna Letters to the Debate
on Jerusalem's Political Position in the Tenth Century B.C.E.," *BASOR* 304 (1996):
17–27. For a concise overview of the subject of the Amarna letters, see idem,
"Amarna Letters," *ABD* 1:174–81. For current English translations of the Amarna

The Amarna letters demonstrate that Late Bronze Age Canaan was divided into a network of kingdoms of various sizes and strengths led by local rulers who were regarded by Pharaoh merely as municipal rulers like Egyptian mayors but were regarded both by their subjects and by the rulers of neighboring cities as kings who ascended their thrones through the dynastic principle and who, in turn, passed their thrones on to their heirs. Although the Amarna letters contain few details about the internal structure of the kingdoms, they demonstrate that the king's palace served as the center of government and that the bureaucratic apparatus operated either in the palace or in its immediate vicinity. They demonstrate that the capital cities were surrounded by tracts of agricultural fields cultivated by the city's inhabitants and that the peripheral areas contained villages and hamlets each with its own fields and pasture lands. The Amarna letters also demonstrate that internal affairs in Canaan were influenced by the ambitions of local rulers, the power of the nonurban elements, and the readiness of Egypt to interfere in local disputes. Because the six letters written by Abdi-heba refer to the "land of Jerusalem" and to its "towns," the consensus of scholarly opinion is that during the Late Bronze Age Jerusalem served as capital of an Egyptian vassal city-state the size and strength of which was comparable to other like entities in the region.[66] The fact that structures such as those unearthed in Kenyon's Square A/I and Shiloh's Area G continued to stand directly on the bedrock in the Late Bronze Age as in the previous Early and Middle Bronze Ages suggests that the occupational character of the Late Bronze Age settlement did not differ significantly from the occupational character of the preceding periods. The Late Bronze Age represents, however, the final phase during which the physical profile of the area excavated by Kenyon as Area A and Trench I and by Shiloh as Area G conformed to the natural contours of the bedrock. Although the Late Bronze Age ended with the collapse of the Egyptian Empire and the destruction of many city-states, the archaeological record has not produced any evidence that Jerusalem suffered a destruction at this time.

Iron Age I

During the transition to the subsequent Iron Age, the region witnessed the arrival of new population groups, including the Sea Peoples, who settled along the Mediterranean coast, and the Israelites, who—tradition holds—settled in the hilly regions both east and west of the Jordan River.

---

letters, see William L. Moran, *The Amarna Letters* (Baltimore: Johns Hopkins University Press, 1992).

[66] Na'aman, "Contribution of the Amarna Letters," 17–27.

At a time when settlement in the central hill country consisted solely of unfortified villages, a massive, technically complex stepped rampart was built on the City of David's eastern slope above the Gihon Spring. Construction of the stepped rampart permanently altered the local topography and freed subsequent builders from constraints imposed by nature.

The stepped rampart is a massive structure—the boundaries of which have yet to be determined—consisting of a substructure and a superstructure linked by a rubble core. The substructure is composed of a series of interlocking terraces formed by north-south spine walls and closely spaced east-west rib walls that, together, created rows of interlocking, rectangular compartments. Each compartment contained two layers of fill: the upper layer consisted of compacted soil that began flush with the tops of the walls retaining them; the lower layer consisted of loosely packed boulders. The substructural terraces were capped by a rubble core that keyed them to a superstructural mantle. The mantle was constructed of roughly dressed, limestone boulders laid in stepped courses rising from east to west at an approximately 45-degree angle toward the crest of the hill. Portions of the stepped rampart have been investigated by Macalister and Duncan, Kenyon, Shiloh, and, possibly, Bahat.[67]

MACALISTER AND DUNCAN. In their Fields 5 and 7, Macalister and Duncan revealed at least two portions of the stepped mantle and the rubble core used to key the mantle to the substructural terraces beneath; they also appear to have revealed portions of five substructural terrace walls.[68] In Field 5, which encompassed the western edge of both Kenyon's Area A and Shiloh's Area G, Macalister and Duncan uncovered the twenty-three uppermost courses of the stepped mantle that they referred to variously as the "Jebusite Ramp" and the "North Bastion."[69] On the eastern edge of

---

[67] Results of the Macalister and Duncan, Kenyon, and Shiloh excavations are surveyed below. For a suggestion that excavations conducted by Dan Bahat in 1998 on the hill crest above Shiloh's Area G yielded remains of the stepped rampart, see Bahat, "City of David Excavations 1998," 23–24.

[68] Macalister and Duncan, *Excavations on the Hill of Ophel,* plan facing p. 49.

[69] Ibid., 51–55. Macalister and Duncan's interpretation of the structure as Jebusite was based on their belief that it had served as a foundation for the fortification wall standing above it (Shiloh's W. 309). Although they recognized that this fortification wall contained masonry of various periods, they believed its earliest parts were pre-Davidic—and, hence, Jebusite—because it was founded on the bedrock. As the stepped rampart necessarily coexisted with the Jebusite fortification wall, Macalister and Duncan maintained that it, too, was Jebusite. Subsequent excavators have, however, reassessed Macalister and Duncan's dating and concluded that the fortification wall standing above it (Shiloh's W. 309) is the

their Field 7, in an area identical to squares X24–25 of Shiloh's Area G, Macalister and Duncan uncovered an additional segment of the stepped rampart that they called the "South Bastion." The plans and photograph of the South Bastion published by Macalister and Duncan depict fragments of at least eight courses of stepped masonry that closely resemble those of the stepped rampart. Moreover, these courses of stepped masonry appear to have been laid above a mass of boulders and soil similar to that identified here as the stepped rampart's rubble core. Macalister and Duncan interpreted the South Bastion as a distinct architectural feature, contemporary with the North Bastion or Jebusite Ramp.[70] In addition, Macalister and Duncan exposed five closely spaced parallel walls located immediately beneath founding courses of a tower that they identified as "Solomonic" but that Kenyon and Shiloh both dated to the Hellenistic period.[71] These five walls appear to represent substructural rib walls that were subsequently re-exposed by both Kenyon and Shiloh.[72]

KENYON. Kenyon located her squares AI–III and XXIII and Trench I in close proximity to Macalister and Duncan's Fields 5 and 7 for the specific purpose of adducing stratigraphic evidence for dating features of the city's fortifications that Macalister and Duncan had exposed along the eastern edge of the hill crest.[73] During the course of her excavations, Kenyon exposed additional segments of the stepped rampart's mantle, rubble core, and substructural terraces.[74]

First Wall described by Josephus that is presumed to have been constructed in the Hasmonean period, ca. second century B.C.E. See, e.g., Shiloh, *Excavations at the City of David I*, 20, 30.

[70] Macalister and Duncan, *Excavations on the Hill of Ophel*, 60–61, plan facing p. 49, pls. II and XXIV.

[71] Ibid., 57–58.

[72] See Steiner, *Excavations in Jerusalem III*, 24–39; Kenyon, "Excavations in Jerusalem, 1962," pls. VIA–B; idem, "Excavations in Jerusalem, 1964," pls. IIA–IIIB; idem, *Jerusalem*, pls. 12–13, IV; idem, *Digging Up Jerusalem*, pls. 27–28, 31–32; and Shiloh, *Excavations at the City of David I*, pl. 27:2, depicting Tower Wall 310 and the substructural terrace walls found beneath it.

[73] Steiner, *Excavations in Jerusalem III*, 1; Kenyon, *Digging Up Jerusalem*, 47–48.

[74] See Steiner, *Excavations in Jerusalem III*, 28–37 (substructural fills), 42–50 (stepped mantle); idem, "The Jebusite Ramp of Jerusalem: The Evidence from the Macalister, Kenyon and Shiloh Excavations," in *Biblical Archaeology Today, 1990: Proceedings of the Second International Congress on Biblical Archaeology* (ed. A. Biran and J. Aviram; Jerusalem: Israel Exploration Society, 1993), 585–88. Note, however, that Kenyon and Steiner have both identified the substructural terraces and the stepped mantle as distinct architectural features separated in time

Squares AI–III and XXIII. Kenyon encountered remains of the stepped rampart's substructural terraces in her squares AI–III and XXIII during several seasons of excavation.[75] In Squares AI–III these remains consisted of a series of retaining walls that supported fills stabilized and compartmentalized by a number of narrow rib walls.[76] Single faced, one stone wide, and set at close intervals, these rib walls were built on a batter.[77] In addition, Kenyon found that the fills between the rib walls consisted of two distinct elements: an upper element of compact soil; and a lower element of loosely packed boulders.[78] In places, Kenyon managed to reach the

by centuries. Consequently, neither Kenyon nor Steiner uses the terms "substructural terraces," "rubble core," or "mantle" to identify the component parts of the stepped rampart.

[75] Kathleen M. Kenyon, "Excavations in Jerusalem, 1961," *PEQ* 94 (1962): 72–89, esp. 76–82, pls. XX–XXIA; idem, "Excavations in Jerusalem, 1962," 12–13, pls. V–VIIA and VIIIA; idem, "Excavations in Jerusalem, 1964," 12–14, pls. II, IIIB, and IV. For additional photos and descriptions of these finds, see also Kenyon, *Jerusalem,* pls. 12–13, 29–30, 46, and IV; and idem, *Digging Up Jerusalem,* 94–96, 100–103, pls. 27–28, 30–34. For the layout of individual squares in Kenyon's Area A, which included Trench I, see Franken and Steiner, *Excavations in Jerusalem II,* 4.

[76] Steiner, *Excavations in Jerusalem III,* 28–30; Kenyon, "Excavations in Jerusalem, 1962," 12, pls. VI–VIIA; idem, "Excavations in Jerusalem, 1964," 13, pls. IIa and IIIB; idem, *Jerusalem,* pls. 12–13, 29–30, 46, and IV; idem, *Digging Up Jerusalem,* 95, pls. 27–28, 31–32.

[77] Steiner, *Excavations in Jerusalem III,* 27, fig. 4:4; Kenyon, "Excavations in Jerusalem, 1962," 12–13, pl. VIA; idem, *Jerusalem,* 32; idem, *Digging Up Jerusalem,* 95.

[78] Kenyon's descriptions of the substructural terrace fills varied slightly from publication to publication. In 1963 she wrote: "The fill of the compartments varied; in some cases it was completely of loose rubble, in some of earth, and in some of a striated fill that looks in section like turves or mud-bricks (except that the striations are much too extensive and have no firm terminations like mud-bricks) and which is difficult to interpret" (Kenyon, "Excavations in Jerusalem, 1962," 13). In 1965 Kenyon differentiated between the fill that she attributed to the core structure and described as being comprised "mainly of loose stones of medium size with pockets of earth at intervals" (Kenyon, "Excavations in Jerusalem, 1964," 13) and the fill that she attributed to subsequent repairs and rebuilds, about which she stated: "earth and clay were used for the most part instead of a stone filling" (ibid., 13). The "loose stones of medium size" described by Kenyon are identical to the loosely packed boulder fill comprising the lower level of the rampart's substructural terrace fills, while the "earth and clay" described by Kenyon as characteristic of the structure's "rebuilds" are identical to the compact soil fill comprising the upper level of the rampart's substructural terrace fills. Confirmation for this conclusion appears in

base of these rib walls and fills, which allowed her to conclude that they were preserved to heights of at least 6 m.[79] Moreover, in Square A/I, Kenyon found that the rib walls and fills had been built over remains of stratigraphically earlier walls that were founded on the bedrock.[80] Although Kenyon interpreted the earlier walls founded on the bedrock as remnants of dwellings that she dated variously to the Middle Bronze Age and to the transitional period between the Middle and Late Bronze Ages, the ceramic assemblage recovered from the floor between them included fragments of two collar-neck pithoi, five cooking pots with everted, triangular rims, and one krater with an upright rim—vessels that are all indicative of the Late Bronze Age II.[81] Although Kenyon's efforts to date

---

Kenyon's last publication devoted entirely to Jerusalem, where she describes a photograph depicting (from bottom to top) the substructural stone fill, the substructural soil fill, and the rubble core used to link the substructural terraces to the superstructural mantle as showing: "[A]t the base on the right the original stone filling with above it the earth fill and above again the filling of larger stones." (Kenyon, *Digging Up Jerusalem,* 101, pl. 31). The photograph published as pl. 31 in *Digging Up Jerusalem* appears in a larger format in Kenyon, *Jerusalem,* pl. 13. A section drawing of the elements pictured in these photographs appears in Steiner, *Excavations in Jerusalem III,* 27, fig. 4.4. Although Steiner identifies Wall 70, a wall with two faces located at the southern edge of Kenyon's Square A/I, as a free-standing wall that served as the southern boundary of the stone-filled terraces, the continuation of the stone fill south into Square A/XXIII seems to contradict this identification. See Steiner, *Excavations in Jerusalem III,* 29 (identifying Wall 70 as the southern edge of the terrace fill), and 45, fig. 5.4 (photograph depicting continuation of the stone fill south of Wall 70 into Square A/XXIII).

[79] Kenyon, "Excavations in Jerusalem, 1964," 13; idem, *Digging Up Jerusalem,* 95. See also Kenyon, *Jerusalem,* 32, where she speculates: "It is probable that the total height of the stone filling nowhere survives. The maximum exposed was 6 meters, but a little way off the upper part of a compartment belonging to the same complex was uncovered, and this stood some 4.45 meters *higher.* It is quite possible that this particular platform stood at least to that height." See also Steiner, *Excavations in Jerusalem III,* 28, fig. 4.7 (schematic section of substructural terraces).

[80] Kenyon, "Excavations in Jerusalem, 1962," 14; idem, "Excavations in Jerusalem, 1964," 13, pl. IIIB; idem, *Digging Up Jerusalem,* 94, pls. 31–32. These are Walls 55 and 56 belonging to the structure recovered in Square A/I identified here as having belonged to a building used during the Late Bronze Age II. See Steiner, *Excavations in Jerusalem III,* 24.

[81] Kenyon, "Excavations in Jerusalem, 1962," 14 (Middle Bronze Age); idem, "Excavations in Jerusalem, 1964," 13 (Middle or Early Late Bronze Age); idem, *Digging Up Jerusalem,* 94–95 (Middle Bronze Age). For a suggestion that the building remains found on the bedrock beneath the terraces should be redated to the Iron Age I, see Steiner, "Re-dating the Terraces of Jerusalem," 14–15; for

the rib walls and fills were hindered by the small quantity of pottery and other artifacts recovered from them, she dated them variously to the fourteenth century B.C.E. and to the fourteenth–thirteenth centuries B.C.E. based on the presence of imported Mycenaean and Cypriot pottery.[82]

At the southern edge of Square A/XXIII, Kenyon found that the soil and stone fills of the substructural terraces ran up to an architectural feature that appears to be a continuation of the stepped rampart's superstructural mantle.[83] Kenyon identified this architectural feature as a retaining wall associated with the substructural fills that she had excavated immediately to the north. Following expansion of the excavation area farther to the south, however, Kenyon discovered that the retaining wall had been "laid back against the sloping collapse of the earlier fill to the north ... in regular horizontal courses which extended beyond the excavated area to the south."[84] She also observed that "each course tended to overlap that below"[85] and that "the stones of each [lower] course project more and more to the east."[86] Because this steplike structure extended farther south, beyond the limits of her excavation area, Kenyon stopped excavating without reaching either its base or the substructural fills beneath it.[87]

The horizontal courses of massive stones, rising in a steplike fashion from east to west discovered by Kenyon in Square A/XXIII, are strongly reminiscent of the stepped rampart's superstructural mantle excavated farther to the north both by Macalister and Duncan and by Shiloh.[88] These remains excavated by Kenyon are, therefore, cautiously identified as an additional segment of the stepped rampart's mantle.[89] This identification

---

"the transitional period of the Late Bronze Age and the Iron I Period," see idem, *Excavations in Jerusalem III*, 24. The pottery found on the floor surface associated with these building remains appears in Steiner, *Excavations in Jerusalem III*, 28, fig. 4.5.

[82] Kenyon, "Excavations in Jerusalem, 1962," 13; idem, "Excavations in Jerusalem, 1964," 13.

[83] Kenyon, "Excavations in Jerusalem, 1964," 13–14, pl. IV; idem, *Jerusalem*, pls. 29–30; idem, *Digging Up Jerusalem*, pls. 33–34.

[84] Kenyon, "Excavations in Jerusalem, 1964," 13.

[85] Ibid.

[86] Kenyon, *Digging Up Jerualem*, 101.

[87] Ibid., 101–2; idem, "Excavations in Jerusalem, 1964," 13.

[88] Macalister and Duncan, *Excavations on the Hill of Ophel*, 51–55; Shiloh, *Excavations at the City of David I*, 16–17.

[89] For a similar suggestion, see Hendricus Jacobus Franken, "The Excavations of the British School of Archaeology in Jerusalem on the South-East Hill in the Light of Subsequent Research," *Levant* 19 (1987): 129–35, esp. 130–31.

appears to be corroborated by Kenyon's discovery of large quantities of rubble immediately beneath the horizontal courses of stepped masonry, rubble that appears to belong to the rubble core used to key the mantle to the substructural terrace fills.[90] As with the substructural fills, Kenyon's ability to date the stepped retaining wall was hampered by the meagerness of the cultural remains found associated with it; nonetheless, she concluded that it should be ascribed to the Iron Age and that it probably dated to the tenth century B.C.E.[91]

Trench I. East of squares AI–III and XXIII, at the western end of Trench I (Shiloh's squares X5–7), Kenyon appears to have revealed yet another segment of the rampart's stepped mantle.[92] Like the mantle segment that she unearthed at the southern edge of Square A/XXIII, Kenyon found that the segment cleared in Trench I had been constructed of large limestone boulders laid in regular horizontal courses, each tending to overlap the one below it, that its horizontal courses rose steplike from east to west following the slope of the hill, and that the horizontal courses of stepped masonry were built against an underlying fill of loose stones.[93] In

---

[90] Kenyon, "Excavations in Jerusalem, 1964," 13, pls. IIA, IIIB; idem, *Digging Up Jerusalem,* 101–3, pls. 28, 31–32.

[91] Kenyon, "Excavations in Jerusalem, 1964," 13; idem, *Digging Up Jerusalem,* 103. See also Steiner, *Excavations in Jerusalem III,* 43, dating remains of the stepped stone structure found by Kenyon in Square A/XXIII to the tenth century "on [the basis of] its connection with other parts of the structure."

[92] Steiner, *Excavations in Jerusalem III,* 46–47; Kenyon, "Excavations in Jerusalem, 1961," 77, 82, pl. XXIIB; idem, *Digging Up Jerusalem,* 103, 161, pl. 64.

[93] Kenyon, "Excavations in Jerusalem, 1961," 77, 82, pl. XXIIB; idem, *Jerusalem,* pl. 45; idem, *Digging Up Jerusalem,* 103, pl. 64; Steiner, *Excavations in Jerusalem III,* 46, fig. 5.6. Although the same photograph appears in each publication listed in this note, due to the quality of the printing the stony nature of the fill underlying this segment of the stepped mantle is not clearly visible in each. The clearest and best image appears in Kenyon, *Jerusalem,* pl. 45; the worst image appears in Steiner, *Excavations in Jerusalem III,* fig. 5.6. From studying the photograph published by Kenyon in "Excavations in Jerusalem, 1961," pl. XXIIB; *Jerusalem,* pl. 45; and *Digging Up Jerusalem,* pl. 64, Franken concludes that the point in the lower left-hand corner is the structure's southeastern corner (Franken, "Excavations of the British School," 130–31). He then hypothesizes the existence of a passageway or an entrance there. The evidence published to date mitigates against identifying an entrance into the structure there. See Steiner, *Excavations in Jerusalem III,* 46: "As there was no drawing of this part of the section, it remained unclear why there was an 'opening' here." The break in the masonry Franken identifies as an entrance appears simply to be a damaged portion of the superstructure, similar to the line of broken masonry discovered along the B–C square coordinates in Shiloh's Area G.

character and composition the structure that Kenyon unearthed in Trench I is identical to the other segments of the stepped mantle and substructural terraces exposed farther to its north and west. Despite the massiveness of its underlying fills, Kenyon succeeded in penetrating through them to reach earlier levels. As in Squares AI–III and XXIII, she found the structure to have been built on top of stratigraphically earlier structures that were founded on the bedrock.[94] Although Kenyon initially surmised that the structure continued farther downslope, she did not find it preserved in the vicinity of the fortification wall.[95] Kenyon ascribed the structure to the Iron Age but continually refined her assessment of its specific date within that period. Following its discovery, she confidently asserted that "it certainly belongs to the 10th century B.C."[96] Subsequently, however, after studying relevant ceramic evidence, Kenyon cautiously proposed redating it to the time of Hezekiah, approximately the eighth century B.C.E.[97]

SHILOH. During the course of Shiloh's excavations in Area G an additional thirty-five courses of stepped mantle were added to the twenty-three courses unearthed by Macalister and Duncan. Nevertheless, none of the mantle's original boundaries were identified. Thus in Area G alone the stepped mantle consists of fifty-eight courses of masonry standing close to 17 m high (see fig. 1.3).[98] Like Kenyon, Shiloh dated the mantle's construction to the tenth century B.C.E.[99] Also like Kenyon, Shiloh investigated parts of the rampart's underlying terrace fills, which he dated to the Late Bronze Age.[100] Assuming that the stepped masonry unearthed by Kenyon in her Trench I is correctly identified as part of the stepped rampart, then the rampart's preserved height increases to approximately 30 m.[101] Moreover,

---

[94] Kenyon, "Excavations in Jerusalem, 1962," 14. These earlier remains date to the Middle Bronze Age; see Steiner, *Excavations in Jerusalem III*, 13, fig. 3.4 (W52, W53, and W54) and 16.

[95] Kenyon, "Excavations in Jerusalem, 1961," 82. Contra Steiner, *Excavations in Jerusalem III*, 46–47, who identifies these remains as a "tower" that supported the base of the stepped rampart and was founded—at least in part—on bedrock.

[96] Kenyon, "Excavations in Jerusalem, 1962," 14.

[97] Kenyon, *Digging Up Jerusalem*, 103.

[98] See Shiloh, *Excavations at the City of David I*, 17.

[99] Ibid., 16–17, 27.

[100] Ibid., 16.

[101] For corroboration both of this identification of the stepped masonry found by Kenyon at the western end of Trench I and of the estimated height of the structure's preserved components, see Steiner, *Excavations in Jerusalem III*, 46–47; idem, "Jebusite Ramp of Jerusalem," 587.

Fig. 1.3. Air view of stepped rampart. Photographer: Zev Radovan

assuming that Kenyon correctly concluded that the stepped masonry continued to descend downslope, the only structural remains substantial enough to have supported the stepped rampart would have been the city's fortification wall.[102] If so, the stepped rampart would have stretched from the fortification wall, which was founded on bedrock at 660 m above sea level, to the top of the hill crest, where its preserved height was measured during Shiloh's excavations at 697.53 m above sea level, for a total height of at least 37.5 m.[103]

Macalister and Duncan attributed the stepped rampart to the Jebusites because they recognized it as one of the earliest architectural elements on the slope. Kenyon and Shiloh each interpreted the substructural terraces as a free-standing architectural unit that they ascribed to the Late Bronze Age

---

[102] For evidence that Kenyon seems to have reached this conclusion herself, see Kenyon, "Excavations in Jerusalem, 1961," 82.

[103] For the level of bedrock beneath the fortification wall, see Steiner, *Excavations in Jerusalem III*, 37, fig. 4.18. For a schematic indication of the stepped rampart's upper level, see Shiloh, *Excavations at the City of David I*, 55, fig. 17.

and dated either to the fourteenth or thirteenth century B.C.E. on the basis of imported pottery found inside the terrace fills and (apparently) of Kenyon's discovery of building remains containing Middle Bronze Age pottery beneath them. Kenyon and Shiloh each interpreted the stepped mantle as a buttress added to the terraces during the tenth century B.C.E. on the basis of pottery found directly above it. Although Kenyon never described the pottery on which she based her date for the stepped mantle, Shiloh based his date on the discovery of red-slipped, hand-burnished pottery that since Albright's excavations at Tell Beit Mirsim has been interpreted as a chronological indicator for the period of the united monarchy.[104] Because, however, the soil fills containing this pottery covered and, therefore, postdated the mantle, the ceramic material in them provides only a *terminus ante quem* date for the mantle's last use and no indication of when it was built. Better evidence for dating the stepped mantle's construction comes from two segments of its lowest courses that were removed during the Shiloh excavations. In Square C5 mantle stones covering an area approximately 3 m long and nine courses wide were removed and a rectangular probe was dug (see figs. 1.4–5). In Square B4 mantle stones were removed and a vertical section was cut (see figs. 1.6–7). These probes yielded both architectural evidence demonstrating that the stepped mantle and the substructural terraces were built together as a single architectural unit and ceramic evidence providing a *terminus post quem* date for the rampart's construction at the transition between the Late Bronze Age II and the Iron Age I.

---

[104] Shiloh, "Jerusalem, City of David, 1982," 130. William F. Albright, *The Excavation of Tell Beit Mirsim, vol. III, The Iron Age* (AASOR 21–22; New Haven: American Schools of Oriental Research, 1943), 152–54. Long considered to be a chronological indicator of the tenth century B.C.E. and the period of the united monarchy, red-slipped, hand-burnished pottery does seem to have made its first appearance in the late eleventh or early tenth century B.C.E. See Amihai Mazar, "On the Appearance of Red Slip in the Iron Age I Period in Israel," in *Mediterranean Peoples in Transition: Thirteenth to Early Tenth Centuries BCE* (ed. S. Gitin et al.; Jerusalem: Israel Exploration Society, 1998), 368–78. Nevertheless, use of red-slipped, hand-burnished pottery as a tool for dating ceramic assemblages has been complicated by recent studies indicating that the transition from hand to wheel burnishing occurred gradually, "taking place at a different time and in a different manner in each region." See, e.g., Orna Zimhoni, "Lachish Level V and IV: Comments on the Material Culture of Judah in the Iron II in the Light of the Lachish Pottery Repertoire," in idem, *Studies in the Iron Age Pottery of Israel: Typological, Archaeological and Chronological Aspects* (Tel Aviv Occasional Publications 2; Tel Aviv: Institute of Archaeology, Tel Aviv University, 1997), 57–178, esp. 121.

Fig. 1.4. Before view of rectangular probe. Photographer: Isaac Harari

Fig. 1.5. After view of rectangular probe. Photographer: Sylvia Owen
For figs. 1.4 and 1.5, see also the photographs in Jane M. Cahill, "David's Jerusalem: Fiction or Reality? It Is There: The Archaeological Evidence Proves It," *BAR* 24/4 (1998): 34–41 and 63, esp. 36–37.

Fig. 1.6. Before view of vertical section.   Fig. 1.7. After view of vertical section.
Photographer: Yigal Shiloh   Photographer: Yigal Shiloh

    The vertical section cut in Square B4 revealed a fill of large and small
fieldstones sloping down from west to east that ended at the top of a substructural soil fill. Its excavation showed that the stepped mantle capped and
sealed the rubble core, which in turn capped and sealed the soil- and stone-
filled terraces. The rectangular probe was excavated from an architectural
seam that marked the junction between a segment of the substructural spine
wall and the stepped mantle to an artificial line marked by the southern wall
of the Burnt Room House, which was built on top of the stepped rampart
during the Iron Age II (see below). Like the vertical section, the rectangular
probe revealed a fill of large and small fieldstones sloping down from west
to east that is best interpreted as part of the rubble core used to key the
stepped mantle to the substructural terraces. The rectangular probe also
revealed that in this area the stone fill found immediately beneath the mantle steps was bonded (i.e., structurally integrated) with stone fill retained by
the substructural spine wall. The rectangular probe ended when stones too
large to extract from this small area were reached.
    The ceramic assemblage recovered from both the vertical section and
the rectangular probe is identical in character and composition to that
recovered from the stone and soil fills of the substructural terraces. During

Shiloh's excavations a corpus of approximately 500 sherds was retrieved from loci ascribed to the stepped rampart. This corpus is comprised of roughly 100 sherds from the stone fills, roughly 350 sherds from the soil fills, and roughly 50 sherds from the rubble core (see figs. 1.8–10).[105]

Although the corpus includes some sherds originating from virtually all earlier periods of the site's occupation and a few sherds representing vessel forms currently considered to be diachronic markers of the Iron Age I, the vast majority of the sherds represent locally familiar forms characteristic of the Late Bronze Age II. Sherds representing earlier periods of occupation include a ledge handle characteristic of the Early Bronze Age, pierced-rim cooking pots characteristic of the Middle Bronze Age IIA, pithoi with profiled rims characteristic of the Middle Bronze Age IIB, and a ledge-rim cooking pot, a Bichrome vessel, and a Chocolate-on-White vessel all characteristic of the transitional period between the Middle and Late Bronze Ages and/or the Late Bronze Age I. The Late Bronze Age II period is represented by sherds from imported Mycenaean and Cypriot vessels as well as by sherds from virtually all local vessel forms typical of the period, including platter bowls; carinated bowls; painted chalices; bi-conical jugs and/or kraters; cooking pots with everted, triangular rims; and folded-rim storage jars. Sherds representing forms considered to be diachronic markers of the Iron Age I include one rim of a "Manassite bowl," one rim of a possible cyma-profile bowl, and several fragments of collar-neck pithoi.[106] Collar-neck pithoi are now known to have been in use during the Late Bronze Age II, and the Manassite and cyma-profile bowl sherds are only isolated examples of these typically Iron Age I vessel forms.[107] While study

---

[105] Although Shiloh did not typically save all pottery retrieved during the excavation because his research design did not include quantitative analysis of the ceramics, he saved all the pottery from the various components of the stepped rampart (with the exception of undecorated body sherds) because Kenyon had specially noted the meagerness of the ceramic material found in the terrace fills and because the quantity of ceramic material found in these features was indeed significantly less than that recovered from other features excavated in Area G.

[106] "Manassite bowl" is a term coined by Adam Zertal for rounded, thick-walled bowls commonly found at sites located in the tribal territory of Manessah dating to the Iron Age I. See Adam Zertal, "'To the Lands of the Perizzites and the Giants': On the Israelite Settlement in the Hill Country of Manasseh," in *From Nomadism to Monarchy: Archaeological and Historicl Aspects of Early Israel* (ed. I. Finkelstein and N. Naʾaman; Jerusalem: Israel Exploration Society, 1994), 47–69, esp. 51–52.

[107] The collar-neck pithos "is a type long considered a *fossile directeur* for both the Iron I period and the Israelite presence within it. It has recently been shown, however, that the type begins to appear in the LB II ... and is found also outside the Israelite settlement sphere in Iron I.... Thus, its significance lies not in its mere

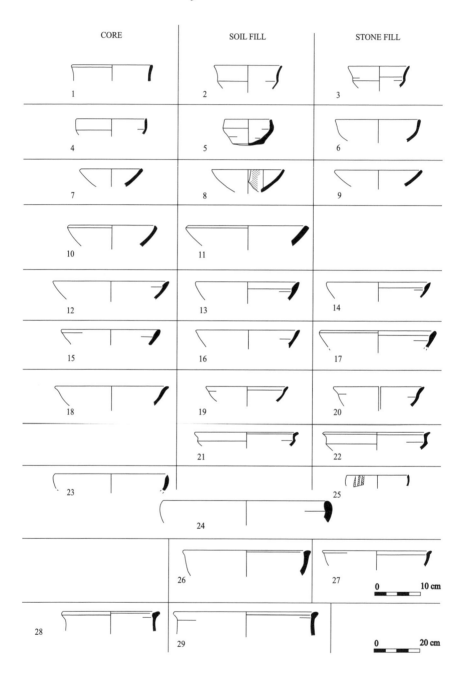

Fig. 1.8a. Bowls and kraters from inside the stepped rampart (see also fig. 1.8b)

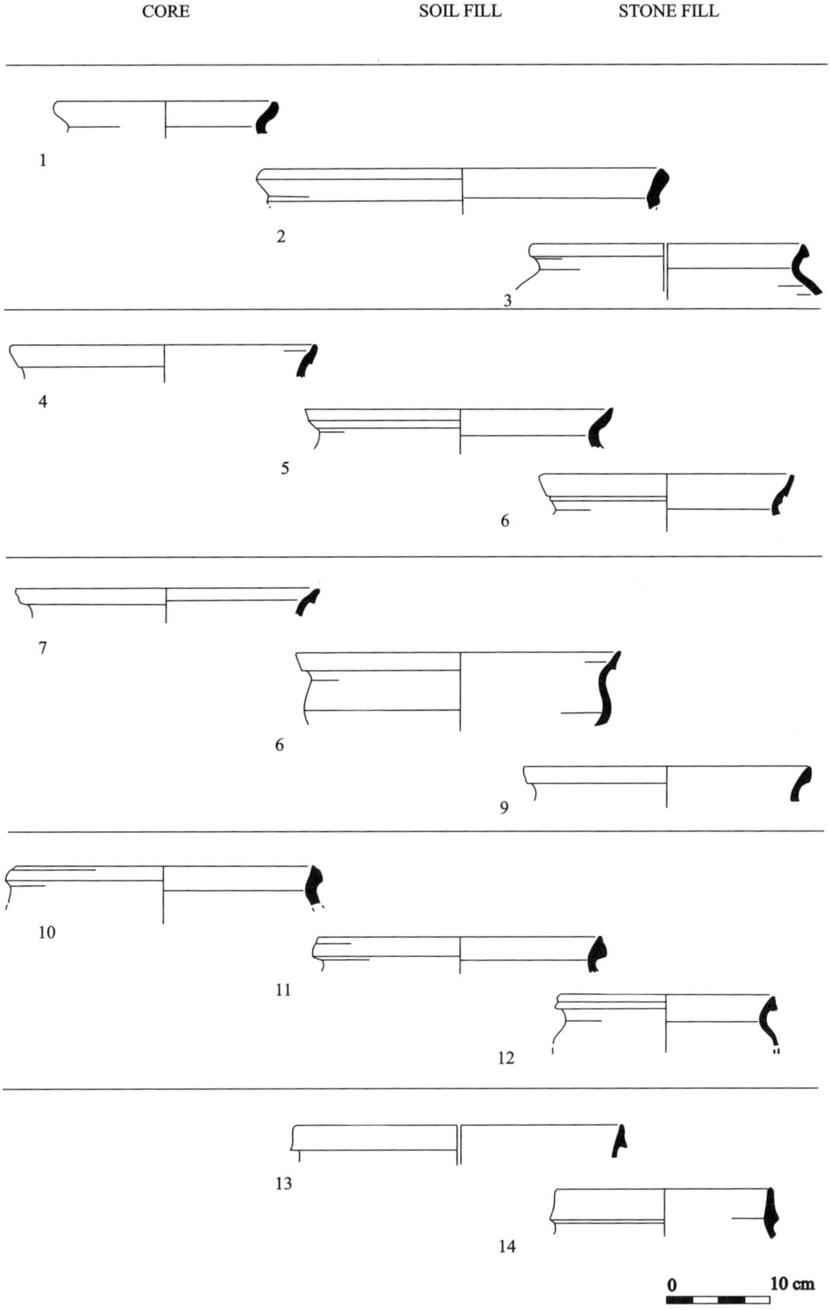
CORE
SOIL FILL
STONE FILL
1
2
3
4
5
6
6
7
9
10
11
12
13
14
0
10 cm

Fig. 1.9a. Cooking pots from inside the stepped rampart (see also fig. 1.9b)

Fig. 1.8b: Bowls and kraters from inside the stepped rampart

#	NUMBER	LOCUS	IDENTITY	DESCRIPTION	
				WARE	SURFACE TREATMENT
1	G17574-2	1116	Rubble Core	Light Reddish Brown 2.5 YR 6/4	Interior and exterior self slipped
2	G11144-2	917	Soil Fill	Light Reddish Brown 2.5 YR 6/4	Interior and exterior self slipped
3	G15450-1	1113	Stone Fill	Pink 7.5 YR 7/3	Interior and exterior self slipped
4	G17507-2	1116	Rubble Core	Pink 7.5 YR 7/3	Exterior slip Pinkish White 7.5 YR 8/2
5	G11043-3	910	Soil Fill	Pink 7.5 YR 7/3	Interior and exterior self slipped
6	G15481-3	1117	Stone Fill	Pink 7.5 YR 7/3	Interior and exterior self slipped
7	G17563-1	1111	Rubble Core	Pink 7.5 YR 7/4	Interior and exterior self slipped
8	G11262-1	915	Soil Fill	Light Red 10R 6/4	Interior and exterior slipped Pinkish White 7.5 YR 8/2; Rim and cross painted Light Reddish Brown 2.5 YR 6/4
9	G15476-2	1113	Stone Fill	Not Available	Not Available
10	G15497-3	1116	Rubble Core	Pink 7.5 YR 7/4	None
11	G11274-1	910	Soil Fill	Light Red 10 R 6/4	Interior and exterior slipped Pinkish White 7.5 YR 8/2
12	G15461-1	1111	Rubble Core	Pink 7.5 YR 7/4	None
13	G11392-3	910	Soil Fill	Not Available	Not Available
14	G11464-3	961	Stone Fill	Light Brown 7.5 YR 6/3	Interior and exterior slipped Pinkish White 7.5 YR 8/2
15	G11056-2	907	Rubble Core	Light Brown 7.5 YR 6/3	Interior and exterior slipped Pinkish White 7.5 YR 8/2
16	G11349-2	915	Soil Fill	Light Brown 7.5 YR 6/3	Interior and exterior slipped Pinkish White 7.5 YR 8/2
17	G11441-2	961	Stone Fill	Light Red 2.5 YR 6/6	None
18	G17563-2	1111	Rubble Core	Pink 7.5 YR 7/4	Interior self slipped
19	G11180-1	915	Soil Fill	Pink 7.5 YR 7/4	Interior self slipped
20	G8115-3	864	Stone Fill	Pinkish Gray 5 YR 6/2	Interior and exterior slipped Pink 7.5 YR 7/3

21	G11274-3	910	Soil Fill	Light Brown 7.5 YR 6/3	Interior and exterior slipped Pinkish White 7.5 YR 8/2
22	G15472-1	1113	Stone Fill	Light Red 10R 6/6	Rim and exterior burnished; Interior and exterior slipped Pinkish White 7.5 YR 8/2
23	G11181-1	907	Rubble Core	Light Reddish Brown 2.5 YR 6/4	None
24	G11274-5	910	Soil Fill	Light Reddish Brown 2.5 YR 6/4	None
25	G15450-8	1113	Stone Fill	Light Brown 7.5 YR 6/3	Interior and exterior self slipped; paint on exterior and rim Dark Brown 7.5 YR 3/2
26	G11409-2	910	Soil Fill	Light Brown 7.5 YR 6/3	Interior and exterior slipped Pinkish White 7.5 YR 8/2
27	G8138-1	864	Stone Fill	Light Brown 7.5 YR 6/3	Interior and exterior slipped Pinkish White 7.5 YR 8/2
28	G15451-3	1111	Rubble Core	Light Reddish Brown 2.5 YR 6/4	Interior and exterior self slipped
29	G11180-5	915	Soil Fill	Gray 5 YR 6/1	None

Fig. 1.9b: Cooking pots from inside the stepped rampart

#	NUMBER	LOCUS	IDENTITY	DESCRIPTION	
				WARE	SURFACE TREATMENT
1	G17507-1	1116	Rubble Core	Reddish Brown 2.5 YR 5/4	Self slipped
2	G8242-7	845	Soil Fill	Red 2.5 YR 5/6, Pinkish Gray 5 YR 6/2	Self slipped
3	G15450-2	1113	Stone Fill	Reddish Brown 2.5 YR 5/4	Self slipped
4	G15405-1	1111	Rubble Core	Reddish Brown 2.5 YR 5/4	Self slipped
5	G11163-2	910	Soil Fill	Reddish Brown 2.5 YR 5/4	Self slipped
6	G15476-1	1113	Stone Fill	Reddish Brown 2.5 YR 5/3	Self slipped
7	G15451-1	1111	Rubble Core	Not Available	Not Available
8	G11047-1	909	Soil Fill	Reddish Brown 2.5 YR 5/4	Self slipped
9	G11441-5	961	Stone Fill	Reddish Brown 2.5 YR 5/4	Self slipped
10	G17574-1	1116	Rubble Core	Not Available	Not Available
11	G11163-1	910	Soil Fill	Reddish Brown 2.5 YR 5/4	Self slipped
12	G15481-2	1117	Stone Fill	Reddish Brown 2.5 YR 5/4	Self slipped
13	G11230-1	910	Soil Fill	Reddish Brown 2.5 YR 5/4	Self slipped
14	G17654-1	1147	Stone Fill	Reddish Brown 2.5 YR 5/4	Self slipped

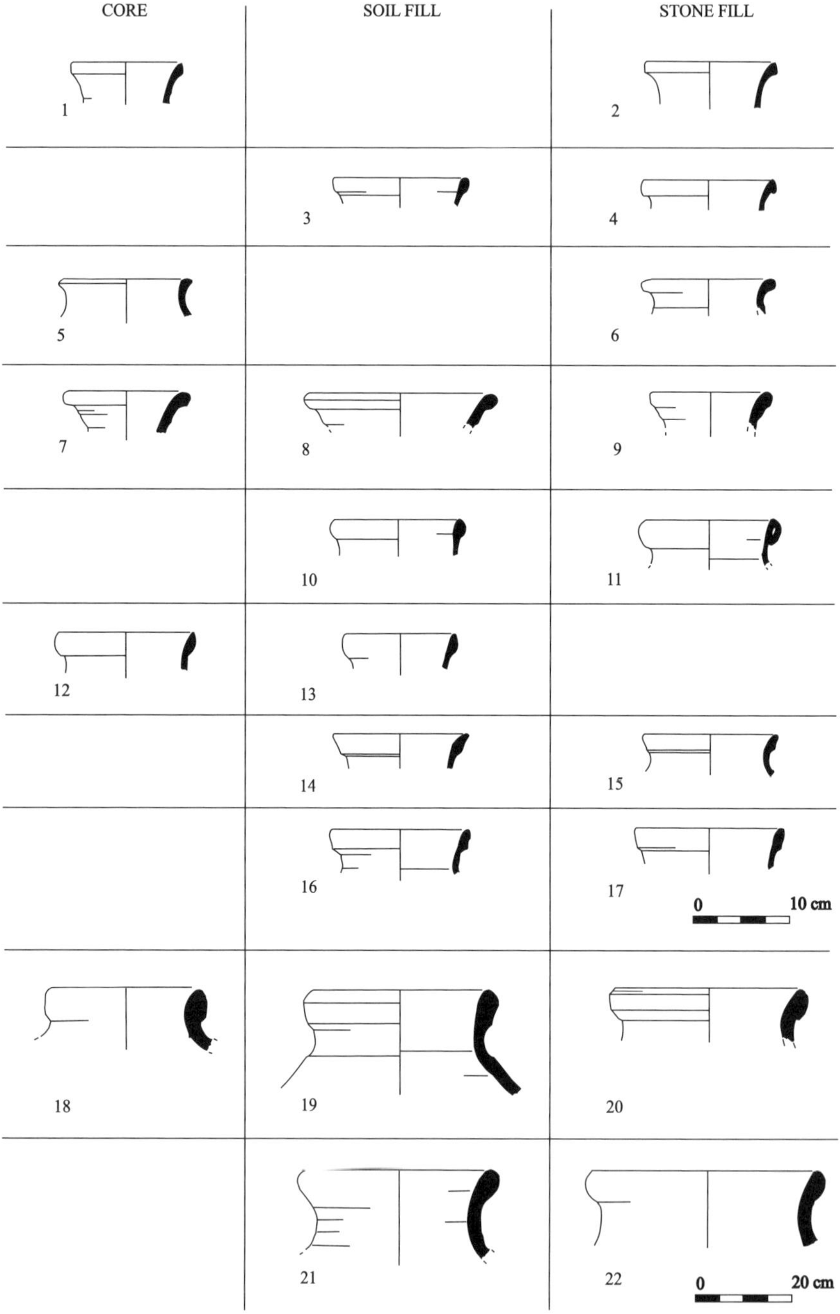

Jane M. Cahill

Fig. 1.10a. Jugs, jars, and pithoi from inside the stepped rampart

Fig. 1.10b: Jugs, jars, and pithoi from inside the stepped rampart

#	TYPE	NUMBER	LOCUS	IDENTITY	DESCRIPTION	
					WARE	SURFACE TREATMENT
1	Jug	G15451-2	1111	Rubble Core	Not Available	Not Available
2	Jug	G15460-1	1113	Stone Fill	Pinkish Gray 5 YR 6/2	Exterior slipped white 10 YR 8/2
3	Jug	G11204-4	909	Soil Fill	Gray 5 YR 6/1	Exterior slipped white 10 YR 8/2
4	Jug	G15450-12	1113	Stone Fill	Light Gray 10 YR 7/2	Exterior slipped white 10 YR 8/2
5	Jar	G17563-5	1111	Rubble Core	Gray 5 YR 6/1	Exterior self slipped; traces of dark painted band around neck
6	Jar	G8115-3	864	Stone Fill	Pinkish Gray 5 YR 6/2	Interior and exterior slipped pink 7.5 YR 7/3
7	Jar	G17563-4	1111	Rubble Core	Light Brown 7.5 YR 6/3	Interior and exterior slipped pink 7.5 YR 7/3
8	Jar	G11369-2	910	Soil Fill	Gray 5 YR 6/1	Exterior self slipped
9	Jar	G8138-2	864	Stone Fill	Light Gray 10 YR 7/2	Exterior slipped white 10 YR 8/2
10	Jar	G11043-8	910	Soil Fill	Light Red 2.5 YR 6/6	None
11	Jar	G15481-4	1117	Stone Fill	Not Available	Not Available
12	Jar	G11056-1	907	Rubble Core	Gray 5 YR 6/1	Exterior slipped white 10 YR 8/2
13	Jar	G11419-1	915	Soil Fill	Light Red 2.5 YR 6/6	Exterior slipped white 7.5 YR 8/2
14	Jar	G11047-4	909	Soil Fill	Pinkish Gray 5 YR 6/2	Exterior slipped white 10 YR 8/2
15	Jar	G17600-2	1118	Stone Fill	Light Red 2.5 YR 6/6	None
16	Jar	G11349-6	915	Soil Fill	Not Available	Not Available
17	Jar	G11441-6	961	Stone Fill	Pinkish Gray 5 YR 6/2	Interior and exterior slipped pink 7.5 YR 7/3
18	Pithos	G15497-1	1116	Rubble Core	Not Available	Not Available
19	Pithos	G11038-1	909	Soil Fill	Not Available	Not Available
20	Pithos	G15482-2	1118	Stone Fill	Light Brown 7.5 YR 6/4	None
21	Pithos	G11187-2	910	Soil Fill	Not Available	Not Available
22	Pithos	G17512-1	1117	Stone Fill	Not Available	Not Available

of the ceramic corpus is not yet complete, it is advanced enough to state with confidence that it is comparable to the ceramic corpora from Lachish VI, Tell Beit Mirsim B1 and B2, Gezer XIV–XIII, Izbet Sartah III, and Giloh.

The problem of dating the construction of monumental stone structures on the basis of underlying fills is complex and controversial.[108] Nevertheless, analysis of both the stratigraphic and the ceramic evidence suggests that the stepped rampart was built during the transition from the Late Bronze Age II to the Iron Age I. Analysis of the stratigraphic evidence demonstrates that the

---

appearance, but rather in its relative frequency in the assemblage." See Raphael Greenberg, "New Light on the Early Iron Age at Tell Beit Mirsim," *BASOR* 265 (1987): 55–80, esp. 71. For discussions concerning the early appearance of collar-neck pithoi in the final phase of the Late Broze Age II, see, e.g., Pirhiya Beck and Moshe Kochavi, "A Dated Assemblage of the Late 13th Century B.C.E. from the Egyptian Residency at Aphek," *TA* 12 (1985): 29–42; Larry G. Herr, "The History of the Collared Pithos at Tell el-ʿUmeiri, Jordan," in *Studies in the Archaeology of Israel and Neighboring Lands in Memory of Douglas L. Esse* (ed. S. R. Wolff; Chicago: Oriental Institute of the University of Chicago; Atlanta: American Schools of Oriental Research, 2001), 237–50; Ann E. Killebrew, "The Collared Pithos in Context: A Typological, Technological, and Functional Reassessment," in Wolff, *Studies in the Archaeology of Israel,* 377–98, esp. 379; and Avner Raban, "Standardized Collared-Rim Pithoi and Short-Lived Settlements," in Wolff, *Studies in the Archaeology of Israel,* 493–518, esp. 496–500. For the possibility that the collar-neck pithos made its initial appearance prior to the final phase of the Late Bronze Age, see Francis W. James and Patrick E. McGovern, *The Late Bronze Egyptian Garrison at Beth–Shan: A Study of Levels VII and VIII* (Philadelphia: University Museum, 1993) 5, 43, 74–75, fig. 32:4 (pithos with well-defined ridge in the collar recovered from Egyptian-style building at Beth Shean dated to the first half of the thirteenth century B.C.E.); and Michal Artzy, "Incense, Camels and Collared Rim Jars: Desert Trade Routes and Maritime Outlets in the Second Millennium," *OJA* 13/2 (1994): 121–47, esp. 136 (fragments of collar-neck pithoi recovered at Tel Nami from pits that preceded construction of the rampart ascribed to the thirteenth century B.C.E.). For discussions concerning the late appearance of collar-neck pithoi in the Iron Age II, see, e.g., Israel Finkelstein, "The Archaeology of the United Monarchy: An Alternative View," *Levant* 28 (1996): 177–87, esp. 182; Piotr Bienkowski, "The Beginning of the Iron Age in Edom: A Reply to Finkelstein," *Levant* 24 (1992): 167–69; and Israel Finkelstein, "Stratigraphy, Pottery, and Parallels: A Reply to Bienkowski," *Levant* 24 (1992): 171–72. For a general discussion concerning the continuity of Late Bronze Age II material culture into the Iron Age I, see Amihai Mazar, "The Iron Age I," in *The Archaeology of Ancient Israel* (ed. A. Ben-Tor; New Haven: Yale University Press, 1992), 258–301, esp. 260–62; and William G. Dever, "Ceramics, Ethnicity, and the Questions of Israel's Origins," *BA* 58 (1995): 200–213.

[108] For a recent discussion of the issue citing earlier treatments, see Shlomo Bunimovitz and Zvi Lederman, "The Iron Age Fortifications of Tel Beth Shemesh: A 1990–2000 Perspective," *IEJ* 51 (2001): 121–47, esp. 134–36.

stepped rampart stands directly above structures ascribable to the Late Bronze Age II and directly below structures ascribable to the first phase of the Iron Age II (ca. tenth century B.C.E.; see below). Analysis of the ceramic evidence in light of data currently available from other excavations demonstrates that the latest possible date for the ceramic assemblage recovered from the rampart's underlying fills is the early Iron Age I, approximately the twelfth century B.C.E.[109] Moreover, probes cut through the stepped mantle demonstrate both that it capped and sealed the rubble core, and that the rubble core was, in at least the area probed, bonded to stone fill retained by a substructural spine wall. Consequently, the stepped mantle, the rubble core, and the interlocking substructural terraces must have been contemporary and should be identified as component parts of a single structure. That such extraordinary architectural phenomena would be preserved within similar boundaries, contain identical pottery, and yet represent the remains of two distinct structures separated in time by three to four centuries, as advocated by Kenyon and Shiloh, is very unlikely.

Although the full extent of the stepped rampart and its substructural terraces have yet to be determined, the size and complexity of this monumental structure suggests that it was an integral part of the city's fortification system and that, as such, it may reasonably be reconstructed as having stretched east to the fortification wall located at mid-slope. Although, to date, remains contemporary to the stepped rampart have not been found on the crest of the hill above it, the rampart's size and structural complexity suggest that it skirted a fortress or citadel that housed the city's administrative-religious complex—that is, a feature that can reasonably be reconstructed as having occupied the highest point in town. The construction of the stepped rampart in Jerusalem during the transition from the Late Bronze Age II to the Iron Age I distinguishes Jerusalem from other hill-country settlements, invites comparison with sites such as Tel Miqne/Ekron in the Shephelah, El-Ahwat

---

[109] Other archaeologists familiar with the ceramic corpus recovered from the stepped rampart's underlying fills have also concluded that it should be ascribed to the Iron Age I, roughly the twelfth century B.C.E. See, e.g., Steiner, *Excavations in Jerusalem III*, 29; idem, "Re-dating the Terraces," 15; and comments made by Avi Ofer and Amihai Mazar at the Second International Congress on Biblical Archaeology in "Discussion," in Biran and Aviram, *Biblical Archaeology Today, 1990*, 628–30. Although absolute dates for the transition from the Late Bronze to the Iron Age have been notoriously difficult to establish, Ussishkin's discovery that Stratum VI at Lachish lasted at least until the days of Ramesses III indicates that the transition did not predate the twelfth century B.C.E. See David Ussishkin, "Levels VII and VI at Tel Lachish and the End of the Late Bronze Age in Canaan," in *Palestine in the Bronze and Iron Ages: Papers in Honour of Olga Tufnell* (ed. J. N. Tubb; London: Institute of Archaeology, University of London, 1985), 213–30, esp. 218–19.

near Wadi ʿAra, and Tell el-ʿUmeiri in Transjordan, where similarly dated—albeit not similarly constructed—fortifications have recently been revealed.[110] Construction of the monumental stepped rampart in the City of David at the dawn of the Iron Age set the stage for Jerusalem's future development as capital of the united monarchy.

DEVELOPMENT DURING THE PERIOD OF THE UNITED MONARCHY

The Old Testament account of Jerusalem's emergence as capital of the united monarchy names and describes various constructions that were either extant or added to the city, including the citadel of Zion, the temple, and the royal precinct. While the location of the temple and the royal precinct can reasonably be surmised and even their appearance can reasonably be reconstructed based on excavated remains from other sites, no archaeological remains in Jerusalem can be identified confidently with any of the structures named in the Bible.[111] Consequently, in recent years some scholars have challenged both the existence of the kings of the united monarchy as historical figures and the ascription of *any* archaeological remains in Jerusalem to the period of their rule.[112]

---

[110] For descriptions of the fortification wall found at Tel Miqne/Ekron, see, e.g., Trude Dothan, "Tel Miqne-Ekron: An Iron Age I Philistine Settlement in Canaan," in *The Archaeology of Israel: Constructing the Past, Interpreting the Present* (ed. N. A. Silberman and D. Small; JSOTSup 237; Sheffield: Sheffield Academic Press, 1997), 96–106, esp. 99; idem, "The Arrival of the Sea Peoples: Cultural Diversity in Early Iron Age Canaan," in *Recent Excavations in Israel: Studies in Iron Age Archaeology* (ed. S. Gitin and W. G. Dever; AASOR 49; Winona Lake, Ind.: Eisenbrauns, 1989), 1–22, esp. 6. For description of fortifications found at El-Ahwat, see Adam Zertal, "The 'Corridor-Builders' of Central Israel: Evidence for the Settlement of the 'Northern Sea Peoples'?" in *Defensive Settlements of the Aegean and the Eastern Mediterranean after c. 1200 B.C.: Proceedings of an International Workshop Held at Trinity College Dublin* (ed. V. Karageorghis and C. E. Morris; Nicosia: Anastasios G. Leventis Foundation, 2001), 215–32. For descriptions of the fortification system built at Tell el-ʿUmeiri, see, e.g., Larry G. Herr, "Tell el-ʿUmayri and the Madaba Plains Region during the Late Bronze-Iron Age I Transition," in Gitin et al., *Mediterranean Peoples in Transition,* 251–64; idem, "Tell al-ʿUmayri and the Reubenite Hypothesis," *ErIsr* 26 (1999): 64*–77*.

[111] For current discussions of the ability to locate and reconstruct the Jerusalem temple, see Avigdor Horovitz, "The Temple of Solomon" [Hebrew], in Ahituv and Mazar, *History of Jerusalem,* 131–54; and Ze'ev Herzog, "The Temple of Solomon: Its Plan and Archaeological Background" [Hebrew], in Ahituv and Mazar, *History of Jerusalem,* 155–74.

[112] See, e.g., Steiner, "Jerusalem in the Tenth and Seventh Centuries BCE," 283: "Based on the archaeological evidence Jerusalem of the tenth/ninth century BCE

Most doubts concerning the existence of David and his progeny as truly historic figures have been dispelled by discovery of stela fragments bearing an inscription written in Old Aramaic at Tel Dan.[113] The first and largest fragment was discovered in 1993 beneath a wall dated to the eighth century B.C.E.; two additional pieces were found in 1994.[114] Apparently raised by an Aramean ruler identified by Biran and Naveh as Hazael, king of Damascus, the stela's author boasts of victories over enemies.[115] Biran and Naveh reconstruct lines 7 through 9 of the inscription to assert: "[I killed Jeho]ram son of [Ahab] king of Israel, and [I] killed [Ahaz]iahu son of [Jehoram kin]g of the House of David."[116] Jehoram, king of the northern kingdom of Israel, and Ahaziah, king of the southern kingdom of Judah, were contemporaries whose reigns overlapped during the mid-ninth century B.C.E.[117] The inscription's reference to the "House [or dynasty] of David" suggests that the kings of Judah traced their descent back to an actual David. Synchronisms between the Bible and the historical records of Egypt and Assyria allow the reign of David (and his successor Solomon) to be dated to the tenth century B.C.E.[118] Although fragmentary and largely unpublished, stratigraphic evidence for the uninterrupted occupation of Jerusalem from the Iron Age I to the early Iron

---

can be described as a small town, occupied mainly by public buildings.... What is more significant: this centre was a new foundation. There had not been, in the centuries before the tenth/ninth, a town there at all.... [I]n the tenth or, more likely, the ninth century BCE a new town was founded [in Jerusalem], a town with impressive public buildings, but without large residential quarters, indicating that it functioned as a regional administrative centre or as the capital of a small, newly established state"; see also Ussishkin, "Jerusalem during the Period of David and Solomon," 57–58; and Israel Finkelstein, "The Rise of Jerusalem and Judah: The Missing Link," *Levant* 33 (2001): 105–15, esp. 105, where he states, "[I]n the tenth century BCE ... Jerusalem was no more than a small settlement limited to the old Bronze Age mound of the City of David," and argues that the stepped rampart's construction should be dated to the ninth—or possibly even the eighth—century B.C.E. [Editors' note: See also the essays by Ussishkin and Finkelstein in this volume.]

[113] Avraham Biran and Joseph Naveh, "An Aramaic Stele Fragment from Tel Dan," *IEJ* 43 (1993): 81–98.

[114] Avraham Biran and Joseph Naveh, "The Tel Dan Inscription: A New Fragment," *IEJ* 45 (1995): 1–18.

[115] Ibid., 17–18.

[116] Ibid., 13.

[117] Gershon Galil, *The Chronology of the Kings of Israel and Judah* (Leiden: Brill, 1996), appendix A.

[118] Ibid., 15–16. See also Kenneth A. Kitchen, "The Sheshonqs of Egypt and Palestine," *JSOT* 93 (2001): 3–12.

Age II (ca. twelfth/eleventh–tenth/ninth century B.C.E.) has come to light in almost every area excavated by Shiloh on the City of David's eastern slope but has not been found elsewhere in Jerusalem.

CITY OF DAVID

Stratified remains ascribable to the early Iron Age II have been found throughout the City of David's eastern slope, including, especially, Shiloh's Areas B, D, E, and G. In these areas this period is represented by at least three—and possibly four—stratigraphic phases, 15, 14, 13, and possibly 12, ascribed respectively to the twelfth/eleventh, tenth, ninth, and early eighth centuries B.C.E. The remains of these four phases evidence a secure period during which the city prospered and outgrew its previous boundaries.

AREA G

Analysis of the cultural and stratigraphic evidence from Area G suggests that soil fills found covering the stepped rampart contain pottery and artifacts that span the Iron Age I and that the two most extensively excavated Iron Age structures, the four-room House of Ahiel and the Burnt Room House, were both built on top of the stepped rampart early in the Iron Age II. Cultural evidence from Area G includes the remains of a cultic stand bearing the figure of a naked man with a pointed beard and long, flowing hair. Based on analogies to scenes depicted on North Syrian reliefs from Carchemish and Tell Halaf, the figure on this stand has been identified as Humbaba and the stand has been interpreted as depicting a specific Syrian version of the Mesopotamian myth of his slaying by the hero Gilgamesh.[119] Cultic stands bearing figurative reliefs are characteristic of the of the Iron Age I and early Iron Age II periods.[120] Stratigraphic evidence from Area G includes the disposition of the House of Ahiel and the Burnt Room House. In some places the foundations of these two structures were laid directly on top of the stepped mantle, in other places the foundations were laid directly on top of the rubble core, and in still other places directly on top of the rib walls and fills of the soil- and stone-filled substructural terraces. The disposition of these Iron Age structures demonstrates that the stepped rampart had been partly removed at the time they were built and suggests that it was purposely *dismantled* to

---

[119] Pirhiya Beck, "On the Identification of the Figure on the Cultic Stand from the City of David" [Hebrew], *ErIsr* 20 (1989): 147–48, 199* (English summary).

[120] Pirhiya Beck, "The Cult-Stands from Ta'anach: Aspects of the Iconographic Tradition of Early Iron Age Cult Objects in Palestine," in Finkelstein and Na'aman, *From Nomadism to Monarchy,* 352–81.

Fig. 1.11. Air view of houses built on top of stepped rampart. Photographer: Sylvia Owen. See also the photograph in Cahill, "David's Jerusalem," 40.

accommodate their construction—presumably after it had ceased serving a strategic function (see fig. 1.11).[121]

The earliest floor surface in the Burnt Room House is ascribed to Stratum 14 of Shiloh's stratigraphic sequence.[122] It yielded fragments of a Phoenician bichrome flask and an assemblage of local pottery that includes both unslipped, hand-burnished vessels and red-slipped, hand-burnished vessels (see figs. 1.12–13).[123] Immediately above the floor ascribed to

---

[121] For a similar proposal, see Franken, "Excavations of the British School," 133.

[122] For an explanation of the stratigraphic scheme employed for Shiloh's excavations, see Donald T. Ariel, *Excavations at the City of David 1978–1985 Directed by Yigal Shiloh, vol. II, Imported Stamped Amohora Handles, Coins, Worked Bone and Ivory, and Glass* (Qedem 30; Jerusalem: Institute of Archaeology, Hebrew University of Jerusalem, 1990), xi–xii.

[123] For recent discussions of Phoenician bichrome pottery, see Ayelet Gilboa, "The Dynamics of Phoenician Bichrome Pottery: A View from Tel Dor," *BASOR* 316 (1999): 1–22; idem, "Iron I–IIA Pottery Evolution at Dor—Regional Contexts and the Cypriot Connection," in Gitin et al., *Mediterranean Peoples in Transition,* 413–25; idem, "New Finds at Tel Dor and the Beginning of Cypro-Geometric

Fig. 1.12. Stratum 14 floor. Photographer: Sylvia Owen

Stratum 14 lay a floor ascribed to Stratum 13. It yielded fragments of a Cypro-Phoenician Black-on-Red juglet and an assemblage of local pottery typologically similar to that found on the Stratum 14 floor (see fig. 1.14). Above the Stratum 13 floor lay still another floor ascribed to Stratum 12b. While the neighboring House of Ahiel appears to have produced a sequence of only two floors spanning the same period of time as the three floors found in the Burnt Room House, the earliest of these two floors is ascribed to Stratum 14 based both on its stratigraphic position immediately above remains of the stepped rampart and on the accompanying ceramic assemblage.

The stratigraphic evidence from both the Burnt Room House and the House of Ahiel demonstrates that rather than having been built at the time of David and Solomon, as suggested by Kenyon and Shiloh, the stepped rampart was partly removed and new structures were built over it.[124] The

Pottery Import to Palestine," *IEJ* 39 (1989): 204–18. For a recent discussion of red-slipped and burnished pottery citing earlier literature, see Mazar, "On the Appearance of Red Slip," 368–78.

[124] The recent publication of Kenyon's excavations in Squares AI–III and XXIII and Trench 1 appears to corroborate this conclusion. See Steiner, *Excavations in*

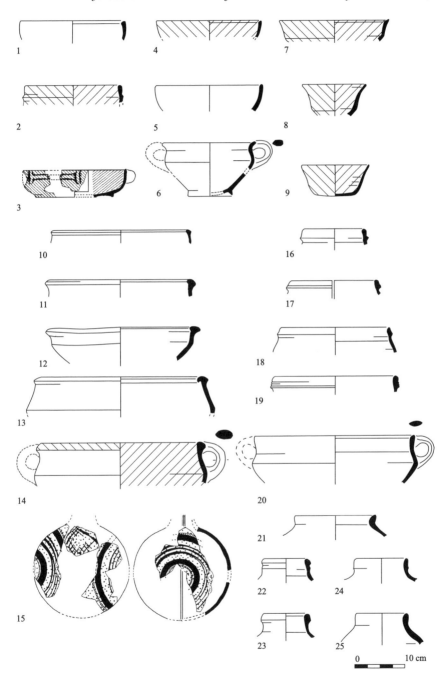

Fig. 1.13a. Pottery from Stratum 14 floor (see also fig. 1.13b)

Fig. 1.13b: Pottery from Stratum 14 floor

#	TYPE	NUMBER	LOCUS	ARAD STRATUM 12 COMPARISON*	DESCRIPTION	
					WARE	SURFACE TREATMENT
1	Bowl	G17648-7	1146	fig. 1:1	Reddish Brown 2.5 YR 5/4	Interior and exterior self slipped; interior and exterior horizontal hand burnish
2	Bowl	G4839-3	829	fig. 1:9	Light Reddish Brown 5 YR 6/4	Interior and exterior slipped Light Red 10 R 6/6 and horizontal hand burnish
3	Bowl	G17646-3	1146	None	Light Reddish Brown 2.5 YR 6/4	Interior and exterior slipped Red 10 R 4/6 and Reddish Brown 5 YR 5/4 and interior hand burnished
4	Bowl	G17648-2	1146	figs. 5:4-6	Light Reddish Brown 2.5 YR 6/4	Interior and exterior slipped Red 10 R 5/6 and horizontal hand burnish
5	Bowl	G11855-6	983	figs. 5:4-6	Reddish Brown 2.5 YR 5/4	Interior and exterior self slipped and horizontal hand burnish
6	Krater	G17644-3	1146	None	Light Reddish Brown 2.5 YR 6/4	Interior and exterior slipped White 10 YR 8/2
7	Bowl	G11741-5	987A	figs. 5:1-2	Light Reddish Brown 2.5 YR 6/4	Interior and exterior slipped Red 10 R 5/6 and horizontal hand burnish
8	Goblet	G17648-3	1146	None	Light Reddish Brown 2.5 YR 6/4	Interior and exterior slipped Red 10 R 4/6 and hand burnished to high gloss
9	Bowl	G11741-6	987A	None	Light Brown 7.5 YR 6/4	Interior and exterior slipped Light Reddish Brown 2.5 YR 6/4; interior horizontal hand burnish
10	Bowl	G17648-15	1146	figs. 1:6, 15, 17	Light Reddish Brown 2.5 YR 6/4	Interior and exterior self slipped; interior and rim hand burnished

#	TYPE	NUMBER	LOCUS	ARAD STRATUM 12 COMPARISON	DESCRIPTION	
					WARE	SURFACE TREATMENT
11	Krater	G17644-6	1146	fig. 1:5	Reddish Brown 2.5 YR 5/4	Interior and exterior self slipped
12	Krater	G11741-1	987A	fig. 1:19	Pink 7.5 YR 7/3	Interior and exterior self slipped; interior and rim hand burnished
13	Krater	G11741-4	987A	fig. 1:7	Reddish Brown 2.5 YR 5/4	Self slipped
14	Krater	G17666-1	1146	None	Pink 5 YR 7/4	Interior, rim and handle slipped Pale Red 10 R 6/4 and horizontal hand burnish
15	Flask	G17646-9	1146	None	Light Reddish Brown 5 YR 6/4	Exterior slipped White 10 YR 8/1; Paint: Dark Gray 5 YR 4/1 and Yellowish Red 5 YR 5/6
16	Cooking Pot	G17646-4	1146	fig. 2:1	Reddish Brown 2.5 YR 5/4	Self slipped
17	Cooking Pot	G17652-1	1149	figs. 2:4; 5:10	Reddish Brown 2.5 YR 4/3	Self slipped
18	Cooking Pot	G17653-1	1150	figs. 2:8; 5:10	Brown 7.5 YR 5/3	Self slipped
19	Cooking Pot	G17648-4	1146	fig. 2:2	Light Reddish Brown 5 YR 6/4	Self slipped
20	Cooking Pot	G4769-3	820	fig. 2:16	Weak Red 10 R 5/4	Self slipped
21	Store Jar	G11855-4	983	figs. 3:9; 5:15	Light Reddish Brown 2.5 YR 6/3	Self slipped
22	Store Jar	G17651-1	1146	None	Pale Red 10 R 6/4	Self slipped
23	Store Jar	G11855-5	983	fig. 3:11	Light Reddish Brown 5 YR 6/4	Exterior slipped Pink 7.5 YR 7/3
24	Store Jar	G11741-3	987A	fig. 3:12	Light Reddish Brown 5 YR 6/4	Self slipped
25	Store Jar	G11741-2	987A	fig. 3:10	Light Reddish Brown 5 YR 6/4	Self slipped

* Miriam Aharoni, "The Pottery of Strata 12–11 of the Iron Age Citadel at Arad," [Hebrew], *ErIsr* 15 (1981): 181–204, 82* (English summary).

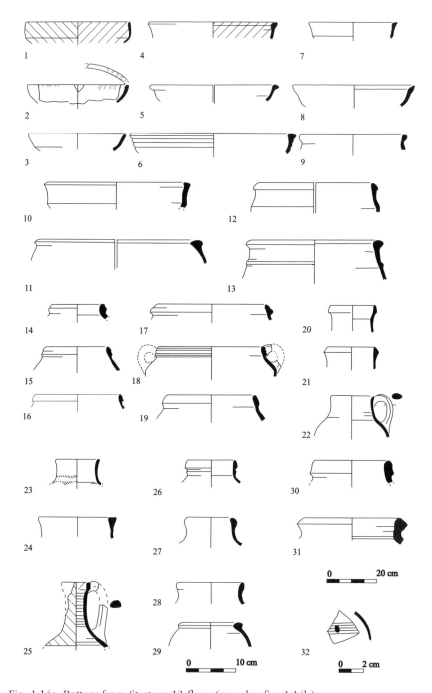

Fig. 1.14a. Pottery from Stratum 13 floor (see also fig. 1.14b)

Figure 1.14b: Pottery from Stratum 13 floor

#	TYPE	NUMBER	LOCUS	ARAD* LACHISH V** COMPARISON	DESCRIPTION	
					WARE	SURFACE TREATMENT
1	Bowl	G11639-3	962	1:14 (12) 3.10:1, 6	Light Reddish Brown 2.5 YR 6/4	Interior and exterior slipped Red 2.5 YR 4/6 and hand burnish
2	Bowl	G11783-6	972	6:2-3 (11) 3.5:1	Light Reddish Brown 2.5 YR 6/4	Interior and exterior self slipped and hand burnished; rim parallel lines of paint Weak Red 10 R 4/3
3	Bowl	G11294-7	972	6:4-6 (11) 3.5:2; 3.19:6	Reddish Brown 2.5 YR 5/4	Self slipped
4	Bowl	G11584-35	962	1:19 (12) 3.13:7; 3.17:1	Light Brown 7.5 YR 6/3	Interior slipped Pink 7.5 YR 7/3 and horizontal hand burnish
5	Bowl	G11584-8	962	6:13 (11) 3.17:4	Interior: Red 2.5 YR 5/6; Exterior: Pinkish Gray 7.5 YR 6/2	Interior and rim self slipped and hand burnished
6	Bowl	G11760-1	972	None 3.8:12, 19	Reddish Brown 2.5 YR 5/4	Interior and exterior self slipped and hand burnished
7	Bowl	G17604-4	1139	10:1 (11) 3.11:1	Reddish Brown 2.5 YR 5/4	Interior and exterior self slipped and hand burnished
8	Bowl	G11584-3	962	6:9, 11 (11) 3.8:20	Light Reddish Brown 2.5 YR 6/4	Interior and rim self slipped and hand burnished
9	Bowl	G11468-2	962	None None	Pink 7.5 YR 7/4	Interior and exterior slipped White 10 YR 8/2
10	Krater	G11468-3	962	6:17 (11) 3.17:5	Pink 7.5 YR 7/3	Interior and exterior self slipped and rim hand burnished
11	Krater	G11760-3	972	1:6, 15,17 (12) 3.26:5	Pink 7.5 YR 7/3	Interior and exterior self slipped; interior and rim hand burnished

#	TYPE	NUMBER	LOCUS	ARAD LACHISH V COMPARISON	DESCRIPTION	
					WARE	SURFACE TREATMENT
12	Krater	G17604-2	1139	None 3.26:7	Pale Red 10 R 6/4	Interior and exterior self slipped and hand burnished
13	Krater	G11760-2	972	8:9, 13 (11) 3.30:2; 3.31:1	Pink 7.5 YR 7/3	None
14	Cooking Pot	G17612-3	1139	2:3 (12) 3.39:3	Reddish Yellow 5 YR 6/6; Reddish Brown 2.5 YR 5/4	Interior and exterior self slipped
15	Cooking Pot	G11783-5	972	2:12 (12) 3.38:1	Not Available	Not Available
16	Cooking Pot	G17611-2	1139	2:9 (12) 3.40:2	Reddish Yellow 5 YR 6/6; Reddish Brown 2.5 YR 5/4	Interior and exterior self slipped
17	Cooking Pot	G11783-8	972	7:2 (11) 3.38:3	Red 2.5 YR 5/6; Very Pale Brown 10 YR 8/2	Interior and exterior self slipped
18	Cooking Pot	G11804-4	977	10:2 (11) 3.38:4	Reddish Yellow 5 YR 6/6; Reddish Brown 2.5 YR 5/4	Interior and exterior self slipped
19	Cooking Pot	G11742-3	972	7:1 (11) None	Reddish Yellow 5 YR 6/6; Reddish Brown 2.5 YR 5/4	Interior and exterior self slipped
20	Cooking Jug	G17604-8	1139	5:7 (12) 3.44:4	Reddish Brown 2.5 YR 5/4	Self slipped
21	Cooking Jug	G11584-41	962	7:3-4 (11) 3.44:11	Reddish Brown 2.5 YR 5/4	Self slipped
22	Cooking Jug	G17612-4	1139	7:5 (11) 3.44:16	Reddish Brown 2.5 YR 5/4	Self slipped
23	Amphoriskos	G11584-6	962	7:8; 9:10 (11) None	Light Reddish Brown 5 YR 6/4	Self slipped; two horizontal bands Weak Red 10 R 4/3
24	Jug	G11522-6	962	8:1 (11) None	Pinkish Gray 7.5 YR 7/2	Red paint on neck 10 R 4/2

#	TYPE	NUMBER	LOCUS	ARAD LACHISH V COMPARISON	DESCRIPTION	
					WARE	SURFACE TREATMENT
25	Jug	G11742-1	972	None / None	Light Reddish Brown 2.5 YR 6/4	Exterior and inside of rim slipped Light Red 2.5 YR 6/6 and exterior vertical hand burnish
26	Store Jar	G11584-5	962	None / 3.53:1	Reddish Brown 2.5 YR 5/4	Self slipped
27	Store Jar	G11552-2	962	3:13; 4:3 (12) / None	Pale Red 10 R 6/4	Exterior self slipped
28	Store Jar	G11639-16	962	8:7 (11) / 3.46:1- 2	Pink 7.5 YR 7/3	Exterior self slipped
29	Store Jar	G11804-6	977	8:10 (11) / 3.54:3	Light Reddish Brown 5 YR 6/4	Exterior self slipped
30	Pithos	G11639-2	962	8:11 (11) / None	Pink 7.5 YR 7/3	Exterior self slipped
31	Pithos	G11783-14	972	8:8 (11) / None	Pinkish Gray 7.5 YR 7/2	Exterior self slipped
32	Black on Red Juglet	G11639-6	962	None / None	Light Reddish Brown 2.5 YR 6/4	Exterior slipped Red 5/6 and painted Black 2.5 YR N2.5/

Aharoni, "Pottery of Strata 12–11," 181–204, 82 (English summary). The first number refers to the figure in Aharoni; the number in parentheses refers to the stratum.

**Orna Zimhoni, "Lachish Levels V and IV: Comments on the Material Culture of Judah in the Iron Age II in the Light of the Lachish Pottery Repertoire," in idem, *Studies in the Iron Age Pottery of Israel: Typological, Archaeological and Chronological Aspects* (Tel Aviv Occasional Publications 2; Tel Aviv: Institute of Archaeology, Tel Aviv University, 1997), 57–178.

new structures are ascribed to Stratum 14 and dated, on the basis of the ceramic evidence, to the first phase of the Iron Age II, roughly the tenth century B.C.E.[125] Remains ascribed to Stratum 13 are dated to the ninth century B.C.E., and remains ascribed to Stratum 12b are dated to the early eighth century B.C.E. Although analysis of the ceramic corpus recovered from each of these strata is not yet complete, it is advanced enough to state that the local pottery ascribed to Stratum 14 appears to be closely comparable to that reported from Arad XII, a stratum that all commentators agree dates to the tenth century B.C.E.[126] The pottery from Stratum 13 appears closely comparable to that from Arad XI and Level V at Lachish, and the pottery ascribed to Stratum 12b appears closely comparable to that from Level IV at Lachish. Above the floors ascribed to these strata, another series of floor surfaces spans the second half of the Iron Age II period from approximately the late eighth/early seventh to the sixth century B.C.E. (Strata 11–10).

Areas B, D, and E

An early Iron Age stratigraphic sequence comparable to that discerned in Area G has also been discerned in Shiloh's Areas B, D, and E in places that were located both inside and outside the city's fortification wall.

Jerusalem III, 54–88 (reporting the discovery of structural remains dated to the Iron Age II built directly on top of either the mantle and/or the substructural fills of the stepped rampart), esp. 58 (reporting that these structural remains included floors bearing pottery attributable to the tenth century B.C.E.).

[125] For evidence that Yigal Shiloh had also reached this conclusion, see Yigal Shiloh, "Jerusalem: The Early Periods and the First Temple Period," *NEAEHL* 2:698–712, esp. 703, where, in discussing the stepped rampart, he wrote: "[P]arts of its [i.e., the stepped rampart's] base are buried under masonry and thin earth layers dating to the ninth century, *perhaps even to the end of the tenth century BCE*" (emphasis added).

[126] For the Arad pottery, see Miriam Aharoni, "The Pottery of Strata 12–11 of the Iron Age Citadel at Arad" [Hebrew], *ErIsr* 15 (1981): 181–204, 82* (English summary); and Ze'ev Herzog et al., "The Israelite Fortress at Arad," *BASOR* 254 (1984): 1–34. Even Israel Finkelstein, the chief proponent of the low chronology for the Iron Age II, maintains that "Arad seems to provide the only firm chronological landmark in the south between the early-twelfth and late-eighth centuries B.C.E. … [and that] … Stratum XII at Arad is therefore the only level in southern Israel, [and] possibly in the entire country, which can safely be dated, on its own merits, to the tenth century" (Finkelstein, "United Monarchy," 181). As observed by Amihai Mazar ("Iron Age Chronology: A Reply to I. Finkelstein," *Levant* 29 [1997]: 157–67, esp. 161), Finkelstein cannot rationally maintain that the ceramic assemblage from Arad XII dates to the tenth century B.C.E. but that all comparable assemblages date to the ninth century B.C.E.

INSIDE THE FORTIFICATION WALL

The best evidence of this stratigraphic sequence found inside the fortification wall comes from Area E1, where Stratum 15 of the Iron Age I is represented by accumulations of debris and poorly built walls containing pottery that is mostly datable to the eleventh century B.C.E.[127] Evidence of the subsequent Stratum 14 includes a multiroom building with pebble floors and small area interpreted as a cultic corner found containing the lower half of a fenestrated offering stand as well as two ceramic chalices.[128] In Stratum 13, the floors of the multiroom building were raised. Additional remains ascribed to Stratum 14 were also unearthed in Area E3 immediately north of Area E1.[129] As in Area G, the ceramic assemblages from Strata 14 and 13 in Area E1 are typologically similar and include vessels that are both unslipped and hand burnished, and red slipped and hand burnished.

OUTSIDE THE FORTIFICATION WALL

The best evidence of this stratigraphic sequence found outside the fortification wall comes from Areas B and D1, located south of Area E1 in an area that was partially excavated by Weill.[130] On a rock ledge in Area D1 located immediately east of a natural cave excavated by Weill, a series of five superimposed layers of debris almost 2 m deep was found containing large quantities of animal bones and pottery ascribed to Stratum 15. Above these layers of debris, distinguished by their color, texture, and content, were two layers of fill (L. 430 and L. 432) topped by the fragmentary remains of a beaten earth floor and a clay oven—all of which have been ascribed to Stratum 14.[131] Immediately north of this floor lay two additional Stratum 14 deposits: one in which a complete storage jar was found broken in a large cupmark (L. 423); and another in which a complete lamp was found (L. 426).[132]

In Area B located immediately east of Area D1, a sparse occupational level consisting of poorly built walls was ascribed to Stratum 14.[133] These

---

[127] Shiloh, "Jerusalem: The Early Periods," 2:702. For reference to architectural remains from this period found in Area E1, see Shiloh, *Excavations at the City of David I*, 26.

[128] Shiloh, *Excavations at the City of David I*, 12, pl. 21:2; idem, "Jerusalem, City of David, 1984," *IEJ* 35 (1985): 65–67, esp. 66; idem, "Jerusalem, City of David, 1982," 130.

[129] Shiloh, "Jerusalem, City of David, 1984," 67.

[130] For Area B, see Ariel and Lender, "Area B," 1–32. For Area D, see Ariel et al., "Area D1," 33–72.

[131] Ariel et al., "Area D1," 37–39.

[132] Ibid., 40–41, 119, fig. 14:8–9.

[133] Ariel and Lender, "Area B," 4–7.

walls and their associated floors were built close to three openings in the east wall of Channel II, at least two of which appear to have been blocked to facilitate their construction.[134] Ceramic and stratigraphic evidence recovered from each of these areas demonstrate that the extramural quarter was founded in the eleventh or tenth century B.C.E. and abandoned at the end of the eighth century B.C.E.[135] In contrast to the House of Ahiel and the Burnt Room House (Area G), the structural remains unearthed in the extramural quarter consisted of thin walls built of small fieldstones enclosing floors and fills containing ceramic assemblages consisting primarily of kitchenware. The quality of both these structural remains and their associated ceramic assemblages suggests that structures built in the extramural quarter served as dwellings for Jerusalem's less-affluent residents.[136] While evidence from the extramural quarter demonstrates that the city spread beyond its fortification walls on the southeast at least as early as the tenth century B.C.E., possibly even earlier, the time at which the city expanded to the north and west is still unclear and very controversial.

Temple Mount

Biblical tradition holds that David bought a threshing floor located outside the city and that Solomon built the temple there, on the hill located north of the City of David and known ever after as the Temple Mount. Kenyon discovered stratified remains that she interpreted as evidence for the Solomonic expansion of the city in three areas, all of which were located only a short distance north of the stepped rampart: Square A XVIII, Site H, and Site M.[137] In Square A XVIII Kenyon discovered a palmette (i.e., Proto-Aeolic) capital and a number of ashlar blocks that she dated to the tenth century "at the foot of the scarp on the eastern crest of the eastern ridge."[138] Despite the fact that Kenyon found the capital and ashlar blocks in destruction debris that could only have resulted from the Babylonian

---

[134] Ibid., 9, plan 4:106–4 and 106–6.

[135] Ariel and De Groot, "Iron Age Extramural Occupation," 158.

[136] See Alon De Groot and Donald T. Ariel, "Ceramic Report," in Ariel, *Excavations at the City of David V,* 91–154, esp. 93–94, 103, fig. 7:19–26, 113–21 figs. 11–15. Although Reich and Shukron have recently found the remains that they identify as a second fortification wall located closer to the floor of the Kidron Valley than the wall previously excavated by Kenyon and Shiloh at the mid-slope, they attribute their wall's construction to Hezekiah, ca. eighth century B.C.E. See Reich and Shukron, "Wall from the End of the First Temple Period," 14–16.

[137] Kenyon, *Digging Up Jerusalem,* 107–28; idem, *Jerusalem,* 54–62.

[138] Kenyon, *Jerusalem,* pl. 20; idem, "Excavations in Jerusalem, 1962," 16, pl. VIIIB; Steiner, *Excavations in Jerusalem III,* 48, 50.

conquest of 587/6, Steiner dates the capital and ashlars to the ninth century.[139] In Site H Kenyon discovered a short segment of a wall that she interpreted as part of a casemate fortification wall.[140] In Site M Kenyon discovered a layer of soil containing pottery ascribable to the tenth century B.C.E.[141] Kenyon dated the casemate fortification wall to the period of Solomon and interpreted it and the tenth-century pottery from Site M as evidence that the Solomonic expansion of the city to the Temple Mount (i.e., Mount Moriah) was confined to the hill crest.[142] Because details of Kenyon's discoveries remained unpublished for many years, and because no other evidence of contemporary occupation has been recovered from the City of David's hill crest, most scholars have long regarded Kenyon's interpretations of the remains that she dated to the tenth century B.C.E. from Sites H and M skeptically. A notable exception is Eilat Mazar, who has argued that Kenyon's discoveries indicate that David's palace was located in the vicinity of Kenyon's Site H.[143]

---

[139] Steiner, *Excavations in Jerusalem III*, 50, citing Yigal Shiloh, *The Proto-Aeolic Capital and Israelite Ashlar Masonry* (Qedem 11; Jerusalem: Institute of Archaeology, Hebrew University of Jerusalem, 1979), 11. Shiloh's date derived from his comparison of the Jerusalem capital to capitals found at Ramat Rahel, many of which were found in destruction debris dated to the sixth century B.C.E. (Shiloh, *The Proto-Aeolic Capital,* 21). Although Steiner uncritically accepts Shiloh's suggested date for the capital and discusses it in the chapter devoted to the tenth–ninth centuries B.C.E., she describes its find spot as follows: "In debris from the destruction of the city in square A/XVIII, Kenyon found some ashlars as well as fragments of a capital." Although Steiner does not discuss any finds from Square A/XVIII in the chapter dedicated to the Iron II Period (ca. ninth–sixth centuries B.C.E.), her "Phasing of all squares" dates the destruction debris found in Square AXVIII to 587 B.C.E. (Steiner, *Excavations in Jerusalem III*, 6, table 1.3). Additional evidence for ascribing the destruction debris containing the capital and the ashlar blocks to the Babylonian conquest is found in Kenyon's description of the capital's find spot as located immediately "beneath the 5th–3rd century deposits" (Kenyon, "Excavations in Jerusalem, 1962," 16).

[140] Kenyon, *Digging Up Jerusalem*, 115, pl. 37 (photograph); Steiner, *Excavations in Jerusalem III*, 48 (section drawing).

[141] Kenyon, *Digging Up Jerusalem,* 116.

[142] Ibid., 114–19.

[143] Eilat Mazar, "Excavate King David's Palace!" *BAR* 23/1 (1997): 50–57, 74; idem, "The Undiscovered Palace of King David in Jerusalem: A Study in Biblical Archaeology" [Hebrew], in Faust, *New Studies on Jerusalem: Proceedings of the Second Conference,* 9–20. Steiner's recent publication of Kenyon's discoveries includes a section drawing of the casemate wall but no pottery and does not include any information about the remains discovered in Site M (Steiner, *Excavations in Jerusalem III,* 48). While the section drawing published by Steiner

Similarly unclear is the construction date of monumental architecture found in excavations directed by Benjamin Mazar and Eilat Mazar immediately south of the Temple Mount. The earliest floors in building remains interpreted by Eilat Mazar as an Iron Age gateway leading into the royal precinct contained pottery dating to the eighth century B.C.E.[144] However, E. Mazar found a small black juglet sheltered between stones of the structure's foundation courses.[145] The handle attached to the center of the juglet's narrow neck, its small round body, and its button base all suggest that both the juglet and the construction date of the building remains in which it was found predate the eighth century B.C.E. Although the presence of this lone juglet in a foundation course is not sufficient to say with certainty by how long these building remains predate the eighth cenury B.C.E., the juglet itself is a type traditionally dated to the tenth century B.C.E. that is commonly found only at northern sites demonstrating connections with the Phoenician coast.[146]

WESTERN HILL

Similarly difficult to date is the time that the city expanded onto the western hill. Nahman Avigad's discovery of a fortification wall in the Jewish Quarter ascribable to the late eighth century B.C.E. proved conclusively that the western hill was not only occupied but fortified at that time. Nevertheless, his discovery that the wall was built over earlier structural remains left unresolved the question of when that occupation began. The stratigraphic report of excavations in Area A recently published by Geva and Reich demonstrates that the structures beneath the fortification wall exhibit more than one phase of occupation. Although the ceramic material from these structures has not yet been published, Geva and Reich

---

presents a plausible depiction of a casemate wall, the photograph of the same remains published by Kenyon is less convincing (Kenyon, *Digging Up Jerusalem,* pl. 37). If, however, Steiner has correctly identified the structural remains found on the bedrock in Squares H/II–III as components of the Middle Bronze Age fortification wall, then the structural remains found on the bedrock in Square H/I may plausibly be identified as an additional segment of the Middle Bronze Age fortification wall (Steiner, *Excavations in Jerusalem III,* 12–14, and 16 [Walls 50 and 51]).

[144] See discussion of Wall 4 in Eilat Mazar and Benjamin Mazar, *Excavations in the South of the Temple Mount: The Ophel of Biblical Jerusalem* (Qedem 29; Jerusalem: Institute of Archaeology, Hebrew University of Jerusalem, 1989), 9–12, photo 13.

[145] Ibid., 34 photos 61; 87, pl. 13:1.

[146] For a brief discussion of this type of juglet, see Zvi Gal and Yardenna Alexandre, *Horbat Rosh Zayit: An Iron Age Storage Fort and Village* (IAA Reports 8; Jerusalem: Israel Antiquities Authority, 2000), 66.

have concluded that occupation of the western hill did not predate the eighth century B.C.E.[147]

CONCLUSIONS

Archaeological evidence adduced from excavations in Jerusalem suggest the following reconstruction of how the city looked at the end of the period of the united monarchy. The focal point of the city would have been the temple built on the Temple Mount, adjoined by a precinct of royal and administrative buildings, none of which have been revealed, at least arguably because the Temple Mount is strictly off limits to archaeologists. To the south, the City of David would have retained many features from earlier periods to which new features were added. Features retained from earlier periods were infrastructural in nature. They included the Gihon Spring, the pool from which its waters were drawn, and its guard towers. Reich and Shukron's discovery of at least one floor surface dating to the final phase of the Iron Age built up to the exterior wall of one of these towers proves undisputedly that at least one of these towers remained standing until then.[148] The fortification wall built during the Middle Bronze Age also remained standing throughout the period of the united monarchy until it was superseded by later construction during the Iron Age II. Proof that the Middle Bronze Age fortification wall remained standing comes from Shiloh's discovery that large sections of it were incorporated into the fortification wall built during the Iron Age II and from Kenyon's discovery that structures were built up to its outer face during the Iron Age II. So, too, Channel II, which carried water from the Gihon Spring to agricultural terraces located along the City of David's eastern slope and ultimately to a reservoir located at the southern tip of the city, remained in use from at least the Middle Bronze Age through the period of the united monarchy—when some of its openings appear to have been blocked to facilitate the construction of dwellings along the City of David's eastern

---

[147] Hillel Geva and Ronny Reich, "Area A—Stratigraphy and Architecture, IIa. Introduction," in *Jewish Quarter Excavations in the Old City of Jerusalem Conducted by Nahman Avigad, 1969–1982* (ed. H. Geva; Jerusalem: Israel Exploration Society and Institute of Archaeology, 2000), 37–43, esp. 42. See also Alon De Groot et al., "Iron Age II Pottery," in *Jewish Quarter Excavations in the Old City of Jerusalem Conducted by Nahman Avigad, 1969–1982, vol. II* (ed. H. Geva; Jerusalem: Israel Exploration Society and Institute of Archaeology, 2003), 1–49.

[148] Reich (oral communication). See also Reich and Shukron, "Light at the End of the Tunnel," 32.

slope. Because only some but not all of its openings appear to have been blocked at this time, Channel II seems to have remained operable at least until Hezekiah's Tunnel was developed in roughly the eighth century B.C.E.

Also retained from an earlier period, but redesigned to serve a new function during the period of the united monarchy, is the stepped rampart. Presumed to have supported a citadel or palace-temple complex in the previous Iron Age I, the stepped rampart appears to have been purposely dismantled during the period of the united monarchy to facilitate the construction of a new residential quarter. The size of the houses known as the House of Ahiel and the Burnt Room House, the quality of their construction, and the presence of imported Cypro-Phoenician pottery on one of their floors suggest that these houses were built and occupied by Jerusalem's more affluent residents. Indeed, the size, quality of construction, and contents distinguish the dwellings built on top of the stepped rampart from those founded contemporaneously in the extramural quarter farther downslope. These differences suggest a stratification of early Iron Age society not previously evidenced in Jerusalem's archaeological record. Moreover, the disfigurement of the stepped rampart and the development of two new residential quarters, one on the skirts of the city's citadel or palace-temple complex and the other outside the city's fortification wall in proximity to its irrigated agricultural terraces, suggest developmental pressures caused by a growing population and a shift in the city's security requirements, pressures that appear to have been stimulated by an increasingly stable environment and expansion or relocation of the city's administrative-religious center farther north—or uphill—to the Temple Mount.

In sum, the archaeological evidence demonstrates that during the time of Israel's united monarchy, Jerusalem was fortified, served by two water-supply systems, and populated by a socially stratified society that constructed at least two new residential quarters—one located inside and the other located outside—the city's fortification wall. The administrative and economic strength required both to generate and to support the city evidenced by the archaeological record is best identified with the period of the united monarchy rather than with the subsequent period during which rulers of the rump state of Judah struggled to maintain their autonomy. The raised floor levels ascribed to Strata 13 and 12 of Shiloh's stratigraphic sequence evidenced in houses constructed during Stratum 14 are best interpreted as evidence of this subsequent period. Consequently, Stratum 14 of Shiloh's excavations in the City of David appears to evidence the time during which Jerusalem emerged as capital of Israel's united monarchy in the mid-to-late tenth century B.C.E.

POSTSCRIPT

Because nothing presented thus far engages recently proposed theories for down-dating remains traditionally associated with the period of the united monarchy at other sites—most notably Gezer, Megiddo, and Hazor—to the period of the Omride dynasty that ruled the northern kingdom of Israel during the ninth century B.C.E., one of the most topical issues pertaining to the period of the united monarchy remains unaddressed: How do the new theories advanced primarily by Israel Finkelstein and David Ussishkin of Tel Aviv University impact the current interpretation of Jerusalem's historical development?[149] The short answer, and the conclusion that should be drawn from the archaeological evidence outlined above is, they do not. Although the long answer will not and cannot be fully asserted until publication of both past and present excavations—in Jerusalem in general and the City of David in particular—is completed, the principle underlying the long answer is simple and relevant to all types of archaeological interpretation: theories based on negative evidence should never be preferred to theories based on positive evidence. Stated another way: absence of evidence is not evidence of absence, especially at sites such as Jerusalem that are located in hilly terrain.

Theories for down-dating archaeological remains traditionally associated with the period of the united monarchy at other sites are based, in large part, on arguments advanced by Israel Finkelstein regarding the development of Philistine pottery and the similarity evidenced by pottery recovered from the floor of the great compound at Tel Jezreel and level VA–IVB at Megiddo.[150] Theorizing that the evolution of Philistine pottery from its Mycenaean IIIC:1b-related monochrome origins through its bichrome apex and ultimate disappearance stretched from the late twelfth to the mid-tenth century B.C.E., Finkelstein concludes that the first Iron Age levels postdating its disappearance represent the period of the united monarchy dating to the mid-to-late tenth century B.C.E.[151] Based on the Bible's description of Jezreel as having been built by Ahab and destroyed during the course of Jehu's coup d'état, Finkelstein concludes that pottery recovered from the floors of the great compound excavated there under the direction of David Ussishkin and John Woodhead should

---

[149] See, e.g., Finkelstein, "Rise of Jerusalem and Judah," 105–15; Ussishkin, "Jerusalem during the Period of David and Solomon," 57–58 [Editors' note: see articles by Finkelstein and Ussishkin in this volume.]

[150] Finkelstein, "Archaeology of the United Monarchy," 177–87.

[151] Ibid., 179–80.

be dated to the mid-ninth century B.C.E.[152] Based on Zimhoni's observation that the pottery recovered from those floors was comparable to the pottery recovered from level VA–IVB at Megiddo, Finkelstein concludes that level VA–IVB at Megiddo—as well as comparable levels excavated at other sites such as Gezer and Hazor—should be down-dated from the mid- to late tenth to the mid-ninth century B.C.E.[153] Applying these chronological conclusions to the historical record, Finkelstein infers that Israel did not exist as a distinct ethnic entity in the Iron I period, that no Israelite state existed before the ninth century B.C.E., and that no Judahite state existed before the late eighth century B.C.E.[154] Using these conclusions to rewrite the occupational history of virtually every major site in Israel, Finkelstein has rocked the archaeological community by challenging the consensus of scholarly opinion regarding the historicity of the united monarchy.[155]

Previous challenges to the historicity of the united monarchy have been based primarily on historical-literary criticism of the Hebrew Bible.[156] Advocates of historical-literary criticism maintain that the stories of early Israel are literary rather than historical texts that were composed during either the Persian (ca. sixth–fourth century B.C.E.) or the Hellenistic period (ca. fourth–second century B.C.E.); to the extent that they possess any historical content, that content pertains to the Persian and/or Hellenistic periods.[157] Extreme advocates of historical-literary criticism maintain that to the extent stories of early Israel possess any historical content, that conent pertains only to the periods in which they were written. In other words, because the Hebrew Bible was composed during the postexilic period, the Hebrew Bible *does not and cannot* contain historical information about the preexilic period. Extreme advocates of historical-literary criticism argue that ancient Israel is not a historic reality but

---

[152] Ibid., 183.

[153] Ibid., 183–85.

[154] Israel Finkelstein, "State Formation in Israel and Judah: A Contrast in Context, A Contrast in Trajectory," *Near Eastern Archaeology* 62/1 (1999): 35–52.

[155] See Haim Watzman, "Biblical Iconoclast: Israel Finkelstein Tilts with Colleagues over the History of Early Iron Age Palestine," *Arch* 54/4 (2001): 30–33.

[156] See, e.g., William G. Dever, "Save Us from Postmodern Malarkey," *BAR* 26/2 (2000): 28–35, 68–69, citing earlier literature; Watzman, "Biblical Iconoclast," 30–33.

[157] See Richard Elliott Friedman, *Who Wrote the Bible?* (2d ed.; San Francisco: Harper San Francisco, 1987); William G. Dever, *What Did the Biblical Writers Know and When Did They Know It? What Archaeology Can Tell Us about the Reality of Ancient Israel* (Grand Rapids: Eerdmans, 2001).

rather a fictitious myth invented by biblical writers.[158] Extremists also argue that while archaeology may be a putative source of historical information, in practice archaeology is largely mute because archaeological data is scant, archaeological methodology is imprecise, and interpretation of archaeological data is subjective.[159]

Whether relying primarily on the interpretation of archaeological data or on critical interpretation of the Hebrew Bible, modern writers who have challenged the historical existence of the united monarchy cite archaeological evidence from Jerusalem—or rather a supposed lack thereof—in support of their historical conclusions.[160] In most cases, these citations are either grossly misleading, illogical, disingenuous, or all three.

Examples of grossly misleading citations to Jerusalem's archaeological record include assertions by various authors that the City of David was wholly unoccupied during the Late Bronze Age. In light of the six Amarna letters written by Abdi-heba, king of Jerusalem, these assertions have led to published articles proposing the Mount of Olives, the Temple Mount, and even sites located farther afield as the true location of Late Bronze Age Jerusalem.[161] Similarly misleading assertions have also been made regarding early Iron Age Jerusalem. The most extreme example of these assertions are those made by David Ussishkin, who maintains that following approximately 150 years of intense archaeological excavation Jerusalem has failed to produce any evidence of an occupational stratum, a fortification wall, or even of pottery ascribable to the period of the united monarchy. From these and similar assertions, Ussishkin and others conclude that the archaeological evidence contradicts the biblical descriptions of Jerusalem at the time of the united

---

[158] See, e.g., Philip R. Davies, *In Search of "Ancient Israel"* (JSOTSup 148; Sheffield: Sheffield Academic Press, 1992); Keith W. Whitelam, *The Invention of Ancient Israel: The Silencing of Palestinian History* (New York: Routledge, 1996); Niels Peter Lemche, *The Israelites in History and Tradition* (Louisville: Westminster John Knox, 1998); Thomas L. Thompson, *The Mythic Past: Biblical Archaeology and the Myth of Israel* (New York: Basic Books, 1999); V. Phillips Long, ed., *Israel's Past in Present Research: Essays on Ancient Israelite Historiography* (Winona Lake, Ind.: Eisenbrauns, 1999).

[159] Dever, "Save Us from Postmodern Malarkey," 28–29.

[160] See, e.g., David W. Jamieson-Drake, *Scribes and Schools in Monarchic Judah: A Socio-Archaeological Approach* (SWBA 9; JSOTSup 109; Sheffield: Sheffield Academic Press, 1987), 136–59; Finkelstein, "State Formation in Israel and Judah," 35–52; and idem, "Rise of Jerusalem and Judah," 105–15. For an alternative view, see Dever, *What Did the Biblical Writers Know.*

[161] See, e.g., Franken and Steiner, "Urusalim and Jebus," 110–11; Knauf, "Jerusalem in the Late Bronze and Early Iron Ages," 75–90.

monarchy.[162] These assertions—and the conclusions drawn from them—are not only grossly misleading because virtually every archaeologist to have excavated in the City of David claims to have found architecture and artifacts dating to these periods, but they are also illogical and disingenuous because they purposely ignore the limited contexts available for archaeological investigation in Jerusalem, sound principles of stratigraphic interpretation, site formation processes characteristic of all hill-country sites, and contradictory conclusions reached by archaeologists familiar not only with the published record but with the entire corpus of excavated material.

CONTEXTS AVAILABLE FOR ARCHAEOLOGICAL INVESTIGATION

Conclusions that Jerusalem was wholly unoccupied or—at most—the site of an impoverished village during the Late Bronze and early Iron Ages are grounded on assertions that Jerusalem's archaeological record has not produced monumental architecture constructed during these periods.[163] While Kenyon, Shiloh, and members of Shiloh's staff have long pointed to the stepped rampart—and/or its component parts—as monumental architecture constructed in Jerusalem during either (or both) the Late Bronze or the early Iron Age, the areas of Jerusalem in which one would except to find monumental architecture from these periods are either unexcavated or compromised by later building activity. The Temple Mount, the acropolis of Jerusalem throughout both the First and Second Temple periods, remains strictly off limits to archaeological investigation because it now supports Islamic monuments built during the late seventh century C.E. Unlike the Temple Mount, the area located above the stepped rampart— where the acropolis of the pre-Israelite city is thought to have been located—has been extensively excavated. However, this area has been heavily compromised by structures dating to the Roman, Byzantine, and early Islamic periods that have been found both on and *in* the bedrock. Kenyon found the City of David's hill crest so heavily compromised by

---

[162] Ussishkin, "Jerusalem during the Period of David and Solomon," 57–58; Steiner, "Jerusalem in the Tenth and Seventh Centuries BCE," 280–88.

[163] Ussishkin, "Jerusalem during the Period of David and Solomon," 58. See also Finkelstein, "Rise of Jerusalem and Judah," 105. The archaeological record in Jerusalem does not include palaces or city gates built of ashlar masonry like those ascribed to the period of the united monarchy at Gezer, Megiddo, and Hazor. If, however, suggestions to down-date the ashlar masonry at Gezer, Megiddo, and Hazor to the ninth rather than to the tenth century B.C.E. are correct, then there is no reason to expect ashlar masonry in Jerusalem during the tenth century B.C.E., and its absence cannot cogently be used as a reason for rejecting Jerusalem as capital of the united monarchy.

later building and quarrying that she lamented: "For all we know, the original height of the eastern ridge may have been appreciably above that of the surviving rock."[164]

STRATIGRAPHIC INTERPRETATION

Conclusions that Jerusalem could not have served as the capital of a united monarchy are grounded on assertions that Jerusalem's archaeological record has produced only meager—as opposed to significant—remains from the Late Bronze and the early Iron Ages despite the fact that it has been excavated extensively and significant remains from other periods have been found (i.e., the Middle Bronze Age II and the Iron Age II). Reasoning that significant remains from the Late Bronze and early Iron Ages would have been found had occupation during these periods been significant, Ussishkin, Finkelstein, and others conclude that the meager remains from the Late Bronze Age and the early Iron Ages preserved in Jerusalem's archaeological record prove that the occupation of the site throughout these periods was also meager. Yet, the so-called "meager" remains from the Late Bronze and early Iron Ages are comparable to and consistent with the remains of *every* other period evidenced in Jerusalem prior to the final phase of the Iron Age II. With the possible exception of the Early Bronze Age houses unearthed in Shiloh's Area E1, no complete building plan has been discerned for any structure except the House of Ahiel, which—according to the interpretation promulgated here—was built during the period of the united monarchy. The Early Bronze Age houses were preserved because they were built in a bedrock hollow that was subsequently bridged, and therefore sealed, by the Middle Bronze Age fortification wall. Apart from the sections of the Middle Bronze fortification wall cleared by Parker, Kenyon, and Shiloh and fragments of the Middle Bronze Age towers recently cleared by Reich and Shukron, building remains from the Middle Bronze Age consist solely of a few fragmentary beaten earth floors not unlike those recovered from the Late Bronze Age. Moreover, like the Early Bronze Age structures that Shiloh found in Area E1, the Middle Bronze Age floor surfaces found in that same area were preserved only because they were built in dips and hollows in the bedrock that were subsequently bridged, and therefore sealed, by buttressing added to the fortification wall during the course of the Middle Bronze Age. Structural remains from the Late Bronze Age are also fragmentary, built directly on bedrock, and preserved only when sheltered by outcroppings of bedrock and sealed by later construction of monumental architecture, such as the stepped rampart.

---

[164] Kenyon, *Digging Up Jerusalem,* 94.

The best preserved remains found on the City of David's eastern slope are those from the final phase of the Iron Age II. These remains are well preserved because they are remains of the last buildings constructed on the City of David's eastern slope prior to modern times. Following the destruction of Iron Age II Jerusalem by the Babylonians in 587/6 B.C.E., the buildings constructed on the eastern slope collapsed downslope, blanketing the hillside with loose stones.[165] During the subsequent Persian period, the stones of this collapse were covered by soil-filled terraces that sealed and preserved remains of the collapsed Iron Age II structures. Despite the fact that the City of David was not the only area of Jerusalem intensely developed during the Iron Age II, Iron Age II remains comparable to those found on the City of David's eastern slope have not been preserved anywhere else in Jerusalem because all other areas of the city experienced—and continue to experience—intense occupation in subsequent periods of history.[166]

SITE FORMATION PROCESSES

The topographic features that make comparisons between hill-country sites and lowland sites difficult also impact the significance that negative evidence should be accorded in hill-country sites. Prior to Shiloh's excavations, evidence for the earliest occupation in Jerusalem consisted solely of a few tombs and small quantities of Early Bronze Age pottery found on and near the bedrock in the vicinity of the Gihon Spring. Today the consensus of scholarly opinion is that settlement in Jerusalem began at least one thousand years earlier during the Chalcolithic period and that the Early Bronze Age settlement included rectangular broad-room houses like those found at many other contemporary sites. Although remains of an Early Bronze Age fortification wall have not been found, the existence of such walls at the hill-country sites of ʿAi and Tell el-Farah North and the discovery that segments of the city's Middle Bronze Age fortification wall were incorporated into the fortification wall built during the Iron Age II suggest that an Early Bronze Age wall might eventually be discerned in Jerusalem. Until recently, the consensus of scholarly opinion regarding Channel II and the Warren's Shaft water systems was that they were constructed during the Iron Age, but based on stratigraphic evidence revealed

---

[165] Kenyon, *Jerusalem,* pl. 9.

[166] Although substantial remains from the Iron Age II—including elements of the city's fortification system—have been found outside the Temple Mount, in the Jewish Quarter, and on Mount Zion, none of these areas has produced either a complete structure or floor surfaces bearing large assemblages of complete vessels comparable to those unearthed in the City of David.

during Reich and Shukron's recent excavations, the consensus of scholarly opinion now is that both water systems were used during the Middle Bronze Age, approximately one thousand years earlier than commonly believed only a few years ago!

CONCLUSIONS OF ARCHAEOLOGISTS FAMILIAR WITH THE FULL RECORD

Although some authors argue that Jerusalem has produced no occupation stratum, no fortification wall, and not even any pottery ascribable to the Late Bronze and early Iron Ages, virtually every archaeologist who has excavated in the City of David claimed to have found such remains. While detailed discussion of the stratigraphic and ceramic evidence for the City of David's occupation during these periods appears in the preceding pages, recent assertions that Jerusalem remained unfortified from the end of the Middle Bronze Age to the late Iron Age II remain to be addressed. Kenyon and Shiloh each excavated various segments of the city's fortification wall that they independently concluded had been built during the Middle Bronze Age and had remained in use until the Iron Age II. Their conclusions concerning the wall's longevity were based on their discovery of stratified ceramic assemblages containing Middle Bronze Age pottery associated with the wall's lower courses and stratified ceramic assemblages containing Iron Age pottery associated with the wall's upper courses. Although Kenyon theorized that evidence for use of the fortification wall during the intervening Late Bronze and early Iron Ages was lost to erosion, debris originating during these periods is more likely to have been purposely removed to allow for the wall's continued use. Kenyon and Shiloh each based the conclusion that the wall remained in use on intimate knowledge both of exigencies imposed by physical properties of the steep slope and of the published and the unpublished archaeological record. For example, Kenyon and Shiloh were each well aware that exigencies imposed by the steep slope produced archaeological strata that are similarly sloped, that are notoriously difficult to disentangle, and that—more often than not—preserve evidence only of an architectural feature's first and last periods of use. Ussishkin's conclusion that Jerusalem remained unfortified during the Late Bronze and early Iron Ages is diametrically opposed to Kenyon and Shiloh's conclusion that the Middle Bronze Age wall continued in use throughout the intervening periods. However, unlike Kenyon and Shiloh, who based their conclusion on sound principles of stratigraphic and ceramic interpretation, Ussishkin, without stating any reasons, cursorily rejects their conclusion as "unconvincing."[167] Examples of structures that have remained in use for

---

[167] Ussishkin, "Jerusalem during the Period of David and Solomon," 57–58.

hundreds, if not thousands, of years abound even in modern Jerusalem, such as the walls surrounding the Temple Mount, the Church of the Holy Sepulchre, the Islamic monuments on the Temple Mount, and the walls of the Old City. Conclusions reached by seasoned stratigraphers such as Kenyon and Shiloh, who were intimately acquainted with all the archaeological evidence, that infrastructural features of the ancient city such as the fortification wall and the underground water systems remained in use for long periods of time should not be rejected without either reasoned argument or any attempt to engage the vast quantities of unpublished data that all scholars know exist.[168]

Thus, the conclusions to be drawn from roughly 150 years of archaeological excavation in Jerusalem are twofold: (1) the absence of evidence is largely meaningless; and (2) evidence from new excavations in Jerusalem will always influence the development of new theories more than the development of new theories will influence the understanding of Jerusalem's development.

---

[168] Kathleen M. Kenyon, Benjamin Mazar, and Nahman Avigad all began their excavations in Jerusalem late in their careers, and all died without publishing the results of their excavations. Although Yigal Shiloh began his excavations in Jerusalem early in his career, he, too, died without publishing the results. Neither these excavators nor the institutional bodies that sponsored their excavations planned or prepared for the exigencies incumbent in publishing the results of their work posthumously. For an analysis of this need and the archaeological profession's failure to address it, see Jane M. Cahill, "Who Is Responsible for Publishing the Work of Deceased Archaeologists?" in *Archaeology's Publication Problem* (ed. H. Shanks; Washington, D.C.: Biblical Archaeology Society, 1999), 2:47–57. See also Steiner, *Excavations in Jerusalem III*, xv, describing some of the exigencies incumbent in publishing Kenyon's Jerusalem excavations.

The Rise of Jerusalem and Judah: The Missing Link[*]

Israel Finkelstein
Tel Aviv University

If one needs to summarize over a century of explorations in Jerusalem, the proper statement regarding the Bronze and Iron Ages would be that archaeology revealed evidence for major building activity in two periods only: the Middle Bronze II–III and the late Iron II (the eighth–seventh centuries B.C.E.). In both periods the site was heavily fortified, and measures were undertaken to provide it with a proper water supply.[1] The interval between these periods, which covers the Late Bronze, the Iron I, and the early Iron II (ca. 1550–750 B.C.E.), provides indications of habitation but almost no signs of monumental building operations.

The archaeology of Jerusalem in the intervening time span and the historical interpretation of the finds vis-à-vis the textual material have recently become a focus of fierce disputes.[2] In what follows I wish to present my own views on this subject, based on a fresh analysis of the

---

[*] This essay is a slight revision and expansion of an article that first appeared in *Levant* 33 (2001): 105–15.

[1] See, e.g., Hendricus Jacobus Franken and Margreet L. Steiner, *Excavations by Kathleen M. Kenyon in Jerusalem 1961–1967, vol. II, The Iron Age Extramural Quarter on the South-East Hill* (British Academy Monographs; Oxford: Oxford University Press, 1990); Yigal Shiloh, *Excavations at the City of David I, vol. I, 1978–1982: Interim Report of the First Five Seasons* (Qedem 19; Jerusalem: Institute of Archaeology, Hebrew University of Jerusalem, 1984), 26–29; Hershel Shanks, "Everything You Ever Knew about Jerusalem Is Wrong (Well, Almost)," *BAR* 25/6 (1999): 20–29; Ronny Reich and Eli Shukron, "The System of Rock-Cut Tunnels Near Gihon in Jerusalem Reconsidered," *RB* 107 (2000): 5–17.

[2] See, e.g., Hendricus Jacobus Franken and Margreet L. Steiner, "Urusalim and Jebus," *ZAW* 104 (1992): 110–11; Nadav Na'aman, "The Contribution of the Amarna Letters to the Debate on Jerusalem's Political Position in the Tenth Century B.C.E.," *BASOR* 304 (1996): 17–27; Margreet Steiner, "David's Jerusalem: Fiction or Reality? It's Not There: Archaeology Proves a Negative," *BAR* 24/4 (1998): 26–33, 62–63; Jane M. Cahill, "David's Jerusalem: Fiction or Reality? It Is There: The Archaeological Evidence Proves It," *BAR* 24/4 (1998): 34–41, 63.

fragmentary data that has thus far been published[3] and on adapting the finds to the low-chronology system for the Iron Age strata.[4] A prominent part of my analysis will be devoted to a reevaluation of the question of state formation in Iron Age Judah.

INTRODUCTION: FROM CHIEFDOM TO STATEHOOD

There is no question that in the second half of the eighth century B.C.E. the built-up area of Jerusalem expanded from the City of David to the Western Hill and the city reached its maximal size in biblical times.[5] At the same time dozens of settlements of all size ranks—from regional towns to small villages and tiny farmsteads—appeared in the hill country of Judah to the south of Jerusalem.[6]

There were several reasons for the sudden demographic growth of Judah. First, it seems that torrents of refugees who escaped the horrors of the Assyrian liquidation of the northern kingdom in 720 B.C.E. and the devastation of the Judahite Shephelah by Sennacherib in 701 B.C.E. settled in the highlands of Judah—both in the capital[7] and in the countryside. Second, in the 730s B.C.E., Judah (under King Ahaz) made a bold decision to

---

[3] The finds from the three major modern projects at the City of David (the excavations of Kathleen Kenyon, Yigal Shiloh, and Ronny Reich and Eli Shukron) have not yet been fully published. This is a major obstacle in any attempt to deal with the history of Bronze and Iron Age Jerusalem. [Editors' note: see the essays by Cahill, Steiner, Reich, and Shukron in this volume, where some of this material is published for the first time.]

[4] Israel Finkelstein, "The Archaeology of the United Monarchy: An Alternative View," *Levant* 28 (1996): 177–87; idem, "Bible Archaeology or Archaeology of Palestine in the Iron Age? A Rejoinder," *Levant* 30 (1998): 167–74. To avoid confusion, I have marked my dating of the finds (according to the low-chronology system) "LC" and other scholars' views (according to the conventional dating system) "CC." The chronology debate encompasses the strata of the eleventh–ninth centuries; there is no dispute over the eighth-century material. The reader should be aware that my tenth- and ninth-century strata have generally been dated to the eleventh and tenth centuries respectively. My Iron I also covers the tenth century B.C.E.

[5] Magen Broshi, "The Expansion of Jerusalem in the Reigns of Hezekiah and Manasseh," *IEJ* 24 (1974): 21–26; Nahman Avigad, *Discovering Jerusalem* (Nashville: Nelson, 1983), 31–60.

[6] Avi Ofer, "'All the Hill Country of Judah': From a Settlement Fringe to a Prosperous Monarchy," in *From Nomadism to Monarchy: Archaeological and Historical Aspects of Early Israel* (ed. I. Finkelstein and N. Na'aman; Washington, D.C.: Biblical Archaeology Society; Jerusalem: Israel Exploration Society, 1994), 92–121.

[7] See Broshi, "Expansion of Jerusalem," 21–26.

cooperate with Assyria,[8] and it was integrated into the Assyrian economic sphere. Possibly the most important result of this strategic move was to ensure that Judah played an important role in the southern trade network. As a result, the Beer-sheba Valley experienced a significant change and went from a sparsely settled fringe area to a relatively densely settled and well-protected region of the Judahite state. Third, as long as the northern kingdom prospered, Judah remained a marginal entity—a sort of client state—to its south. The fall of Israel and the establishment of direct Assyrian rule in the north of the country opened the way for the rise of Judah as one of the major players in the affairs of the Levant.

There is also no doubt that the situation in the tenth century B.C.E. was utterly different. Jerusalem was no more than a small settlement limited to the old Bronze Age mound of the City of David.[9] The finds from this period—according to both conventional and low dating—are meager and do not show any sign of Jerusalem being a prosperous capital of a large empire. The Judahite hill country was also relatively empty, inhabited by a small number of people who lived in a limited number of villages.

These have been the reasons for my recent proposal[10] that Judah reached full-blown statehood only in the late eighth century B.C.E., about a century and a half later than the northern kingdom.[11] But this theory, even if valid in the broad outline, faces two difficulties. First, it is illogical that Judah sprang into life from a void; there must have been a transition

---

[8] E.g., see Nadav Na'aman, "Hezekiah and the Kings of Assyria," *TA* 21 (1994): 235–54.

[9] David Ussishkin, "Solomon's Jerusalem: The Text and the Facts on the Ground," in this volume; Steiner, "David's Jerusalem," 26–33, 62–63. For a different interpretation of the finds that, apart from the polemical language, is *not* in total contradiction, see Cahill, "David's Jerusalem," 34–41, 63.

[10] Israel Finkelstein, "State Formation in Israel and Judah, A Contrast in Context, A Contrast in Trajectory," *Near Eastern Archaeology* 62/1 (1999): 35–52; Israel Finkelstein and Neil A. Silberman, *The Bible Unearthed: Archaeology's New Vision of Ancient Israel and the Origin of Its Sacred Texts* (New York: Free Press, 2001), 229–50.

[11] For Judah, see also David W. Jamieson-Drake, *Scribes and Schools in Monarchic Judah: A Socio-Archaeological Approach* (SWBA 9; JSOTSup 109; Sheffield: Sheffield Academic Press, 1991); Ernst Axel Knauf, "King Solomon's Copper Supply," in *Phoenicia and the Bible: Proceedings of the Conference Held at the University of Leuven on the 15th and 16th of March 1990* (ed. E. Lipiński; OLA 44; Studia Phoenicia 11; Leuven: Departement Oriëntalistiek; Peeters, 1991), 167–86; Hermann M. Niemann, *Herrschaft, Königtum und Staat: Skizzen zur soziokulturelle Entwicklung im monarchischen Israel* (FAT 6; Tübingen: Mohr Siebeck, 1993), 50–56.

phase between the two stages: the sparsely settled tenth century and the densely settled late eighth century. Second, certain finds in the Shephelah and the Beer-sheba Valley do not fit this scenario. I refer mainly to the massive building activity in Beth-shemesh (see below); to Lachish IV, the forerunner of Lachish III, which should apparently be dated to the second half of the ninth century;[12] and to the fortified sites of Beer-sheba V and Arad XI, which also date to the ninth century B.C.E.[13] There are two options here. (1) These sites belonged to Judah. In this case, the periphery of the kingdom would have shown signs of statehood prior to the late eighth century. (2) These sites were not part of the southern kingdom. With this scenario, we would need to find an alternative territorial formation that could have been responsible for their construction. Since I see no such alternative (below), there is no way out of the notion that we seem to be missing a link in the chain of events that led to the development of Judah into full statehood.

THE STONE TERRACES AND THE STEPPED STONE STRUCTURE

Before I start paging through the periods, I wish to comment briefly on two construction elements uncovered on the eastern slope of the City of David. I refer to the system of stone terraces, unearthed by both Kenyon[14] and Shiloh,[15] and to the "stepped stone structure" first excavated by Macalister in the 1920s, which partially covers the terraces.[16] Both have been mentioned time and again in relation to one or more of the "interval" periods; clarification of the confusion regarding their relationship— whether they were built together or in two different periods—and date is key for any discussion of the archaeology of Jerusalem from the Late Bronze to the early Iron II.

---

[12] For the remains, see David Ussishkin, "Excavations at Tel Lachish 1978–1983: Second Preliminary Report," _TA_ 10 (1983): 171–73; for the pottery, see Orna Zimhoni, _Studies in the Iron Age Pottery of Israel: Typological, Archaeological and Chronological Aspects_ (Tel Aviv Occasional Publications 2; Tel Aviv: Tel Aviv University Press, 1997), 57–178.

[13] LC; Finkelstein, "United Monarchy," 181.

[14] Kathleen M. Kenyon, _Digging Up Jerusalem_ (London: Benn, 1974), 95–96.

[15] Shiloh, _Excavations at the City of David I,_ 16.

[16] Margreet Steiner, "The Jebusite Ramp of Jerusalem: The Evidence from the Macalister, Kenyon and Shiloh Excavations," in _Biblical Archaeology Today, 1990: Proceedings of the Second International Congress on Biblical Archaeology_ (ed. A. Biran and J. Aviram; Jerusalem: Israel Exploration Society, 1993), 585–88.

Cahill and Tarler argued that the two were built together in the thirteenth–twelfth centuries B.C.E.,[17] while Kenyon, Shiloh, and Steiner proposed that they were built in two different periods. Kenyon[18] and Shiloh[19] dated the stone terraces to the Late Bronze Age and the stepped stone structure to the tenth century B.C.E. (CC). Steiner dated the stone terraces to the thirteenth–twelfth century and the stepped stone structure to the tenth or ninth century B.C.E. (CC).[20]

The following points are crucial for resolving the confusion:

1. A house with an Iron I collared-rim jar on its floor was uncovered *under* the stone terraces.[21]
2. A large quantity of Iron I sherds (in addition to a limited number of Late Bronze sherds) was retrieved from the construction of the stone terraces.[22] No tenth-century sherds (CC) were found there.
3. The stepped stone structure that covers the stone terraces yielded sherds from the tenth–ninth century.[23] It seems that the number of earlier sherds found between its layers was limited.
4. The earliest floor surfaces built above the stepped stone structure yielded tenth-century sherds.[24]

There are two options of interpretation here: if the two structures were built together, the ninth century B.C.E. (LC) is the only option for the construction date.[25] Yet the pottery assemblages retrieved from the two structures are utterly different: no ninth-century sherds (LC) were found in

---

[17] Jane M. Cahill and David Tarler, "Response to Margreet Steiner—The Jebusite Ramp of Jerusalem: The Evidence from the Macalister, Kenyon and Shiloh Excavations," in Biran and Aviram, *Biblical Archaeology Today, 1990*, 625–26.

[18] Kenyon, *Digging Up Jerusalem,* 95–103.

[19] Shiloh, *Excavations at the City of David I,* 16–17.

[20] Steiner, "Jebusite Ramp," 585–88; idem, "Re-dating the Terraces of Jerusalem," *IEJ* 44 (1994): 13–20.

[21] Steiner, "Re-dating the Terraces of Jerusalem," 13–20.

[22] Steiner, "David's Jerusalem," 29, 62 n. 5.

[23] CC—Steiner, "Re-dating the Terraces of Jerusalem," 19; idem, "David's Jerusalem," 30.

[24] CC—Cahill, "David's Jerusalem," 39.

[25] There is one difficulty here: Steiner, "Re-dating the Terraces of Jerusalem," 19, compared the "9th century" sherds (CC) from the stepped stone structure to the pottery of Kenyon's Phase 2 (Franken and Steiner, *Excavations in Jerusalem II,* 10–30), which should be dated, in the main, to the eighth century B.C.E. A verdict will be possible only with the full publication of the pottery.

the stone terraces, and only a few Iron I sherds were discovered in the stepped stone structure. This seems to indicate that the two were built separately. In that case, I would opt for an Iron I date for the stone terraces and a ninth (LC) or even eighth-century date for its renovation—the stepped stone structure.

THE LATE BRONZE AGE (CA. 1550–1150 B.C.E.)

It is difficult to estimate the size and nature of Late Bronze Age Jerusalem. Archaeologically, the meager Late Bronze pottery reported from the ridge of the City of David[26] is enough to indicate that the site was settled at that time.[27] But architectural remains from the Late Bronze Age have not yet been uncovered. Textually, we know that in the fourteenth century B.C.E. Abdi-heba ruled from Jerusalem over the entire southern hill country.[28] South of modern Hebron, Jerusalem dominated the sparsely settled hills, including the area around the second largest Late Bronze site in the southern hill country, Khirbet Rabûd.[29] The western border of Jerusalem ran along the slopes of the highlands, with the towns of the longitudinal valley of the eastern Shephelah (e.g., Qiltu/Keilah = Khirbet Qila) clearly belonging to the city-states of Lachish and Gath. It is reasonable to assume that in the north, Bethel belonged to the territory of Shechem, while Jericho was ruled by Jerusalem.[30] According to this reconstruction, Jerusalem

---

[26] Shiloh, *Excavations at the City of David I,* 26; Cahill, "David's Jerusalem," 34–35.

[27] Contra Franken and Steiner, "Urusalim and Jebus," 110–11.

[28] Israel Finkelstein, "The Territorial-Political System of Canaan in the Late Bronze Age," *UF* 28 (1996): 221–55.

[29] For the identification of this site with biblical Debir, see Moshe Kochavi, "Khirbet Rabûd = Debir," *TA* 1 (1974): 2–33. Nadav Naʾaman ("Canaanite Jerusalem and Its Central Hill Country Neighbours in the Second Millennium B.C.E.," *UF* 24 [1992]: 275–91) argued that the southern part of the central highlands was an independent entity, with its center at Debir. But apart from the fact that Debir is not mentioned in the Amarna archive, archaeological surveys indicate that it had no sedentary hinterland. It is also doubtful whether it was inhabited in the Amarna phase of the Late Bronze Age (see Shlomo Bunimovitz, "The Land of Israel in the Late Bronze Age: A Case Study of Socio-Cultural Change in a Complex Society" [Hebrew] [Ph.D. thesis, Tel Aviv University, 1989], 135). In any case, the excavations indicate that at most the Late Bronze settlement was small, sparsely built, and unfortified (see Kochavi, "Khirbet Rabûd = Debir," 2–33).

[30] A key town for the delineation of the borders of Jerusalem is Bit NIN.URTA of EA 290. For the different possibilities, see Finkelstein, "Territorial-Political System," 235 and bibliography.

controlled a territory of approximately 2,400 km². Only eight settlements have been recorded in this area, covering an estimated (Late Bronze Age) built-up area of less then 8 ha, that is, a population of about 1,500 sedentary people. This was the most sparsely settled region in Late Bronze Canaan. Abdi-heba ruled over a dimorphic countryside, with a mixed population comprised of a few sedentary communities and a large number of pastoral groups.

With no archaeological evidence available, one can only speculate that Jerusalem's built-up area did not comprise much more than a modest palace for the ruling family (apparently mentioned in EA 287),[31] an adjacent temple, and a few more houses for the local elite.[32] The dimorphic chiefdoms of the highlands in the Late Bronze Age—Jerusalem and Shechem—were different from the lowlands city-states both territorially and demographically,[33] so we should not expect their centers to have been big cities with massive monuments. The idea that major Late Bronze remains were completely destroyed by later occupational activity[34] should be rejected, since earlier monuments, mainly the Middle Bronze fortifications,[35] survived later building operations.

THE IRON I (CA. 1150–925/900 B.C.E.)

Iron I pottery, including collared-rim jars, found under and inside the terrace system on the eastern slope[36] and in other parts of the southeastern ridge,[37] indicates that settlement activity in the City of David was quite

---

[31] William L. Moran, *The Amarna Letters* (Baltimore: Johns Hopkins University Press, 1992), 327–29.

[32] Knauf's appealing proposal (Ernst Axel Knauf, "Jerusalem in the Late Bronze and Early Iron Ages: A Proposal," *TA* 27 [2000]: 75–90) that the core of the Late Bronze and Iron I settlement should be sought on the highest point of the ridge—the Temple Mount—cannot be accepted, since excavations around it to the west and south did not yield any sign for Late Bronze activity.

[33] Israel Finkelstein, "The Sociopolitical Organization of the Central Hill Country in the Second Millennium B.C.E.," in *Biblical Archaeology Today, 1990, Precongress Symposium: Population, Production and Power* (ed. A. Biran and J. Aviram; Jerusalem: Israel Exploration Society, 1993), 119–31.

[34] Na'aman, "Contribution of the Amarna Letters," 17–27; Cahill, "David's Jerusalem," 36.

[35] See, e.g., Shanks, "Everything You Ever Knew," 20–29.

[36] Steiner, "Re-dating of the Terraces of Jerusalem," 13–20; idem, "David's Jerusalem," 29.

[37] Shiloh, *Excavations at the City of David I,* 26.

intensive. According to my new analysis of the ceramic chronology,[38] the Iron I pottery of the highlands probably covers most of the tenth century as well.[39] The stone terraces on the eastern slope could have been built anytime between the late twelfth and the early tenth century (LC). They probably functioned as a support for a significant construction effort up-slope. Ironically then, the low-chronology system provides more evidence for tenth-century Jerusalem than the conventional dating of the Iron Age strata.[40]

It is reasonable to assume that the Jerusalem of the Iron I, like the fourteenth-century stronghold of Abdi-heba, continued to rule over the dimorphic southern highlands. The only difference is a modest though meaningful growth in the number of settlements, both to the south of the city, where the number of sites doubled to almost twenty,[41] and even more so to its north, where a relatively large number of sites had newly been established.[42] Most of the area to the south of Jerusalem was still comprised of woodlands and steppelands that were exploited by pastoral groups.

Textually, we have little reliable information about Iron I Jerusalem. The story of the conquest of Jebus by David cannot be considered a straightforward historical testimony. Most probably, ancient folktales, the core of which are impossible to trace, were manipulated by the Deuteron-omistic Historian in order to describe the way in which the Davidic dynasty established itself in Jerusalem.[43] The biblical description of Jerusalem in

---

[38] Finkelstein, "United Monarchy," 177–87; idem, "Bible Archaeology," esp. 171–72.

[39] I refer to the collared-rim jars and more so to several types that are described as "Iron I–II" in Israel Finkelstein et al., *Highlands of Many Cultures: The Southern Samaria Survey: The Sites* (Monograph Series of the Sonia and Marco Nadler Institute of Archaeology 14; Tel Aviv: Institute of Archaeology, Tel Aviv University, 1997), 18. Note that this publication still uses the conventional dating system.

[40] Needless to say, the finds debated by Cahill, "David's Jerusalem," 34–41, 63, and Steiner, "David's Jerusalem," 26–33, 62–63, as representing the tenth century should stand for the ninth century B.C.E. (see below).

[41] See Ofer, "Hill Country of Judah," 102 for the Iron I.

[42] Israel Finkelstein and Izchak Magen, *Archaeological Survey of the Hill Country of Benjamin* (Jerusalem: Israel Antiquities Authority, 1993).

[43] Even if the *ṣinnôr* of 2 Sam 5:8 should be translated as "water tunnel," "water conduit," or "shaft" (for the latest and bibliography, see Svend Holm-Nielsen, "Did Joab Climb 'Warren's Shaft'?" in *History and Traditions of Early Israel* [ed. A. Lemaire and B. Otzen; Leiden: Brill, 1993], 38–49), it only means that the people of late monarchic Jerusalem knew the water systems on the east slope of the City of David.

the days of Solomon as an illustrious capital of a glamorous empire should be seen as a picture of an idyllic golden age. As such, they are wrapped in later theological and ideological goals and thus based on very little original material.[44] At the same time, the fact that David was the founder of the dynasty in Jerusalem cannot be challenged, since the Tel Dan Stela refers to Judah as "the house of David."[45]

Yet the settlement and demographic picture that emerges from the cycle of stories about the activity of David and his band in the south does contain, so it seems, valuable information. These narratives certainly reflect a pre-eighth-century fringe landscape in southern Judah. In late monarchic times this area had already been densely settled, so there was no way for the Deuteronomistic Historian to portray this kind of activity in the periphery of the Judean hills. I would therefore propose that these stories represent early materials—probably preserved as oral folktales—that were incorporated into the later text.[46] Although they were adjusted to the goals of the later writers, we may still be able to identify in them the action of a local chieftain who moves with his gang to the south of Hebron, in the Judean Desert and in the Shephelah, far from the control of central government in the highlands farther to the north. David takes over Hebron, the second most important Iron Age town in the highlands of Judah[47] and

---

[44] See, e.g., John Van Seters, *In Search of History: Historiography in the Ancient World and the Origins of Biblical History* (New Haven: Yale University Press, 1983), 307–12; J. Maxwell Miller, "Separating the Solomon of History from the Solomon of Legend," in *The Age of Solomon: Scholarship at the Turn of the Millennium* (ed. L. K. Handy; Leiden: Brill, 1997), 1–24; Hermann M. Niemann, "The Socio-Political Shadow Cast by Biblical Solomon," in Handy, *Age of Solomon,* 252–95.

[45] Avraham Biran and Joseph Naveh, "An Aramaic Stele Fragment from Tel Dan," *IEJ* 43 (1993): 93.

[46] On pre-Deuteronomistic layers in the Deuteronomistic History (which include the rise of David narratives), see, e.g., Alexander Rofé, "Ephraimite versus Deuteronomistic History," in *Storia e tradizioni di Israele* (Brescia: Paideia, 1991), 221–35; Bruce C. Birch, *The Rise of the Israelite Monarchy: The Growth and Development of 1 Samuel 7–15* (SBLDS 27; Missoula, Mont.: Scholars Press, 1976); P. Kyle McCarter, *I Samuel* (AB 8; Garden City, N.Y.: Doubleday, 1980), 18–20; idem, *II Samuel* (AB 9; Garden City, N.Y.: Doubleday, 1984), 6–8 (the latter two date these materials to the second half of the eighth century); and Anthony F. Campbell, *Of Prophets and Kings: A Ninth Century Document (1 Samuel 1–2 Kings 10)* (CBQMS 17; Washington, D.C.: Catholic Biblical Association of America, 1986), dating them somewhat earlier.

[47] There has always been a major center in the southern fringe area of the Judean highlands: Khirbet et-Taura in the Early Bronze, Hebron in the Middle Bronze, Khirbet Rabûd in the Late Bronze, and Hebron again in the Iron Age. In

the center of his theater of operations, then expands to the north and conquers Jerusalem, the traditional center of government in the southern hill country. David, according to these stories, is a typical Apiru leader who manages to establish a new dynasty in Jerusalem. But the change of dynasty did not change the character of Jerusalem or the nature of the territory to its south. In the tenth century we are still facing an Amarna-like situation of a sparsely settled dimorphic chiefdom. David was no more than another Abdi-heba.

A very different demographic process took place at the same time in the northern part of the central highlands. This area had a denser settlement system and was by far more mature in nature. This maturity can been seen in fact that the settlements were not limited to one type but rather consisted of sites from almost all size of hierarchies.[48] This dichotomy—between a more developed north and the less developed south—provides the background for the developments that will take place in these two regions in the next century.

Farther away, in the northern valleys, the tenth century is characterized by a revival of the Canaanite cultural and territorio-political system of the second millennium B.C.E. The main centers in this landscape—which I have recently labeled "New Canaan"[49]—were (LC terms) Megiddo (Stratum VIA), Dor, Tel Rehov, and Kinneret (Stratum V). They probably served as centers of territorial entities, city-states, for all practical purposes. Almost all features of their material culture—pottery, metallurgical, and architectural traditions; layout of the main cities; and settlement patterns in the countryside—show clear continuation of second-millennium traditions.[50] The idea that poor tenth-century Jerusalem, with its sparsely settled hinterland, ruled over the faraway, rich, and prosperous city-states of the northern valleys is therefore absurd.[51]

---

my opinion, these sites served, each in its time, as a "second city" to the more dominant center in Jerusalem. Naʾaman ("Canaanite Jerusalem," 275–91) interprets them as centers of independent entities.

[48] See the list and map in Finkelstein et al., *Highlands of Many Cultures*, 896–97, 950 respectively; the classification "Iron I–II" of the conventional chronology used there fits the tenth–ninth centuries of the low chronology.

[49] Israel Finkelstein, "City States and States: Polity Dynamics in the 10th–9th Centuries BCE," in *Symbiosis, Symbolism and the Power of the Past: Ancient Israel and Its Neighbors from the Late Bronze Age through Roman Palestine, Proceedings of the W. F. Albright Institute of Archaeological Research and the American Schools of Oriental Research Centennial Symposium* (forthcoming).

[50] Ibid.

[51] On this question, see also Knauf, "King Solomon's," 167–86; Hermann M. Niemann, "Megiddo and Solomon—A Biblical Investigation in Relation to Archaeology,"

Archaeology does not supply the slightest clue for the real extent of the Jerusalem territory in the days of the founders of the Davidic dynasty. From the long-term perspective it is reasonable to assume that it dominated the traditional territory of second-millennium Jerusalem, from Bethel to the southern fringe of the highlands. The biblical description of a far-reaching united monarchy represents, more than anything else, the territorial ambitions of seventh-century Judah. The mythical united monarchy is a literary construct of Josianic times, aimed to provide the ideological platform for the claim of the Davidic kings to the lands and people of the vanquished northern kingdom.[52] The only clue in the biblical narrative—if there is a clue—is the appeal of the Deuteronomistic Historian to the collective memory of his compatriots, that in the distant past the founders of the Davidic dynasty had ruled over a territory larger than the traditional boundaries of late monarchic times, including areas that were later incorporated into the northern kingdom. In other words, for a while in the tenth century Jerusalem could have dominated areas in the northern hill country, possibly near Bethel and maybe even farther to its north, hence the idea of a great united monarchy. We can say no more.

A short while later, the history of the highlands returned to flow in its normal course. A competing dynasty emerged in the north, and Jerusalem's rule was once more restricted to its traditional territories in the southern hill country. Again, as in the second millennium B.C.E., the settlement system, agricultural potential, and trade networks in the north were much

---

TA 27 (2000): 59–72. The tenth-century settlement systems in the northern highlands and in the northern valleys were the ones that faced the campaign of Pharaoh Shishak in 926 B.C.E. The results of this campaign and the question of whether Shishak destroyed the city-state system in the northern valleys are beyond the scope of this paper. As for the southern highlands, the Shishak relief in Karnak does not mention Jerusalem or any other Judahite settlement in the highlands south of Gibeon, while 1 Kgs 14:25–27 refers to his threat to Jerusalem. Most scholars have interpreted this source as a genuine historical testimony that originated from a chronicle of the temple or the palace (e.g., Benjamin Mazar, "The Campaign of Pharaoh Shishak to Palestine," in *Volume du congrès: Strasbourg, 1956* [VTSup 4; Leiden: Brill, 1957]: 58). But the poverty of tenth-century Jerusalem, the demographic sparseness of Judah, and the complete lack of any evidence for writing at that time makes it difficult to accept the notion of archive keeping in tenth-century Jerusalem. Whether the seventh-century Deuteronomistic Historian knew about the Shishak campaign from vague memories that were transmitted orally or from late seventh-century Saite propaganda, he usurped the data on a campaign in the northern highlands and used it in his theological scheme of transgression (of Rehoboam) and retribution (better presented in the Chronicler version in 2 Chr 12:2–12).

[52] See in detail Finkelstein and Silberman, *Bible Unearthed.*

more developed. Hence, Israel grew to be the dominant state in the region, while Judah remained isolated, sparsely settled, and in a way dependent on its northern neighbor.

THE NINTH CENTURY B.C.E.: THE OMRIDE CONNECTION

Archaeologically, ninth- and early eighth-century B.C.E. Jerusalem is represented by the meager "tenth-century" pottery (CC) found in the City of David.[53] The most important construction effort that may be connected to the ninth-century settlement is the stepped stone structure on the eastern slope. As mentioned above, the pottery found within its courses and on top of it should apparently be dated to the ninth century (LC). This monumental construction must have supported a major building. A clue for the nature of this building may have been found immediately to the north of Shiloh's Area G. Kenyon[54] uncovered a pile of ashlar blocks there, including a Proto-Aeolic capital[55]—both characteristic of the ninth-century finds at Samaria and Megiddo.[56] The blocks were found at the foot of a scarp, under fifth- to third-century B.C.E. deposits; they probably collapsed from a building up-slope. There is no way to date the original building within the Iron II. The capital is better executed than the Megiddo and Samaria ones and resembles the Ramat Rahel capitals that were in use in a seventh-century building. This stylistic distinction may be attributed to chronological differences[57] but also to functional or even regional variations. From the location point of view, the blocks were found immediately to the north and at the foot of the stepped stone structure.[58] The blocks,

---

[53] See Cahill, "David's Jeruslem," 34–41, 63; Shiloh, *Excavations at the City of David I*, Stratum 14. One of the great shortcomings of the conventional dating has been the difficulty in isolating the material culture of the ninth century, especially in the south (see Finkelstein, "United Monarchy"; idem, "Bible Archaeology," 167–74). This is well demonstrated in the case of Jerusalem, where the ninth-century finds (CC) are summarized in three meaningless lines (Shiloh, *Excavations at the City of David I*, 27).

[54] Kathleen M. Kenyon, "Excavations in Jerusalem, 1962," *PEQ* 95 (1963): 16, pl. VIIIB.

[55] For the latter, see Yigal Shiloh, *The Proto-Aeolic Capital and Israelite Ashlar Masonry* (Qedem 11; Jerusalem: Israel Exploration Society, 1979), 10–11.

[56] LC—Israel Finkelstein, "Omride Architecture," *ZDPV* 116 (2000): 114–38.

[57] See Phillip P. Betancourt, *The Aeolic Style in Architecture* (Princeton, N.J.: Princeton University Press, 1977), 38, 44–45; Kay Prag, "Decorative Architecture in Ammon, Moab, and Judah," *Levant* 19 (1987): 126. Both date the Jerusalem capital to the eighth–seventh century B.C.E.

[58] Kenyon's Square XVIII; see Shiloh, *Excavations at the City of David I*, fig. 3.

then, may have collapsed from a building that stood on top of the stepped stone structure.[59]

In the hill country to the south of Jerusalem, the ninth century is characterized by another growth in the number of settlements: from almost twenty in the Iron I (including the tenth century) to thirty-four in the ninth century (LC; "Iron IIA" in CC terms).[60] Though I have reservations about the ability to identify subphases of the late Iron I and Iron II according to survey material in sites that yield a limited number of sherds, I accept the trend represented in Ofer's finds: the number of sites in the southern hill country gradually grew from a minimum in the Late Bronze, through the Iron I and the early Iron II, to a peak in the late Iron II.

To sum up this point, though the ninth-century finds in Jerusalem and the hill country of Judah indicate some development from the previous centuries, they do not mark a breakthrough from the state-formation point of view. But this is the first time in the history of the Jerusalem territorio-political entity that we are forced to look beyond the boundaries of the southern hill country. I refer to the finds in the Beer-sheba Valley and the Shephelah that I mentioned in the beginning of this essay as the stimulants for a new investigation of state formation in Judah.

The Beer-sheba Valley witnessed a major transformation in the transition from the Iron I to the early Iron II. The late eleventh- to tenth-century system of Tel Masos II–I and Beer-sheba VII declined and was replaced, after a short while, by the ninth-century system (LC) of the fortified administrative center of Beer-sheba V and the fort of Arad XI.[61] These two worlds are quite different in nature. The first shows no sign of central administration and no clue of being part of a larger, out-of-desert territorial formation and was probably related to the Philistine coast and to the people on the southern fringe.[62] The latter was clearly administrative in nature and connected to a central government outside the valley. There is no alternative

---

[59] The section of the "casemate wall" uncovered by Kenyon in her Area H ("Excavations in Jerusalem, 1962," 17–18) is too small to allow chronological or architectural conclusions.

[60] For the number, see Ofer, "Hill Country of Judah," 102–4.

[61] The pottery of Arad XI is close to that of Lachish IV (Zimhoni, *Studies in the Iron Age Pottery of Israel,* 206–7). Therefore, it may date somewhat later than Beer-sheba V.

[62] Israel Finkelstein, *Living on the Fringe: The Archaeology and History of the Negev Sinai and Neighbouring Regions in the Bronze and Iron Ages* (Monographs in Mediterranean Archaeology 6; Sheffield: Sheffield Academic Press, 1995), 103–26; Knauf, "Jerusalem in the Late Bronze and Early Iron Ages," 75–90.

but to identify this government with Judah. Suffice it to say that in both cases the site continued to develop in the same layout and same material culture into the eighth century B.C.E.

In the Shephelah, the key site is Lachish. After a long occupational gap that followed the destruction of Stratum VI in the mid-twelfth century B.C.E.,[63] the site was reoccupied in the ninth century (LC; Stratum V).[64] Tufnell assigned to this stratum the construction of Palace A (on Podium A),[65] a view that was supported at the time by Ussishkin,[66] who now proposes that the Lachish palace was first built in Stratum IV (on Podia A+B).[67] The latter city, with its elaborate palace and massive fortifications,[68] was established in the second half of the ninth century B.C.E.[69] Both Strata V and IV must be affiliated with Judah. The town of Stratum V developed, apparently uninterruptedly, into the fortified city of Stratum IV, which is the forerunner of the great late-eighth-century Judahite city of Stratum III, the city that was besieged by Sennacherib in 701 B.C.E.

Beth-shemesh also features a massive, early Iron II construction effort, which includes the large building in Area B and the elaborate water reservoir with its monumental entrance.[70] These elements were built on top of the Iron I layer and under the terminal eighth-century stratum.

With these data in mind, we should now turn to the north. In the beginning of the ninth century a powerful dynasty emerged in Israel. The Omride state was established on the solid foundations of a highly developed settlement and demographic system in the northern highlands, a system that was lacking in the area of Jerusalem. The Omrides had an ambitious agenda; they opted for expansion into the lowlands and beyond and the creation of

[63] David Ussishkin, "Levels VII and VI at Tel Lachish and the End of the Late Bronze Age in Canaan," in *Palestine in the Bronze and Iron Ages: Papers in Honour of Olga Tufnell* (ed. J. N. Tubb; London: Institute of Archaeology, 1985), 213–28.

[64] See the assemblage of pottery in Yohanan Aharoni, *Investigations at Lachish: The Sanctuary and the Residency (Lachish V)* (Publications of the Institute of Archaeology; Tel Aviv: Gateway, 1975), pls. 41–43.

[65] Olga Tufnell, *Lachish (Tell ed-Duweir), vol. III, The Iron Age* (London: Oxford University Press, 1953), 52–53.

[66] David Ussishkin, "Excavations at Lachish—1973–1977, Preliminary Report," *TA* 5 (1978): 28–31.

[67] David Ussishkin, "Excavations and Restoration Work at Tel Lachish 1985–1994: Third Preliminary Report," *TA* 23 (1996): 35 n. 4.

[68] Ussishkin, "Excavations at Tel Lachish 1978–1983," 171–73.

[69] For the pottery, see Zimhoni, *Studies in the Iron Age Pottery of Israel*, 173.

[70] Shlomo Bunimovitz and Zvi Lederman, "Beth-shemesh: Culture Conflict on Judah's Frontier," *BAR* 23/1 (1997): 46–47, 75–77.

a large territorial, "multiethnic" state. To that end, they embarked on military expansionism combined with diplomatic maneuvers. The Tel Dan Stela [71] discloses that in the far north the northern kingdom expanded into territories that were perceived by Hazael as having belonged previously to the Arameans. In the east the Omrides conquered territories later claimed by King Mesha of Moab. In the northwest they establish a political-commercial alliance with the Phoenicians, which was strengthened by the diplomatic marriage of Ahab to Jezebel.[72] All this made the northern kingdom at the time of the Omrides a potent regional state. It controlled both the olive oil–producing lands of the highlands and the fertile dry-farming lands of the valleys; it dominated some of the most important trade routes in the region; and it commanded large and diverse resources of manpower, which could be deployed in military build-up and building activities.

There can be no doubt that in the south the Omrides had the power to take over the marginal, demographically depleted kingdom of Judah. Yet they opted for military and political cooperation backed by diplomatic marriage (of Jehoram and Athaliah). Instead of deposing the Davidic dynasty, they decided to take it over from within. This was not an act between equal entities, like the relationship between Israel and the Phoenicians, but rather a sheer dominance of the northern kingdom over the small client-state (or better, chiefdom) to its south.[73] Both the biblical text and the Dan Inscription tell us that in the next decades the Judahite kings served the military ambitions of the Omrides. In a way, these were the true days of a united monarchy—one that was ruled from Samaria, not from Jerusalem.

It seems to me that the "missing link" in the development of the southern kingdom—the initial steps toward full statehood—can be identified in this period. The Omride influence in Jerusalem and Judah did not stop at diplomatic and military domination. It probably extended to economic and cultural dominance as well.

Based primarily on Samaria and Jezreel (and supported by less-comprehensive evidence from Hazor, Megiddo, and Gezer) I have recently

---

[71] Biran and Naveh, "Stele Fragment," 81–98; idem, "The Tel Dan Inscription: A New Fragment," *IEJ* 45 (1995): 1–18.

[72] On the power of the Omrides, see, e.g., Stefan Timm, *Die Dynastie Omri: Quellen und Untersuchungen zur Geschichte Israels im 9. Jahrhundert vor Christus* (FRLANT 124; Göttingen: Vandenhoeck & Ruprecht, 1982); J. Maxwell Miller and John H. Hayes, *A History of Ancient Israel and Judah* (Philadelphia: Westminster, 1986), 250–88.

[73] See also Herbert Donner, "The Separate States of Israel and Judah," in *Israelite and Judaean History* (ed. J. H. Hayes and J. M. Miller; Philadelphia: Westminster, 1977), 391; Knauf, "Jerusalem in the Late Bronze and Early Iron Ages," 81.

Israel Finkelstein

tried to delineate the characteristics of monumental Omride architecture.[74] Their government compounds at Samaria, Jezreel, and possibly Hazor featured the construction of a big podium, which involved massive operations of leveling and especially filling in order to create a flat platform for a royal quarter. A casemate compound was established on the podium. It was sparsely inhabited, comprised of large open spaces surrounding a palace. The palace—the focus of the compound—was probably of the *bit-hilani* plan. Viewed from the elaborate gate that led into the compound, the palace was located at the far end, slightly off the main axis. Viewed from the axis of the gate, the rectangular compound was either longitudinal (at Samaria) or a broad complex (at Jezreel). The Omride government centers served the administration of the state as well as the propaganda and legitimacy needs of the dynasty. According to Williamson, at Jezreel—in the heartland of the "Canaanite" valley—the idea was to overawe, even intimidate the local population, which, I would add, was incorporated into the Omride state not long before.[75] At Samaria—in the heartland of the Israelite population—the aim was to impress.

Wightman suggested that the layout of the Jerusalem tenth-century palace-temple compound was similar to the Omride compound at Samaria.[76] Ussishkin took a more daring stand, proposing that a Samaria-like government compound, which included a palace and a temple, was built on the Temple Mount in Jerusalem in the ninth century B.C.E.[77] This idea cannot be examined archaeologically, since the huge Herodian construction completely eradicated or buried any sign of earlier buildings. Still, if we follow this idea we can envision a Samaria-like longitudinal, rectangular casemate compound covering an area of 2.5–4 ha (the size of the Samaria and Jezreel compounds respectively,[78] compared with the ca. 15-ha Herodian platform), built on a podium and entered through an elaborate gate in the south.[79] In Jerusalem, like Samaria, the compound

---

[74] Finkelstein, "Omride Architecture," 114–38; see also David Ussishkin, "Jezreel, Samaria, and Megiddo: Royal Centers of Omri and Ahab," in *Congress Volume: Cambridge, 1995* (ed. J. A. Emerton; VTSup 66; Leiden: Brill, 1997), 351–64.

[75] Hugh G. M. Williamson, "Tel Jezreel and the Dynasty of Omri," *PEQ* 128 (1996): 41–51.

[76] Gregory J. Wightman, *The Walls of Jerusalem from the Canaanites to the Mamluks* (Mediterranean Archaeology Supplement 4; Sydney: University of Sydney, 1993), 29–31.

[77] See the article by Ussishkin in this volume.

[78] Much smaller than Wightman's reconstruction (*Walls of Jerusalem,* 31).

[79] The structure excavated by Mazar to the south of the Temple Mount and identified as a gate (Eilat Mazar and Benjamin Mazar, *Excavations in the South of the*

was crowned by a palace and a temple (for the house of Baal in Samaria, see the biblical testimony in 2 Kgs 10).[80]

Temple Mount: The Ophel of Biblical Jerusalem [Qedem 29; Jerusalem: Institute of Archaeology, Hebrew University of Jerusalem, 1989], 13–28, 58–60) is situated where Wightman (*Walls of Jerusalem,* 31, fig. 7:11) would locate the gate into the temple-palace compound. The structure, if indeed a gate, is oriented at a different angle than Wightman's proposal, though it could have served as an outer gate of a more elaborate complex. In any event, the meager finds do not allow to date its construction within the Iron II framework.

[80] Speaking about the possibility that an Omride-like compound was built in Jerusalem, one cannot ignore the nearby site of Ramat Rahel (Yohanan Aharoni, *Excavations at Ramat Rahel: Seasons 1959 and 1960* [Rome: Centro di studi semitia, 1962]; idem, *Excavations at Ramat Rahel: Seasons 1961–1962* [Rome: Centro di studi semitia, 1964]). A palatial casemate compound measuring 75 x 50 m, with a large courtyard, was built there. The construction involved leveling and filling operations (Aharoni, *Ramat Rahel: Seasons 1961–1962,* 119). This layout recalls the Omride compounds at Samaria and Jezreel, though on a much smaller scale. Proto-Aeolic capitals were found at the site. A wall of ashlar blocks laid in the headers and stretchers method at Ramat Rahel (the only such construction that has been found in the southern kingdom) is identical to the Inner Wall at Samaria (compare ibid., pl. 24:1–2 to John W. Crowfoot et al., *Samaria-Sebaste, vol. I, The Buildings at Samaria* [London: Palestine Exploration Fund, 1942], pl. XIII:1–2; for the similarity to Samaria, see Yohanan Aharoni, "Excavations at Ramat Rahel 1954: Preliminary Report," *IEJ* 6 [1956]: 138, 140; Yigael Yadin, "The 'House of Baal' of Ahab and Jezebel in Samaria, and that of Athalia in Judah," in *Archaeology in the Levant: Essays for Kathleen Kenyon* [ed. R. Moorey and P. Parr; Warminster, U.K.: Aris & Phillips, 1978], 127–35; Ze'ev Herzog, *Archaeology of the City: Urban Planning in Ancient Israel and Its Social Implications* [Monograph Series of the Sonia and Marco Nadler Institute of Archaeology 13; Tel Aviv: Emery and Claire Yass Archaeology Press, Institute of Archaeology, Tel Aviv University, 1997], 250). The finds retrieved at the Ramat Rahel compound (Stratum VA) clearly date to the late seventh century B.C.E. A large number of *lmlk* seal impressions found at the site (mainly in fills) were assigned to an earlier casemate compound (Stratum VB) that was inhabited in the late eighth century B.C.E. Eighth-century pottery was also found in a later excavation conducted at the site by Gabriel Barkay ("Ramat Rahel," *NEAEHL* 4:1267). Aharoni raised the possibility that the site was founded a bit earlier, in the ninth century (e.g., Aharoni, *Ramat Rahel: Seasons 1961–1962,* 119–22). Yadin ("House of Baal," esp. p. 132) was more daring, arguing that the palatial casemate compound (of Stratum VA) was originally built in the ninth century B.C.E. He connected it to the period of Omride interregnum in Jerusalem. The earliest pottery published dates to the late eighth century, though the final reports (Aharoni, *Ramat Rahel: Seasons 1959 and 1960;* idem, *Ramat Rahel: Seasons 1961–1962*) do not supply sufficient information for a detailed analysis of the finds. Only large-scale excavations utilizing modern methods may clarify the complex stratigraphic and chronological problems related to Ramat Rahel.

Both archaeologically and textually there is no way to decide if the Jerusalem temple was built in the tenth century, as the Deuteromimistic Historian insists, if an earlier temple was renovated in the tenth century,[81] or if the temple was built later. I would tend to support one of the former possibilities because of the strong tradition in the biblical text that the Jerusalem temple was built in the early days of the Davidic dynasty. On this, the Deuteronomist must have echoed the tradition known to the people of late-monarchic Jerusalem.[82] There is also no way to tell the exact date of construction of the Jerusalem palace. But here we may have a clue. If one accepts Ussishkin's idea, that the description of the temple in 1 Kgs 7 refers to a *bit hilani,* it would be impossible to assign it to the tenth century.[83] The *bit hilani* concept—originally a Late Bronze design[84]— reemerged in Syria only in the early ninth century[85] and was imported to Palestine by the Omrides in the first half of that century (e.g., Palace 6000 at Megiddo [LC]).[86] There is no way to envision the construction of a *bit hilani* in remote, marginal Jerusalem prior to the appearance of its prototypes in Syria. In other words, if indeed the palace was of the *bit hilani* type, the late-monarchic author of 1 Kgs 7 describes a building that could not have been built before the ninth century B.C.E.

All this leads me to suggest that in the first half of the ninth century, under the influence of the Omrides, Jerusalem made the first steps in its development from a small, Amarna-type government stronghold to an elaborate capital. This was also the beginning of the rise of Judah as a

---

[81] Konrad Rupprecht, *Der Tempel von Jerusalem: Gründung Salomos oder jebusitisches Erbe?* (BZAW 144; Berlin: de Gruyter, 1977); Knauf, "Jerusalem," 78.

[82] Accepting the historicity of the date of the construction of the temple and rejecting the historicity of a great and glamorous united monarchy may be labeled a "double standard." Yet I see a great difference between memories regarding the foundation of a specific building still standing in seventh-century Jerusalem and narratives on far-away territories that had not been ruled by the Davidic dynasty at that time or in the preceding centuries.

[83] David Ussishkin, "King Solomon's Palace and Building 1723 in Megiddo," *IEJ* 16 (1966): 174–86.

[84] Henri Frankfort, "The Origin of the Bit Hilani," *Iraq* 14 (1952): 120–31.

[85] For the Tell Halaf palace, the most important building for dating the appearance of the Iron Age *hilani,* see, e.g., Irene J. Winter, "North Syrian Ivories and Tell Halaf Reliefs: The Impact of Luxury Goods upon 'Major' Arts," in *Essays in Ancient Civilization Presented to Helene J. Kantor* (ed. A. Leonard and B. E. Williams; Studies in Ancient Oriental Civilization 47; Chicago: Oriental Institute of the Unversity of Chicago, 1989), 321–32; contra William F. Albright, "The Date of the Kapara Period at Gozan (Tell Halaf)," *AnSt* 6 (1956): 75–85.

[86] Finkelstein, "United Monarchy," 177–87.

state. As I have already mentioned, the economy must have been an important component in this process, with the lucrative desert trade playing a major role in these developments.

The association of the northern kingdom with Phoenicia on one hand and the southern trade on the other hand is evident in the finds from Kuntillet ʿAjrûd in northeastern Sinai,[87] dated to the early eighth century B.C.E.[88] This kind of activity could have started a bit earlier. The evidence for this comes from the meaningful change in the Beer-sheba Valley, from the tenth-century system centered around Tel Masos (which may have declined as a result of Shishak's campaign), to the ninth-century system of Beer-sheba V and Arad XI (LC). The latter sites seem to represent an effort by Judah, probably under the auspices of the Omrides, to take control of the trade routes that passed through the Beer-sheba Valley. The story in 1 Kgs 22:48–49 on Jehoshaphat's attempt to engage in southern trade with the help of the northern kingdom (the Chronicler's version [2 Chr 20:35–36] is preferable here, even if presenting an ideal Jehoshaphat),[89] even if grossly exaggerated,[90] may represent a vague echo of this period.

This was also the first time that Judah expanded into the Shephelah. In the tenth century this region was dominated by the Philistine city-states, especially Ekron and Gath. We have no archaeological information for Gath (Tell es-Safi) yet. Ekron (Stratum IV) was "totally destroyed"[91] in the late tenth century (LC), perhaps in the course of the Shishak campaign. A few decades later, possibly with the help of the Omrides, Judah expanded into the rich agricultural land of the Upper Shephelah. This move is represented by the construction of the city of Strata V and mainly IV at Lachish and the early Iron II stratum at Beth

---

[87] Pirhiya Beck, "The Drawings from Horvat Teiman (Kuntillet ʿAjrud)," *TA* 9 (1982): 3–68; André Lemaire, "Date et origine des inscriptions paléo-hébraîque et phéniciennes de Kuntillet ʿAjrud," *SEL* 1 (1984): 131–43; Eitan Ayalon, "The Iron Age II Pottery Assemblage from Horvat Teiman (Kuntillet ʿAjrud)," *TA* 22 (1995): 192–95.

[88] Radiocarbon dates put the site in the range of ca. 800–770 B.C.E. (Irina Carmi and Dror Segal, "14C Dating of an Israelite Biblical Site at Kuntillet ʿAjrud (Horvat Teiman): Correction, Extension, and Improved Age Estimate," *Radiocarbon* 38 [1996]: 385–86).

[89] For a discussion, see Miller and Hayes, *History of Ancient Israel,* 277–80.

[90] Etzion Geber, for instance, had not yet been inhabited in the ninth century B.C.E. See Gary D. Pratico, *Nelson Glueck's 1938–1940 Excavations at Tell el-Kheleifeh: A Reappraisal* (Atlanta: Scholars Press, 1993).

[91] Trude Dothan and Moshe Dothan, *People of the Sea: The Search for the Philistines* (New York: Macmillan, 1992), 252.

Shemesh. The link of the Omrides to the Shephelah may explain two otherwise peculiar notes in the Deuteronomistic History. The first is 2 Kgs 12:18, which relates that in the course of his assault on Israel, Hazael, king of Aram Damascus, campaigned as far south as Gath in the Shephelah[92] and even tried to assault Jerusalem. Hazael's campaign in the Shephelah should be explained as an attempt to gain control over the southern trade,[93] which was at least partially dominated by the Omride-Judah alliance. The second is 2 Kgs 1, which describes King Ahaziah of Israel's call on Baal-zebub the god of Ekron.[94]

In the 830s, with the Jehu coup and the liquidation of the Omride dynasty in Samaria, and the weakening of the northern kingdom under the pressure of Aram Damascus, the dominance of Israel over Judah was waning. A coup in Jerusalem eliminated the remaining influence of the Omride dynasty in the Judahite capital.[95]

---

[92] The identification of this place with another Gath, such as Gittaim (Benjamin Mazar, "Gath and Gittaim," *IEJ* 4 [1954]: 227–35) has been rejected by most scholars (e.g., Anson F. Rainey, "The Identification of Philistine Gath—A Problem in Source Analysis for Historical Geography," *ErIsr* 12 [1975]: 63*–76*; William M. Schniedewind, "The Geopolitical History of Philistine Gath," *BASOR* 309 [1998]: 69–77).

[93] Also John Gray, *I and II Kings: A Commentary* (2d ed.; OTL; Philadelphia: Westminster, 1970), 589; Gosta W. Ahlström, *The History of Ancient Palestine from the Paleolithic Period to Alexander's Conquest* (Minneapolis: Fortress, 1993), 610.

[94] Some scholars see this story, or parts of it, as a legend (e.g., Gray, *I and II Kings,* 459; Alexander Rofé, *The Prophetic Stories: The Narratives about the Prophets in the Hebrew Bible, Their Literary Types and History* [Jerusalem: Magnes, 1988], 34; Burke O. Long, *2 Kings* [FOTL 10; Grand Rapids: Eerdmans, 1991], 16), but the question remains: Why the reference to Ekron? Rofé's proposal, that the story was inserted into the book of Kings in postexilic times (*Prophetic Stories,* 35–40; see also Steven L. McKenzie, *The Trouble with Kings: The Composition of the Book of Kings in the Deuteronomistic History* [Leiden: Brill, 1991], 91–92), has been rejected by other scholars (e.g., Mordechai Cogan and Hayim Tadmor, *II Kings: A New Translation* [AB 11; Garden City, N.Y.: Doubleday, 1988], 28). Though a place named Accaron is mentioned in the Hellenistic period (Yoram Tsafrir et al., *Tabula Imperii Romani Iudaea Palaestina* [Jerusalem: Israel Academy of Sciences and Humanities, 1994], 56), Tel Miqne was not inhabited after the early sixth century (Trude Dothan and Seymour Gitin, "Miqne, Tel (Ekron)," *NEAEHL* 3:1056–58). It is thus difficult to understand this narrative on a postexilic background.

[95] For a detailed examination of the 2 Kgs 11 story, which may have two different sources in it, see Gray, *I and II Kings,* 565–83. The story is highly ideological, aiming to delegitimize Athaliah in particular and Omride rule in Jerusalem in general as an anomaly and a deviation from God's promise to David

SUMMARY

Within a few decades in the ninth century, Jerusalem in particular and Judah in general went through a significant transformation, from an Amarna-type dimorphic entity to the first steps toward full statehood. This transitional phase in the history of Judah—the missing link that I was looking for—was achieved under Omride dominance. According to this scenario, Judah as an early state is an outcome of the Omride political and economic ambitions. In the period of the dynasty of Jehu, especially in the days of Joash and Jeroboam II, Judah continued to live in the shadow of Israel. But it now had the necessary infrastructure to make the big leap forward in the second half of the eighth century B.C.E. This last step to full statehood came with the destruction of Israel and the incorporation of Judah into the Assyrian world system.

---

and to legitimize the accession of Jehoash to the throne (see, e.g., Mario Liverani, "L'histoire de Joas," *VT* 24 [1974]: 438–45; Long, *2 Kings*, 155). However, its basic historicity is not disputed.

Solomon's Jerusalem: The Text and the Facts on the Ground[*]

David Ussishkin
Tel Aviv University

The biblical text is the sole written source describing King Solomon's glorious reign and his capital, Jerusalem. It presents Jerusalem of that time as a large and rich city, befitting its role as the capital of a great and prosperous kingdom and king. We are told that Solomon extended the small town or citadel that he inherited from his father, known as the "stronghold of Zion" or the "City of David" and incorporated the Temple Mount in the extended city (fig. 3.1). There he built a large royal palace (1 Kgs 7:1–12) and a smaller but magnificent temple beside it. We are also told that Solomon blocked the "breaches" of the city of David (1 Kgs 11:27) and surrounded Jerusalem with a city wall (1 Kgs 9:15). He also built a *millo,* apparently a structure or structures based on constructional fills (1 Kgs 9:15, 24; 11:27). The text emphasizes the luxury and extravagance of everything that king Solomon desired to build in Jerusalem (1 Kgs 9:19). The best expression of the luxury and extravagance of the king and whatever he did is given in the story of the visit by the Queen of Sheba (1 Kgs 10:4–5): "And when the queen of Sheba had seen all Solomon's wisdom, and the house that he had built, and the meat of his table, and the sitting of his servants, and the attendance of his ministers, and their apparel, and his cupbearers, and his ascent by which he went up unto the house of the Lord, *there was no more spirit in her.*"

The scholarly difficulties and problems of evaluating and using the biblical texts describing the united monarchy period (i.e., their reliability and historicity) are well known, so there is no need to discuss them here. These difficulties also apply to the descriptions of Solomonic Jerusalem and their interpretation. In light of the problems of relying on the information given

---

[*] This article is based on the text of a paper presented at a session of the Society of Biblical Literature conference in Boston in November 1999, chaired by Ann E. Killebrew and Andrew G. Vaughn, with minor additions and alterations.

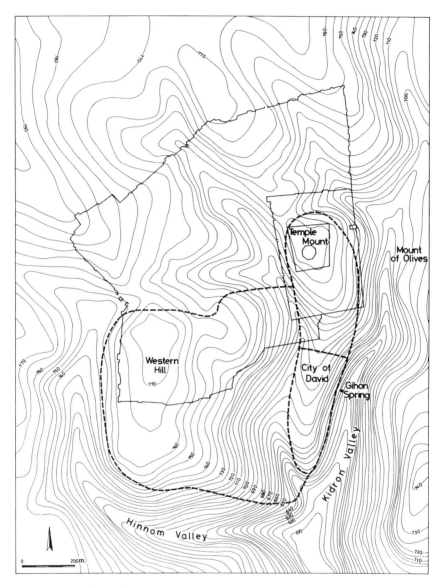

Fig. 3.1. Map of Jerusalem in the First Temple period

in the biblical texts and the absence of any other external written sources, the archaeological data regarding Jerusalem are of prime importance for understanding and reconstructing the city of Solomon's time.

Turning to the archaeological evidence, we see that intensive and systematic archaeological investigations have been carried out in Jerusalem for more than 150 years. Let me start by briefly summarizing the results of these investigations, with special reference to the period of King Solomon.

Settlement in Jerusalem started in the Chalcolithic and Early Bronze periods on the eastern side of the southeast hill, that is, the "City of David," to the south of the Temple Mount. The settlement was founded in this particular area due to the location here of the Gihon Spring, which was its main source of water (fig. 3.1).

In the following millennia until the end of the Iron Age we have in fact two intensive settlement periods or strata. The earlier settlement is a fortified settlement dating to the Middle Bronze Age II period, that is, to the first half of the second millennium B.C.E. Impressive remains were uncovered on the eastern slope of the City of David in the successive excavations of Kenyon and Shiloh and recently in the excavation of Reich and Shukron in the area of the Gihon Spring. A massive segment of a city wall, possibly part of a tower or a gate tower, was uncovered by Kenyon.[1] A long segment of the city wall, as well as the houses of the settlement built adjacent to its inner side, were discovered by Shiloh.[2] Remains of a massive tower constructed of huge boulders were found near the Gihon Spring by Reich and Shukron.[3] They also convincingly showed that the rock-cut tunnel enabling access to the spring known as "Warren's Shaft" also dates to the Middle Bronze Age.

The second major settlement period of biblical Jerusalem, as evidenced by the archaeological remains, dates to the latter part of the Iron Age (eighth–seventh centuries B.C.E.). At that time Jerusalem was the capital of the Judahite kingdom, and it was destroyed in 588/6 B.C.E. by the Babylonian army of Nebuchadnezzar. During this period Jerusalem extended in size, becoming a metropolis, the central city in Judah. Jerusalem of that time spread over the entire City of David, the Temple Mount, and the Western Hill, now the area of the Jewish and Armenian Quarters in the Old City (fig. 3.1). The city was heavily fortified. Its city wall was uncovered by Kenyon and Shiloh along the eastern slope of the City of David, extending along and above the stump of the earlier stone city wall dating to Middle Bronze Age II.[4] Another wall segment was

---

[1] Kathleen M. Kenyon *Digging Up Jerusalem* (London: Benn, 1974), 76–97.

[2] Yigal Shiloh, *Excavations at the City of David I, 1978–1982: Interim Report of the First Five Seasons* (Qedem 19; Jerusalem: Institute of Archaeology, Hebrew University of Jerusalem, 1984), 12, 26.

[3] Ronny Reich and Eli Shukron, "Light at the End of the Tunnel," *BAR* 25/1 (1999): 22–33, 72.

[4] Kenyon, *Digging Up Jerusalem,* 144–47; Shiloh, *Excavations at the City of David I,* 28.

uncovered farther to the north by Eilat Mazar.[5] Further, segments of lower or outer city walls were uncovered by Reich and Shukron to the south of the Gihon Spring.[6] Finally, massive fortifications were discovered by Avigad on the western hill, proving that the entire Judahite metropolis was heavily fortified.[7]

The evidence of the pottery indicates that this large city was established no later than the eighth century B.C.E. The pottery found here is similar to that of Level III at Lachish. Tel Lachish—in the excavation of which I spent many of the best years of my life—is the key site for the Iron Age in Judah. Level III was destroyed by the Assyrian army of Sennacherib in 701 B.C.E.[8] Hence the large pottery assemblage buried beneath the destruction debris is well dated and helps us in dating similar pottery assemblages at other sites. Of particular interest in the Lachish Level III pottery are the many stamped royal Judahite storage jars, known as *lmlk* storage jars.[9] They were possibly part of the preparations by the government of King Hezekiah to meet the Assyrian invasion.[10] Hundreds of stamped handles of such storage jars were also found in various parts of Jerusalem.[11] The Lachish Level III type pottery and the *lmlk* storage jars prove that Jerusalem had already reached its larger dimensions during the course of the eighth century B.C.E. This was the city of Hezekiah's time, which was challenged by the Assyrian army of Sennacherib in 701 B.C.E.[12]

We shall now turn to consider the archaeological data regarding Jerusalem in the period between the end of the Middle Bronze Age in the

---

[5] Eilat Mazar and Benjamin Mazar, *Excavations in the South of the Temple Mount: The Ophel of Biblical Jerusalem* (Qedem 29; Jerusalem: Institute of Archaeology, Hebrew University of Jerusalem, 1989).

[6] Hershel Shanks, "Everything You Ever Knew about Jerusalem Is Wrong (Well, Almost)," *BAR* 25/6 (1999): 20–29.

[7] Nahman Avigad, *Discovering Jerusalem* (Nashville: Nelson, 1983), 23–60.

[8] David Ussishkin, "The Destruction of Lachish by Sennacherib and the Dating of the Royal Judean Storage Jars," *TA* 4 (1977): 28–60.

[9] Ibid.

[10] Nadav Naʾaman, "Sennacherib's Campaign in Judah and the Date of the *lmlk* Stamps," *VT* 29 (1979): 61–81; see recent discussion in Andrew G. Vaughn, *Theology, History and Archaeology in the Chronicler's Account of Hezekiah* (SBLABS 4; Atlanta: Society of Biblical Literature, 1999).

[11] Vaughn, *Theology, History and Archaeology,* 166.

[12] David Ussishkin, "The Water Systems of Jerusalem during Hezekiah's Reign," in *Meilensteinen: Festgabe für Herbert Donner* (ed. M. Weippert and S. Timm; Wiesbaden: Harrassowitz, 1995), 289–92.

sixteenth century and the eighth century B.C.E., that is, in the period between the two fortified settlements discussed above. This important chapter in the history and archaeology of Jerusalem was recently the subject of a series of studies by Na'aman, Steiner, and Cahill.[13] There is no need to discuss it all over again here. The archaeological evidence indicates that during the entire period between the end of the Middle Bronze Age and the eighth century B.C.E. Jerusalem was not abandoned, and there are the remains of some human activity, of a small settlement on the eastern slope of the City of David, centered in the area above the Gihon Spring (fig. 3.1).

Of special interest is a strange and unique structure, labeled by Shiloh "the stepped stone structure." Based on stone terraces supported by constructional fills, it is a kind of a retaining wall supporting the eastern, rocky steep slope of the City of David above the spring.[14] The whole structure is enigmatic and was used and rebuilt for many generations. Shiloh, Steiner, and Cahill and Tarler attempted to fix its exact date on the basis of pottery in the fills.[15] It seems that this structure (or parts of it) originated in the end of the Late Bronze Age—that is, in the thirteenth–twelfth centuries B.C.E.—and was in use until the Second Temple period. Its original function is unclear, and nothing was discovered on the summit above it. At this point one cannot say if it was a retaining wall originally crowned by a fortress or whether it had some other function.

Beyond that, only small amounts of unstratified pottery and some remains of flimsy walls and floors have been uncovered dating to this general period.[16] In addition, a few Late Bronze Age tombs outside the

---

[13] Nadav Na'aman, "The Contribution of the Amarna Letters to the Debate on Jerusalem's Political Position in the Tenth Century B.C.E.," *BASOR* 304 (1996): 17–27; Margreet L. Steiner, "David's Jerusalem: Fiction or Reality. It's Not There, Archaeology Proves a Negative," *BAR* 24/4 (1998): 26–33, 62–63; Jane Cahill, "David's Jerusalem: Fiction or Reality. It Is There, The Archaeological Evidence Proves It," *BAR* 24/4 (1998): 34–41.

[14] Shiloh, *Excavations at the City of David I,* 15–17.

[15] Ibid.; Margreet L. Steiner, "The Jebusite Ramp of Jerusalem: The Evidence from the Macalister, Kenyon and Shiloh Excavations," in *Biblical Archaeology Today, 1990: Proceedings of the Second International Congress on Biblical Archaeology* (ed. A. Biran and J. Aviram; Jerusalem: Israel Exploration Society, 1993), 585–88; idem, "Re-dating the Terraces of Jerusalem," *IEJ* 44 (1994): 13–20; Jane M. Cahill and David Tarler, "Response to Margreet Steiner—The Jebusite Ramp of Jerusalem: The Evidence from the Macalister, Kenyon and Shiloh Excavations," in Biran and Aviram, eds., *Biblical Archaeology Today,* 625–26

[16] Cahill, "David's Jerusalem," 34–41.

city proper were found, including a large tomb excavated on the Mount of Olives.[17]

Some—but not all—of the pottery of the earlier part of the Iron Age found by Kenyon and Shiloh has been published.[18] When evaluating the pottery of this period, one must remember that its chronology in general is problematic and controversial.[19] The pottery chronology was decided on the basis of sites located in the valleys and in the Shephelah, and we know very little of what happens in the hills of Judea and Samaria. The main chronological pivots are the pottery assemblage of Level VI at Lachish, the last Canaanite city destroyed by a terrible fire in the third quarter of the twelfth century B.C.E.,[20] and the above-mentioned pottery assemblage of Level III at Lachish, destroyed in 701 B.C.E. The chronology of the pottery between these two dates is problematic: one scholar talks of twelfth-century pottery, while a colleague might ascribe the same piece of pottery to the eleventh century B.C.E.

The following anecdote illustrates the difficulties involved. I remember discussing the Jerusalem pottery chronology with Alon De Groot, at the time Shiloh's assistant in the City of David excavations, who told me that he could show me "trays of tenth-century B.C.E." red irregularly burnished Iron Age pottery found in the excavations. When I commented that what he defines as tenth-century pottery is probably ninth-century pottery according to the "low chronology" concept, he happily answered that in that case he would provide me with "other trays of earlier pottery." When I asked Israel Finkelstein, who leads the crusade for lowering Iron Age pottery chronology, what kind of pottery we have to expect, in his view, in tenth-century Jerusalem, he said that "we are not sufficiently familiar with the pottery of this hilly region in this period to answer that question."

---

[17] Sylvester J. Saller, *The Excavations at Dominus Flevit (Mount Olivet, Jerusalem), part II, The Jebusite Burial Place* (Publications of the Studium Biblicum Franciscanum 13; Jerusalem: Franciscan Press, 1964).

[18] See recently Alon De Groot and Donald T. Ariel, "Ceramic Report," in *Excavations at the City of David 1978–1985 Directed by Yigal Shiloh, vol. V, Extramural Areas* (ed. D. T. Ariel; Qedem 40; Jerusalem: Institute of Archaeology, Hebrew University of Jerusalem, 2000), 93–94, figs. 7, 11–15.

[19] Israel Finkelstein, "The Archaeology of the United Monarchy: An Alternative View," *Levant* 28 (1996): 177–87; Amihai Mazar, "Iron Age Chronology: A Reply to I. Finkelstein," *Levant* 29 (1997): 157–67.

[20] David Ussishkin, "Levels VII and VI at Tel Lachish and the End of the Late Bronze Age in Canaan," in *Palestine in the Bronze and Iron Ages: Papers in Honour of Olga Tufnell* (ed. J. N. Tubb; London: Institute of Archaeology, 1985), 213–28; Roff Kraus, "Ein wahrscheinlicher Terminus post quem für das Ende von Lachish VI," *MDOG* 126 (1994): 123–30.

But we need not dwell here on the complex chronological questions. The evidence is sufficient to conclude that a settlement in the general area above the Gihon Spring existed between the sixteenth century and the eighth century B.C.E., possibly with some breaks in habitation during this long period of time.

The above analysis, which indicates the existence of a small settlement above the Gihon Spring at the beginning of the Iron Age and the existence of a large fortified city in the eighth century and later, raises another cardinal problem. Many of the Judahite towns that are familiar to us in the eighth and seventh centuries B.C.E. were already extensively settled in the ninth century, if not before. Turning again to Lachish, the key site of Judah, we see that Level III, which was destroyed by the Assyrians in 701 B.C.E., was a strong royal fortress. This level was in fact a rebuilding of an earlier city-level, Level IV, which marks the beginning of the strongly fortified city. Level IV was preceded by Level V, which was an unfortified, extensive settlement founded on the Canaanite abandoned site. The dates of Levels V and IV are difficult to establish; they preceded Level III, which was destroyed in 701 B.C.E., and this is the only fixed chronological datum we possess. For various reasons, mainly the pottery analysis carried out by Zimhoni, it seems that Levels V and IV date to the ninth and the beginning of the eighth centuries B.C.E.[21] This is of course one of the pivots in Finkelstein's suggestion to lower the Iron Age chronology. Other scholars would date these levels earlier.[22] One way or another we have at Lachish Level IV a large and heavily fortified Judahite stronghold dating to the ninth century B.C.E. Can we accept the presently available archaeological evidence that Jerusalem the capital was so poor and small in comparison to Lachish, the provincial center, as well as to other cities in Judah? It thus follows that Iron Age II Jerusalem, which—based on the archaeological evidence—was already a great metropolis in the later part of the eighth century B.C.E., had in fact been founded already in the ninth century, in parallel to Lachish Level IV. We can assume that an in-depth study of the Jerusalem pottery, in particular that found by Avigad in the western hill, will uncover also many Lachish Level IV type sherds, which will prove the above point.

When turning to focus our attention on Jerusalem of the united monarchy period, it is clear that the available archaeological evidence, when

[21] Orna Zimhoni, *Studies in the Iron Age Pottery of Israel: Typological, Archaeological and Chronological Aspects* (Tel Aviv Occasional Publications 2; Tel Aviv: Tel Aviv University Press, 1997), 172–74.

[22] Yigael Yadin, "A Rejoinder," *BASOR* 239 (1980): 23; William G. Dever, "Late Bronze Age and Solomonic Defenses at Gezer: New Evidence," *BASOR* 262 (1986): 33 n. 35.

evaluated independently, indicates that a settlement, apparently limited in size and importance, possibly including a small fort, existed in the City of David, in the area above the Gihon Spring. Scholars are divided in their interpretation of this evidence into two distinct groups.

Most scholars—such as recently Shiloh, Shanks, Mazar, and Cahill— assume that the biblical description of Solomonic Jerusalem is reliable; hence, it is the "starting point" of their understanding of the city.[23] They assume that the Solomonic city was a magnificent capital, protected by a massive city wall, densely populated, and crowned by a large royal palace and temple. Into this picture the real finds uncovered in the field are fitted like pieces in a jigsaw puzzle. In other words, they conclude: the city at that time was as described in the biblical text, but, due to one reason or other, only some poor finds were uncovered on the slope above the Gihon Spring, and these poor finds fit well into the general picture.

Some archaeologists—such as recently Franken and Steiner, Finkelstein, and myself—strongly believe that the starting point for an archaeological evaluation should be the data collected on the ground, analyzed in an objective and unbiased manner.[24] This principle naturally also applies to the case of Solomonic Jerusalem. When studying the data using this approach, we observe that the extant remains indicate the existence of a small settlement at that time rather than a large magnificent capital.

This conclusion is strongly supported by four arguments, detailed below.

THE QUESTION OF FORTIFICATIONS. As discussed above, two systems of fortifications were uncovered in Jerusalem, one dating to the Middle Bronze Age II and one dating to the eighth century B.C.E. and later. As related above, on the eastern slope of the City of David these two city walls extended in parallel to one another and were partly superimposed. No fortifications dating to the period between the Middle Bronze and eighth century B.C.E. have been found. Kenyon's suggestion, that the Middle Bronze Age wall continued to be in use until the eighth century lacks any factual basis and should be rejected.[25] Ariel and De Groot argued recently that "the archaeological 'gap' between the two periods is most

---

[23] Shiloh, *Excavations at the City of David I*, 27; Hershel Shanks, *Jerusalem: An Archaeological Biography* (New York: Random House, 1995), 47–49, esp. figure on 74–75; Amihai Mazar, *Archaeology of the Land of the Bible, 10,000-586 B.C.E.* (ABRL; New York: Doubleday, 1990), 375–79; Cahill, "David's Jerusalem," 34–41.

[24] Hendricus J. Franken and Margreet L. Steiner, "Urusalim and Jebus," *ZAW* 104 (1992): 110–11; Steiner, "David's Jerusalem," 26–33, 62–63; Israel Finkelstein, "The Rise of Jerusalem and Judah: The Missing Link," *Levant* 33 (2001): 105–15.

[25] Kenyon, *Digging Up Jerusalem,* 130–44.

likely the result of preservational and stratigraphical factors, and related to the steep slope on which the fortification line was situated."[26] But it seems unlikely that the earlier and later city walls were so well preserved and only the city wall of the interim period disappeared in its entirety. It thus seems clear that the settlement that existed in Jerusalem in the tenth century B.C.E. was not surrounded by a proper city wall.

THE SETTLEMENT REMAINS NEAR THE GIHON SPRING. The spring was undoubtedly the focus of settlement activity during the Bronze and Iron Ages. In the recent excavations carried out near the spring by Reich and Shukron, massive fortifications as well as pottery from the Middle Bronze Age II as well as rock-cut remains, debris, and pottery from the later Iron Age were found. However, nothing was discovered here representing the periods in between.

THE QUESTION OF POTTERY. It is usually argued that our lack of evidence for the tenth-century settlement also results from the fact that no investigations can be carried out on the Temple Mount. But here we should raise the question of pottery. Pottery vessels usually have a short life span, and then they eventually break to pieces. These pottery sherds do not decay, nobody sweeps them away, and they remain in the debris of the site. Assuming that a large settlement existed in Jerusalem in the tenth century with its focal point on the Temple Mount, we would have expected to find, collect, and identify many thousands of contemporary pottery sherds in the debris all over the place, in particular in the area surrounding the Temple Mount. But this is not the case. More important, in the vast areas uncovered by Benjamin Mazar, and later by Eilat Mazar, to the west and south of the Temple Mount not a single pottery sherd of the tenth–ninth centuries B.C.E. was identified. Twenty-one *lmlk* stamped storage jar handles form the earliest pieces of datable Iron Age pottery discovered here.[27]

THE QUESTION OF FUTURE EXCAVATIONS. In all similar cases we are used to hearing the argument that "things were not found until now, but future excavations will uncover them!" Naturally, this could also apply to

---

[26] Donald T. Ariel and Alon De Groot, "The Iron Age Extramural Occupation at the City of David and Additional Observations on the Siloam Tunnel," in Ariel, ed., *Extramural Areas,* 160.

[27] Yonatan Nadelman, "Hebrew Inscriptions, Seal Impressions, and Markings of the Iron Age II," in Mazar and Mazar, *Excavations in the South of the Temple Mount,* 131–32.

Solomonic Jerusalem. However, every inch of biblical Jerusalem, except for the Temple Mount, was turned over and over again during the many excavations that took place there since de Saulcy's pioneering work in 1851.[28] There is no other cardinal site in the Holy Land that has so intensively been investigated.[29] The recent excavations of Reich and Shukron near the Gihon Spring indeed proved that new, important discoveries can still be made in excavations in Jerusalem; however, it is unlikely that the present overall picture, crystallized by the finds of long, continuous, and intensive archaeological investigations, will radically change in the future. In other words, being realistic I am afraid that evidence regarding the magnificent Solomonic capital was not discovered because it is nonexistent, not because it is still hidden in the ground.

The conclusion that Jerusalem of Solomon's time was a settlement limited in size, located in the City of David above the Gihon Spring, brings to the fore the question of the royal acropolis on the Temple Mount, which according to the biblical text was built by Solomon. The royal compound included the king's magnificent palace (1 Kgs 7:1–12) and the adjacent temple. The palace complex included a ceremonial wing probably built as a *bit-hilani* in north-Syrian style,[30] a residence for Solomon's wife, the Egyptian princess, and a royal treasury labeled "The house of the forest of Lebanon." Both palace and temple were situated in the middle of enclosed courtyards. This royal compound was in continuous use until the end of the Judahite kingdom, when it was destroyed by the Babylonian army.

The royal acropolis was probably smaller than the compound built here by King Herod in the first century B.C.E., whose shape is presently preserved in the Muslim Haram esh-Sharif. Many graphic restorations portray the outlines of the rectangular Haram esh-Sharif, and inside, the smaller Iron Age compound is marked by curving lines.[31] On the other hand several scholars, notably Kenyon and Ritmeyer, believe that the Herodian walls follow, at least in part, the lines of the earlier Iron Age walls. Hence the walls of the earlier compound extended in straight rather than curved lines.[32]

---

[28] L. Félicion J. C. de Saulcy, *A Narrative of a Journey Round the Dead Sea and in the Bible Lands in 1850 and 1851,* vol. 2 (London: Bentley, 1854).

[29] Yigal Shiloh, "Jerusalem: The Early Periods and the First Temple Period," *NEAEHL* 2:702.

[30] David Ussishkin, "King Solomon's Palace and Building 1723 in Megiddo," *IEJ* 16 (1966): 174–86; idem, "King Solomon's Palaces," *BA* 36 (1973): 78–105.

[31] E.g., Mazar, *Archaeology of the Land of the Bible,* 418, fig. 10.8; see also fig. 3.1 here.

[32] Kenyon, *Digging Up Jerusalem,* 111–14, fig. 22; Leen Ritmeyer, "Locating the Original Temple Mount," *BAR* 18/2 (1992): 24–45.

Wightman compared the Solomonic compound to that of Omride Samaria, also restoring its walls in straight lines.[33]

In following this line of thought it can be assumed that the royal compound of the kings of the house of David in Jerusalem was based in plan and character on the same model as the royal Omride compounds in Samaria and Jezreel.[34] Both these compounds portray a common, crystallized concept and plan. In both Samaria and Jezreel the compound was founded on the summit of a hill, with bedrock forming much of the surface. In both places the compound was rectangular and surrounded by a casemate wall. Large amounts of soil and debris were dumped as constructional fills against the casemate walls, turning the compound into a podium with a horizontal surface. The inside of the Jezreel compound was hardly excavated; in Samaria several buildings as well as large open courtyards were found inside the compound.

This royal acropolis can be easily understood—from the point of view of town-planning—in the context of the later metropolis of the eighth and seventh centuries B.C.E. At that time it was located in the highest point of the city, with two of its sides (on the west and south) flanking settled quarters of the city and two sides (on the east and north) forming the edge of the city and joining its city wall (fig. 3.1). This is the topographical situation that forms the background to the appearance of Rabshakeh in front of the city wall and the royal palace to present his ultimatum to King Hezekiah.[35] We can recall many other capitals in the ancient Near East where the royal acropolis was situated in a similar position, such as Tell Halaf, the site of Aramean Gozan, Nimrud, the site of Assyrian Kalah, Ras Shamra, the site of Canaanite Ugarit, and Canaanite Megiddo.

However, the situation in Jerusalem in the tenth century B.C.E. was quite different. If indeed the settlement was small and located above the Gihon Spring, as indicated by the archaeological data, the addition of a large royal compound, much larger than the settlement itself and at a distance from it, would be rather anomalous. There are in fact four alternative possibilities for reconstructing the history of the royal acropolis of the house of David on the summit of the Temple Mount. Since it is impossible

---

[33] Gregory J. Wightman, *The Walls of Jerusalem from the Canaanites to the Mamluks* (Mediterranean Archaeology Supplement 4; Sydney: University of Sydney, 1993), 29–31.

[34] John W. Crowfoot et al., *Samaria-Sebaste I: The Buildings at Samaria* (London: Palestine Exploration Fund, 1942); David Ussishkin and John Woodhead, "Excavations at Tel Jezreel 1994-1996: Third Preliminary Report," *TA* 24 (1997): 11, fig. 4.

[35] Ussishkin, "Water Systems of Jerusalem," 289–92.

to conduct proper archaeological investigations there, these alternatives are based not only on topographical and archaeological grounds but mainly on the interpretation and evaluation of the biblical text and on historical interpretation. The four alternatives are as follows.

First, as recently suggested by Knauf, the cultic and secular center of both the Late Bronze and Israelite cities was on the Temple Mount.[36] However, there are no textual or archaeological indications to support this theory.

Second, the royal acropolis was built as a separate entity by Solomon as described in the biblical text, and it was incorporated in the expanding city in a later period.

Third, Solomon erected a temple on the Temple Mount, "though on a much smaller scale than the one built in the late monarchical period," as suggested by Na'aman[37] The same may possibly apply to a modest version of the adjacent secular palace.

Fourth, the royal acropolis was constructed as described in the biblical text but in a later period, when the modest tenth-century B.C.E. settlement became a large, fortified city.

The above summary of Jerusalem during the reign of Solomon as presented above is shown purely from the point of view of the archaeologist and summarizes the archaeological evidence. The interpretation and evaluation of this evidence is naturally left to the historians and biblical scholars. The first eminent scholar to have taken the challenge was Na'aman.[38] On the basis of the archaeological evidence he defined tenth-century Jerusalem as a "highland stronghold" and the kingdom of Judah in the late tenth–ninth centuries B.C.E. as "a peripheral small and powerless kingdom."[39]

Finally, the historical evaluation of Jerusalem brings to the fore another interesting point. One reads in 1 Kgs 14:25–28 (also 2 Chr 12:2–12) that Pharaoh Shishak came to Jerusalem in the fifth year of King Rehoboam "and took away the treasures of the house of the Lord, and the treasures of the king's house; he even took away all; and he took away all the shields of gold that Solomon had made." How can we understand this piece of information in view of what we know of the city of this time? This problem is in fact associated with another question: Shishak's campaign was recorded in his inscription in Karnak, but nothing is said there about

---

[36] Ernst Axel Knauf, "Jerusalem in the Late Bronze and Early Iron Ages: A Proposal," *TA* 27 (2000): 75–90.

[37] Na'aman, "Contribution of the Amarna Letters," 23.

[38] Ibid., 17–27.

[39] Ibid., 24.

a campaign to Judah in general and Jerusalem in particular. Na'aman, the most recent scholar who has analyzed Shishak's campaign, concluded that the appearance of Gibeon in the Karnak list is associated with the tribute of the king of Judah.[40] In any case, the question of Jerusalem and Shishak's campaign should be considered in view of the archaeological evidence regarding Jerusalem of the tenth century B.C.E.

---

[40] Nadav Na'aman, "Shishak's Campaign to Palestine As Reflected by the Epigraphic, Biblical and Archaeological Evidence" [Hebrew], *Zion* 63 (1998): 247–76, esp. 269–70.

The United Monarchy in the Countryside: Jerusalem, Judah, and the Shephelah during the Tenth Century B.C.E.

Gunnar Lehmann
Ben-Gurion University of the Negev

Jerusalem of the united monarchy is under debate. What was once viewed as a magnificent capital, displaying the splendor of the mighty united monarchy, is now challenged by some claiming that Jerusalem during the tenth century B.C.E. was no more than a village-like, small settlement.[1] Scholarly opinions have been so forceful that Nadav Naʾaman asks if proponents of this new interpretation would have Jerusalem reduced to the status of a "cow town"?[2] While most contributions in this volume address the many historical and archaeological problems involved in the history of the city itself, this essay looks to the countryside around Jerusalem. The essay does not ignore those other facets of the discussion, but it strives to avoid an increasingly sterile attitude that hands out labels such as "minimalism" or "maximalism." In fact, the best contributions in this debate were never simply minimalist or maximalist, labels that are facile and misleading. In recent years, archaeology and history have developed well beyond this dead-end street, and new agendas are evolving. Staring spellbound at yesterday's struggle by reformulating the same point over and over certainly does not help to overcome the deadlock of minimalism versus maximalism.

---

[1] For a summary of mostly traditional views of biblical Jerusalem, see Shmuel Ahituv and Amihai Mazar, eds., *The History of Jerusalem: The Biblical Period* [Hebrew] (Jerusalem: Yad Izhak Ben-Zvi, 2000). In recent years, an increasing number of scholars are challenging the conventional interpretation of Jerusalem; see, e.g., Ernst Axel Knauf, "Jerusalem in the Late Bronze and Ealy Iron Ages: A Proposal," *TA* 27 (2000): 75–90; and Israel Finkelstein, "The Rise of Jerusalem and Judah: The Missing Link," *Levant* 33 (2001): 105–15.

2 Nadav Naʾaman, "Cow Town or Royal Capital? Evidence for Iron Age Jerusalem," *BAR* 23/4 (1997): 43–47, 67.

This essay thus addresses the problems associated with Jerusalem by moving out into the countryside. Specifically, the essay examines the southern mountains of Hebron and Judah and the western hills of the Shephelah during Iron Age IIA (fig. 4.1). Because the essay focuses on Jerusalem and its biblical importance, the examination of the countryside starts with Jerusalem and, in its bias, thus will return to Jerusalem in the end. The main purpose of this essay is to discuss the implications of the settlement history in Judah and the Shephelah during the tenth century B.C.E. and subsequently to investigate the significance of the evidence for the city of Jerusalem.

Much of the basis for our discussion is found in two unpublished theses of Tel Aviv University. The first one is Yehuda Dagan's "The Shephelah during the Period of the Monarchy," written by one of the most experienced archaeological surveyors of Israel.[3] The second thesis is Avi Ofer's

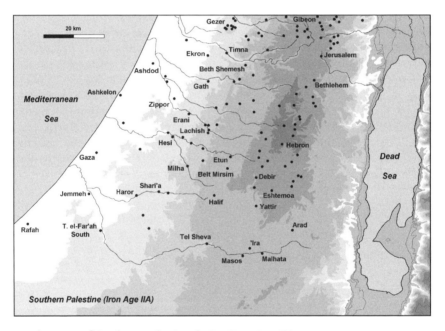

Fig. 4.1. Map of Southern Palestine during Iron Age IIA

---

[3] Yehudah Dagan, "The Shephela during the Period of the Monarchy in Light of Archaeological Excavations and Survey" [Hebrew] (M.A. thesis, Tel Aviv University, 1992). See also idem, *The Shephelah of Judah: A Collection of Articles* [Hebrew] (Tel Aviv: Tel Aviv University, 1982); idem, *Map of Lakhish (98)* (Archaeological Survey of Israel; Jerusalem: Israel Antiquities Authority, 1992); idem, "Cities of the Judean Shephelah and Their Divison into Districts Based on Joshua 16," *ErIsr* 25 (1996): 136–46.

"The Highland of Judah during the Biblical Period." Ofer's doctoral thesis is a comprehensive survey report and settlement study of the Judean highland.[4] While these two theses represent the bulk of the evidence, the essay compares a number of other studies with the studies of Dagan and Ofer, making corrections and additions where necessary (see fig. 4.2).[5]

Our goal is hampered by the fact that there are two major uncertainties concerning the settlement pattern of Judah during the tenth century B.C.E. First, there is an ongoing debate concerning Iron Age chronology. The traditional chronological system has been challenged by

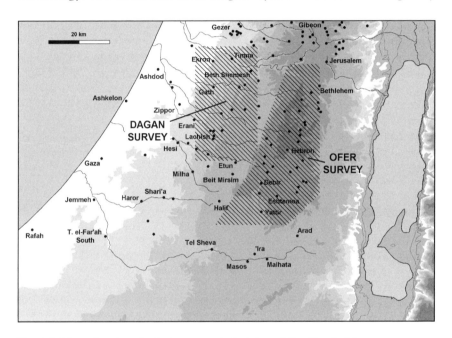

Fig. 4.2. Map of archaeological surveys in Judah and the Shephelah

---

[4] Avi Ofer, "The Highland of Judah during the Biblical Period" [Hebrew] (Ph.D. diss., Tel Aviv University, 1993).

[5] Jack D. Elliott, "Lahav Research Project Regional Survey, 1993," *Lahav Research Project, 1993 Season: Report Part II* (unpublished); Israel Finkelstein et al., *Highlands of Many Cultures: The Southern Samaria Survey: The Sites* (Monograph Series of the Institute of Archaeology, Tel Aviv University 14; Tel Aviv: Sonia and Mario Nadler Institute of Archaeology, 1997); Amos Kloner, *Survey of Jerusalem: The Southern Sector* [Maps 105 and 106] (Archaeological Survey of Israel; Jerusalem: Israel Antiquities Authority, 2000); Alon Shavit, "The Ayalon Valley and Its Vicinity during the Bronze and Iron Ages" [Hebrew] (M.A. thesis, Tel Aviv University, 1992); idem, "Settlement Patterns in the Ayalon Valley in the Bronze and Iron Ages." *TA* 27 (2000): 189–230.

Israel Finkelstein and others, and a proposal for a new "low chronology" has been made. Proponents of the low chronology suggest that the end of the Iron Age I and the Iron Age IIA should be dated some eighty to one hundred years lower than the traditional chronology. This debate is far from over,[6] although for the time being radiocarbon dates seem to favor the low chronology.[7] Yet the results are preliminary at present, and much will depend on the results of an ambitious radiocarbon project conducted by Ayelet Gilboa, Ilan Sharon, and Elisabetha Boaretto.[8] Dozens of Iron Age radiocarbon dates are currently being processed as part of an effort to solve the chronology deadlock. Because the debate has not been resolved, this essay refers to the traditional dates more out of convenience than out of conviction.

The second problem stems from recent research by Avi Faust, who claims that many settlements, especially in the central Judean highlands, were abandoned in Iron Age IIA.[9] In his view, the expansion of very small settlements during Iron Age I was followed by a contraction of the settlement pattern. During the tenth century B.C.E., the population of the many small Iron Age I villages became more concentrated in a fewer number of villages. The result was an abandonment of many small villages during the

---

[6] Amnon Ben-Tor and Dror Ben-Ami, "Hazor and the Archaeology of the Tenth Century B.C.E," *IEJ* 48 (1998): 1–37; Israel Finkelstein, "The Archaeology of the United Monarchy: An Alternative View," *Levant* 28 (1996): 177–87; idem, "The Philistine Countryside," *IEJ* 46 (1996): 225–42; idem, "Bible Archaeology or Archaeology of Palestine in the Iron Age? A Rejoinder," *Levant* 30 (1998): 167–74; idem, "Philistine Chronology: High, Middle, or Low?" in *Mediterranean Peoples in Transition: Thirteenth to Early Tenth Centures BCE: In Honor of Trude Dothan* (ed. S. Gitin et al.; Jerusalem: Israel Exploration Society, 1998), 140–47; idem, "Hazor and the North in the Iron Age: A Low Chronology Perspective," *BASOR* 314 (1999): 55–70; Ernst Axel Knauf, "The 'Low Chronology' and How Not to Deal with It," *BN* 101 (2000): 56–63; Amihai Mazar, "Iron Age Chronology: A Reply to I. Finkelstein," *Levant* 29 (1997): 157–67.

[7] Still unpublished radiocarbon dates from Dor and Megiddo seem to favor the low chronology of Finkelstein; a low-chronology interpretation is also possible for the radiocarbon dates of Tel Rehov (Tell es-Sarem near Sheikh er-Rihab, south of Beth-shean). See Ayelet Gilboa and Ilan Sharon, "Early Iron Age Radiometric Dates from Tel Dor: Preliminary Implications for Phoenicia, and Beyond," *Radiocarbon* 43 (2001) 1343–52; and Amihai Mazar, "The 1997–1998 Excavations at Tel Rehov: Preliminary Report," *IEJ* 49 (1999): 1–42.

[8] Ayelet Giloboa, University of Haifa; Ilan Sharon, the Hebrew University of Jerusalem; and Elisabetha Boaretto, Weizman Institute at Rehovot.

[9] Avi Faust, "From Hamlets to Monarchy: A View from the Countryside on the Formation of the Israelite Monarchy" [Hebrew], *Cathedra* 94 (1997): 7–32.

Iron IIA and an increase in size of the few villages that remained. Faust especially challenges survey results such as that of Judah by Avi Ofer. While the results of the Shephelah survey by Yehudah Dagan seem to support Faust's views, Ofer has proposed an expansion of the settlement pattern in Judah during Iron Age IIA. Faust based his claims exclusively on excavation results, studying a sample of forty sites. He holds that some of the sites in the highlands were not permanently settled, even though very small amounts of Iron Age IIA pottery were found there.[10] He explains this pottery as seasonal agricultural outposts of the remaining villages, a phenomenon well known in Ottoman Palestine in Arabic as *ʿizba* (plural *ʿizab*).[11]

Faust explains that the abandonment of the small villages during Iron Age IIA was due mainly to increasing defense needs, which could be found only in the larger settlements. In response to the need for protection, inhabitants of the numerous smaller villages abandoned their settlements and moved to the larger villages, resulting in their growth in size and population. Faust argues that during the Iron Age IIB these settlements became the nucleus of the beginning urbanization in the mountain regions.

It is currently impossible to test Faust's theory. The present political situation simply does not permit for a reinvestigation of the relevant sites in Judah and the West Bank. Even if Faust is correct, there may be some observations in addition to his that could explain the phenomenon.

Faust's data may suggest that the situation in Judah is comparable to some extent with developments in Greece during the Geometric and Archaic periods, the formation of the *polis*. The early Greek *polis* was far from being a city; it was an alliance of villages with a common cult center and a fortified place for defense, often an acropolis. Cities developed only during the seventh and sixth centuries B.C.E. Until then the *polis* was a rural constitution rather than an urban settlement.[12] The Greek city came into

---

[10] Personal communication.

[11] An *ʿizba* is a seasonal settlement that is connected to a nearby larger village; the meaning of the word is "country estate, farm, rural settlement." See Moshe Brawer, "Frontier Villages in Western Samaria" [Hebrew], in *Judaea and Samaria* (ed. A. Shmueli et al.; Jerusalem: Bet hotsaah Kenaan, ha-hafatsah ha-Hotsaah le-or Misrad ha-bitahon, 737/1977), 411–12; David Grossman, "The Relationship between Settlement Pattern and Resource Utilization: The Case of the North-Eastern Samaria," *Transactions of the Institute of British Geographers* 6/1 (1981): 34. The word goes back to the root *ʿazaba,* "to be far."

[12] Among the many titles on this subject, see Frank Kolb, *Die Stadt im Altertum* (Munich: Beck, 1984), 58–95; Robin Osborne, *Greece in the Making, 1220–479 B.C.* (Routledge History of the Ancient World; London: Routledge, 1996); Anthony M. Snodgrass, *Archaic Greece: The Age of Experiment* (London: Dent & Sons, 1980).

being during the seventh century B.C.E. when many of the villages of the *polis* alliances were abandoned. The population moved closer to their spiritual centers, where fortifications and an agora provided defense and an institutionalized forum for political representation. This process is called *synoikism* in Greek history. Although there was no *polis* formation in ancient Israel, village alliances and eventually early urbanism in Judah may have been formed through *synoikism*.

According to Faust, the phase of settlement contraction during Iron Age IIA was followed by a settlement expansion in Iron Age IIB. Based on this founding of new settlements and agricultural areas, Faust concludes that this expansion must have caused competition and conflicts. It would have been necessary to develop strategies to legitimate such claims on the land. Similar processes were observed in Greece, where a growing population clashed over land rights. One form of legitimizing land ownership was hero-cults.[13] A large number of Bronze Age tombs were found during the Geometric period by local farmers due to the increased intensification of land use, which led to increased competition for agricultural areas. As a result, Bronze Age tombs found in these rural areas were claimed as burials of ancestors and past heroes, confirming rights of land ownership. Such invented traditions may have occurred also in Iron Age Israel, where tombs of ancestors, judges, and patriarchs were revered.

Another phenomenon of Greek *polis* formation may have occurred in ancient Israel, even though a *polis* in the Greek sense of the word did not develop there. According to François de Polignac, the eighth-century B.C.E. *poleis* that would become city-states of classical Greece were defined as much by the boundaries of "civilized" space as by their urban centers. The cults organized social space and articulated social relationships. The city took shape through "religious bipolarity," not only at the central sanctuaries in the city—the acropolis—but also in rural sanctuaries on the edges of the settlement's territory. Sanctuaries "in the wild" identified the *polis* and its sphere of influence, its "civilized" space. These rural sanctuaries were also places for initiation rites and as such instrumental in the formation of the status of *polis* citizens. Together with the urban cults, they gave rise to the concept of the state as a territorial unit distinct from its neighbors. Frontier sanctuaries were therefore often the focus of disputes between emerging communities.[14]

Rural sanctuaries and high places in ancient Israel may have had such functions in certain periods. An example would be Bethel and Luz.

---

[13] Snodgrass, *Archaic Greece,* 37–40.

[14] François de Polignac, *Cults, Territory, and the Origins of the Greek City-State* (Chicago: University of Chicago Press, 1995).

The city Luz had a sanctuary *extra muros,* Bethel. During the Iron Age the city became increasingly identified with the name of its sanctuary, Bethel, which eventually replaced the old name of the settlement, Luz.[15] Similar cases of rural sanctuaries attached to an emerging city may be Gibeon–Nabi Samwil,[16] Ephrata–Bethlehem, Laish–Dan and perhaps Zorah–Beth-shemesh.[17]

Regardless of how one interprets Faust's data, his hypothesis forces one to question just how heavily one can rely on survey results if such plausible and fundamental criticism can be made. Views such as that of Faust have led to a bias that still causes much unfounded doubt and general rejection of surveys in Palestinian archaeology. Certainly, settlement maps drawn with survey data are incomplete. A number of sites have been overlooked, and the estimate of the settlement size is sometimes imprecise. On the other hand, archaeological inspections by government departments are strict in Israel and Palestine, and many sites have been reported and excavated in salvage operations before constructions and developments were started. In addition, many research excavations were conducted in the area of survey investigation. Finally, archaeologists carefully combed the Palestinian landscapes in numerous surveys. Judah and the Shephelah are regions with limited alluvium or aeolian sediments such as loess, which may cover an ancient site. Here erosion damages the sites and exposes artifacts. Thus, except for areas with intensive terracing,[18] the conditions are good for what has been called "site visibility." The density of survey research in both Judah and the Shephelah, as well as in Palestine in general, is exceptionally good and unparalleled in the Near East. Thus, there is a reliable sample of Iron Age sites in the area of investigation. These sites are known from both excavations and from surveys. This sample allows some generalizations and statistical statements.[19]

---

[15] Othmar Keel and Max Küchler, *Geographisch-geschichtliche Landeskunde* (vol. 1 of *Orte und Landschaften der Bibel;* Zürich: Benziger; Göttingen: Vandenhoeck & Ruprecht, 1982–84), 299.

[16] Joseph Blenkinsopp, *Gibeon and Israel: The Role of Gibeon and the Gibeonites in the Political and Religious History of Early Israel* (SOTSMS 2; Cambridge: Cambridge University Press, 1972), 7.

[17] Gunnar Lehmann et al., "Zora und Eschtaol: Ein archäologischer Oberflächensurvey im Gebiet nördlich von Bet Schemesch," *UF* 28 (1996): 401–2.

[18] Shimon Gibson et al., "The Sataf Project of Landscape Archaeology in the Judaean Hills: A Preliminary Report on Four Seasons of Survey and Excavation (1987–89)," *Levant* 23 (1991): 29–54.

[19] For a detailed discussion of site visibility and survey methodology, see Riccardo Francovich and Helen Patterson, eds., *Extracting Meaning from Ploughsoil*

Thus, there are four possibilities to continue with this essay.

1. The conventional chronology is correct and Faust is wrong: the Iron Age IIA sites recorded by Ofer in Judah date to the tenth century and were not abandoned in that period.
2. The low chronology is correct and Faust is wrong: Ofer's settlement pattern of the late Iron Age I represents in fact the situation of the Iron Age IIA. What Ofer dated to the eleventh century B.C.E. has to be dated to the tenth century B.C.E. Likewise, Ofer's Iron Age IIA sites should be dated to the ninth century.
3. The conventional chronology and Faust are correct: with Faust and contra Ofer there are a limited number of large settlements in Judah during the tenth century B.C.E.
4. The low chronology and Faust are correct. In this case Ofer's settlement pattern of the late Iron Age I represents in fact the situation of the tenth century B.C.E. Faust does not claim that the sites with these pottery styles were abandoned. In this scenario, the abandonment of the Iron Age IIA villages according to Faust is thus not a process of the tenth century B.C.E. but of the ninth century B.C.E. Thus, as far as the tenth century B.C.E. is concerned, case 4 equals case 2.

Since the radiocarbon study of the Iron Age chronology is still underway and because it is currently impossible to test Faust's hypothesis in the Palestinian areas of Judah and the West Bank, a compromise must be found in order to write this essay. Our solution will be to discuss only scenarios 1 and 2 in depth. Options 3 and 4 will be discussed shortly in the conclusions of this essay.

This essay will thus present the evidence for both Iron Age I and Iron Age IIA. Followers of the traditional chronology will understand the Iron Age I data as evidence for the time before the tenth century B.C.E., while adherents of the low chronology will date the end of Iron Age I to the tenth century B.C.E.

Assemblages (vol. 5 of *The Archaeology of Mediterranean Landscapes;* Oxford: Oxbow, 1999); Gibson et al., "Sataf Project of Landscape Archaeology," 29–54; Mark Gillings et al., eds., *Geographical Information and Systems and Landscape Archaeology* (vol. 3 of *The Archaeology of Mediterranean Landscapes;* Oxford: Oxbow, 1999); Philippe Leveau et al., eds., *Environmental Reconstruction in Mediterranean Landscape Archaeology* (vol. 2 of *The Archaeology of Mediterranean Landscapes;* Oxford: Oxbow, 1999); Marinella Pasquinucci and Frederic Trément, eds., *Non-Destructive Techniques Applied to Landscape Archaeology* (vol. 4 of *The Archaeology of Mediterranean Landscapes;* Oxford: Oxbow, 1999).

The map in figure 4.1 (p. 118) illustrates the settlement distribution of what is conventionally assumed to be the tenth century B.C.E. in southern Palestine. The settlements on that map should have been occupied at some point during the tenth century B.C.E. Although there are more theoretical attempts to deal with the difficult question of how many archaeological sites of one period were in fact contemporary,[20] the most convincing method is the retrieval of precisely datable artifacts from those sites. In the case of the settlements in Judah and the Shephelah, Ofer and Dagan explain their criteria of dating explicitly.[21] The dating of the rest of the sites indicated in figure 4.1, which were not surveyed by Dagan or Ofer, relies mainly on excavation results. The surveys conducted by scholars other than Dagan and Ofer unfortunately do not usually specify the precise period of the Iron Age II during which a site was occupied.[22] General statements such as "Iron Age II," a period that spans the tenth to sixth centuries B.C.E., do not allow a more precise dating to any century within the Iron Age. Ben-Gurion University; Claremont Graduate University, California; and Rostock University, Germany, are currently carrying out a survey of pre-Hellenistic settlements in southwest Israel, which may allow the drawing of more detailed settlement maps in the future.[23]

MEDITERRANEAN LANDSCAPES

The traditional method of archaeology in Israel and Palestine was to concentrate on settlement remains at tells. However, archaeological research during the past twenty-five years increasingly incorporates all relics of human activity in the landscape, thus providing more data for an investigation of ancient agriculture, land use, and environmental studies. This essay applies an approach of "landscape archaeology," which works with Fernand Braudel's paradigm of Mediterranean landscapes, in order to

---

[20] Robert Dewar, "Incorporating Variation in Occupation Span into Settlement-Pattern," *American Antiquity* 56 (1991): 604–20.

[21] Ofer, "Highland of Judah," 36–40, pl. 9 with pottery dated by him to Iron Age IIA. In the case of the Shephelah, Dagan used the pottery comparisons from Lachish Stratum V for his dating of a site to the tenth century B.C.E. (Dagan, "Shephelah during the Period of the Monarchy," 252–55).

[22] For example, Jack D. Elliott, "Preliminary Report on the Lahav Regional Survey, 1992 Field Season," *Lahav Research Project, 1992 Season: Report Part II*, 292–323; or Shavit, "Settlement Patterns in the Ayalon Valley," 189–230.

[23] This survey is directed by Tammi J. Schneider, Hermann M. Niemann, and the author.

test its validity for the landscapes under investigation here. Braudel distinguished between coastal plains and wide plainlike valleys, hill-country and mountain areas.[24] As in most Mediterranean regions, the plains of Palestine are characterized by fertile alluvial or, in the south, loess soils. Rainfall and streams are sufficient for agriculture without irrigation. However, in many areas of the Mediterranean the water was not always a blessing. If not drained, the plains were a spectacle of misery and desolation. Where the plain is very flat and the water flow is confronted with obstacles such as sand dunes, swamps and wetlands were formed. These areas had high rates of malaria and other related diseases. Such conditions exist in the coastal Sharon and Akko Plain, as well as in the Jezreel Valley. Swamps are less common, however, in southwest Palestine, in the land of the Philistines.

In northern Palestine, cash crops apparently played an important role in the development of the necessary investment capacity and were financed by an influx of profits from long-term and large-scale trade.[25] In times of political stability and prosperity, profitable products were cultivated for export and the safe investment of profits made in risky sea trade.

It is especially intriguing to compare the Phoenician economy with that of the Philistines. During the Iron Age I and IIA, the Phoenician mercantile and agricultural economy was able to develop what might be called "investment capacities." *Capital* in the modern sense existed only in rudimentary form in the Iron Age. It was already possible to "invest" and secure profits made in the high-risk sea trade in business, which was less risky. Wealth permitted the employment of large numbers of workers in workshops producing textiles and other craft products. The few less valuable raw materials available in the land of the Phoenicians were turned into value-added craft products such as luxury items. The Phoenician economy was able to "invest" and to employ experts well versed in the necessary technologies. The Phoenicians were also able to invest in their fleet and to man them with trained sailors. The wood required for building the ships must have been imported from the hill country and the mountains. The sea trade made accessible additional raw materials that were not available in the immediate hinterland of the Phoenicians or Philistines. These materials formed an integral part of the Phoenician

---

[24] Fernand Braudel, *The Mediterranean and the Mediterranean World in the Age of Philip II* (London: Fontana, 1972).

[25] Gunnar Lehmann, "Phoenicians in Western Galilee: First Results of an Archaeological Survey in the Hinterland of Akko," in *Studies in the Archaeology of the Iron Age in Israel and Jordan* (ed. A. Mazar; JSOTSup 331; Sheffield: Sheffield Academic Press, 2001), 65–112.

industry. To what extent is it possible to translate such structures to the land of the Philistines?

In agriculture, the Philistine wealth permitted the production of cash crops such as wine and oil and the maintenance of the necessary manpower. As before, value-added production and expertise were part of the business. Nevertheless, as with the Phoenicians, the Philistine economy was not "capitalism." There was no dynamic investment in the modern sense, and the "financial" system was primitive.[26] On the other hand, the Philistine trade and landownership certainly produced profits for a certain class.[27]

According to Braudel the largest settlements, the cities, are also found in the plain. Even though urbanism is a phenomenon of the plain, the predominant form of settlement in the plain is still the village, some of them large "village-towns." The presence of large villages and cities means that the Mediterranean plain is commonly characterized by a relatively large population, especially in comparison to the neighboring hill country or mountainous regions.

The agricultural basis for all of these populations is grain production. In contrast to the villages of the hill country, the wealthy mercantile cities had the capacity to produce and invest profits, and these capacities often led to wealthy landowners and poor peasants. All of these characteristics meant that in the plain the gap between rich and poor widened rapidly. In times of prosperity, the rich became even wealthier while the benefit to the poor was marginal.

If this hypothesis is accepted, the Philistines would have been able to produce in large quantities and to employ both experts and considerable numbers of less-trained workers. As a result, production would have been of a high quality and, of course, profitable. The more significant question for the purposes of our study is not whether the Philistines managed, as the Phoenicians, to integrate trade, manufacture, and agriculture into one economic system. Rather, we must be more concerned with determining if private initiative played a role in this system and to what extent the state(s) controlled economic activities.

In Braudel's paradigm, the developments in the plain described above contrast with the developments in the hill country. In comparison to the plain, the hill country was underdeveloped. The main reason for this lack of development was that the investment cost of development was much higher than in the plains. Not only were the soils poorer in quality than

---

[26] See Moses I. Finley, *The Ancient Economy* (London: Hogarth, 1985), esp. ch. 5.

[27] Ibid., 188–91.

those in the plains, but the land development in the hill country required wood and brush clearing as well as terracing.

The plain's "investment capacity" may have had a significant influence on these economically underdeveloped areas. It may have profited from the exploitation of such "underdeveloped" areas as the hill country with its agricultural potential for value-added agricultural production in oil and wine, especially since the hill country was easily accessible, bordering immediately on the territory of the plain's city-states. Developed technology and "investment capacity" went together with cheap labor, raw materials, and rich agricultural land in the plain. This dynamic economic potential of the plain is in contrast to the limited resources and population in the hill country.

Throughout history, the Mediterranean hill-country regions typically were easy prey for kings, soldiers, and pirates. In times of efficient government in the plain, the hills were usually integrated into the plain's economy and polities. In light of this reconstruction, it is difficult to see the population of Judah during Iron Age I and IIA efficiently competing with the Philistines for control of the Shephelah. These low hills of the Shephelah were most probably in the hands of the Philistine city-states. The agriculture of this region was characterized by a combination of grain production in limited suitable areas and terraced crops such as olives, wine, and tree orchards. Often forest clearing took place for the large demands of the plain. The predominant form of settlement in the hills was the small village, although there were a few larger settlements in the Shephelah during the Iron Age, such as Beth-shemesh or Lachish.

The Mediterranean mountains, the third major landscape in Braudel's system, have even less agricultural area available for grain production than the low hills (that is, the Shephelah). Production there is usually characterized by a subsistence economy. The mountain farmers typically would have limited grain production that was complemented by wine, olives, and fruit trees. The mountain pastures are used for sheep and goat herds, and these herds would produce milk and meat products. The predominant form of settlement is the hamlet. The limited resources often caused the Mediterranean mountains to be relatively overpopulated, while the absolute number of the population was small. While relying on subsistence farming, mountain farmers were usually in economic contact with the plain. They exchanged meat, milk products, cash crops, and timber with the advanced craft and food production of the plain.

Applying Braudel's paradigm to the Palestinian mountains, one observes that the Judean hill country is not as large, remote, elevated, and extended as other mountain landscapes in the Mediterranean. Wagstaff describes Judah as an area of mid-latitude position in the region and of moderate elevation.[28] The area was thus less remote than other Mediterranean mountain regions, such as Moab or Edom in Transjordan. On the other hand, another of Braudel's features seems to fit Judah well: the poverty of the region in comparison with the urban centers of the plain. While the gap between rich and poor increased in the plain during times of relative prosperity, in the mountains there was a shared sense of equality among the poor.

Despite the limited resources and subsequent subsistence lifestyle in the mountains, there is one advantage: the terrain provides "mountain freedom."[29] The mountains were less accessible and desirable than the plains and the hill country, so the mountains served as a refuge from the kings, soldiers, and pirates who plagued the hills. Thus, during the early Iron Age the valleys and slopes, together with dense woods and shrubs, created a distance between the mountains and the plain, with its control and taxes. Being free from the cities' control, the mountaineers were viewed by the inhabitants of the plains as local bandits and robbers. These "mountain people" were people difficult to control, wild, and independent.

This feature is well illustrated by young David and his resistance to Saul. It is clear that David and his wanderings in the Judean mountains were more than an individual and random event but rather were based on structural conditions. Comparisons can be made with the description of Grisafi, a Sicilian mafia leader from 1917, who dwelled in the mountains. The account reads like the biblical description of David:

> The outlaw Grisafi, a mountain-dweller of thirty-six years of age, originally a shepherd, who commanded the armed band, was a consummate bandit. Fierce and cautious, most redoutable, up to all tricks and stratagems of guerilla warfare, and protected by a thick net of local favour strengthened by terror.... He had set up in the western part of the province of Agrigento a kind of special domain over which he ruled absolutely, interfering in every kind of affair, even the most intimate, making his will felt in every field, including levying tolls and taxes, blackmailing and committing crimes of bloodshed without stint. Aided not only by his boldness but by constant luck, and being a good shot, he had always succeeded in escaping from the toils of the police; he had escaped unhurt from several conflicts.[30]

---

[28] John Malcolm Wagstaff, *The Evolution of Middle Eastern Landscapes: An Outline to A.D. 1840* (London: Croom Helm, 1985), 53.

[29] Lawrence E. Stager, "The Archaeology of the Family in Ancient Israel," *BASOR* 260 (1985): 5.

[30] Cesare Mori, *The Last Struggle with the Mafia* (London: Putnam, 1933), 130–32.

Obviously, it is not a charismatic personality alone but also geographical and environmental conditions that contribute to a phenomenon such as David. Some of the mountain rulers such as Labayu of the Amarna letters and Saul of the books of Samuel bear much similarity with each other. The mountains encourage certain political structures, and, as one observes with both Labayu and Saul, it is dangerous for mountain rulers to leave their territory and to enter the plain.

In the case of David, the biblical tradition (of whatever period) identifies some sites of his activities in the wilderness.[31] These sites are located at the southeastern edge of the Judean settlements of Iron Age IIA (fig. 4.3), in an area that was increasingly settled in the tenth century B.C.E., according to Ofer.[32] Despite this expansion of settlement during or immediately after the time of David, for the authors and readers of 1 Sam 23:14–26; 25, David's wilderness years represented a convincing scenario. The outlaws following David are characterized by their mobility, their local social coalitions, and the difficult accessibility of the terrain with which biblical David was well acquainted, hiding in a desert environment.

POPULATION SIZE

It is beyond the scope of this study to test the entire Braudelian paradigm. Instead, I will concentrate on some aspects of spatial organization of Judah during the tenth century B.C.E. and discuss the results against the background of a structural history as outlined above. In order to address issues of spatial organization, we should begin with an attempt to estimate the ancient population of Judah in the tenth century B.C.E. Estimating the population size of archaeological sites is one of the most important tasks of settlement archaeology, since the population size is, as in the case of estimating village endogamy, one of the most important keys to an archaeology that is concerned with social and cultural dynamics.

While these numbers will be essential for most of the analyses applied in this essay, one recognizes that estimates of ancient populations are notoriously difficult to make. However, there are a number of important recent studies on estimating the population of ancient societies that make our task more manageable.[33] The population of Palestine during the

---

[31] Baruch Halpern, *David's Secret Demons: Messiah, Murderer, Traitor, King* (Grand Rapids: Eerdmans, 2001), 284–87.

[32] Ofer, "Highland of Judah."

[33] For methodology, see Magen Broshi, "Methodology of Population Estimates: The Roman-Byzantine Period As a Case Study," in *Biblical Archaeology Today, 1990: Proceedings of the Second International Congress on Biblical Archaeology*

nineteenth and early twentieth centuries, especially the statistics and census of the British Mandate Government in Palestine in the 1930s and 1940s, is a key for the estimates used here.[34] Some of these data were summarized by Biger and Grossman.[35] They concluded that the density per built-up hectare for Palestine as a whole was an average of 250 persons.

(ed. A. Biran and J. Aviram; Jerusalem: Israel Exploration Society, 1993), 420–25; Magen Broshi and Ram Gophna, "The Settlements and Population of Palestine during the Early Bronze Age," *BASOR* 253 (1984): 41–53; C. D. De Roche, "Population Estimates from Settlement Area and Number of Residences," *Journal of Field Archaeology* 10 (1983): 187–92; George E. Harmon, "Floor Area and Population Determination" (Ph.D. diss., Southern Baptist Theological Seminary, 1983); Fekri A. Hassan, "Demographic Archaeology," *Advances in Archaeological Method and Theory* 1 (1978): 49–103; idem, "Demography and Archaeology," *Annual Review of Anthropology* 8 (1979): 137–60; idem, *Demographic Archaeology* (New York: Academic, 1981); Carol Kramer, "Estimating Prehistoric Populations: An Ethnoarchaeological Approach," in *L'Archeologie de l'Iraq du début de l'époque néolithique a 333 avant notre ère: Perspectives et limites de l'interprétation anthropologique des documents, Colloque Internationaux, Paris 1978* (Paris: Centre National de la Recherche Scientifique, 1980), 315–34; Leon Marfoe, "Review of Early Arad I, by Ruth Amiran," *JNES* 31 (1980): 317–21; John Nicholas Postgate, "How Many Sumerians Per Hectare? Probing the Anatomy of an Early City [Tell Abu Salabikh]," *Cambridge Archaeological Journal* 4 (1994): 47–65; Yigal Shiloh, "The Population of Iron Age Palestine in the Light of a Sample Analysis of Urban Plans, Areas, and Population Density," *BASOR* 239 (1980): 25–35; Jeffrey R. Zorn, "Estimating the Population Size of Ancient Settlements: Methods, Problems, Solutions, and a Case Study," *BASOR* 295 (1994): 31–48. Most recently: Israel Finkelstein, "Ethno-Historical Background: Land Use and Demography in Recent Generations," in Finkelstein et al., *Highlands of Many Cultures,* 109–30; John Bintliff and Kostas Sbonias, eds., *Reconstructing Past Population Trends in Mediterranean Europe (3000 BC–AD 1800)* (vol. 1 of *The Archaeology of Mediterranean Landscapes;* Oxford: Oxbow, 1999).

[34] J. B. Barron, comp., *Report and General Abstracts of the Census of 1922 Taken on 23rd of October, 1922* (Britain: Government of Palestine, 1922); E. Mills, ed., *Census of Palestine 1931* (2 vols.; Alexandria: Government of Palestine, 1933); Office of Statistics, *Village Statistics, Jerusalem 1938* (Jerusalem: Government of Palestine, 1938); Office of Statistics, *Village Statistics, Jerusalem 1945* (Jerusalem: Government of Palestine, 1945); Government of Palestine, Office of Statistics, "Survey of Social and Economic Conditions in Arab Villages, 1944," *General Monthly Bulletin of Current Statistics* (1945): 426–47, 509–17, 559–67, 745–64; (1946): 46–56, 554–73.

[35] Gideon Biger and David Grossman, "Village and Town Populations in Palestine during the 1930s–1940s and Their Relevance to Ethnoarchaeology," in *Biblical Archaeology Today, 1990: Proceedings of the Second International Congress on Biblical Archaeology, Jerusalem, June–July 1990, Supplement* (ed. A. Biran and J. Aviram; Jerusalem: Israel Exploration Society, 1993), 19–30.

Yet there were significant regional differences. In the mountain areas, the density was 160–260 per hectare, while in the coastal plain it was as high as 260–400 persons per hectare.

In this paper a density factor of 150–300 persons per built-up hectare is assumed. The estimate is thus considerably imprecise, but this assumption enables us to operate at least within a certain dimension of population size. While an estimate of 150–300 persons in a village may seem rather inaccurate, it makes clear that there were not 600 or 1,000. Two maps are used in this essay to present the estimates of the population of Judah in the tenth century B.C.E. Figure 4.3 represents the settlement map of what is conventionally assumed to be the tenth century B.C.E. Figure 4.4 shows the settlements of the tenth century B.C.E. according to the proposed low chronology, which date to Iron Age I according to the traditional chronology.

According to the available data, the built-up area of the Judean mountains south of Jerusalem—Jerusalem not included—was almost 18.1 ha in Iron Age I, while it reached 33.7 ha in Iron Age IIA. As a comparison, the

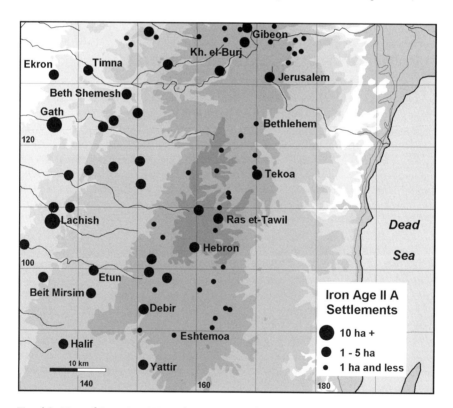

Fig. 4.3. Map of Iron Age IIA settlements in Judah and the Shephelah

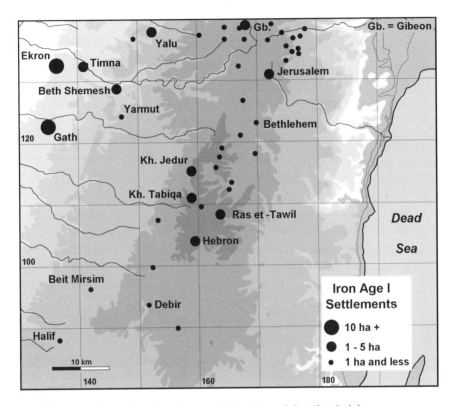

Fig. 4.4. Map of Iron Age I settlements in Judah and the Shephelah

built-up area on the two maps here north of Jerusalem—including the city—was 7.9 ha in Iron Age I and almost 19.2 ha in Iron Age IIA. The area north of Jerusalem includes only the immediate hinterland of that city. In addition there are data for the Shephelah, where 39.9 ha were built up in Iron Age I, 95 ha in Iron Age IIA.

Table 4.1. Estimate of built-up area and population in Judah, the Jerusalem area, and the southern Shephelah during Iron Age I and IIA

	built-up area (ha) Iron I	built-up area (ha) Iron IIA	population estimate Iron I	Population estimate Iron IIA
Iron Age I Shephelah	39.9	95.0	5,985–11,970	14,250–28,500
Iron Age I south of Jerusalem (without Jerusalem)	18.1	33.7	2,715–5,430	5,055–10,110
Iron Age I north of Jerusalem (incl. Jerusalem)	7.9	19.2	1,185–2,370	2,880–5,760
Total	65.9	147.9		

As the Braudelian paradigm of Mediterranean landscapes predicted, the mountain regions are less populated than the lower hill country. The built-up area in the Shephelah is twice as large as the Judean in Iron Age I and even three times larger in Iron Age IIA. Most of this built-up area is concentrated in two cities, Ekron (20 ha) and Gath (15 ha). Both cities account for 87.7 percent of the total built-up area in the Shephelah. In addition, there are only six more small villages in that area. This hyper-integration into an urban framework characterizes the Philistine countryside in this period and will be discussed below.

Another interesting point is the fast growth of areas north of Jerusalem in general and in the areas represented here on the maps in particular. Here, in Benjamin, the built-up area grows by more than 243 percent. The population density in this region during Iron Age IIA is much higher than in Judah. In the Judean mountains, the built-up area grew only slowly from Iron Age I to Iron Age IIA. While the growth factor was 2.4 in the Shephelah and 2.4 in the region north of Jerusalem, it was just 1.9 in Judah.

The city of Jerusalem was apparently rather small in both periods, Iron Age I and IIA. For the reconstruction we depend on the distribution of pottery from the particular periods, as well as on the few architectural remains of that time. Domestic architecture and residential evidence of the tenth century B.C.E. (conventional chronology) was found mostly in the eastern part of the City of David.[36] The remains were found inside the fortified areas as well as outside of the wall, with evidence of social stratification.[37] The only monumental, nondomestic architectural complex excavated is the so-called "stepped structure." This structure and its two components consist of a substructure with a system of stone terraces and an overlying superstructure with rubble core and a stepped mantle of stones.[38] I understand this structure as a fortification at the weakest topographical point of the City of David, the northern front.[39] Against Knauf,[40] I interpret the stepped structure as the northeast corner of the city. Where exposed in Area G, it is clearly visible that the stepped structure runs south–northward

---

[36] Alon De Groot, "The 'Invisible City' of the Tenth Century B.C.E." [Hebrew], in *New Studies on Jerusalem: Proceedings of the Seventh Conference, December 2001* (ed. A. Faust and E. Baruch; Ramat Gan: Bar-Ilan University, 2001), 29–34 .

[37] Jane M. Cahill, "Jerusalem at the Time of the United Monarchy: The Archaeological Evidence" [Hebrew], in Faust and Baruch, *New Studies on Jerusalem: Proceedings of the Seventh Conference,* 21–28.

[38] For a summary, see David Tarler and Jane M. Cahill, "David, City of," *ABD* 2:52–67.

[39] For previous interpretations, see the summary in ibid.

[40] Knauf, "Jerusalem in the Late Bronze and Early Iron Ages," 75–90.

in the direction of the Temple Mount but turns west in Area G, providing an elevated terrace to the City of David in front of the saddle between the City of David and the Temple Mount.[41]

The date of the terraces and the mantle of the stepped structure are debated, with archaeologists generally opting for one of three options.

1. They might have been built together in the thirteenth–twelfth century.[42]
2. The terraces might be from the Late Bronze Age and the mantle from the tenth century.[43]
3. The terraces date to the thirteenth–twelfth century and the superstructure to the tenth or ninth century.[44]

With Finkelstein, I would opt cautiously for the following scenario: sub- and superstructures were not built together.[45] Several factors point to this conclusion: (1) the pottery assemblages in both sub- and superstructure are different; (2) an Iron Age I house with a collared-rim jar on its floor was found *under* the substructure; (3) no tenth-century pottery was found in the substructure, while tenth–ninth century pottery was present in the superstructure. Therefore, it seems reasonable to conclude that the substructure with its terraces was the first fortification attempt in Jerusalem during Iron Age I. The superstructure with its stepped stone mantle completed these fortification efforts in the tenth century (or ninth century in the low chronology). Most important in the context of this study is the size of the City of David that is included by both the sub- and superstructure. In both phases Jerusalem would have been a small city of maximal 450 x 120 m = 5.4 ha. According to the modest architectural and pottery evidence, the size of Jerusalem may be estimated to some 2 ha during Iron

---

[41] For a photograph of this situation, see Tarler and Cahill, "David, City of," 2:56.

[42] Ibid., 2:52–67. See also Cahill's essay in this volume.

[43] Kathleen Kenyon, *Digging up Jerusalem* (London: Benn, 1974), 95–103; Yigal Shiloh, *Excavations at the City of David, vol. I, 1978–1982: Interim Report of the First Five Seasons* (Qedem 19; Jerusalem: Institute of Archaeology, Hebrew University of Jerusalem, 1984), 16–17.

[44] Margreet Steiner, "The Jebusite Ramp of Jerusalem: The Evidence from the Macalister, Kenyon, and Shiloh Excavations," in Biran and Aviram, *Biblical Archaeology Today, 1990,* 585–88; idem, "Redating the Terraces of Jerusalem," *IEJ* 44 (1994): 13–20.

[45] Finkelstein, "Rise of Jerusalem and Judah," 106. He does not rule out the possibility that both structures might have been built separately. Finkelstein assigns to the strata his low-chronology dates.

Age I and some 4 ha during Iron Age IIA. Applying our population factor, there would have been a population of 300–600 in Iron Age I and 600–1,200 in Iron Age IIA in Jerusalem.[46]

SOCIAL MOVEMENTS: ENDOGAMY AND MARRIAGE ALLIANCES

The settlements in Iron Age Judah had contacts with each other, and, although mobility was limited, some movements occurred on a regular basis. One such movement was a social one, contracting marriages between villages, or village exogamy. This village exogamy was necessary in order to avoid incest. There is a relationship between village size and village exogamy. The larger the settlement population, the more marriage partners are available in the village without running the risk of incest; in other words, village endogamy will be predominant. In smaller villages, on the other hand, more people are closely related to each other and thus have to look for a partner outside of their small community; that is, they have to engage in exogamy. This has important implications for ancient village societies such as the early Iron Age villages in the central highlands of Palestine. Most of these settlements are very small, often not larger than one hectare.[47] Thus, exogamy must have been extensive.

In a comprehensive study, Adams and Kasakoff collected data on marriages from studies of nonindustrial societies from all over the world in order to investigate the range of sizes of endogamous groups and the reasons of variations that exist within this range. They thus discussed the forces that serve to confine the social horizon of a people.

Exogamy plays an important role in the social interaction of villages with each other. Although it is widely underestimated in the local traditions,[48]

---

[46] Compare this with Tarler and Cahill, "David, City of," 2:65, who quote other estimates. This essay excludes the Temple Mount as a settlement area and minimizes the extent of occupation on the western slopes of the City of David. In my view, nothing justifies an assumed 10 ha settlement area on the Temple Mount in the Solomonic period.

[47] Stager, "Archaeology of the Family," 23–24.

[48] The local traditions often exaggerate the amount of endogamy in their community. The statistics, however, show clearly the differences between the local opinion and the factual behavior. Exogamy is considered to be "bad," but it is widely practiced. Among the many references for this observation are Hilma Natalia Granquist, *Marriage Conditions in a Palestinian Village* [Artas] (2 vols.; Helsingsfors: Societas Scientiarum Fennica; 1931–35), 1:92; Louise Elizabeth Sweet, *Tell Tooqan: A Syrian Village* (Anthropological Papers of the Museum of Anthropology of the University of Michigan 14; Ann Arbor: University of Michigan Press, 1960), 176; Jeremy Boissevain, *Hal-Farrug: A Village in Malta* (New York: Holt, Rinehart

exogamy is in fact one of the key factors of social change, communication, and territorial organization of nonstate societies. With an increase in exogamy propinquity, more people in a particular region are related to each other and more people communicate with each other. As a result, groups in different villages with increasing family relationships form marriage alliances, systems of interlocking subgroups that extend over their territories. These groups and their spatial interaction are instrumental in the formation of tribes and tribal coalitions, shaping the social and political landscape on nonstate societies.

These observations and considerations have been developed and advanced for archaeological research by Reinhard Bernbeck. In his study of early Mesopotamian villages and their modes of production, Bernbeck developed a formula that could estimate the endogamy within an ancient settlement.[49] His formula is drawn from the societies mentioned by Adams and Kasakoff.[50] In other words, Bernbeck uses anthropological data to explain ancient social interaction. In my study of twenty villages of different nonindustrial societies, I utilized the methodology from the studies of Adams, Kasakoff, and Bernbeck.[51] As a result, I propose to estimate village endogamy with a modified formula (E = village endogamy, pop = population of the settlement): E = 15.047 Ln(pop) - 37.174.

Exogamy is clearly related to a spatial pattern. In all observed communities people tried to marry in the immediate neighborhood if they married out. Such regional patterns existed also in the traditional Palestinian society. Proximity is an essential factor in exogamous marriages. Anthropological data from Palestine during the 1930s and 1940s demonstrate that 80 percent of all village marriages were contracted with spouses within the village and from adjacent or neighboring villages.[52]

An example of this observation is Artas, a Palestinian village in Judah a few kilometers south of Bethlehem. In this village an ethnographer, Hilma

---

& Winston, 1969), 37; Edmund Ronald Leach, *Pul Eliya—A Village in Ceylon: A Study of Land Tenure and Kinship* (Cambridge: Cambridge University Press, 1961), 168; John Gulick, *Social Structure and Culture Change in a Lebanese Village* [al-Munsif] (New York: Viking Fund Publications, 1955), 129–30.

[49] Reinhard Bernbeck, *Die Auflösung der häuslichen Produktionsweise* (Berliner Beiträge zum Vorderen Orient 14; Berlin: Reimer, 1994), 39–40.

[50] John W. Adams and Alice B. Kasakoff, "Factors Underlying Endogamous Group Size," in *Regional Analysis 2: Social Systems* (ed. C. A. Smith; New York: Academic, 1976), 157.

[51] For details of the method, see Gunnar Lehmann, "Reconstructing the Social Landscape of Early Israel: Marriage Alliances in a Rural Context" *TA* (in press).

[52] Breuer, *Social and Economic Conditions,* 430–31.

Granquist, studied marriage customs in the traditional Palestinian society.[53] In 1927 Granquist recorded a population of 530 in the village and
335 marriages, which encompass all marriages of this village with a
research depth of one hundred years. During these one hundred years
there were 151 marriages in Artas in which both partners were born in
Artas (endogamy in the village 45.1 percent). In 113 marriages one partner came from another village (exogamy in the village 33.7 percent); in
71 cases a member of the village left Artas to marry outside (exogamy outside the village 21.2 percent). The 335 marriages that Granquist recorded
involved 670 persons. Of these, 184 either left or joined the village. In
other words, in one hundred years Artas exchanged 184 persons, that is,
27.5 percent of all married persons, with its neighboring villages. In a
patrilocal society such as the traditional Palestinian communities, the people moving are almost exclusively women, who move into the household
of the groom.

Of the 264 endogamous and exogamous village marriages in Artas[54]
recorded by Granquist, 57.2 percent were endogamous in the village. If the
marriages with villages within a radius of 5 km around Artas are included,
80.3 percent of the village marriages are accounted for. If we extend this
radius to 10 km distance, 88.3 percent of marriages are included; in 15 km
distance, 94.3; and in 30km distance, 97.3 percent (see fig. 4.5). When the
findings from this village are combined with the findings from eight other
communities, the trend line is seen to be a logarithmic function. On the
bases of these findings, many more examples from the Middle East, and
from other parts of the world,[55] we have good reason to assume that the
spatial distribution of exogamy around a village is predictable by a logarithmic function.

Just as individual villages have an "80 percent field of marriage interaction" around them, whole regions exchange around 80 percent of their
marriage spouses with each other.[56] Such regions or "80 percent groups of
endogamous regions," defined by the intermarriage of some 80 percent of
their marriages, play an important role in the spatial organization of social
interaction, including the formation of political units. Such an exchange
between the villages may be called "intervillage endogamy." Through this
process, the villages form a semiclosed group, exchanging most of their
spouses within the confinements of this unit. Such 80-percent groups can

---

[53] Granquist, *Marriage Conditions in a Palestinian Village*.

[54] The seventy-one marriages of Artas women leaving the village are not included
here.

[55] Lehmann, "Reconstructing the Social Landscape."

[56] Adams and Kasakoff, "Factors Underlying Endogamous Group Size," 155–56.

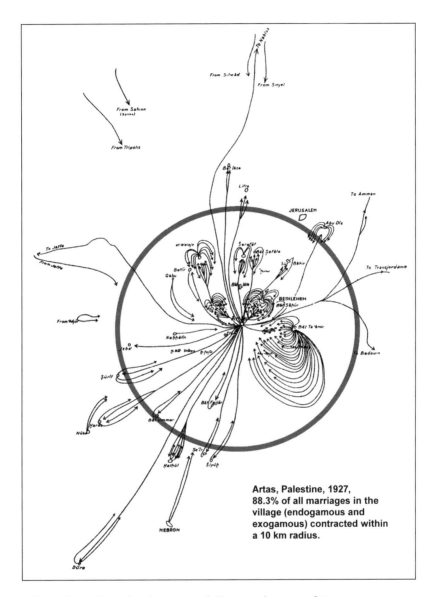

Artas, Palestine, 1927,
88.3% of all marriages in the
village (endogamous and
exogamous) contracted within
a 10 km radius.

Fig. 4.5. Relationship of endogamy and distance: the case of Artas

be recognized by the fact that after the rate of endogamy that defines this group is reached, the size of the population involved increases almost astronomically for only a very small increase in rates of marriages, that is, endogamy (see the example of Artas above).

Eighty-percent groups are semiautonomous social microcosms within which a large portion of daily interaction occurs. For pastoralists, the 80-percent group is typically the "tribe."[57] In the highlands of New Guinea, it is a valley. In peasant societies, it might be a set of small villages close to each other or in the neighborhood of a larger settlement.

Adams and Kasakoff have found that marriages contracted outside an 80-percent group are often made by individuals of high status or by immediate neighbors of an 80-percent group.[58] However, villages that belong to an 80-percent group usually try to marry within the borders of their group. The 80-percent groups thus appear to be discrete. Geographical and cultural factors may influence the social fabric of the groups. Although they are defined by the marriage interaction in the first place, alliances and coalitions may arise from the daily interaction and the propinquity that results from their marriage ties.

The areas within which these processes take place are geographically *fields of movement* or *fields of interaction.*[59] These fields of interaction have no absolute limits, and their borders are open to influences from outside. The limits of movement within the geographical *fields of interaction* may serve to define the territory of marriage alliances. As demonstrated, there are fewer marriages over increasing distances. The 80-percent margin of marriage proved to be a useful limit to the more intensive exchange between residential groups. This is Haggett's *mean field* of movement.[60] It specifies the area beyond which marriage becomes increasingly unlikely.

In order to isolate 80-percent fields of marriage interaction in Iron Age Judah, I defined groups of villages whose settlements are connected by topography (accessibility) and shared resources (land and water) and that are divided from other nearby villages and their 80-percent groups by wadis, mountains, or other topographical features. In addition, all the villages in such a group should be within a day's walking distance from each other. The populations of these settlements are added until an 80-percent group of marriage probability is reached. In other words, a group of villages is reconstructed that would exchange 80 percent of its

---

[57] The problem is the definition of "tribe." Although Emanuel Marx (*The Bedouin of the Negev* [New York: Praeger, 1967]) has defined the tribe as a territorial unit, others see it as a political unit. People residing in a tribal territory need not be members of the tribe, but people residing in a village are always members of the village and as such are counted within the village endogamy.

[58] Adams and Kasakoff, "Factors Underlying Endogamous Group Size," 155–56.

[59] See Peter Haggett, *Locational Analysis in Human Geography* (London: Arnold, 1965), 40–55.

[60] Ibid., 41.

marriages among each other, that is, the mean field of marriage movements. The result of this procedure for Judah during the Iron Age I and Iron Age IIA is illustrated in this essay in two maps (figs. 4.6 and 4.7).[61]

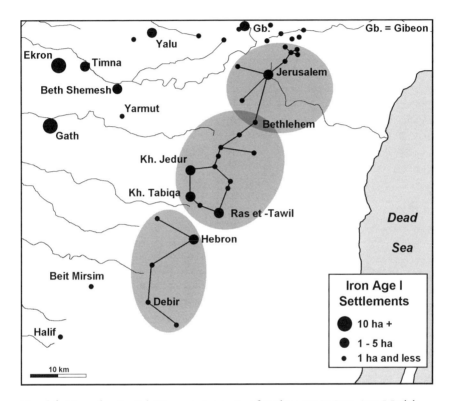

Fig. 4.6. Map of potential 80-percent groups of endogamy in Iron Age I Judah

According to the equation of village endogamy, a population of approximately 2,300 persons constitutes an 80-percent group. However, empirical data show that there are societies with 80-percent groups ranging from a population of 700 to 6,000 people. This essay assumes a total population of approximately 5,000 to 10,000 in the Iron Age IIA Judah.[62]

---

[61] For a comparable analysis of villages, village territory, and mean fields of interaction around them, see Hermann M. Niemann, "Stadt, Land und Herrschaft: Skizzen und Materialien zur Sozialgeschichte im monarchischen Israel" (D.S.T. diss., Universität Rostock, 1990).

[62] Israel Finkelstein, *The Archaeology of the Israelite Settlement* (Jersualem: Israel Exploration Society, 1988), 193, uses a density factor of 250 persons per hectare, a

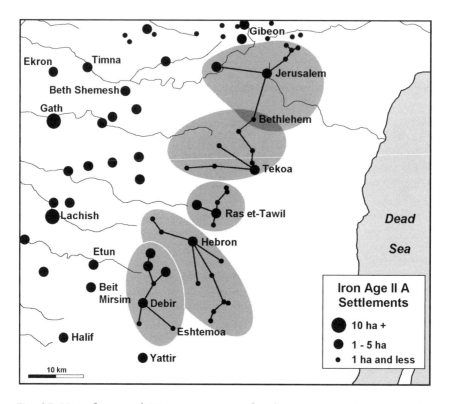

Fig. 4.7. Map of potential 80-percent groups of endogamy in Iron Age IIA Judah

The threshold for 80-percent groups ranges between 500 to 2,000 persons in most societies, with a total population up to 10,000.[63] When all of these factors are taken into consideration, the village-endogamy equation for

---

number that might be a little too large compared with the 200 persons per hectare in a typical early twentieth-century Palestinian village in a rural mountain area (Mills, *Census of Palestine 1931,* vol. 1; Moshe Brawer, "Transformation in Pattern, Dispersion, and Population Density in Israel's Arab Villages" [Hebrew], *ErIsr* 17 [1984]: 8–15).

[63] Note in this connection Adams and Kasakoff, "Factors Underlying Endoga-mous Group Size," 158: "There appears to be an upper as well as a lower limit on endogamous group size. Even in societies where it is possible to come in contact with a very large number of people, as is the case in the more densely populated areas of our sample, and even where such contact is actually maintained through markets and the like, the marriage universe is probably limited to groups of 10,000 at the most."

Iron Age IIA Judah suggests that a size range of 1,200–2,400 people for an 80-percent group seems to be close enough to the limits of actual marriage movements in early Iron Age Judah.

Under this method, I reconstructed the 80-percent groups by adding the population of villages that were the closest neighbors and that shared topographical boundaries, taking high mountains and deep valleys as geographical barriers of movement. Once the number of such a group of villages was large enough to form an 80-percent group, a limit of this mean field is looked for. It has to be emphasized that these fields are open systems without an absolute border and that still some 20 percent of all marriages within these fields are contracted with communities beyond the limits of the mean field.

This method was applied to early Iron Age Judah, and the results are presented on maps of potential 80-percent field of endogamous marriage interaction (figs. 4.6 and 4.7). The Iron Age inhabitants of the fields marked on the maps may have shared 80 percent of their marriages with each other. The Iron Age I population had to walk longer distances than in the following Iron Age IIA. Due to the sparse population and settlement in Iron Age I, it was more difficult to find a partner for marriage in the immediate neighborhood. The three fields of interaction are the marriage group around Jerusalem; the group in central Judah with Khirbet Jedur, Khirbet Sabiqa, and Ras et-Tawil; and the third group around Hebron. The central group and the Hebron group are separated by the Hebron mountains north of that city in the area of Mamre and Jebel Jalis.

In Iron Age IIA the social landscape became more complex. There were now five groups. The Jerusalem territory did not change much. But in central Judah the Iron Age I marriage group may have separated into two groups centered around the largest villages, one around Tekoa and the other around Ras et-Tawil. Both groups had almost the same population: the Tekoa group, 1,020–2,040 persons; the Ras et-Tawil group, 1,110–2,220 persons. The population growth here could have caused the establishment of two marriage groups both covering a territory of a day's walk.

The same process took place in southern Judah. The population of the Iron Age I Hebron group grew and allowed the differentiation of two potential 80-percent fields of endogamous marriage interaction. The settlement expanded southeastward, while there were also new and large villages southwest of Hebron. The population was now large enough to form two separate marriage groups. One could potentially have been around Debir, while the other one might have used Hebron as a center.

It is unrealistic to assume that an anthropological and geographical model such as a potential 80-percent field of endogamous marriage interaction can be exactly identified with a certain type of ancient family organization, such as the *mišpāḥâ* of the Bible. Yet the fields of interaction did influence human behavior in space and doubtless found an expression in the Iron Age culture of Judah. Although it is difficult to find out to what extent ancient family organization reflected this interaction, it is probable that 80 percent of the marrying women did not leave this territory and that the resulting endogamy that could be established within these fields of interaction stabilized the conditions of land ownership, making sure that family members from within the field of interaction inherited the family land.

In spite of the difficulties in establishing the extent of interaction of ancient *mišpāḥôt,* I would like to venture a few speculations regarding these territories based on the above findings. Hebron was identified as the city of the Calebites, a *mišpāḥâ* that settled in this area. Could Kiriath-arba have been an early coalition (including marriage alliances?) of four villages around Hebron as a center? Iron Age I Debir (Kiriath-sepher) was clearly within the territory of Caleb (see Josh 15:15–17; Judg 1:11–13), but note that by the Iron Age IIA there were enough people living southwest of Hebron to form an independent 80-percent field of endogamous marriage interaction. Do these observations provide a new context for the discussion of Othniel, the son of Kenaz, the younger brother of Caleb, who took possession of the city of Debir (Josh 15:15–19)?[64] This could only be a consideration if we assume that these texts reflect in any way events of the early Iron Age rather than later traditions, maybe even related to the penetration of Judah by the Edomites/Idumaeans.[65]

According to 1 Chr 2:24 and 4:5, Tekoa was formerly under the control of the Calebites. Based on our findings, one should ask if the new field of marriage interaction around Tekoa in Iron Age IIA observed above reflects in any way the detachment from Calebite supremacy. The village of Bethlehem presents a particular problem in the attempt to answer this question. This site is very small in both periods, Iron Age I (0.5 ha) and Iron Age IIA (0.6 ha). The settlement may have included a small village, Ephrath, and an adjacent sanctuary, Bethlehem.[66] In the fields of interaction illustrated on the maps in figures 4.6 and 4.7, Bethlehem seems to be

---

[64] See Avi Ofer, "'All the Hill Country of Judah': From a Settlement Fringe to a Prosperous Monarchy," in *From Nomadism to Monarchy: Archaeological and Historical Aspects of Early Israel* (ed. I. Finkelstein and N. Naʾaman; Jerusalem: Israel Exploration Society, 1994), 112.

[65] In the genealogical lists concerning Judah (1 Chr 2:3; 4:23) a remarkable number of names occur also in Edom (see ibid., 116). To which period do these resemblances belong? Is any influence from later Idumaean traditions excluded?

[66] For such double names and double functions, see Keel et al., *Orte und Landschaften der Bibel,* 1:298–300 (discussing the case of Bethel-Luz).

part of the Jerusalem marriage group. While the centers of the 80-percent field of endogamous marriage interaction here were Ras et-Tawil and later Tekoa, Bethlehem played an important role in the tradition of the families here, the clans of Ephrath.[67]

Thus Bethlehem is either at the periphery of the Ras et-Tawil group or at the periphery of the Jerusalem group. The site may have been more important as a sanctuary than as a settlement. There are a number of clues that there was a cult of a female deity in the Bethlehem area. Most important in this context are the inscribed arrowheads found near al-Khadr, dating to Iron Age I.[68] The name inscribed on the arrowhead is ABDLB'T, the servant of the lioness, the animal being the attribute of the goddess. The arrowheads themselves are apparently an offering, perhaps in a rural sanctuary.

In conclusion, in accordance with the biblical tradition, we may have evidence in Iron Age I Judah for two major family groupings, which are interpreted here as 80-percent groups of endogamous marriage interaction. One is the Caleb-group in southern Judah, the other the Ephrath-group in central Judah. Both groups may have split up into two subgroups as early as Iron Age IIA.[69] Both groups were also in contact with each other and other groups beyond their 80-percent field of endogamous marriage interaction, since 20 percent of all marriages within these fields are contracted with communities outside the limits of the mean field. Especially in Iron Age Judah with its limited population, nomadic groups may have played an important role in marriage alliances.[70] In this context of family and tribal

---

[67] Aaron Demsky, "The Clans of Ephrath: Their Territory and History," *TA* 13–14 (1986–87): 46–59.

[68] For references, see *KAI*, nos. 21, 29. Note also the tomb of Rachel, a rural sanctuary of a mother figure north of Bethlehem (Keel et al., *Orte und Land-schaften der Bibel*, 1:606–10), and the nearby Byzantine church, called Cathisma, commemorating the pregnant Mary resting on a rock on her way to Bethlehem (Kloner, *Survey of Jerusalem*, 90* site no. 92, with references). There was an Adonis cult at Bethlehem during the Roman period. Henri Cazelles discussed the possibility that Lahmu was in fact a vegetation deity like Adonis, being connected to a goddess ("Bethlehem," *ABD* 1:714). The modern name of the settlement al-Khadr, "location of the arrowheads," apparently reflects the worship of Adonis (Keel et al., *Orte und Landschaften der Bibel*, 2:736).

[69] Similarly, see Ofer, "Hill Country of Judah," 112–14.

[70] Almost 11 percent of the marriages of the village Artas in the neighborhood of Bethlehem were made between the village and the nearby nomadic tribe of the Bet Tacamir, which settled in the 1920s approximately 5 km east of Artas and which Granquist calls "half bedouin" (Granquist, *Marriage Conditions in a Palestinian Village*, 14 n. 4, 91, 97–98). This is even more remarkable, since Artas and the Bet

alliances, the use of a tribal name such as "Judah" is somewhat problematic, since "the concept of a 'tribe' Judah lacks any concrete content, and seems to be a late, artificial application to the history of the families which settled in the Land of Judah."[71]

SETTLEMENT PATTERN

The survey data from Judah and the Shephelah shows an expansion of the settlement in that area from Iron Age I to Iron Age IIA. It is exactly this process that is challenged by Faust, a challenge that is currently impossible to test for the settlement pattern of Judah.[72] If one accepts the survey data, an expansion of the settlement pattern emerges (table 4.2).

Table 4.2. Number of sites in Judah, the Jerusalem area, and the southern Shephelah during Iron Age I and IIA[73]

	Iron I	Iron IIA
sites in the Shephelah	6 sites	19 sites
sites in Judah (without Jerusalem)	18 sites	32 sites
sites north of Jerusalem (including Jerusalem)	19 sites	15 sites

---

Even if these data are accepted, a number of problems remain unsolved. Were all sites of one pottery period in fact settled at the same time? The ability to date pottery is usually quite broad and does not provide a conclusive answer. In a similar manner, one should ask if all of the sites were settlement permanent sites. It is possible that some of them might have been seasonal settlements? Again, no definite answers are possible.

Tacamir used to be enemies in the nineteenth century. The marriages included thirty women of the Bet Tacamir marrying into Artas, while only six women from Artas married men of the Bet Tacamir. According to Granquist, it was considered to be an indignity for Artas women to marry into the bad living conditions of the Bet Tacamir (ibid., 98). There are no other figures of intermarriage between pastoralists and village populations in pre-modern Palestine available to me.

[71] Ofer, "All the Hill Country of Judah," 117.

[72] Faust, "From Hamlets to Monarchy," 7–32.

[73] Main sources: Dagan, "Shephelah during the Period of the Monarchy"; Israel Finkelstein and Izchak Magen, eds., *Archaeological Survey of the Hill Country of Benjamin* (Jerusalem: Israel Antiquities Authority, 1993), maps 83–83/1–83/2–83/12–101–102; and Ofer, "Highland of Judah."

The factors of settlement localization include availability of natural resources, conditions of communication and transportation, political organization, land tenure, security conditions, and other cultural factors.[74]

The Dead Sea east of Judah caused the major transport routes to bypass the area either at the north or at the south. The only major route was the north-south road close to the line of watershed in Judah. Many settlements in Judah during the Iron Age I and IIA, including the more important ones, are lined up along this road. On the map in figure 4.8 the road network of Iron Age IIA is reconstructed according to the topography

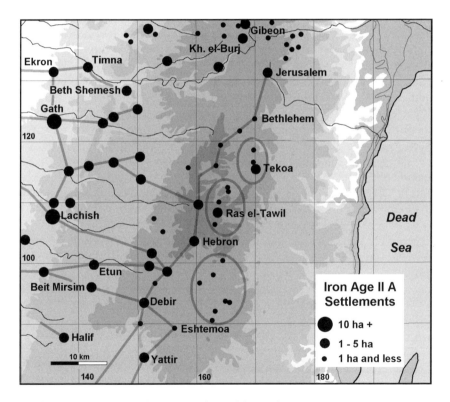

Fig. 4.8. Iron Age IIA settlements and possible roads

---

[74] See, e.g., David Charles Hopkins, *The Highlands of Canaan: Agricultural Life in the Early Iron Age* (SWBA 3; Sheffeld: JSOT Press, 1985), 159; Ian Hodder and Clive Orton, *Spatial Analysis in Archaeology* (Cambridge: Cambridge University Press, 1976), 229–36; Steven E. Falconer and Stephen H. Savage, "Heartlands and Hinterlands: Alternative Trajectories of Early Urbanization in Mesopotamia and the Southern Levant," *American Antiquity* 60 (1995): 38–44.

of Judah, the roads of the nineteenth and twentieth centuries C.E., and the road network proposed for the Iron Age by Dorsey.[75]

The settlement pattern in Judah in these periods appears as north-south situated chains of sites. This is in obvious contrast to the east-west chains of settlements in the coastal plain and the Shephelah. This settlement pattern in the Shephelah was probably caused by expansion of coastal urban centers that expanded to the east instead of north or south. Those centers were lined up at or near the coast in north-south directions. An expansion to the south or north by one of the coastal centers would thus have resulted in conflicts and competition with the neighboring centers. An expansion in the direction of the hill and mountain areas was apparently less difficult to establish and was faced with less resistance.

The main road in Judah led from Jerusalem to the south. As the road went south, it passed Bethlehem, Hebron, and Debir, and it eventually reached the Plain of Beer-sheba. Three "pockets" of settlements are situated east of this road and are bypassed by it: the area of Tekoa, the area of Ras et-Tawil, and the small villages southeast of Hebron. All three areas border the Judean Desert and, being rural and somewhat remote, were not directly connected with any trade and transport passing through Judah.

The settlement continuity between Iron Age I and Iron Age IIA is remarkably high: 72.2 percent of the Iron Age I sites are also settled in Iron Age II. The few abandoned Iron Age I sites lay mostly in the area of Ras et-Tawil. Sites founded in Iron Age IIA were spread out over most parts of Judah. There were important changes, however, in the region southeast of Hebron. While this area was uninhabited in Iron Age I, in Iron Age II seven new sites were established. These seven sites formed the "pocket" of sites southeast of Hebron, which lay off the main north-south road. It was in this area and further east of it that David spent his years in the wilderness.

The Iron Age I sites that continue to be inhabited in Iron Age IIA constitute only some 40 percent of the settlements of that period. Almost 60 percent of the Iron Age IIA villages are new foundations. Thus, there is a considerable settlement continuity and expansion between Iron Age I and Iron Age IIA.

Most of the Iron Age I and Iron Age IIA villages lay on a mountain or a hilltop. Such settlement positions account for 61.2 percent of the Iron Age I settlements and 56.2 percent of the Iron Age II settlements. While the middle range of mountain slopes accounted for only 16.6 percent of sites during the Iron I, in Iron Age II this position became more frequent. In the Iron II, 31.3 percent of the villages were built on a middle slope. Of the

---

[75] David Alden Dorsey, *The Roads and Highways of Ancient Israel* (Baltimore: Johns Hopkins University Press, 1991).

Iron Age IIA sites built on a middle slope, seven out of ten villages were new foundations in that period. Clearly, the settlement expansion in Iron Age IIA favored such a lower position more than the settlement pattern in the previous period. It seems safe to conclude that the population felt safe enough to leave the high lookouts on the mountain and hilltops and decided to settle in areas that were more advantageous agriculturally. If this is indeed the case, then this phenomenon contradicts Faust's claim that the security situation worsened in the Iron Age IIa.

Settlement hierarchy was underdeveloped in both the Iron Age I and IIA. As observed above, Jerusalem may have occupied four hectares of built-up area. Hebron, Ras et-Tawil, and Tekoa all had three hectares of built-up areas. In addition, Jerusalem is situated at the periphery of Judah, while the other three large villages were all well within the settlement pattern of the region. While it is common to argue that Jerusalem was the supreme center of the united monarchy and that Hebron, Ras et-Tawil, and Tekoa were regional centers, the data presented here make it difficult to see Jerusalem as such a central place. As a settlement, it had just the size of a large village, being in the same size class as the three assumed Judean subcenters.

This is obvious when the sites are plotted in a rank-size diagram (see figs. 4.9–10).[76] The settlements appear in a wide bow. If Judah would have been a well-integrated region in Iron Age I and IIA, one would expect that the line of the ranked sites would have been straight. One does not observe a straight line in either the Iron Age I or IIA. The Iron Age I seems to have been even better integrated than the later period, Iron Age IIA. The settlement pattern of Iron Age IIA was apparently divided in three subregions, each of them internally well-integrated groups of small villages with a central larger village. Among the three larger villages, Hebron, Ras et-Tawil, and Tekoa, Hebron was apparently the most important one. The village alliances emerging in this scenario were most probably based on kinship groups and tribal coalitions, similar to the ones in Transjordan from the same time periods.[77]

As repeatedly observed, Iron Age I sites in the mountain areas often inhabit marginal locations.[78] The surrounding topography is often rugged,

---

[76] For rank-size analysis, see Hodder and Orton, *Spatial Analysis in Archaeology,* 69–73; and Haggett, *Locational Analysis in Human Geography,* 101–3.

[77] Oystein Sakala LaBianca and Randall W. Younker, "The Kingdoms of Ammon, Moab and Edom: The Archaeology of Society in Late Bronze/Iron Age Transjordan (ca. 1400–500 BCE)," in *Archaeology of Society in the Holy Land* (ed. T. E. Levy; London: Leicester University Press, 1995), 399–415.

[78] Hopkins, *Highlands of Canaan,* 161.

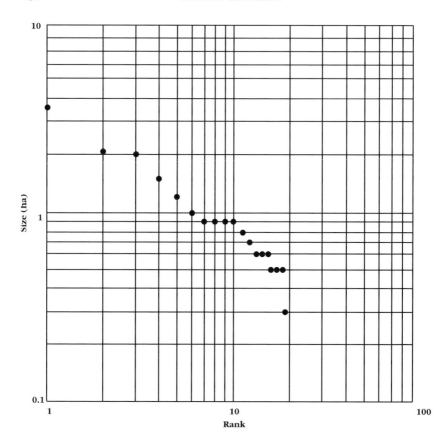

Fig. 4.9. Rank-size Iron Age I Judah

fresh-water supply is limited, and the available soils are often not of the best quality required for grain production. As pointed out above, the villages lay on isolated mountains and hills or at the end of low ridges. During Iron Age IIA this situation changed to some extent. Villages with a total of 9.1 ha built-up area Iron Age lay on middle slopes, 28.4 percent of the total built-up area in Judah in that period. While it seems to have been more important to live closer to the grain fields in the bottom of the valleys, still some 71 percent of the population lived on mountain and hill tops. Security may have been the main reason for the choice of this settlement position. This location was chosen over considerable disadvantages. Long walks for water supply from distant springs and to the fields in the valleys and the terraces on the slopes and back into the village were the daily strains of the farmers.

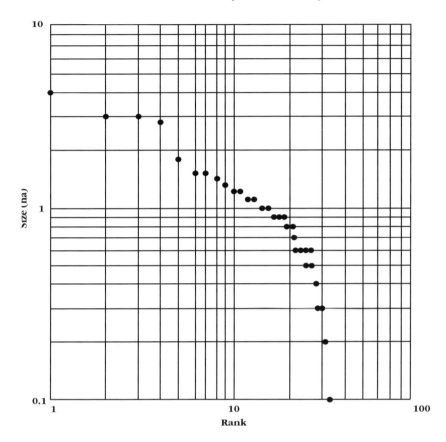

Fig. 4.10. Rank-size Iron Age IIA Judah

Agriculture in Judah is hampered by unfavorable conditions. Rainfall is limited to 300—500 mm a year and reaches 600—700 mm only in areas of more than 1,000 m elevation. Good soils are available only in the valleys and never in larger continuous expanse.[79] The maps in figures 4.11 and 4.12 illustrate the distribution of soils with a good quality for grain production. Areas of horticulture in 1931 are indicated in figures 4.13 and 4.14.[80]

[79] Werner Richter, *Israel und seine Nachbarräume: Ländliche Siedlungen und Landnutzung seit dem 19. Jahrhundert* (Erdwissenschaftliche Forschung 14; Wiesbaden: Steiner, 1979), 323.

[80] Grossman, "Relationship between Settlement Pattern," fig. 4 with soils grade 1 for western Judah, complemented in eastern Judah by Meron Benvenisti and

Gunnar Lehmann

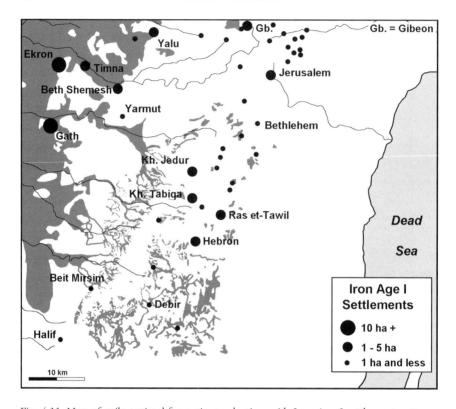

Fig. 4.11. Map of soils optimal for grain production with Iron Age I settlement pattern

Using modern soil and land-use maps does not imply that the conditions in the Iron Age were exactly those of the Ottoman period or the early twentieth century. This data can be used, however, to formulate explicit hypotheses on ancient agriculture, which may then be tested. In general, this essay assumes that the agriculture in Judah was largely a subsistence economy, as it was still in the 1930s.[81]

The soil maps in figures 4.11 and 4.12 show clearly that the soils best suited for grain production are limited in Judah. Although these areas were sufficient for most of the small villages in Iron Age I and IIA,

---

Shlomo Khayat, *The West Bank and Gaza Atlas* (Jerusalem: West Bank Data Base Project, 1988), map 24, permanent cultivation in 1967. Regarding the Shephelah, see Ron Adler et al., eds., *Atlas of Israel* (Jerusalem: Survey of Israel, 1970), with nonirrigated cultivation in 1931.

[81] Richter, *Israel und seine Nachbarräume,* 139.

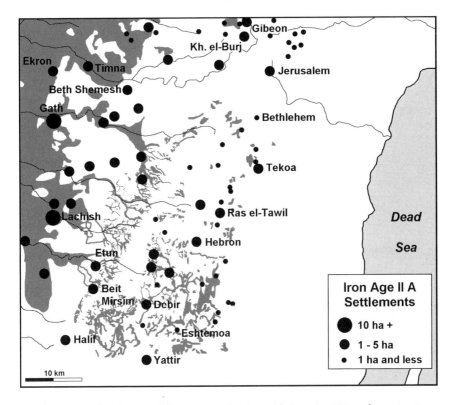

Fig. 4.12. Map of soils optimal for grain production with Iron Age IIA settlement pattern

they did not provide a surplus comparable to that in Samaria or Philistia. As a result, Judah was in most periods of its settlement history only sparsely settled, especially in relation to its northern and western neighbors. The maps in figures 4.11 and 4.12 illustrate the wider but still limited valleys in the Shephelah west of Judah with areas of grain growing. More to the west the beginning vast areas of grain cultivation in the coastal plain of the Philistines are visible. Although only part of this Philistine plain is shown on the maps, they still indicate the much larger agricultural potential of that area. The grain surplus produced in the Philistine plain provided investment capacities (see above) there that were lacking in Judah.

There are some larger valleys and soil pockets southeast of Hebron; these are precisely the areas that were settled in Iron Age IIA. Yet the agricultural capacities of these areas are limited by low rainfall. Agriculture crops were risky in these areas in any year, and during a dry year the result could be disastrous. In the Ottoman period and in the early

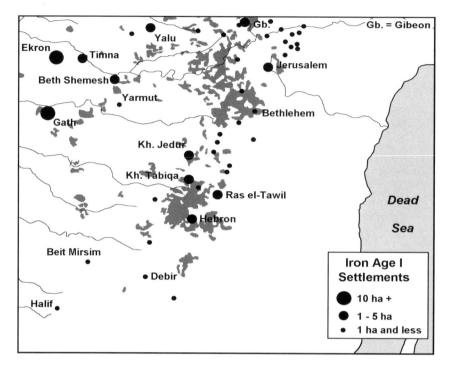

Fig. 4.13. Map of areas with horticulture (situation 1967) Iron Age I settlement pattern

twentieth century a complementary economic system was in use, attempting to make the best use of the diverse highland and lowland environment. As a result, the population practiced a modified form of transhumance.[82] Transhumance in Judah was different from such economies in other parts of the Mediterranean, primarily by the fact that Judah is a small mountain area. It is of mid-latitude position with moderate elevation.[83] Herding took place only a few hours away from the main village, for example, in the rocky zone west of modern Dura[84] or in the dry southern regions of Judah. Thus, traditional agriculture in Judah demanded space and expansion. During the nineteenth century this often created local competition, feuds, and violence. The bedouin

---

[82] David Grossman, "The Expansion of the Settlement Frontier on Hebron's Western and Southern Fringes," *Geographical Research Forum* 5 (1982): 65.

[83] Wagstaff, *Evolution of Middle Eastern Landscapes,* 53.

[84] Grossman, "Expansion of the Settlement Frontier," 65.

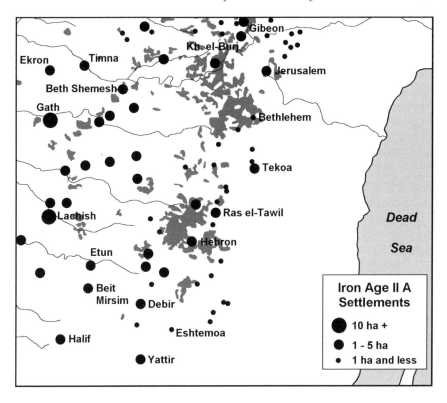

Fig. 4.14. Map of areas with horticulture (situation 1967) Iron Age IIA settlement pattern

have played a part in this insecurity, but their threat has probably been overestimated in the past.[85]

In recent centuries, nomadic pastoralists lived around and between the villages and were in constant contact with the settled population. This may have been the case also in the periods under discussion here. In a recent article Finkelstein stressed the coexistence of sedentary populations and pastoral nomadism in Judah during the Late Bronze Age and the early Iron Age.[86] It is impossible to estimate the number or the impact of nomadic pastoralists in Iron Age Judah. Dever estimates the percentage of pastoral nomads among the sedentary population in the Bronze and Iron Ages at

---

[85] Richter, *Israel und seine Nachbarräume,* 139; Grossman, "Expansion of the Settlement Frontier," 67–69.

[86] Finkelstein, "Rise of Jerusalem and Judah," 107–8.

no more than 10–15 percent, applying in fact the number of pastoral nomads in all of Palestine during the nineteenth and early twentieth century.[87] As a comparison, the British census of 1931 listed 3 percent of the population in the Hebron district as "nomadic."[88]

Horticulture was practiced extensively in Judah. The maps found in figures 4.13 and 4.14 show the extension of terraces with olive, grape and fruit-tree cultivation around 1967. Horticulture was also an important part of ancient Judean agriculture.[89] According to Finkelstein, horticulture spread in the area of his Ephraim survey only during the later parts of Iron Age I and especially during Iron Age II.[90] Building terraces for horticulture was a considerable investment, implying a sedentary population that was prepared to wait years before harvesting the first fruits of its plantations.[91] Thus, horticulture required a regional economic cooperation to provide the necessary economic security for such an investment. The social organization of the tribal societies in Judah during Iron Age I and IIA would have been able to provide this requirement.

BACK TO JERUSALEM: A CONCLUSION

As long as the chronological problems of early Iron Age Palestine are not solved, it is difficult to integrate data reflecting social and economic change, the dimension of Braudel's *histoire conjoncturelle*, with a history of events in Iron Age I and IIA. In some sense most scholars today agree on a "minimalist" point of view in this regard. It does not seem reasonable any longer to claim that the united monarchy ruled over most of Palestine and Syria. The question today is, To what degree are we cutting back the dimensions of the united monarchy and Jerusalem as its capital?

---

[87] William G. Dever, "Israelite Origins and the 'Nomadic Ideal': Can Archaeology Separate Fact from Fiction?" in Gitin et al., *Mediterranean Peoples in Transition*, 225, quoting Nadav Naʾaman, "The 'Conquest of Canaan' in the Book of Joshua and in History," in Finkelstein and Naʾaman, *From Nomadism to Monarchy*, 233, and the references there.

[88] Mills, *Census of Palestine 1931*.

[89] Oded Borowski, *Agriculture in Iron Age Israel* (Winona Lake, Ind.: Eisenbrauns, 1987), 101–33; Hopkins, *Highlands of Canaan*, 227–32; for modern Judah, see Richter, *Israel und seine Nachbarräume*, 333–37.

[90] Finkelstein, *Archaeology of the Israelite Settlement*, 199.

[91] John Boardman, "The Olive in the Mediterranean: Its Culture and Use," in *The Early History of Agriculture: A Joint Symposium of the Royal Society and the British Academy* (ed. J. Hutchinson; Oxford: Oxford University Press, 1977), 189.

As a means of conclusion, I will attempt to make at least a modest contribution to this complex question about the character of the united monarchy in general and Jerusalem of David and Solomon in particular. I will focus the summary on three points: demographic, economic, and sociopolitical processes.

DEMOGRAPHY

One of the most intriguing phenomena discussed here is the low population estimate of Judah during both the Iron Age I and IIA. No matter which chronology one follows, the population in the homeland of David and Solomon was very low. Whether there were eighteen villages according to the low chronology or thirty-two according to the conventional chronology, it is doubtful that the three thousand (minimum) or ten thousand (maximum) inhabitants of Judah could have subjugated all of Palestine, not to speak of Syria as well. Moreover, the unlikelihood of domination by Judah is increased because the population of the coastal plain and the inland valleys was much denser and larger.

It is this proportional discrepancy that is significant. Further, although there may have been an increase of the population in Iron Age IIA,[92] it did not result in an "abundance of manpower" that "enabled David to mobilize a great army and to conquer large areas."[93]

ECONOMY

Agricultural production in early Iron Age Judah was limited, especially in comparison with the coastal plain and the area of the northern tribes in Samaria. How could Jerusalem have ruled over city-states far away in the densely populated northern valleys and hills when the capital itself was only of modest size with a sparsely settled hinterland? Another indicator of a weak Judah was the expansion of territory and settlement of the Philistine city-states. These city-states avoided conflicts with each other and expanded up the wadis into the hill and mountain country. Apparently the political opponents in the hills and mountains were unable to prevent this expanse into the Shephelah. The Philistine city-states were able to increase their territory and the diversity of their agricultural area, integrating plain and hill slopes into their economy. This expansion into the hill country provided them with additional areas for grain production and horticulture, including wine and olive-oil production. There was nothing in Judah with its limited soils for grain growing and lacking sur-

---

[92] A point challenged by Faust, "Hamlets to Monarchy," 7–32.

[93] Nadav Naʾaman, "The Contribution of the Amarna Letters to the Debate on Jerusalem's Political Position in the Tenth Century B.C.E.," *BASOR* 304 (1996): 23.

plus that matched the scale and expanse of the Philistine economy. The investment capacities of the cities in the coastal plain outdid anything comparable in the mountain areas.

Blakely and Horton have suggested that the tripartite pillared buildings at Tell el-Hesi as well as other such buildings in Palestine were structures serving a governmental and economic function on the borders of Israel and Judah.[94] They observed that these buildings appear in a large circle surrounding Israel and Judah, but none of them occur in Transjordan. It is further argued that for much of the tenth and ninth centuries, Tell el-Hesi served as some sort of Judahite governmental center on the main road from Gaza to Hebron and Jerusalem. This interpretation with an emphasis on the Judeans operating the center is apparently based partly on Blakely and Horton's implicit understanding of the united monarchy as a state with a "central government"[95] and partly on the observation that there is "no Philistine pottery except for a few sherds," thus excluding the possibility that Philistines organized the center.

Blakely and Horton's observation of the spatial distribution of tripartite pillared buildings around the central hill country is certainly very important. However, I would argue that centers such as the one in Tell el-Hesi on the main road from Gaza to Hebron and Jerusalem were in the hands of the Philistines. It is doubtful that the absence of Philistine pottery is enough evidence for Judean presence. During the survey of the Philistine countryside currently conducted by the writer,[96] Philistine pottery was found on sites east of Tell el-Hesi, such as Tel Qeshet (Tell Qunaytra). If pots represent peoples, Philistines may very well have been in the area.

But pots are not that significant in this matter. The social and economic relationships between plain and mountains should be given weight as we seek to answer this question. The Philistines had both the means and the profit from operating trading centers on the borders of their territory, thus extending their economic influence in the direction of the tribal mountain regions. In this explanation, the function served by Philistines in Tell el-Hesi in the tenth century B.C.E. was transferred in the ninth century to neighboring Lachish, which was probably in Judean territory. This was achieved when the political powers in the mountains

---

[94] Jeff A. Blakely and Fred L. Horton, "On Site Identifications Old and New: The Example of Tell el-Hesi," *NEA* 64 (2001): 28–29.

[95] Ibid, 28.

[96] On behalf of Ben-Gurion University, with the co-directors Tammi J. Schneider, Claremont Graduate University, California, and Hermann M. Niemann, University of Rostock, Germany.

were indeed in control of the Shephelah. It remains to be seen whether these powers in the ninth century B.C.E. were in fact Judeans.

SOCIOPOLITICAL DEVELOPMENTS

The lack of settlement hierarchy and integration of the Judean villages in both Iron Age I and IIA do not point to a well-developed state with urban central places.[97] The society was rather organized in kinship groups and tribal alliances,[98] based on groups of endogamy, which this study localizes as 80-percent fields of marriage interaction in the Judean landscape. This reconstruction as well as the underdeveloped settlement hierarchy reveal a settlement pattern of village-like small centers. Jerusalem was just one of them, and there are few indications that it was the most important. The most remarkable evidence for a more important role for Jerusalem emerges not from regional settlement archaeology but from excavations within the city. The impressive stepped structure, whether of the tenth (conventional chronology) or the ninth (low chronology) century B.C.E., was the most monumental building in Judah during this time.[99]

---

[97] Recently there has been some progress in Palestinian archaeology to define a state. In archaeology and history, see Shlomo Bunimovitz, "Problems in the 'Ethnic' Identification of the Philistine Material Culture," *TA* 17 (1990): 210–22; idem, "The Study of Complex Societies: The Material Culture of Late Bronze Age Canaan as a Case Study," in Biran and Aviram, *Biblical Archaeology Today, 1990,* 443–51; Israel Finkelstein, "State Formation in Israel and Judah: A Contrast in Context, A Contrast in Trajectory," *NEA* 62 (1999): 35–52; Volkmar Fritz and Philip R. Davies, eds., *The Origins of the Ancient Israelite States* (JSOTSup 228; Sheffield: Sheffield Academic Press, 1996); David W. Jamieson-Drake, *Scribes and Schools in Monarchic Judah: A Socio-Archeological Approach* (SWBA 9; JSOTSup 109; Sheffield: Sheffield Academic Press, 1991); Hermann M. Niemann, *Herrschaft, Königtum und Staat: Skizzen zur soziokulturellen Entwicklung im monarchischen Israel* (FAT 6; Tübingen: Mohr Siebeck, 1993); in anthropology and sociology, note Stefan Breuer, *Der Staat: Entstehung, Typen, Organisationsstadien* (Hamburg: Rowohlt, 1998); Henri J. M. Claessen and Peter Skalnik, eds., *The Early State* (The Hague: Mouton, 1978); idem, *The Study of the State* (The Hague: Mouton, 1981); Timothy K. Earle, *How Chiefs Come to Power: The Political Economy in Prehistory* (Stanford, Calif.: Stanford University Press, 1997); Jonathan Haas, *The Evolution of the Prehistoric State* (New York: Columbia University Press, 1982); Werner Leuthäusser, *Die Entwicklung staatlich organisierter Herrschaft in frühen Hochkulturen am Beispiel des Vorderen Orients* (Frankfurt am Main: Lang, 1998); Charles Keith Maisels, *The Emergence of Civilization: From Hunting and Gathering to Agriculture, Cities, and the State in the Near East* (London: Routledge, 1990).

[98] For a similar scenario in contemporary Transjordan, see LaBianca and Younker, "Kingdoms of Ammon, Moab and Edom," 399–415.

[99] Cahill ("Jerusalem at the Time of the United Monarchy," 26–27) claims that there is archaeological evidence for a socially stratified society that occupied

It is difficult to imagine that the poor economy of the mountain areas, especially in Judah, could have been the backbone of an expansive united monarchy. However, Halpern rejects this argument, stressing that the size of demography or of social and economic infrastructure as observable in archaeology is not significant.[100] According to Halpern, arguments based on population size are so frequently contradicted by reality as to be all but useless as a starting point of analysis. Contra Halpern, I would like to maintain that size and the structural analysis of demography as well as social and economic infrastructure provides valuable data for reconstructing the past. In all historical cases quoted by Halpern as contradicting the argument of size, including Sparta, there were social and political entities that managed to operate with their shortcomings. But precisely those shortcomings eventually sealed their fate, a good example again being Sparta. In other words, there are charismatic personalities such as Alexander of Macedonia who conquer the world with a few thousand soldiers. But how long can a society function against the odds of their meager population size and resources?

David and Solomon may have been such charismatic personalities struggling against the odds. The observations of this essay throw strong doubts on the concept of a fully developed monarchy with a complex territorial state-organization in the hill country during the tenth century B.C.E. Lacking a centralized settlement structure, Judah was apparently organized in local kinship groups. The structural analysis does not suggest any regional framework that integrated these groups in a long-term process of statehood. At best there was an alliance of kinship groups and villages. Against this background, could David and Solomon have ruled over large parts of Palestine in a way that corresponds to the biblical narrative? The evidence is compatible, if one interprets these kings as leaders of temporary tribal and village coalitions with limited resources.

They could have been successful in a limited region over a limited period, establishing an ad hoc reign in the manner of a leader such as the bedouin ruler Dhahir al-ʿUmar in the eighteenth century C.E.[101] Dhahir al-ʿUmar's rule in Galilee was built on his charisma and energetic personality, not on an elaborated state organization, and it fell apart with the death of Dhahir. In a similar way, David and Solomon may have been able to

---

residential quarters inside and outside the fortification wall. See also Cahill's essay in this volume.

[100] Halpern, *David's Secret Demons,* 211–12.

[101] Hermann M. Niemann, "The Socio-Political Shadow of the Biblical Solomon," in *The Age of Solomon: Scholarship at the Turn of the Millennium* (ed. L. K. Handy; Leiden: Brill, 1997), 265–67.

establish a territorial rule during their lifetimes, making optimal use of their military and diplomatic options. *Contra* Halpern, I maintain that in the long term their rule would have suffered from a lack of internal state organization and the weak integration of its main components, the local kinship groups, as outlined above. *With* Halpern, I see a crucial role of Tyre and the Phoenicians in promoting a more efficient production and delivery in their agricultural hinterland, in Israel. This commercial encouragement may have been instrumental in supporting the political power of the united monarchy and helped eventually to create a fully developed state in Israel.[102]

As for the size of the united monarchy's territory, Halpern's detailed analysis of David's "empire" confines the northern and eastern borders of the united monarchy to a territory similar to the one of the kingdom of Israel in the ninth century B.C.E.[103] His arguments are based almost exclusively on his textual and historical analysis. While Halpern insists on a central state organization in the united monarchy, the territory of this monarchy did not, in his view, extend into Syria. Other scholars, such as Herbert Donner, have suggested that the northwestern borders were dictated by Tyre,[104] resulting in the cession of the land of Kabul that may have been in fact only recognition of Phoenician claims on western Galilee. Thus, the territorial extension of the united monarchy is severely limited by scholars who are above any suspicion of being minimalists.

Apparently the Braudelian paradigm of Mediterranean landscapes and their interdependencies fits our data. But if this is indeed the case, it must be explained how Judah, this backward mountain region, gained possession of the Shephelah. Both traditionalists and adherents of the low chronology agree that this acquisition was impossible without the support of the northern tribes. For traditionalists, the union with the northern tribes during the united monarchy created the political power to expand down into the hill country. In contrast, Finkelstein explains the Judean presence in the Shephelah by means of the influence and backing that the vassal kingdom of Judah received from its masters, the Omrides of the northern kingdom in the ninth century B.C.E.[105] It is indeed difficult to explain this process without the support of the northern tribes and/or kingdom.

---

[102] For Dhahir al-ʿUmar's dependence on cotton production and its export to France in the eighteenth century C.E., see Halpern, *David's Secret Demons,* 210.

[103] Ibid., 107–226.

[104] Herbert Donner, "The Interdependence of Internal Affairs and Foreign Policy during the Davidic-Solomonic Period (with Special Regard to the Phoenician Coast)," in *Studies in the Period of David and Solomon and other Essays* (ed. T. Ishida; Winona Lake, Ind.: Eisenbrauns, 1982), 205–14.

[105] Finkelstein, "Rise of Jerusalem and Judah," 105–15.

Thus, in contrast to the biblical tradition, a modest Jerusalem emerges from the archaeological record. Whether one follows the conventional chronology or the low chronology, there was no splendid Jerusalem before the eighth century B.C.E. However, it was apparently more than a "cow town," although cattle certainly roamed there. The tenth-century B.C.E. Jerusalem was fortified with an impressive defense, the stepped structure. The city may not have been the capital of a powerful empire; it might not have been even a city but rather a fortified stronghold with a small town. Still, it is possible that the masters of Jerusalem ruled in some form over the central hill country and even beyond. They did this, however, only in accordance and agreement with the kinship alliances of the communities in the hill country. As soon as this consent was withdrawn, the united monarchy collapsed. The land of Judah, the home base of David and Solomon, was neither rich nor densely populated in the tenth century B.C.E. Finally, while most, even minimalist, scholars, agree today on the historicity of David and Solomon, the social and economic environment of these men must have been modest. The tremendous power and great wealth that was ascribed to David and Solomon was a product of much later times that longed for an earlier golden age of a united monarchy.

Solomon's Jerusalem and the Zion Tradition

J. J. M. Roberts

Princeton Theological Seminary

Over the last twenty-six years, I have written extensively about the interconnected complex of religious and political ideas and ideals that make up the so-called Zion tradition.[1] The existence of such a tradition had been suggested by other scholars before me, though at the time I began writing on the topic it was generally held that this tradition complex was a pre-Israelite creation and that David simply took over this tradition

---

[1] J. J. M. Roberts, "The Davidic Origin of the Zion Tradition," *JBL* 92 (1973): 329–44; idem, "The Religio-Political Setting of Psalm 47," *BASOR* 221 (1976): 129–32; idem, "Zion Tradition," *IDBSup*, 985–87; idem, "The King of Glory," *PSB* NS 3/1 (1980): 5–10; idem, "A Note on Isaiah 28:12," *HTR* (1981): 49–51; idem, "Isaiah in Old Testament Theology," *Int* 36 (1982): 130–43; idem, "Zion in the Theology of the Davidic-Solomonic Empire," in *Studies in the Period of David and Solomon and Other Essays* (ed. T. Ishida; Tokyo: Yamakawa-Shuppansha, 1982), 93–108; idem, "The Divine King and the Human Community in Isaiah's Vision of the Future," in *The Quest for the Kingdom of God: Studies in Honor of George E. Mendenhall* (ed. H. B. Huffmon et al.; Winona Lake, Ind.: Eisenbrauns, 1983), 127–36; idem, "Isaiah 33: An Isaianic Elaboration of the Zion Tradition," in *The Word of the Lord Shall Go Forth* (ed. C. L. Meyers and M. O'Connor; Winona Lake, Ind.: Eisenbrauns, 1983), 15–25; idem, "Isaiah and His Children," in *Biblical and Related Studies Presented to Samuel Iwry* (ed. A. Kort and S. Morschauser; Winona Lake, Ind.: Eisenbrauns, 1985), 193–203; idem, "Isaiah 2 and the Prophet's Message to the North," *JQR* 75 (1985): 290–308; idem, "Yahweh's Foundation in Zion (Isa 28:16)," *JBL* 106 (1987): 27–45; idem, "In Defense of the Monarchy: The Contribution of Israelite Kingship to Biblical Theology," in *Ancient Israelite Religion: Essays in Honor of Frank Moore Cross* (ed. P. D. Miller et al.; Philadelphia: Fortress, 1987), 377–96; idem, "The Meaning of *ṣemaḥ bᵓ* in Isaiah 4:2," in *Haim M. I. Gevaryahu Memorial Volume* (ed. J. J. Adler; Jerusalem: World Jewish Bible Center, 1990), 110–18; idem, "The Old Testament's Contribution to Messianic Expectation," in *The Messiah: Developments in Earliest Judaism and Christianity* (ed. J. H. Charlesworth; Minneapolis: Fortress, 1992), 39–51.

from the Jebusites after his capture of Jerusalem.[2] This dominant position was only beginning to be challenged by a few critical voices, most of whom wanted to date the formation of the tradition quite late in Israel's history, after the time of Isaiah of Jerusalem.[3] In my 1973 *JBL* article, "The Davidic Origin of the Zion Tradition," while accepting Rohland's analysis of this tradition, I tried to demonstrate that both the dominant "Jebusite" position and its "late" critics were wrong. By appealing to comparative Near Eastern material, I tried to show that, while it might have used earlier Canaanite motifs, this tradition complex was a genuinely Israelite creation and that the Davidic-Solomonic era of the united monarchy was the most likely period for its formation. Some years later I returned to the topic to offer my own constructive analysis of the tradition. This was presented orally at a conference on the period of David and Solomon held in Tokyo in 1979, and it was published in the conference volume in 1982 under the title, "Zion in the Theology of the Davidic-Solomonic Empire." Since then, I have had occasion in the context of numerous articles, particularly on the book of Isaiah, to refer to the importance of this tradition as a formative influence on the Judahite theology of the late eighth century B.C.E., but this is the first opportunity I have had to critically reevaluate my earlier position.

Nonetheless, despite major shifts in scholarly fashions in the intervening years, I am generally pleased with my earlier treatment of the topic. I am aware of the current penchant among some biblical scholars for the late dating of biblical sources or archaeological strata that have traditionally been associated with the united monarchy. In particular, I remain unconvinced by the attempts of Israel Finkelstein, David Usshishkin, and others to lower the dating of the archaeological levels that provided archaeological support for the existence of the united monarchy.[4] Similiarly, I have

---

[2] Note especially the dissertation by Edzard Rohland, "Die Bedeutung der Erwählungstraditionen Israels für die Eschatologie der alttestamentlichen Propheten" (Ph.D. diss., Heidelberg, 1956), cited extensively by Gerhard von Rad, *The Theology of Israel's Prophetic Traditions* (vol. 2 of *Old Testament Theology;* New York: Harper & Row, 1965), 116, 156.

[3] Note especially Gunther Wanke, *Die Zionstheologie der Korachiten in ihrem traditionsgeschichtlichen Zusammenhang* (BZAW 97; Berlin: Töpelmann, 1966).

[4] See especially the interchange between Israel Finkelstein and Amihai Mazar: Israel Finkelstein, "The Archaeology of the United Monarchy: An Alternative View," *Levant* 28 (1996): 177–87; Amihai Mazar, "Iron Age Chronology: A Reply to I. Finkelstein," *Levant* 30 (1998): 157–67; Israel Finkelstein, "Biblical Archaeology or Archaeology of Palestine in the Iron Age? A Rejoinder," *Levant* 30 (1998): 167–73; Amihai Mazar and John Camp, "Will Tel Rehov Save the United Monarchy?" *BAR* 26/2 (2000): 38–51, 75.

not found compelling arguments presented by the radical minimalists who deny the existence of a historical David, a united monarchy, and the origin of the Israelite state in the tenth century B.C.E.[5] None of these arguments have been able to present a more coherent interpretation of the data, and most scholars continue to concur with the earlier interpretations.[6] I remained convinced that the Zion tradition was formulated by Israelite court theologians in the period of the Davidic-Solomonic empire and that its creation is in part a reflection of Israel's, and thus Yahweh's, rise to imperial power. The one glaring gap that I see in my earlier treatment of the Zion tradition is a failure to treat adequately the position of the Davidic monarch within that tradition, a gap that I hope to remedy now, as I review my earlier outline.

The fundamental theologoumenon in the Zion tradition is that Yahweh is the great king (מלך רב [Ps 48:3]; גדול [Ps 47:3]; עליון [Pss 46:5; 47:3]), the suzerain, not only over Israel, but over the other nations and their gods as well. Such an imperialistic claim is explicit in Ps 82, where Israel's God puts the gods of the other nations on trial for injustice and threatens to remove them from office. It is also presupposed by Ps 2's treatment of the kings hostile to Jerusalem as rebellious vassals.

Isaiah's inaugural vision and its reflection in his later message shows that this theologoumenon was already a fixed part of the tradition prior to 738 B.C.E. In Isa 6 the prophet sees Yahweh as a gigantic king seated on a very high throne. That throne is probably a reference to the fifteen-foot-high cherubim throne that Solomon installed in the temple (1 Kgs 6:23–28), and the seraphim most likely reflect the existence in the temple of a pair of very tall pole-mounted winged serpents,[7] such as are represented embossed on the rim of one of the bronze bowls taken as booty from Palestine to Assyria by Tiglath-pileser III following his campaign in

---

[5] Some of the major works of this group in which one can find citations of earlier literature include Philip Davies, *In Search of "Ancient Israel"* (JSOTSup 148; Sheffield: JSOT Press, 1992); Keith W. Whitelam, *The Invention of Ancient Israel: The Silencing of Palestinian History* (London: Routledge, 1996); Niels Peter Lemche, *The Israelites in History and Tradition* (Louisville: Westminster John Knox, 1998); Thomas L. Thompson, *The Mythic Past: Biblical Archaeology and the Myth of Israel* (New York: Basic Books, 1999).

[6] For an even more recent exchange between the minimalist Philip Davies and the more traditional William G. Dever, see Philip Davies, "What Separates a Minimalist from a Maximalist? Not Much," *BAR* 26/2 (2000): 24–27, 72–73; and William G. Dever, "Save Us from Postmodern Malarkey," *BAR* 26/2 (2000): 28–35, 68.

[7] The form שרפים is just the plural of שרף, a word found two other times in Isaiah in the expression שרף מעופף, "flying seraph," in contexts where it clearly refers to a winged serpent (Isa 14:29; 30:6).

734–732.[8] One should note that winged serpents are associated with thrones in Egyptian iconography,[9] and two of them are found on a model limestone sanctuary from Syria, one behind each of the cherubim that form the two sides of the throne.[10] *Nehushtan,* the bronze serpent mounted on a pole, purportedly by Moses, and not removed from the Jerusalem temple until the time of Hezekiah's reform, is probably to be identified as such a pole-mounted winged seraph.[11] Seraphim in Egyptian art and on Hebrew seals from the eighth century function as guardians and protective deities for the enthroned deity,[12] and the seraphim in Isa 6 occupy precisely the same position above and behind the throne as their Egyptian parallels,[13] but in Isaiah's vision the protective function of these figures is significantly altered. Instead of spreading out their wings to protect Yahweh, the seraphim use their wings to protect themselves from Yahweh's majesty.[14]

---

[8] A drawing of this object is already found in Austen Henry Layard, *A Second Series of the Monuments of Nineveh Including Bas-Reliefs from the Palace of Sennacherib and Bronzes from the Ruins of Nimroud from Drawings Made on the Spot, during a Second Expedition to Assyria* (London: John Murry, 1853), pl. 68, top row, second drawing; see also Richard D. Barnett, "Layard's Nimrud Bronzes and their Inscriptions," *ErIsr* 8 (1967): 1*–7*.

[9] Note the winged cobras on the throne of Tutankhamun (Martin Metzger, *Königsthron und Gottesthron: Tronformen und Throndarstellungen in Ägypten und in Vorderen Orient im dritten und zweiten Jahrtausend vor Christus und deren Bedeutung für das Verständnis von Aussagen über den Thron im Alten Testament* [AOAT 15/1–2; Neukirchen-Vluyn: Neukirchener Verlag, 1985], 2:71, no. 253).

[10] See the unfortunately obscure picture in ibid., 2:239, no. 1193.

[11] 2 Kgs 18:4. See also Num 21:6–9.

[12] See the illustrations and discussion in Othmar Keel, *Jahwe-Vision und Siegelkunst: Eine neue Deutung der Majestätsschilderungen in Jes 6, Ez 1 und 10 und Sach 4* (SBS 84/85; Stuttgart: Katholisches Bibelwerk, 1977).

[13] Note particularly Metzger, *Königsthron und Gottesthron,* 2:67, no. 236; and Keel, *Jahwe-Vision und Siegelkunst,* 89, nos. 48–49.

[14] The antecedent to which the third masculine singular suffix on פָּנָיו and רַגְלָיו refers back is to לְאֶחָד, "each of the seraphim," not the more distant לוֹ, referring to God. Each seraph covers his own face and "feet," not Yahweh's face and feet, contra Susan Niditch, *Ancient Israelite Religion* (New York: Oxford University Press, 1997), 44. They are not blocking Yahweh's view and covering Yahweh's private parts; they are protecting their own face and private parts from God's glory. The image is analogous to that of Moses wrapping his face in his mantel before walking out of the cave into the presence of Yahweh (1 Kgs 19:13). Just as humans are threatened by a direct, unfiltered view of the divine presence (Isa 6:5), so even the awesome seraphim must protect themselves from such a direct view.

Both the portrayal of Yahweh as a gigantic God who will not fit in the temple and the portrayal of his glory as frightening even to the fearsome seraphim underscore for Isaiah the point that Yahweh is a great suzerain who will brook no rival, for whom every high and exalted would-be rival must be abased (Isa 2:11–17). He alone will be exalted, and he alone should be one's object of fear (Isa 8:13). The other nations are mere tools in Yahweh's hand for carrying out his own plans (Isa 10:5–15). Of course, the imagery of a deity as oversized is not limited to Israel. There are many Near Eastern parallels to this motif, but one of the most striking is found in the Iron Age Syrian temple at ʿAin Dārā, which is contemporary with Solomon's temple and structurally quite similar.[15] It has footprints almost a meter long carved into the pavement and tracking into the sanctuary, suggesting a gigantic deity with a stride of more than 10 m and a height of at least 20 m.[16]

The second major element in the Zion tradition was the claim that Yahweh had chosen David and his dynasty (בית דויד) as his anointed regents. I find the omission of this point in my earlier treatment surprising, since the sources specifically link the choice of David and his line with the choice of Jerusalem (Pss 2:6; 78:68–70; 132:11–17): "I have set my king on Zion, my holy mountain." This choice of the Davidic house was formalized by the tradition of a covenant of grant issued to David by Yahweh (2 Sam 7; 23:5; Pss 2:7; 89:29; 132:10–12), and the Davidic ruler's special relationship to Yahweh was elaborated in terms of the language of sonship and inheritance. The Davidic king was to enter into and exercise the rule of Yahweh, controlling the powers of chaos just as Yahweh had done (Ps 89:10–19, 26). The Davidic ruler was expected to trust in Yahweh's promise, to rule with Yahweh's justice, and to build up and maintain Yahweh's city (Ps 101:8). This element is reflected in Isaiah's appropriation of the tradition where his appeal to Ahaz and the house of David is clearly dependent on the tradition of Yahweh's twin choice of David and David's city, Jerusalem (Isa 7:1–17). One should note that Isaiah assumed that David was a real king who captured Jerusalem (Isa 29:1), the city of David (Isa 22:9), founded the Judahite royal house, the בית דויד (Isa 7:13; 22:22), and originally ruled over Ephraim as well as Judah before the division of the northern and southern kingdoms (Isa 7:17).

---

[15] See John Monson, "The New ʿAin Dārā Temple, Closest Solomonic Parallel," *BAR* 26/3 (2000): 20–35, 67; and Lawrence E. Stager, "Jerusalem As Eden," *BAR* 26/3 (2000): 36–47; as well as idem, "Jerusalem and the Garden of Eden," *ErIsr* 26 (1999): 183*–94*.

[16] Monson, "New ʿAin Dārā Temple," 27; Stager, "Jerusalem and the Garden of Eden," 183*–94*.

The third major element in the Zion tradition was the claim that Yahweh had chosen Zion for his own dwelling place. Since my earlier work gives an adequate treatment of this element, the topic is only surveyed briefly here. David's movement of the ark of the covenant into Jerusalem presupposes an oracle announcing such a divine choice of Jerusalem, and Solomon's construction of the temple in Jerusalem would have required further oracles confirming Yahweh's approval of Solomon's building project. Indeed, the theological tradition can claim Solomon's work as Yahweh's own doing, "He [Yahweh] chose the tribe of Judah, Mount Zion which he loved; he built his sanctuary like the heights, he founded it forever like the earth" (Ps 78:68–69). This motif was dear to Isaiah's heart. For him Yahweh had founded Zion (Isa 14:12), dwelt in Mount Zion (Isa 8:18), and was laying the foundation stone of his sanctuary there (Isa 28:16).

This claim that Yahweh, the imperial God, chose Zion, founded it, and lives in it, leads to several subsidiary motifs. If the divine suzerain lives in Zion, its topography must fit such a divine dwelling. So Mount Zion is envisioned as a high mountain, identified with Baal's Mount Ṣapon, and seen as the source of the river of paradise. As Lawrence Stager has shown in his two recent articles on Jerusalem as the garden of Eden, Solomon's decoration of the temple and his horticultural work planting exotic gardens along the slopes of the Kidron Valley symbolically represented Jerusalem as God's primeval garden.[17] Such motifs are also present in Isaiah, who envisions the mountain of the house of Yahweh as the tallest of the mountains (Isa 2:2) and who regards the enemy king's disparagement of the mountain of daughter Zion (Isa 10:32) as tantamount to a vain and haughty attempt to set up his throne on the heights of Ṣapon, thus rivaling Elyon (Isa 14:13–14). One should also note his odd vision of Jerusalem as a place of broad rivers (Isa 33:20–21).

The claim also suggests that Yahweh's presence in Jerusalem provides the city with security. Neither the mythological powers of chaos nor their embodiment in hostile human kings can threaten God's city. At his rebuke the enemy will melt away. The only negative side to this motif is that Zion's inhabitants must be of the right sort to live in the presence of such a terrifying deity. Again, all these elements are found in Isaiah (Isa 8:9–10; 14:12, 17:12–14; 29:1–8; 31:4–5; 33:10–16).

Finally, the other nations must recognize Yahweh's imperial rule, bring their tribute to him and his king, and come to the suzerain for arbitration of their disputes. One finds this motif in Isa 2:1–4 and 11:10.

---

[17] Stager, "Jerusalem As Eden," 36–47; idem, "Jerusalem and the Garden of Eden," 183*–94*.

In short, all the elements of the Zion tradition are present in the work of Isaiah of Jerusalem in a way that suggests he was making use of a preexisting tradition. He does not argue for this theology so much as he presupposes it. He simply calls upon his audience to take this royal Zion theology, long cultivated in Jerusalem's court and temple, with utmost seriousness.

If this analysis is even partially correct, it raises very serious questions about the attempt to dismiss the united monarchy as a historical fiction. The rise of deities to imperial prominence in the ancient Near East is usually associated with the actual political rise of the deity's city or country. It is not unusual to find a linkage between the rise of the deity to divine kingship, the election of his human king, and the elevation of his royal city. A classic example is the elevation of Marduk, Hammurabi, and Babylon in the prologue to the Code of Hammurabi. One could also think of the elevation of Inanna, Sargon, and Akkad in the earlier period. Imperial ideologies are easily created in times of political success, and they may be maintained long after those glory days have passed, but one would like to see some proof that such ideologies were ever created in the ancient Near East in a period of abject weakness. The most likely period for the creation of such an imperial ideology in Israelite history would be in the time of imperial expansion and consolidation under David and Solomon, when, if the Israelite accounts of this period in the books of Samuel and Kings have any merit, Yahweh did appear to dominate the gods of the surrounding nations and when the surrounding nations did in fact pay tribute to the Davidic king and his God.

Finkelstein pretends that one can simply ignore these literary documents since they have not been preserved as inscriptions contemporary with the events they describe. He wants to rewrite Israel's history simply on the basis of contemporary archaeological remains. Indeed, he excoriates other archaeologists as methodologically flawed if they allow these documents the slightest influence on their archaeological judgments. However, these literary documents cannot be ignored in any serious reconstruction of Israelite history. They represent a body of evidence that must be taken into account. One must analyze these documents, isolate any earlier sources in these documents, and evaluate them in light of what else one knows of ancient Near Eastern history. One should not dismiss them as historically irrelevant without providing a plausible literary and historical explanation for their composition and historical setting that would justify such a dismissal. Finkelstein's literary allies, the radical minimalists, have provided no such plausible explanation. In order to support their conclusions, they are forced to date all this material late, in the exilic period at the earliest. Yet this simplistic reading of the biblical narratives results in an interpretation that is unable to explain the presence of such a major difference between the Hebrew of traditionally early narratives and traditionally late works. They are also unable to provide a plausible explanation and thus must deny the apparent apologetic thrust of much of the narrative in Samuel and Kings, since that apologetic seems directed against persons and to situations that no longer existed and that no longer constituted any threat to anyone in the late period to which they assign the composition of these narratives. They also provide no plausible explanation for the relative accuracy of the biblical accounts when there is synchronic information from Akkadian, Moabite, Aramean, or Egyptian sources.

In my earlier article, I have an extended discussion of Ps 68, where

> one already has the motif of Yahweh choosing Mount Zion as the high mountain on which he desires to dwell and where his temple in Jerusalem is to stand (68:16–17, 30). The poem also tells of his victory over mythological powers as well as over enemy kings, and it mentions Yahweh's thunder against his foes, as well as the plunder which results from the flight of the enemy. Finally, it mentions the tribute of the nations and Yahweh's exaltation in the world.[18]

I gave a number of stylistic, lexical, and contextual reasons for dating this text to the time of Solomon, and if this dating is correct, it suggests a very early date for the Zion tradition.

Even if one rejects an early date for this and other relevant psalms, one cannot so easily dismiss the evidence of the eighth-century prophets by a late dating. In the prophetic literature from the last half of the eighth century one finds references to the house of David and other historical allusions that suggest an acquaintance with just such historical traditions as are found in the books of Samuel and Kings. This is less than two hundred years from the end of Solomon's purported reign, and given the continuity in both the Judahite ruling house and in its state capital, it is difficult to envision that the eighth-century inhabitants of Jerusalem had no sense for the real history of their state. If a half-educated modern American can be assumed to have at least a vague outline knowledge of the formation of this country in the last decades of the eighteenth century, why should one doubt that members of the Judahite elite would have had at least a comparable knowledge of the real beginnings of their own state?

---

[18] Roberts, "Zion in the Theology of the Davidic-Solomonic Empire," 105–7, esp. 107.

Solomon and the Great Histories

Richard Elliott Friedman
University of California, San Diego

One of our field's central battles almost from the beginning has been early versus late. When De Wette heard the idea that the Priestly law was late, from the Second Temple period, he said that this view "suspended the beginnings of Hebrew history not on the grand creations of Moses, but on airy nothings." But that view, the lateness of the majority of the Pentateuch, has been the majority view of the field for over a hundred years. The linguistic evidence never supported it. And in recent years the work of scholars such as Robert Polzin, Gary Rendsburg, Ziony Zevit, and especially Avi Hurvitz has produced a mass of evidence that reveals that the works J, E, P, and the Court History through Solomon all were composed in Classical (preexilic) Hebrew.[1] One would think either that this would settle it or that there would be a rush of responses. But wait! This is biblical scholarship, so a number of scholars responded by dating everything later.[2] Not only is P postexilic, but so is virtually the entire Deuteronomistic

---

[1] Robert Polzin, *Late Biblical Hebrew: Toward an Historical Typology of Biblical Hebrew Prose* (Atlanta: Scholars Press, 1976); Gary Rendsburg, "Late Biblical Hebrew and the Date of P," *JANESCU* 12 (1980): 65–80; Ziony Zevit, "Converging Lines of Evidence Bearing on the Date of P," *ZAW* 84 (1982): 502–9; Avi Hurvitz, "The Relevance of Biblical Hebrew Linguistics for the Historical Study of Ancient Israel," in *Proceedings of the Twelfth World Congress of Jewish Studies: Jerusalem, July 29–August 5, 1997* (ed. R. Margolin; Jerusalem: World Union of Jewish Studies, 1999), 21–33; idem, "The Evidence of Language in Dating the Priestly Code," *RB* 81 (1974): 24–56; idem, *A Linguistic Study of the Relationship between the Priestly Source and the Book of Ezekiel* (CahRB; Paris: Gabalda, 1982); idem, ללשון בין לשון (Jerusalem: Bialik Institute, 1972); idem, "Continuity and Innovation in Biblical Hebrew—The Case of 'Semantic Change' in Post-Exilic Writings," in *Studies in Ancient Hebrew Semantics* (ed. T. Muraoka; AbrNSup 4; Leuven: Peeters, 1995): 1–10; idem, "The Usage of שש and בוץ in the Bible and Its Implication for the Date of P," *HTR* 60 (1967): 117–21.

[2] See Erhard Blum, *Die Komposition der Vatergeschichte* (WMANT 57; Neukirchen-Vluyn: Neukirchener Verlag, 1984); idem, *Studien zur Komposition*

History. So is J.[3] And E does not exist—but it is late, too.[4] I was in a session with two leading late-dating scholars, John Van Seters and Erhard Blum, at the Society of Biblical Literature annual meeting in 1995. They did not mention the linguistic evidence. So I asked them, "What about the linguistic evidence?" In their responses they just went on and did not answer. Avi Hurvitz asked the same question of Thomas Thompson at a session in Jerusalem in 1998. And Thompson responded, "Now here I'm going to have to plead mea culpa." But he said he would get to it sometime. Redating biblical texts without addressing the evidence of language is like working on a revolutionary new view of diabetes without taking into account sugar.

---

des Pentateuch (BZAW 189; Berlin: de Gruyter, 1990); see also John Van Seters, *Abraham in History and Tradition* (New Haven: Yale University Press, 1975); idem, *In Search of History: Historiography in the Ancient World and the Origins of Biblical History* (New Haven: Yale University Press, 1983); idem, *Prologue to History: The Yahwist As Historian in Genesis* (Louisville: Westminster John Knox, 1992); idem, *The Life of Moses: The Yahwist As Historian in Exodus-Numbers* (Louisville: Westminster John Knox, 1994).

[3] Other works relating to the late dating of J include Hans Heinrich Schmid, *Der sogenannte Jahwist* (Zurich: Theologischer Verlag, 1976); Rolf Rendtorff, *The Problem of the Process of Transmission in the Pentateuch* (trans. J. Scullion; JSOTSup 89; Sheffield: Sheffield Academic Press, 1990); idem, *Das Überlieferungsgeschichtliche Problem des Pentateuch* (Berlin: de Gruyter, 1977); Martin Rose, *Deuteronomist und Jahwist: Beruhrungspunkte beider Literaturwerke* (Zurich: Theologischer Verlag, 1982). For bibliographies and analyses, see David M. Carr, "Controversy and Convergence in Recent Studies of the Formation of the Pentateuch," *RelSRev* 23 (1997): 22–31; Albert de Pury, "Yahwist ('J') Source," *ABD* 6:1016–20; Ernest W. Nicholson, "The Pentateuch in Recent Research: A Time for Caution," in *Congress Volume: Leuven, 1989* (VTSup 43; Leiden: Brill, 1991), 10–21; Thomas B. Dozeman, "The Institutional Setting of the Late Formation of the Pentateuch in the Work of John Van Seters," *Society of Biblical Literature: 1991 Seminar Papers* (ed. E. H. Lovering; Missoula, Mont.: Society of Biblical Literature, 1991), 253–64; and the group of discussions in *JSOT* 3 (1977).

[4] Van Seters, *Abraham in History and Tradition;* idem, *In Search of History;* idem, *Prologue to History;* idem, *The Life of Moses;* idem, "The Pentateuch," in *The Hebrew Bible Today* (ed. S. McKenzie and M. P. Graham; Louisville: Westminster John Knox, 1998), 3–49; Rose, *Deuteronomist und Jahwist;* Blum, *Die Komposition der Vatergeschichte;* idem, *Studien zur Komposition des Pentateuch;* Andrew D. H. Mayes, *The Story of Israel between Settlement and Exile* (London: SCM, 1983), 139–49; Joseph Blenkinsopp, *The Pentateuch: An Introduction to the First Five Books of the Bible* (ABRL; Garden City, N.Y.: Doubleday, 1992). For an alternative view, see recently Robert K. Gnuse, "Redefining the Elohist?" *JBL* 119 (2000): 201–20.

It is a strange phenomenon in scholarship: once a model becomes successful, most scholars are not out there trying to prove it any longer. So the unusual models are the ones in which scholars are doing projects and creating a buzz. And then people say: the majority of scholars *working on the question* no longer accept the dominant model! So it has been with Freud. People say, "No one accepts Freud anymore," while thousands of analysts practice the Freudian model every day. And so with the Documentary Hypothesis: People have said to me, "The majority of scholars working on the question no longer accept it." But that is because the battle has been won, so most of our colleagues are not exactly working *on* the question. They are working *within* the dominant model of the solution to the question. And, meanwhile, our colleagues with the new, unusual models, hold SBL sessions and publish a torrent of articles and books, but, to this day, they have not addressed the full evidence that brought us to the dominant model in the first place.

What is the result? Scholarship, at its best, is supposed to be a search for the truth. But this is turning it more than ever into a battle for consensus. And scholarship at its best is a joy. It is even fun. But this is turning it into a bore.

So let me turn back to the days of yesteryear, when we were step-by-step recognizing the antiquity of our texts. First, Martin Noth identified the Deuteronomistic History, telling the story from Moses in Deuteronomy to the exile at the end of 2 Kings.[5] Then, Frank Cross and many others among us argued that the Deuteronomistic History was largely composed before the exile, at the time of Josiah, which moved back about 95 percent of the work from the exile to Josiah.[6] Then, some of us concentrated on the Deuteronomistic Historian's sources, which moved about 80 to 90 percent of the work back well before Josiah.[7] Which brings me to the material of

---

[5] Martin Noth, *Überlieferungsgeschichtliche Studien* (Tübingen: Niemeyer, 1943).

[6] Frank Moore Cross, *Canaanite Myth and Hebrew Epic: Essays in the History of the Religion of Israel* (Cambridge: Harvard University Press, 1973), 274–325; Richard Elliott Friedman, *The Exile and Biblical Narrative*, (HSM 22; Atlanta: Scholars Press, 1981); idem, "From Egypt to Egypt: Dtr[1] and Dtr[2]," in *Traditions in Transformation: Turning-Points in Biblical Faith* (ed. B. Halpern and J. D. Levenson; Winona Lake, Ind.: Eisenbrauns, 1981), 167–81; Richard D. Nelson, *The Double Redaction of the Deuteronomistic History* (JSOTSup 18; Sheffield: Sheffield Academic Press, 1981).

[7] Richard Elliott Friedman, *Who Wrote the Bible?* (2d ed.; San Francisco: Harper San Francisco, 1997), 101–49; idem, "The Deuteronomistic School," in *Fortunate the Eyes That See: Essays in Honor of David Noel Freedman in Celebration of His Seventieth Birthday* (ed. A. B. Beck et al.; Grand Rapids: Eerdmans, 1995), 70–80; Baruch Halpern, *The First Historians* (San Francisco: Harper & Row, 1988); P. Kyle McCarter Jr., *1 Samuel* (AB 8; New York: Doubleday, 1980); Anthony Campbell, *Of*

this paper: sources. This concerns two large source-works of the biblical historians, both of which are centered in Solomon's Jerusalem. They were probably written there, and they culminate there.

I have discussed the first of these sources in recent papers and a book.[8] I contended that the source known to us as J is just the first part of a lengthy work of prose that continues past the death of Moses at the end of the Torah and includes portions of Joshua, Judges, 1 Samuel, practically all of 2 Samuel, and the first two chapters of Kings. I call it by the title *In the Day* because it begins with the words ביום עשות יהוה ארץ ושמים. My colleagues and students have started calling it Greater-J or Super-J. It tells a story from the creation of the world to the establishment of Solomon's kingdom. I will give just a brief summary of the lines of evidence here.

First, a bank of terminology lines up uniquely in this particular group of texts. Its frequency and consistency rule out coincidence as an explanation, and it crosses too many lines of genre and subject matter to be explained as deriving from mere convergence of such things. As a sampling: Abigail says of her foolish husband Nabal, "As his name is, that's how he is!" There are ten occurrences of the term נָבָל or נְבָלָה in all of biblical prose. And all ten are in this group of texts. Jacob says to Laban, "Why did you deceive me?" (למה רמיראי). So also says Joshua to the Gibeonites, Saul to Michal, and the woman of Endor to Saul. Of seven occurrences of למה רמיתני and במרמה in biblical prose, all are in this group of texts. Of seven occurrences of the expression "to wash the feet," in biblical prose, all are in this group. All nine references to Sheol in biblical prose are in this group of texts.[9] All nine occurrences of the term for shearing (גזז) are in this group. The phrase for "those who live in the land" (יושב הארץ) applies to the Canaanite inhabitants of the land but refers to them in the singular. This formulation occurs six times in biblical prose. All

---

Prophets and Kings: A Ninth Century Document (1 Samuel 1–2 Kings 10) (CBQMS 17; Washington, D.C.: Catholic Bible Association of America, 1986); Steven L. McKenzie, *The Chronicler's Use of the Deuteronomistic History* (HSM 33; Atlanta: Scholars Press, 1985).

[8] Richard Elliott Friedman, "The First Great Writer," unpublished paper read at the Biblical Colloquium (1986) and in colloquia at Cambridge (1900), Yale (1991), Hebrew University of Jerusalem (1997), University of California, Berkeley (1998), and University of California, San Diego (1998); idem, *The Hidden Book in the Bible* (San Francisco: Harper, 1998).

[9] For a discussion of the potential significance of this, see Richard Elliott Friedman and Sawna D. Overton, "Death and Afterlife: The Biblical Silence," in *Judaism in Late Antiquity Part 4: Death, Life-after-Death, Resurrection and the World-to-Come in the Judaisms of Antiquity* (ed. A. J. Avery-Peck and J. Neusner; Leiden: Brill, 2000).

six are in this group (Gen 50:11; Exod 34:12, 15; Num 14:14; Judg 11:21; 2 Sam 5:6). The expression for old age (זקן בא בימים) is applied to Abraham, Isaac, Joshua, and David—all in this group. Similar observations can be made about the use of other terminology in this group: the root בשׂר—"to bring news"—eleven of twelve occurrences; the term "to lie with" (שׁכב) with sexual connotation—thirty-two cases in biblical prose, thirty of them in this group; the expression "faithfulness and truth" (ואמת חסד)—all seven occurrences in biblical prose; the word "spies" (מרגלים)—all twelve occurrences in the Hebrew Bible.

Now, it is not just that there is this recurring bank of terms and phrases in this collection of texts. It is also that the texts in which this bank of terms and phrases occur are connected. For example, in the last J passages in the Pentateuch, Israel is located at Shittim (Num 25:1–5), which is where Joshua is when the lexical affinities begin in the book of Joshua (Josh 2:1; 3:1). Likewise, the material in 1 Samuel, known as the Samuel B source, connects back to the conclusion of Judges. Judges 21 ends with the taking of wives from Shiloh, and Samuel begins in Shiloh (1 Sam 1). And the account in Judg 11:40 reports that Israelite women would go out "regularly" (מימים ימימה) to commemorate Jephthah's daughter. The account later reports in Judg 21:19 that the wifeless Benjaminites captured women who went out on the occasion of the regular holiday at Shiloh. They say, "Here's a holiday of YHWH in Shiloh מימים ימימה." And then Samuel B begins with the notation that Elkanah would go up to sacrifice "מימים ימימה at Shiloh" (1 Sam 1:3; 2:19). And these are the only occurrences of this expression in biblical narrative.[10] And then the end of the Samuel B material flows integrally into the Court History.

Now it is not just that the terms recur and that the texts in which this happens are connected. It is also that the recurring terms and phrases are *meaningfully* related. Thus, for example, the text in J notes that Cain kills Abel when they are in the field. What is the significance of informing us that they are in a field at the time? Even early biblical commentators searched for the meaning of this seemingly inconsequential detail. But later in this corpus, there is the story of another fratricide: Absalom has his brother Amnon killed (for raping Tamar). In an attempt to get David to pardon Absalom the "wise woman of Tekoa" tells David that one of her two sons has killed the other. And she mentions a seemingly unrelated detail: the brothers fought "in the field" (2 Sam 14:6).[11] The same term,

---

[10] It occurs in a passage of law in Exod 13:10.

[11] Joseph Blenkinsopp noted the parallel references to "field" in Gen 4:8 and 2 Sam 14:6 in "Theme and Motif in the Succession History (2 Sam xi 2ff.) and the Yahwist Corpus," in *Volume du Congrès: Genève, 1965* (VTSup 15; Leiden: Brill,

which is an extraneous detail, occurring in both stories of brother killing brother is suspect. And there is further evidence of their linkage, because references to *field* occur in other sibling-rivalry stories in these texts. In the episode of Jacob's appropriation of Esau's birthright, Esau comes to Jacob "from the field" (Gen 25:29). Indeed, Esau is introduced as an אִישׁ שָׂדֶה (25:27). Similarly, Joseph begins his report of his dream to his brothers with the words: "Here we were binding sheaves in the field" (Gen 37:7, 19–20), which prompts his brothers to propose fratricide a few verses later, saying, "Here comes the dream-master! And now, come on and let's kill him!" The story of the war between Benjamin and the rest of the Israelite tribes is also presented in terms of brothers killing brothers (Judg 20:13, 23, 28; 21:6); and there, too, the word *field* comes up twice.

The theme of fratricide recurs repeatedly in this work. It begins with Cain and Abel and ends with Solomon executing Adonijah, and in between we read of Jacob and Esau, Joseph and his brothers, Abimelech killing seventy of his brothers, the war between Benjamin and the other Israelite tribes, the struggle between Israel and Judah (which likewise is cast in terms of brothers) (2 Sam 2:26–27), and Absalom and Amnon. But it is not just the fact of the ongoing theme. It is that the recurring language is meaningfully selected and distributed throughout this corpus. And it is not merely the fratricide theme that culminates in Solomon. At the beginning of the story, four rivers flow from Eden, one of which is the Gihon. And we know that the choice of the Gihon was purposeful because the author puns on its name, as the curse on the snake is: "you'll go on your belly [גְּחֹנְךָ]." Finally, at the conclusion of the story, Solomon is made king at the Gihon (1 Kgs 1:33).

The work begins with the pairing of the tree of life and the tree of knowledge of good and bad. To have one is to lose the other. The work ends with the account of Solomon's treatment of the last threat to the Davidic throne: Shimei, but the words *knowledge, good, bad,* and *death* fill it, occurring fifteen times. And the two words for *life* used in the beginning of the work (חי and נֶפֶשׁ) occur ten times in the last two chapters. And the formulation of God's command to the first human reappears here in the formulation of King Solomon's command to Shimei: God says, "In the day you eat from it you will die" (Gen 2:17; repeated in 3:4); Solomon says, "In the day you go out … you will die" (1 Kgs 2:37; repeated in 2:42). And this formulation ("In the day you do X … you will die") occurs nowhere else in the Hebrew Bible. At the beginning, the symbolic moment that conveys father-son succession in J is when Jacob bows to his son Joseph on

1966), 51. He also pointed out a number of additional parallels of theme between J and the Court History.

his deathbed (Gen 47:31). At the conclusion, David bows to his son Solomon on his deathbed (1 Kgs 1:47). There is the theme of the security of the country. Promised to Abraham near the beginning of the work, it is fulfilled through Joshua near the middle. It is promised to David for his son (2 Sam 7:12: "I will make his kingdom secure"), and then it is achieved through Solomon at the end. The work's last words are והממלכה נכונה ביד שלמה. From Gihon to Gihon, from Eden to Sinai to Jerusalem, all of these things have their denouement in Solomon in the last two chapters of the Court History. The first portion of this work, as far as Moses, was used as a source by the redactor of the Torah. The latter part, as far as Solomon, was used by the Deuteronomistic Historian. The Deuteronomistic Historian then went into the history of the kings of Judah and Israel. The language and connections in the accounts of those two kingdoms are so different that it is clear that the historian used different sources for Israel and for Judah. Baruch Halpern demonstrated twenty years ago that the main source for Judah was a work that told the story from Solomon to Hezekiah—and that this source-work was used by both the Deuteronomistic Historian and the Chronicler.[12]

The evidence of this includes both key terms, formulas, and themes that disappear after Hezekiah in Chronicles and an inclusio of Solomon and Hezekiah bookending the work. In accession formulas, the queen mother's name is given through Hezekiah, and then it disappears. Most burial notices in Chronicles and all in Kings have burial "in the city of David" up to Hezekiah, but none have it after Hezekiah. Kings has the notice of there being no king as great as Hezekiah but then says that there was no king as great as Josiah before him or after him. The rest motif disappears after Hezekiah. In Chronicles there is a formulaic use of the verb חזק, usually in the *hitpaʿel,* with almost every Judahite king to Hezekiah, but after Hezekiah it is never used this way and never in the *hitpaʿel.* And, after all, it is the root of the name Hezekiah.

The Solomon-to-Hezekiah inclusio is manifest in a range of connections. Hugh Williamson had noted the parallel emphasis on Solomon's and Hezekiah's wealth, on bringing tribute to both, and on the seven-plus-seven days' length of their festivals of temple dedication.[13] Halpern added

---

[12] Baruch Halpern, "Sacred History and Ideology: Chronicles' Thematic Structure—Indications of an Earlier Source," in *The Creation of Sacred Literature: Composition and Redaction of the Biblical Text* (ed. R. E. Friedman; University of California Publications Near Eastern Studies 22; Berkeley and Los Angeles: University of California Press, 1981), 35–54.

[13] Hugh G. M. Williamson, *Israel in the Books of Chronicles* (Cambridge: Cambridge University Press, 1977), 120–25.

that Chronicles describes the people's response to Hezekiah's leadership at his Passover as follows: "And there was great joy in Jerusalem; there had been nothing like it in Jerusalem *since the days of King Solomon*" (2 Chr 30:26). The sacrificial duties of the priests are described in the same words in the Solomon and Hezekiah texts (2 Chr 2:3; 8:13; 31:3). The priests are described as going through a process of sanctification (התקדשו) only in the Solomon and Hezekiah treatments (2 Chr 5:11; 29:15, 34). Chronicles declares that the king succeeded in everything that was in his heart to do with regard to the temple only in the cases of Solomon and Hezekiah (2 Chr 7:11; 31:21). There is an obvious concentration on temple and tabernacle in Solomon and Hezekiah. I would add that the משכן is mentioned only with regard to these two—and not figuratively or symbolically: In both the Solomon and the Hezekiah accounts, the tabernacle is a real structure housed in the temple (2 Chr 5:5; 29:6–7). But after Hezekiah the tabernacle disappears.

Thus we have two great histories, works that were used as sources for the Torah and the Deuteronomistic History: one that went from creation to Solomon and one that went from Solomon to Hezekiah. The first included twelve generations from Abraham to Solomon. The second included twelve generations from Solomon to Hezekiah. The question is: Why is Solomon the turning-point of both? In the case of the latter work: If it was a history of the kings of Judah, why start with Solomon and not Rehoboam? Or if it was a history back to a united monarchy, why start with Solomon and not David? And in the case of the former work, why go to Solomon? It is not because Solomon builds the temple, because this work ends with Solomon's accession and executions and never gets to the temple.

It may be that Solomon was of no importance in and of himself for the writer of that work. The point is just to establish that the promises to David came true. So it stops as the kingdom is established. Alternatively, my teacher Frank Cross used to say that the most banal solution is usually the right one, so let me suggest this banal solution: the work stops at Solomon because that is who was king when the author wrote it. This is the view of my colleague David Noel Freedman that I have been resisting for years: it was written at the time of Solomon, so it goes to the author's own day. And perhaps the author of the Solomon-to-Hezekiah source knew the creation to Solomon work (*In the Day*) and so he decided to start where that work left off. And he went down to Hezekiah because that was who happened to be king when *he* was writing.

That is neat and simple, but we have to take into account the literary connections of themes and wording between Solomon and Hezekiah. And we have to take into account the historical and political connections between them, particularly with regard to the report of how these two kings connected with and empowered the priesthood. Solomon and

Hezekiah are the two great kings for the Zadokite, Aaronide priesthood. Solomon inherits from David two chief priests, Zadok and Abiathar, but he removes Abiathar, who is said to have supported Solomon's brother and opponent for the throne, Adonijah. Zadok and the Aaronides are in; the others, whether you call them Mushites, Shilonites, or non-Aaronides, are out. And Hezekiah, according to Chronicles, establishes the distinctions between priests and Levites, so that non-Aaronides are no longer considered priests (2 Chr 31:2). Solomon built the temple; Hezekiah centralized religion at that temple. Ironically, Sennacherib gave Hezekiah and the Aaronides their victory, making it possible to centralize and control the priestly establishment. And so the author of the Solomon-to-Hezekiah source-work, presumably a partisan—if not a member—of the priestly establishment, saw a natural continuum in the two monarchs who were the heroes and benefactors of that establishment.

Meanwhile Solomon is more than just the last king in the work that flows from creation to the Judahite court. He is the focus of the work. It is constructed to culminate in Solomon no less than the other work is constructed to culminate in Hezekiah, the king like whom there was no other. Maybe that is why it starts with fratricide, Cain's killing of Abel, and maintains it as a theme: because it is *aiming* to get to Solomon's killing of Adonijah. And presumably that is why it starts at the Gihon: because its trajectory is to Solomon's anointing at the Gihon. And it starts with man clinging to woman, so that Adonijah will be understood, like Shechem, to fall because of his attachment to a woman. And it starts with woman's subordination to man, but it ends with Solomon, the most powerful male, bowing to Bathsheba when she enters the room. In short, all the things that are now denouements and culminations and climaxes were actually, originally, the starting points, the focuses of the work.

What makes Solomon so complex a biblical figure? In each of these source-works Solomon was originally good, but then both works came into the hands of an editor—or more correctly, a historian. The Deuteronomistic Historian made Solomon bad. His work cast him as breaking the Deuteronomic law of the king. It has been common in our field to claim that the law of the king was composed to denigrate Solomon: to take the very things Solomon had done and to make them forbidden: lots of horses, lots of women, lots of wealth. But the more likely scenario is that the historian, wanting to make a case against Solomon, accused him of breaking the law.[14] When David defeated Aram, he hamstrung the thousands of horses he captured, but Solomon kept his horses, violating the law of the

---

[14] Baruch Halpern, *The Constitution of the Monarchy in Israel* (HSM 25; Chico, Calif.: Scholars Press, 1981).

king. Those who tell political history today do the same thing: claiming that it is not that the president met that woman in his office or that his opponents detested him, but rather that he broke the law. In any case, whether the law was written to make Solomon look bad or Solomon's story was written to emphasize that he broke the law, the outcome was the same: the Deuteronomistic Historian was rewriting Solomon. Josiah, the hero of the Deuteronomistic History, destroys Solomon's altars. The Chronicler, meanwhile, takes the same material and makes Solomon pretty good.

Why does the Deuteronomistic Historian do this? This seems to be consistent with other evidence that the Deuteronomistic Historian came from the excluded priesthood. Call it Shilonite, Mushite, or Levite. It is the prophet Ahijah of *Shiloh* who opposes Solomon. The same acts that made Solomon attractive to the Aaronides made him the nemesis of the excluded priests. David moves the ark to Jerusalem, but Solomon builds the temple and begins the process that moved the full religious establishment there. So Solomon forever impacted the focus of the Bible's narration of history, and Solomon's Jerusalem forever governed its picture.

PART 2

THE RISE AND FALL OF JERUSALEM
AT THE END OF THE JUDAHITE KINGDOM

Western Jerusalem at the End of the First Temple Period in Light of the Excavations in the Jewish Quarter

Hillel Geva
The Hebrew University of Jerusalem, Israel Exploration Society

INTRODUCTION

The settlement of Jerusalem goes back to at least as early as the Early Bronze Age, when the City of David on the southern part of the eastern ridge was settled. Later, according to the biblical account, David seized the Canaanite-Jebusite walled city whose area at the time was some 50 dunams (approximately 13 acres) and made it into the capital of his kingdom. During the reign of Solomon, the Bible describes the city's expansion and the construction of a royal acropolis with temple on Mount Moriah (today's Temple Mount). By the tenth and ninth centuries B.C.E., the view is that the settlement in ancient Jerusalem covered the entire eastern ridge (City of David, Ophel, and Mount Moriah), including an area of 160 dunams (some 40 acres). This was the extent of the city on the eve of its expansion to the southwestern hill, a step that was to determine the city's limits at the end of the First Temple period and in generations to come.

The southwestern hill is located to the west of the eastern ridge, with the Central Valley (or Tyropoeon) in between. The hill is higher than the eastern ridge and wider in area. It is well-protected on its west and south sides by the deep and wide Hinnom Valley. To the north it is bounded by the Transversal Valley that descends from the area of the present-day Jaffa Gate in the west wall of the Old City toward the Temple Mount on the east (along today's David Street and its continuation, Street of the Chain). This shallow valley did not provide the hill with a sufficient natural defense on this side. Two secondary summits can be discerned on the hill: the higher, western peak is located in today's Armenian Quarter, and the slightly lower, eastern one is in the center of the Jewish Quarter. Between the two peaks a short, shallow valley descends northward (along today's Ha-Yehudim Street) toward the Transversal Valley. The topography of the

183

hill has determined the course of the city walls ever since the end of the First Temple period.

THE DEBATE IN THE PAST BETWEEN "MINIMALISTS" AND "MAXIMALISTS"

Historically, researchers of ancient Jerusalem have been divided regarding the question of when the fortified area of the city expanded out from the eastern ridge to include the southwestern hill as well. Until the large-scale excavations in the Jewish Quarter following the reunification of the city in 1967, these differences of opinion stemmed from the dearth of archaeological evidence from the southwestern hill in the past, conflicting interpretations of the biblical descriptions of Jerusalem, and the credibility of Josephus's testimony that the First Wall that encompassed the

Fig. 7.1. Map of the Jewish Quarter showing the location of the excavations areas

southwestern hill had been built in the days of David and Solomon (in other words, during the First Temple period; *War* 5.4.2).[1]

According to the "minimalist" view (known also as the "one-hill theory"), the area of the Jerusalem in biblical times was limited to the eastern ridge: the City of David and Mount Moriah. Proponents of this approach viewed the topographical descriptions of Jerusalem in the Bible as consistent with a small city. As to Josephus's testimony concerning the time of the First Wall's construction, it was dismissed as unrealistic in light of the fact that the surviving remains of this wall uncovered on the southwestern hill were not older than the Second Temple period. This was the prevalent view among archaeological experts on Jerusalem in the mid-twentieth century, among them Michael Avi-Yonah, Nahman Avigad,[2] and Kathleen Kenyon (see below).

The "maximalist" view (known also as the "two-hills theory") held that the biblical city already encompassed the southwestern hill within its bounds. The proponents of this view disagreed among themselves as to precisely when the expansion took place (in Jebusite times, during the united kingdom, or later during the days of the kingdom of Judah). It was their opinion that only a large city covering both hills could have served as the capital of the kingdom of Israel and Judah. They also claimed that the detailed description in the Bible of the lengthy wall of Jerusalem reconstructed by Nehemiah (3:1–32) could only fit a large city that included the southwestern hill as well. These scholars pointed also to Josephus's statement concerning the construction of the First Wall around the southwestern hill by David and Solomon (meaning the First Temple period) as providing support for their view. Among the well-known scholars who supported the maximalist view (until Kenyon's excavations in Jerusalem in the 1960s) were Frederick Bliss and Archibald Dickie, Gustaf Dalman, Jan Simons, Louis-Hugues Vincent,[3] and Ruth Amiran (see below).

---

[1] For summaries of the debate, see Jan Simons, *Jerusalem in the Old Testament: Researches and Theories* (Leiden: Brill, 1952), 226–29; Michael Avi-Yonah, "Topography" [Hebrew], in *Sefer Yerushalayim* (*The Book of Jerusalem*) (ed. M. Avi-Yonah; 2 vols.; Jerusalem: Bialik Institute and Dvir, 1956), 1:157–60; Hillel Geva, "The Western Boundary of Jerusalem at the End of the Monarchy," *IEJ* (1979): 84–85; Gabriel Barkay, "Jerusalem of the Old Testament Times: New Discoveries and New Approaches," *BAIAS* (1985–86): 33–34 and list on 40–41.

[2] Michael Avi-Yonah, "The Walls of Nehemiah: A Minimalist View," *IEJ* (1954): 239–48; Nahman Avigad, "Archaeology" [Hebrew], in Avi-Yonah, *Sefer Yerushalayim,* 1:145–55.

[3] Frederick J. Bliss and Archibald C. Dickie, *Excavations at Jerusalem 1894–1897* (London: Palestine Exploration Fund, 1898), 290, 320–22; Gustaf Dalman, *Jerusalem und sein Gelände* (Gutersloh: Bertelsmann, 1930); Simons, *Jerusalem in*

Between these two extreme opinions there was also an intermediate view according to which the eastern part of the southwestern hill had been incorporated into the city already in First Temple times.[4]

The advantage the minimalists enjoyed, which was at the same time the disadvantage of the maximalists, was the perceived lack of archaeological finds on the southwestern hill dated to the First Temple period. This, however, was not entirely true. Some pottery of this period had been found in past excavations on Mount Zion, albeit not much and quite sporadic, both on the southern slope and in the southwest corner of the hill.[5] Further, Cedric N. Johns in the 1930s and 1940s first found a clear layer of earth fill dating from the end of the First Temple period in the "Tower of David" citadel. He even noted the possibility that the segment built of field stones incorporated in the Second Temple First Wall in the citadel might date from the end of the days of the kingdom of Judea.[6] These sporadic and partial pieces of evidence did not receive the attention they deserved. The state of research in the 1950s was described accurately by Jan Simons:

> The excavations hitherto made on the Southwestern Hill are too few in number, on too small a scale or too obscure in their results to play a decisive part in the main question raised by this hill, viz., what was its original relation to the settlement on the Southeastern ridge representing the earliest nucleus of the city, and when did it become an organic unity with this nucleus, such as it was at all events during the Herodian period?[7]

A significant contribution to the debate was made by Ruth Amiran when she published the contents of two tombs from the end of the First Temple

---

the Old Testament, 229; Louis-Hugues Vincent and P. M.-A. Stéve, *Jérusalem de L'ancien testament: recherches d'archéologie et d'histoire* (Paris: Gabalda, 1954–56), 1:89, 637–39.

[4] Kurt Galling, "Jerusalem" and "Palast," *BRL*. Another proposal was that biblical Jerusalem consisted of two separate areas, Zion in the City of David and Jerusalem on the southwestern hill. See Otto Proksch, "Das Jerusalem Jesajas," *PJ* 26 (1930): 12–40; and also R. Pearce S. Hubbard, "The Topography of Ancient Jerusalem," *PEQ* 98 (1966): 137–41.

[5] Bliss and Dickie, *Excavations at Jerusalem 1894–1897*, pls. XXV:1, XXVII: 1–2; see also Shimon Gibson, "The 1961–67 Excavations in the Armenian Garden," *PEQ* 119 (1987): 83; Richard W. Hamilton, "Note on Excavations at Bishop Gobat School, 1933," *PEFQS* (1935): 141–43.

[6] Cedric N. Johns, "Excavations at the Citadel, Jerusalem, 1934–9," *PEQ* 72 (1940): 15, 21; idem, "The Citadel, Jerusalem: A Summary of Work since 1934," *QDAP* 14 (1950): 129–34; and see Geva, "Western Boundary of Jerusalem," note 1.

[7] Simons, *Jerusalem in the Old Testament*, 226.

period found across from the Jaffa Gate in the upper part of the Hinnom Valley, to the west of the southwestern hill. Amiran perceived a geographical-historical link between the location of these tombs and the expansion of the city toward the southwestern hill and believed that it provided evidence in favor of the maximalists.[8]

We can thus summarize the state of affairs up to this point by saying that while past excavations on the southwestern hill did yield certain finds from the First Temple period, they were neither of a quantity nor of a quality to have made it possible to provide a definitive answer to the question of whether or not Jerusalem had already expanded to that hill at the time. The evidence did point to the direction in which future research should proceed in order to arrive at such an answer, namely, extensive archaeological excavations on the southwestern hill.

In order to obtain new evidence on this issue, Kenyon's expedition conducted excavations in several places on the southwestern hill during the years 1961–67. Excavations in areas B, DI, DII, and E on the hill's eastern slope did not yield any finds from the end of the First Temple period.[9] However, in the excavation that Kenyon and Tushingham conducted in the Armenian garden (area L) in the western part of the southwestern hill (to the south of the citadel and the Jaffa Gate), several segments of walls with earth fills from the end of the First Temple period were found. These were interpreted by the excavators as indications of quarrying in the area, not as proof of permanent settlement.[10] Tushingham was of the opinion that the earth fill from this period was brought to the Armenian garden from elsewhere (from somewhere in the Jewish Quarter or perhaps even from an area to the north of the southwestern hill) when the podium for Herod's palace was being built.[11] However, the results of subsequent excavations throughout the southwestern hill have voided the excavators' interpretation of their finds in the Armenian garden.[12]

---

[8] Ruth Amiran, "The Necropolis of Jerusalem in the Time of the Monarchy" [Hebrew], in *Judah and Jerusalem: The Twelfth Archaeological Convention* (Jerusalem: Israel Exploration Society, 1957), 65–72 .

[9] Kathleen M. Kenyon, *Jerusalem: Excavating Three Thousand Years of History* (London: Thames & Hudson, 1967), 70–71.

[10] Kathleen M. Kenyon, *Digging Up Jerusalem* (London: Benn, 1974), 147; A. Douglas Tushingham, *Excavations by Kathleen M. Kenyon in Jerusalem, 1961–1967, vol. I* (Toronto: Royal Ontario Museum, 1985), 12–16.

[11] Tushingham, *Excavations in Jerusalem I*, 9–24; idem, "The Western Hill of Jerusalem: A Critique of the 'Maximalist Position,'" *Levant* 19 (1987): 137–38.

[12] See Gibson, "The 1961–67 Excavations," 81–87; and the answer: A. Douglas Tushingham, "The 1961–67 Excavations in the Armenian Garden, Jerusalem: A Response," *PEQ* 120 (1988): 142–45.

Kenyon believed that the "negative" results of her excavations on the southwestern hill constituted conclusive proof for the minimalist view that this area was not part of Jerusalem during the First Temple period (although it should be pointed out that she did modify her view after finds from this period were discovered in the Jewish Quarter excavations; see below). The results of her excavations appeared indeed to decide the debate in favor of the minimalists: the southwestern hill apparently was not part of the urban area of Jerusalem during the First Temple period.

Thus matters stood on the eve of Avigad's excavations in the Jewish Quarter, in which impressive and surprising finds, of settlement and fortification, from the end of the First Temple period were discovered.

REMAINS OF THE SETTLEMENT AT THE END OF THE FIRST TEMPLE PERIOD IN THE JEWISH QUARTER

Between the years 1969 and 1982 extensive excavations were conducted by the late Nahman Avigad in the Jewish Quarter, situated in the southeastern part of today's Old City—the eastern part of the southwestern hill. This was the most extensive excavation project ever conducted on the southwestern hill. Twenty-two different areas in all parts of the Jewish quarter were excavated, some 20 dunams (5 acres) in all (fig. 7.1). The results of these excavations proved crucial for an understanding of the history of the settlement of this part of the city.

The remnants dating to the end of the First Temple period found on the natural bedrock are the earliest finds in the stratigraphic array unearthed in the Jewish Quarter. The intensive building activities of the continuous period of settlement during Second Temple times and later caused great damage to structures of the First Temple period and in most cases left only very sporadic remnants in its wake. Still, the evidence that has survived is enough to provide a picture of the nature and fortifications of the settlement that existed there toward the end of the First Temple period.[13]

In several places in the Jewish Quarter, remains of stone quarries were found underneath the remnants from the First Temple period. The finds on

---

[13] A more detailed description of the finds from the Jewish Quarter can be found in Nahman Avigad, *Discovering Jerusalem* (Nashville: Nelson, 1983); and in the final report: Hillel Geva, ed., *Jewish Quarter Excavations in the Old City of Jerusalem Conducted by Nahman Avigad, vol. I, Architecture and Stratigraphy: Areas A, W and X-2, Final Report* (Jerusalem: Israel Exploration Society, 2000).

the west side of the hill, in the Armenian garden excavated by Kenyon and Tushingham (area L),[14] testify to the nature and size of the quarries on the southwestern hill during the First Temple period. That quarry continued also along the hill's west slope outside today's city walls, to the south of the Jaffa Gate. The cliffs formed by the quarrying activity were used later in the same period for hewing burial tombs.[15] Evidence of quarrying was found also inside the citadel ("Tower of David"), on the northwestern corner of the hill.[16] Presumably the stone for Iron Age construction in the Jewish Quarter was quarried in the nearby slopes to the north and east. It should be mentioned that the natural stone occurring inside Jerusalem and in its vicinity was quarried during all periods but is most characteristic of the sites of the Iron Age.[17]

The First Temple period remnants in the Jewish Quarter include sections of impressive fortifications, remnants of private houses, earth fill, and many small objects. The archaeological strata of the period have accumulated to a height of 2 m, and occasionally several architectural stages can be discerned. In some areas excavated in the Jewish Quarter, no layers from the end of the First Temple period were found, these having apparently all been removed during the intensive construction activity of later periods. (In other areas it was impossible to continue digging under the remains of later structures, either because these structures were marked for preservation or because the depth of accumulated archaeological layers and modern debris was such as to prevent any further digging.) Still, it is worth mentioning that even in these areas potsherds and other small objects dated to the First Temple period were found in the later strata.

---

[14] Kenyon, *Digging Up Jerusalem,* 147; Tushingham, *Excavations in Jerusalem I,* 9–12, 16, 19–20; see Gibson, "The 1961–67 Excavations," 81–85.

[15] Magen Broshi et al., "Two Iron Age Tombs below the Western City Wall" [Hebrew], *Cathedra* 28 (1983): 17–32; Magen Broshi and Shimon Gibson, "Excavations along the Western and Southern Walls of the Old City of Jerusalem," in *Ancient Jerusalem Revealed* (ed. H. Geva; Jerusalem: Israel Exploration Society, 1994), 147–50.

[16] Johns, "Excavations at the Citadel," 127, fig. 5; Renee Sivan and Giora Solar, "Excavations in the Jerusalem Citadel, 1980–1988," in Geva, *Ancient Jerusalem Revealed,* 176.

[17] Moshe A. Avnimelech, "Influence of the Geological Conditions on the Development of Jerusalem," *BASOR* 181 (1966): 24–31; Yigal Shiloh and Aharon Horowitz, "Ashlar Quarries of the Iron Age in the Hill Country of Israel," *BASOR* 217 (1975): 37–48.

Domestic Construction

The walls of the houses from the First Temple period are well built. They are made of hard field stones or dressed soft limestone. The floors were made of a thin layer of crushed and pressed limestone, with an occasional layer of plaster on top. The small finds from this period, typical of Judean culture of the time, are of a domestic nature and include pottery vessels (fig. 7.8) as well as figurines (fig. 7.2) and *lmlk*, rosette, and private stamp-seal impressions.

Building L.363 (Area A) is the largest and most complete structure found on the site and provides a good example of the kind of buildings erected here in First Temple times (fig. 7.3). On its north side was a row of rooms that was exposed for a length of 16 m; its east and south sides were destroyed when the Broad Wall was built. L.116 (Area A) is an example of a rectangular, rock-hewn, and plastered installation that was used for processing agricultural produce or for the storage of liquids in jars (fig. 7.4).

Remains from the end of the First Temple period were discovered in excavations that had been conducted earlier on the southwestern hill (see above). Various finds from this period were unearthed by Kenyon in the 1960s (Area F), at the bottom of the southeastern slope of the hill,

Fig. 7.2. Israelite fertility figurine

to the west of the Central Valley (on a massive wall that was found here; see below), including a well-built water channel.[18] Since the 1970s further remains from the end of the First Temple period (in addition to those found in the Jewish Quarter) have been found on the southwestern hill. Remains of a building with an assemblage of complete vessels were found in excavations on Mount Zion.[19] Other remains were found in the citadel, in renewed excavation in the Armenian garden, on the eastern slope of

---

[18] Kathleen M. Kenyon, "Excavations in Jerusalem, 1961," *PEQ* 94 (1962): 85; idem, "Excavations in Jerusalem, 1962," *PEQ* 95 (1963): 19; idem, "Excavations in Jerusalem, 1963," *PEQ* 96 (1964): 11; idem, "Excavations in Jerusalem, 1964," *PEQ* 97 (1965): 15–16.

[19] Magen Broshi, "Excavations on Mount Zion 1971–1972," *IEJ* 26 (1976): 81–82.

Fig. 7.3. Area A, Building L.363, looking westward

Mount Zion outside the Old City walls, and in the excavations conducted by Shiloh (Area H) at the bottom of the hill's east slope.[20] Interestingly, an (industrial?) structure was uncovered on the hill's west slope, outside the walls of today's Old City to the south of the Jaffa Gate, in an area that all agree was outside the western wall of the city even at the end of the First Temple period (see below).[21]

---

[20] Ruth Amiran and Avraham Eitan, "Excavations in the Courtyard of the Citadel, Jerusalem, 1968–1969: Preliminary Report," *IEJ* 20 (1970): 9–10, 15; Giora Solar and Renee Sivan, "Citadel Moat," *ESI* 3 (1984): 48; Dan Bahat and Magen Broshi, "Excavations in the Armenian Garden," in *Jerusalem Revealed: Archaeology in the Holy City, 1968–1974* (ed. Y. Yadin; New Haven: Yale University Press, 1976), 56; Meir Ben-Dov, "Excavations and Architectural Survey of the Archaeological Remains along the Southern Wall of Jerusalem," in Geva, *Ancient Jerusalem Revealed,* 311–12; Florentino Díez, "Jerusalem, Church of St. Peter in Gallicantu: 1998–1999," *Hadashot Arkheologiyot* 112 (2000): 84*–85*; Alon De Groot and Dan Michaeli, "Area H: Stratigraphic Report," in *Excavations at the City of David 1978–1985 Directed by Yigal Shiloh, vol. III, Stratigraphcal, Environmental and Other Reports* (ed. A. De Groot and D. T. Ariel; Jerusalem: Institute of Archaeology, Hebrew University of Jerusalem, 1992), 50–51.

[21] Broshi and Gibson, "Excavations along the Western and Southern Walls," 150.

Fig. 7.4. Area A, Installation L.116

THE FORTIFICATIONS

Three impressive well-preserved segments of fortifications from the end of the First Temple period were found in excavations in the northern part of the Jewish Quarter (fig. 7.5). These are remnants of the First Wall described by Josephus, which protected the southwestern hill from the north. The wall's foundations are in the bedrock, and for their construction earlier buildings from this period had to be torn down (see Isa 22:10). The fortifications are made of large field stones, among which occasional large dressed stones are interspersed. The corners of the fortifications were made of particularly large, well-dressed blocks of stone. The stones were placed in courses along both faces, and the spaces between them were filled with small stones.

A section of wall W.555, the Broad Wall (Area A), 65 m in length was exposed (see fig. 7.6). The wall survived mostly to a height of one to three courses, but eight to nine survived at its northern end, reaching a total height of approximately 4 m. What makes this wall special is its great thickness, some 7 m, which is very unusual among the fortifications of the period. The wall lies in a northeasterly-southwesterly direction and then

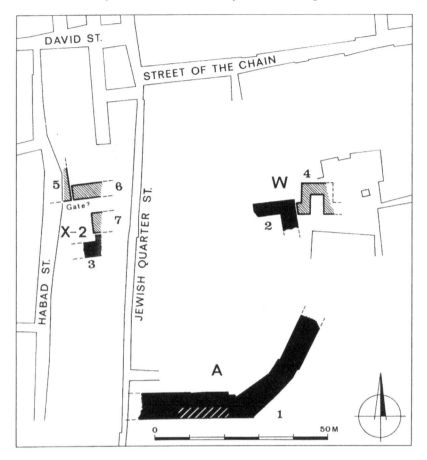

Fig. 7.5. Plan of the fortification remains uncovered at the northern side of the Jewish Quarter: (1) Wall W.555, the Broad Wall (Area A); (2) Tower W.4006–4030, the Israelite Tower (Area W); (3) Fortification W.4220–W.4221 (Area X–2)

turns due west. The reason for the wall's serpentine course and great thickness lies in the fact that it follows the contour of the topography in this area, circling the small valley separating the southwestern hill's two peaks from the south. This area suffers from topographical inferiority and is a weak point in the fortification line; this weakness was corrected by constructing a particularly massive wall in this sector. Avigad proposed identifying this wall with the "Broad Wall" mentioned in Neh 3:8.[22]

---

[22] Avigad, *Discovering Jerusalem,* 62; see also Rafi Grafman, "Nehemiah's 'Broad Wall,'" *IEJ* 24 (1974): 50–51.

Fig. 7.6. Area A, wall W.555, the Broad Wall, general view looking northeast

Fortified corner W.4006–W.4030—the Israelite Tower (Area W), which was discovered slightly north of the Broad Wall—is undoubtedly one of the most impressive fortification remains from biblical times to have been found in the land of Israel (see fig. 7.7). The structure consists of two perpendicular walls, one going from east to west for a distance of 12 m and one going from north to south, of which only 8 m were exposed. The walls are some 4 m wide and are preserved to a maximal height of approximately 7 m. This element of fortification was identified by Avigad as the corner of a four-chambered gatehouse, which stood in part of Jerusalem's north wall. Reconstructing the gate so that part of it stood out from the fortification line poses a certain difficulty, since city gates during the Iron Age were located inside the wall. Avigad identifies this gate with the "Middle Gate" mentioned in Jer 39:3, in relation to the capture of the city by the Babylonians in 587–586 B.C.E.[23]

Fortification W.4221–W.4222 (Area X-2) was found 40 m to the west of Area W. Only a small section of wall and the corner of a tower projecting northward from the wall were discovered there. The wall is some 4 m wide and has been preserved to a height of up to 7 m.

DATING THE SETTLEMENT ON THE SOUTHWESTERN HILL AND THE CONSTRUCTION OF THE FORTIFICATIONS

The finds discovered in the Jewish Quarter excavations and the other excavations as well indicate that toward the end of the First Temple period, since the second half of the eighth century B.C.E., the urban area of Jerusalem began for the first time to expand from the eastern ridge toward the southwestern hill.[24]

Indirect evidence for the date of the settlement on the southwestern hill during this period can be found in several groups of tombs that have been excavated since the 1970s in the upper Hinnom Valley to the west of the southwestern hill (in addition to the contents of the two tombs that Amiran had published earlier).[25] These tombs were hewn at the same time as the city expanded westward, for the inhabitants then apparently

---

[23] Avigad, *Discovering Jerusalem,* 49–54.

[24] The shapes of the pottery vessels found in the earliest strata and their typical wheel burnish are typologically identical with stratum III at Lachish, which is generally accepted as having been destroyed by the Assyrian king Sennacherib on his campaign to Judea in 701 B.C.E. See Orna Zimhoni, *Studies in the Iron Age Pottery of Israel: Typological, Archaeological and Chronological Aspects* (Tel Aviv Occasional Publications 2; Tel Aviv: Institute of Archaeology, Tel Aviv University, 1997), 118–21.

[25] Amiran, "Necropolis of Jerusalem," 65–72.

Fig. 7.7. Area W, corner of fortification W.4006–W.4030, the Israelite Tower

Fig. 7.8. Group of ceramic vessels from the end of the First Temple Period

preferred hewing tombs on that side of the city instead of in the traditional burial grounds to the east of the City of David.[26] In several of the tombs excavated in the Hinnom Valley pottery assemblages and other finds were discovered, which testify to their having been in use during the eighth–seventh centuries B.C.E.[27] Another tomb, discovered in Ketef Hinnom, contained a particularly rich assemblage of finds from the seventh and

---

[26] David Ussishkin, *The Village of Silwan: The Necropolis from the Period of the Judean Kingdom* (Jerusalem: Israel Exploration Society, 1993). Also worth mentioning are the rock-hewn rooms exposed by Benjamin Mazar on the east slope of the southwestern hill (opposite Robinson's Arch at the Temple Mount), which he identified as Phoenician-style tombs of the ninth to eighth centuries B.C.E. See further Benjamin Mazar, "The Excavations in the Old City of Jerusalem Near the Temple Mount: Second Preliminary Report, 1969–1970 Seasons" [Hebrew], *ErIsr* 10 (1971): 22–23; Meir Ben-Dov, *In the Shadow of the Temple: The Discovery of Ancient Jerusalem* (San Francisco: Harper & Row, 1985), 35–42. However, these are apparently not tombs. Even the publishers of the find are uncertain as to whether they were used for storage or for burial. See Eilat Mazar and Benjamin Mazar, *Excavations in the South of the Temple Mount: The Ophel of Biblical Jerusalem* (Qedem 29; Jerusalem: Institute of Archaeology; Hebrew University of Jerusalem, 1989), 50–55.

[27] Amos Kloner and Dave Davis, "A Burial Cave of the Late First Temple Period on the Slope of Mount Zion," in Geva, *Ancient Jerusalem Revealed,* 107–10; Ronny Reich, "The Ancient Burial Ground in the Mamilla Neighborhood, Jerusalem," in Geva, *Ancient Jerusalem Revealed,* 111–15.

beginning of the sixth centuries B.C.E.[28] It would thus appear that the use of the tombs to the west of the southwestern hill is in complete chronological agreement with the dating of the settlement of the residential quarter on that hill.[29]

The three sections of fortifications found in the Jewish Quarter belong to the north wall of Jerusalem in First Temple times. They were built in two separate but successive stages. First the Broad Wall was built by Hezekiah king of Judea at the end of the eighth century B.C.E. as part of fortifying Jerusalem against the coming Assyrian invasion. The biblical account relates the story of the fortification of the city together with the king's construction of a water-supply system (2 Chr 32:1–8). "Hezekiah's Tunnel" led the water of the Gihon Spring in the Kidron Valley to the east and outside of the City of David to the Siloam Pool at the southern, lower end of the Central Valley, to the west and outside of the City of David. The wall that encircled the southwestern hill descended eastward on the southern slope of Mount Zion above the Hinnom Valley and joined the wall of the City of David at its south end, south of the Siloam Pool. The pool was thus enclosed by the city wall, providing its inhabitants with water even in times of siege. Hezekiah's two important construction projects, building a wall around the southwestern hill and digging the tunnel, are closely connected. Together they created a complex and effective defensive array whose efficacy was proved when the Assyrian army besieged Jerusalem in 701 B.C.E. and failed to capture the city (2 Chr 32:21–24).

The finds indicate that the Broad Wall fell into disuse shortly after its construction, perhaps because of damage it may have sustained during the

---

[28] Gabriel Barkay, "Excavations at Ketef Hinnom in Jerusalem," in Geva, *Ancient Jerusalem Revealed,* 93–106.

[29] Granted, some scholars proposed pushing the beginning of the settlement of the southwestern hill back to the ninth century B.C.E. (Gabriel Barkay, "The Iron Age II–III," in *The Archaeology of Ancient Israel* [ed. A. Ben-Tor; Tel Aviv: Open University of Israel, 1992], 367) or advancing the settlement of the western part of the hill to the seventh century B.C.E. (Magen Broshi, "The Expansion of Jerusalem in the Reigns of Hezekiah and Manasseh," *IEJ* 24 [1974]: 21–23; Tushingham, "Western Hill of Jerusalem," 138; idem, *Excavations in Jerusalem I,* 20; William G. Dever, "Book Review—Tushingham, 1985," *AJA* 93 [1989]: 611). However, neither of these proposals has any archaeological evidence to support it at the moment. Please note that the date given by Kenyon and Tushingham for the beginning of the settlement in this region, the seventh century B.C.E., is based on their view that Stratum III at Lachish was destroyed in 597 B.C.E., whereas today it is generally accepted that it was destroyed by Sennacherib in 701. See David Ussishkin, "The Destruction of Lachish by Sennacherib and the Dating of the Royal Judean Storage Jars," *TA* 4 (1977): 28–60.

attack of the Assyrian army against the walls of Jerusalem in 701 B.C.E.[30] The fact that Jerusalem was besieged from the north certainly showed the defenders that the long and winding course of the Broad Wall circling the short valley between the two peaks of the southwestern hill was a weak point in the city's defense system. In its stead a new wall was built during the seventh century B.C.E., to the north of the old wall. This wall crossed the valley in a short, straight line between gate tower 4006–4030 in the east and fortification segment W.4220–W.4221 in the west, creating a more effective defensive array with a well-defended gate (Area W). After the new fortification line was completed, the Broad Wall to the south ceased functioning and remained within the walls of the city. Its stones were taken to be reused already during the First Temple period, and its remaining foundations were later covered by the foundations of buildings in the Second Temple period.

A new line of fortification defended Jerusalem from the north during the Babylonian siege of 587–586 B.C.E. On a surviving portion of a beaten earth road that passed along the outside of the fortified tower in Area W, several arrowheads were found in a layer of ashes. This is clear evidence of the battle over the walls of Jerusalem that ended with the city's destruction by the Babylonians. One of the arrowheads is of a "Scythian" type whose earliest appearance in the land of Israel is not earlier than the mid-seventh century B.C.E. Its location at the foot of the fortification in a layer of destruction is what makes it possible to date the military event that led to it being left there to the end of the First Temple period, when the Babylonians besieged Jerusalem. Jerusalem was captured and completely destroyed by the Babylonian army. Additional physical evidence for the destruction was found in the Ophel and the City of David.[31] This evidence is consistent with the biblical account (2 Kgs 25:8–10) of the complete destruction of Jerusalem during the Babylonian conquest and sheds further light on it.

---

[30] The assault on the wall of Jerusalem was directed from the northern side, which was always, because of the higher topographical elevation here, the weakest point in the defense line of the wall. Josephus mentioned the location of the Assyrian camp on the northern side of Jerusalem. See David Ussishkin, "The 'Camp of the Assyrians' in Jerusalem," *IEJ* 29 (1979): 137–42.

[31] E. Mazar and B. Mazar, *Excavations in the South of the Temple Mount,* 21, 43, 59; Yigal Shiloh, *Excavations at the City of David, vol. I, 1978–1982: Interim Report of the First Five Seasons* (Qedem 19; Jerusalem: Institute of Archaeology, Hebrew University of Jerusalem, 1984), 18–19.

THE QUESTION OF THE WALL'S CONTINUATION WESTWARD

The sections of fortification found in the Jewish Quarter belonged to the northern part of the wall that protected the southwestern hill at the end of the First Temple period. This is the wall that Josephus called the "First Wall" (*War* 5.4.2). Remnants of the First Wall dating from the Second Temple period exposed by the excavations show its course. The wall went from the Temple Mount on the east to the western end of the hill (near today's Jaffa Gate and the citadel). There it turned south and continued along the western slope of the hill over the Hinnom Valley (following the course of the western Old City wall), circled (today's) Mount Zion from the south and descended eastward to the southern end of the City of David. The course of the wall thus encompassed the entire southwestern hill so that its whole area was within the fortified city (see fig. 7.9). Several sections of the fortifications that were excavated along the wall made it clear that well-preserved remnants of fortifications from the First Temple period were integrated into the Second Temple–period wall. Avigad believes that this evidence points to the wall from the end of the First Temple period having encompassed the entire hill.[32] The long course surrounding the whole hill is logical from a topographical-strategic point of view as well, since it would have included the western and highest peak (in today's Armenian Quarter) of the hill inside the fortified area.[33] The finds that were discovered also corroborated Josephus's testimony: the First Wall was indeed first built already in the First Temple period.

---

[32] Avigad reconstructed the continuation of the line of the wall from the Jewish Quarter straight eastward to the Temple Mount. Another view, which cannot be proved, claims that the wall continued northward and crossed the Transversal Valley. See, e.g., Benjamin Mazar, "Jerusalem in the Biblical Period" [Hebrew], in *Cities and Districts in Eretz-Israel* (ed. B. Mazar; Jerusalem: Bialik, 1975), map on p. 39; Ruth Amiran, "The First and the Second Walls of Jerusalem Reconsidered in the Light of the New Wall," *IEJ* 21 (1971): 166–67. For a section of a massive wall uncovered northeast of the Jewish Quarter, see Amos Kloner, "Rehov Hagay," *ESI* 3 (1984): 57–59.

[33] Avigad, *Discovering Jerusalem,* 57, fig. 36. Avigad published two earlier proposals for the line of this wall that do not enclose the entire southwestern hill. See idem, "Excavations in the Jewish Quarter of the Old City of Jerusalem, 1970 (Second Preliminary Report)," *IEJ* 20 (1970): fig. 3; idem, "Excavations in the Jewish Quarter of the Old City of Jerusalem, 1971 (Third Preliminary Report)," *IEJ* 22 (1972): fig. 2. With the progress of the excavations in the Jewish Quarter and the new discoveries made, Avigad adopted the maximalist view, that the wall enclosed the entire hill.

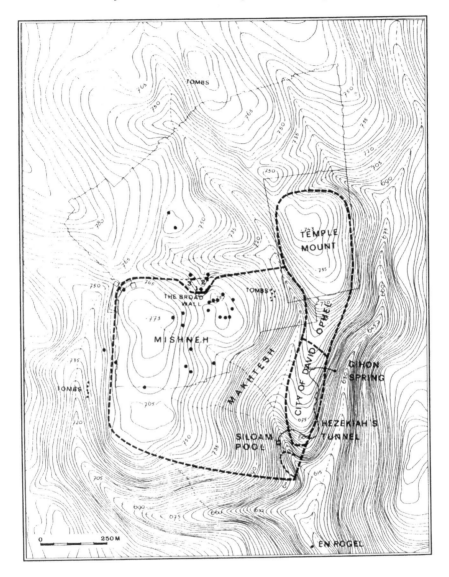

Fig. 7.9. Map of Jerusalem at the end of the First Temple period (eighth to seventh centuries B.C.E.)

I have attempted to demonstrate the correctness of Avigad's view by pointing attention to the massive constructions found in the past on the hill's west side, in the citadel by Johns and Amiran-Etan and by Kenyon-Tushingham in the Armenian garden (Area L), which I believe are unrecognized but clear remnants of the western part of the wall from the First Temple period.[34] Possibly also a section of an ancient fortification consisting of a row of chambers that was integrated into the Second Temple–period wall and that was discovered by Bliss and Dickie on the southern slope of Mount Zion was suggested as another remnant of the First Temple–period wall.[35] Another section of construction several meters wide made of large field stones was discovered by Kenyon (in Area F) at the southeast end of the hill to the west of the southern edge of the Central Valley.[36] Kenyon dated this construction to the beginning of the first century C.E., but it may well be, as Avigad suggests, another remnant of the wall from the end of the First Temple period.[37]

Avigad's ("neomaximalist") opinion has been accepted by the majority of scholars.[38] However, there are those who believe that only the eastern side of the hill was inside the wall (the "neominimalist" approach). Kenyon, who claimed at first, following her excavations, that the hill was not settled during the First Temple period (see above), changed her mind after the Broad Wall was found in the Jewish Quarter and came to believe that the wall encompassed only the area of today's Jewish Quarter.[39] A different "neominimalist" opinion claims that the wall

---

[34] Geva, "Western Boundary of Jerusalem," 84–91; Amiran, "Necropolis of Jerusalem," 71–72; see also, concerning the section of the city wall in the citadel, Hillel Geva, "Excavations in the Citadel of Jerusalem, 1979–1980: Preliminary Report," *IEJ* 33 (1983): 56–58.

[35] Bliss and Dickie, *Excavations at Jerusalem 1894–1897*, plan I; Amiran, "Necropolis of Jerusalem," 72.

[36] Kenyon, "Excavations in Jerusalem, 1963," 11, pl. V; idem, "Excavations in Jerusalem, 1964," 15–16; idem, *Digging Up Jerusalem*, 246–47, pl. 95.

[37] Avigad, "Excavations in the Jewish Quarter of the Old City of Jerusalem, 1970," 134 n. 13.

[38] B. Mazar, "Jerusalem in the Biblical Period," 42; Ussishkin, "Camp of the Assyrians," 138–41; Barkay, "Jerusalem of the Old Testament," 38; Yigal Shiloh, "Jerusalem: The Early Periods and the First Temple Period," *NEAEHL* 2:707–9. Hillel Geva, "Respondent," in *Biblical Archaeology Today, 1990: Proceedings of the Second International Congress on Biblical Archaeology* (ed. A. Biran and J. Aviram; Jerusalem: Israel Exploration Society, 1993), 620–24; Ronny Reich, "The Topography and Archaeology of Jerusalem in the First Temple Period," in *The History of Jerusalem, The Biblical Period* (ed. S. Ahituv and A. Mazar; Jerusalem: Yad Izhak Ben-Zvi, 2000), 117 and map. See also Ernest Marie Laperrousaz, "Jérusalem la Grande," *ErIsr* 24 (1993): 138*–47*.

[39] Kenyon, *Digging Up Jerusalem*, 28, fig. 26; supported also by Graeme Auld and Margreet Steiner, *Jerusalem I: From the Bronze Age to the Maccabees* (Cities of the Biblical World; Cambridge: Lutterworth, 1996), 40.

enclosed the entire eastern half of the hill, including its slope opposite the City of David.[40]

There also exists an intermediate opinion that wishes to reconstruct the course of the wall in the west as passing beneath today the Armenian Quarter or, in other words, somewhat to the east of the course proposed by Avigad (east of today's Old City wall).[41]

Since these various opinions were published, new segments of fortifications from the end of the First Temple period have come to light at the western end of the hill, both in the citadel's eastern moat and in the southwestern corner of Mount Zion.[42] These provide new, important evidence that, added to the other facts (mentioned above), proves that the wall at the end of the First Temple period reached the Hinnom Valley in the west and encompassed the entire southwestern hill.

Summary: The Character of the Settlement on the Southwestern Hill

The finds from the excavations in the Jewish Quarter and in other parts of the southwestern hill have shown that this area had been settled since the mid-eighth century B.C.E. and was in fact surrounded by a defensive wall. It was the archaeological research that, as expected, provided the evi-

---

[40] Dan Bahat, with Chaim T. Rubinstein, *The Illustrated Atlas of Jerusalem* (trans. S. Ketko; New York: Simon & Schuster, 1990), map on p. 25; idem, "Was Jerusalem Really That Large?" in Biran and Aviram, *Biblical Archaeology Today, 1990*, 581–84; Broshi, "Excavations on Mount Zion," 81; idem, "Iron Age Remains in the Chapel of St. Vartan in the Church of the Holy Sepulcher," in Geva, *Ancient Jerusalem Revealed*, 84. See also Pierre Benoit, "Recension de N. Avigad: Hᶜyr Hᶜlywnh šl Yrwšlym," *RB* 88 (1981): 251–53.

[41] Tushingham relies on the supposed existence of a natural small valley, which he assumes existed in today's Armenian Quarter, a few dozen meters east of the Old City wall (A. Douglas Tushingham, "The Western Hill under the Monarchy," *ZDPV* 95 [1979]: 39–55; idem, *Excavations in Jerusalem I*, 9–16); Shimon Gibson has the wall running closer to today's Old City wall, approximately at the eastern edge of the Armenian garden (Gibson, "The 1961–67 Excavations," 87); Wightman also supports this reconstructed course of the west wall at the end of the First Temple period. However, he thinks that the northwest corner of the wall reached today's citadel and from there continued in a southeasterly direction into today's Armenian Quarter (Gregory J. Wightman, *The Walls of Jerusalem from the Canaanites to the Mamluks* [Mediterranean Archaeology Supplement 4; Sydney: University of Sydney, 1993], 50–51, 58–59, fig. 11).

[42] Solar and Sivan, "Citadel Moat," 48; Doron Chen et al., "Mount Zion: Discovery of the Iron Age Fortifications below the Gate of the Essenes," in Geva, *Ancient Jerusalem Revealed*, 80–81.

dence that resolved the long-standing debate concerning the size of biblical Jerusalem in favor of the maximalist view. The city's expansion made an indelible impression on the people at the time and is echoed in Ps 122:2–3: "Our feet are standing in your gates, O Jerusalem. Jerusalem is built like a city that is closely compacted together." In the later biblical literature two new suburbs of Jerusalem are mentioned, *mišneh* and *maktēš* (2 Kgs 22:14; Zeph 1:10–11). The word *mišneh* ("secondary") probably refers to the new residential quarter on the southwestern hill, whereas *maktēš* ("mortar") was apparently the name of the Central Valley between the two hills on which the city was built in those days.

The expansion of Jerusalem toward the end of the First Temple period was part of a more general growth process that occurred in the kingdom of Judea at the time, with towns and villages growing and many new settlements being founded.[43] The growth in population and the number of settlements was unprecedented in the history of Judea and its capital Jerusalem. In Jerusalem this process was particularly evident for the urban area, which grew within a short time to 600 dunams, making Jerusalem for the first time in biblical times into the city with the largest area in the land of Israel. With the growth in area, the agricultural hinterland of the city expanded as well. New plots of land were made arable in terraces built on the hill slopes, and scores of small farms were established. These provided the economic base on which the city's growing populace and expanding area depended.[44]

Various explanations have been given for the growth of the population in Judea during the eighth century B.C.E.[45] Broshi believes that it was caused by the arrival of refugees from the kingdom of Israel and

---

[43] Moshe Kochavi, ed., *Judaea, Samaria and the Golan: Archaeological Survey 1967–1968* [Hebrew] (Jerusalem: Archaeological Survey of Israel, 1972), 20–22; Avi Ofer, "The Judean Hills in the Biblical Period" [Hebrew], *Qad* 115 (1998): 46–48; more recently, see idem, "The Monarchic Period in the Judean Highland: A Spatial Overview," in *Studies in the Archaeology of the Iron Age in Israel and Jordan* (ed. A. Mazar; JSOTSup 331; Sheffield: Sheffield Academic Press, 2001), 14–37.

[44] Avraham Faust, "The Impact of Jerusalem's Expansion in the late Iron Age on the Farms of Rural Settlement in Its Vicinity" [Hebrew], *Cathedra* 84 (1997): 53–62 and bibliography there; Zvi Greenhut, "The Periphery of Jerusalem in the Bronze and Iron Ages—New Discoveries" [Hebrew], in *New Studies on Jerusalem: Proceedings of the Second Conference* (ed. A. Faust; Ramat Gan: Bar-Ilan University, 1996), 3–8.

[45] For discussion and bibliography, see Avraham Faust, "The Social Structure of the Israelite Society during the 8th–7th Centuries BCE according to the Archaeological Evidence" [Hebrew] (Ph.D thesis, Bar-Ilan University, 1999), 21–33.

from the Shephelah region of Judea during the Assyrian campaigns of conquest.[46] Stager tends to ascribe it to an economic motive: after all available agricultural lands had been utilized and no more surplus land was available, the populace began moving from the country into the towns in search of livelihood.[47] Herr is of the opinion that it was Judea and Jerusalem's developing economy, offering opportunities for employment and commerce, that attracted many new inhabitants.[48] Halpern claims that on the eve of Sennacherib's campaign it became the official policy of the kings of Judea to transfer population to the cities in order to facilitate the construction of fortifications.[49] It would thus appear that a complex array of conditions existing simultaneously during the eighth century B.C.E. was behind the observed urban growth. The political stability and security that the kingdom of Judea enjoyed during the eighth century (according to the biblical account, from the days of King Uzziah), in conjunction with economic growth and Jerusalem's central position in the cult, all made the settlement of the southwestern hill possible at that time. Perhaps this was even a step taken on official initiative out of political and military considerations, or at least one that received official blessing. The additional populace very likely originated in the natural growth of the population and internal migration. However, one cannot dismiss the possibility that, as a result of the Assyrian threat and in the aftermath of the Assyrian campaign, some of the inhabitants of the kingdom of Israel and the Shephelah region immigrated to the kingdom of Judah.

The settlement of the southwestern hill occurred within a relatively short time span. The city boundary very likely expanded westward in an organic manner without any central planning. The remnants uncovered in the Jewish Quarter and in other parts of the hill are too few in number and too sporadic to provide a clear picture of the urban nature of this residential quarter at the time. Still, these remnants do tell us that the hill as a whole was quite sparsely settled, with most residents occupying the upper part. Some parts of the hill, especially on its east slope, perhaps

---

[46] Broshi, "Expansion of Jerusalem," 21–26.

[47] Lawrence E. Stager, "The Archaeology of the Family in Ancient Israel," *BASOR* 260 (1985): 1–35.

[48] Larry G. Herr, "The Iron Age II Period: Emerging Nations," *BA* 60 (1997): 155–57.

[49] Baruch Halpern, "Jerusalem and the Lineage in the Seventh Century BCE: Kinship and the Rise of Individual Moral Liability," in *Law and Ideology in Monarchic Israel* (ed. B. Halpern and D. W. Hobson; JSOTSup 124; Sheffeld: Sheffeld Academic Press, 1991), 25–26.

remained unsettled and were used for agriculture, for growing fruit trees and seasonal crops. It is very difficult to estimate the number of the south-western hill's inhabitants at the end of the First Temple period. The city's overall area at the time was some 600 dunams, of which approximately 450 dunams were on the southwestern hill (including its east slope overlooking the Tyropoeon Valley). A very conservative estimate would put the permanent population of Jerusalem at the height of its development at the end of the eighth century B.C.E. at around six to seven thousand people at the most, of whom about half lived on the southwestern hill, and only very few north of it. This number takes into consideration the resources and needs of the inhabitants, most of whom were engaged in terrace agriculture in the hills surrounding the city, while others earned their livelihood in the service of the royal administration and the temple. The fixed quantity of water available from the Gihon Spring was also a factor limiting the population of the city (no water installations dating to this period were found on the southwestern hill).[50]

The buildings on the southwestern hill were simple and of a domestic nature; no remnants of elaborate official construction were found. The wealthy established population certainly continued to live in the City of David near the water source; this remained Jerusalem's urban center to the end of the First Temple period. Evidence of this is provided by the quality of housing construction in that area: in the northern part of the City of David ashlars, a Proto-Aeolic capital, and sophisticated tiered construction were found, in addition to the rich finds discovered inside the houses, including stone altars, remnants of wooden furniture, and a collection of

---

[50] Magen Broshi, ("Le population de l'ancienne Jérusalem," *RB* 82 [1975]: 5–14) estimates that Jerusalem's population during the eighth century B.C.E. (when it reached an area of 500 dunams) was approximately 20,000, which grew to 24,000 when the city attained its greatest area (including the western part of the south-western hill) in the seventh century B.C.E. Broshi's study has now been republished in English: "Estimating the Population of Ancient Jerusalem," in idem, *Bread, Wine, and Scrolls* (JSPSup 36; London: Sheffield Academic Press, 2001), 110–20. Shiloh's estimate of the city's population at the end of the First Temple period is close to that of Broshi (Yigal Shiloh, "The Population of Iron Age Palestine in the Light of a Sample Analysis of Urban Plans, Areas and Population Density," *BASOR* 239 [1980]: 30; see also Magen Broshi and Israel Finkelstein, "The Population of Palestine in 734 BCE" [Hebrew], *Cathedra* 58 [1990]: 3–24). However, the data indicate that population density decreases clearly and consistently as a settlement's area increases (Gideon Biger and David Grossman, "Village and Town Population in Palestine during the 1930s–1940s and Their Relevance to Ethnoarchaeology," in *Biblical Archaeology Today, 1990, Supplement* (ed. A. Biran and J. Aviram; Jerusalem: Israel Exploration Society, 1993), 19–30.

bullae.[51] No quality construction or finds of this nature were discovered on the southwestern hill.

The city's expansion during the eighth century B.C.E. did not stop at the southwestern hill but continued on to the hills to the north (in today's Christian and Muslim Quarters). In this area stone quarries were located, such as the one found in the area of the Church of the Holy Sepulchre in the Christian Quarter.[52] The most common finds in the northern areas of Jerusalem are potsherds, all indicating that the inhabitants here were few and probably concentrated mostly on the upper part of the Central Valley. Barkay identifies the city's northern quarters with *Gareb* and *Goah* mentioned in Jeremiah (31:38).[53] When the Broad Wall was built in the days of Hezekiah at the end of the eighth century B.C.E., the city's fortifications encompassed the entire area of the southwestern hill; the quarters farther to the north were apparently left unfortified.

The residential development of the city's western quarters had not yet reached full urban status when it was cut short by Sennacherib's siege in 701 B.C.E. During the seventh century until the Babylonian destruction, the population remained only within the bounds of the walled part of the southwestern hill. The unfortified residential areas on the northern hills were certainly greatly damaged during the siege of Sennacherib and were deserted. At this event the extramural residential quarter established at the end of the eighth century B.C.E. on the low eastern slope of the City of David was also destroyed and deserted.[54] Judea was too exhausted after the siege to provide the economic and manpower resources for further developing the city. This had an adverse effect also on the inhabitants of

---

[51] Kenyon, *Jerusalem,* pl. 20; Shiloh, *Excavations at the City of David I,* 17–20, pls. 34–35.

[52] Magen Broshi and Gabriel Barkay, "Excavations in the Chapel of St. Vartan in the Holy Sepulchre," *IEJ* 35 (1985): 108–19.

[53] Barkay, "Jerusalem of the Old Testament," 39.

[54] Kenyon, *Digging Up Jerusalem,* 137–43; Shiloh, *Excavations at the City of David I,* 28–29; Donald T. Ariel and Alon De Groot, "The Israelite Settlement outside the Walls of City of David," in *New Studies on Jerusalem: Proceedings of the Third Conference* (ed. A. Faust and E. Baruch; Ramat Gan: Bar-Ilan University, 1997), 9–12; Donald T. Ariel, ed., *Excavations at the City of David 1978–1985 Directed by Yigal Shiloh, vol. V, Extramural Areas* (Qedem 40; Jerusalem: Institute of Archaeology, Hebrew University of Jerusalem, 2000); Ronny Reich and Eli Shukron, "The Excavations at the Gihon Spring and Warren's Shaft System in the City of David," in *Ancient Jerusalem Revealed: Expanded Edition 2000* (ed. H. Geva; Jerusalem: Israel Exploration Society, 2000), 337–39.

southwestern hill who were not yet sufficiently entrenched there.[55] Interestingly enough, however, despite the kingdom's much-reduced political status and human and economic resources, Jerusalem in the seventh century B.C.E. occupied a much more central position than it did during the eighth century.[56] But this is perhaps a wrong impression based upon the biblical account and a matter of relativity: the enhanced status Jerusalem enjoyed toward the end of the First Temple period may only seem high when compared to the rest of the kingdom's abysmal state during most of the seventh century B.C.E.

The residential quarter established toward the end of the First Temple period on the southwestern hill was completely destroyed by the Babylonians and remained in ruins during the Persian and Early Hellenistic periods (sixth to second centuries B.C.E.). The area became slowly populated again only from the middle of the second century B.C.E. in the Hasmonean period. During this period the First Wall was rebuilt around the southwestern hill. It reached its period of greatest splendor in the days of Herod, when it was known as the Upper City.

---

[55] A decrease in the number of settlements is evident throughout the kingdom of Judea during the Iron Age IIc (the seventh century B.C.E.). See Avi Ofer, "The Highland of Judah during the Biblical Period" [Hebrew], (Ph.D thesis, Tel Aviv University, 1993), 127–41. For the importance of Jerusalem in the seventh century B.C.E., see Margreet Steiner, "Jerusalem in the Tenth and Seventh Centuries BCE: From Administrative Town to Commercial City," in Mazar, ed., *Studies in the Archaeology of the Iron Age,* 284–86.

[56] On social and economic developments between the eighth and seventh centuries B.C.E., see Faust, "Social Structure of the Israelite Society," 32–33; Jane Cahill, "Rosette Stamp Seal Impression," in *Jewish Quarter Excavations in the Old City of Jerusalem Conducted by Nahman Avigad, 1969–1982, vol. II, The Finds from Areas A, W and X–2, Final Report* (ed. H. Geva; Jerusalem: Israel Exploration Society, 2003), 85–98.

The Urban Development of Jerusalem in the Late Eighth Century B.C.E.

Ronny Reich* and Eli Shukron**

* Univeristy of Haifa and Israel Antiquities Authority
** Israel Antiquities Authority

The discoveries made in the Jewish Quarter of Jerusalem by the archaeological expedition headed by Nahman Avigad brought a dramatic change in our knowledge of the city's topography in the late Iron Age II. Avigad's excavations showed conclusively that the fortifications and settlement of Jerusalem extended to the western hill. Recently, the first volume of the final report of the excavations has been published.[1] This final report describes in detail the fortifications and architecture of the city during this period.[2]

One of the primary conclusions from Avigad's excavations was that the city expanded its perimeter considerably to the west during the late Iron Age II. The earliest stratum in almost every area of the excavations revealed remains of domestic architecture and other signs of human occupation dating to the eighth and seventh centuries B.C.E.[3] This new quarter of the city was fortified by a massive city wall, which was labeled the "Broad Wall" because of its massive size.[4]

The beginning of this expansion to the western hill was correlated to the pottery retrieved from these earlier strata and dated to the eighth century B.C.E.[5] It was also found that the occupation of the western parts of the city lasted throughout the late Iron Age II, until the destruction of

---

[1] Hillel Geva, ed., *Jewish Quarter Excavations in the Old City of Jerusalem Conducted by Nahman Avigad, 1969–1982, vol. I, Architecture and Stratigraphy: Areas A, W and X-2, Final Report* (Jerusalem: Israel Exploration Society, 2000).

[2] Nahman Avigad and Hillel Geva, "Iron Age II, Strata 9–7," in Geva, *Jewish Quarter Excavations I*, 44–82.

[3] Nahman Avigad, *Discovering Jerusalem* (Nashville: Nelson, 1983), 23–60.

[4] Avigad and Geva, "Iron Age II, Strata 9–7," 45–61.

[5] Avigad, *Discovering Jerusalem*, 49, 55.

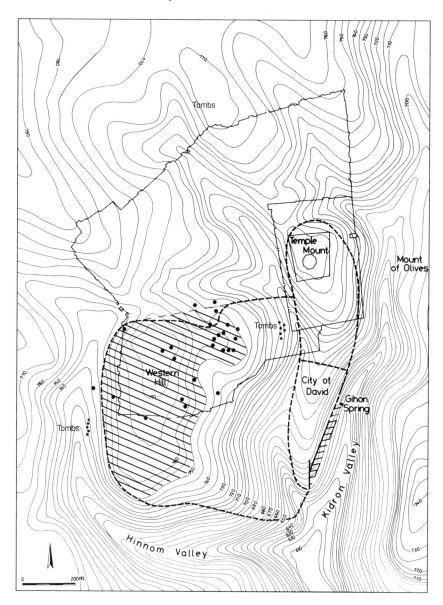

Fig. 8.1. Map of Jerusalem in the First Temple period. The slashes represent areas that experienced new settlement during the late eigthth century.

the city by the Babylonians in 586 B.C.E.[6] The date of the western expansion of Jerusalem at some point during the eighth century B.C.E. also coincides with the dates of the earliest tombs found in the adjacent cemeteries, discovered to the west of the city—namely those of Kettef Hinnom[7] and of Mamilla.[8]

Recent excavations by the present authors revealed that the western part of the city was not the only area to be heavily fortified during the late Iron Age II period. The present authors were fortunate to discover well-preserved segments of a city wall on the southeastern hill of the City of David. This wall is located to the east of and parallel to the main eastern city wall, which was exposed previously during the excavations of Kenyon[9] and Shiloh.[10] We were somewhat surprised that the new wall was exposed on the lowermost part of the eastern slope of the hill, just above the bottom of the Kidron Valley.

A well-preserved segment of the wall was encountered in Area J of our excavations, located approximately 100–120 m due south of the Gihon Spring.[11] Other, smaller segments of the wall were found in some of the squares excavated in 1995, Area A in our excavations. These are located further to the south, at a distance between 200–240 m from the spring.[12] This newly discovered line of fortification encloses an area that was appended on the eastern side of the city. During the course of Yigal Shiloh's excavations, several houses were uncovered in this area (Areas D and E from Shiloh's excavations).[13] The present authors extended the exposure of these houses farther to the south.[14] Because these houses

---

[6] Ibid., 53–54.

[7] Gabriel Barkay, "Excavations at Ketef Hinnom in Jerusalem," in *Ancient Jerusalem Revealed* (ed. H. Geva; Jerusalem: Israel Exploration Society, 1994), 105.

[8] Ronny Reich, "The Ancient Burial Ground in the Mamilla Neighbourhood, Jerusalem," in Geva, *Ancient Jerusalem Revealed,* 111–15.

[9] Kathleen Kenyon, *Digging Up Jerusalem* (London: Benn, 1974), 83, 144–47.

[10] Yigal Shiloh, *Excavations at the City of David, vol. I, 1978–1982: Interim Report of the First Five Seasons* (Qedem 19; Jerusalem: Institute of Archaeology, Hebrew University of Jerusalem, 1984), 28; pl. 10, W163, 201; pls. 14, 15, W219.

[11] Ronny Reich and Eli Shukron, "Jerusalem, City of David," *Hadashot Arkheologiyot* 112 (2000): 82*–83*, figs. 150–51.

[12] Ronny Reich and Eli Shukron, "Jerusalem, City of David," *ESI* 18 (1998): 91.

[13] Shiloh, *Excavations at the City of David I,* 7, 9–10; Donald T. Ariel et al., "Area D1: Stratigraphic Report," in *Excavations at the City of David 1978–1985 Directed by Yigal Shiloh, vol. V, Extramural Areas* (ed. D. T. Ariel; Qedem 40; Jerusalem: Institute of Archaeology, Hebrew University of Jerusalem, 2000), 42–59.

[14] Reich and Shukron, "Jerusalem, City of David," 92.

were located to the east of the main eastern city wall (the Kenyon-Shiloh wall), Shiloh had previously suggested[15] that these houses were part of an eastern extramural quarter. Since the newly discovered eastern lower wall from our excavations encloses this eastern neighborhood, one must reevaluate Shiloh's earlier conclusion that these settlements were extramural and not located inside a fortified section of the city.

The remains of the houses excavated in this quarter were dated by Shiloh to the eighth century B.C.E.[16] During Shiloh's excavations, it was discovered that the residential strata contained pottery with parallels to Lachish Level III, so what he identified as the extramural settlement was dated to the eighth century B.C.E. We also found pottery with parallels to Lachish Level III in our excavations in both the residential strata and in the strata associated with newly discovered line of fortifications. We thus dated the origination of the residential settlement and the new fortifications to the eighth century B.C.E.

In terms of dating the end of this residential settlement that was enclosed by the newly discovered line of fortifications, one should note that no pottery from the end of the Iron Age (i.e., from the seventh–sixth centuries B.C.E.) was found in either Shiloh's or our excavations. The later Iron Age II pottery was absent from both the domestic areas and the newly discovered fortifications. The present authors thus conclude that this area of domestic settlement to the southeast of Jerusalem was both settled and fortified during the eighth B.C.E. and then abandoned before the end of the seventh century B.C.E.

With the newly discovered city wall from our excavations, it is seen clearly that these domestic areas from Shiloh's excavation were located inside a fortified area and were not extramural settlements, as Shiloh previously concluded. However, despite the new discoveries, the extramural theory is still held by Donald Ariel and Alon De Groot of the Shiloh expedition. As the discovery of the newly found eastern wall cannot be evaded, they simply say: "this fortification occurred well after the neighborhood was already in existence."[17] This statement by De Groot and Ariel implies that the newly discovered wall from our excavations was constructed some time (several decades or more) after the inhabitants of the city decided to build a group of houses outside their city's fortifications in the eighth century B.C.E.

---

[15] Shiloh, *Excavations at the City of David I,* 7, 10.

[16] Ibid., 7, 10.

[17] Donald T. Ariel and Alon De Groot, "The Iron Age Extramural Occupation of the City of David and Additional Observations on the Siloam Channel," in Ariel, *Excavations at the City of David V,* 164.

This assumption of settlement before the presence of the forifications is highly unlikely. Even though Ariel and De Groot might point to a lack of stratigraphic connections between the domestic houses and the newly found eastern city wall, there is circumstantial evidence that points to the correlation of the two finds. Based on the ceramic assemblages associated with both the domestic structures and city wall, the present authors maintain that there is no significant chronological gap between the time when the houses were built and the construction of the city wall. The similarity of the pottery suggests that if a chronological gap did indeed exist between the building of the residential quarter and the wall, it must have been of a very short duration and the result of technical reasons.[18]

A good parallel for this type of short gap between the construction of domestic settlements and the new city wall can be found in the city's expansion to the western hill. The archaeological data from Avigad's excavations show clearly that the process of expansion to the west took place over an extended period of time and that stratigraphic data exists for this. Some of the private houses built on the western hill were found cut by the course of the Broad Wall, which was built somewhat later.[19] Such a stratigraphic relation does not exist in the eastern part of the City of David, so the present authors conclude that the period of time between domestic settlement and the construction of the new city wall must have been shorter than was the case on the western hill (see below).

Before this issue of chronological relationship between the new domestic settlement and the newly discovered wall can be further explored, it is helpful to examine the possibility that the city of Jerusalem expanded to the west and to the east at the same time during the eighth century B.C.E. Table 8.1 (p. 214) presents some helpful data that relate to these two expansions of the city, westward and eastward.

One can see clearly from even a cursory glance at these data that the nature of the expansions is quite different. These differences become even greater when one undertakes even a rough estimation of the human labor required for these undertakings. A densely populated ancient city of 40 dunams could house approximately 2,000 people.[20] Based on these calculations, the newly planned eastern quarter would have housed approximately 150 people. The similarity in the pottery from our excavations suggests that

---

[18] The present authors conclude that this short gap between the domestic construction and the construction of the eastern city wall is likely, as will be demonstrated below.

[19] Avigad, *Discovering Jerusalem*, 55–56, fig. 35.

[20] We use the number 25 persons per dunam as a coefficient.

all of the houses in this eastern area were built at approximately the same time. Such a conclusion is not surprising, since this task would have been relatively simple to undertake in a short period for only 150 inhabitants.

Table 8.1

	Western extension[21]	Eastern extension
Measurements of added area (minimal estimate)	550 x 550 m (excluding slopes)	30 x 200
Estimated area added to the city (only level area, excluding slopes)	300	6
Amount of urban expansion (%) related to the original site	900 percent	15–20 percent
Date of urban expansion	early eighth to sixth century B.C.E.	eighth century B.C.E.
Width of city wall (meters)	7	2
Length of city wall (meters)	1,900	300
Estimate of volume of construction (in cubic meters, at 5 m of average height)	66,500	3,000
Nature of terrain of expanded part	mostly level	slope

After the completion of the houses, the citizens of the city would likely have considered it necessary to complete the extension of the city wall. The present authors estimate that the community would have needed to employ a couple scores of builders for this operation. At most, fifty workers would have been needed. It is further reasonable to assume that a single construction worker can build one cubic meter of a wall per day. Therefore, 3,000 cubic meters of wall (see table) require two to three months of work. We thus conclude that the entire eastern quarter could have been built and fortified within three to four months. As will be seen below, the amount of time needed to complete the expansion on the Western Hill was much greater.

The estimates for the western expansion are more difficult and less precise because the numbers of unknowns are greater. The most significant unknown datum is whether the new Broad Wall encompassed a new quarter that had already been built densely or that included some (many?)

---

[21] Avigad, *Discovering Jerusalem,* fig. 36.

open spaces during its beginning. The present authors opt for the second possibility (based on the probable origin of the inhabitants for both quarters; see below). For this reason, the present authors are conservative and posit a density coeffect of only ten persons per dunam, for a total of 3,000 persons. The average time required to build the entire new quarter would have been, again, one month, regardless of the number of houses, since each family could build its own house and all the houses could be built simultaneously. However, the construction of the city wall of this newly added western quarter was of a totally different magnitude. While it is difficult to estimate precisely how long the construction would have taken, the following data make it clear that the construction would have taken much longer than the expansion in the eastern part of the city.

The main question is whether all these newcomers were present at the city gate at the same time or, alternatively, arrived over a longer period of time, perhaps several months or even a couple of years. This is an important factor because we have to minimize the estimation for the available working force for the Broad Wall. While all the working force was available right from the beginning for the eastern expansion (see below), in the west we cannot assume that a similar percentage of the population could have been involved in this task. If in the east we assumed that a third of the population was involved in constructing the city wall (50 out of 150), in the western part of the city, we can assume only that a sixth of the population took part in the construction (500 out of 3,000). The number of construction workers might even have been lower. The working force of the initial group of newcomers could conceivably have allocated only about 500 persons to start and to construct a broad wall of 66,500 cubic meters, which would have taken them some five to six months.

This rough exercise given above demonstrates that the time span between initial steps to add a new quarter to the city and the completion of the work, manifested by the completion of the wall, was considerably different between both new quarters. Yet in both instances it is possible to conclude that we are speaking of a relatively short time.

At the first sight, the eastern expansion seemed to be a contemporary, albeit smaller, version of the western urban expansion. The figures given in the table clearly indicate that these urban expansions point to much more complicated processes. We have here archaeological evidence that points to two fortified extensions of the city in the eighth century B.C.E. An expansion of the city to the western hill added an extremely large area to the relatively modest size of the southeastern hill (City of David). To a former fortified site of roughly 35–40 dunams of the southeastern hill (excluding the northern area of the so-called "Ophel") a large and vast area was added. This included the elevated, plateau-like area of the western hill and Mount Zion (excluding the slopes to the south and east). This urban expansion was of at least 300 dunams, which marks an addition of approximately 900 percent to the urban area. This is an enlargement of almost two orders of magnitude.

An extension to the east added only a narrow strip of fortified urban space. This new area was only approximately 30 m wide, extending eastward from the older city wall (the Kenyon-Shiloh Wall). The new quarter was built midway down the slope, up to the newly founded wall built on the lower part of the slope. The length of this area is more difficult to establish. To date we have encountered the eastern wall in two excavation areas (A and J). It seems also that at its southern edge the newly discovered eastern wall abutted the high rock scarp that is located roughly 200 m south of the spring. On the other hand, we have no data whatsoever from the area north of the Gihon. The measurements of the eastern extension of the city seem now to be known for an area of 6 dunams (30 x 200 m). This is a small-size expansion of roughly 15–20 percent.

Comparison between these two urban expansions poses several difficulties and questions. Did these expansions occur simultaneously? If not, which one was first? Were both expansions undertaken for the same reasons? Was the nature of these expansions the same? Are these expansions in correlation with the needs and the capability of the population?

We wish to present the following scenario in the history of the urban development of the city of Jerusalem in the eighth century B.C.E. The perimeter of the city was indeed extended twice in this century. These expansions did not occur simultaneously. One extension followed the other, with a rather short interval between them, perhaps of several decades. During the late ninth and earlier parts of the eighth century B.C.E., the population of Jerusalem grew steadily due to the natural growth of its population, augmented by the fact that the city attracted outsiders because it was the main city of the kingdom of Judah.

At a particular moment this growth, although slow, exceeded a certain "critical mass," and a group of inhabitants initiated an extension of the fortified area of the city. The area for the extension was chosen on the lower eastern slope of the city. It seems that the low topographical location was not considered a dangerous disadvantage, and perhaps the proximity to the water source was more attractive.

This extension enabled the much-needed addition of fortified living space. Several scores of houses could have been added. This action was undertaken in a rather organized way, as the layout of the excavated houses of this area show. The construction of the additional city wall was of a magnitude (mainly constructed out of field stones) that could be met in a reasonable time by the current labor force of the city. This expansion seems to be a logical phase in the natural development of the life of a city.

In contrast to the eastern extension, the western expansion of the city seems extraordinary in every respect. It certainly cannot reflect any type of a continuing additional natural growth to the city. It undoubtedly was caused by an artificial growth, which was caused by an external addition of population.

When Avigad proved the expansion of the city westward in the eighth century, two possible sources of this extensive addition of population were noted.[22] One option is the destruction of the neighboring kingdom of Israel and its capital Samaria by the Assyrians under Sargon II in 722 B.C.E. The Hebrew Bible mentions an invitation that was extended to the northern brethren to come to Jerusalem (2 Chr. 30:1–9). It is logical to assume that a large number of refugees arrived in Judah and specifically Jerusalem as a result of the catastrophe in the north. A second option is the conquest of the Judean Shephelah by Sennacherib of Assyria in 701 B.C.E., in which he claimed the capture of forty-six towns and the siege and capture of Lachish, the main city of that region. One must assume that refugees of those battles and actions, who fled east, also reached Jerusalem.

By logical reasoning we suggest that the eastern extension of Jerusalem slightly predated the extension of the city's perimeter to the west. Had the western expansion occurred before the eastern, it would likely have given enough living space for a large number of newcomers as well as a solution for the crowded southeastern hill. In short, no additional expansions to the east would have been needed. The existence of the eastern expansion makes sense only if it preceded the western expansion.

This scenario, we believe, might explain the odd fact that the small, newly founded eastern quarter of the city not only was created in the eighth century B.C.E. but was also soon abandoned, while the western fortified areas were occupied to the very end of the Iron Age. The eastern quarter was established and fortified due to the urban needs of the city, without any notion of the future population problems. Later, when the large immigration waves arrived, the city was enlarged westward. At that point the inhabitants of the eastern quarter abandoned their relatively new fortified quarter, with its obvious topographical disadvantages, for the benefits and advantages of the larger, level, and fortified western spaces. What they could not do earlier with their modest numbers and small labor force, and perhaps did not envisage at all, became a reality that encouraged them to move from the eastern to the western quarters. The eastern wall, however, continued to stand abandoned, exposed to a

---

[22] Magen Broshi, "The Expansion of Jerusalem in the Reigns of Hezekiah and Manasseh," *IEJ* 24 (1974): 21–26.

considerable height. Only in the first century C.E. was it finally covered by the growing amounts of the city garbage that was dumped down the eastern slope of the southeastern hill.

Egypt's Role in the Events of 701 B.C. in Jerusalem

James K. Hoffmeier
Trinity International University—Divinity School

The Assyrian invasion of Judah by Sennacherib in 701 B.C. is one of the most dramatic events in biblical history and one of the most studied by scholars over years. There are a number of reasons for the plethora of scholarly discussions of this campaign (or campaigns, if there were two, as suggested by some). First, there are well-known epigraphic sources that offer the Assyrian perspective. Second, the Bible (2 Kgs 18:13–19:37; Isa 36:1–37:38; 2 Chr 32:1–23) provides the Judahite perspective on the crisis of 701 B.C. Moreover, archaeological evidence from this campaign includes Hezekiah's Tunnel with its late eighth-century inscription, the defensive walls associated with his building effort in anticipation of the Assyrian onslaught (2 Kgs 32:5), and the indications of the Assyrian siege at Lachish. King Hezekiah, of whom it is reported in 2 Kgs 18:5 "that there was none like him among all the kings of Judah after him, nor among those who were before him," and the role of Isaiah the prophet in these events have captured the interest of generations of biblical scholars. Finally, there is the role of Egypt in the events at the end of the eighth century. Specifically, 2 Kgs 19:9 and Isa 37:9 make almost passing reference to Taharqa (Tirhakah), *melek kûš*, joining the fray against Sennacherib. However, questions continue to be raised about the historicity of this reference. Donald Redford has recently asserted, "to take the reference to Taharqa in 2 Kings 19:9 seriously ... is unwarranted and produces misleading results."[1] Even more recently, William Gallagher stated, "We cannot merely assume that II K. 19:9 is reliable."[2] Consequently, this problem—if the biblical statements about the involvement of Egypt in the affairs of Judah should be considered factual—will be discussed below in the context of investigating the rising power of the Kushite dynasty in Egypt.

---

[1] Donald B. Redford, *Egypt, Canaan, and Israel in Ancient Times* (Princeton, N.J.: Princeton University Press, 1992), 353 n. 163.

[2] William Gallagher, *Sennacherib's Campaign to Judah* (New Studies in the History and Culture of the Ancient Near East 18; Leiden: Brill, 1999), 221.

The purpose of the present study is to examine the political develop-ments in the late eighth century B.C. in Egypt through an examination of the Kushite takeover of Egypt. In the process of this examination, I will offer an explanation of why they became entangled in Western Asia (and thus in the affairs of Judah) in 701. My thesis is that the reason for the Kushite strike against Assyria in 701 B.C. can be discerned by studying (1) the principles of Kushite succession and (2) the Kushite policy toward con-trolling Egypt.

Unlike the situation with the Assyrian sources, there is presently lim-ited textual evidence from Egypt for this period. This paucity of inscriptions thus presents the biggest challenge for the attempt to under-stand the role of all the players from Egypt in the events. The Kawa Stela IV, discovered at Napata, may offer some background information to Taharqa's rise to his military position in 701 B.C. In 2 Kgs 18:20–21 the Rab-shakeh asks Hezekiah, "On whom do you now rely, that you have rebelled against me?" He then answers his own question with the charge, "Behold, you are relying on Egypt?" This accusation indicates that the Assyrians were convinced that Hezekiah would not have made such a bold move without securing Egypt's support. However, determining who (Ekron, Judah, or both) called on Egypt for military aid in the Assyrian sources is difficult owing to grammatical uncertainties;[3] however, following the read-ing of Mordechai Cogan and William Gallagher,[4] it seems that Ekron alone summoned Egyptian support, and not Hezekiah.

Sennacherib's Annals, both on the Taylor Prism and Rassam Cylinder, report that Hezekiah was complicit in the Levantine revolt for receiving the deposed Padi of Ekron.[5] However, the Rassam version states that it was "the officials, the nobles and the people of Ekron who had overthrown Padi, their king, (who was) under oath and obligation to Assyria."[6] Evi-dently the Ekronites were the chief instigators of the rebellion that prompted Sennacherib's invasion into Philistia, not Hezekiah's act of receiving the deposed Padi. The Annals describe Padi as being "under oath and obligation to Assyria,"[7] making Ekron's revolt especially egregious.

---

[3] I am indebted to my colleague Lawson Younger for discussing his essay with me and for sharing his valuable notes on this text with me.

[4] "Sennacherib's Siege of Jerusalem," translated by Mordechai Cogan (*COS* 2.119B:303); and Gallagher, *Sennacherib's Campaign to Judah,* 116.

[5] "The Siege of Jerusalem," translated by A. Leo Oppenheim (*ANET,* 287); for another translation of this critical line, see that of Donald J. Wiseman, in *Documents from Old Testament Times* (ed. D. W. Thomas; London: Nelson, 1958), 66–67.

[6] "Sennacherib's Siege of Jerusalem," *COS* 2:119B.303.

[7] Ibid.

Returning to the biblical text, the juxtaposition of the Rabshakeh's charge of Hezekiah's rebellion against Sennacherib in 2 Kgs 18:7 and the reference to his march on Philistia "as far as Gaza" in 18:8 suggests that Hezekiah may have supported the popular rebellion. This support would thus explain the receipt of the deposed Padi.

As mentioned above, no extant Egyptian texts inform us about the campaign involving Taharqa. To make matters worse, historical records in general concerning the final decade of the eighth century are, in Redford's words, "spotty."[8] In spite of this situation, several recent works by biblical scholars, like those of Paul Ash[9] and Bernard Schipper,[10] have attempted to reopen some of the chronological problems surrounding this period. As Kenneth Kitchen has already addressed and shown the shortcomings of their arguments and the resulting historical problems, the discussion below does not address these works in detail.[11]

KASHTA, FATHER OF THE TWENTY-FIFTH DYNASTY

As stated above, a study of Kushite succession is instructive for understanding the reasons for the involvement in the affairs of Judah in 701 B.C. As we review this history, one observes that the rise to power of the Egyptianized, Kushite, Twenty-Fifth Dynasty in Egypt in the latter third of the eighth century can be traced back to Egypt's New Kingdom (ca. 1550–1070 B.C.). With the ouster of the Hyksos from the Delta by King Ahmose, Egypt's imperial interest turned north to Canaan and south into Nubia. In fact, the textual evidence from Ahmose through Thutmose II suggests that Nubia was the principal theater of Egypt's interest.[12] Egypt maintained firm

---

[8] Donald B. Redford, "A Note on the Chronology of Dynasty 25 and the Inscription of Sargon II at Tang-i Var," *Or* 68 (1999): 58–60.

[9] Paul Ash, *David, Solomon and Egypt: A Reassessment* (JSOTSup 297; Sheffield: Sheffield Academic Press, 1999).

[10] Bernd Ulrich Schipper, *Israel und Ägypten in der Königszeit: Die kulturellen Kontakte von Salomo bis zum Fall Jerusalems* (OBO 170; Fribourg: Universitätsverlag; Göttingen: Vandenhoeck & Ruprecht, 1999).

[11] I am grateful to Professor Kitchen for providing me with advance copies of review articles that treat these two works and that of Gallagher. See Kenneth A. Kitchen, "Ancient Israel, from Abraham to the Roman Destruction of the Temple—A Review Article," *Them* 25 (2000): 93–94. For another and more thorough review of Schipper's work by Kitchen, see idem, review of Bernd Ulrich Schipper, *Israel und Ägypten in der Königszeit, BO* 58 (2001): 376–85.

[12] James K. Hoffmeier, "Egypt's Foreign Policy in the Eighteenth Dynasty," in *Egypt, Israel, and the Ancient Mediterranean World: Essays in Honor of Donald B. Redford* (ed. G. Knoppers; forthcoming).

control of this region through a network of forts, administrative centers, and temples, which represented a return to the Nubian policy of the Twelfth Dynasty (1973–1795 B.C.).[13] Throughout the New Kingdom, Egypt's interests in Nubia were under the supervision of the "Viceroy of Kush," under whom were the Deputies of Wawat and Kush.[14] Furthermore, Egyptian temples flourished during the New Kingdom in Nubia, from Sebua and Amada in the north to Napata/Gebel Barkal in the south. Consequently, the cult of Amun (Re) pervaded Nubia and was embraced by the forebears of the Twenty-Fifth Dynasty rulers who hailed from Napata.[15]

The demise of the New Kingdom (ca. 1070 B.C.) did not result in the immediate loss of Egyptian influence in Nubia. The Twenty-First Dynasty Theban priest-king, Heri-Hor (1080–1074 B.C.) had been the "Viceroy of Kush"[16] (*imy r ḫȝswt rsyt, sȝ nsw kȝš*), and, surprisingly, Nesi-Khonsu (A) wife of Pinudjem II (ca. 990–969 B.C.) bore this title.[17] Such titles may have been purely honorific or may have meant that she, in her capacity as the "First Chief of the Harim of Amun," may have been the recipient of taxes from Nubia.[18] The last attested Viceroy of Kush was Pamiu (ca. 775–750 B.C.), of whom László Török, the Polish Nubiologist, has recently suggested that "His office, if not entirely formal, was limited to the administration of the estates of the Lower Nubian temples under Theban authority, especially the Chnum temple at Elephantine."[19]

The departure of this last vestige of Egyptian colonialism may well have paved the way for Kashta of Napata to extend his influence north to the First Cataract region, judging from a stela erected by the Nubian on Elephantine Island.[20] Kashta bears traditional pharaonic titles: "King of Upper

[13] Kenneth A. Kitchen, "The Historical Chronology of Ancient Egypt: A Current Assessment," in *Absolute Chronology: Archaeological Europe 2500–500 BC* (ed. K. Randsborg; Acta Archaeologica 67; Copenhagen: Munksgaard, 1996), 11.

[14] Bruce G. Trigger et al., *Ancient Egypt: A Social History* (Cambridge: Cambridge University Press, 1983), 208–9.

[15] László Török, *The Kingdom of Kush: Handbook of the Napatan-Meroitic Civilization* (HO 31; Leiden: Brill, 1997), 53–130; David O'Connor, *Ancient Nubia: Egypt's Rival in Africa* (Philadelphia: University Museum, 1993), 58–69.

[16] Kenneth A. Kitchen, *The Third Intermediate Period in Egypt—1100–650 BC* (3d ed.; Warminster, U.K.: Aris & Phillips, 1995), §§14–16.

[17] Ibid., §232.

[18] Ibid.

[19] Török, *Kingdom of Kush*, 144.

[20] Tormod Eide et al., *Fontes Historiae Nubiorum: Textual Sources for the History of the Middle Nile Region between the Eighth Century BC and the Sixth Century AD*, vol. 1 (Bergen: University of Bergen, 1994), text no. 3.

and Lower Egypt, Ny-Maat-Re, Lord of the Two Lands, Kashta, Son of Re, Lord of the Two Lands" (*nsw-bity, ny-mꜣʿt-rʿ, sꜣ rʿ nb tꜣwy Kꜣ-š-t*). Kashta, possibly meaning "the Kushite," adopted the prenomen of Amenemhet III, the longest-reigning monarch of the Twelfth Dynasty. Provisional dates for Kashta's reign are 760–747 B.C.

Kashta's legitimacy as King of Upper Egypt, Török believes, was established by associating himself with the Amun cult at Thebes and appointing his daughter, Amenirdis I, as "God's Wife of Amun."[21] Kitchen, however, posits that it is more likely that Pi(ankh)y appointed his sister to this post.[22] Regardless of the extent of Kashta's rule over Upper Egypt, he was the father of Pi(ankh)y and Shabako, the first indisputable kings of Egypt's Twenty-Fifth Dynasty. The legitimacy of these kings is surely attributable to Kashta's policies.

PI(ANKH)Y, CONQUEROR OF EGYPT

Little can be said about the nature of Pi(ankh)y's control of Egypt during his first twenty years. The salient historical document of his reign is his great triumphal stela that was discovered at his capital, Napata. The stela vividly recounts the military conquest of Upper and Middle Egypt.[23] Dated to his twenty-first regnal year (ca. 727 B.C.), the stela specifies that the Kushites considered Egypt to be their domain. Tefnakht, whom the stela calls "The Chief of the West" and not "King" (*nsw*), indicates that Pi(ankh)y considered himself to be the only legitimate pharaoh.[24] While Pi(ankh)y seems initially indifferent toward Tefnakht's mastering control of the Delta, his sortie into Upper Egypt was clearly regarded as an invasion of Napatan turf. Until Tefnakht's move south, the fragmented Delta posed no threat to nominal Kushite control of Middle Egypt. Line 8 mentions that Pi(ankh)y writes to his military officers in Middle Egypt. The two

---

[21] Török, *Kingdom of Kush*, 149–51.

[22] Kitchen, *Third Intermediate Period*, §122 n. 289. These dates are accepted by Török (*Kingdom of Kush*, 144).

[23] The fullest study of this stela is that of Nicolas C. Grimal, *La Stèle Triomphale Pi(ankh)y au Musée du Caire* (Cairo: Institut Français d'Archaeologie Orientale du Caire, 1981). See also "The Victory Stela of King Piye," *AEL* 3:66–84. A slightly revised edition of Lichtheim's translation in *AEL* is now available: "The Victory Stela of King Piye [Piankhy]," *COS* 2.7:42–51.

[24] Tefnakht's name does not ever occur in a cartouche, whereas the names of Namart (line 17), Osorkon (line 18), and Iuput (line 18) are written within a cartouche, and they are called "king" (*nsw*), while the cartouche of Peftuaubast is called "ruler" (*ḥkꜣ*) (line 70). None but Pi(ankh)y is called *nsw-bity* and "pharaoh."

names recorded, Purem and Lemersekny, are not Egyptian. The former is thought to be Nubian, while the latter might be Libyan.[25] This suggests that Pi(ankh)y had troops under his command in Middle Egypt, who may well have been Nubian contingents or, at least, Egyptian forces under Nubian command. It appears that, in addition to having garrisons in Egypt, the Kushites drafted treaties with some of the rulers of Upper and Middle Egypt. When Namart of Hermopolis changed his allegiance to the advancing Tefnakht, he is said to have "rejected the water of his majesty," according to Miriam Lichtheim.[26] The idiom to be "on the water" (*ḥr mw*) of another means to be loyal.[27] Hence, Grimal's translation, "infidèle à son allégeance à Sa Majesté," is preferable.[28] This reference suggests that a system of treaties with monarchs was used to control Upper and Middle Egypt prior to 727 B.C.

Pi(ankh)y's campaign ended after marching to Memphis, Heliopolis, and Athribis (the northernmost location attained). In Athribis he received the submission and tribute of the other Delta dynasts and Libyan chieftains (lines 107–126), and he received a message from Tefnakht in Sais, who wanted to take a divine oath (lines 139–140). Although Tefnakht never appeared before Pi(ankh)y in person, envoys went to Sais to hear the oath of allegiance and receive tribute. With this concession, the Delta appeared securely under Nubian control and Pi(ankh)y returned victoriously to Napata, where he erected his famous stela to commemorate the triumph. Kushite interests in Egypt were likely governed from Thebes (and not Memphis) by the "God's Wife of Amun," Amenerdis, and by such high-ranking Nubian officials as Harwa, the High Steward.[29] In 720 B.C., Pi(ankh)y installed his daughter, Shepenwepet II, to the prestigious post, the "God's Wife of Amun." Tefnakht, however, was never really subdued and regained control of the Delta and continued south to Memphis after Pi(ankh)y's return to Nubia.[30] This means that the Nubians really did not control all of Egypt and certainly not the Delta. Moreover, this conclusion concurs with Assyrian records that make no mention of Kush (*melubba*) until the Yamani affair.

---

[25] Grimal, *La Stèle Triomphale Pi(ankh)y*, 22 n. 55

[26] "The Kadesh Battle Inscriptions of Ramses II," *AEL* 2:69.

[27] Raymond O. Faulkner, *A Concise Dictionary of Middle Egyptian* (Oxford: Oxford University Press, 1962), 105.

[28] Grimal, *La Stèle Triomphale Pi(ankh)y*, 18 and 21 n. 52.

[29] Török, *Kingdom of Kush*, 164.

[30] Kitchen, *Third Intermediate Period*, §332.

SHABAKO (716–702 B.C.)

Pi(ankh)y's death is fixed at 716 B.C., and he was succeeded by his brother Shabako, following the Nubian practice of collateral succession rather than the Egyptian patrilinear system. Shabako, best known for his role in the preservation of the "Memphite Theology," reigned till 702.[31] He built extensively in the Thebaid and as far north as Memphis and Athribis in the Delta.[32] His building activity in the north was likely made possible by his campaign to regain (or really gain) control of the Delta, which might be commemorated on a large scarab now in the Royal Ontario Museum.[33] His move north must have occurred early in his reign, to judge from an inscription dated to his year two associated with an Apis burial at Sakkara.[34] The fact that Tefnakht survived Pi(ankh)y's conquest, and was succeeded by his son Bakenrenef (Bocchoris), suggests that Sais remained a dominant force in the Delta. This may explain Shabako's relocation to Memphis, effectively making it his capital.[35] Shabako (if the Manethonian tradition is to be accepted) apparently captured and executed Bakenrenef shortly after his move to Memphis.[36] If this was the case, the Nubians thereby were able finally to master all of Egypt. This apparently had been Shabako's goal, to judge from his "Egypto-centric" royal titulary,[37] such as his Golden Horus name: *Sb(3)ḳ-t3wy* (He-Who-Blesses or Refreshes-the-Two-Lands).[38]

---

[31] Török, *Kingdom of Kush,* 166; Donald B. Redford, "Sais and the Kushite Invasions," *JARCE* 22 (1985): 13 (suggests Shabako's reign continued as late as 698 B.C.).

[32] Nicholas C. Grimal, *A History of Ancient Egypt* (Oxford: Blackwell, 1992), 343–45.

[33] Samuel Mercer, "A Scarab of Shabaka, First King of the 25th or Ethiopic Dynasty of Egypt," *Bulletin of the Royal Ontario Museum of Archaeology* 10 (May 1931): 2–5. See also, Redford, "Sais and the Kushite Invasions," 6–8.

[34] Jean Vercoutter, "The Napatan Kings and Apis Worship (Serapeum Burials of the Napatan Period)," *KUSH* 8 (1960): 62–76. See especially pp. 65–67. There is also a year-two date for Shabako at Karnak that could predate the Apis inscription (ibid., 66 n. 27).

[35] Since Shabako recorded an inscription in year two at the burial of an Apis bull at Sakkara that had been buried Bakenrenef (Vercoutter, "The Napatan Kings and Apis Worship," 62–76) shows that his move north occurred quite early in his reign.

[36] Anthony J. Spalinger, "The Year 712 BC and Its Implication for Egyptian History," *JARCE* 10 (1973): 96, speculates that Bocchoris was killed for his hostile stance vis-à-vis the Assyrians, Shabako preferring a more moderate foreign policy.

[37] Kitchen, *Third Intermediate Period,* §§337–40.

[38] Török, *Kingdom of Kush,* 167 n. 280; Kitchen, *Third Intermediate Period,* §339 n. 766.

Another factor for Shabako's more active role in the Delta may have been the rise of Assyrian power in nearby Israel and Philistia during the reigns of Shalmaneser V and Sargon II.[39] In 720 B.C. Sargon II campaigned in Philistia, pushing south to Raphia, where an Egyptian-Philistine force was encountered and defeated.[40] The Egyptian force was led by Re'e, likely a general of one of the Delta kings,[41] who, according to Sargon's records, was sent fleeing to Egypt.[42] In 716 B.C., the putative accession year of Shabako, Osorkon IV, the ruler of Tanis, sent a diplomatic gift of twelve horses to Sargon in Philistia, showing he had no interest in tangling with the might of Assyria.[43] This show of goodwill was most certainly motivated by Sargon's activity in north Sinai in which he settled deportees on the Brook of Egypt,[44] not far from Tanis. Furthermore, if indeed Osorkon IV is "So" of 2 Kgs 17:4, as I believe, he may have wanted further to pacify Sargon. Osorkon IV's blip disappears from the "radar screen" of history in 715 B.C. as "the last vestige of the 22nd Dynasty as a sovereign power," observes Kitchen.[45]

Shabako and his court were no doubt alarmed by the threat Assyria posed to Egypt. Nevertheless, it appears that Shabako also did not want to cross Sargon either, as reflected by the extradition of Yamani the rebellious king of Ashdod who had fled to Egypt for sanctuary in 712/11 B.C. Assyrian records from Khorsabad agree that Yamani abandoned his city and family when he escaped to Egypt. The Great "Summary" Inscription records the incident in Sargon's own words:

> I marched to Ashdod. Now when this Yamani heard from afar the approach of my campaign he fled to the border area of Egypt which is on the border with Melluḫḫa (Nubia).... The king of Meluḫ[ḫa]—who in ///

---

[39] Török, *Kingdom of Kush*, 166. Assyrian domination of Philistia can be traced back to 734 B.C., when Tiglath-pileser III conquered Gaza (see *COS* 2.117C:288; Hayim Tadmor, "Philistia under Assyrian Rule," *BA* 39 [1966]: 86–90). Tadmor believes that the Assyrians' move on Philistia was motivated by their desire to control trade along the Levantine coast, having already taken over Phoenicia (ibid., 88). See also Younger's essay in this volume for a discussion of Assyrian involvement in the Levant during the latter half of the eighth century B.C.

[40] Tadmor, "Philistia under Assyrian Rule," 91; Gallagher, *Sennacherib's Campaign to Judah*, 113–15.

[41] Kitchen, *Third Intermediate Period*, §333.

[42] Tadmor, "Philistia under Assyrian Rule," 91.

[43] Ibid., 92.

[44] Gallagher, *Sennacherib's Campaign to Judah*, 114–15.

[45] Kitchen, *Third Intermediate Period*, §336.

land of U[r]izzu, an inaccessible place, a way [/// who]se ancestors [from the] distant [past] until now had nev[er se]nt their messengers to the kings, my ancestors, in order to inquire about their well-being—heard from af[ar] of the might of the gods [Ass]ur, [Nabu], (and) Marduk. The [fear]ful splendor of my majesty overwhelmed him and panic overcame him. He put him (Yamani) in handcuffs and manacles, [fe]tters of iron, and they brou[ght] (him) the long journey to Assyria (and) into my presence.[46]

The 1999 publication of Sargon II's inscription from Tang-i Var in Western Iran (lines 19–21) provides a new and important datum on the Yamani episode.[47] In addition to stating that "He fled to the region of Meluḫḫa and lived (there) stealthfully (lit. like a thief)," it identifies the king of Meluḫḫa as Shapataku, that is, Shabataka (Shebitku), not Shabako as might be expected.[48] Grant Frame, who published this material, immediately recognized the challenge this reference creates for chronology, but he perhaps overreacts by declaring that this "will require Egyptologists to revise their current absolute chronology of Egypt's twenty-fifth dynasty."[49] As already noted, Sargon's Philistine campaign against Ashdod is usually dated to 712/11,[50] only a few years after Shabako is thought to have acceded the throne in 715 B.C. Since the Tang-i Var text reports military activities in 706 and Sargon died in 705 B.C., the dating of this new inscription is indisputable.[51] Redford, who added a note in the same volume of *Orientalia* on the implications of this new information, suggests that Shabako's dates might be lowered to 713 to 699 B.C. or that a co-regency existed between Shabako and Shabataka.[52] This second option would remove the need for altering the chronology. The possibility of a co-regency between these monarchs has been discussed by some in the past but not widely accepted.[53] Recently, however, and

---

[46] "The Great 'Summary' Inscription," translated by K. Lawson Younger Jr. (*COS* 2.118E:296–97). The Small "Summary" Inscription (translated by K. Lawson Younger Jr. in *COS* 2.118F:297) provides a nearly identical report.

[47] Grant Frame, "The Inscription of Sargon II at Tang-I Var," *Or* 68 (1999): 31–57. For another recent translation, see that of K. Lawson Younger Jr. in *COS* 2.118J: 299–300.

[48] Frame, "Inscription of Sargon II," 36, 40.

[49] Ibid., 52.

[50] Ibid., 52; Tadmor, "Philistia under Assyrian Rule," 94; Kitchen, *Third Intermediate Period*, §341.

[51] Frame, "Inscription of Sargon II," 51.

[52] Redford, "A Note on the Chronology of Dynasty 25," 58–60.

[53] William Murnane, *Ancient Egyptian Coregencies* (Chicago: Oriental Institute, 1977), 189–90; Frank Yurco, "Sennacherib's Third Campaign and the Coregency of

before the discovery of the Tang-i Var text, the association of Shabako and Shabataka has once again been championed by Frank Yurco.[54] Reference to Shabataka in 706 B.C. certainly bolsters the case for a co-regency between these monarchs.

If the Tang-i Var inscription is correct in assigning Shabataka as the Kushite leader who returned Yamani to Sargon, it is curious that it is Shabako's name that occurs on clay seal impressions found at Nineveh by Layard.[55] This would suggest that Shabako was the king responsible for official diplomatic communiqués. In his comprehensive study of Egyptian co-regencies, the late William Murnane observed that during the Twelfth Dynasty the junior partner in a co-regency was "the executive, dynamic force in the duumvirate inside Egypt, although foreign rulers continued to correspond with the senior partner."[56] Perhaps this was the case in the Twenty-Fifth Dynasty.

It is also worth noting that there is no evidence for contact between Kush and Assyria prior to the return of Yamani, since Sargon's claims that no earlier Kushite had sent messengers to Assyria.[57] In this regard, one is reminded of the reference in Isa 18 that mentions the arrival of Kushite ambassadors to western Asia. Perhaps it was after Shabako's move to the Delta,[58] and around the time of the Assyrian assault on Ashdod, that the Kushite embassy came to the Levant as reported in Isa 18. This proposal is supported in Isaiah's oracle in Isa 20 that is dated to Sargon's campaign against Ashdod. It warned Judah against reliance on the Nubians, an exhortation I believe was taken seriously even in 701 B.C. Prior to the reference to the king of Meluḫḫa in texts reporting on the Yamani affair, Egypt's leaders were called "Pharaoh (*pirʿu*) or "king" (*šar*) of Egypt. This

---

Shabaka and Shebitku," *Serapis* 6 (1980): 221–40; Grimal, *History of Ancient Egypt,* 346; Kitchen, *Third Intermediate Period,* §§556–57.

[54] Frank Yurco, "The Shabaka-Shebitku Coregency and the Supposed Second Campaign of Sennacherib against Judah: A Critical Assessment," *JBL* 110 (1991): 35–45.

[55] Austin Henry Layard, *Discoveries among the Ruins of Nineveh and Babylon; with Travels in Armenia, Kurdistan, and the Desert: Being the Result of a Second Expedition Undertaken for the Trustees of the British Museum* (New York: Harper & Brothers, 1853), 156 59.

[56] Murnane, *Ancient Egyptian Coregencies,* 240.

[57] "The Small 'Summary' Inscription," *COS* 2.118F:297. On this being the earliest reference to Kush by the Assyrians, see Spalinger, "Year 712 BCE," 99; see also Gallagher, *Sennacherib's Campaign to Judah,* 122.

[58] Isaiah 18:7 refers to the Kushites as "a nation mighty and conquering." This would hardly be true prior to Shabako's advance on the north.

factor raises the question as to whom the Rabshakeh had in mind when he accused Hezekiah of relying on Egypt (2 Kgs 18:20–21; Isa 36:4–5), an intriguing question that will be addressed below.

The possibility of a co-regency is now more attractive, given the fact that Shabako had moved his court to Memphis and that Napata, the Nubian capital, was around two thousand miles away. Shabataka may well have been ruling from Napata, whence he was able to apprehend Yamani and initiate his extradition.[59] In doing so, the Kushites were likely following the New Kingdom practice of the pharaoh ruling from Memphis while the "Viceroy of Kush" governed Nubia.[60] In the case of the Nubians, the idea of the "Viceroy of Kush" would take on special meaning, since the title in Egyptian is *imy-r ḫȝswt rsywt, sȝ nsw kȝš*—"the Overseer of southern, foreign lands, King's son of Kush." In this case it was the king's son who ruled in Kush (unlike in New Kingdom times, when nonroyal officials held the office). If this scenario is correct, it may explain the title used by Sargon, *šar Meluḫḫa,* for Shabataka at this early date. It should be noticed that he is neither called "pharaoh" (*pirʿu*) nor "king of Egypt" (*šar muṣri*), and certainly the diplomatic gesture of returning Yamani to Sargon assured continued peaceful relations with Assyria for another decade and may have convinced the Assyrians that they had nothing to fear from the Kushites.

SHABATAKA (SHEBITKU) 702–690 B.C.

Shabako died in Memphis around 702 B.C.,[61] and most likely before 701 B.C., and was succeeded by his nephew, the elder son of Pi(ankh)y, the aforementioned Shabataka. Egyptologists agree that the accession of this new monarch marked the beginning of a more hostile stance toward Assyria. Nicholas Grimal, the French Egyptologist and expert in the Nubian archaizing practices,[62] observes: "in his foreign policy Shebitku adopted a considerably more aggressive stance than his predecessors. The

---

[59] It should be noted that the Assyrian records give no indication how long Yamani was a refuge in Egypt-Nubia, but since the two Summaries and the Kang-i Var texts come from the very end of his life, it may be that the extradition took place closer to 705 than 712/1. This consideration would significantly shorten a co-regency.

[60] Trigger et al., *Ancient Egypt,* 208–29.

[61] Kitchen, *Third Intermediate Period,* §345.

[62] See Grimal, *La Stèle Triomphale Pi(ankh)y,* 257–302; idem, "Bibliothèques et propagande royale à l'époque éthiopienne," in *Livre du centenaire, 1880–1980* (ed. J. Vercoutter; Cairo: Institut français d'archéologie orientale, 1980), 37–48.

concessions made by Shabako to Sargon II had provided Egypt with about fifteen years of respite."[63] The reason for this about-face is not clear.

The archaistic royal titulary of this monarch tells its own story and, perhaps, signals Shabataka's militaristic aspirations. "Strong Bull, crowned in Thebes" (*ḫˁ m wȝst*), the epithet made popular by the Thutmoside kings of the Eighteenth Dynasty, is adopted, as well as the Two Ladies name "of Mighty Respect in All Lands" (*ˁȝ šfi m ȝw nbw*) and the Golden Horus name "of Mighty Strong Arm Who Smites the Nine Bows" (*ˁȝ ḫpš ḥwi pḏt psḏ*).[64] Kitchen labels this development as "a sudden reversion to the imperial style,"[65] while Török goes even further, suggesting that Shabataka's regal title "conveys an aggressive message, announcing the ruler's preparations for the unavoidable clash with Assyria."[66] While textual evidence of Shabataka's policies from his own reign are lacking, we may glean some information from the Kawa stelae of Taharqa, and this will lead us to the events of 701 B.C. in Judah.

TAHARQA AND THE EVENTS OF 701 B.C.

Kawa Stela IV, which was published by Macadam in 1949, is dated to the sixth regnal year of Taharqa (ca. 685 B.C.).[67] Now in the Cairo Museum, it reports on Prince Taharqa, son of Pi(ankh)y, being summoned north to Thebes, along with other princes, to join King Shabataka. No reason, however, is offered for the king's directive, but the mention of "the army of his majesty" (*mšˁ ḥm.f*) accompanying the northward-bound convoy might be suggestive of the military nature of the mission. Taharqa recalls that he was twenty years old when this happened (not twenty in his fifth regnal year, as Macadam misunderstood!)[68] and that he emerged as the favorite of Shabataka. Török observes:

> Presumably due to the lack of a male heir and in view of the aggressive policy decided by the new ruler of the double kingdom, Taharqo was at

---

[63] Grimal, *History of Ancient Egypt,* 346.

[64] Török, *Kingdom of Kush,* 169 n. 298. Henri Gauthier, *Le Livre des Rois d'Égypte IV* (Cairo: Institut français d'archéologie orientale, 1916), 12–26.

[65] Kitchen, *Third Intermediate Period,* §345.

[66] Török, *Kingdom of Kush,* 169.

[67] M. F. Laming Macadam, *Temples of Kawa: The Inscriptions* (Oxford: Oxford University Press, 1949), 1:7–10.

[68] His error was pointed out many years ago by Kenneth A. Kitchen in *Ancient Orient and the Old Testament* (Downers Grove, Ill.: InterVarsity, 1966), 82–83; idem, "Late-Egyptian Chronology and the Hebrew Monarchy," *JANESCU* 5 (1973): 95–101.

the same time declared heir apparent. This also conforms, in turn, with the Egyptian tradition of the appointment of the crown prince as commander-in-chief of an expeditionary force.[69]

This is a salient point that may answer why in 701 B.C. Taharqa (Tirhakah) is called *melek kûš* in 2 Kgs 19:9 and Isa 37:9. By Esarhaddon's day, when Taharqa was sole ruler and pharaoh, he is called "King of Egypt and Kush," in the Zinjirli Stela (RS 37–38).[70] Whether or not he was co-regent, the heir to Pharaoh often led military expeditions, especially for a more senior king. A classic example of this is documented in Sinuhe, where we are informed: "Now then his majesty dispatched his army to Libya [*tmḥw*], his eldest son being commander of it, the good god, Senusert (I). . . . It is he who subdued foreign lands while his father was in the palace."[71] Ramesses II is known to have received the title "Commander-in-Chief of the Army" as a young lad and to have accompanied his father on Levantine campaigns while yet in his mid-teens,[72] and Ramesses likewise regularly included his sons on military campaigns. The princes of Ramesses II, in turn, are shown to have been active on military campaigns.

Some have tried to suggest that in 701 B.C. Prince Taharqa would have been only a child, since the reference to his age, twenty in Kawa Stela IV, points to the first year of his reign in 690 B.C. at the death of Shabataka.[73] Only a misreading of the text by Macadam could possibly lead to this conclusion,[74] and this reading has been erroneously used to support the

---

[69] Török, *Kingdom of Kush,* 170.

[70] Riekele Borger, *Die Inschriften Asarhaddons Königs von Assyrien* (AfOB 9; Graz: self-published, 1956), 98–99, lines RS 37–38.

[71] Lines R 12–13, 50. Translation my own, text in Aylward M. Blackman, *Middle Egyptian Stories and the Shipwrecked Sailor* (Bibliotheca Aegyptiaca 2; Leiden: Brill, 1932), 4–5, 19.

[72] Kenneth A. Kitchen, *Pharaoh Triumphant: The Life and Times of Ramesses II* (Warminster: Aris & Phillips, 1982), 24–25.

[73] Redford (*Egypt, Canaan, and Israel,* 353 n. 163) claims that "in 701 Taharqa was still a lad in Nubia, and his first trip to Egypt proper lay years in the future." He also rejects the notion of Kitchen (and consequently that subsequently held by Török) that the reference in Kawa Stela IV to Taharqa's call north by Shabataka had anything to do with military matters. Jürgen von Beckerath likewise believes that Taharqa could not have been in Judah in 701 B.C. ("Ägypten und der Feldzug Sanheribs im Jahre 701. V. Chr.," *UF* 24 [1992]: 3–8).

[74] Cf. Kitchen, "Late-Egyptian Chronology," 95–101; idem, *Third Intermediate Period,* §§128–29. In support of Kitchen's reading of the text over against that of Macadam, see Anson F. Rainey, "Taharqa and Syntax," *TA* 3 (1976): 38–41.

two-campaign hypothesis.[75] It must be recalled that Pi(ankh)y, Taharqa's father, died in 716 B.C., meaning that Taharqa was minimally fourteen to fifteen in 701 B.C. if he was sired on Pi(ankh)y's deathbed![76] More likely, Taharqa was conceived four to five years before Pi(ankh)y's demise, making him twenty in 702/1 B.C., as the Kawa Stela asserts.

CONCLUDING THOUGHTS

Let us now consider some implications of the foregoing discussion on Hezekiah's Judah in 701 B.C.

1. After Shabako's conquest of the Delta, there was no plan to tangle with the Assyrians, despite their proximity to Egypt during Sargon's reign. A policy of pacification was adopted. Because he ruled from Memphis, Shabako appointed Shabataka as crown prince or co-regent to govern Nubia from Napata. Shabataka, in turn, did the same in appointing Taharqa around 702.

2. The accession of Shabataka marked a shift in the former policy. While our sources do not explain the reason for this change, two suggestions present themselves: (1) Shabataka had become wary of the Assyrian military presence operating within striking distance of the Delta; and (2) as the imperialistic titles he assumed suggest, Shabataka wanted to return Egypt to its former glory, controlling the Levant. In either case, the Assyrians posed a threat to Egypt's security or its imperial designs.

3. Ekron's rebellion and call on Egypt to help provided Shabataka with the opportunity he sought to take on the Assyrians. The crown prince or co-regent, Taharqa, represented Kushite interests, as was often the case in military matters in Pharaonic Egypt.

4. The Assyrians thought that the petty Delta rulers (i.e., Egypt the broken reed) might be able to send a token force to Philistia in response to Ekron's call, but they still thought of the Kushites as an ally, thanks to Shabako and Shabataka's friendly treatment toward Assyria by the extradition of Yamani. Consequently, Sennacherib was caught off guard when he heard that Taharqa, the Kushite, was marching out against him (2 Kgs 19:9; Isa 37:9).

---

[75] William F. Albright, *From the Stone Age to Christianity* (2d ed.; Garden City, N.Y.: Doubleday, 1957), 314; John Bright, *A History of Israel* (2d ed.; Philadelphia: Westminster, 1972), 296–308; William H. Shea, "Sennacherib's Second Palestinian Campaign," *JBL* 104 (1985): 401–18.

[76] Kitchen has also made this observation in *Third Intermediate Period,* §132; and idem, "Late-Egyptian Chronology," 229.

5. While Hezekiah supported the anti-Assyrian rebellion fomented by Ekron, he was not involved in calling on Egypt, a point I suggested some years ago.[77] My reason for proposing this is that the biblical text does not condemn him for this action, a point that would not be lost on Isaiah. To be sure, Hezekiah was censured by Isaiah for his defensive building program prior to the Assyrian invasion of Judah (Isa 22:8b–11).

The oracles of Isa 30:1–5 and 31:1–3 are thought to be an invective threat (a woe) against those who seek aid from Egypt and are dated to Hezekiah's day by many Old Testament scholars.[78] There is, however, nothing within these texts that point to 701, as I have argued elsewhere.[79]

The following considerations militate against these oracles dating to 701 B.C., as is widely held. First, they give no knowledge of the Kushites who ruled from Memphis. Second, the only geopolitical clue offered in these two oracles that might assist in dating them is the reference to Tanis and Hanes in Isa 31:4 as the place where Pharaoh is contacted. Tanis, present-day San el-Hagar, is known to be the dominant city of the east Delta, which was situated on the Pelusiac branch of the Nile. It was the seat of the Twenty-First Dynasty and continued to be economically, militarily, and politically significant through most of the Third Intermediate Period. However, as mentioned above, after 715 B.C., Osorkon IV is not mentioned again in Egyptian sources, and little is known about its political significance in 702/1. Hanes has been identified with modern Ahnasyia, ancient Heracleopolis (*H*[*wt nni*]*nsw*), 80 km south of Memphis.[80] This location makes absolutely no sense during the Third Intermediate Period. More likely is the suggestion Wilhem Spiegelberg made nearly a century ago, that there was a location in the Delta by the same name as the one

---

[77] James K. Hoffmeier, "Egypt As an Arm of Flesh: A Prophetic Response," in *Israel's Apostasy and Restoration: Essays in Honor of Roland K. Harrison* (ed. A. Gileadi; Grand Rapids: Baker, 1988), 88–89.

[78] Brevard S. Childs, *Isaiah and the Assyrian Crisis* (London: SCM, 1967), 32–33; Arthur S. Herbert, *The Book of the Prophet Isaiah, Chapters 1-39* (Cambridge: Cambridge University Press, 1973), 180; Otto Kaiser, *Isaiah 13–39* (OTL; Philadelphia: Westminster, 1978), 283–84; Klaus Koch, *The Assyrian Period* (trans. M. Kohl; vol. 1 of *The Prophets;* Philadelphia: Fortress, 1978), 128–29.

[79] Hoffmeier, "Egypt As an Arm of Flesh," 88–89. Shmuel Aḥituv has recently called Isa 31:1–3 "perhaps the earliest" of the oracles against reliance upon Egypt but does not offer a date (Shmuel Aḥituv, "Egypt That Isaiah Knew," in *Jerusalem Studies in Egyptology* [ed. I. Shirun-Grumach; ÄAT 40; Weisbaden: Harrassowitz, 1998], 3).

[80] Henry O. Thompson, "Hanes," *ABD* 3:49–50.

located in Middle Egypt.[81] A more attractive proposal has been offered by Kitchen, who suggests that Hebrew *Hanes* is the vocalization for Egyptian *ḥ(wt) nsw*, "house of the king," that is, the palace.[82] The parallelism of 30:4 would suggest that Zoan and Hanes are one and the same and, hence, points to the palace at Tanis.[83] Given this scenario, I would argue that Tanis is the logical place for Israel or Judah to send for help in 722, but not 701. Hence I agree with John Hayes and Stuart Irvine that these oracles in Isa 30 and 31 are directed at Hoshea of Samaria, who sent envoys to "So" (Osorkon IV) king of Egypt for help, as reported in 2 Kgs 17:4, and have no bearing on the events of Hezekiah's day.[84]

I maintain this because the book of Isaiah contains no indictment of Hezekiah for calling on Egypt for help, and because, moreover, no such judgment is found in 2 Kings and 2 Chronicles (both books give high praise rather than condemnation for this godly monarch; see 2 Kgs 18:5; 2 Chr 32:1–23). I thus believe that the Kushites joined in battle against the Assyrians because they understood that if Philistia and Judah were to be defeated, Egypt would be the next theater of operations by the empire-minded Assyrians. In as much as Esarhaddon invaded Egypt in 671 and fought against Taharqa,[85] they were right in trying to make a preemptive strike against the lone superpower of the day. Whatever hopes Judah had that Kush would be a help against Assyria in 711, Isaiah's condemnation (Isa 20) of such reliance put an end to a pro-Kushite policy, which I propose carried over to 701 B.C.

---

[81] Wilhem Spiegelberg, *Aegyptologische Randglossen zum Alten Testamentum* (Strassburg: Schlesier & Schweikhardt, 1904), 36–38. This view would agree with Herodotus, who located Heracleopolis parva in the Delta.

[82] Kenneth A. Kitchen, "Hanes," *NBD*[2], 452–53.

[83] If Hanes refers to the palace at Tanis, then Isaiah is far more informed about Egypt's geopolitical realities than Ahituv has recently suggested ("Egypt That Isaiah Knew," 3–7). His claim of Isaiah's complete ignorance of Nubia, as reflected in Isa 18, has been soundly refuted in a recent study (Meir Lubetski and Claire Gottlieb, "Isaiah 18: The Egyptian Nexus," in *Boundaries of the Ancient Near Eastern World: A Tribute to Cyrus H. Gordon* [ed. M. Lubetski et al.; JSOTSup 273; Sheffield: Sheffield Academic Press, 1998], 264–303) that appeared around the same time as Ahituv and was, therefore, not a response to his article in *Jerusalem Studies in Egyptology*.

[84] John Hayes and Stuart Irvine, *Isaiah the Eighth-Century Prophet: His Times and His Preaching* (Nashville: Abingdon, 1987), 338–48.

[85] See Anthony Spalinger, "Esarhaddon and Egypt: An Analysis of the First Invasion of Egypt," *Or* 43 (1974): 295–326.

Assyrian Involvement in the Southern Levant at the End of the Eighth Century B.C.E.

K. Lawson Younger Jr.
Trinity International University—Divinity School

The purpose of this study is to examine the impact of Assyrian activities in the southern Levant at the end of the eighth century B.C.E., especially as these affected the kingdom of Judah and its capital city, Jerusalem.[1] The two Assyrian monarchs conducting military operations in the southern Levant during the last two decades of the 700s were Sargon II and his son Sennacherib. Sargon campaigned in the region three times (although in one instance he was not physically present); Sennacherib campaigned only once. But both effected significant changes throughout the entire eastern Mediterranean coast.

In the last few years, a number of important studies have addressed the questions of Assyrian involvements in the Levant during this period. Just works published in 1999–2000 devoted to the third campaign of Sennacherib against Hezekiah, or some aspect of it, present a daunting task to anyone interested in understanding what happened during this invasion. The complexity of all the various issues related just to this score of years ought to humble even the most self-assured historian and warns us to be cautious in our reconstructive efforts. In a real sense, this is quite ironic,

---

[1] Thus this study will deal primarily with the relevant Assyrian materials. For the archaeology of the period, see Ephraim Stern, *The Assyrian, Babylonian, and Persian Periods 732–332 BCE* (vol. 2 of *Archaeology of the Land of the Bible;* ABRL; New York: Doubleday, 2001), 3–214. For the biblical materials, see Richard S. Hess, "Hezekiah and Sennacherib in 2 Kings 18–20," in *Zion, City of Our God* (ed. R. S. Hess and G. J. Wenham; Grand Rapids: Eerdmans, 1999), 23–41; Raymond F. Person Jr., "II Kings 18–20 and Isaiah 36–39: A Text Critical Case Study in the Redaction History of the Book of Isaiah," *ZAW* 111 (1999): 373–79; and Francolino J. Gonçalves, "2 Rois 18,13–20,19 Par. Isaïe 36–39. Encore une fois, lequel des deux livres fut le premier?" in *Lectures et relectures de la Bible: Festschrift P.-M. Bogaert* (ed. J.-M. Auwers and A. Wénin; BETL 144; Leuven: Leuven University Press, 1999), 27–55.

since the invasion of Sennacherib is unquestionably the most well-attested event in all the Hebrew Bible (or in the New Testament too, for that matter). Amazingly, it is, at the same time, the most detailed description of an Assyrian campaign to the west in the cuneiform sources.[2]

It is also certainly an irony of history that today one of the major exemplars of Sennacherib's Annals that attests to his attack on Hezekiah, the Jerusalem Prism,[3] is housed in the city of Jerusalem! I wonder what Sennacherib would think? Moreover, it is an interesting and perhaps ironic fact that it is *only* during the reign of King Hezekiah that Jerusalem is explicitly mentioned in the cuneiform documents from Mesopotamia. Of course, it was mentioned much earlier in the Amarna correspondence, but this is far removed from the context of this essay.

Not only is it the case with the city of Jerusalem, but it is also the case that the nation-state of Judah is only mentioned for the first time in the Assyrian royal inscriptions during the latter portion of the eighth century. The lateness of Judah's mention in the Assyrian texts (Jerusalem as well, of course) should not be understood as an indication of Judah's insignificance in size and wealth, as is sometimes done. Since Judah had been beyond Assyrian interest before 734–732 B.C.E., it is not surprising that the capital city of this southern Levantine state received no mention in Assyrian inscriptions. Tiglath-pileser III's reference to Ahaz, the ruler of this southern Levantine state,[4] is purely a function of the expansion of the Assyrian Empire. As this empire expanded, it came into contact with nations and peoples with which it had not previously had contact. In fact, this is a common motif developed in the Assyrian royal inscriptions to emphasize the present significance of the reigning king and his achievements as over against his predecessors.[5] Thus the relatively late mention of Judah is

---

[2] Hayim Tadmor, "Sennacherib's Campaign to Judah: Historical and Historiographical Considerations" [Hebrew], *Zion* 50 (1985): 65–80, esp. 66.

[3] Pnina Ling-Israel, "The Sennacherib Prism in the Israel Museum—Jerusalem," in *Bar-Ilan Studies in Assyriology Dedicated to Pinhas Artzi* (ed. J. Klein and A. J. Skaist; Ramat Gan: Bar-Ilan University, 1990), 213–48 and pls. i–xvi.

[4] See Hayim Tadmor, *The Inscriptions of Tiglath-Pileser III, King of Assyria* (Jerusalem: Israel Academy of Sciences, 1994), 170–71, Summary Inscription 7.11; see also *COS* 2.117D:289.

[5] See Hayim Tadmor, "World Dominion: The Expanding Horizon of the Assyrian Empire," in *Landscapes: Territories, Frontiers and Horizons in the Ancient Near East* (ed. L. Milano et al.; HANEM 3/1; Padova: Sargon, 1999), 55–62. For another example, see the mention of Meluḫḫa in Sargon's Great Summary Inscription (lines 109b–112; *COS* 2.118E:297). Even more minor kings could employ this motif to heighten their royal image. See, e.g., Ninurta-kudurrī-uṣur—Suḫu Annals no. 2 (lines ii.1–29a; iv.1'–9a'; iv.26b'–38'), *COS* 2.115B:280–81.

purely a function of the process of the expanding Assyrian Empire, giving no indication of the size and wealth of each of the newly mentioned states. Obviously this also applies to the city of Jerusalem.

Judah is next mentioned in the Assyrian royal inscriptions in Sargon II's Nimrud Inscription.[6] Here Sargon describes himself as "the subduer of Judah, which lies far away" (*mu-šak-niš* KUR *Ia-ú-du šá a-šar-šú ru-ú-qu*). Now this could be a hollow claim, but the intriguing parallel in the Nimrud Prisms in which Sargon describes himself as the "subduer of the distant Medes" (*mu-šak-niš* KUR *Ma-da-a-a ru-qu-ú-ti*) suggests that the claim has substance. In fact, this parallel demonstrates that it is entirely possible that some kind of military action was taken by Sargon against the kingdom of Judah.[7] But if this occurred, when did it occur, and what kind of action was it? How did it impact Jerusalem?

Sargon's first military action in the west was in 720 B.C.E.. This campaign's first objective was the defeat of a western coalition led by Yau-bi'di (Ilu-bi'di) of Hamath that included the cities of Arpad, Simirra, Damascus, Hatarikka, and Samaria. Sargon defeated this coalition decisively at the battle of Qarqar (the same site where Shalmaneser III had fought a western alliance in 853 B.C.E.). Sometime soon after this battle Sargon besieged and quickly captured Samaria.[8] Continuing south, he defeated an Egyptian army at Raphia and reconquered Gaza. Eight different inscriptions, as well as possibly some of Sargon's reliefs (see discussion below), witness to this campaign.[9] Could this be the context for Sargon's subduing of Judah?

Nadav Na'aman has recently argued for dating the Nimrud Inscription to late 717 or early 716 B.C.E.[10] This argument seems convincing, since it is based on both the content and the structure of the historical section. Therefore, it is most likely that the "subduing of Judah" referred to in the Nimrud

---

[6] See Hugo Winckler, *Die Keilschrifttexte Sargons* (Leipzig: Pfeiffer, 1889), 168–73; and *COS* 2.118I:298–99.

[7] K. Lawson Younger Jr., "Sargon's Campaign against Jerusalem—A Further Note," *Bib* 77 (1996): 108–10.

[8] K. Lawson Younger Jr., "The Fall of Samaria in Light of Recent Research," *CBQ* 61 (1999): 461–82.

[9] Zechariah 9:1–5 may also allude to this campaign (William W. Hallo and William K. Simpson, *The Ancient Near East: A History* [2d ed.; Fort Worth: Harcourt Brace College Publishers, 1998], 135).

[10] Nadav Na'aman, "The Historical Portion of Sargon II's Nimrud Inscription," *SAAB* 8 (1994): 17–20; for similar arguments, see also Eckart Frahm, *Einleitung in die Sanherib-Inschriften* (AfOB 26; Vienna: Institut für Orientalistik der Universität, 1997), 231.

Inscription took place in 720 B.C.E. The text's reference simply cannot refer to any later campaign after 716 B.C.E. Moreover, this may be further supported by Nimrud letter 16,[11] which appears to date from between 720 and 715 B.C.E. and reports the arrival of emissaries from the west in Calah, bringing tribute, including emissaries from Judah. Thus it seems certain that 720 B.C.E. was the year of Sargon's subjugation of Judah.

Two other sources may refer to this campaign: Isa 10:27–32 and/or the Azekah Inscription. Recently Marvin Sweeney has argued that Isa 10:27–32 pertains to the campaign of Sargon II in 720.[12] If he is correct, then Sargon approached Jerusalem from the north in an apparently successful attempt to reassert control over Judah, which had probably stopped tribute payments to Assyria after the death of Tiglath-pileser III.

One of the more important Assyriological contributions for the study of the latter part of the eighth century is undoubtedly the work of Nadav Naʾaman that he published in 1974.[13] He demonstrated that a fragment (K 6205) that had been attributed up to that time to Tiglath-pileser III, in fact, belonged with another fragment (BM 82-3-23, 131) that had been attributed to Sargon II, recovering a document that has come to be known as the "Azekah Inscription." The reference to the Judahite city of Azekah in line 5', as well as the name of Hezekiah (partially restored), demonstrate that part of the military action that the inscription portrays is set in Judah. Another city, whose name is not preserved, is described

---

[11] Henry W. F. Saggs, "The Nimrud Letters, 1952—Part II," *Iraq* 17 (1955): 126–54, esp. 134–35, pl. xxxiii; Mordechai Cogan, *Imperialism and Religion: Assyria, Judah and Israel in the Eighth and Seventh Centuries B.C.E.* (SBLMS 19; Missoula, Mont.: Scholars Press, 1974), 118; and esp. J. Nicholas Postgate, *Taxation and Conscription in the Assyrian Empire* (Studia Pohl: Series Maior; Rome: Biblical Institute Press, 1974), 117–18 (for the date of the letter and collation); Simo Parpola, *Letters from Assyria and the West* (part 1 of *The Correspondence of Sargon II;* SAA 1; Helsinki: Helsinki University Press, 1987), 92–93, no. 110, lines r. 4–13. See also Alan Millard, "Assyrian Involvement in Edom," in *Early Edom and Moab: The Beginning of the Iron Age in Southern Jordan* (ed. P. Bienkowski; Sheffield Archaeological Monographs 7; Sheffield: Collis, 1992), 35–39, esp. 36. Note as well a list of wine allocations from Nimrud. See Stephanie Dalley and J. Nicholas Postgate, *The Tablets from Fort Shalmaneser* (CTN 3; Oxford: Oxford University Press, 1984), no. 135. See *COS* 3.96:245.

[12] Marvin A. Sweeney, "Sargon's Threat against Jerusalem in Isaiah 10,27–32," *Bib* 75 (1994): 457–70; idem, *Isaiah 1–39, with an Introduction to Prophetic Literature* (FOTL 16; Grand Rapids: Eerdmans, 1996); see also Younger, "Sargon's Campaign against Jerusalem," 108–10.

[13] Nadav Naʾaman, "Sennacherib's 'Letter to God' on his Campaign to Judah," *BASOR* 214 (1974): 25–39.

in line 11' as a "royal city of Philistines, which [Hezek]iah had captured and strengthened for himself." The biblical text alludes to Hezekiah's activity in Philistia in 2 Kgs 18:8. Na²aman suggested the Philistine city of Gath (Tell eṣ Ṣafi), but recently Galil has proposed the city of Ekron.[14] Nevertheless, the city's description (if lines 12'–20' continue with a description of the city mentioned in line 11') does not seem to fit particularly well with Ekron.[15]

Unfortunately, the text is very fragmentary, making it difficult to date. In fact, the following dates have been proposed: 720, 715, 712, 701, and 689 B.C.E.[16] Recently Eckart Frahm has discussed the text and suggested a date of 720 B.C.E.[17] If he is correct, then this has certain implications for biblical chronology, since Hezekiah, who seems to be named in the inscription, would have been king of Judah at this time. But the evidence, built mainly on an attribution of the inscription to Sargon, which is based primarily on literary allusions and negative evidence for other possible dates, is hardly firm.[18] And if Isa 10:27–32 is describing Sargon's

---

[14] Gershon Galil, "Judah and Assyria in the Sargonid Period" [Hebrew], *Zion* 57 (1992): 111–33; idem, "Conflicts between Assyrian Vassals," *SAAB* 6 (1992): 55–63; idem, "A New Look at the 'Azekah Inscription,'" *RB* 102 (1995): 321–29. Na²aman now concurs with this suggestion (personal communication).

[15] Moreover, Ekron was a mere ten acres in 701 with a population of approximately sixteen hundred inhabitants. The identification of the city as Ekron would fit either with Sargon's 720 campaign or with Sennacherib's 701 campaign. The best fit historically is the latter.

[16] The last date is based on the theory of two western campaigns of Sennacherib. See most recently William H. Shea, "Jerusalem under Siege: Did Sennacherib Attack Twice?" *BAR* 25/6 (1999): 36–44, 64. The theory misunderstands the reference to Taharqa/Tirhakah in 2 Kgs 19 (see Hoffmeier's discussion in this volume) as well as some of the other material. There is no extrabiblical source that even hints at a later campaign. See Paul-Eugène Dion, "Sennacherib's Expedition to Palestine," *EgT* 20 (1989): 12 n. 38, 15–18.

[17] Frahm, *Einleitung in die Sanherib-Inschriften,* 229–232; see also Andreas Fuchs, *Die Inschriften Sargons II. aus Khorsabad* (Göttingen: Cuvillier, 1994), 314–15.

[18] The statement in line 5' is also problematic: [. . .] ᵁᴿᵁ*A-za-qa-a* É *tuk-la-te-šú šá ina bi-ri*[*t? mi-i*]*ṣ-ri-ia u* ᴋᵁᴿ *Ia-u-di* [. . .] "[. . .] the city of Azekah, his stronghold, which is between my [bo]rder and the land of Judah[. . .]." Na²aman ("Sennacherib's 'Letter to God,'" 26) restored: *šá ina bi-ri*[*t mi-i*]*-ri-ia u* ᴋᵁᴿ *Ia-u-di* "which is between my [bo]rder and the land of Judah." Galil ("New Look at the 'Azekah Inscription,'" 322) reads: ina ˹*bi-rit?*˺ [*áš*]*-ri-ia u* ᴋᵁᴿ.*Ia-u-di* "which is located between my [la]nd and the land of Judah." This reading follows Riekele Borger, *BAL*² 1:134, who reads: ˹*áš*˺*-ri-ia*. Frahm rejects this reading and suggests [*ki*]-[*i'ṣ-ri-ia*, thus "which is between my troop contingent and the land of Judah."

720 campaign, then it seems less likely that Sargon attacked Judah from both the north and the west.

In 716 or 715 B.C.E., Sargon campaigned again in Philistia, as recorded in some prism fragments from Ashur and Nineveh.[19] Unfortunately, the events of this campaign are, for the most part, very sketchy. Apparently deportees were settled on the Brook of Egypt, being assigned to the sheikh of Laban. Sargon may have wanted to create a clearly defined border between his empire and Egypt and have a local chief be responsible for it. With the Assyrian army in the region, Šilkanni, the king of Egypt (Osorkon IV), felt compelled to send Sargon twelve magnificent horses as a gift. These were probably Kushite horses from the Dongola Reach area, already an important horse-breeding center at this time.[20] This campaign was probably more commercial than military.[21] Although it is likely that Sargon replaced the king of Ashdod at this time (i.e., Azuri with Aḫimiti), there is no clear evidence to confirm this. While Becking has ascribed the Azekah Inscription to this campaign,[22] arguing for an incursion into Judah against Hezekiah, the evidence is quite insufficient and hence unlikely.

The next reference to Judah is found in Sargon's Nineveh Prism fragments.[23] A translation of the relevant lines follows:

VII.a: Sm 2022,II' (lines 13–16)
In my ninth regnal year, I [marched] against [the city of Ashdod, which is on the coast] of the Great Sea. [. . .] [the city] of Ashdod [. . .][. . .]

---

[19] Newly edited by Andreas Fuchs, *Die Annalen des Jahres 711 v. Chr. nach Prismenfragmenten aus Ninive und Assur* (SAAS 8; Helsinki: Neo-Assyrian Text Corpus Project, 1998), 28–29.

[20] Lisa A. Heidorn, "The Horses of Kush," *JNES* 56 (1997): 105–14.

[21] Gerald L. Mattingly, "An Archaeological Analysis of Sargon's 712 Campaign Against Ashdod," *NEASB* 17 (1981): 47–64, esp. 47; A. Kirk Grayson, "Assyria: Tiglath-Pileser III to Sargon II (744–705 B.C.)," in *The Assyrian and Babylonian Empires and Other States of the Near East, from the Eighth to the Sixth Centuries B.C.* (ed. J. Boardman et al.; 2d ed.; CAH 3/2; Cambridge: Cambridge University Press, 1991), 89.

[22] Bob Becking, *The Fall of Samaria: An Historical and Archaeological Study* (SHANE 2; Leiden: Brill, 1992), 54.

[23] Fuchs, *Annalen des Jahres 711 v. Chr.,* 44–46, 73–74, 124–31; Zdzislaw J. Kapera, "Was Ya-ma-ni a Cypriot?" *FO* 14 (1972): 207–18; idem, "The Ashdod Stele of Sargon II," *FO* 17 (1976): 87–99; idem, "The Oldest Account of Sargon II's Campaign against Ashdod," *FO* 24 (1987): 29–39; Nadav Na'aman, "Ahaz's and Hezekiah's Policy toward Assyria in the Days of Sargon II and Sennacherib's Early Years" [Hebrew], *Zion* 59 (1994): 5–30 ; idem, "Hezekiah and the Kings of Assyria," *TA* 21 (1994): 235–54.

VII.b: K.1668 + col. IV' (lines 1–8a)
Because [he (Azuri) committed crimes . . .] from As[hdod . . .] Aḫimiti [. . .]
I promoted his favorite brother (Aḫimiti) ov[er the people of Ashdod] and
I [placed him on the throne of his father]. I imposed on him tribute and
tax[es . . .] as [former] kings [. . .].

(lines 8b–25a)
Now they, the evil [Hittites], in [. . .] plotted evil [. . .] to withhold tribute.
[Against] their princes they started a rebellion (and) insur[rection]; and
they caused him (Azuri) to get out [of Ashdod] like a shedder of blood.
Yamani, a *ḫupšu* man, [. . .] [. . .] [they plac]ed over them [. . .] They
caused [him] to sit [on the throne] of his lord. Their city [. . .] [. . .] battle
[. . .] [. . .] [. . .] [. . .] in its vicinity, a moat [. . .] 20 cubits (8.88 meters)
in depth [they dug] that reached ground water.

(lines 25b–33a)
To the [kings] of Philistia, Judah, E[dom], Moab, who live by the sea, bear-
ers of tri[bute and] gifts to Ashur, my lord, <they sent> words of falsehood
(and) treacherous speech to incite enmity with me.[24] To Pharaoh, king of
Egypt, a prince who could not save them, they brought their goodwill
gifts and implored his alliance.

(lines 33b–48)
(But) I Sargon, the legitimate ruler, who fears the oath of Shamash (and)
Marduk, who observes the commands of Ashur, I caused my troops to
cross over the Tigris (and) Euphrates Rivers at full springtime flood as
though on dry land. Now Yamani himself, their king, who trusted in his
own power, (and) did not submit to my lordship, heard the advance of
my troops from afar, and the radiance of Ashur, my lord, overwhelmed
him; and [. . .] on the bank of the river [. . .] deep water [. . .] he took?
[. . .] [. . .] far away [. . .] he fled [. . .] [. . . A]shdod [. . .] [. . .]

Here Judah is mentioned in connection with other southern Levantine
states to whom seditious messages were sent by the leaders of a rebellion
in Ashdod who had installed a *ḫupšu* man,[25] Yamani, as their new king.
These same leaders had also sent their goodwill gifts (*šul-man-na-šú-nu
iš-šu-ú-ma*) to Pharaoh, king of Egypt (*ᵐPi-ir-ʾu-u š[á]r* KUR *Mu-uṣ-ri*),
most likely Shabako, and implored his alliance (*e-ter-ri-šu-uš ki-it-ra*) (lines

---

[24] For this difficult sentence, see Fuchs, *Annalen des Jahres 711 v. Chr.,* 74; and
K. Lawson Younger Jr., "Recent Study on Sargon II, King of Assyria: Implications
for Biblical Studies," in *Mesopotamia and the Bible* (JSOTSup 341; ed. M. W.
Chavalas and K. L. Younger Jr.; Sheffield: Sheffield Academic Press, 2002), 288–329.

[25] For *ḫupšu,* see Richard S. Hess, "The Bible and Alalakh," in Chavalas and
Younger, *Mesopotamia and the Bible,* 208–20.

30b–33a). Thus the leaders of the rebellion in Ashdod were attempting to create a *kitru*-alliance, just as the leaders of Ekron attempted to do in the days of Sennacherib (see the discussion of this motif below).

However, no alliance formed, and none of these states supported the rebels in Ashdod, except for the Philistine city of Gath (Gimtu), which may have been simply part of Ashdod's territory (at least this is how the reference in Sargon's Great Summary Inscription is understood by many scholars). In fact, a few years earlier "Azuri, the king of Ashdod, plotted in his heart to withhold tribute, and he sent (messages) to the neighboring kings, hostile to Assyria" (Annals, lines 249–250; Great Summary Inscription, lines 90–92). But there was no support forthcoming in this instance, and Sargon states rather matter of factly that he simply removed Azuri and replaced him with Aḥimiti.[26] In any case, Sargon dealt with the Yamani rebellion apparently through his *turtānu* besieging and conquering Ashdod, Gath (Gimtu), and Ashdod-Yam.[27] These are the only places specifically mentioned in connection with this campaign against Ashdod.[28] The only biblical text to mention Sargon by name is Isa 20:1, which refers to this military action, stating: "In the year that the commander-in-chief [*tartān*], who was sent by King Sargon of Assyria, came to Ashdod and fought against it and took it" (NRSV). This is confirmed by the Eponym Chronicle, which notes that Sargon stayed "in the land."[29]

In his landmark article of 1958, Hayim Tadmor argued that the Assyrian army conquered Gath, Gibbethon, and Ekron on its way to Ashdod and Ashdod-Yam and that after the capture of Ashdod, Azekah was assaulted and captured.[30] Tadmor based his argument on two reliefs in Sargon's

---

[26] See Andreas Fuchs, "Aḫi-Mīti," *PNA* 1:65.

[27] See the Annals (lines 258b–259a) and the Great "Summary" Inscription (lines 103b–105a). See Fuchs, *Die Inschriften Sargons II,* 197, 185; *COS* 2.118A:293–94; 2.118E:296–97.

[28] Both Ashdod and Ashdod-Yam show clear evidence of conquest. At Ashdod, approximately three thousand individuals were excavated in several mass burials in Stratum VIII within Area D. Some of these skeletons display evidence of decapitations, a not uncommon Assyrian practice after the capture of rebellious cities. See Moshe Dothan, *Ashdod II–III: The Second and Third Seasons of Excavations 1963, 1965, Soundings in 1967* (ʿAtiqot English Series 9–10; Jerusalem: Department of Antiquities and Museums in the Ministry of Education and Culture; Department of Archaeology, Hebrew University; Israel Exploration Society, 1971), 1:92–94, 101, 212–14; idem, "Ashdod," *NEAEHL* 1:93–102; Jacob Kaplan, "Ashdod-Yam," *NEAEHL* 1:102–3.

[29] Alan Millard, *The Eponyms of the Assyrian Empire 910–612 BC* (SAAS 2; Helsinki: Neo-Assyrian Text Corpus Project, 1994), 47, 60.

[30] Hayim Tadmor, "The Campaigns of Sargon II of Assur: A Chronological-Historical Study," *JCS* 12 (1958): 22–40; 77–100, esp. 80-85; idem, "Philistia under

palace: Gabbutunu (Gibbethon) and ʿAmqarruna (Ekron) (Room V, reliefs 5, 10). That the epigraphs identify these two cities is clear; that they belong to the 712 campaign rather than the 720 campaign is not clear. In fact, in contrast to Tadmor, in the most recent study of this matter, John Russell argues in favor of the one-campaign-per-room hypothesis that understands the reliefs of Gabbutunu and ʿAmqarruna to date to the 720 campaign.[31]

Recently it has been suggested that the Azekah Inscription depicts events in the context of Sargon's campaign against Ashdod in 712/711 B.C.E.[32] However, as stated above, there is no evidence that the campaign of 712 in any way involved Judah. Moreover, as noted above, Isa 20:1 refers to the Assyrian action against Ashdod in 712/711. Surely the prophet would have mentioned the Assyrian conquest of the Judahite city of Azekah if it had actually occurred in this context, since it would have served as a more powerful object lesson than the Philistine city of Ashdod.[33] As already argued above, the Nimrud Inscription's record of Judah's subjugation, based on the inscription's date, refers to the 720 B.C.E. campaign. Thus there is really no evidence of Judah's involvement in Ashdod's rebellion with the resultant, typical Assyrian reprisal.

Fortunately, the recent publication of the Tang-i Var inscription by Grant Frame has clarified one important item about this campaign.[34] Yamani, the rebel king of Ashdod, had fled at the very first sign of the Assyrian army to the border of Egypt and Ethiopia (Meluḫḫa), where he consequently lived "like a thief." Prior to the publication of the Tang-i Var

---

Assyrian Rule," *BA* 29 (1966): 92–95; idem, "On the Use of Aramaic in the Assyrian Empire: Three Observations on a Relief of Sargon II" [Hebrew], *ErIsr* 20 (1989): 249–52.

[31] John M. Russell, *The Writing on the Wall: Studies in the Architectural Context of Late Assyrian Palace Inscriptions* (Winona Lake, Ind.: Eisenbrauns, 1999), 114–23. See also Younger, "Fall of Samaria," 475–76 with bibliography; and Beatrice André-Salvini, "Remarques sur les inscriptions des reliefs du palais du Khorsabad," in *Khorsabad, le palais de Sargon II, roi d'Assyrie: Actes du colloque organisé au musée du Louvre par le Service culturel les 21 et 22 janvier 1994* (ed. A. Caubet; Louvre conférences et colloques; Paris: La documentation Française, 1995), 15–45.

[32] Galil, "Judah and Assyria in the Sargonid Period," 111–33; idem, "Conflicts between Assyrian Vassals," 55–63; idem, "New Look at the 'Azekah Inscription,'" 321–29. The argument for this date is based on the attribution of the inscription to Sargon II rather than to Sennacherib and on the problematic reading in line 5' (see note 18 above). See also Younger, "Recent Study on Sargon II," 316–17. For a translation of the Azekah inscription, see *COS* 2.119:300–305.

[33] See Frahm, *Einleitung in die Sanherib-Inschriften,* 231.

[34] Grant Frame, "The Inscription of Sargon II at Tang-i Var," *Or* 68 (1999): 31–57 and pls. i–xviii.

inscription, all we knew was that the king of Ethiopia had been "overwhelmed" by the fearful splendor of Sargon's majesty and in panic had chained Yamani and sent him to Sargon (Great Summary Inscription, lines 109b–112; Small Summary Inscription, line 14). But now, with the publication of this new inscription, we know that the king who returned Yamani to Sargon was Shabataka/Shebitku (written Šapataku᾽). Thus the Tang-i Var inscription indicates that Shabataka/Shebitku was already ruler by 706, at least four years earlier than has generally been thought.[35]

In 706, Sargon completed his new capital, Dūr-Šarrukin, requiring the western kings to attend its dedication.[36] Hezekiah may very well have made the trek to visit this impressive new capital. However, a year later Sargon was suddenly and unexpectedly killed on the battlefield while campaigning in Anatolia. His death rocked the ancient world. Outside of Assyria, the impact was so great that the song of Isa 14:4b–21, applied secondarily to a king of Babylon,[37] asserted that his fall was heard in the very depths of Sheol and roused the Rephaim into sarcastic rejoicing.[38] Thus, almost immediately revolts occurred throughout the empire.

Within Assyria there was great consternation, not only because Sargon was the first and only Assyrian king killed on the battlefield, but also because he had not received a proper burial (his body was either in enemy

---

[35] Ibid., 52–54; and Donald B. Redford, "A Note on the Chronology of Dynasty 25 and the Inscription of Sargon II at Tang-i Var," *Or* 68 (1999): 58–60. For a possible co-regency of Shabako and Shabataka, see Hoffmeier's essay in this volume; Frank J. Yurco, "The Shabaka-Shebitku Coregency and the Supposed Second Campaign of Sennacherib against Judah: A Critical Assessment," *JBL* 110 (1991): 35–45; Kenneth A. Kitchen, "Regnal and Genealogical Data of Ancient Egypt (Absolute Chronology I). The Historical Chronology of Ancient Egypt, A Current Assessment," in *The Synchronisation of Civilisations in the Eastern Mediterranean in the Second Millennium B.C.: Proceedings of an International Symposium at Schloss Haindorf, 15th–17th of November 1996 and at the Austrian Academy, Vienna, 11th–12th of May 1998* (ed. M. Bietak; Vienna: Österreichischen Akademie der Wissenschaften, 2000), 29–42, esp. 40–41.

[36] Great Summary Inscription, lines 177–179; Fuchs, *Die Inschriften Sargons II,* 355.

[37] Isaiah himself may have called Sargon king of Babylon, since Sargon spent 710–707 B.C.E. ruling in Babylon—even reckoning his regal years on this basis (Cyprus Stela, lines 21–22; see Winckler, *Die Keilschrifttexte Sargons,* 180–81). Although this is possible, the original taunt seems to be used in the present context of Isaiah as a prophetic judgment on Babylon.

[38] Harold L. Ginsberg, "Reflexes of Sargon in Isaiah after 715 B.C.E.," in *Essays in Memory of E. A. Speiser* (ed. W. W. Hallo; New Haven: American Oriental Society, 1968), 47–53; William R. Gallagher, "On the Identity of Hêlēl Ben Šāḥar of Isa. 14:12–15," *UF* 26 (1994): 131–46.

hands or lost on the battlefield). This provoked an inquiry by Sennacherib through extispicy concerning "Sargon's Sin"[39] in order to determine what had caused him to be killed and not buried in his home. The result was the abandonment of Sargon's new capital of Dūr-Šarrukin and the strengthening of the opponents of his Babylonian policies.

This brings us to Sennacherib's invasion of 701 B.C.E. From the Assyriological side, we are happily in a much better situation to study this invasion than we were even just five years ago. First, there is a very helpful new study of Sennacherib's inscriptions by Eckart Frahm that also gives us an edition of the Rassam Cylinder, which dates to 700 B.C.E., only a year after the invasion itself.[40] Second, we have the new translations of Mordechai Cogan of the Rassam Cylinder and the Azekah Inscription in the second volume of *The Context of Scripture* (*COS* 2.119:300–305). Third, we have an excellent new monograph by William Gallagher that gives us the most recent full-length study devoted specifically to Sennacherib's Third Campaign.[41]

The accession of Sennacherib symbolized in many ways the start of a new phase of the Assyrian impact on western Asia.[42] In fact, as William Hallo has observed:

> No longer did the Assyrian army march annually toward new conquests. Only eight campaigns, plus two conducted by his generals, marked the twenty-four years of his reign, and the royal annalists made no attempt

---

[39] See Hayim Tadmor et al., "The Sin of Sargon and Sennacherib's Last Will," *SAAB* 3 (1989): 3–51, esp. 9–24; and Alasdair Livingstone, *Court Poetry and Literary Miscellanea* (SAA 3; Helsinki: Helsinki University Press, 1989), 77–79.

[40] The exemplars of Sennacherib's Annals arranged according to date are: the Rassam Cylinder (700 B.C.E.; Frahm, *Einleitung in die Sanherib-Inschriften,* 47–61); Cylinder C (697 B.C.E.; ibid., 66–68 [= Cylinder T]); the Heidel Prism (694 B.C.E.; Alexander Heidel, "The Octogonal Sennacherib Prism in the Iraq Museum," *Sumer* 9 [1953]: 117–88); the King Prism (694 B.C.E.; Leonard W. King, *Cuneiform Texts 26* [London: British Museum, 1909], pls. 1–39); the Jerusalem Prism (691 B.C.E.; Ling-Israel, "Sennacherib Prism," 213–48 and pls. i–xvi); the Taylor Prism (691 B.C.E.; see the Chicago Prism); and the Chicago Prism (689 B.C.E.; Riekele Borger, *BAL*[2] 1:64–88, 132–40, esp. 73–77). See also Louis D. Levine, "Preliminary Remarks on the Historical Inscriptions of Sennacherib," in *History, Historiography and Interpretation: Studies in Biblical and Cuneiform Literatures* (ed. H. Tadmor and M. Weinfeld; Jerusalem: Magnes, 1983), 58–75; and Mario Liverani, "Critique of Variants and the Titulary of Sennacherib," in *Assyrian Royal Inscriptions: New Horizons in Literary, Ideological and Historical Analysis* (ed. F. M. Fales; Orientis Antiqui Collectio 17; Rome: Istituto per l'oriente, 1981), 225–57.

[41] William R. Gallagher, *Sennacherib's Campaign to Judah: New Studies* (SHCANE 18; Leiden: Brill, 1999).

[42] Jana Pečírková, "Assyria under Sennacherib," *ArOr* 61 (1993): 1–10.

to edit the record (as they had with Sargon) in order to make it appear otherwise.[43]

Except for this campaign, Sennacherib did not personally initiate any campaign of expansion in the west.[44] The only campaign of expansion resulting in territorial annexation (his second campaign) was in the east, in the mountainous land of the Kassites. Thus Tadmor concludes: "All and all, Sennacherib was overtly not an expansionist. Throughout his reign, the Assyrian borders remained more or less the same. In some places (such as Philistia) they even shrank slightly."[45]

Hence the new *pax Assyriaca* stabilized the relations of Assyria and her western vassals to some extent. Whereas there were no less than six major Assyrian campaigns to the west in the preceding forty years prior to Sennacherib's accession, there were only three of comparable magnitude in the nearly sixty years that followed: Sennacherib's invasion of the Levant in 701, Esarhaddon's capture of Sidon in 677, and the more or less continuous decade of warfare in and against Egypt by Esarhaddon and Ashurbanipal (673–663).[46]

There can be no doubt that one of the significant impacts of Assyria on Judah in the late eighth century was literary. The very literature of the Hebrew Bible reflects this impact at various points. Many of these, especially in the context of First Isaiah, have been convincingly demonstrated by Peter Machinist.[47] Space does not allow for rehearsing all of them again here.

Gallagher's study is especially important as it reminds us of two things: first, the importance of studying Sennacherib's campaign against Judah in the larger context of his third campaign as well as his inscriptions in general; and second, the importance of studying the various literary aspects of the Assyrian inscriptions. Biblical scholars have, in numerous instances, ignored these two important factors. Often they read only the portion of the third campaign directly addressing Sennacherib's dealings with Hezekiah (plethora are the commentaries and

---

[43] Hallo and Simpson, *Ancient Near East,* 137.

[44] Tadmor, "World Dominion," 61. In order to suppress revolts in the northwestern regions of the empire, Sennacherib's generals led two military operations (one to Cilicia, especially aimed at Tarsus, in 696; the other to the border of Tabal in 695).

[45] Ibid.

[46] Hallo and Simpson, *Ancient Near East,* 138.

[47] Peter Machinist, "Assyria and Its Image in First Isaiah," *JAOS* 103 (1983): 719–37.

textbooks that quote only this portion of Oppenheim's now-outdated translation from *ANET*), and frequently these scholars employ a reading strategy that simplistically accepts Sennacherib's account; while at the same time, they employ a critical reading to the biblical material.[48] More sophisticated readings need to be applied to both the Annals and the biblical material.

The Assyrian royal inscriptions, like the biblical texts, use impositional structures to emplot their narratives. When the entire third campaign is taken into consideration (see table 10.1 below), it is clear that there are two phases, with the first phase setting the stage for the second. The first phase, directed against Phoenicia, clarified who was loyal and disloyal among the kings of the west, for at the end of this phase only three rebels remained in the southern Levant: Ṣidqa of Ashkelon, the noblemen of Ekron, and Hezekiah of Judah. The second phase—the remainder of the third campaign—was directed at defeating these remaining rebels.

Moreover, there are a number of clear interlinks between the phases. For example, Luli, the king of Sidon—the first king mentioned in the third campaign—is personally overwhelmed by the fear of the splendor of Sennacherib's lordship (*pul-ḫi me-lam-me be-lu-ti-ia is-ḫu-pu-šu-ma;* Rassam 32b) and Hezekiah, the Judahite—the last ruler mentioned in the third campaign—is personally overwhelmed by the fear of the splendor of Sennacherib's lordship (*pu-ul-ḫi me-lam-me be-lu-ti-ia is-ḫu-pu-šu-ma;* Rassam 55a). Thus the two episodes concerning Luli and Hezekiah (the Sidon Episode * A and the Judahite Episode * A; see table 10.1) form an *inclusio* for the narration of the entire campaign and reinforce the message that the fear of the splendor of Sennacherib's lordship is overwhelming to his enemies.

In addition, there are three episodes (one in phase one, two in phase two) that utilize three thematic elements to build up the narrative: A (personal effect on the enemy king), B (capture of cities), and C (governmental change and imposition of tribute). The threefold repetition of these elements (never in the same order) emphasizes the power of the Assyrian king to overcome enemy kings (Luli, Phoenician; Ṣidqa, Philistine; Hezekiah, Judahite) and impose his will upon each region. The second episode of phase one is unique within the campaign, since it records the submission of the eight kings of Amurru with their payment of four years' back tribute. The second episode of phase two is also unique in that it describes a rebellion

---

[48] See Ian W. Provan, "In the Stable with Dwarves: Testimony, Interpretation, Faith and the History of Israel," in *Congress Volume: Oslo, 1998* (ed. A. Lemaire and M. Sæbø; VTSup 80; Leiden: Brill, 2000), 281–319, esp. 311–12.

Table 10.1: Structure of the Third Campaign

Phase One: Phoenicia (Rassam, 32–38)
1. The Sidon Episode (Rassam, 32–35)
*   A   *Personal effect on the enemy king:* Luli's personal fear (Rassam 32)
            Focus: Luli's personal fear overwhelms him (Rassam, 32a)
            Result: he flees into the midst of the sea (Rassam, 32b)
        B   *Capture of cities:* Luli's cities are overwhelmed (Rassam, 33–34)
        C   *Governmental change and imposition of tribute:* the installation of
            Tuba'alu with tribute imposed (Rassam, 35)
2. The Vassal King Episode (Rassam, 36–38)—at Ushu (Bull 4, 19–20)
    Submission of the eight kings of Amurru with their gifts (four years'
    back tribute)

Phase Two: Southern Levant: Philistia and Judah (Rassam, 39–58)
1. The Ashkelon Episode (Rassam, 39–41)
        A   *Personal effect on the enemy king:* Ṣidqa's removal and deportation
            (Rassam, 39)
        C   *Governmental change and imposition of tribute:* the installation of
            Šarru-lu-dari with tribute imposed (Rassam, 40)
        B   *Capture of cities:* Ṣidqa's cities are captured and plundered (Rassam,
            41)
2. The Ekron Episode (including Egyptian involvement) (Rassam, 42–48)
        D   *Ekronite rebellion:* officials, nobles and people remove Padi (Rassam,
            42–43a)
        E   *Egyptian involvement·* the battle of Eltekeh (Rassam, 43b–46a)
        D   *Ekronite rebellion crushed:* officials, nobles and people punished;
            Padi restored and imposition of tribute (Rassam, 46b–48)
3. The Judahite Episode (Rassam, 49–58)
        B   *Capture of cities:* Hezekiah's cities captured and plundered (Rassam,
            49–51)
            Focus on Hezekiah: conquest of his 46 cities (Rassam, 49–50)
            Result: plundering of these cities (Rassam, 51)
        C   *Governmental change and imposition of tribute:* Hezekiah's capital—
            Jerusalem (Rassam, 52–54)
            Focus on Hezekiah: siege of his capital city—Jerusalem (Rassam,
            52)
            Result: reduction of his land and tribute imposed (Rassam,
            53–54)
*   A   *Personal effect on the enemy king:* Hezekiah's personal fear (Rassam,
            55–58)
            Focus on Hezekiah: personal fear overwhelms him (Rassam, 55a)
            Result: Hezekiah's tribute is sent after Sennacherib (Rassam,
            55b–58)

against a legitimate king with the alliance of another power. This presents a special problem that the Assyrian king also overcomes so that right order is restored and proper tribute is once again imposed. Interestingly, it is this theme of "tribute" (spelled out by the use of various different Assyrian terms) that is found in all five episodes and thus unifies the campaign.

Phase two is clearly demarcated by the chiastic structuring of the elements A, C, B in the Ashkelon Episode and B, C, A in the Judahite Episode. The middle episode is structured so that issues of the Ekronite rebellion (D, D) are narrated on either side of the centered account of the Egyptian involvement and the battle of Eltekeh (E). The placement of this account here at the very center of phase two serves to heighten the achievement of victory of the Assyrian monarch in this "superpower" open-field battle.

While the overall chronology of the "third campaign" follows the general outline of events, it is not strict (i.e., some events are presented out of order).[49] In fact, Tadmor has argued that the scribes developed the account of the third campaign in stages from the easy victories to the harder ones.[50] This order of events created a literary effect, slowly increasing the tension by progressing from the easy to the difficult. It also placed all the incidents showing the Assyrian king's invincibility together, thus impressing this all the more onto the minds of readers.[51] This is helpful to keep in mind as one comes to the longer and climactic account of Hezekiah at the end of the campaign.[52]

---

[49] Two examples can be cited. It is obvious that Sennacherib could not have exiled Ṣidqa, king of Ashkelon, before he arrived in Philistia, but the account of Ṣidqa's stubbornness is introduced first, just after the submission of the other rulers from Amurru. The point is that these others hastened to pay their tribute and thus avoided disaster while Ṣidqa did not. The text goes on to recount how Sennacherib's army conquered Joppa and its immediate hinterland, territory subservient to Ṣidqa. Another example is the return of Padi to his throne. This would hardly have been accomplished right after the conquest of Ekron; it must have taken place after Hezekiah had already seen the handwriting on the wall and decided to placate the invader.

[50] Tadmor, "Sennacherib's Campaign to Judah," 71, 73.

[51] Gallagher, *Sennacherib's Campaign to Judah,* 117.

[52] Elnathan Weissert ("Creating a Political Climate: Literary Allusions to *Enūma Eliš* in Sennacherib's Account of the Battle of Halule," in *Assyrien im Wandel der Zeiten* [ed. H. Waetzoldt and H. Hauptmann; RAI 39; Heidelberger Studien zum alten Orient 6; Heidelberg: Heidelberger Orientverlag, 1997], 191–202, esp. 195) points out that the siege of Jerusalem (the third campaign), the passage to Mount Nipur (the fifth campaign), and the account of the battle of Halule (the eighth campaign) are the major rhetorical peaks in Sennacherib's Annals.

In the final, climactic Judahite episode, there is a threefold division in which the focus is squarely on Hezekiah, introduced by the phrases: *ša* ^m*Ḫazaqiau* (line 49), *šâšu* (line 52), and *šū* ^m*Ḫazaqiau* (line 55). Each division stresses a different item with a corresponding result: the conquest of his forty-six cities with resultant plundering (lines 49–51), the siege of Jerusalem with resultant reduction of his land and imposition of tribute (lines 52–54), and the personal fear of Hezekiah with the resultant tribute sent after Sennacherib (lines 55–58).

As many scholars have pointed out, in the process of interpretation it is important to consider the ideological and propagandistic elements of the Assyrian royal inscriptions. It is also important to consider the narrative's emplotment along cultural and religious lines.[53]

For example, in Sennacherib's Annals, the entire Ekron episode (including the battle of Eltekeh) is loaded with religious phrases that cast the conflict into the cosmic realm. This is primarily accomplished by a number of literary allusions to the Legend of Etana.[54] Thus there is a significant contrast built between two alliances: one, holy; the other, unholy. A holy oath and covenantal alliance (*adê* and *māmītu*) had been established by the

---

[53] Technically, the term *ideology* would include cultural and religious world-view orientations. But *ideology* is often used with a purely *political* nuance. For a recent discussion, see Michael Freeden, "Ideology, " in *Routledge Encyclopedia of Philosophy* (ed. E. Craig; 10 vols.; London: Routledge, 1998), 4:681–85. The interrelationship between Assyrian political and religious aspects is summed up by A. Kirk Grayson ("Assyrian Rule of Conquered Territory in Ancient Western Asia," *CANE* 2:962): "Thus, ideologically the continued expansion of Assyria's rule of foreign territory became an essential part of the political structure of the Neo-Assyrian Empire. Linked very closely with this motivation was religious zeal. The king was the vice-regent of the state god Asshur, and all the king's acts, including his military achievements, were carried out on behalf of the god. Thus when the monarch conquered a new territory, he did so 'with the support of the god Asshur.'" On the divine royal interchange, see Beate Pongratz-Leisten, "The Interplay of Military Strategy and Cultic Practice in Assyrian Politics," in *Assyria 1995: Proceedings of the Tenth Anniversary Synoposium of the Neo-Assyrian Text Corpus Project Helsinki, September 7–11, 1995* (ed. S. Parpola and R. M. Whiting; Helsinki: Neo-Assyrian Text Corpus Project, 1997), 245–52; idem, *Herrschaftswissen in Mesopotamien* (SAAS 10; Helsinki: Neo-Assyrian Text Corpus Project, 1999); Frederick M. Fales and Giovanni B. Lanfranchi, "The Impact of Oracular Material on the Political Utterances and Political Action in the Royal Inscriptions of the Sargonid Dynasty," in *Oracles et prophéties dans l'antiquité: actes du colloque de Strasbourg 15–17 juin 1995* (ed. J.-G. Heintz; Travaux du Centre de Recherche sur le Proche-Orient et la Grèce Antiques 15; Paris: De Boccard, 1997), 99–114.

[54] As pointed out by Gallagher (*Sennacherib's Campaign to Judah*, 120–21).

king of Assyria with Padi the king of Ekron.[55] Such oaths had divine sanction, and violating them was a sacrilegious transgression with serious consequences for the desecraters. Thus the rulers of Ekron committed *anzillu* ("an abomination") by disregarding this holy alliance and removing Padi. The term *anzillu* is normally found in magical texts, wisdom literature, and penitential psalms, but it occurs here for the first time in Assyrian royal inscriptions. In the *Šurpu* incantations[56] and the Legend of Etana,[57] it describes the breaking of oaths (*māmītu*). In the legend (see *COS* 1.131:453–57), an eagle and a snake swear an oath (*māmītu*) before Shamash to be friends and to help one another. But after a period of mutual benefit, the eagle "plotted evil in its heart." In spite of warnings from its own young of the terrible consequences of breaking the oath of Shamash, the eagle then commits *anzillu* by breaking the oath and eating the snake's young. The eagle is said to have "harbored evil against his friend" (*mukīl lemutti ana ibrišu*). Grief-stricken, the snake prays to Shamash, the warrior, for justice in responding to the eagle's breach of the oath, and Shamash helps the snake take revenge on the eagle. Thus, like the eagle, the Ekronites have committed an *anzillu,* "an abomination," a sacrilegious transgression against the oath, and like the eagle they have betrayed friendship by handing Padi over to Hezekiah "like an enemy" (*nakriš*).

Having committed this sacrilege against a holy alliance, the Ekronites establish, in contrast, an unholy alliance between themselves and the Egyptians/Ethiopians (denoted by the use of the verb *katāru*).[58] Such

---

[55] Padi is now well attested. In addition to Sennacherib's inscriptions, two inscriptions from Tel Miqnê/Ekron attest to this king. The first is the now-famous Ekron Inscription of Akhayus (see *COS* 2.42:164). Another inscription from Ekron reads: *lbʿl wlpdy* "for Baʿal and for Padi." See Seymour Gitin and Mordechai Cogan, "A New Type of Dedicatory Inscription from Ekron," *IEJ* 49 (1999): 193–202. Padi (Pidi of Ekron) is apparently also mentioned in a docket for some silver from Nineveh. It was presumably attached as a label to the silver. See Frederick M. Fales and J. Nicholas Postgate, *Provincial and Military Administration* (part 2 of *Imperial Administrative Records;* SAA 11; Helsinki: Helsinki University Press, 1995), 42 (text no. 50).

[56] Erica Reiner, *Šurpu: A Collection of Sumerian and Akkadian Incantations* (AfOB 11; Graz: n.p., 1958), 43.

[57] J. V. Kinnier Wilson, *The Legend of Etana* (Warminster: Aris & Phillips, 1985), 32, I/C, line 4.

[58] Rassam 43 presents an interpretive difficulty in determining the subject of the verb *ikterūnimma*. There are three possibilities. (1) The subject is LUGAL.MEŠ-*ni*(*šarrānī*) KUR *Mu-ṣu-ri* "The kings (var. the king) of Egypt assembled the bowmen, chariots, and horses of the king of Meluhha, an army without number, and came to their assistance" (Nadav Naʾaman, "Sennacherib's Campaign and the

unholy alliances (*kitru*)[59] are usually depicted with the enemies coming together against the Assyrian king. The weaker party (here the Ekronites) often pays the stronger one with a "bribe" or "voluntary gift." Unlike the *adê,* the *kitru* alliance is unholy since it is based on selfish motives. It always reflects misplaced "trust."[60] In contrast, the Assyrian king "trusts" in Ashur. The *kitru* alliance normally consists of chaotic elements with unimaginable numbers of troops. The Assyrian king, who administers order, stands against it alone. The contrast between the two alliances means that the outcome is inevitable. Sennacherib, having his "trust" in Ashur, the protector of the *adê,* would easily defeat his overwhelming, numerically superior enemies and vanquish the *kitru* alliance.

Obviously, the story of the siege of Jerusalem in 2 Kgs 18–19 utilizes some of the same religious impositional structures as in the literary emplotment of the Ekron episode in Sennacherib's Annals. The religious overtones

---

Lmlk Stamps," *VT* 39 [1979]: 65; Anthony J. Spalinger, "Notes on the Military in Egypt during the XXVth Dynasty," *SSEAJ* 11 [1981]: 53). (2) The subject is LUGAL.MEŠ-*ni*(*šarrānī*) KUR *Mu-ṣu-ri* ˡúERIM.MEŠ(*ṣābī*) ᴳⁱˢBAN(*qašti*) ᴳⁱˢGIGIR.MEŠ(*narkabāti*) ANŠE.KUR.RA.MEŠ (*sīsî*) *ša* LUGAL KUR *Me-luḫ-ḫa* "the kings of Egypt, (and) the bowmen, chariot corps, and cavalry of the kings of Ethiopia assembled a countless force and came to their (i.e., the Ekronites') aid" (Cogan, *COS* 2.119B:303). (3) The subject is ˡúGÌR.ARAD.MEŠ(*šakkanakki*) ˡúNUN.MEŠ(*rubê*) *ù* UN.MEŠ(*nišī*) ᵁᴿᵁ*Am-qar-ru-na* "(As for) the city officials, rulers and people of Ekron ... their hearts became afraid ... and against me they banded together with the kings of Egypt, the troops, bowmen, chariots, and horses of the king of Meluhha, a force without number, and they went to their (the Ekronites') aid" (Gallagher, *Sennacherib's Campaign to Judah,* 116). He argues (ibid., n. 16): "Liverani 1982:43–66 showed that the party in trouble usually enlists the aid of a stronger party. Since the Ekronites are in trouble here, they are the subject of *katāru.*"

A point in favor of this third understanding is the analogy of Rassam 45, which reads: ˡúEN(*bēl*) ᴳⁱˢGIGIR.MEŠ(*narkabāti*) *ù* DUMU.MEŠ(*māri*) LUGAL.MEŠ KUR *Mu-ṣu-ra-a-a a-di* ˡúEN(*bēl*) ᴳⁱˢGIGIR.MEŠ(*narkabāti*) *ša* LUGAL KUR *Me-luḫ-ḫa bal-ṭu-su-un i-na* MURAB₄(*qabal*) *tam-ḫa-ri ik-šu-da* ŠU.II(*qātā*)-*a-a* "My hands captured alive in the midst of the battle the charioteers and princes of the kings of Egypt, together with the charioteers of the king of Ethiopia." Note the contrast: "they (the Ekronites) allied together X, Y, etc." :: "my hands (Sennacherib) captured X, Y, etc." Basically, the same direct object is fronted in both sentences.

[59] For *kitru* alliances, see Mario Liverani, "*Kitru, Katāru,*" *Mesopotamia* 17 (1982): 43–66.

[60] On the theme of the enemy's misplaced trust, see Chaim Cohen, "Neo-Assyrian Elements in the First Speech of the Biblical Rab-Shaqeh," *IOS* 9 (1979): 32–48, esp. 39–41; and Francolino J. Gonçalves, *L'expédition de Sennachérib en Palestine dans la littérature hébraïque ancienne* (EBib 7; Paris: Gabalda; Leuven: Peeters, 1986), 410–12.

with the issue of "trust in the deity"[61] playing a significant role in each demonstrate the inherent religious or theological flavor of all ancient Near Eastern history writing.

Interestingly, the Annals blame the Ekronite rulers for the *kitru* alliance, even though Hezekiah is clearly involved. Not only is he mentioned in connection with the Ekron episode, but the use of the term *ikkibu* to describe Jerusalem as a type of "taboo" place in the description of the siege of the city (Rassam, line 52) is a subtle literary connection back to the *anzillu* ("abomination") of the rulers of Ekron, since the two terms are sometimes paired. According to Malku IV 71–74, *ikkibu* is equated with *anzillu,* and in *Šurpu* VIII 79 NíG.GIG(*ikkibu*) equals *anzillu.* Thus the Hezekiah episode is subtly linked to the Ekron episode and the *kitru* alliance.

It is clear that Hezekiah was a major leader (if not the major leader) in the rebellion in the west, for according to the Assyrians he had meddled in Philistine affairs. It may be significant that the Rassam Cylinder lacks the phrase "who had not submitted to my yoke" for Hezekiah (found later in the Chicago/Taylor prisms, line 19). He was in a different category of enmity with Sennacherib than merely refusing to pay tribute.[62] Through the imprisonment of Padi and his attacks on pro-Assyrian cities in Philistia,[63] Hezekiah had made himself Sennacherib's public enemy number one.

Yet it was the rulers of Ekron who experienced the worst possible fate after the capitulation of their city, while Ṣidqa and especially Hezekiah were punished relatively mildly. By literarily heightening the significance of the rulers of Ekron to the formation of the *kitru* alliance and by emphasizing the punishment meted out upon them, Sennacherib's scribes were able to demonstrate the severe consequences of defying an Assyrian oath and forming a *kitru* alliance without having to explain the lack of such severe punishment upon the primary opponent, Hezekiah.

Ironically, while the rulers of Ekron received the worst punishment, the remainder of the Ekronites received pardon. In addition, the archaeological evidence makes it abundantly clear that Ekron prospered during the next century of Assyrian rule.[64] In contrast, while Hezekiah escaped the

---

[61] John W. Olley, "'Trust in the Lord': Hezekiah, Kings and Isaiah," *TynBul* 50 (1999): 59–77.

[62] Gallagher, *Sennacherib's Campaign to Judah,* 38.

[63] See Siegfried Mittmann, "Eine prophetische Totenklage des Jahres 701 v. Chr. (Micha 1:3–5a.8–13a.14–16)," *JNSL* 25 (1999): 31–60.

[64] Seymour Gitin, "The Neo-Assyrian Empire and Its Western Periphery: The Levant, with Focus on Philistine Ekron," in Parpola and Whiting, *Assyria 1995,* 77–103.

worst that Sennacherib could have meted out to him personally, the state of Judah did not fare as well—certainly not experiencing the economic growth that Ekron did.[65]

While the ideological, propagandistic elements of another episode in Sennacherib's Annals is well known,[66] namely, the account of the battle of Halule, religious overtones are clearly manifest in that episode too. In a recent article, Elnatan Weissert has convincingly demonstrated that the scribes of the eighth campaign prism edition[67] transfigured the episode into the cosmic realm through five strong literary allusions to *Enuma Elish*. Thus the writer literally "demonizes" the enemy,[68] the inhabitants of Babylon and their unworthy leader Mushezib-Marduk. Through these allusions, the episode is transferred into the cosmic realm in which the Babylonians and Mushezib-Marduk parallel monstrous Tiamat and Kingu respectively,

---

[65] Whether the figure 200,150 in Sennacherib's Annals is accurate or not, the economic, social, religious, and psychological impact on Judah and Jerusalem must have been pronounced. Moreover, whatever the case with the figure, this appears to have been an unidirectional deportation (similar to Tiglath-pileser III's deportations in the northern kingdom; see K. Lawson Younger Jr., "The Deportations of the Israelites," *JBL* 117 [1998]: 201–27). For different approaches to this figure's nature and accuracy, see David M. Fouts, "Another Look at Large Numbers in Assyrian Royal Inscriptions," *JNES* 53 (1994): 205–11; Antti Laato, "Assyrian Propaganda and the Falsification of History in the Royal Inscriptions of Sennacherb," *VT* 45 (1995): 198–223; Walter Mayer, *Politik und Kriegskunst der Assyrer* (ALASP 9; Münster: Ugarit-Verlag, 1995); Alan Millard, "Large Numbers in the Assyrian Royal Inscriptions," in *Ah, Assyria . . . : Studies in Assyrian History and Ancient Near Eastern Historiography Presented to Hayim Tadmor* (ed. M. Cogan and I. Eph'al; ScrHier 33; Jerusalem: Magnes, 1991), 213–22; Na'aman, "Ahaz's and Hezekiah's Policy," 5–30; idem, "Hezekiah and the Kings of Assyria," 235–54; Bustenay Oded, "History vis-à-vis Propaganda in the Assyrian Royal Inscriptions," *VT* 48 (1998): 423–25; Marco de Odorico, *The Use of Numbers and Quantifications in the Assyrian Royal Inscriptions* (SAAS 3; Helsinki: Neo-Assyrian Text Corpus Project, 1995). The same type of numeric problem is found in the 185,000 figure of 2 Kgs 19:35 given for the Assyrian casualties ending Sennacherib's attack on Jerusalem.

[66] Antti Laato, "Hezekiah and the Assyrian Crisis in 701 B.C.," *SJOT* 1 (1987): 49–68; idem, "Assyrian Propaganda," 198–223.

[67] Weissert, "Creating a Political Climate," 191–202. The Chicago, Taylor, and Jerusalem prisms generally fall into Weissert's category, with the battle of Halule as the climax. The Walters Art Galley account, while not a prism, also records this eighth campaign, with Halule as its climax. For the battle tactics, see JoAnn Scurlock, "Neo-Assyrian Battle Tactics," in *Crossing Boundaries and Linking Horizons: Studies in Honor of Michael C. Astour on His Eightieth Birthday* (ed. G. D. Young et al.; Bethesda, Md.: CDL, 1997), 491–517.

[68] Describing them as *gallê lemnūti* "wicked demons."

who threaten cosmic law and order. These *Enuma Elish*–like characters are easily overcome by the hero, King Sennacherib.

However, there is an important twist. The Sargonid scribes equated their national god Ashur with the Babylonian primeval deity, Anshar, so that Ashur is frequently written AN.ŠAR. Behind this scribal innovation lies an ideological coup.[69] Thus the Assyrians showed that Ashur was not interchangeable with Marduk but superior to him, since Anshar was the older deity—and older is better; yet they did so within the Babylonian system of theogony. In this way, the Assyrians, as Machinist puts it, succeeded in "out-Babylonizing" the Babylonians.[70] Thus interestingly, Sennacherib does not parallel the hero of the Babylonian version of *Enuma Elish* (i.e., Marduk) but the hero of the Assyrianized version of *Enuma Elish,* the god Ashur-Anshar. This Assyrian version probably sees its completion in the latter part of Sennacherib's reign.[71] A form of this ideology is stated in the Marduk Ordeal: "It is said in *Enūma Eliš:* When heaven and earth were not yet created, Aššur (AN.ŠAR) came into being."[72] Finally, since the human Assyrian king conducting the battle of Halule is elevated to the status of divine hero fighting monstrous adversaries, it is only fitting and necessary that his instruments of war be likewise lifted to the rank of divine royalty.[73]

In light of Weissert's discussion, it is worth noting that there is a clear literary allusion to *Enuma Elish* in the narration of Sennacherib's third campaign. In the description of the chaotic elements of the *kitru* alliance (discussed above), the narrative describes the Egyptians' preparations for the battle of Eltekeh, stating that they "sharpened their weapons" (*uša⁾⁾alū kakkıšun,* line 44). As Gallagher has noted,[74] in *Enuma Elish* IV.92, the

---

[69] As pointed out by Livingstone, *Court Poetry and Literary Miscellanea,* xvii. See also Wilfred G. Lambert, "Göttergenealogie," *RlA* 3:469–71.

[70] Peter Machinist, "The Assyrians and Their Babylonian Problem: Some Reflections," *Wissenschaftskolleg zu Berlin, Jahrbuch* (1984): 353–64.

[71] Ibid., 356. It is possible that the Assyrian version was complete in the days of Sargon II, since there are clear allusions to *Enuma Elish* in his inscriptions (see Johannes Renger, "Neuassyrische Königsinschriften als Genre der Keilschriftliteratur— Zum Stil und zur Kompositionstechnik der Inschriften Sargons II von Assyrien, " in *Keilschriftliche Literaturen* (ed. K. Hecker and W. Sommerfeld; RAI 32; BBVO 6; Berlin: Reimar, 1986): 109–28, esp. 127 and n. 52). See Tadmor et al., "The Sin of Sargon," 3–51.

[72] Livingstone, *Court Poetry and Literary Miscellanea,* 82–86, text 34, line 54. There are two versions of the Marduk Ordeal, one from Ashur and the other from Nineveh and Calah (ibid., nos. 34 and 35).

[73] Weissert, "Creating a Political Climate," 196–97.

[74] Gallagher, *Sennacherib's Campaign to Judah,* 121.

gods who are allied with Tiamat also sharpen their weapons before her battle with Marduk (*u ilāni ša tāḫāzi ušaʾʾalūšunu kakkēšun*). Gallagher concludes: "The undertones of the king fighting against the forces of chaos were thus clear to those who knew Mesopotamian literature."[75]

The only open-field battle in the third campaign was the battle of Eltekeh.[76] There are two interrelated questions about this battle that are not clearly answered in the sources: When during the campaign did this battle occur? What, if any, is the relationship between the battle as recounted in Sennacherib's Annals and the report of Taharqa/Tirhakah in 2 Kgs 19:9?

The Assyrian account implies that the battle of Eltekeh occurred before the attack on Judah. However, if the report of Taharqa's approach in 2 Kgs 19:9 is connected with the battle, then the battle may have occurred after the Assyrian invasion of Judah had begun, as seemingly implied by the biblical text. This is the way some scholars have understood the order of events.

For example, Aharoni asserted the priority of the biblical text over Sennacherib's Annals.[77] For him the Annals are "more of a summary than a chronological account," and therefore "there can be no doubt that the biblical sequence is the more accurate." Thus while Sennacherib met the Egyptians on the plain of Eltekeh and claimed a great victory, since the biblical account credits the divine deliverance of Jerusalem at this point, the Annals may well be covering up for the true disaster (i.e., the defeat by the Egyptians under Taharqa/Tirhakah).[78]

---

[75] Ibid.

[76] Ibid. Gallagher suggests that the Judahites probably took part in it. This is not improbable, since participation in this battle by all the allies with their Egyptian partners certainly gave the alliance their best opportunity to defeat the Assyrians.

[77] Yohanan Aharoni, *The Land of the Bible: A Historical Geography* (trans. A. F. Rainey; rev. ed.; Philadelphia: Westminster, 1979), 388.

[78] Ibid., 392–93. On the chronological issues, see, on the one hand, Jurgen von Beckerath, "Ägypten und der Feldzug Sanheribs im Jahre 701 v. Chr.," *UF* 24 (1992): 3–8; idem, "Über chronologische Berührungspunkte der altägyptischen und der israelitischen Geschichte," in *"Und Mose schrieb dieses Lied auf": Studien zum Alten Testament und zum Alten Orient. Festschrift für Oswald Loretz zur Vollendung seines 70. Lebensjahres mit Beiträgen von Freunden, Schülern und Kollegen* (ed. M. Dietrich and I. Kottsieper; AOAT 250; Münster: Ugarit-Verlag, 1998), 91–99; and Leo Depuydt, "The Date of Piye's Egyptian Campaign and the Chronology of the Twenty-Fifth Dynasty," *JEA* 79 (1993): 269–74. On the other hand, see Kitchen, "Regnal and Genealogical Data"; and esp. Hoffmeier's essay in this volume. Also see Anson F. Rainey, "Taharqa and Syntax," *TA* 3 (1976): 38–41; Yurco, "The Shabaka-Shebitku Coregency," 35–45; Laszlo Török, *The Kingdom of Kush: Handbook of the Napatan-Meroitic Civilization* (HO 31; Leiden: Brill, 1997), 170–71.

However, for both the Assyrian annals and the biblical text, the question may be to what extent the chronological order has been rearranged for topical reasons. Galil feels that the attack on Philistia followed by the attack on Judah is an artificial distinction of the annals and that, in fact, operations against both Philistia and Judah were conducted simultaneously.[79]

Gallagher counters: "to some extent this is true, but I do not believe that the distinction between the invasion of Philistia and the invasion of Judah is completely artificial. I have assumed that the main Assyrian thrust was first against Philistia, then against Judah. Galil's reasoning led him to infer that the battle of Eltekeh occurred at a later stage of the campaign than the annals claim."[80] He lists five convincing reasons why the battle of Eltekeh must have occurred earlier in the campaign.[81] First, when the Annals diverge from the chronological order there is usually a good literary reason for doing so; those who hold that the chronological order of the annals has been so drastically altered do not give any reason for this rearrangement by the scribes. Second, if Eltekeh is Tell esh-Shallaf,[82] the battle was probably not fought there later in the war, since this would be too far north for the Assyrian army to have allowed the Egyptian army to penetrate at this point. The Assyrians would have wanted to intercept the Egyptians earlier in their northward progression. Third, there is no evidence that a battle with Taharqa/Tirhakah even occurred after the report of him reached Sennacherib. Fourth, if the Egyptians intervened later in the war, then they and their allies were incompetent strategists, or Egypt had a vacillating policy for Judah and Philistia. Having had ample time to prepare for the Assyrian invasion (705–701 B.C.E.), if the Egyptian intervention is connected to the report of Taharqa's approach, the Egyptians had waited until Lachish had been conquered, Ashkelon had capitulated, Ekron was being besieged or had been destroyed, and an Assyrian army was just outside Jerusalem. Neither Hezekiah nor the Philistines would have wanted the invasion to go this far, so why did Egyptian help arrive so late? Fifth, the Rabshakeh declares in his first speech that Egypt is a crushed reed (2 Kgs

---

[79] Gershon Galil, "Sennacherib versus Hezekiah: A New Look at the Assyrian Campaign to the West in 701 BCE" [Hebrew], *Zion* 53 (1988): 1–12, esp. 9.

[80] Gallagher, *Sennacherib's Campaign to Judah,* 11, 123–25.

[81] Ibid., 123–25.

[82] Eltekeh is identified with Tell esh-Shallaf or with Tell Melât. See Benjamin Mazar, "The Cities of the Territory of Dan," *IEJ* 10 (1960): 65–77, esp. 72–77; and Nadav Naʾaman, *Borders and Districts in Biblical Historiography* (Jerusalem Biblical Studies 4; Jerusalem: Simor, 1986), 108 n. 49. Eltekeh is part of the Danite allotment (Josh 19:40–48). Being listed independently in Sennacherib's Annals with Timnah reinforces the listing in Josh 19:43–44.

18:21), which is a phrase equivalent to Akkadian *qanâ ḫaṣāṣu/ḫuṣṣuṣu,* which occurs in similes of defeated enemies. It is possible that the scribes placed Ṣidqa's captivity before the conquest of Jaffa and the battle of Eltekeh so that the battle narrations would be less disrupted.[83]

Therefore, since the statements in Sennacherib's Annals and 2 Kgs 19:9 seem to refer to separate events, Kitchen has posited two Egyptian armies: one that fought and lost at Eltekeh and another under Taharqa/Tirhakah that approached the Philistine coast but retreated and did not engage the Assyrians.[84] This seems to be the most even-handed way to deal with the two different statements in the Assyrian and biblical records.[85]

Finally, what was the precise outcome of the battle? Gallagher feels that since the Assyrian victory over the Egyptians is expressed in standard, dry phrases (*ittišun amdaḫiṣma, aštakan dabdâšun*), perhaps the Assyrian victory was not as decisive as the annals claim.

> The account is meager compared to Sennacherib's account of his battle against Merodach-baladan and pursuit of the enemy is not mentioned at all, but rather the capture of two unimportant towns: Eltekeh and Timnah. The battle of Eltekeh was not a defeat for the Assyrians, but it destroyed some of their manpower and decreased morale. Perhaps calling the battle a stalemate would be more accurate.[86]

In other words, the battle of Eltekeh was tactically a victory, but strategically it was not. In this sense, perhaps the battle was a victory in an analogous way to the later Assyrian victory at the battle of Halule. The battle of Eltekeh was enough of a victory that the Assyrians consolidated their hold on the region. But it was a limited victory in that it did not provide a basis for any follow-up and exploitation beyond the immediate region; certainly it provided no basis for the invasion of Egypt. Further, the Egyptians,

---

[83] According to Tadmor, "Sennacherib's Campaign to Judah," 73. He also noted that the conquest of the four cities serves as a bridge to the next episode.

[84] Kenneth A. Kitchen, "Egypt, the Levant and Assyria in 701 B.C.," in *Fontes atque Pontes: Eine Festgabe für Hellmut Brunner* (ed. M. Görg; AAT 5; Wiesbaden: Harrassowitz, 1983), 243–53; idem, *The Third Intermediate Period in Egypt (1100–650 BC)* (2d ed.; Warminster, U.K.: Aris & Phillips, 1986), 154–61.

[85] Of course, if 2 Kgs 19:9 is anachronistic or the result of a confused author of the B1 source, then one only needs to deal with the chronological issues in the Assyrian annals (see Dion, "Sennacherib's Expedition to Palestine," 23–24; Anthony J. Spalinger, "The Foreign Policy of Egypt Preceding the Assyrian Conquest," *CdÉ* 53 [1978]: 22–47). But in light of the Egyptian evidence, it seems more likely that 2 Kgs 19:9 is proleptic. See Hoffmeier's essay in this volume.

[86] Gallagher, *Sennacherib's Campaign to Judah,* 121.

although defeated and unable to intervene in the deliverance of their allies from the bulk of the Assyrian onslaught, were not so badly defeated that they could not still exert influence in the region, so that the very "rumor" of an Egyptian advance still caused great concern for Sennacherib.

Another area in which religious influence can be detected in Sennacherib's Annals, specifically in the narration of the campaign against Hezekiah, comes from the genre of "queries to the sungod (Shamash)." As Assyria gained military supremacy, only rarely did her enemies dare to confront her in an open-field battle. As noted above, the battle of Eltekeh is the only such battle recorded for the third campaign. On account of Assyria's military superiority, her enemies were compelled to devise strategies for forcing the Assyrian army to conquer numerous cities in order to subjugate more territory.[87] But the Assyrian army developed various means of coping with these cities in order to conquer them quickly and efficiently.[88] This meant the development of many different techniques of accomplishing a breakthrough—whether through manpower, military equipment, or the like—as well as many other procedures for obtaining the capitulation of these resistant cities. Studying the Assyrian genre of "queries to the sungod (Shamash)," Israel Eph'al has observed that these texts often utilize a more or less comprehensive list of assorted techniques for conquering a city.[89] This was apparently done in order to cover the various contingencies as the Assyrians attempted to divine the outcome of their siege of a particular city. The compilation on page 260 is based on the queries.[90]

It is very interesting that both Sennacherib's Annals and the Azekah Inscription list a number of these techniques and are perhaps drawn from the formulaic lists in the "queries to the sungod (Shamash)." Undoubtedly, a number of sheep donated their livers for examination in order to ensure Sennacherib's success in the conquest of the forty-six Judahite cities.[91]

---

[87] For the Judahite strategy, see Baruch Halpern, "Jerusalem and the Lineages in the Seventh Century BCE: Kinship and the Rise of Individual Moral Liability," in *Law and Ideology in Monarchic Israel* (ed. B. Halpern and D. W. Hobson; JSOTSup 124; Sheffield: Sheffield Academic Press, 1991), 18–59.

[88] Israel Eph'al, "Ways and Means to Conquer a City, Based on Assyrian Queries to the Sungod," in Parpola and Whiting, *Assyria 1995,* 49–53, esp. 50.

[89] Ibid., 51.

[90] Ivan Starr, *Queries to the Sungod: Divination and Politics in Sargonid Assyria* (SAA 4; Helsinki: Helsinki University Press, 1990).

[91] For these Judahite sites, see Andrew G. Vaughn, *Theology, History, and Archaeology in the Chronicler's Account of Hezekiah* (SBLABS 4; Atlanta: Scholars Press, 1999), 19–58. Interestingly, there are thirty-nine towns in the Shephelah districts (Josh 15:33–44). See Anson F. Rainey, "The Biblical Shephelah of Judah," *BASOR* 251 (1983): 1–22.

Table 10.2: Ways of Conquering a City
Based on Neo-Assyrian Queries
(based on Eph'al, "Ways and Means to Conquer a City," 49–53)

Technique	**Phrase(s) and Citations**
friendliness or peaceful negotiations	*ina* KA(*pî*) DÙG.GA(*ṭâbi*) *u salīm ṭubbāti* (SAA IV 30:6; 43:9; 44:10; 63:7–8; 267:5)
	ina dibbī ṭâbūti (SAA IV 101:5')
fearfulness (of the defenders of the attacking troops)	*puluḫtu* (SAA IV 29:5')
pressure	*siʾūtu* (SAA IV 43:6; 44:8; 102:7')
force	*danānu* (SAA IV 43:6; 63:6; 102:6')
famine, hunger, and want	*bubūtu* (SAA IV 29:4'; 30:7; 44:9)
	ḫušaḫḫu (SAA IV 29:4'; 31:8; 43:8; 102:5)
	sunqu (SAA IV 29:4')
thirst	*ṣūmu* (SAA IV 102:6')
waging war	*ina* DÙ-*eš* (*epēš*) GIŠ.TUKUL(*kakki*) MURUB₄(*qabli*) *u* MÈ(*tāḫāzi*) (SAA IV 31:6–7; 43:7; 44:8; 63:5; 102:3'; 267:5, rev. 10)
powerful weapon	*ina* GIŠ.TUKUL(*kakki*) *danni* (SAA IV 102:5')
(scaling) ladders	GIŠ.Ì.DIB//GIŠ.I.BAL(*simmiltu*) (SAA IV 30:8; 43:7; 44:9; 102:4')
ramps	*arammu* SAA IV 29:3'; 43:8; 44:9; 63:7; 101:6'; 102:4')
battering rams	*šubû* (SAA IV 29:3; 43:8; 44:10; 63:7; 101:7; 102:4)
breach	GAM(*pilšu*) (SAA IV 31:7; 43:7; 44:9; 102:4')
tunnel	*niksu* (SAA IV 30:7; 31:7; 43:7; 63:6; 102:4')
water that softens [bricks]	*mê maḫāḫi* (SAA IV 102:5')[92]
negligence (of the defenders)	*šēṭūtu* (SAA IV 102:7')
lack (of soldiers in the city)	*mēkūtu* (SAA IV 29:2'; 30:7; 102:7')
	mēkūtu ša ERIM.MEŠ(*ummanāti*) *šá* ŠÀ(*libbi*) URU(*āli*) (SAA IV 31:8)
insurrection, rebellion, revolt	ḪI.GAR(*bārtu*) (SAA IV 63:8)
	sīḫu (SAA IV 63:8)
	KI.BAL(*nabalkattu*) (SAA IV 43:7)
any ruse of capturing a city	*mimma šipir nikilti ša* DIB(*ṣabāt*) URU(*āli*) *mal* GÁL-*ú*(*bašû*) (SAA IV 30:10–11; 43:10; 44:11; 102:8'; 267 rev. 11)

---

[92] *CAD* (M 1:49 s.v. *maḫāḫu*) cites another context (a *tamītu* text): "will the city be conquered [*ina iṭ-ṭ*]*e-e ma-ḫa-ḫi* by softening bitumen?"

In the description of Sennacherib's seventh campaign as recorded in the later edition of Sennacherib's Annals (Chicago Prism, IV.61–78a), a campaign conducted against Elam, the scribes list the thirty-four Elamite cities besieged and conquered, utilizing the same summary phraseology that they use in their description of the third campaign. Thus, based on analogy with the first and seventh campaigns, it appears very likely that there was some kind of account listing all of these forty-six Judahite cities captured during the third campaign by name, from which the scribes could have drawn in the formulation of the Annals but for whatever reasons chose not to utilize. While the biblical account mentions only Lachish and Libnah, Sennacherib's palace reliefs picture only Lachish, clearly identified by an epigraph.[93] This epigraph is the only time that Lachish is mentioned in the Assyrian sources. Interestingly, however, only three of the cities mentioned in the relief epigraphs are definitely included in his Annals. The six remaining cities (plus one fragmentary name) mentioned in the epigraphs are mentioned by Sennacherib only in his epigraphs. According to Russell,[94] this lack of overlap between the annals and the epigraphs makes it clear that the known editions of the Annals could not have been the source for the campaign episodes depicted in the wall reliefs. There must have been a more detailed written source or sources on which both the verbal and visual accounts were based, and in the case of Sennacherib's third campaign this may have been the fragmentary Azekah Inscription.[95] An early account of the first campaign against Merodach-baladan as recorded in the Bellino Cylinder (lines 39–50) reinforces this possibility.[96]

Several of these techniques for conquering a city would fall under the more general heading of propaganda. As Ephʿal points out, an integral part of the interparty contact during a siege was negotiation, which might be conducted at almost any stage of the siege.[97] At the first stage, the purpose of the negotiation was to try to reach agreement without the need for actual fighting, which would result in exertion, casualties, and damage on both sides. With the manpower shortage that the Assyrian army constantly faced, the capture of a city without the expenditure of any forces was always a preference. Thus "however, one may evaluate the present form

---

[93] Richard D. Barnett et al., *Sculptures from the Southwest Palace of Sennacherib at Nineveh* (2 vols.; London: British Museum Press, 1998).

[94] Russell, *Writing on the Wall,* 140.

[95] Ibid., 141.

[96] See further Frahm, *Einleitung in die Sanherib-Inschriften,* 42–45; Cogan, *COS* 2.119:300–302.

[97] Ephʿal, "Ways and Means," 51.

of the (*rab šaqe*) speeches, the historical reality behind the tactic they represent is confirmed by the report of similar embassies in Assyrian sources, such as that during Tiglath-pileser III's siege of Babylon in 729 B.C.E."[98] This is reinforced by Gallagher's studies.[99]

CONCLUSION

The full consideration of the literary, ideological, and religious features of both the Assyrian royal inscriptions and the biblical texts should serve as a caution to those who assume the historicity of these texts without giving due consideration to this feature of ancient Near Eastern narrative emplotment. Conversely, it should also serve as a warning to those who too quickly dismiss the historicity of the biblical material by accusing the biblical text of being "theological," when, in fact, this is standard fare for all ancient Near Eastern history writing. Taking the literary, ideological, and religious aspects into consideration will provide better exegesis of the Assyrian sources in the process of the reconstruction of the historical events.

Thus it becomes evident that neither the Assyrian nor the biblical source is so objective as to be free of the biases imposed by its own ideological agendas.[100] Both accounts are ideological and religious—it could not be otherwise. The miraculous deliverance of Jerusalem according to the book of Kings (and Isaiah) can be reconciled with the limited victory claimed by the Assyrians if these biases are taken into account. The task of the historian remains the same: to weigh the comparative evidence point by point in order to discover, if possible, the nature of its convergence with the biblical data and the reasons for its divergence.[101] Concerning the literariness of both accounts, Amelie Kuhrt concludes:

> Both accounts are probably "true"; but the differing emphases in the two—
> the deliberate omission of a setback in Sennacherib's account; placing the

---

[98] Machinist, "Assyria and Its Image," 729. For the text, see Saggs, "The Nimrud Letters," 21–56, esp. 23–34, 47. See also Cohen, "Neo-Assyrian Elements," 32–48; Dion, "Sennacherib's Expedition to Palestine," 13–14; and Peter Machinist, "The *Rab šāqēh* at the Wall of Jerusalem: Israelite Identity in the Face of the Assyrian 'Other,'" *IIS* 41 (2000): 151–68.

[99] William R. Gallagher, "Assyrian Deportation Propaganda," *SAAB* 8 (1994): 57–65; idem, *Sennacherib's Campaign to Judah*, 162–220.

[100] William W. Hallo, "Jerusalem under Hezekiah: An Assyriological Perspective," in *Jerusalem: Its Sanctity and Centrality to Judaism, Christianity, and Islam* (ed. L. I. Levine; New York: Continuum, 1999), 36–50, esp. 38.

[101] Ibid., 45.

abortive Jerusalem siege at the culmination of the campaign in the account of 2 Kings—provide exactly the effect each side wanted to create: the merciful raising of the siege in response to humble submission by an already defeated king who had suffered much territorial loss in Sennacherib's case; a divine delivery, which saves the sacred city with its temple at the last moment and frustrates the conqueror's ambitions in the perspective of the Deuteronomist.[102]

Thus the outcome of the invasion might be summed up as follows: while Judah was not reduced to the status of a puppet state or, even worse, a province of the Assyrian Empire (as happened to Samaria to the north), it remained in vassalage to Assyria, having suffered significant political, economic, and military loss.

However, ultimately, as powerful as these two Assyrian monarchs were and as much as they caused great stress in Jerusalem, neither brought the kind of impact and long-term repercussions on Jerusalem that Nebuchadnezzar II did over a century later, for neither king captured and destroyed Jerusalem. The stereotypical verbal trio *appul aqqur ina išāti ašrup* "I razed, I destroyed, I burned with fire" was never employed by either of these Assyrian emperors to describe their military actions with respect to the Judahite royal city.

---

[102] Amelie Kuhrt, *The Ancient Near East, c. 3000–330 BC* (2 vols.; London: Routledge, 1997), 2:478; see also Alan Millard, "Sennacherib's Attack on Hezekiah," *TynBul* 36 (1985): 61–77.

Egypt, Assyria, Isaiah, and the Ashdod Affair:
An Alternative Proposal

J. J. M. Roberts
Princeton Theological Seminary

The essays in this volume by James K. Hoffmeier and K. Lawson Younger Jr. are both major contributions to the ongoing discussion of the role Egypt and Assyria played in southern Palestine in the late eighth century B.C.E. Younger's treatment of the Assyrian material is particularly welcome. He clearly demonstrates his major thesis that the Assyrian sources are just as subject to ideological shaping as the biblical sources; his extensive bibliographical references are very helpful; and his historical reconstructions seem more responsive to new evidence and less problematic than Hoffmeier's. Before addressing details of the two men's reconstructions, however, it may prove useful to review the evidence for Egyptian interaction with Palestine from the time of Tiglath-pileser III through the end of the eighth century.

The Deuteronomistic History offers relatively little information on Egypt's role during this period. It mentions that Hoshea, the last king of Israel, sent messengers to So, king of Egypt, and that this provoked Shalmaneser V, Hoshea's Assyrian overlord, to remove Hoshea and besiege Samaria (2 Kgs 17:3–4). It also has a high Assyrian official suggest during Sennacherib's siege of Jerusalem that Hezekiah was relying on Pharaoh king of Egypt and his chariots and horsemen to save Judah from the Assyrians (2 Kgs 18:21, 24). Finally, it mentions a report that the Assyrian king Sennacherib received warning that Taharqa/Tirhakah, king of Nubia, had set out to fight against him (2 Kgs 19:9). In contrast, the references to their southern neighbors in Hosea and Isaiah are far more numerous but in general less clear and chronologically less precise.[1]

---

[1] Hosea does not mention Nubia, but he complains about Israel making treaties with Assyria and Egypt (Hos 7:11, 16; 12:2). He threatens Israel with a return to Egyptian bondage (8:13; 9:3, 6), and he suggests that they will be divided between Egypt and Assyria (11:5), from where God will eventually recall them (11:11). Just

Nor are the Egyptian and Nubian sources as helpful as one might wish. The great victory stela of the Nubian king Pi(ankh)y does provide important information about the identify of the Delta rulers at the time of Pi(ankh)y's campaign north from Nubia to the Delta region sometime in the 720s B.C.E., when all of the Delta rulers eventually paid homage to him. Osorkon IV was ruling at Tanis in the eastern Delta, and Tefnakhte was ruling at Sais in the western Delta. Pi(ankh)y apparently returned home to Napata in Nubia after his successful campaign without any serious attempt at restructuring the political arrangements in the Delta region. This left Tefnakht free to reassert his hegemony in the western Delta and southward to Memphis, while Osorkon IV appears to have been left in control of the eastern Delta, but neither king has left direct inscriptional evidence of contact with Palestine or Assyria. Tefnakht was succeeded by Bakenranef, and sometime during his reign Shabako, Pi(ankh)y's Nubian successor, marched north from Nubia to resubjugate his Egyptian vassals. By Shabako's second year he controlled Memphis, and several donation stela from various sites in the Delta region from years two to six suggest that he was generally recognized as overlord by the Delta rulers.[2] There is a late tradition in Manetho that he burned Bakenranef alive. It is not clear, however, how many, if any, of the other Delta dynasts he actually eliminated. Kitchen cites a commemorative scarab issued by Shabako as an indication of the "firmness and dispatch" with which the Nubian "took effective control of all Egypt right up to the Asiatic frontier,"[3] but one may

---

what appeals to Egypt Hosea has in mind is not clear. Hoshea's appeal to So is probably one, though one may suspect that there were other appeals in the troubled period after the death of Jeroboam II, particularly in the years immediately prior to Tiglath-pileser's campaign against Israel. Isaiah also has numerous references to Egypt and a number of references to Nubia. The geographical designation מצרים, "Egypt," occurs some forty-eight times in Isa 1–39. While four of these references to Egypt can be dismissed as irrelevant to the question at hand, since they refer to much earlier traditions about Egypt (Isa 10:24, 26; 11:15, 16), the rest of the references to Egypt seem to deal with the state contemporary with the writer. One also finds six occurrences of the geographical designation כוש, "Nubia," in the same corpus (11:11; 18:1; 20:3–5; 37:9). In addition, צען, "Tanis," occurs three times (19:11, 13; 30:4), and חנס, "*Aḥnâs* south of Memphis" (30:4), פתרוס, "land of the south, Upper Egypt" (11:11), and נף, "Memphis" (19:13), all occur one time. There are also six occurrences of the word פרעה, "Pharaoh" (19:11; 30:2, 3; 36:6), though it is not immediately apparent to which ruler or rulers of Egypt this title refers.

[2] Kenneth A. Kitchen, *The Third Intermediate Period in Egypt (1100–650 B.C.)* (3d ed.; Warminster, U.K.: Aris & Phillips, 1996), 378–79.

[3] Ibid., 379.

wonder if the text will bear the weight Kitchen hangs on it. In Kitchen's translation the text merely says:

> (Titles of:) Shabako, given life, more loved by Amun than any king who has existed since the founding of the land. He has slain those who rebelled against him in both South and North, and in every foreign land. The Sand-dwellers are faint because of him, falling for (very) fear of him—they come of themselves as captives and each among them seized his fellow—for he (the king) had performed benefactions for <his> father (Amun), so greatly does he love him.[4]

The claims of the text are actually quite vague and not easy to translate into concrete historical detail. It neither names nor gives the number of those who rebelled against Shabako and thus provides no clear evidence for the extent of the change of rulers in the Delta resulting from this campaign. The text does imply some kind of control over the border between the eastern Delta and its approaches from Palestine, but it provides no detail on how this oversight was administered, and it does not require the assumption of Shabako's direct rule in the eastern Delta. Kitchen proposes that Tanis was a royal fief under Shabako, but even he must admit that at best this was a "brief lapse," that "the finds at Tanis suggest that ... the local line of hereditary rulers had soon re-established themselves."[5] Moreover, the Egyptian material in itself cannot fix the precise date of Shabako's accession to the throne or of his march north. Shabako was succeeded by Shabataka, and, according to Kitchen, his throne names suggest a more aggressive stance toward his enemies in Syria-Palestine. The Kawa inscriptions of Taharqa/Tirhakah, who succeeded Shabataka in 690 B.C.E., suggests that Shabataka, sometime after becoming king, sent Taharqa/Tirhakah and other royal siblings together with a Nubian army north into Lower Egypt. Kitchen plausibly interpreted this as an indication that Shabataka was preparing for war with Assyria, particularly when this information was combined with the biblical reference to Taharqa/Tirhakah as Sennacherib's enemy in 701 B.C.E. However, without help from the Assyrian sources this Egyptian and Nubian material could not be chronologically fixed. Kitchen dated Shabataka's accession to 702 B.C.E., but a recently published Assyrian inscription shows that he was already king in 707/6 B.C.E.[6]

---

[4] Ibid.

[5] Ibid., 396.

[6] Grant Frame, "The Inscription of Sargon II at Tang-i Var," *Or* 68 (1999): 31–57. See also Donald B. Redford, "A Note on the Chronology of Dynasty 25 and the Inscription of Sargon II at Tang-i Var," *Or* 68 (1999): 58–60. This information is incorporated in the discussion by Bernd Ulrich Schipper, *Israel und Ägypten in der*

One is on more solid chronological ground when one turns to the references from Assyrian sources, though the Assyrian scribal practice of filling empty years with a glorious deed of the king, even if that meant moving an event earlier in a king's reign, does create some disturbing variants in the dating of particular events.[7] Fuchs's explanation of these variants seems compelling, and I will follow Fuchs in his attribution of events that have variant datings to particular years. There are notices mentioning Egypt or Nubia in 734, 722, 720, 716, 715, 711, and 701.

In 734 B.C.E., when Tiglath-pileser III marched down the Philistine coast, Hanunu of Gaza fled from his city and took refuge in Egypt, but sometime following the fall of Gaza to the Assyrians, Hanunu returned from Egypt and submitted, and Tiglath-pileser reinstalled him in Gaza.[8] In the same year Tiglath-pileser also appointed Idibi'ilu as the gatekeeper facing Egypt,[9] a move that appears to have been in the nature of an early warning system against the possibility of an Egyptian attack on the Assyrian holdings in Palestine. Tiglath-pileser also set up a royal stela in the city of the Brook of Egypt,[10] and while the inscriptions recording this event are fragmentary, an Egyptian king may have paid tribute to Tiglath-pileser in the same year.[11]

In 722 B.C.E., in the accession year of Sargon II, Sargon claims to have opened up the closed trading station of Egypt and to have mixed the people of Egypt and Assyria together so that they could carry out trade.[12] There is some suspicion, however, that this notice has been placed here to make the early part of Sargon's reign seem more impressive. Tadmor has suggested that it should be associated with the events in Sargon's sixth or seventh year, that is, 716 or 715 B.C.E.[13]

Königszeit: Die kulturellen Kontakte von Salomo bis zum Fall Jerusalems (OBO 170; Fribourg: Universitätsverlag; Göttingen: Vandenhoeck & Ruprecht, 1999), 204–5.

[7] Andreas Fuchs, *Die Annalen des Jahres 711 v. Chr. nach Prismenfragmenten aus Nineve und Assur* (SAAS 8; Helsinki: Neo-Assyrian Text Corpus Project, 1998), 81–96.

[8] Hayim Tadmor, *The Inscriptions of Tiglath-Pileser III, King of Assyria* (Jerusalem: Israel Academy of Sciences and Humanities, 1994), 138–41:8'–14'; 177:14'–19'; 189:8–16.

[9] Ibid., 143:34'; 169:6'; 179: 22'; 203:16'.

[10] Ibid., 179:18'.

[11] Ibid., 191:23–25.

[12] Andreas Fuchs, *Die Inschriften Sargons II. aus Khorsabad* (Göttingen: Cuvillier, 1994), 88:17–18.

[13] Hayim Tadmor, "The Campaigns of Sargon II of Assur: A Chronological-Historical Study," *JCS* 12 (1958): 35.

In 720 B.C.E., apparently in conjunction with the widespread revolt against Assyria led by Ilu-bi'di of Hamat, Hanunu of Gaza also revolted, and a certain Re'e, a high official (*turtannu*) of an Egyptian king, came to Hanunu's support. Sargon defeated the Egyptian army, Re'e fled from the battle, Sargon captured Hanunu, took him in chains to Asshur, burned down the city of Rapiḫu, and exiled over nine thousand of its inhabitants.[14]

In 716 B.C.E., according to the "Annals from the Year 711,"[15] after Sargon had carried out an action, probably against Arabs, on the border of the city of the Brook of Egypt, Shilkanni king of Egypt paid Sargon a tribute of twelve large horses.[16] It is now generally agreed that Shilkanni could only be Osorkon IV, the Libyan ruler of Bubastis and Tanis.[17]

In 715 B.C.E., according to the annals from Khorsabad, following the account of a victory over various Arab tribes, Pharaoh, king of Egypt, is listed along with a number of Arab rulers who paid tribute to Sargon.[18] The parallels between these two references, associated in one textual tradition with 716 and with 715 in the other, suggest that they actually refer to one and the same event and that Shilkanni and Pharaoh are one and the same person. The prism puts the Egyptian tribute before the Mannean campaign, while the annals place it after that campaign, but the difference is probably a literary difference rather than a historical one. I would be inclined to date the event to 715 B.C.E.

In 711 B.C.E., following Fuchs's analysis of the variant datings, falls the Assyrian conquest of the Philistine city of Ashdod, to which we will return. Finally, in 701 B.C.E. is the notice in Sennacherib's Annals that Ekron called the Egyptian kings (LUGAL.MEŠ *māt Mu-ṣu-ri*) and the bowmen, chariots, and horses of the king of Nubia (LUGAL *māt Me-luḫ-ḫi*) to come to their aid.

---

[14] Fuchs, *Inschriften Sargons II,* 90:53–57.

[15] For this designation of the version of the annals reconstructed from the Prism a+b and the remarkablly similar tablet fragment A 16947 and prism fragment VA 8424, see Fuchs, *Annalen des Jahres 711,* 3–4. Fuchs makes a very convincing case that these annals were written in 711 B.C.E.

[16] Ibid., 28–29. This text had been published earlier by E. F. Weidner, "Šilkan(ḫe)ni, König von Muṣri, ein Zeitgenosse Sargons II. Nach einem neuen Bruchstück der Prisma-Inschrift des assyrischen Königs," *AfO* 14 (1941–44): 40–56.

[17] Kitchen, *Third Intermediate Period,* 143. The name *Wsrkn* is formed from the Libyan name element *šrkn/šlkn* and the initial element *w*. The Assyrian transcription of the final element reflects the normal correspondence of consonants, and the lack of the initial element is not unexpected. The initial *w* can be lost, as the Hebrew rendering of *W3b-ib-Rᶜ* as חפרע shows. See William F. Albright, "Further Light on Synchronisms between Egypt and Asia in the Period 935–685 B.C.," *BASOR* 141 (1956): 24; and most recently, Schipper, *Israel und Ägypten,* 156.

[18] Fuchs, *Die Inschriften Sargons II,* 110:123–25.

In addition to these references to Egyptian meddling in southern Palestine, one should also note the relatively few references to Judah in the Assyrian sources prior to Sennacherib's third campaign. An inscription of Tiglath-pileser III mentions Jehoahaz (Ahaz) of Judah among those who paid tribute to him. A Nimrud inscription of Sargon II has Sargon refer to himself as "the subduer of Judah, which lies far away" (*mu-šak-niš* KUR *Ya-ú-du šá a-šar-šú ru-ú-qu*). Another Sargonic inscription mentions the ruler of Judah among other southern Palestinian rulers who received letters from Yamani of Ashdod trying to entice them to join Ashdod's revolt against Assyria. Finally, there is the fragmentary Azekah Inscription, which appears to mention Hezekiah of Judah.

Younger is probably correct when he associates this relative lack of Assyrian references to Judah to Assyria's lack of prior contact with Judah rather than to Judah's contemporary unimportance. He is probably also correct when he dates Sargon's subjugation of Judah to 720 B.C.E., thus associating it with the suppression of the general revolt in the west during that year. His further assumptions about that subjugation are less convincing. Younger assumes that this rare epithet of Sargon implies a real campaign of Sargon against Judah, and he looks for other sources that may refer to this "campaign." He refers to Marvin Sweeney's view that Isa 10:27–32 reflects a campaign of Sargon against Jerusalem,[19] saying that if Sweeney "is correct, then Sargon approached Jerusalem from the north in an apparently successful attempt to reassert control over Judah, who had probably stopped tribute payments to Assyria after the death of Tiglath-pileser III." Younger also mentions the Azekah Inscription as possibly referring to this "campaign" but then dismisses it, in my opinion correctly, because he thinks it dates to the time of Sennacherib's campaign. Even if one accepts Younger's dating of Sargon's subjugation of Judah to 720, as I do, there is no reason to create a "campaign" of Sargon against Judah unmentioned in Sargon's Annals. It appears that Ahaz, who was still king of Judah at that time,[20] remained loyal to Assyria during this revolt, but it

---

[19] Marvin A. Sweeney, "Sargon's Threat against Jerusalem in Isaiah 10,27–32," *Bib* 75 (1994): 457–70.

[20] There is a well-known discrepancy in the biblical sources about the date of Hezekiah's accession to the throne. According to the stereotypical regnal résumé in 2 Kgs 18:1, Hezekiah came to the throne in the third year of Hoshea of Israel. Since Tiglath-pileser III's inscriptions fix Hoshea's accession to ca. 732 B.C.E., that would put Hezekiah's accession in ca. 729 B.C.E. Likewise, 2 Kgs 18:9–10, which calculates on the basis of the regnal résumé in 2 Kgs 18:1, puts Hezekiah's accession in 729 B.C.E. In contrast, 2 Kgs 18:13, which is independent of the regnal résumé, dates Sennacherib's 701 campaign against Judah to Hezekiah's fourteenth year, a synchronism that would place Hezekiah's accession in 715 B.C.E. How does one resolve

would have been very difficult for him, if not impossible, to have sent his tribute to Assyria during that troubled time, when all the territories between him and Assyria were at war with Assyria.[21] As soon as Assyria crushed the revolt, Ahaz no doubt appeared before the Assyrian king with his back tribute and reaffirmed his uninterrupted loyalty to Sargon.[22] That would be all the justification Sargon would need for coining the epithet "the subduer of Judah." There is no compelling reason to connect Isa 10:27–32 with Sargon. The line of march reflected in Isa 10:27–32, with its avoidance of Judah's northern border fortifications on the main north-south road from Samaria, suggests a surprise attack on Jerusalem that fits well with the Syro-Ephraimite attack on Jerusalem in 732 B.C.E. but does not correspond with anything we actually know about Sargon's activities. Moreover, it is embedded in a larger body of material in Isa 10 that shows clear signs of being reworked material originally composed during the Syro-Ephraimite crisis.[23]

Despite this minor difference with Younger, I find his historical reconstructions generally convincing. He clearly recognizes that Hezekiah was

---

this internal biblical conflict? Jeffrey Rogers, in a 1992 dissertation at Princeton Theological Seminary, made a careful comparative study of all the regnal résumés and synchronisms found in 1–2 Kings in the MT, OG, Kaige, and Lucianic recensions. He discovered that the text of the regnal résumés was very fluid, that "no fewer than six introductory résumés lack a synchronism in at least one textual witness" (Jeffrey S. Rogers, "Synchronism and Structure in 1–2 Kings and Mesopotamian Chronographic Literature" [Ph.D. diss., Princeton Theological Seminary, 1992], 259). He suggested that these synchronisms were in fact added to the relatively late framework in intensive redactional activity that took place on the Hebrew text after the separation between MT and the Hebrew *Vorlage* behind OG. In contrast, the text of the synchronisms standing outside the regnal résumés were more stable in textual transmission and show far less evidence of late systematic, postexilic redaction (ibid., 258, 298–303). On the basis of his work, it seems safer to trust the synchronism in 2 Kgs 18:13 that stands outside the influence of the highly redacted regnal résumé and thus to date Hezekiah's accession to 715 B.C.E.

[21] Booty being sent from the provinces to Assyria was always subject to attack, as the letter mentioning an Arab attack on booty being sent from Damascus indicates (Simo Parpola, *Letters from Assyria and the West* [part 1 of *The Correspondence of Sargon II;* SAA 1; Helsinki: Helsinki University Press, 1987], 136, no. 175).

[22] There is a letter mentioning emissaries from Egypt, Gaza, Judah, Moab, and Amon with their tribute, as well as the Edomite, Ashdodite, and Ekronite, but the letter is not dated (ibid., 92, no. 110). The mention of Egypt along with the Ashdodite could make one think of 720 or 715 B.C.E., but the reference to work on bull colossi for the royal residence might make one think of an even later date.

[23] See my discussion in J. J. M. Roberts, "Isaiah and His Children," in *Biblical and Related Studies Presented to Samuel Iwry* (ed. A. Kort and S. Morschauser; Winona Lake, Ind.: Eisenbrauns, 1985), 193–203.

the major leader in the rebellion against Sennacherib in the west, in contrast to Hoffmeier, who wants to play down Hezekiah's role and make the
Ekronites the chief instigators in the plot. Younger's much more sophisticated literary reading of Sennacherib's account helps to explain the
particular treatment given to the Ekronites in the document,[24] while still
giving full weight to the information that Hezekiah rebelled against
Assyria and campaigned against Philistia (2 Kgs 18:7–8) and that the Ekronites turned over their deposed King Padi to Hezekiah. These details, for
which Hoffmeier has no adequate explanation, clearly suggest that
Hezekiah was a major player behind the Philistine revolt. Younger also
takes seriously the information in the Tang-i Var inscription that Shabataka
was the Nubian king who extradited Yamani, which implies that he had
already ascended the throne by 706 B.C.E. Hoffmeier, on the other hand,
seems so wedded to Kitchen's chronology, constructed prior to the publication of the Tang-i Var inscription, that he has difficulty accommodating
the disturbing new evidence. He appears to suggest that the inscription
may be wrong, but even if it is correct, it cannot require him to abandon
the chronology that has Shabako on the throne until 702. Thus there must
have been a co-regency in which the younger Shabataka was appointed
to rule in Nubia while Shabako remained on the throne at Memphis in
Egypt. Such a co-regency is certainly possible, but one wonders whether
it is really required by the evidence or whether it is simply created in
order to maintain a shaky chronology that has become increasingly dubi-
ous in the light of new evidence.

Two other elements in Hoffmeier's reconstruction also appear to me
very problematic. Apparently assuming that Shabataka extradited Yamani
in 711 B.C.E., Hoffmeier argues that Shabako followed a policy of appease-
ment toward Assyria and that Shabataka did not alter that policy until 702
B.C.E., when he became sole ruler, and that Shabataka put this new policy
in effect only after the revolt of Ekron, thus surprising Assyria with this
unexpected hostility from Nubia. He also argues, largely on the basis of the
Deuteronomistic Historian's positive evaluation of Hezekiah, that Hezekiah
never called on Egypt for aid against the Assyrians and that the anti-Egyptian
oracles in Isa 30–31 date to an earlier period. The weaknesses in both
these elements of his reconstruction can be seen by taking a closer look at
Assyrian and biblical evidence for the Ashdod affair of 711 B.C.E.

---

[24] On the other hand, Younger's treatment of the *kitru* alliance as always
"unholy" and always reflecting "misplaced 'trust'" seems to fall into the danger of
overinterpreting a vocabulary item. The word is sometimes used with regard to aid
the Assyrian king sends to his vassal or that is requested by his vassal (*CAD*, K,
467), and, as such, it hardly carries the negative overtones that Younger seems
always to associate with the word.

Fuchs, on the basis of a close comparison of Sargon's Annals from 711 with the later inscriptions of 707 and 706, set up a list of nine elements to represent the event as presented in these sources, but Fuchs's list must be supplemented because of the new information provided by the Tang-i Var inscription. I present those elements below in a slightly revised form.

1. Azuri, the king of Ashdod, planned to withhold his tribute and sent letters to the surrounding kings trying to stir up hostility toward Assyria. Because of the evil Azuri had done, Sargon removed him from Ashdod and replaced him with Azuri's favored brother, Ahimeti.

2. The inhabitants of Ashdod hated Ahimeti's rule and drove him out of Ashdod like a criminal. In his place they raised up a certain commoner, Yamani or Yadna, to be their king.[25]

3. They then fortified Ashdod against Assyrian attack and began sending letters to the surrounding states, including the kings of the Philistines, Judah, Edom, Moab, and those who dwell by the sea—all vassals of Assyria—encouraging them to join the revolt.

4. They also sent their present to Pharaoh king of Egypt, a ruler who could not save them, and kept asking him for military support.

5. Sargon and a relatively small Assyrian army made a forced march on Ashdod in 711 B.C.E., crossing the Euphrates at the height of the spring flood as on dry ground.

6. Yamani heard of the approach of the Assyrian army and fled by sea well before its arrival at Ashdod.

7. Yamani eventually ended up in the territory of Egypt that is on the border of Nubia, where he was no longer seen or where he lived like a thief.

8. The Assyrians captured Ashdod and two nearby cities, plundered them, deported the population, resettled the cities with exiles from other areas, and appointed an Assyrian governor over them.

9. Awed by Sargon's military might, Shabataka (*ša-pa-ta-ku-u'*), the king of Nubia (*šar mat me-luḫ-ḫa*), who was in Upper Egypt, put Yamani in chains and had him brought before Sargon in Assyria.

The annals from 711, written in the same year as the conquest of Ashdod, clearly have the most expanded account of this incident. It is the only

---

[25] There has been a great deal of inconclusive discussion about the individual's name. Yamani has been explained as a gentilic *yawanî*, "the Greek," while Yadna has been explained as "the Cypriot," from Yadnana, "Cyprus," but this interpretation has not won general acceptance.

account that mentions the fortification of Ashdod, the messages of Yamani to the named surrounding states, the payment of money and repeated requests for help to the Egyptian king, and Yamani's flight by sea. Unfortunately, in this fragmentary text there is an unreconstructable break near the beginning of the account and another in the section describing the fortification of Ashdod. Moreover, after a fragmentary description of Yamani's flight to a distant location and a few traces that begin the account of the conquest of Ashdod, the text completely breaks off. Despite this break, Fuchs makes a convincing case that this text contained no information about the ultimate fate of Yamani. By contrast, the small and large display inscriptions from 707 B.C.E. and the Tang-i Var inscription from 706 B.C.E. contain an account of Yamani's flight to Upper Egypt, where he lived like a thief or where his place was not seen. Then the display inscriptions from 707 B.C.E. contain an account of the reorganization of the conquered territory of Ashdod that is lacking in the Tang-i Var inscription, followed by an account also found in the Tang-i Var inscription of the extradition of Yamani. The Tang-i Var inscription identifies the Nubian king who extradited Yamani as Shabataka but otherwise is much briefer than the display inscriptions. Especially the large display text expands on this event as extraordinary in ways that suggest that it happened not long before the inscription was written. In the fragment numbered 81-7-23,3, the prism fragment from 706, the extradition of Yamani is mentioned, but it is now placed before the reorganization of the conquered territory of Ashdod. Finally, in the Khorsabad annals there is no mention of any flight; the illegitimate king of Ashdod, called Yadna in this text, is simply captured along with the people of his land at the conquest of Ashdod.

It is clear that everything recorded in this account did not happen in the single year 711. The whole account is placed under this year because that is the year in which the campaign against Ashdod took place, but that is no guarantee that the events that led up to the campaign or the events that followed the successful conquest of Ashdod all took place in the same year. Since the mention of the spring flood suggests that the campaign began early in the year, the disturbances that led up to the campaign must have taken place in the preceding year or years. Azuri was discovered to be writing letters to the surrounding countries courting revolt, and he was replaced by Ahimeti, but the population then removed Ahimeti and replaced him with Yamani. There then passed sufficient time for Ashdod to work on some major fortifications, including the digging of a deep, wet moat,[26] and to send letters to the surrounding countries, including

---

[26] According to the annals of 711, they dug this moat twenty cubits deep, at which point they hit ground water (*mê naqbi*). Larry Stager, the excavator of

repeated messages to an Egyptian king. This suggests an extended period. The Assyrian removal of Azuri suggests the presence of an Assyrian force sufficient to impose its will on the rebellious city, and it is difficult to imagine the populace removing the new Assyrian appointee while that force was still in the vicinity of Ashdod. That raises the question when such a force was present, and two possibilities suggest themselves: 720, when Sargon fought at Gaza; and 715, when an Assyrian detachment was present near the city of the Brook of Egypt.[27]

If the events leading up to the campaign took time, one must also assume that the reorganization of the territory extended over a lengthy period. It is very unlikely that a small mobile unit on a forced march would have brought with them exiles from the eastern mountains to settle in Ashdod. Both the deportation of the inhabitants of Ashdod and the resettlement of a new population brought from the distant eastern mountains is unlikely to have been completed overnight. Finally, the extradition of Yamani appears not to have taken place until sometime around 707 B.C.E., almost four years after the fall of Ashdod.

With these preliminary remarks on the Near Eastern sources for this affair, let us now turn to the biblical account in Isa 20. The text begins with the notice: "In the year that the *tartān* came to Ashdod, when Sargon the king of Assyria sent him, and fought against Ashdod and took it." The notice provides information not found in any of the Assyrian accounts of this affair, the information that Sargon himself did not lead this expedition but that it was carried out by the Assyrian *tartān* or field marshal, one of the highest Assyrian officials. Since it was not particularly unusual in the Assyrian annals for an Assyrian king to claim to have led a campaign when in fact he was not present, Fuchs and, I think, most Assyriologists would agree that the biblical information on this point is probably more reliable than the claims in Sargon's royal inscriptions. After all, the people in Philistia and Judah knew with whom they were dealing; if Sargon himself had been present, the writer would hardly have omitted that fact.

Ashkelon, informs me that this is a remarkably accurate description of the depth at which ground water is to be found in the whole coastal region of Philistia to this day.

[27] This has traditionally been identified with the Wadi el-Arish, but Naʾaman has argued rather convincingly that it should be identified with the Brook Beṣor located just south of Gaza and slightly north of Rapiḫu (Nadav Naʾaman, "The Brook of Egypt and Assyrian Policy on the Border of Egypt," *TA* 6 [1979]: 68–90). Wadi el-Arish is located much farther south, and there is no evidence of settlement along it in the period in question.

This observation also suggests that the account in Isa 20 is from a relatively early and historically reliable source.[28] It is a narrative about the prophet that embeds a prophetic oracle, rather than simply an oracle or collection of oracles. In this regard it is comparable to the narrative in Isa 7:1–25 and the more extended collection of such stories in Isa 36–39. One may wonder if at one time there was a larger collection of such stories that made up a separate literary work and whether Isa 20 as well as Isa 7:1–25 were simply abstracted from this larger collection and inserted into the collection of Isaianic oracles at their present locations.

The text continues with a second temporal expression, and I would translate the rest of the passage prior to textual corrections as follows:

> At that time Yahweh spoke through Isaiah the son of Amoz, saying, "Go, remove the sackcloth from upon your loins, and your sandals remove from upon your feet." And he did so, going about naked and barefoot. And Yahweh said, "As my servant Isaiah has gone naked and barefoot for three years as a sign and a portent against Egypt and against Nubia, thus the king of Assyria shall lead away the captives of Egypt and the exiles of Nubia, young men and old, naked and barefoot, with butts uncovered, the nakedness of Egypt. And they will be dismayed and ashamed of Nubia to whom they looked and of Egypt their boast. And the inhabitant of this seacoast will say in that day, 'Look what happened to the one to whom we looked, to whom we fled for help to be saved from the king of Assyria! How then can we escape?'"

There are several difficulties in the text. The one that has provoked the most discussion has been Isaiah's dress or, rather, the lack of it. Reams have been written trying to keep Isaiah's private parts at least partially covered, but the mention of the bare butts in 20:4 seems to undercut these attempts. I do not understand this apologetic concern, since prophets were known to do outrageous things as symbolic actions. One need only think of the embarrassingly weird actions of a Hosea or an Ezekiel. Moreover, the text need not imply that Isaiah spent twenty-four hours of every day for three years buck naked. It may mean no more than that Isaiah made a brief "full monty" appearance each day in front of the palace where the royal counselors were discussing their response to the letters from Ashdod. Wildberger claims that the climate in Palestine would preclude Isaiah from going completely unclothed for that length of period, but if his symbolic appearances were limited to a few hours each day, the Palestinian climate

---

[28] The Assryian title *tartān* occurs only one other time in the biblical record, in connection with the account of the officers that Sennacherib sent to negotiate with Hezekiah for the surrender of Jerusalem in 701 B.C.E. (2 Kgs 18:17).

would no more preclude it than the northern Italian climate precluded the medieval German emperor Henry IV from standing barefoot in the snow for three days seeking Pope Gregory VII's absolution.

It should be noted that the clothes that Isaiah was asked to remove were sackcloth from his loins and sandals from his feet. The mention of sackcloth has provoked more discussion. Sackcloth was not the normal dress in Palestine. For ordinary people the wearing of sackcloth normally signaled some kind of mourning, and it was apparently worn next to the bare skin without undergarments (1 Kgs 21:27). On the other hand, some scholars assume that sackcloth (שַׂק) was the normal attire of prophets. The only evidence to support this claim, however, is two passages that use a different vocabulary for the garment in question. One is the vague reference to Elijah's appearance as "the owner of a hair garment that he girded around his loins with a leather girdle" (בַּעַל שֵׂעָר וְאֵזוֹר עוֹר אָזוּר בְּמָתְנָיו; 2 Kgs 1:8), and the other is Third Zechariah's reference to a "hair mantel" (אַדֶּרֶת שֵׂעָר) as something characteristically worn by prophets in his day (Zech 13:4). If sackcloth was not the normal dress of Isaiah, it suggests that Isaiah was already dressing in a way that suggests a symbolic action prior to the command mentioned in Isa 20:2. The narrative as we have it may have been shortened from a longer, more detailed account in which Isaiah originally appeared in sackcloth, symbolizing the mourning that would befall the Philistine city. If so, the shift from sackcloth to bare skin would represent a significant upping of the ante in the prophet's symbolic action.

Though it may have provoked less discussion, a far more critical difficulty in elucidating this text is clarifying the temporal sequence. It is clear that the two temporal expressions with which the passage begins cannot be understood as implying that everything in the account took place in the same year that the *tartān* came to Ashdod. The reference to the three years of Isaiah's weird prophetic behavior rules that out. The dating of this extended process to this particular year is rather similar to the Assyrian practice of dating extended historical actions to the particular year in which a relative climax is reached. It is also similar to the dating of the events narrated in Isa 7:1–25. While the introductory remarks in 7:1–2 suggest a setting in the time of the Syro-Ephraimite attack on Jerusalem, it is clear that Isaiah's symbolic actions and interpretive oracles during this period imply an extended period of at least several years. Isaiah gives three of his children symbolic names relating to the Syro-Ephraimite war, at least two of whom are born during this period, and the time limits attached to the names of the children for the temporal end of the crisis suggest that Isaiah kept prophesying about this issue for several years.[29]

---

[29] See Roberts, "Isaiah and His Children," 192–203.

To return to Isa 20, one could ask whether Isaiah's prophetic sign activity preceded the coming of the *tartān* or followed it. Either would be possible in the abstract, but the logic of the situation suggests it preceded the *tartān*'s arrival. We know that Ashdod sent messages to the king of Judah and the other surrounding kings encouraging them to join the revolt. Isaiah's extended public display is most logically interpreted as his attempt to discourage the Judahite court from being swayed by such messengers. There is a good probability that the oracle in Isa 14:28–32 that is dated to the year of Ahaz's death comes from this same period. After a warning to the Philistines, it raises the question, "What will one answer the messengers of the nation?" It goes on to answer the question with a statement that implies Judah should trust in Yahweh's commitment to Zion and stay away from such rebellious alliances being proposed by Ashdod. By the time the *tartān* had arrived on the scene and Yamani, the king of Ashdod, had already fled, it is unlikely that anyone in the Judahite court would still have been pushing a treaty with Ashdod.

The NRSV assumes this anterior temporal sequence and, following the RSV, tries to make it clear by a pluperfect translation, "at that time the LORD had spoken to Isaiah the son of Amoz, saying, 'Go and loose the sackcloth from your loins and take your sandals off your feet,' and he had done so, walking naked and barefoot. Then the LORD said...." The NRSV translation will not work, however. It makes God's command to Isaiah to carry out a symbolic act and Isaiah's carrying out of that symbolic act pluperfects but God's explanation of the act a simple perfect. This suggests that Isaiah walked around naked for three years but only in the third year offered an interpretation for his strange behavior. On the face of it this seems unlikely. If Isaiah's strange behavior had no self-evident meaning and he offered no explanation of the actions, how could they influence the Judahite court? More damning, however, is a detail in the text that the NRSV glosses over. Verse 2 actually says, "Yahweh spoke by the hand of Isaiah" (בְּיַד יְשַׁעְיָהוּ), not "Yahweh spoke to Isaiah." The expression implies that Yahweh was speaking to others through Isaiah, which means one cannot separate this statement temporally from the following statement in verse 3, where the revelation is communicated to the people. Even if one rejects the pluperfect translation, however, the expression שָׁלֹשׁ שָׁנִים is awkwardly placed. It still sounds as if the explanation for the symbolic act was not offered until three years after the activity had begun. The improbability of this led Gray to suggest that this interpretation was in fact a new interpretation of the symbolic act introduced by Isaiah at the very end of this period of symbolic action.[30]

---

[30] George Buchanan Gray, *A Critical and Exegetical Commenatry on the Book of Isaiah, I–XXXIX* (ICC; Edinburgh; T&T Clark, 1912), 346.

He suggested that originally the symbolic action may have been inter-preted as a threat to the Judahite leaders but that at the end of the period Isaiah reinterpreted it as a threat to the real powers behind the revolt, Egypt and Nubia. This seems ingenious but strained and quite hypotheti-cal. Another suggestion Gray mentions seems less strained and no more hypothetical; that is, why not simply assume a mechanical vertical dis-placement of the phrase from the preceding verse? That would yield, "At that time Yahweh spoke through Isaiah the son of Amoz saying, 'Go and loose the sackcloth from your loins and take your sandals off your feet,' and he did so, walking naked and barefoot for three years. And Yahweh said, 'As my servant Isaiah has walked naked and barefoot as a sign and portent against Egypt and against Nubia, thus the king of Assyria shall lead away....'" With this textual correction, the expression "three years" indi-cates the period of the symbolic action, but the verbal explanation of the action could be understood as accompanying the symbolic action from the very beginning.

As the symbolic action is explained, the threat is explicitly directed against Egypt and Nubia. The reference to Nubia has generated a great deal of historical discussion, some of it misleading because of a mistaken identification of Pharaoh king of Egypt in certain Assyrian texts as the Nubian Shabako. A close reading of the Assyrian sources shows that they distinguish clearly between Pharaoh king of Egypt and the king of Nubia. Since the king of Nubia does not enter the picture in the Assyrian sources until the extradition of Yamani from Upper Egypt, an event that can hardly be earlier than 707 B.C.E., on the basis of the Assyrian sources alone one could question Nubian interference in Palestine prior to 707 B.C.E. Isaiah's oracle, however, suggests that Egypt and Nubia were the two major pow-ers that Ashdod looked to for military help against Assyria. Since Isaiah was on the scene in Jerusalem and appears to have been aware of the purpose of the messengers from Ashdod, it is just as difficult to dismiss this refer-ence to Nubia as unhistorical as it is to dismiss as unhistorical the notice about the *tartān* being the leader of the Assyrian expedition. However, if the people of Ashdod were promoting the vain hope of Nubian interven-tion, one may legitimately ask from where this vain hope arose. Osorkon IV paid tribute to Sargon after Assyrian intervention in the Brook of Egypt region in 715 B.C.E., which may have been the same time that the Assyri-ans removed Azuri from the throne of Ashdod. However, Osorkon's gift to Sargon need not be interpreted as anything more than a temporary expe-dient to avoid immediate conflict. Within a year or two of Osorkon's tribute, Ashdod was plotting revolt with the clear expectation that the king of Egypt, presumably this very Osorkon, would come to their aid. From Isaiah it seems clear that the messengers from Ashdod were also promis-ing help from Nubia. Such a promise suggests that Shabako's move north to impose his overlordship on the Delta rulers, whatever its precise date, had by 714 B.C.E. impressed the inhabitants of southern Palestine with the strength of Nubia. It is not impossible that Shabako was using his vassal Osorkon to encourage revolt in southern Palestine. If Shabako's scarab referring to the fear he inspired in the sand dwellers is anything more than empty boasting, it may reflect some joint Nubian-Egyptian activity on the frontier sufficient to encourage revolt but insufficient to merit mention in the Assyrian annals. There is certainly no indication that Shabako was desperate to maintain peace with Assyria in the years 714–708 B.C.E. While neither Shabako nor his client king in Tanis sent the expected military assistance to Ashdod, the long delay in the extradition of Yamani suggests that Shabako originally harbored the fugitive, a hostile action toward Assyria, as the provision for the extradition of fugitives in the Near Eastern treaty tradition clearly indicates. Shabako probably hoped to use Yamani in the future to stir up affairs in Philistia.[31] Shabataka's extradition of Yamani is probably to be dated shortly after Shabataka's accession to the throne, but it should not be taken as an indication of a desperate desire for peace with Assyria, since a few years later Shabataka sent Nubian and Egyptian troops against Sennacherib. There are other more likely reasons for Shabataka's actions. It probably became clear to Shabataka that Yamani had lost his credibility in Philistia and thus his usefulness for Nubia's designs on Philistia. Extraditing Yamani would provide a pretext for Nubian officials to gather intelligence in the heart of Assyrian territory and allow Shabataka to avoid a premature conflict with Assyria for which Nubia was not yet prepared.

Some scholars have taken the reference to the captivity of the Egyptians and the exile of the Nubians in Isa 20:4 as an indication that this passage stems from a later date, after the invasions of Egypt by Esarhaddon and Ashurbanipal, when numerous exiles from Egypt and Nubia were led away to Assyria. The difficulty with this interpretation, however, is the response of the Philistines to this supposed invasion of Egypt and Nubia. If an Assyrian army had already marched deep into Egypt, Ashdod and the other Philistine cities through which such an army must have already passed would hardly still be discussing how they might be saved. Their fate would have been long decided. It makes more sense to understand this reference to Egyptian and Nubian captives as referring to the Egyptian and Nubian soldiers who made up the relief force that had apparently been promised by Egypt and that Ashdod expected to appear in Philistia

---

[31] Similar reasons lay behind Pharaoh Shishak's harboring of the fugitives Hadad the Edomite (1 Kgs 11:14–22) and Jeroboam the Ephraimite (1 Kgs 11:40) in the time of David and Solomon.

to help them fend off the Assyrian attack. Apparently the Judahite court and Isaiah also expected such a relief force to appear, just as an Egyptian relief force had appeared earlier in 720 in support of Hanuna of Gaza. Isaiah, however, threatened that this relief force would itself be captured by the Assyrians and its members marched away into exile stripped naked. The expression "young and old" is to be taken as a merismus indicating that the whole force would be captured and so humiliated. If the text refers to the defeat of a combined Egyptian-Nubian relief force in a pitched battle in the vicinity of Ashdod, then the following remarks by the Philistines make perfect sense. The Philistines, besieged in their cities, having watched from their city walls the cataclysmic defeat of their Egyptian and Nubian allies in the open field, could well express their dismay at what they knew was coming next—their own destruction. The defeat of a relief force in the open field usually led to the surrender and often destruction of the besieged city or cities that the relief force was trying to save, as the fate of Gaza and Rapiḫu in 720 B.C.E. so clearly illustrate.

There has been some discussion of the identity of the subject of the verbs in verse 5, since the subject is not named. Given the context, however, in which Ashdod was sending letters to its neighbors trying to persuade them to join in the revolt, it is most logical to assume that the Philistines of Ashdod and its environs are the understood subject. They are the ones who will be dismayed at and ashamed of Egypt and Nubia, to whom they looked for help. The subject in verse 6, "the inhabitant of this seacoast" (יֹשֵׁב הָאִי הַזֶּה), could be taken as synonymous, or it could be taken as referring to a somewhat broader circle. The Assyrian annals of 711 clearly distinguish between the kings of the inland states of Judah, Edom, and Moab, the kings of the land of Philistia, and another group, "those who dwell by the sea." It may be this latter group that Isaiah makes the subject of the complaint in verse 6.

The expression in verse 6, אֲשֶׁר־נַסְנוּ שָׁם, "where we fled," is sometimes taken as an indication that the speakers were an exiled community that had fled to Egypt and that it was there in Egypt that the Assyrians threatened them, but the usage of the verb נוס in Isaiah does not support this interpretation. A comparison of Isa 30:16 and 31:1 suggests that the verb does not always carry the negative overtone of "flee" but can have the more neutral or even positive sense of "run" or "move swiftly." The sense of verse 6 is not that the Philistines fled Philistia and settled in Egypt but that the Philistines ran down to Egypt for help, just as the Judahites went down to Egypt to get horses for the conflict in 701 (Isa 30:2; 31:1).

Of course, in a technical sense Isaiah's prophecy was not fulfilled. The king of Assyria did not lead the Egyptian and Nubian troops away naked because the Egyptian and Nubian relief force never showed up.

The failure of Isaiah's prophecy to be fulfilled in this precise way, however, is hardly proof that Isaiah did not make this prediction. The prophets often prophesied things that never came to pass precisely as they threatened. The Philistines of Ashdod and any of the inhabitants of the seacoast who joined them in revolting against Assyria were no doubt dismayed by and ashamed of their Egyptian and Nubian allies, who failed to come to their assistance, thus sealing their fate. However, in a more profound sense this prophecy of Isaiah appears to have been successful, because it succeeded in its main goal of persuading Hezekiah not to join the revolt. There is no indication that Judah or any of the other inland states responded to Ashdod's letters by joining the revolt.

Still, Nubia and its Egyptian vassals were not done meddling in Palestinian affairs. The shocking death of Sargon in 705 B.C.E. provided the new opportunity for Nubian intervention for which Shabataka had apparently been waiting and planning. This time Isaiah was unable to stem the enthusiasm for revolt in the Judahite court. It is clear from both the archaeological evidence[32] and Isa 22:8–11 that Hezekiah was preparing for revolt against Assyria. Isaiah 39:1–8 indicates that he received an embassy from Merodach-baladan of Babylon, Assyria's archenemy, and the most likely explanation for this is that Merodach-baladan was trying to get Hezekiah to join Babylon in a common revolt against Assyria. The identity of these people and their reason for being in Jerusalem had apparently been kept secret from Isaiah, a point reflected in his complaints about Judah's leaders making plans without consulting Yahweh (29:15; 30:1–2).[33] If Hezekiah were plotting revolt against Assyria, and if in pursuing this policy he were willing to entertain a treaty with Babylon, it would be very odd if he did not also look for support from Egypt, the traditional counterbalance to Assyria in southern Palestine. Isaiah 30:1–7 and 31:1–3 specifically mention an appeal to Egypt, and the reference to the treaty with death in 28:15 probably alludes to a treaty with Egypt. Hoffmeier denies that Isa 30:1–7 and 31:1–3 date to the time of Hezekiah, but his argument is unconvincing. The oracle about the treaty with death is clearly addressed to the rulers of Jerusalem (28:14), not Samaria, and

---

[32] See Andrew G. Vaughn, *Theology, History, and Archaeology in the Chronicler's Account of Hezekiah* (SBLABS 4; Atlanta: Scholars Press, 1999).

[33] See J. J. M. Roberts, "Blindfolding the Prophet: Political Resistance to First Isaiah's Oracles in the Light of Ancient Near Eastern Attitudes toward Oracles," in *Oracles et Prophéties dans l'Antiquité, Actes du Colloque de Strasbourg 15-17 juin 1995* (ed. J.-G. Heintz; Université des Sciences Humaines de Strasbourg, Travaux du Centre de Recherche sur le Proche-Orient et la Grèce Antiques 15; Strasbourg: De Boccard, 1997), 135–46.

the continuation of 31:1–3 in 31:4–5 suggests that this anti-Egyptian oracle was likewise directed to the royal court in Jerusalem. Whatever its
precise date, 18:1–6 also appears to be a warning to the Hezekian court
not to rely on Egypt for deliverance. Moreover, since the Assyrian Rabshakeh specifically refers to Hezekiah's reliance on Egypt (2 Kgs 18:21), it
makes little sense to deny that Hezekiah had been negotiating with Egypt
and its Nubian masters.

Egypt's Role in the Events of 701 B.C.: A Rejoinder to J. J. M. Roberts

James K. Hoffmeier
Trinity International University—Divinity School

The present volume represents the collaboration of a number of biblical scholars and archaeologists, with Jerusalem as the focal point. In keeping with the interdisciplinary nature of contemporary biblical scholarship, my contribution reflected my academic expertise, Egyptology. Specifically, my interest concentrated on the interface between Egypt (and Nubia) and Hezekiah and the events of 701 B.C. Professor J. J. M. Roberts, a distinguished senior scholar, was invited by the editors to offer a critique of my paper and that of my colleague, K. Lawson Younger. They were kind enough to give me the opportunity to respond—I am delighted to offer a brief rejoinder.

Roberts's paper is largely his reconstruction of the events leading up to 701 B.C. rather than being a genuine review of our studies. He does, however, praise Younger's excellent study, though he finds my reconstruction "problematic" (in another place he calls it "very problematic") in at least three major points. Rather than offer a critique of his reconstruction, I will limit myself to responding to the points where he differs with me, namely, the chronological implications of the recently discovered Tang-i Var inscription of Sargon II, the role Hezekiah played in the rebellion that precipitated Sennacherib's invasion in 701 B.C., and my dating of Isa 30:1–2 and 31:1 to around or just prior to 722 B.C. If my dating is correct, this would mean that Isaiah the prophet did not rebuke Hezekiah for summoning Egypt for help, because Hezekiah did not summon them.

The Tang-i Var inscription of Sargon II is an important one, and I acknowledged that. Roberts states that Younger "takes seriously the information" it provides, while he alleges of me that "he appears to suggest that the inscription may be wrong" (272). It is helpful to review what I actually said. First, I noted that the dating of the text was "indisputable." Second, I did, however, suggest that Grant Frame, who published this text, "perhaps overreacts" when he says that it "will require Egyptologists to revise their current absolute chronology of Egypt's twenty-fifth dynasty."[1] Never did I suggest that there is an error in reading the text or that anything is wrong with it, as Roberts implied.

The issue has to do with Shabataka being named as the Kushite king who sent Yamani of Ashdod from his sanctuary in Nubia to Sargon in Assyria. The previously known Small and Great Summary inscriptions of Sargon, on the other hand, had only generally identified the King of Meluḫḫa as extending the favor.[2] Hence the new datum is most welcomed and demands that the previous understanding of this event be reassessed, which is exactly what I did. Frame, and obviously Roberts, believe that the appearance of "Shapataku, king of the land of Meluḫḫa (i.e., Kush)" in this text *can only* mean that Shabataka had become king before 705/6 B.C., thus requiring the moving of the accession of this king from approximately 702 to 706 B.C. A recent article by Dan'el Kahn has also come to this conclusion, which forces him to push back the date of Shabako's accession to 721 B.C.[3]

Roberts seems to think that my motivation for rejecting what he believes are the chronological implications of the reference to Shabataka was to support Kitchen's chronology that predates the discovery of the new information regarding Shabataka. Indeed, I do accept Kitchen's chronology, as most people do. However, the bulk of my historical reconstruction was based on László Török's impressive and comprehensive monograph, which is conspicuous by its absence in Roberts's reconstruction of the eighth century.[4] True, this work predates Tang-i Var, but he too accepts Kitchen's chronology. There is no reason to defend anyone's chronology in the light of new compelling evidence. The problem is that the new reference to Shabataka can be interpreted in more than one way.

In the same issue of *Orientalia* in which Frame's publication of the Tang-i Var text appeared, my mentor Donald Redford considered the implications of the new discovery for Twenty-Fifth Dynasty chronology. He rightly sees two options: lower Shabataka's accession date to approximately 705 B.C. (which Roberts apparently favors) or posit a co-regency between Shabako and Shabataka.[5] A decade before the publication of the

---

[1] Grant Frame, "The Inscription of Sargon II at Tang-I Var," *Or* 68 (1999): 52.

[2] See K. Lawson Younger's translation in *COS* 2.118E:296–97.

[3] Dan'el Kahn, "The Inscription of Sargon II at Tang-I Var and the Chronology of Dynasty 25," *Or* 70 (2001): 1–18.

[4] László Török, *The Kingdom of Kush: Handbook of the Napatan-Meroitic Civilization* (HO 31; Leiden: Brill, 1997).

[5] Donald B. Redford, "A Note on the Chronology of Dynasty 25 and the Inscription of Sargon II at Tang-i Var," *Or* 68 (1999): 58–60.

Tang-i Var inscription, Frank Yurco made a good case for a co-regency between these two Kushite rulers.[6] The reference to Shabataka at this earlier date would further support Yurco's argument. In my view, the co-regency option makes good sense because it takes into account the problems of ruling a kingdom that stretched around two thousand miles along the Nile. When Shabako relocated from Napata to Memphis, it made sense to establish Shabataka as co-regent back in Napata, where he was able to apprehend Yamani. If this interpretation of Tang-i Var is correct, it is supported by the title given to Shabataka as *šar meluḫḫa,* king of Kush, and not king of Egypt or pharaoh (*pirʿu*). This identification of Shabataka, I argued in my essay, would parallel that of Taharqa in Isa 37:7 and 2 Kgs 19:9, where he is called *melek kûš* in 701 B.C. prior to his accession in 690 B.C., when he would have been called pharaoh, not just king of Kush.

It is thus inaccurate for Roberts to say that I do not take the Tang-i Var inscription seriously. Rather, I prefer to take seriously the co-regency option that Redford recognized as one way of interpreting the new datum (the Tang-i Var inscription).

Kitchen has now addressed the chronological implications of the reference to Shabataka in 706 B.C.[7] He allows for the possibility that Shabataka could be sole monarch in 706, which would require only a four-year adjustment to his chronology.[8] However, he cautions that the Assyrian use of the title *šar* is no indicator that the person bearing the title is a king (Eg. *nsw*), since it is often used indiscriminately of nonroyal figures.[9] Consequently, Kitchen prefers to see Shabataka, as I do, as being the "ruler of Kush," not pharaoh of Egypt. This view also accords with Török's view that Shabataka had been accorded authority in Napata as crown prince, as Taharqa was by 701 B.C.

The second point where Roberts disagrees with me is on Hezekiah's role in the revolt that led to Sennacherib's invasion. Roberts explains that

---

[6] Frank Yurco, "The Shabaka-Shebitku Coregency and the Supposed Second Campaign of Sennacherib against Judah: A Critical assessment," *JBL* 110 (1991): 35–45.

[7] Kenneth A. Kitchen, "Regnal and Geneological Data of Ancient Egypt (Absolute Chronology I): The Historical Chronology of Ancient Egypt, A Current Assessment," in *The Synchronisation of Civilisations in the Eastern Mediterranean in the Second Millennium B.C.* (ed. M. Bietak; Vienna: Verlag der Öesterreichischen Akademie der Wissenschaften, 2000), 39–52. He actually made this observation some years earlier in the preface to idem, *The Third Intermediate Period in Egypt—1100–650 BC* (3d ed.; Warminster, U.K.: Aris & Phillips, 1995), xxvii.

[8] Kitchen, "Regnal and Geneological Data," 50.

[9] Ibid.

I "play down Hezekiah's role and make the Ekronites the chief instigators in the plot" (272). In fact, I do not "make" Padi of Ekron the ringleader of the rebellion. Rather, Sennacherib (and not me) makes the claim. He is particularly disturbed that the Ekronites had violated his *kitru*-oath.[10] No such charge is leveled against Hezekiah in the Assyrian sources. Obviously, when Hezekiah received the deposed Padi he was inviting Assyrian retribution, but that alone, in my view, does not mean that Hezekiah called upon the Kushite king for help. Isaiah castigated Hezekiah for his building program in anticipation of Sennacherib's invasion rather than relying on God (Isa 22:8b–11), but he says nothing about calling upon Egypt for help. The Deuteronomistic Historian likewise does not charge Hezekiah with relying on Egyptian chariots (see 2 Kgs 17–19). This silence, I propose, should be taken seriously.

Roberts also rejects my suggestion that Isa 30:1–2 and 31:1, woes against trusting Egypt for help, were directed against the northern kingdom and should be assigned to the period around the fall of Samaria, roughly 723/2. He finds my arguments "unconvincing" and points to Isa 28:14 as evidence that the rulers of Jerusalem, not Samaria, are the target of the "woes" in 30:1 and 31:1. The fact that 28:14 is so far removed from 30:1 is not, in my opinion, a very compelling argument for identifying the audience of the later oracles. Furthermore, the real problem for Roberts's use of 28:14 is that 28:1–6 specifically mentions Ephraim, often used in prophetic writings for the northern kingdom (e.g., thirty-seven occurrences in Hosea).

Brevard Childs has recently affirmed that "it is clear that the main thrust of this invective is directed against Samaria."[11] Earlier on, Donner claimed, "It is beyond doubt that the oracle derives from the period between 733/32 and 722. It probably falls in the period around 724, when king Hoshea of Ephraim began to offer resistance to Assyria."[12] In 701, when Roberts now wants to date these oracles, a reference to Ephraim would make little sense.

In a study published in 1987, Roberts himself recognized that 28:1–6 was directed against Samaria and dated it to the Syro-Ephraimite war (ca. 735/4 B.C.).[13] He further opined that 28:1–13 and 28:14–22 share the same

---

[10] Cf. Mordechai Cogan's translation in *COS* 2.119B:303.

[11] Brevard S. Childs, *Isaiah* (OTL; Louisville: Westminster John Knox, 2001), 205.

[12] Herbert Donner, *Israel unter den Volkern: Die Stellung der klassischen Propheten des 8. Jahrhunderts v. Chr. zur Aussenpolitik der Konige von Israel und Juda* (VTSup 11; Leiden: Brill, 1964), 77, quoted in Otto Kaiser, *Isaiah 13–39: A Commentary* (trans. R. A. Wilson; OTL; Philadelphia: Westminster, 1974), 237.

[13] J. J. M. Roberts, "Yahweh's Foundation in Zion (Isa 28:16)," *JBL* 106 (1987): 37.

theme and thus "may stem from the same historical setting."[14] However, he thinks that Isaiah "reused" these passages at a later time, which he broadly dated to "the Assyrian period to introduce his oracle against the Judean leaders."[15] The first part of his argument is sound, because of the reference to Ephraim, but his proposal that the oracle is reused at a later date is highly speculative. Needless to say, there is nothing in the text of Isa 28–31 to date these oracles to the end of the eighth century, as Roberts apparently now believes. Toward the end of his response in the present volume, he suggests that the oracle concerning Kush in 18:16 "also appears to be a warning to the Hezekian court not to rely on Egypt for deliverance" (283). I agree, and I believe that Hezekiah took it seriously and did not summon the Kushites for assistance.

---

[14] Ibid. 38.
[15] Ibid. 37.

Jerusalem in Conflict: The Evidence for the Seventh-Century B.C.E. Religious Struggle over Jerusalem

Lynn Tatum
Baylor University

INTRODUCTION

In what follows, I will focus on the late eighth century down to the destruction of Jerusalem by the Babylonians. That is, I will deal with the era from King Hezekiah down through the fall of Judah. I will not, however, attempt to summarize the archaeological material, which is too extensive to cover in a short paper. Nor will I rehearse the biblical data, which is, unfortunately, not so very extensive. What I intend to do here is to look at the biblical and archaeological data with a particular theoretical agenda in mind.

It is my contention that Jerusalem's biblical and archaeological data can best be understood if they are incorporated into a theoretical framework that has two foci. First, I believe the data provide a clear picture of what can be termed "secondary state collapse." Second, I believe the seventh-century evidence reveals an intense polity struggle in Jerusalem between those advocating a strong, centralized monarchy and those championing a traditional, segmentary societal structure.

SECONDARY STATE COLLAPSE

First, let me make a few comments on the issue of secondary state collapse. Most scholars have been content to understand the fall of Israel in 722 and the fall of Judah in 586 as being simple examples of states collapsing as the result of foreign invasion. I have argued elsewhere, however, that the collapse of Judah and Israel should be seen as exemplars of a more universal phenomenon, secondary state collapse.[1]

---

[1] Lynn Tatum, "From Text to Tell: King Manasseh in the Biblical and Archaeological Record" (Ph.D. diss., Duke University, 1988).

Anthropologists have long focused on the phenomenon of cultural change. Colin Renfrew has even proposed that a taxonomy of cultural change should be developed. Noting certain common elements in the process of cultural change, he has suggested that there are not only cross-cultural commonalities of status (e.g., chiefdoms, centralized states, etc.) but that there are also cross-cultural commonalities of transition. That is, there are many cultures that go through the same types of transformations. These transformations Renfrew calls "allactic forms."[2] In one study, Renfrew focused on a particular type of allactic form: the state collapse in early state societies.[3] For convenience, I will refer to this phenomenon as "secondary state collapse." Renfrew derived much of his theoretical base from "catastrophe theory," which was developed by the French mathematician Rene Thom.[4] Drawing upon anthropological work on such varied cultures as the Hittites, the classic Maya, the Minoan palace civilization, and Tiahuanaco, Renfrew utilized catastrophe theory to develop an explanatory model for state collapse. All of these cultures, as well as others, exhibit common features in the process of their decline and collapse as state entities. Renfrew not only left open the possibility that other cultures could be subsumed under his allactic form but also positively asserted that such should be the case. I argue that Renfrew's model is applicable to the decline and collapse of Jerusalem and the Judahite monarchy.

In Renfrew's model, state collapse refers to more than just the final days of a state system. Rather, it is a period of cultural transition that operates on the order of a century before the final mutation occurs. In the case of ancient Judah, this would include, of course, the seventh century.

SECONDARY STATE COLLAPSE: TRAITS

In discussing secondary state collapse, Renfrew compiled a list of the common features that distinguish the precollapse state from its successor.[5] Many of these features can be discerned, he asserted, in the

---

[2] Colin Renfrew, "Transformations," in *Transformations: Mathematical Approaches to Culture Change* (ed. C. Renfrew and K. L. Cooke; New York: Academic Press, 1979), 16–17.

[3] Colin Renfrew, "Systems Collapse As Social Transformation: Catastrophe and Anastrophe in Early State Societies," in Renfrew and Cooke, *Transformations,* 481–505.

[4] Rene Thom, *Structural Stability and Morphogenesis* (trans. D. H. Fowler; Reading, Mass.: Benjamin, 1975).

[5] Renfrew, " Systems Collapse As Social Transformation," 482–85.

archaeological record. Here are just a few of the chief traits of second-ary state collapse:

1. Disappearance of the state's central administrative organization. The precollapse state will show evidence of centralized administration. However, during the postcollapse era, the central temples disappear, the old military organization vanishes, public works cease, the old central storage centers are abandoned, and palaces and administrative centers are deserted.
2. Disappearance of the traditional elite class. The precollapse state will provide evidence of social elites. Postcollapse, the elites are gone. Without the state apparatus to accumulate the goods and to redistribute them to the elites, this group must perforce disappear.
3. Economic collapse. With the termination of the centralizing administration, the large-scale economic redistribution network also vanishes.
4. Reversion to subsistence agriculture. Secondary states typically develop out of chiefdoms that are based economically on agricultural production. When the state collapses, it quite naturally will revert to its earlier agrarian organization.
5. Population decline and settlement shifts. The urbanized, nucleated structure of the old centralizing state is no longer adaptive. Without the redistribution infrastructure to bring in food, high population density proves disastrous.

SECONDARY STATE COLLAPSE: DIACHRONIC ASPECTS

Renfrew also suggests that secondary state collapse will exhibit particular diachronic aspects. These manifest themselves over time and operate during and through the process of collapse. It is important to remember that the state collapse is a process and not an event. It takes place over time and has a temporal depth.[6]

1. The collapse of the state polity usually takes place on the order of a century.
2. The period of state collapse generally reveals a pattern of disturbances and conflicts.
3. Collapsing states often show an inability to maintain their boundaries.
4. The collapse is not the result of a "single" obvious cause.

---

[6] Ibid., 484–85.

5. The collapsing state will generally show a pattern of increasing complexity over time, with a sudden and precipitous decline culminating in the collapse of the state system.

SECONDARY STATE COLLAPSE: "AFTERMATH" DEVELOPMENTS
    In his study of state-collapse transition, Renfrew noted that two developments can generally be discerned in the wake of a state's demise.[7]

1. The creation of a "romantic Dark Age myth." The groups behind the inevitable efforts to "reconstitute" the centralized state attempt to establish legitimacy by connecting themselves with the heroic age of the past, the usual method being the composition of genealogies. The new candidates for power claim to be the true descendants of the ancient heroes of old.
2. The state fissions into smaller territories, and society "reverts" back to an earlier segmentary polity. Moreover, this "aftermath" organization can show surprising analogies with the polity seen centuries or millennia earlier in the "formative" stage of the culture. This feature brings me to my second major theoretical category: the centralizing/segmentary conflict.

CENTRALIZING/SEGMENTARY CONFLICT

It is my contention that the evidence from seventh-century Jerusalem can best be understood when viewed from the perspective of a segmentary/centralizing conflict. The term *segmentary society* was first used in ethnographic research in Africa. A segmentary society can be defined as an acephalous (i.e., no king or chief), nonranked society composed of multiple "segments" that are of equal political rank and classification.[8] For the purposes of this essay, this segmentary social organization should be contrasted to the "centralizing" strategy of the Davidic monarchy (i.e., a centralized, hierarchical social organization under the rule of a monarch). Numerous scholars have understood early Israel as a segmentary society and the monarchy as a centralizing strategy, but most have assumed that

---

[7] Ibid., 483–84.

[8] This definition is borrowed from Christian Sigrest: "[eine] akephale (d.h. politisch nicht durch eine Zentralinstanz organisierte) Gesellschaft, deren politische Organisation durch politisch gleichrangige und gleichartig unterteilte, mehr- oder vielstufige Gruppen vermittelt ist" (*Regulierte Anarchie: Untersuchungen zum Fehlen und zur Entstehung politischer Herrschaft in segmentären Gesellschaften Afrikas* [Olten-Frieburg: Walter, 1967], 30).

the segmentary option essentially disappeared with the triumph of the monarchy. I assert, however, that the opposition to the monarchy persisted to the very end of the monarchic era.[9] Moreover, this struggle over polity can help us understand the Jerusalem material.

EVALUATING THE JERUSALEM MATERIAL

In discussing the sociopolitical model of the final century of the Judahite monarchy, I will focus on two aspects. I have asserted that the seventh century can be best understood in light of Renfrew's model of secondary state collapse as well as a conflict revolving around the alternative adaptive strategies of centralization or segmentation. I will now turn to the archaeological evidence and examine it in light of this proposed model.

It must be acknowledged that much of the Jerusalem material remains unpublished (though the situation is improving).[10] Moreover, the absence of clear stratification with corresponding destruction layers makes the Jerusalem datings less precise than at other Judean sites. In addition, the scattered location of the various excavations makes correlation of the various strata difficult.[11] Nevertheless, a general picture of the eighth–seventh

---

[9] Lynn Tatum, "King Manasseh and the Royal Fortress at Horvat 'Uza," *BA* 54 (1991): 138.

[10] The Avigad excavations in the Jewish Quarter are slowly appearing post-humously, and the recent reports on the Yigael Shiloh excavations in the City of David are now providing excellent data for evaluation: Yigal Shiloh, *Excavations at the City of David, vol. I, 1978–1982: Interim Report of the First Five Seasons* (Qedem 19; Jerusalem: Institute of Archaeology, Hebrew University of Jerusalem, 1984); Donald T. Ariel, *Excavations at the City of David 1978–1985 Directed by Yigal Shiloh, vol. II, Imported Stamped Amphora Handles, Coins, Worked Bone and Ivory, and Glass* (Qedem 30; Jerusalem: Institute of Archaeology, Hebrew University of Jerusalem, 1990); Alon De Groot and Donald T. Ariel, eds., *Excavations at the City of David 1978–1985 Directed by Yigal Shiloh, vol. III, Stratigraphical, Environmental, and Other Reports* (Qedem 33; Jerusalem: Institute of Archaeology, Hebrew University of Jerusalem, 1992); Donald T. Ariel and Alon De Groot, *Excavations at the City of David 1978–1985 Directed by Yigal Shiloh, vol. IV, Various Reports* (Qedem 35; Jerusalem: Institute of Archaeology, Hebrew University of Jerusalem, 1994); Donald T. Ariel, *Excavations at the City of David 1978–1985 Directed by Yigal Shiloh, vol. V, Extramural Areas* (Qedem 40; Jerusalem: Institute of Archaeology, Hebrew University of Jerusalem, 2000).

[11] For example, though the distance between the Shiloh excavations and the Mazar excavations is less than a kilometer, correlating the stratigraphy of the two excavations is extremely difficult. In addition, the reports on Benjamin Mazar's excavations south of the Temple Mount are available: Eilat Mazar and Benjamin

century stratigraphy is possible. In addition, the results of these several excavations, when taken as a whole, correspond to what Renfrew's model would anticipate. In periods of centralization, construction and expansion in the central-place capital would be expected; in eras of decentralization, construction should be minimal.

First, let me say a word about the so-called *lmlk* store jars. We will not go into the long debate over the use of the *lmlk* stamps for dating purposes.[12] Both the four-wing and two-wing types have been found in the same loci at Lachish, and their suggested use as indicators of chronological distinction can no longer be maintained. Introduction of all types of the stamp now must be attributed to the reign of Hezekiah.

Many have attributed Hezekiah's introduction of the *lmlk* jars to his preparation for rebellion against Assyria. Implicit in this suggestion is a connection between Hezekiah's centralizing reforms and subsequent revolt against Assyria. I assert, however, that Hezekiah's centralizing reforms should be distinguished from his rebellion against his Mesopotamian overlord. The separation of these two phenomena is confirmed by the biblical chronology. Both Kings and Chronicles place Hezekiah's reforms at the very inception of his tenure. His rebellion takes place, at the minimum, more than a decade later. As for the dating of the *lmlk* jars, it would appear that the most logical interpretation is to connect them with Hezekiah's centralizing reforms at the beginning of his reign.

Now let us turn to an overview of the eighth–seventh century stratigraphy in Jerusalem. Here Shiloh's work on the City of David excavations provides important data for a general reconstruction of Jerusalem's seventh-century developments. Shiloh's Stratum 12 is associated with the pottery horizon of Hezekiah's reign. If this was indeed a period of centralization, we would expect this stratum to provide evidence for construction and expansion, and this is precisely what the stratum revealed. In fact, according to the excavator this stratum was "notable for its widespread building activity" (see 2 Chr 32:3–5).[13] The stratum included the construction of a city wall some five meters thick,[14] and a new residential quarter was founded in the eastern section of the city.[15] In addition, archaeological

---

Mazar, *Excavations in the South of the Temple Mount: The Ophel of Biblical Jerusalem* (Qedem 29; Jerusalem: Institute of Archaeology, Hebrew University of Jerusalem, 1989).

[12] For a convenient summary, see David Ussishkin, "The Destruction of Lachish by Sennacherib and the Dating of the Royal Judean Storage Jars," *TA* 4 (1977): 54–56.

[13] Shiloh, *Excavations at the City of David I,* 28.

[14] See ibid., figs. 11, 15.

[15] That is, in Shiloh's Area E (ibid., 28).

investigation as well as paleographic analysis on the Siloam Inscription have confirmed the Bible's attribution of the new hydraulic tunnel to Hezekiah's era (2 Kgs 20:20; 2 Chr 32:30).

It was almost certainly during Hezekiah's reign that the city expanded to take in the western hill, modern Mount Zion—the diversion of the Gihon Spring into the Siloam Pool only makes sense if the central valley and the western hill were both included in Hezekiah's city. The biblical traditions confirm this, and references to the "second quarter" (המשנה) now begin to appear (2 Kgs 22:14; 2 Chr 34:22; Zeph 1:10–11). Furthermore, Avigad's discovery of the so-called "broad wall" in the Jewish Quarter of the modern walled city of Jerusalem provides additional evidence of the city's expansion during this period.[16]

Most scholars have connected the expansion of Jerusalem to Hezekiah's preparation for the Assyrian rebellion.[17] The connection with his rebellion is unlikely, however, since much of the Stratum 12 construction was nonmilitary.[18] For example, a residential quarter constructed in Area E was marked by nicely stepped alleyways and a plastered drainage channel so well built as to be lined with hewn limestone slabs and covered with flagstones.[19]

It seems, then, that Stratum 12 should not be viewed as an attempt to fortify the king's city in the face of an Assyrian onslaught. It appears more likely that the burgeoning of population associated with the spread of Jerusalem should be connected with the influx of northern refugees in the years following the destruction of Samaria.[20] This would explain the phenomenon of the poor constructions built outside the Jerusalem fortifications during Stratum 12, which were abandoned in subsequent strata.[21] It was perhaps in this context, with a newly expanded client base, that Hezekiah could have attempted the centralization that is reflected by the biblical traditions, the *lmlk* jars, the expansion of Jerusalem, the Jerusalem fortification construction, and the hydraulic project known as Hezekiah's Tunnel.

---

[16] For example, Magen Broshi, "The Expansion of Jerusalem in the Reigns of Hezekiah and Manasseh," *IEJ* 24 (1974): 21–26; Nahman Avigad, *Discovering Jerusalem* (Nashville: Nelson, 1983), 55–56; Shiloh, *Excavations at the City of David I*, 28.

[17] Avigad, *Discovering Jerusalem*.

[18] See, for example, the Lower Terrace House; Shiloh, *Excavations at the City of David I*, 13.

[19] Ibid.

[20] This has also been suggested by Broshi, "Expansion of Jerusalem," 26–27.

[21] Shiloh, *Excavations at the City of David I*, 28; see also the structures underlying Avigad's broad wall; Avigad, *Discovering Jerusalem*, 56, fig. 35.

However, in the immediate post-Hezekiah era, the evidence points to a generalized lapse in construction and expansion at Jerusalem. While the distinction between Strata 11 and 10 is not always clear in Shiloh's presentation, it can be seen that little new construction is associated with Stratum 11. The stratum is "represented by relatively sparse finds, architectural or ceramic."[22] This stratum would be the stratum generally associated with the early years of Manasseh's reign. In Shiloh's Area E there is one new construction, the "ashlar house."[23] Other than this, the main construction consists of alterations and repairs of the major constructions of Hezekiah's Stratum 12.

In the final Iron Age stratum, however, the picture again changes. Stratum 10 is to be associated primarily with the era that stretches from the final years of Manasseh, through the reign of Josiah, down to the end of the monarchy. This stratum shows a renewal in activity and construction. There can be no doubt about the temporal distinction between Stratum 12 and 10 nor of their general dates. Shiloh published photographs of three pottery assemblages, two from Stratum 10 loci and one from a Stratum 12 locus.[24] Even without pottery drawings, the contrasts are clear, and dates can be confirmed.[25] Stratum 10 must belong to the last half of the seventh century.

Several structural innovations and numerous indicators of relative material culture prosperity mark Stratum 10. Shiloh noted that in Stratum 10 "widespread" building activities were taking place. In Area G, for example, two new massive terraces were founded near the acropolis.[26] The "House of the Bullae" was constructed, as were the "House of Ahiel" and the "Burnt Room." All this construction indicates an "expanding [of] the residential area of the city in Stratum 10."[27] The construction here was of excellent quality with quoins and doorways of dressed limestone. Traces of an archive with scores of bullae "point to the public (official?) nature of these structures,

---

[22] Shiloh, *Excavations at the City of David I,* 14.

[23] Ibid., 28.

[24] Ibid., Stratum 10: figs. 24:1 and 30:2; Stratum 12: fig. 22:2.

[25] To mention just one example: note the multiridged deep cooking pot in fig. 22:2, which is typical to the late eighth century; see, e.g., Yohanan Aharoni, ed., *Beer-sheba I: Excavations at Tel Beer-Sheba 1969–1971 Seasons* (Tel Aviv: Tel Aviv University Institute of Archaeology, 1973), fig. 70:10 (Stratum II); see also idem, *Investigations at Lachish: The Sanctuary and the Residency (Lachish V)* (Publications of the Institute of Archaeology; Tel Aviv: Gateway, 1975), pl. 44:6 (Stratum III). This form differs from its seventh-century derivative, the single-ridged deep cooking pot in fig. 24:1. See also idem, *Lachish V,* plate 27:21 (Stratum II). Examples could be multiplied.

[26] Shiloh, *Excavations at the City of David I,* 18.

[27] Ibid., 29.

located in close proximity to the acropolis."[28] Area E3 reveals the construction of a "columbarium" attributed to Stratum 10.[29] In addition, Area E1 testifies to the continuation and repair of the "Ashlar House."[30] In fact, numerous Stratum 10 buildings reveal repair and remodeling, further indicating the relative prosperity (and lengthy duration) of the stratum.[31]

As can be seen, the evidence from the city of Jerusalem comports well with our suggested model. Hezekiah's era, Stratum 12, reveals an expanding and thriving city. Fortifications were undertaken, water supply was improved, residential areas enlarged, and a new quarter was added to the city. In short, the capital city took on a new and unprecedented aspect, well in keeping with the portrait of a centralizing capital.

The subsequent stratum, Stratum 11, is the stratum most closely connected to the post-701 era. Stratum 11 reveals an ebbing of the centralizing movement. Construction lessened, expansion stalled, and, at least for Manasseh's early years, refortification ceased.

In the last half of the seventh century, however, the movement toward centralization reemerged. Construction picked up, both in quantity and quality, as Stratum 10 testifies. When Josiah's reform is viewed in the proper light, as a centralizing reform rather than an anti-Assyrian rebellion, it comes as no surprise that this final phase was *not* marked by the construction of new fortifications. There is neither archaeological evidence nor biblical evidence that Josiah or any of the subsequent kings undertook any major fortification projects in Jerusalem.

This point deserves special attention. Peter Welten has rekindled the old skepticism concerning the veracity of the Chronicler's reports. Welten has focused on the *Festungen* notices in 1 and 2 Chronicles. He dismissed these notices as attempts "theologisch zu qualifizieren" those kings of whom the Chronicler approves.[32] However, in light of the Chronicler's supposed laxness with regard to historical fact, one wonders why the Chronicler did not assign any fortification project to the favored Josiah.[33]

---

[28] Ibid., 29; Margreet Steiner has argued that the archive is "private," since it is found in proximity to cooking pots and some other domestic material. Nevertheless, the archive gives evidence of scribes, officers, and an official Judaean bureaucracy (Margreet Steiner, "The Archaeology of Ancient Jerusalem," *CurBS* 6 [1998]: 159).

[29] Shiloh, *Excavations at the City of David I,* 10.

[30] Ibid., 14.

[31] Ibid., 18.

[32] Peter Welten, *Geschichte und Geschichtsdarstellung in den Chronikbüchern* (WMANT 42; Neukirchen-Vluyn: Neukirchener Verlag, 1973), 34.

[33] It should be mentioned that the Chronicler did mention Josiah's temple remodeling (2 Kgs 22:3–7; 2 Chr 34:8–13).

On the contrary, the Chronicler attributed the refortification of Jerusalem to the *evil* Manasseh (2 Chr 33:14). Welten also denied the veracity of this passage.[34]

Welten must be rejected on this point. It is difficult to understand why the Chronicler would have fabricated a story about the refortification of Jerusalem and then have attributed that refortification to the *evil* king Manasseh. It would appear more likely that the Chronicler was simply reporting information drawn from earlier sources.

In reference to the Chronicler's report on Manasseh's building projects, one final archaeological datum should be mentioned. Kenyon's Area A excavations near the Gihon Spring revealed a defensive wall outside what we now know to be the main defensive line of Hezekiah's era.[35] Since it was not found as part of the City of David excavations, it cannot be precisely tied in with the stratigraphy there. However, the literary traditions preserve only one reference to Jerusalem's refortification in the post-Hezekiah period: the Chronicler's attribution of a fortification wall to Manasseh. The Chronicler describes in 2 Chr 33:14 a "wall outside to the city of David, on the west side of Gihon" [my translation]. The Chronicler's account uses the unusual construction of חיצונה with the preposition ל: הומה חיצונה לעיר־דויד. This strange linguistic construction may correspond to the unusual architectural construction of Kenyon's wall; this wall abuts the exterior of the main defensive wall. The wall is "outside" the Stratum 12 wall of Hezekiah, it is exterior to the "City of David," and it is "west of Gihon in the [Kidron] valley." It is possible, if not likely, that this may in fact be the wall attributed by the Chronicler to Manasseh.[36]

Now I shall attempt to correlate the excavation data described above with Renfrew's state-collapse model. The *traits* he emphasized as being available in the archaeological record include the following. First, the pre-collapse state will show evidence of administrative organization. Here both the biblical and the archaeological data agree. We have archaeological evidence of archives (e.g., the House of the Bullae) as well as biblical references to scribes and scribal activity.[37]

---

[34] Based largely on a supposed lateness of vocabulary, Welten attributed the report to the Chronicler's own era (*Geschichte,* 78). I, of course, reject his argument.

[35] Kathleen Kenyon, *Digging Up Jerusalem* (London: Benn, 1974), 144–47.

[36] This has been suggested by Dan Bahat, "The Wall of Manasseh in Jerusalem," *IEJ* 31 (1981): 235–36.

[37] For a detailed discussion of the evidence for scribal activity, see David Jamieson-Drake, *Scribes and Schools in Monarchic Judah* (SWBA 9; JSOTSup 109; Sheffield: Sheffield Academic Press, 1991).

Second, Renfrew suggested that there will be evidence of elite classes in the precollapse state. The Jerusalem material reveals ample evidence of luxury items. Kenyon found a workshop for bronze.[38] Shiloh found wooden furniture imported from North Syria.[39] Imported wine jars from Cyprus or Greece have also been excavated.[40] The "ashlar house" and residences with "indoor" toilets also give evidence of a rising elite class.[41]

Third, the collapse of the state will be reflected in an economic collapse. In contrast to the poverty of the postcollapse state, the precollapse state will show evidence of a strong economy. Here the evidence of eighth–seventh century Judah reveals a portrait of robust economic health. There is extensive evidence for economic trade matrices, even on an international level. As mentioned above, imported goods include furniture, wine jars (and presumably the wine [from the Aegean]), imported ivory (from Syria?),[42] scarabs (from Egypt), and fine pottery bowls (from Assyria).[43] Shiloh has pointed to the presence of names inscribed in South Arabian script on local pottery as pointing to the likely presence of foreign traders in Jerusalem.[44]

Fourth, the collapse of the state will reveal a transition from a centralized economy to its older agrarian, subsistence form. Clearly, the evidence from Judah's capital reveals that its precollapse form is anything but a subsistence/agrarian community. As mentioned above, the excavations reveal the presence of luxury goods, international exchange matrices, and an administrative infrastructure. The postcollapse status, in contrast, appears to be a simple agrarian economy. This seems to be the situation that lies behind Jeremiah's recollection that only "vine dressers and plowmen" remained after Jerusalem's collapse (Jer 52:16). In addition, Eric and Carol Meyers have noted the sudden increase in agricultural units in the Jerusalem district during the Persian era. This increase occurred despite Jerusalem's relative unsuitability for agricultural purposes.[45]

---

[38] Steiner, "Archaeology of Ancient Jerusalem," 159.

[39] Shiloh, *Excavations at the City of David I,* 19.

[40] Steiner, "Archaeology of Ancient Jerusalem," 160.

[41] Jane Cahill et al., "It Had to Happen: Scientists Examine Remains of Ancient Bathroom," *BAR* 17/3 (1991): 64–69.

[42] Ariel, "Worked Bone and Ivory," in *Excavations at the City of David II,* 124–26.

[43] Steiner, "Archaeology of Ancient Jerusalem," 161.

[44] Yigal Shiloh, "The Material Culture of Judah and Jerusalem in Iron Age II: Origins and Influences," in *The Land of Israel: Crossroads of Civilizations* (ed. E. Lipiński; Leuven: Peeters, 1985), 113–46.

[45] Carol Meyers and Eric Meyers, *Haggai, Zechariah 1–8* (AB 25B; Garden City, N.Y.: Doubleday, 1987), 154–55.

Fifth, the state-collapse transition will reveal population decline and displacement. The precollapse, eighth–seventh century Jerusalem reveals the opposite phenomenon: it is an expanding city with a population that is obviously increasing. While the date of Jerusalem's expansion onto the western hill cannot be determined precisely, it most likely should be attributed to the influx of refugees from the collapse of Israel in 722. Hezekiah's Tunnel and its associated pools are clearly from this period. In short, while Jerusalem's growth shows inevitable fluctuations throughout the eighth–seventh century, the trajectory is clearly one of growth. With the coming of the Babylonians in 586, the population, according to both biblical and archaeological evidence, suffers a precipitous decline.

In terms *diachronic aspects* of state collapse, Renfrew first suggests that it generally takes place over roughly a century. This temporal range is important for our purposes. The process of Jerusalem's demise was not just an early-sixth-century phenomenon; it began much earlier. The process of collapse had its primary genesis in the era of rising Assyrian pressure on the Judahite state, particularly during the reigns of Hezekiah and Ahaz.

Second, the century-long period of state collapse generally reveals a pattern of chronic disturbances and conflicts. Judah's last century comports well with this model: Assyrian invasions, royal assassinations (e.g., King Amon), Egyptian incursions, religious turmoil, and the like.

Third, collapsing states often show an inability to maintain their boundaries. Sennacherib specifically recounted Hezekiah's problems in this regard.[46] In the aftermath of Josiah's death in battle, it appears almost certain that Egypt expanded at the expense of Judah.[47] As to the final days of the Judahite monarchy, references to shrinking borders abound (e.g., Jer. 13:19; 34:7; Obad 10–14). In addition, the work of Cresson and Beit-Arieh in the Negev show an increasing Edomite presence (perhaps even Edomite hegemony) in traditional Judahite territory.

Fourth, the collapse is not the result of a "single" obvious cause. Some may object that the Babylonian invasion of 586 was just such a monocausal factor. However, it should be noted that in the closing 125 years of its existence, Judah was invaded numerous times without the kingdom collapsing. Indeed, the only monarch in the entire last century of Judah's existence to escape the fate of a foreign invasion was Amon, who was assassinated in his second year on the throne.[48]

---

[46] "The Siege of Jerusalem," translated by A. Leo Oppenheim (*ANET,* 287).

[47] So, e.g., Yohanan Aharoni, *Land of the Bible: A Historical Geography* (trans. A. F. Rainey; 2d ed.; Philadelphia: Westminster, 1979), 351.

[48] It should be mentioned that the nature of the death and capture of Jehoiakim is problematic. It is recorded in 2 Kgs 24:6 that "he slept with his fathers"; 2 Chr

Fifth, the collapsing state will usually show a pattern of generally increasing complexity over time with a sudden and precipitous drop, simultaneous with the collapse of the state system. In Judah, this pattern is manifested in the increasingly complex state centralization that reached its apex under Josiah. The textual and archaeological evidence points to the royal maintenance of complex exchange matrices and the property derived from the same. However, the prosperity was transient. With Josiah's violent death, the state began a rapid and precipitous decline.

Finally, let us turn to the "aftermath" developments that Renfrew suggests are typical of collapsing states. Here the processes surrounding Jerusalem's demise comport precisely with Renfrew's model. First of all, we see the creation of a "romantic Dark Age myth"; indeed, the final form of the Deuteronomistic History can be seen as just such a myth. The exploits of David and Solomon or Joshua and Moses are provided as evidence of a long-ago, "golden era." Renfrew suggests that the groups behind the inevitable efforts to "reconstitute" the centralized state attempt to establish legitimacy by connecting themselves with the heroic age of the past, the usual method being the composition of genealogies. These new candidates for power claim to be the true descendants of the ancient heroes of old. Here the Chronicler's material comes to mind, with its lengthy genealogical lists in the opening chapters of 1 Chronicles. Chronicles appears to be trying to depict the postexilic community as the true successor of the old Davidic state.

Second, Renfrew suggests that the postcollapse development typically includes a fissioning into smaller territories and a "reversion" back to an earlier segmentary polity. Moreover, this "aftermath" organization can show surprising analogies with that seen centuries or millennia earlier in the "formative" stage of the culture. Here again the evidence comports with the model: Iron III Judahite society reflects just such a development. The territory controlled by Judah during the Josianic "empire" fissions away. Judahite territory reverts to subsistence, and a "dark age" descends upon Judah as centralized local control and polity evaporates in the face of Babylon's (and subsequently, Persia's) hegemony over the Levantine coast.

36:6–7 asserts he was captured and at least prepared for deportation. Jeremiah, on the other hand, seems to record a violent death, "dragged and cast forth beyond the gates of Jerusalem" (Jer 22:18–19). Both Jeremiah and Chronicles agree on the ignominious end of his reign. See the discussion in Samuel MacLean, "Jehoiakim," *IDB* 2:814.

CONCLUSION

The foregoing presents a picture of eighth–seventh century Jerusalem in a state of conflict. The social conflict and turmoil was not so much the product of religious or nationalistic tensions; rather, it resulted from a struggle over polity. The Davidic monarchy desired to increase power and control over its subject people. Beginning in the last quarter of the eighth century, Hezekiah embarked upon a strategy of consciously drawing the nation's power into Jerusalem. The monarchy's expanding role is indicated by the expansion of Jerusalem as well as the introduction of the *lmlk* jars and the administrative system they represented. However, the monarchic centralizing came to an abrupt halt with the invasion of the Assyrians in 701.

By the end of the Assyrian campaign, every major Judahite city, save Jerusalem, lay in ruins. It appears that the monarchy's centralizing strategy was, at least temporarily, also a casualty of the Assyrian onslaught. The monarchy's centralizing program was largely discredited. It had been unable to protect either its territory or its people. The exchange matrices and administrative infrastructure collapsed with the campaign of the Assyrians. As a result of this collapse, urbanization and agricultural specialization no longer made any sense. In the decades following 701, Judah provided a portrait of a centralized state beginning the process of collapse. Judah's cities were not rebuilt. Even in the capital, Jerusalem, there was little construction. The population abandoned urbanization, apparently opting for the traditional modes of dispersed, self-sufficient agricultural diversification. For the next several decades, the monarchy had neither the power nor the resources to institute any new effort at recentralization. This is almost certainly to be connected to the ebbing of centralization characteristic of the early Manasseh reign.

This changed, however, sometime toward the middle of the seventh century. The Davidic monarchy again embarked on a campaign to establish a strongly centralized state. I suggest that the best evidence indicates that the initial efforts in this recentralization were undertaken in the closing years of Manasseh's reign. First of all, the book of Chronicles testifies to renewed activity during the closing years of Manasseh's reign. Not only is he depicted as improving Jerusalem's fortifications, but he is also credited with placing "commanders of the army in all the fortified cities in Judah" (2 Chr 33:14). Moreover, if the renewed activity discussed above is not attributed to Manasseh's reign, a significant chronological difficulty arises. The short tenure of Manasseh's son Amon precludes considering him as the instigator of the renewed efforts toward centralization. Thus, the only possible alternative candidate is Josiah. However, both Chronicles and Kings give Josiah's age at his accession as eight. One would expect, then, a regency period of at least a decade. Embarking on a major centralizing initiative would seem most unlikely in a regency period.[49] Therefore, it appears that Josiah would have been unable to initiate any major centralizing program prior to about 630, at the earliest. However, the archaeological record points to the renewed centralization as dating closer to the middle of the century.

As evidence for the mid-seventh-century dating of the recentralization, the site of Lachish can be examined. Lachish II is almost certainly to be attributed to this seventh-century centralization. If Josiah were posited as the initiator of this reemergent centralization, then this would demand a seventy-five-year gap between the destruction of Lachish III in 701 and the initial rebuilding of Lachish Stratum II. Judging from the ceramic evidence, the gap between Lachish III and Lachish II must be considerably less than seventy-five years. As further evidence of a mid-seventh-century recentralization, several of the sites, which arose out of the renewed royal activity, show multiple phases (e.g., four phases at both Aroer and Masos). If one dates the foundation of these sites to 630 or later, one must account for the existence of four phases in just four decades. A mid-century date for the foundation of these sites makes much better sense of the data.

If, as the archaeological evidence suggests, Manasseh is properly viewed as the king behind the refortification of Judah, then we should also credit Jerusalem's refortification to this same king. If this is the case, then Chronicles is correct when it asserts that it was Manasseh who built the defensive wall "west of Gihon" (2 Chr 33:14). This wall is most likely to be identified with Kenyon's outer wall. At the very least, it bears an uncanny resemblance to that wall attributed by the Chronicler to Manasseh. Whatever the date of Kenyon's wall, the archaeological evidence testifies to continued and intensive construction and remodeling in Jerusalem throughout the remainder of the seventh century.

In summary, the evidence from Jerusalem comports precisely with the segmentary-centralizing conflict we have suggested. Hezekiah's material reveals an expansion and enhancement of the capital city. In contrast, the ensuing century shows a trajectory of decline as Judah vacillates between brief eras of renewed centralization followed by periods of reemerging segmentary polity. The chief issue was not, despite what many scholars have asserted, anti-Assyrian nationalism. Nor was the struggle primarily religious, though the turmoil clearly had a religious manifestation. The primary locus of conflict was the social struggle over polity adaptation. It is this model of social struggle—centralization versus segmentation—that lies behind the demographic and archaeological evidence in Jerusalem. The

---

[49] My appreciation to Bruce Cresson for pointing out this point.

archaeological material illuminates and reflects the profound struggle in ancient Judah over which of these two polity strategies would prove most effective in the dangerous world of ancient Near Eastern power politics.

"The City Yhwh Has Chosen": The Chronicler's Promotion of Jerusalem in Light of Recent Archaeology

Gary N. Knoppers
The Pennsylvania State University

To speak of the position of Jerusalem in the Chronicler's work is to deal with one of the most consistent and beloved subjects addressed by the biblical author. There is no question that the city plays a central role in his worldview. The subject is truly worthy of a major book, rather than just of a paper.[1] Since this treatment cannot be in any way exhaustive, I will limit myself to three overlapping issues. First, the essay will survey a few of the ways the Chronicler advances Jerusalem's importance in his genealogical introduction and in his portrayal of the united monarchy. Even here, my focus will be largely limited to Jerusalem's cultic identity. Second, the paper will inquire into why the Chronicler, living in the context of the Achaemenid era, feels compelled to promote the cause of Jerusalem to such a great degree. Third, I will explore how the author's depiction of a few incidents pertaining to Jerusalem in the Judahite monarchy may be directed toward the international circumstances of his own time.[2]

THE PRIMACY OF JERUSALEM IN THE UNITED MONARCHY

Within the Chronicler's work, the importance of Jerusalem is already evident within the genealogical prologue (1:1–9:34). The tribal lineages of

---

[1] The reader is referred to the recently published work of Norbert Dennerlein, *Die Bedeutung Jerusalems in den Chronikbüchern* (BEATAJ 46; New York: Lang, 1999). See also the fine treatments of Pancratius C. Beentjes, "Jerusalem in the Book of Chronicles," in *The Centrality of Jerusalem* (ed. M. Poorthuis and C. Safrai; Kampen: Kok Pharos, 1996), 15–28; and Martin Selman, "Jerusalem in Chronicles," in *Zion, City of Our God* (ed. R. S. Hess and G. J. Wenham; Grand Rapids: Eerdmans, 1999), 43–56.

[2] A word about the very difficult issue of nomenclature. In this essay, *Judahite* refers to the population of the preexilic southern monarchy, while *Judean* refers to the population of the postexilic province of Yehud.

1 Chr 2:3–9:1 trace the origins of each Israelite tribe to its eponymous ancestor. Even here, Jerusalem is mentioned in relation to the three major groups of the Chronicler's own time: Judah, Levi, and Benjamin.[3] Conversely, Jerusalem is not mentioned in the context of any of the other Israelite tribal lineages. In the genealogy of Judah, Jerusalem appears as a royal city, the site from which David ruled (1 Chr 3:5).[4] In the lineages of Levi, Jerusalem appears in conjunction with priests who officiated at the temple built by Solomon (1 Chr 5:36, 41)[5] and with the singers appointed by David and traced by the Chronicler to the time of the tabernacle (1 Chr 6:17). Consistent with the tribal allotments of Joshua, which assign Jerusalem to Benjamin (Josh 18:27), the book repeatedly portrays Benjaminites as residing in Jerusalem (1 Chr 8:28 [|| 9:38], 32).[6]

Given the critical status of Jerusalem in the Chronicler's writing, it comes as no great surprise that the narration of the return from exile, appearing at the end of the genealogical prologue, focuses on Jerusalem (1 Chr 9:2–34). Even here, special attention is paid to Jerusalem as a temple city, a place in which priests and Levites serve at the house of Yhwh (9:10–34). In this respect, there is a parallel between the end of the genealogical prologue and the narrative portion of the Chronicler's work.[7] Both the introduction to Israel's tribes and the story of the monarchy end with the Babylonian exile, blame the Babylonian deportations on rebellion (*m'l*) against Yhwh, lack any narration of what happens to the deportees while they are in Babylon, and announce a later return to Jerusalem (1 Chr

---

[3] The Chronicler puts the various tribes of Israel in their place, much as he put the nations in their place within his universal genealogy (1:1–2:2). His work presents a broad understanding of Israel's identity in coordination with the prominent influence of Judah (2:3–4:23), Levi (5:27–6:66), and Benjamin (7:6–11; 8:1–40; 9:35–44) in his own time. The minor genealogies draw attention to the major genealogies.

[4] Jerusalem is not mentioned at all in any of the genealogies of the major Judahite clans (1 Chr 2:3–55; 4:1–23).

[5] In the first case, the anecdote pertaining to Azariah II (1 Chr 5:36) should be transposed to Azariah I (1 Chr 5:35; cf. 1 Kgs 4:2). See further my commentary, Gary N. Knoppers, *I Chronicles* (AB 12; New York: Doubleday, forthcoming).

[6] Jerusalem lay near the border between Judah and Benjamin (Josh 15:8; 18:16), but the tribal allotments situate Jerusalem within Benjamin itself; Zecharia Kallai, *Historical Geography of the Bible: The Tribal Territories of Israel* (Leiden: Brill; Jerusalem: Magnes, 1986), 136–37.

[7] Kings ends with the mercies shown to Jehoiachin in exile (2 Kgs 25:27–30), but Chronicles offers a clearer hope for the future: King Cyrus's decree of an end to exile. As Chronicles repeatedly demonstrates, exile need not be a final conclusion but a condition from which it is possible to return (2 Chr 6:36–39; 7:12–15; 33:12–13). See further below.

9:1–34; 2 Chr 36:12–23). Both mention or allude to Jerusalem's temple.[8] In this way, the author calls attention not only to the indispensability of the land to the ongoing story of Israel but also to the indispensability of Jerusalem to Israelite identity, wherever Israelites might live.

Underscoring the site's great importance, the conquest of Jerusalem is David's first public action upon being made king (1 Chr 11:4–9). Transposing the notice of David's conquest of Jerusalem from the account in 2 Sam 5:6–10 to the very beginning of David's reign and transforming the protagonists from David and his elite troops to David and all Israel, the Chronicler pushes Jerusalem to the front and center of his depiction of the united monarchy.[9] The Chronicler thus commends Jerusalem as the first military, social, and religious priority of the body politic following the disastrous rule of Saul (1 Chr 10:1–14). As in Samuel, part of Jerusalem can be called the "City of David" because of David's role in capturing the town.[10] Bolstering the city's status as the cultic center for all Israelites, the writer makes the first attempt to bring the ark into Jerusalem David's second major action upon being made king (13:1–3).[11] Again, the Chronicler's David does not act alone but proceeds only after consulting with the military and civil leadership of his people (13:1–2). When the first attempt to retrieve the ark fails, David himself intervenes to ensure that the priests and Levites handle the second ascent properly (15:1–16:38). The reign of Israel's reverend king witnesses other efforts to bolster Jerusalem's status. Booty gained in war is brought to Israel's new capital

---

[8] By mentioning various families, officials, and their interrelationships, the author establishes links between the Israel of old (outlined in 1 Chr 2:3–9:1) and the Jerusalem community of his own time; see Manfred Oeming, *Das wahre Israel: Die "genealogische Vorhalle" 1 Chronik 1–9* (BWANT 128; Stuttgart: Kohlhammer, 1990). Consistent with the Chronicler's pan-Israel interest, the text speaks of people from "Ephraim and Manasseh" as living in Jerusalem (1 Chr 9:3). This detail is not found in the partial parallel of Neh 11; Sara Japhet, *I and II Chronicles* (OTL; Louisville: Westminster John Knox, 1993), 208.

[9] Manfred Oeming, "Die Eroberung Jerusalems durch David in deuteronomisticher und chronistischer Darstellung (II Sam 5,6 und 1 Chr 11,4–8): Ein Beitrag zur *narrativen Theologie* de beiden Geschichtswerke," *ZAW* 106 (1994): 404–20.

[10] See 1 Chr 11:5, 7; 15:1. The first two references are taken from the Chronicler's *Vorlage* of 2 Sam 5:7, 9.

[11] I would argue that all of 1 Chr 11:10–12:41 relate to David's rise to power and not to David's reign in Jerusalem; Knoppers, *I Chronicles*. On the Chronicler's use of achronology in configuring David's rise to power and early reign, see Hugh G. M. Williamson, "'We Are Yours, O David': The Setting and Purpose of 1 Chronicles xii 1–23," *OtSt* 21 (1981): 164–76; David Glatt, *Chronological Displacement in Biblical and Related Literatures* (SBLDS 139; Atlanta: Scholars Press, 1993).

(18:7), while donations from Samuel, Saul, Abner, Joab, and others are dedicated to the cause of the future temple (26:26–28).

If the capture of Jerusalem and the establishment of its Yahwistic cultus dominate the early portion of David's reign, organizing a national administration in Jerusalem and preparing for the construction of the long-awaited central sanctuary dominate the latter portion of David's reign (1 Chr 22:1–29:19). The construction of the temple belongs to the age of Solomon, but the Chronicler's David does everything but build the edifice himself. Huram of Tyre provides building materials, and David provides gargantuan amounts of gold, silver, and bronze for the construction effort. Indeed, David throws the full weight of the state behind the project, gives selflessly from his own personal fortune to the effort, and convinces Israel's national leadership to do likewise.[12] Such copious provisions elevate the status of Jerusalem and consolidate its position as the center of all of the Israelite tribes.

The advent of the temple and the centralized worship that it represents lead to the establishment of a system of divisions or courses among the Levites and priests (1 Chr 23:6–26:32). Each division of priests and Levitical singers works its appointed turn in rotation until a round was completed and a new round begun. In this manner, the author ratifies historically institutions that exist in his own time.[13] Part of Jerusalem's administrative reorganization involves the gatekeepers, whom the Chronicler counts as Levites (26:1–19; see also Ezra 2:42, 70; Neh 11:19). Sanctuary guards were active, of course, in David's earlier reign (1 Chr 15:18, 23, 24; 16:38, 42; 23:5), but with the advent of centralization such a temple police force has to become a constituent feature of Jerusalem's economy.[14]

---

[12] There are parallels with Israel's gifts to the tabernacle (Exod 25:1–7; 35:4–9, 20–29).

[13] Although ascribed to David's initiative, this development is attested only in the postexilic period. It persists to the destruction of the Second Temple (Josephus, *Ant.* 7.366; Luke 1:5). See further John W. Wright, "The Legacy of David in Chronicles: The Narrative Function of 1 Chronicles 23–27," *JBL* 110 (1991): 229–42; and Georg Steins, *Die Chronik als kanonisches Abschlußphänomen: Studien zur Enstehung und Theologie von 1/2 Chronik* (BBB 93; Weinheim: Beltz Athenaüm, 1995), although I do not agree with many of his redactional conclusions.

[14] It comes as no great surprise, then, that in the narration of the return from exile found in the genealogical prologue, the gatekeepers appear again as an important component of Jerusalem's corporate life (1 Chr 9:17–32). The situation differs in the partial parallel of Neh 11. On the relationship between these two important texts, see Gary N. Knoppers, "Sources, Revisions, and Editions: The Lists of Jerusalem's Residents in MT and LXX Nehemiah 11 and 1 Chronicles 9," *Text* 20 (2000): 141–68.

The Chronicler's interest in Jerusalem is not limited to the sacred precincts and its officiants. David's reign witnesses the rebuilding of Jerusalem's infrastructure, the erection of David's palace, and the construction of other buildings for David (1 Chr 11:8; 14:1; 15:1). The orderly organization of the military, no less than the restructuring of the priests and the Levites, is part of the administrative reorganization initiated in the last years of David's tenure (27:1–24). The system established—twelve monthly relays of 24,000, each headed by a divisional leader (27:2–16)—provides the ruling king with permanent armed forces to defend Jerusalem against attack.[15] If the establishment of a cultus to attend the ark in the City of David effectively associates the newly won capital with an ancient national relic, the administrative arrangements that mark David's final years establish Jerusalem as Israel's nerve center for centuries to come.

As for Solomon, the divinely chosen successor to David, he does not disappoint. In accordance with his father's instructions, Solomon focuses his energies on constructing the promised sanctuary. Like his predecessor (1 Chr 29:1–5), Solomon is deliberately excessive in providing for the temple (2 Chr 3:8–9). His huge donation of "six hundred talents of fine gold," the equivalent of about 45,000 pounds, dwarfs the amount of tribute that the fifth satrapy was to render to the Achaemenid crown in a year's time![16] Indeed, Dillard has argued that the Chronicler has chiastically arranged Solomon's entire reign to focus on the temple.[17] Although the sanctuary project is initiated by David and completed by Solomon, the Chronicler studiously avoids giving the impression that this shrine was a royal chapel. In portraying the shrine's dedication, the Chronicler, like the Deuteronomist before him, has Solomon promote the importance of this edifice to all Israelites in all sorts of places and conditions.[18] The heart of Solomon's prayer (2 Chr 6:22–40) consists of seven petitions detailing a variety of

---

[15] Compare the standard administrative procedure in 1 Chr 23:6–23; 24:1–19; 25:8–31; 26:1–12.

[16] According to Herodotus (*Hist.* 3.89–95) the annual tribute for the fifth satrapy was 350 talents of silver. The partial parallel to 2 Chr 3:8–9 (*zhb ṭwb lkkrym šš m'wt*) in 1 Kgs 6:19–22 simply speaks of "pure gold" (*zhb sgwr*). On the tribute due the Persians, see Israel Eph'al, "Syria-Palestine under Achaemenid Rule," in *Persia, Greece and the Western Mediterranean c. 525 to 479 B.C.* (ed. J. Boardman et al.; 2d ed.; CAH 4; Cambridge: Cambridge University Press, 1988), 153–54.

[17] Raymond B. Dillard, "The Chronicler's Solomon," *WTJ* 43 (1980): 289–300; idem, "The Literary Structure of the Chronicler's Solomon Narrative," *JSOT* 30 (1984): 85– 93; idem, *2 Chronicles* (WBC 15; Waco, Tex.: Word, 1987), 5–7.

[18] Hugh G. M. Williamson, "The Temple in the Books of Chronicles," in *Templum Amicitae: Essays on the Second Temple Presented to Ernst Bammel* (ed. W. Horbury; JSNTSup 48; Sheffield: JSOT Press, 1991), 15–31.

predicaments in which the nation may find herself, including drought
(6:26–27), defeat by the enemy (6:24–25), open pitched battles (6:34–35),
and exile in another land (6:36–39).[19] In each case the king prays that God
might listen from his heavenly dwelling and be attentive to the prayers of
his people.

Three of the additions the Chronicler makes to his *Vorlage* are particularly illuminating in underscoring Jerusalem's importance in his own
time. The first cites Ps 132:8–10 to conclude Solomon's prayer, tying Yhwh
to the Jerusalem temple cultus and proclaiming this structure as the permanent repository for the ark (2 Chr 6:41–42). The Chronicler thus
underscores a tendency already present in the Deuteronomistic work,
namely, to align the temple with Israel's most ancient cultic institutions
and to advertise the temple as the fulfillment of all those institutions.[20]
The second addition involves the divine consecration of "the burnt offering and the sacrifices" by fire (2 Chr 7:1). The manifestation of Yhwh's
glory and the divine consumption of the sacrifices dramatically confirm
Jerusalem's sanctuary as a divinely approved fixture of Israelite life. Again,
there is a parallel with an older precedent, namely, the manifestation of
Yhwh's glory and the divine consumption of the sacrifices at the tent of
meeting in the time of Moses and Aaron.[21] The third addition involves
lengthening the verbal divine response to Solomon's prayer (2 Chr
7:13–22; 1 Kgs 9:1–9). In the new material, Yhwh directly affirms the
thrust of Solomon's petitions (2 Chr 7:13–15). Should king or people find
themselves in duress, they may respond in four ways: they may "humble

---

[19] In the last case, the Chronicler's text is notably shorter than that of the paral-
lel in 1 Kgs 8:46–53; Steven L. McKenzie, *The Chronicler's Use of the
Deuteronomistic History* (HSM 33; Atlanta: Scholars Press, 1985), 199–205; Gary N.
Knoppers, *The Reign of Solomon and the Rise of Jeroboam* (vol. 1 of *Two Nations
under God: The Deuteronomistic History of Solomon and the Dual Monarchies;*
HSM 52; Atlanta: Scholars Press, 1993), 106–8.

[20] Rudolf Mosis, *Untersuchungen zur Theologie des chronistischen
Geschichtswerkes* (Freiburg: Herder, 1973); Peter Welten, "Lade-Tempel-Jerusalem:
zur Theologie der Chronikbuucher," in *Textgemäss: Aufsätze und Beiträge zur
Hermeneutik des alten Testaments: Festschrift für Ernst Würthwein zum 70. Geburts-
tag* (ed. A. H. J. Gunneweg and O. Kaiser; Göttingen: Vandenhoeck & Ruprecht,
1979), 169–83. With respect to the Deuteronomist's work, see Gary N. Knoppers,
"Prayer and Propaganda: The Dedication of Solomon's Temple and the Deuteron-
omist's Program," *CBQ* 57 (1995): 229–54 (repr., *Reconsidering Israel and Judah:
The Deuteronomistic History in Recent Thought* [ed. G. N. Knoppers and J. G.
McConville; SBTS 8; Winona Lake, Ind.: Eisenbrauns, 2000], 370–96).

[21] Lev 9:24. See also 1 Kgs 18:36–39 (Elijah at Mount Carmel) and 1 Chr 21:26
(David at the threshing floor of Ornan).

themselves" (*nkn⁽*), "pray" (*ḥtpll*), "seek [*bqš*] my face," and "turn [*šwb*] from their wicked ways." For his part, Yhwh "will hear from heaven, forgive their sins, and heal their land" (2 Chr 7:14). In this way, the Chronicler promotes the temple as an appropriate site for divine-human communications not only for members of all the Israelite tribes residing in the land but also for those Israelites residing in the Diaspora.[22]

Considering that the Chronicler is living during the Achaemenid era, his stress on Jerusalem's unique status takes on added significance. The author affirms a variety of objects of divine election (David, Solomon, the Levites, etc.),[23] but of no other site is it said that it is elect of Yhwh (2 Chr 6:34, 38; 12:13; 33:7). The city is the place of which Yhwh said, "In Jerusalem I shall set my name forever" (33:4). The Jerusalem temple is declared to be the place for Yhwh's name (1:18; 2:3; 6:7, 8, 9, 10, 34, 38; 20:8; 33:7). At the shrine's dedication, King Solomon cites the deity's promises to David as stating (*'šr dbr bpyw 't dwyd 'by wbydyw ml' l'mr*): "From the day I brought my people Israel from the land of Egypt I did not choose a city from any of the tribes of Israel to build a house for Yhwh (for) my name to be there,[24] and I did not choose a man to be ruler over my people Israel, but I have chosen Jerusalem for my name to be there, and I have chosen David to be in charge[25] of Israel (6:5–6). Approximately one quarter of all the biblical references to Jerusalem occur in Chronicles.[26] In the book, Yhwh is even referred to as "the God of Jerusalem."[27] The epithet is unique within the Hebrew Scriptures but may be paralleled in one of the Khirbet Beit Lei inscriptions.[28]

---

[22] The temple also has relevance for foreigners who hear of Yhwh's great reputation and journey to Jerusalem for worship (2 Chr 6:32–33 par. 1 Kgs 8:41–43). Although this theme is not a productive concern in the Chronicler's story of the monarchy, he occasionally portrays foreigners as self-confessed agents of Israel's God (e.g., 2 Chr 35:21; 36:22–23); Ehud Ben Zvi, "When the Foreign Monarch Speaks," in *The Chronicler As Author: Studies in Text and Texture* (ed. M. P. Graham and S. L. McKenzie; JSOTSup 263; Sheffield: Sheffield Academic Press, 1999), 109–28.

[23] See Knoppers, *I Chronicles.*

[24] The parallel text of MT 1 Kgs 8:16 evinces a haplography (*homoioteleuton*) from *wl'-bḥrty ... lhywt šmy šm* (*lhywt šmy šm* to *lhywt šmy šm*). See also LXX[B] 1 Kgs 8:16. MT 1 Kgs 8:16, as it stands, contains a non sequitor. Yhwh responds to his previous history of never choosing a city by choosing David.

[25] I am reading with the MT (*lectio brevior*). The Syriac and Targum of 2 Chr 6:6 add *ngyd.*

[26] Beentjes, "Jerusalem," 17.

[27] Albeit by an invading foreigner, Sennacherib (2 Chr 32:19).

[28] Khirbet Bei Lei Burial Cave A inscription (Graffito), line 1. Beentjes provides a good discussion ("Jerusalem," 26–28). Note, however, that the reading is disputed:

WHY PROMOTE JERUSALEM?

On one level, all of this promotion of Jerusalem makes eminent sense. In the time the Chronicler wrote, Jerusalem was pivotal to the economy, social identity, and religious life of Yehud. On another level, this emphasis needs to be explored much more carefully. If Jerusalem's importance was so self-evident, why did the author need to emphasize it so much? Is the author simply restating the obvious? According to Stern, the material remains from Yehud have revealed no figurines, no pagan cults, and no rival sanctuaries to that of the Jerusalem temple.[29] Indeed, many have supposed that the Chronicler lived during a period in which Jerusalem's status was practically unassailable. Does not the Achaemenid era witness the triumph of cultic centralization? Might this be a case in which the Chronicler is preaching to the Levitical choir?

The stress on Jerusalem, the Davidic dynasty, and its temple is so pronounced in the book that some scholars have supposed that the Chronicler's writing must have been composed during the late sixth century, when a movement was afoot to rebuild the temple and some hoped for the reinstitution of the Davidic monarchy.[30] In my youth I was once aligned with this way of thinking, but I am not any longer.[31] A closer look at the larger world in which the Chronicler was a part will show that an author living in the fifth or fourth centuries B.C.E. would have plenty of reason to underscore Jerusalem's value to his people. Far from enjoying a comfortable, if not incomparable, status, the town encountered a variety of internal challenges and a variety of external forms of competition.

Frank Moore Cross, "The Cave Inscriptions from Khirbet Beit Lei," in *Near Eastern Archaeology in the Twentieth Century* (ed. J. A. Sanders; Garden City, N.Y.: Doubleday, 1970), 299–302.

[29] Ephraim Stern, "What Happened to the Cult Figurines?" *BAR* 15/4 (1989): 22–29, 53–54. Note that the same is said to hold true for Samaria: "Up to now, no pagan cult remains have been encountered in Judah or in Samaria" (idem, *The Assyrian, Babylonian, and Persian Periods 732–332 BCE* [vol. 2 of *Archaeology of the Land of the Bible;* ABRL; New York: Doubleday, 2001], 488). This important claim is worthy of further scrutiny.

[30] See, e.g., David Noel Freedman, "The Chronicler's Purpose," *CBQ* 23 (1961): 432–42; Frank Moore Cross, "A Reconstruction of the Judean Restoration," *JBL* 94 (1975): 4–18 (rev. in his *From Epic to Canon: History and Literature in Ancient Israel* [Baltimore: Johns Hopkins University Press, 1998], 151–72); Roddy L. Braun, *1 Chronicles* (WBC 14; Waco, Tex.: Word, 1986), xxviii–xix.

[31] An early date is still possible for the Chronicler's original work, but I no longer see it as the most likely.

In the Chronicler's time Judaism had already become an international religion. Jews lived in Yehud, Egypt, and Babylon. Nevertheless, Jerusalem itself was a little town. During the Achaemenid era, Jerusalem was largely confined to the City of David.[32] Recent archaeological treatments have painted a picture of a small Yehud, smaller and less populous than many previous scholars had thought.[33] The recovery from the devastation wrought by the Babylonian invasions of the early sixth century took centuries to complete. Judaism may have become an international religion, but the heart of that religion was relatively small.

As much as the writer extols the accomplishments of David and Solomon, he lived at a time in which Davidides were not in charge of the political affairs of Yehud. The province of Yehud had its own temple but was subject to the greater authority of the Persian crown. The Second Temple was authorized and aided by a number of Achaemenid kings.[34] The author of the last verses of Chronicles (2 Chr 36:22–23) and the authors of Ezra-Nehemiah uphold this record of Achaemenid patronage, but it is quite conceivable that there were others in Yehud who did not. What is more, the Jerusalem sanctuary, unlike most other temples in the Achaemenid Empire, does not seem to have had its own extensive lands

---

[32] Recent studies have pointed toward the validity of the minimalist theory of Jerusalem's size in the Persian period; see Stern, *Assyrian, Babylonian, and Persian Periods,* 581. In the maximalist line of interpretation (e.g., Frank Michaeli, *Les Livres des Chroniques, d'Esdras et de Néhémie* [CAT 16; Neuchâtel: Delachaux & Nestlé, 1967]), Persian-period Jerusalem extended to much of the western hill. See Hugh G. M. Williamson, "Nehemiah's Walls Revisited," *PEQ* 116 (1984): 81–88; Nicholas A. Bailey, "Nehemiah 3:1–32: An Intersection of the Text and the Topography," *PEQ* 122 (1990): 34–40, and the references listed in these articles.

[33] Avi Ofer, "The Highland of Judah during the Biblical Period" [Hebrew] (Ph.D. diss., Tel Aviv University, 1993); idem, "Judah," *OEANE* 3:253–57; Charles Carter, *The Emergence of Yehud in the Persian Period* (JSOTSup 294; Sheffield: Sheffield Academic Press, 1999).

[34] In making this statement, I am giving some credence to the evidence of the early chapters of Ezra-Nehemiah for reconstructing events in sixth–fifth century Yehud (Ezra 1:1–4, 7–11; 5:13–16; 6:1–12; 7:11–24, 27–28; 8:36; 9:9; Neh 2:8–9, 18; 5:14; 11:23; 13:6). See also Sara Japhet, "The Temple in the Restoration Period: Reality and Ideology," *USQR* 44 (1991): 195–251; André Lemaire, "Histoire et administration de la Palestine à l'époque perse," in *La Palestine à l'époque perse* (ed. E.-M. Laperrousaz and A. Lemaire; Études annexes de la Bible de Jérusalem; Paris: Cerf, 1994), 11–53; Israel Eph'al, "Changes in Palestine during the Persian Period in Light of Epigraphic Sources," *IEJ* 48 (1998): 106–19. For another view, see Peter R. Bedford, *Temple Restoration in Early Achaemenid Judah* (JSJSup 65; Leiden: Brill, 2000).

to support it.[35] This meant that the Jerusalem temple depended on the goodwill of patrons for its maintenance. Persian-period texts paint an uneven picture of support for the temple within Yehud. The author of Isa 66:1–2 casts aspersions on the legitimacy of the Second Temple, questioning whether a transcendent Yhwh really needed this earthly house.[36] The author of Malachi (1:6–14) charges that the priests in Jerusalem were offering lame, sick, and stolen animals as oblations in the temple. The prophet Haggai (2:3) complains that the people of Yehud were not always generous in either the quantity or the quality of their temple offerings. One wonders whether the enthusiasm and wholehearted support with which all the people in Chronicles greeted and unsparingly supported the construction of the temple during the time of David and Solomon are meant to address similar concerns.

If Jerusalem faced a number of internal challenges in the context of Yehud, it also had to deal with a variety of external challenges. The Jerusalem sanctuary was not without rivals. Some scholars have argued for the existence of a Persian-period Judean sanctuary at Lachish.[37] The existence of the shrine itself is not in doubt, but most recent scholars question whether it was Judean in nature.[38] The claim has been made

---

[35] Muhammad A. Dandamaev and Vladimir Lukonin, *The Culture and Social Institutions of Ancient Iran* (Cambridge: Cambridge University Press, 1989), 360–66.

[36] Paul D. Hanson, *The Dawn of Apocalyptic: The Historical and Social Roots of Jewish Apocalyptic Eschatology* (Philadelphia: Fortress, 1979), 170–86.

[37] Yohanan Aharoni, *Investigations at Lachish: The Sanctuary and the Residency (Lachish V)* (Publications of the Institute of Archaeology; Tel Aviv: Gateway, 1975), 5–11, and Geo Widengren, "The Persian Period," in *Israelite and Judean History* (ed. J. H. Hayes and J. M. Miller; London: SCM, 1977), 557, believe that the shrine was Yahwistic. Actually, Aharoni contends for the existence of two successive but architecturally similar shrines at Lachish, the first (Building 10) dating to the Persian age and the second (Building 106), the so-called "Solar-Shrine," constructed at the end of the third century. The evidence for this important claim deserves a thorough reanalysis.

[38] Disputing that the sanctuary at Lachish was Judean, Ephraim Stern argues that the Lachish sanctuary was Edomite. See Ephraim Stern, "The Archaeology of Persian Palestine," in *Introduction; The Persian Period* (ed. W. D. Davies and L. Finkelstein; CHJ 1; Cambridge: Cambridge University Press, 1984), 88–114; and idem, "The Persian Empire and the Political and Social History of Palestine in the Persian Period," in Davies and Finkelstein, *Introduction; The Persian Period,* 70–87. Aharoni contends for a Yahwistic orientation of both sanctuaries (previous note) on the basis of both architectural evidence (e.g., similarities between the plan of the Lachish shrines and those of the Arad temple) and epigraphic evidence (the Aramaic inscription on a Persian-period altar). In my judgment, Aharoni's argument from architecture is stronger than his argument from epigraphy. Aharoni's analysis

that the Yahwistic sanctuary near or at Bethel, along with its priestly cultus, survived into Neo-Babylonian times.[39] The existence of such a sanctuary is well known in the Deuteronomistic denunciations of the failings of the northern kingdom,[40] but its continuation or revival is suggested in the Deuteronomistic peroration on the fall of the northern kingdom (2 Kgs 17:24–28).[41] The Assyrian kings may have succeeded in vanquishing and deporting the human inhabitants of the northern kingdom, but they did not succeed in pacifying all of its animals. According to the biblical writer, the lions of Samaria developed a nasty habit of devouring Assyrian immigrants (2 Kgs 17:24–26). Thanks to the Assyrian king's dispatching of an exiled Israelite priest back to Bethel to teach the colonists how to worship Yhwh, the foreigners from Babylon, Cutha, Avva, Hamath, and Sepharvaim learned to acclimate themselves to the local culture and to adopt Yahwistic practices (2 Kgs 17:27–33). As a result, the lion attacks stopped, and the colonists came to worship both Yhwh and their native deities. Whatever one makes of this cautionary tale, it is highly interesting that the Deuteronomistic

---

of the Aramaic inscription has not won any widespread acceptance; see André Lemaire, "Un nouveau roi arabe de Qedar dans l'inscription de l'autel à encens de Lakish (Planche I)," *RB* 81 (1974): 63–72; Edward Lipiński, *Studies in Aramaic Inscriptions and Onomastics I* (OLA 1; Leuven: Leuven University Press, 1975), 143–45. Further weakening Widengren and Aharoni's case is the fact that according to most recent archaeological studies, Lachish lay outside the boundaries of Yehud.

[39] Joseph Blenkinsopp, "The Judaean Priesthood during the Neo-Babylonian and Achaemenid Periods: A Hypothetical Reconstruction," *CBQ* 60 (1998): 25–43; idem, "Bethel in the Neo-Babylonian Period," in *Judah and the Judeans in the Neo-Babylonian and Persian Periods* (ed. O. Lipschits; Winona Lake, Ind.: Eisenbrauns, forthcoming). The archaeology of the site warrants a careful reexamination; see William G. Dever, "Bethel," *OEANE* 1:300–1.

[40] See 1 Kgs 12:29, 32, 33; 13:1, 4, 10, 11, 32, 33; 2 Kgs 2:2, 3, 23; 10:29.

[41] According to the Deuteronomist, the Bethel altar and sanctuary were desecrated during the reforms of Josiah (2 Kgs 23:4, 15, 17, 19). See Gary N. Knoppers, *The Reign of Jeroboam, the Fall of Israel, and the Reign of Josiah* (vol. 2 of *Two Nations under God: The Deuteronomistic History of Solomon and the Dual Monarchies;* HSM 53; Atlanta: Scholars Press, 1994). The Deuteronomist does not say what came of the shrine at Dan (1 Kgs 12:29, 30; 15:20; 2 Kgs 10:29). Given that the Deuteronomistic coverage of events following the Assyrian exile focuses on Judah, the Deuteronomistic writers do not address the post-Josianic history of Bethel. Bethel is occasionally mentioned in Chronicles (1 Chr 7:28; 2 Chr 13:19), as is Dan (1 Chr 21:2; 2 Chr 16:4; 30:5), but the cult centers at these sites are never directly mentioned (see 2 Chr 13:4–12).

writer concedes that Yahwistic worship continued in the former northern kingdom (2 Kgs 17:33, 41).[42]

Discerning the nature of cultic affairs in the Persian province of
Samaria is difficult. Some suppose that Samarians, lacking a sanctuary of
their own, occasionally journeyed to Jerusalem to worship there.[43] Others
disagree. Stern speaks of there being a seventh-century Samarian sanctuary
attested at Mount Gerizim, while others have thought of a seventh-century
cultic precinct at Samaria.[44] According to Stern, the Gerizim shrine fell into
disuse or was destroyed, but the material remains suggest the construction
of another shrine dating to the fourth century B.C.E., if not earlier.[45] Certainly, the archaeological excavations of Magen attest to the construction
of an impressive city and sacred precinct on Mount Gerizim in Hellenistic
times.[46] Beneath the second-century B.C.E. sacred precinct on Mount Gerizim, Naveh and Magen discovered an older layer, which they date to the
second half of the fifth century and identify as the Samaritan temple mentioned (but misdated) by Josephus.[47] The excavators suggest that each

---

[42] The (later) author of 2 Kgs 17:34 disagrees and asserts that the colonists did
not worship Yhwh.

[43] E.g., Hayim Tadmor, "Judah," in *The Fourth Century B.C.* (ed. D. M. Lewis et
al.; 2d ed.; CAH 6; Cambridge: Cambridge University Press, 1994), 261–96. Tadmor
refers to Jer 41:5, Chronicles, Ezra (4:1, 12–14), and Nehemiah (3:33–34; 4:1–2;
13:28).

[44] Stern, *Assyrian, Babylonian, and Persian Periods,* 52.

[45] Ibid., 427.

[46] Izchak Magen, "Mount Gerizim—A Temple City" [Hebrew], *Qad* 23/3–4
(1990): 70–96; idem, "Mount Gerizim," *NEAEHL* 2:484–92; idem, "Mount Gerizim
and the Samaritans," in *Early Christianity in Context—Monuments and Documents*
(ed. F. Manns and E. Alliata; Studium Biblicum Franciscanum Collectio Maior 38;
Jerusalem: Franciscan Printing, 1993), 91–148; idem, "Mount Gerizim—A Temple
City" [Hebrew], *Qad* 33/2 (2000): 74–118.

[47] Josephus dated its construction to the time of Alexander the Great. See Josephus, *Ant.* 11.302–347; 13.254–256; *War* 1.62–65; Joseph Naveh and Izchak Magen,
"Aramaic and Hebrew Inscriptions of the Second-Century BCE at Mount Gerizim,"
ʿ*Atiqot* 32 (1997): 9*–17*; Izchak Magen et al., "The Hebrew and Aramaic Inscriptions from Mount Gerizim" [Hebrew], *Qad* 33/2 (2000): 125–32. See also Ephraim
Stern and Izchak Magen, "The First Phase of the Samaritan Temple on Mount Gerizim—New Archaeological Evidence," *Qad* 33/2 (2000): 119–24. Jorg Frey thinks
that the outline of the older shrine was not similar to that of the Jerusalem temple; see "Temple and Rival Temple—The Cases of Elephantine, Mt. Gerizim, and
Leontopolis," in *Gemeinde ohne Tempel: Zur Substituierung und Transformation
des Jerusalemer Tempels und seines Kults im Alten Testament, antiken Judentums
und frühen Christentum* (ed. B. Ego et al.; WUNT 118; Tübingen: Mohr Siebeck,

sacred precinct—the Persian-period precinct and the Hellenistic precinct—occupied about five acres on the mountain's summit. If this analysis is sustained, the temple cultus in Jerusalem was faced with a substantial rival at Mount Gerizim already in the fifth century.[48] It is not possible at this time to resolve the issue of whether Persian-period Samaria had other sanctuaries, given the uncertain and sketchy material remains.[49]

In addition to the evidence for a succession of shrines on Mount Gerizim, one should keep in mind the larger socioeconomic realities of Samaria during the Achaemenid period. The material remains from the southern Levant suggest that the Persian province of Samaria was larger, far more populous, and more wealthy than its southern neighbor.[50] The region as a whole does not seem to have suffered a demographic decline from the Iron II period to the Persian period. The Achaemenid era witnesses, in fact, an unprecedented number of sites in Samaria. The Persian period represents, for example, the time in which the northern region of Samaria is the most densely populated (247 sites) of all periods, more than the Iron II period (238 sites) and considerably more than the Hellenistic period (140 sites).[51] When the Jewish community at Elephantine wished

---

1999), 183–86. According to Josephus, it was (*Ant.* 13.256; *War* 1.63). On this question, see the recent comments of Magen, "Mt. Gerizim—A Temple City," 33:97–110 (and pl. 2).

[48] Mary Joan Leith (private communication) calls attention to the recent publication of a fourth-century Samarian coin (# 26) with the name of "Jeroboam" (*yrbʿm*) on the obverse; see Yaakov Meshorer and Shraga Qedar, *The Coinage of Samaria in the Fourth Century B.C.E.* (Beverly Hills: Numismatics Fine Arts International, 1991), 49. On the reverse of this fascinating coin stand two female figures in what may be a shrine. The structure depicted is unknown. One possibility is that it represents a Samarian temple at Mount Gerizim or at Samaria.

[49] This is not to deny that the region of Samaria had such shrines. Rather, one has to acknowledge that no undisputed examples have come to light thus far.

[50] Adam Zertal, "The Pahwah of Samaria (Northern Israel) during the Persian Period: Types of Settlement, Economy, History and New Discoveries," *Transeu* 3 (1990): 9–30; idem, "The Province of Samaria during the Persian and Hellenistic Periods" [Hebrew], in *Michael: Historical, Epigraphical and Biblical Studies in Honor of Professor Michael Heltzer* (ed. Y. Avishur and R. Deutsch; Tel Aviv-Jaffa: Archaeological Centre Publications, 1999), 75*–98*.

[51] Adam Zertal, "The Mount Manasseh (Northern Samarian Hills) Survey," *NEAEHL* 3:1311–12. My focus is with the region of Samaria as a whole. Individual areas differed as to how they fared during the Achaemenid period: Israel Finkelstein, "Southern Samarian Hills Survey," *NEAEHL* 4:1313–14; Zertal, "Pahwah," 11–16; Shimon Dar, "Samaria (Archaeology of the Region)," *ABD* 5:926–31; idem, "The Survey of Western Samaria," *NEAEHL* 4:1314–16.

to rebuild their temple in the late fifth century, they lobbied the authorities in both Jerusalem and Samaria for their support.[52] Certainly the Jews of Elephantine must have felt some affinity with the community of Samaria or they would not have written the Samarian leadership to ask for their assistance. Considering how close Samaria was to Yehud, culturally speaking, these realities cannot but have had an impact on the Chronicler's worldview.[53] There were varieties of Judeans in Yehud, but not all Yahwists were Judeans.

In dealing with the issue of rivals to the Jerusalem temple, one also has to deal with Jewish shrines outside the land of Israel. I have already mentioned the existence of one such Jewish sanctuary at Elephantine.[54] Whether there were also Jewish shrines at Casiphia and elsewhere in the Babylonian Diaspora is disputed.[55] In the second century B.C.E., Jews would build a temple at Leontopolis in Egypt.[56] In short, the reconstruction of the

---

[52] Bezalel Porten and Ada Yardeni, *Letters* (vol. 1 of *Textbook of Aramaic Documents from Ancient Egypt: Newly Copied, Edited and Translated into Hebrew and English;* Jerusalem: Hebrew University of Jerusalem, Department of the History of the Jewish People, 1986), 4.5–4.10.

[53] I hope to deal with this issue in greater depth in a future essay.

[54] Albert Vincent, *La Religion des Judéo-Araméens d'Éléphantine* (Paris: Geuthner, 1937); Bezalel Porten, *Archives from Elephantine* (Berkeley and Los Angeles: University of California Press, 1968); Thomas M. Bolin, "The Temple of יהו at Elephantine and Persian Religious Policy," in *The Triumph of Elohim: From Yahwisms to Judaisms* (ed. D. V. Edelman; CBET 13; Kampen: Kok Pharos, 1995), 127–42.

[55] Some think that the references to "the place" (*hammāqôm*) in Casiphia (Ezra 8:17) and to the "sanctuary" (*miqdāš*) in Ezek 11:16 constitute evidence for the existence of a Jewish sanctuary in Babylonia; see, e.g., Laurence E. Browne, "A Jewish Sanctuary in Babylonia," *JTS* 17 (1916): 400–401; Peter R. Ackroyd, *Exile and Restoration* (OTL; Philadelphia: Westminster, 1968), 34–35; idem, *Israel under Babylon and Persia* (New Clarendon Bible; Oxford: Oxford University Press, 1970), 25–27; Julia H. Chong, "Were There Yahwistic Sanctuaries in Babylon?" *AJT* 10 (1996): 198–217. Joseph Blenkinsopp, *The Pentateuch: An Introduction to the First Five Books of the Bible* (ABRL; Garden City, N.Y.: Doubleday, 1992), 238, speaks of Casiphia as a "cultic establishment ... a center of worship and learning." Others view the biblical references as vague or textually uncertain: James D. Purvis, "Exile and Return," in *Ancient Israel: A Short History from Abraham to the Roman Destruction of the Temple* (ed. H. Shanks; Englewood Cliffs, N.J.: Prentice-Hall, 1988), 158–60. On the construction, *bǝkāsipyā' hammāqôm,* see Hugh G. M. Williamson, *Ezra, Nehemiah* (WBC 16; Waco, Tex.: Word, 1985), 116–17.

[56] Josephus, *Ant.* 12.387–388; 13.62–73; *War* 7.426–427, 436; Jerome, *Expl. Dan.* 3.11.14; Mathias Delcor, "Le Temple d'Onias en Égypte," *RB* 75 (1968): 189–203; Gideon Bohak, *Joseph and Aseneth and the Jewish Temple in Heliopolis* (SBLEJL 10; Atlanta: Scholars Press, 1996), 19–40.

house of God in Jerusalem did not put an end to all other sanctuary construction. In the context of the Persian and Hellenistic periods, the exclusive authority and privilege of the Jerusalem temple could not be taken for granted. Its supporters had to argue their case.

JERUSALEM'S INTERNATIONAL IMPORT IN THE JUDAHITE MONARCHY

Returning to Chronicles, I would like to explore briefly how the author's portrayal of three crises during the Judahite monarchy may be directed toward the international circumstances of the Chronicler's own time. My assumption is that one can learn something about the Chronicler's aspirations for Jerusalem's stature in the late Persian period by examining his depiction of Jerusalem's preexilic past. One of the means by which the author commends Jerusalem's enduring value is through speeches and prayers spoken by major characters in his narration of the Judahite monarchy. Unlike the Deuteronomist, the Chronicler consistently cites Solomon's dedicatory prayer in his work.[57] The reuse of Solomon's prayer is important because it facilitates, among other things, a long-range relationship between people in a variety of locales and circumstances and the Jerusalem temple. When Judahite kings encounter trouble, good things happen to those who petition Yhwh along the lines established by Solomon. In mentioning the critical role played by prayer, I do not wish to diminish the importance of sacrifice.[58] Obviously, the author wanted his audience to be faithful supporters of the temple by journeying to the sanctuary, supporting its cultus, and bringing offerings to its precincts. What the medium of prayer allows, however, is for the author to verbalize the importance of the Jerusalem temple for his readers and to encourage recourse to the temple by those who may reside far away from Jerusalem in other lands. The vehicle of prayer allows Yahwists to support the central sanctuary without having any recourse to the priests, symbols, altars, and courts of other shrines. Three examples will suffice.

When King Jehoshaphat faces a formidable invasion from a coalition of Ammonites, Moabites, and Meunites from the southeast, a group of

---

[57] Mark A. Throntveit, *When Kings Speak: Royal Speech and Royal Prayer in Chronicles* (SBLDS 93; Atlanta: Scholars Press, 1987). The Deuteronomist applies the relevance of Solomon's petitions to the Assyrian crisis faced by Hezekiah, but this is exceptional; see Gary N. Knoppers, "'There was None Like Him': Incomparability in the Books of Kings," *CBQ* 54 (1992): 411–31.

[58] Nor do I wish to imply that the divine promises were absolute. Much like the authors of Deuteronomy (4:23–28; 28:58–64; 30:18), the Chronicler conditions Israel's possession of the land upon its obedience to God. See, e.g., 1 Chr 28:8, in which the addressee is Israel, and 2 Chr 7:17–22.

foes who clearly overlap with some of Yehud's neighbors in the Persian period, the king "sets himself to seek [*drš*] Yhwh" and proclaims a national "fast."[59] The very nations that were spared by God when the Israelites entered the land (Deut 2:1–22) are now threatening Judah's existence within it (2 Chr 20:11–12). In resorting to Jerusalem, the king and people honor the divine directive given at the dedication of the house of God to seek (*bqš*) Yhwh in times of need (2 Chr 7:14). Delivered in the midst of this crisis, Jehoshaphat's prayer calls attention to the universal and particular aspects of Judah's relationship with its God (20:6–12). Yhwh, "the God of our fathers," Jehoshaphat proclaims, is also "the God in the heavens" (*'th-hw' 'lhym bšmym*) and "rules over all of the kingdoms of the peoples" (*w'th mwšl bkl mmlkwt hgwym;* 20:6). There may be no one who can withstand Yhwh, as the king declares, but this deity is still very much connected to a particular place and people.[60] Jehoshaphat's speech, which laments Judah's plight and solicits a divine response, directly alludes to petitions within Solomon's earlier prayer (20:8–9; see 6:28, 34). The explicit reference to the existence of the temple is critical, because this sanctuary was accepted by God as the place where efficacious prayers could be offered (20:8–9; see 7:1–2, 14). Yhwh's incomparable status in no way detracts from the position of Judah and its temple in the divine economy. On the contrary, Yhwh's power as "the God in the heavens" enhances the prospects for a favorable outcome to Jehoshaphat's appeals. In this text, one cannot help but notice a clear declaration in the setting of the Achaemenid era that the God Judeans worship transcends Yehud's borders. Yet the author is quick to underscore the association between Yhwh's name and Jerusalem's temple. In other words, the Chronicler cites Yhwh's incomparability in the divine sphere to reassert the relevance of the central sanctuary for the residents of Judah and Jerusalem.

A second example of the reuse of Solomon's temple dedication to accentuate the significance of Jerusalem is the account of Hezekiah's Passover, found only in Chronicles. In the course of preparing for this festival, construed as a centralized national event in accordance with the dictates of the Deuteronomic law code, Hezekiah appeals to Israelites,

---

[59] See 2 Chr 20:1–4. In 2 Chr 20:1, I am reading "the Meunites" (הַמְּעוּנִים) with LXX[AB]. MT 2 Chr 20:1 reads "the Ammonites" (הָעַמּוֹנִים). The Meunites, a group of disputed origin, are only mentioned in late biblical texts: 2 Chr 20:1 (LXX[AB]); 26:7 (MT), 8 (LXX); Ezra 2:50 (Qere); Neh 7:52. Note with respect to Jehoshaphat's war the repeated association between the Meunites and the hill country of Seir (2 Chr 20:10, 22, 23).

[60] Gary N. Knoppers, "Jerusalem at War in Chronicles," in Hess and Wenham, *Zion, City of Our God*, 57–76.

including the remnant of the northern tribes, and invites them to participate in the Passover.[61] It is important to recall that Chronicles does not include an account of the Assyrian exile. In this respect, the Chronicler's work must be carefully distinguished from that of the Deuteronomists, who posit a massive Assyrian deportation of the residents of the northern kingdom as well as a major influx of immigrants from other parts of the Assyrian Empire into Samaria (2 Kgs 17:1–24).[62] Because the Assyrian exile marks the end of the northern realm, the authors of Kings do not discuss later events in the former northern kingdom.[63] One is left with the impression that the land of the northern tribes, having been emptied of Israelites, was now exclusively populated by foreigners.

The Chronicler's work does not portray a land-emptying northern deportation.[64] To be sure, the author does not directly recount the fall of Israel. Because he regards both the kingdom and the cult of the northern tribes as inherently rebellious, he does not provide an independent history of the northern realm.[65] However, in his narration of Hezekiah's reign, the author provides an indication of his own perspective toward the Assyrian invasions and the Assyrian exile. Hezekiah's letters sent to Ephraim and Manasseh explicitly acknowledge a continuing Israelite presence in the land, "the remnant that is left to you" (*hplyṭh hnš'rt lkm;* 2 Chr 30:6). By speaking of the northerners as "the children of Israel" and by inviting them to return to the God of their fathers, "the God of Abraham, Isaac, and Israel," Hezekiah reaffirms their Israelite identity. In the view of the Chronicler, the northern deportations were not comprehensive. To put matters somewhat differently, Hezekiah would have no one to appeal to attend a national Passover if northern Israelites (Asher, Ephraim, Manasseh, and Zebulun are mentioned by name) no longer remained in the land (2 Chr

---

[61] In earlier legislation the Passover is celebrated as a local, family affair; see Bernard M. Levinson, *Deuteronomy and the Hermeneutics of Legal Innovation* (New York: Oxford University Press, 1997), 53–97.

[62] Bob Becking, *The Fall of Samaria: An Historical and Archaeological Study* (SHANE 2; Leiden: Brill, 1992). The long Deuteronomistic sermon on this series of events (2 Kgs 17:7–41) is, as we have seen, multilayered.

[63] Excepting Josiah's northern reforms (2 Kgs 23:15–20), which undo the damage done by a succession of northern kings from the time of Jeroboam I onward (Knoppers, *Reign of Jeroboam,* 171–222).

[64] The genealogies do mention an Assyrian exile affecting the two-and-a-half Transjordanian tribes (1 Chr 5:23–26).

[65] Gary N. Knoppers, "Rehoboam in Chronicles: Villain or Victim?" *JBL* 109 (1990): 423–40; idem, "'Battling against Yahweh': Israel's War against Judah in 2 Chr 13:2–20," *RB* 100 (1993): 511–32.

30:1–11). The very wording of the invitation unambiguously reaffirms the Israelite character of those who reside in Samaria.

The author acknowledges disasters at the hands of the Assyrian kings stemming from rebellions by "your fathers and your kinsmen" against Yhwh, but the text offers hope to the northern Israelites.[66] If the people are not as stiff-necked as their fathers and kinsmen had been and turn back to Yhwh (*šwb*), Yhwh may turn (*šwb*) his attention back to the survivors (2 Chr 30:6).[67] One sees resonances with one of Solomon's petitions as well as with the theophany of Exod 34:6–7. Like Solomon's appeal dealing with the possibility of foreign exile, Hezekiah's invitation to journey to Yhwh's "sanctuary" (*mqdšw*) plays on the different nuances of the root *šwb* ("to turn, return"). The letter places the onus of responsibility on the addressees. The people's positive response, their returning (*šwb*) to God, may elicit divine compassion for their relatives before their captors in exile, because Yhwh may yet turn (*šwb*) from his fierce anger (2 Chr 30:6–8; see 6:36–39). Being the compassionate, faithful, and merciful God revealed to Moses (Exod 34:6–7), Yhwh may respond to the people's repentance (*šwb*) by returning (*šwb*) their kin and their children to "this land" (2 Chr 30:8–9). The invitation ingeniously appropriates language from earlier texts, while creatively going beyond them. Solomon's petition plays on the prospect of divine mercy toward those exiles who appeal to Yhwh in a foreign land but does not actually mention a return from exile.[68] In a Persian-period context it is surely relevant that the invitation to the northern tribes associates returning to Yhwh with journeying to "his sanctuary that he consecrated forever" (*lmqdšw ʾšr hqdyš lʿwlm;* 30:8). Is it not likely that the Chronicler in expounding this incident is encouraging participation by

---

[66] Indeed, the Chronicler acknowledges that Judah experienced its own share of setbacks. Hezekiah speaks of abandonment of the Jerusalem temple as a reason for the exile of many Judahites during the reign of his predecessor, Ahaz (2 Chr 29:5–11).

[67] A point rightly emphasized by Sara Japhet, *The Ideology of the Book of Chronicles and Its Place in Biblical Thought* (BEATAJ 9; Frankfurt am Main: Lang, 1989); Hugh G. M. Williamson, *Israel in the Books of Chronicles* (Cambridge: Cambridge University Press, 1977); and Roddy L. Braun, "A Reconsideration of the Chronicler's Attitude toward the North," *JBL* 96 (1977): 59–62.

[68] Such a possibility is explicitly raised in Deut 30:1–10, should the exiles turn back (*šwb*) to Yhwh and follow his commands. In Chronicles, the offer meets with an enthusiastic response from Judah and a mixed response from the northern tribes (2 Chr 30:10–14). The national celebration that follows recalls the glory days of the united monarchy (2 Chr 30:15–27); see Mark A. Throntveit, "Hezekiah in the Books of Chronicles," in *Society of Biblical Literature 1988 Seminar Papers* (ed. D. J. Lull; SBLSP 27; Atlanta: Scholars Press, 1988), 302–11.

Yahwists from Samaria and other regions of the former northern kingdom in the Jerusalem cultus of his own time?[69]

A third example of the reapplication of Solomon's dedicatory prayer to underscore Jerusalem's enduring importance is Manasseh's repentance and reform. The Manasseh of Chronicles, like the Manasseh of Kings (2 Kgs 21:1–18), is a wicked tyrant (2 Chr 33:2–9), but the Chronicler's Manasseh suffers divine punishment in the form of deportation to Babylon (33:11), repents, and changes course (33:12–17). During his Assyrian exile in Babylon, the Judahite king entreats the favor of Yhwh (*ḥlh ʾt-pny yhwh*), abjectly humbles himself (*wyknʿ mʾd*) before the God of his fathers, and prays to him (*wytpll ʾlyw*) in accordance with the terms of Solomon's prayer (2 Chr 33:12–13; see 6:36–39). For the Chronicler's audience, it is surely relevant that the text mentions both Assyria and Babylon in connection with Manasseh's exile. My concern in this context is not whether the Chronicler was thinking of a temporary Assyrian capital located in Babylon[70] but with the effect that this story might have had on the Chronicler's readership among the elite in Yehud. The Chronicler's audience would know that the Assyrian and Babylonian deportations were the major exiles affecting the northern and southern tribes. The results of Manasseh's about-face are, therefore, telling. Going beyond his earlier pledge to Solomon, God restores Manasseh to Jerusalem and to his kingdom (33:14; see 7:14). In the Chronicler's work, Manasseh becomes a model of how to deal with self-made adversity. Particularly interesting for our purposes is the fact that Manasseh is living in a foreign land far from Judah when he decides to make amends and reverse course. The fact that Manasseh resides outside the land of Israel, hundreds of miles from Jerusalem, has no effect whatsoever on the efficacy of his prayers.[71] One senses that the Chronicler is making the case that the Jerusalem temple has an enduring relevance for all those who identify with Israel, whether they live in the land of Israel or in the Diaspora.

---

[69] So also Japhet, *I and II Chronicles*, 936–54; Hugh G. M. Williamson, *1 and 2 Chronicles* (NCB; Grand Rapids: Eerdmans, 1982), 360–70.

[70] Most recently, Anson F. Rainey, "The Chronicler and His Sources—Historical and Geographical," in *The Chronicler As Historian* (ed. M. P. Graham et al.; JSOTSup 238; Sheffield: JSOT Press, 1997), 30–72.

[71] Daniel's ritual behavior, while in exile, is another example of the success of this larger strategy of underscoring the critical role played by the Jerusalem temple in the people's life (Dan 6:11).

Conclusions

In the Chronicler's work, the author makes the case that Jerusalem and its institutions are an intrinsic part of Israel's classical heritage. The Chronicler situates Jerusalem's position internationally in his own time by recourse to establishing such a status for the city in preexilic history. Jerusalem appears as the focal point of Judah and Jerusalem, but also with continuing claims on Samaria. Jerusalem is the capital of an international religion centered on the temple. He promotes the value of the Jerusalem temple for all southern and northern Israelites regardless of their particular geographic locations. For those who identify themselves as Israelite, the Jerusalem temple's significance is not confined to Yehud or, for that matter, to the land of Israel. From the perspective of the author of Isa 66:1–2, a transcendent Yhwh did not need the temple in Jerusalem, but from the perspective of the Chronicler such a declaration is largely beside the point. Yhwh had authorized the temple's construction, endorsed its dedication, and repeatedly reaffirmed his relationship to this house of worship. From the Chronicler's perspective, the issue is not whether Yhwh needed this place but how much the people did. Israel's temple city had proven its great value on numerous occasions in the past. The question in the present is whether the people would have recourse to it.

PART 3

BIBLICAL JERUSALEM:
TOWARD A CONSENSUS

Biblical Jerusalem: An Archaeological Assessment

Ann E. Killebrew
The Pennsylvania State University

Jerusalem, as both a spiritual concept and physical reality, has long been the focus of the biblical authors, the theme of theological treatises and interpretations, and the topic of countless scholarly speculations. It is the most extensively excavated ancient site in biblical Israel, a fact that is due in no small measure to its spiritual centrality for the three major monotheistic religions, its contested past, and modern-day concerns of "ownership." For these reasons Andrew G. Vaughn and I selected Jerusalem as the centerpiece of a cross-disciplinary dialogue between biblical scholars, historians, Assyriologists, Egyptologists, and archaeologists within the framework of the Society of Biblical Literature Consultation on "Jerusalem in Bible and Archaeology" held during the Society for Biblical Literature Annual Meetings from 1998 to 2001.

As an archaeologist and a long-time resident of Jerusalem, I deemed any attempt to interpret Jerusalem's past as a foolhardy exercise that was limited by inescapable cultural and personal preconceptions, ideological biases, and circular academic arguments. Though I retain my skepticism regarding the objectivity of archaeology—mute stones do not speak; rather, we translate their words and then interpret them—we should nevertheless attempt the daunting task of reconstructing Bronze and Iron Age Jerusalem based on interdisciplinary dialogue and open debate.

During the past decade in particular, the topic of Jerusalem has provoked especially acrimonious and polemical debates, even as the archaeological evidence, or lack thereof, is being published in increasingly frequent final excavation reports. The focus of the controversy has been the apparent inconsistencies between a literal reading of the biblical account of Jerusalem describing the reigns of David and Solomon and the unimposing archaeological reality of the city during the tenth and ninth centuries B.C.E. Thus, it was with some surprise that with each passing year of our consultation, and during the course of the compilation of this volume, I became increasingly more optimistic that some consensus can be reached regarding Jerusalem's past based on the combined efforts of archaeologists, historians, and biblical scholars, while simultaneously recognizing the personal and professional biases we all bring to the discussion. As this volume demonstrates, archaeology has much to add to this discussion.

In spite of Jerusalem's difficult archaeological record, which has been the topic of many articles and books as summarized in several essays in this volume,[1] I see a coherent image of ancient Jerusalem slowly emerging from the remnants and ruins of ancient Jerusalem, especially from excavations conducted during the past four decades. In addition, numerous well-documented final excavation reports and publications have recently appeared that add significantly to the evidence, with many more primary reports in various stages of preparation.[2] The focus of my archaeological

---

[1] In particular, see the essay by Cahill for a summary of the history of research on Jerusalem as it relates to the united monarchy. See the essays by Geva and Schniedewind for a summary of the history of research as it relates to the end of the Judahite monarchy.

[2] The most relevant and archaeologically well-documented field reports include the excavations on the southeastern hill ("City of David") by Kathleen M. Kenyon (1961–67), excavations in the Jewish Quarter by Nahman Avigad (1969–1982), Benjamin Mazar's (1968–77) and Eilat Mazar's (1986–87) Southern Wall (Ophel) excavations to the south of the Temple Mount, Yigal Shiloh's excavations in the City of David (1978–85), excavations of several Iron II cemeteries at several locales in East Jerusalem, and most recently Ronny Reich's and Eli Shukron's (1995–present) excavations at the base of the eastern slope of the City of David and around the Gihon Spring. The most significant final excavation reports that present relevant primary data for this discussion include the following publications: City of David (Kenyon's final excavation reports): A. Douglas Tushingham, *Excavations in Jerusalem, 1961–1967, vol. I* (Toronto: Royal Ontario Museum, 1985); Hendricus J. Franken and Margreet L. Steiner, *Excavations by Kathleen M. Kenyon in Jerusalem 1961–1967, vol. II, The Iron Age Extramural Quarter on the South-East Hill* (Oxford: Oxford University Press, 1990); Margreet L. Steiner, *Excavations by Kathleen M. Kenyon in Jerusalem 1961–1967, vol. III, The Settlement in the Bronze and Iron Ages* (Copenhagen International Seminar 9; New York: Sheffield Academic Press, 2001); Itzhak Eshel and Kay Prag, eds., *Excavations by Kathleen M. Kenyon in Jerusalem 1961–1967, vol. IV, The Iron Age Cave Deposits on the South-East Hill and Isolated Burials and Cemeteries Elsewhere* (Oxford: Oxford University Press, 1995); City of David (Shiloh's final excavation reports): Yigal Shiloh, *Excavations at the City of David I, 1978–1982: Interim Report of the First Five Seasons* (Qedem 19; Jerusalem: Institute of Archaeology, Hebrew University of Jerusalem, 1984); Donald T. Ariel, *Excavations at the City of David 1978–1985 Directed by Yigal Shiloh, vol. II, Imported Stamped Amphora Handles, Coins, Worked Bone and Ivory, and Glass* (Qedem 30; Jerusalem: Institute of Archaeology, Hebrew University of Jerusalem, 1990); Alon De Groot and Donald T. Ariel, *Excavations at the City of*

audit is the material culture evidence presented in these primary reports, with an emphasis on what has actually been uncovered rather than on speculations regarding what may have (or should have) existed in antiquity.[3] While there are many details that are unknown or remains that are

---

David 1978–1985 Directed by Yigal Shiloh, vol. III, Stratigraphical, Environmental, and Other Reports (Qedem 33; Jerusalem: Institute of Archaeology, Hebrew University of Jerusalem, 1992); Donald T. Ariel and Alon De Groot, eds., *Excavations at the City of David 1978–1985 Directed by Yigal Shiloh, vol. IV, Various Reports* (Qedem 35; Jerusalem: Institute of Archaeology, Hebrew University of Jerusalem, 1994); Donald T. Ariel, ed., *Excavations at the City of David Directed by Yigal Shiloh, vol. V, Extramural Areas* (Qedem 40; Jerusalem: Institute of Archaeology, Hebrew University of Jerusalem, 2000); Donald T. Ariel et al., *Excavations at the City of David 1978–1985 Directed by Yigal Shiloh, vol. VI, Inscriptions* (ed. D. T. Ariel; Qedem 41; Jerusalem: Institute of Archaeology, Hebrew University of Jerusalem, 2000); City of David (Gihon Spring and Lower Southeastern Hill [only preliminary reports]): Ronny Reich and Eli Shukron, "The Excavations at the Gihon Spring and Warren's Shaft System in the City of David," in *Ancient Jerusalem Revealed* (ed. H. Geva; Jerusalem: Israel Exploration Society, 2000), 327–39; Jewish Quarter (Avigad's final excavation reports): Hillel Geva, ed., *Jewish Quarter Excavations in the Old City of Jerusalem Conducted by Nahman Avigad, 1969–1982, vol. I, Architecture and Stratigraphy: Areas A, W and X–2, Final Report* (Jerusalem: Israel Exploration Society, 2000). Southern Wall (Mazars' first final excavation report of the "Millo"): Eilat Mazar and Benjamin Mazar, *Excavations in the South of the Temple Mount: The Ophel of Biblical Jerusalem* (Qedem 29; Jerusalem: Institute of Archaeology, Hebrew University of Jerusalem, 1989); Iron II Cemeteries: Gabriel Barkay, "Northern and Western Jerusalem in the End of the Iron Age" [Hebrew] (Ph.D. diss., Tel Aviv University, 1985); and an updated summary of his dissertation in idem, "The Necropoli of Jerusalem in the First Temple Period" [Hebrew], in *The History of Jerusalem: The Biblical Period* (ed. S. Ahituv and A. Mazar; Jerusalem: Yad Izhak Ben-Zvi, 2000), 233–70; David Ussishkin, *The Village of Silwan: The Necropolis from the Period of the Judean Kingdom* (Jerusalem: Israel Exploration Society, 1993); Ronny Reich, "The Ancient Burial Ground in the Mamilla Neighbourhood, Jerusalem," in *Ancient Jerusalem Revealed: Expanded Edition 2000* (ed. H. Geva; Jerusalem: Israel Exploration Society, 2000), 111–18. For a summary of archaeological research and relevant publications through 1993, see Hillel Geva, "History of Archaeological Research in Jerusalem," *NEAEHL* 2:801–4 and Cahill's essay in this volume.

[3] Although I am focusing on what has been found, it is necessary to note that Mount Moriah (encased in the Temple Mount podium or the Muslim Haram esh-Sharif) has not been excavated due to obvious political and religious considerations. Thus, one of the potentially most promising areas for the exploration of ancient Jerusalem has not and will not be excavated in the foreseeable future. It cannot be ruled out that there may, though not necessarily, be archaeological remains from the Bronze and Iron Ages underneath the present Islamic structures. See Ussishkin's essay in this volume for a discussion of various suggestions regarding a preexilic

no longer preserved, a fairly clear outline of Bronze and Iron Age (ca. 3000–586 B.C.E.) Jerusalem is emerging.

The accumulative archaeological evidence categorically indicates that the ancient city was prominent during two periods—the Middle Bronze Age II (ca. 1800–1550 B.C.E.) and the Iron Age IIC (late eighth–seventh centuries B.C.E.). During the intervening periods (the Late Bronze and the Iron Age I and IIA/early IIB periods),[4] Jerusalem was a far more modest settlement.[5] The most contested period of time, both archaeologically and biblically, relates to our understanding of Jerusalem during the tenth century, specifically the reigns of David and Solomon. Thus far no physical remains have been found in over a century of excavations that come near to matching the biblical magnificence of the Solomon's Jerusalem that served as the capital of a "united monarchy." The core of the debate is not over whether David and Solomon existed but rather over the character of Jerusalem during their reigns: Was it an urban administrative city that could have served as the capital of a united monarchy? Was it an unfortified village? Or was it a unimpressive settlement that served as a regional administrative and/or religious center with some commercial and cultic functions? In this assessment, I discuss the scant archaeological evidence that points to a modest settlement during the fourteenth–ninth centuries B.C.E. Depending on the dating of the infamous "stepped stone structure," Jerusalem either (1) served as a regional administrative hub with some evidence of public structures or (2) was a provincial center that consisted mainly of domestic structures.

Archaeological Consensus: Middle Bronze IIB (ca. 1800–1550 b.c.e.) and Iron IIC (ca. 720–586 b.c.e.)—An Urban Fortified Jerusalem

The Middle Bronze IIB and Iron IIC periods are similar to two bookends: they represent a period of time when Jerusalem was clearly an urban

---

occupation on the Temple Mount. See also Ernst Axel Knauf's proposal in "Jerusalem in the Late Bronze and Early Iron Ages: A Proposal," *TA* 27 (2000): 75–90.

[4] There are several variations on the absolute dating for the Bronze and Iron Ages. I follow Amihai Mazar's suggested chronology and dating for these periods of time: Middle Bronze IIA (2000–1800/1750 B.C.E.), Middle Bronze IIB–C (1800/1750–1550 B.C.E.), Late Bronze I (1550–1400 B.C.E.), Late Bronze IIA–B (1400–1200 B.C.E.), Iron IA–B (1200–1000 B.C.E.), Iron IIA (1000–925 B.C.E.), Iron IIB (925–720 B.C.E.), and Iron IIC (720–586). See Amihai Mazar, *Archaeology of the Land of the Bible 10,000–586 B.C.E.* (ABRL; New York: Doubleday, 1990), 30.

[5] This general conclusion is valid whether one accepts the conventional chronology for dating tenth-century archaeological strata or whether one follows a new "low chronology" for dating these strata. See the essays by Finkelstein and Ussishkin in this volume for a summary of this chronological debate.

and fortified major center of the region. There is an increasing consensus regarding the eighteenth to mid-sixteenth centuries B.C.E. and the eighth to seventh centuries B.C.E. based on the monumental and public structures that have been excavated in Jerusalem. The most important sources of information regarding Middle Bronze Age Jerusalem are Kathleen Kenyon's 1961–67 excavations on the southeastern slope of Silwan village (City of David), Yigal Shiloh's 1978–85 excavations in the City of David, and Ronny Reich's and Eli Shukron's recent work at the Gihon Spring at the foot of the eastern slope of the City of David.[6]

The only final excavation report of the Middle Bronze Age remains in the City of David thus far published is Margreet Steiner's recent volume presenting the results of Kenyon's excavations.[7] Most noteworthy for our discussion is the detailed description of the Middle Bronze IIB fortifications that Kenyon uncovered. The published results provide clear archaeological evidence that this wall was constructed during the second half of the Middle Bronze Age (either at the end of the Middle Bronze IIA or early IIB, ca. 1800 B.C.E.) as a city fortification.[8] A second, later but much broader city wall dating to the eighth–seventh centuries B.C.E. was constructed partially over and occasionally reutilized sections of this Middle Bronze Age wall as its foundations.[9] Both Kenyon's and later Shiloh's excavations revealed that there were clearly two city walls: an earlier Middle Bronze IIB wall and a second but separate Iron IIC wall that reused parts of the Middle Bronze Age wall fortifications. Although in her preliminary reports Kenyon suggests that the city wall remained in use from the "Canaanite-Jebusite" periods and the "greater part of the Jewish Monarchy," she clearly states that there is no archaeological proof for a continued use of this wall following the end of the Middle Bronze Age until the eighth/seventh centuries B.C.E.[10] In agreement with Kenyon, Shiloh also "assumes" in his preliminary report that this wall remained in use from the end of the Middle Bronze Age until it was rebuilt in the late eighth century B.C.E. However, Shiloh notes that there is no archaeological evidence for this assumption and supports it with the statement: "The fact that no other line of fortifications, of any period, was found in the sectional trenches outside and below the existing line, in Areas B, D1 and

---

[6] For a detailed summary and analysis of the results of these excavations, see Cahill in this volume.

[7] Steiner, *Excavations in Jerusalem III,* 10–23.

[8] Ibid., 10–12.

[9] See Yigal Shiloh, *Excavations at the City of David I,* 12, 26.

[10] Kathleen M. Kenyon, "Excavations in Jerusalem, 1962," *PEQ* 94 (1963) 9–10; and see Cahill in this volume.

E2, bolsters this conclusion."[11] Unfortunately this finding would bolster the conclusion that ancient Jerusalem was unwalled and lacked fortifications during the Late Bronze through Iron IIB periods.

In the final excavation report of Kenyon's excavations, and departing from the views of Kenyon and Shiloh, Steiner presents archaeological evidence that the wall went out of use at the end of the Middle Bronze Age and was not in use during the subsequent Late Bronze, Iron I, and Iron IIA/B periods.[12] Not until the late eighth–seventh centuries B.C.E. are there signs of reoccupation to the east (i.e., outside) the Middle Bronze Age city wall. Based on the complete lack of any archaeological or stratigraphic evidence for the continued use of the Middle Bronze Age city wall until the end of the Iron Age, one must reject suggestions that this wall remained in use during the Late Bronze through Iron IIA–B periods. Since no other suitable wall has thus far been uncovered, the only possible conclusion is that ancient Jerusalem from roughly the sixteenth to mid-eighth centuries B.C.E. lacked a city fortification wall. Attempts to explain this absence of archaeological evidence for the continued use of this wall from the fifteenth–late eighth centuries as a result of "erosion" are methodologically unacceptable and lack any proof. The paucity of even sherds dating from the sixteenth–ninth centuries B.C.E. in the fills and slope wash of the eastern slope provides an additional indication that settlement in the City of David was at best modest during the Late Bronze through Iron IIB periods. In particular, I reject suggestions that Jerusalem was fortified in the Late Bronze Age. All evidence indicates that Jerusalem was small and certainly unfortified, matching the general trend of unfortified cities throughout Canaan in the Late Bronze Age. Jerusalem of the Amarna period is hardly likely to have been the exception to this archaeological phenomenon.

Further evidence for a fortified Middle Bronze II settlement includes the recent discovery by Ronny Reich and Eli Shukron of two monumental towers dated to the Middle Bronze IIB period. These towers formed part of a public water system connected to a tunnel that led to the Pool Tower and Spring Tower protecting the Gihon Spring. Their excavations have also revealed that Channel II and Tunnel III are part of this monumental public water system, together with remnants of additional structures dating to this period. Reich and Shukron have convincingly shown that the shaft of "Warren's Shaft" never served as a water system. No less important is their discovery that the tunnel intersecting Warren's Shaft was constructed in

---

[11] Shiloh, *Excavations at the City of David I,* 35 n. 132; see also p. 28.

[12] For a description of the stratigraphic sequence of layers related to Wall 3, see Steiner, *Excavations in Jerusalem III,* 10–12; regarding the lack of evidence for any fortifications during the Late Bronze Age, see ibid., 39.

two phases: the earlier phase dating to the Middle Bronze IIB and the later recutting of the tunnel dating to the eighth–seventh centuries B.C.E.[13] There is no archaeological evidence that the water system remained in use during the Late Bronze through Iron IIA/B periods, especially if the settlements during this six-hundred-year span were unfortified.[14] The recent excavations in the Gihon Spring area provide indisputable support for Jerusalem's importance as a fortified center during the Middle Bronze IIB period.

The late eighth and seventh centuries B.C.E. form the second bookend of preexilic Jerusalem. There is abundant evidence indicating Jerusalem's significance as a major urban center during the late Iron Age. Nearly all excavators working in the City of David, the Ophel, and the Jewish Quarter have uncovered significant remains from the late eighth and seventh centuries. Kenyon's[15] and Shiloh's[16] excavations revealed that the eastern slope of the City of David served as a residential quarter of mixed neighborhoods of affluent and poorer families during the later eighth and seventh centuries B.C.E.

Equally significant are the recent excavations by Reich and Shukron on the eastern slopes of the City of David, where they have uncovered additional sections of the so-called "extramural" residential quarter that are in fact enclosed by several previously unknown eighth–seventh century outer fortification walls (most notably Wall 502). These walls run parallel and down slope from the well-known Iron IIC city wall measuring approximately 5 m wide, the latter uncovered by several Jerusalem excavators,

---

[13] Ronny Reich and Eli Shukron, "Light at the End of the Tunnel," *BAR* 25/1 (1999): 22–33, 72; idem, "Excavations at the Gihon Spring," 327–39; idem, "Jerusalem, City of David," *Hadashot Arkheologiyot* 112 (2000): 82*–83*, figs. 150 and 151; idem, "New Excavations on the Eastern Slope of the City of David" [Hebrew], *Qad* 34/2 (122) (2001): 78–87; idem, "Jerusalem, City of David," *Hadashot Arkheologiyot* 114 (2002): 77*–78*, fig. 118; see also the essay by Cahill in this volume.

[14] In fact, based on the lack of sherds from the Late Bronze through Iron IIB periods, Reich proposes that the Gihon Spring and water systems were not used during the sixteenth–ninth centuries B.C.E. Reich (oral communication, 1 January 2003).

[15] Steiner, *Excavations in Jerusalem III*, 54–111.

[16] For a summary of Shiloh's excavation results, see Shiloh, *Excavations at the City of David I*, 28–29. Only the final excavation report from Area D has been published thus far. See Donald T. Ariel et al., "Area D1: Stratigraphic Report," in Ariel, *Excavations at the City of David V*, 33–72; and Donald T. Ariel and Alon De Groot, "The Iron Age Extramural Occupation at the City of David and Additional Observations on the Siloam Channel," in Ariel, *Excavations at the City of David V*, 155–64.

including Kenyon (Wall 1),[17] Shiloh (Wall 219),[18] as well as Reich and Shukron (Wall 501).[19] The recently discovered walls to the east of the main city wall indicate additional expansions of late Iron II Jerusalem.[20]

Excavations to the south of the Temple Mount in the Ophel area have not revealed any evidence that the area was settled earlier than the ninth century B.C.E. Further, the evidence from the excavations suggests that the biblical Ophel flourished only during the eighth and seventh centuries B.C.E. Charles Warren's 1867 excavations in the Ophel south of Mount Moriah revealed two towers, referred to as Towers A and B. Renewed excavations in this area by Benjamin Mazar (1976) and later by Eilat Mazar (1986–87) uncovered two additional monumental public buildings, designated as Buildings C (a possible gate) and D. Together these structures form a fortified complex that dates to the eighth–early sixth centuries B.C.E., the Babylonians destroying it in 586 B.C.E. Eilat Mazar has suggested that this complex may have been constructed as early as the ninth century, based on the discovery of a complete "black juglet" nestled in the foundation stones of Building D. She posits that the juglet was placed as a foundation deposit, but her suggestion is impossible to prove (or disprove). It should be pointed out that this juglet indicates a *terminus post quem* date (ninth century or later) for the construction of the gate and not necessarily its use. Thus, following the archaeological record in other areas of biblical Jerusalem, these large public structures postdate the period of the united monarchy and were in use during the peak of Jerusalem's biblical history: the eighth–seventh centuries B.C.E.

Evidence for a greatly expanded Jerusalem, outside the boundaries of the City of David and Ophel, is presented in volume I of the Jewish Quarter excavations. The results of these excavations prove conclusively that Jerusalem served as the major center of the southern kingdom of Judah. The highlights of Nahman Avigad's excavations include (in addition to residential structures) the discovery of the Iron IIC western fortification system that comprises a monumental city wall dating to the late eighth century (referred to as the "Broad Wall") together with an impressive tower. The

---

[17] Franken and Steiner, *Excavations in Jerusalem II*, 50–56; Steiner, *Excavations in Jerusalem III*, 89–91.

[18] Shiloh, *Excavations at the City of David I*, 10, 12–13, 28.

[19] See the essay by Ronny Reich and Eli Shukron in this volume for a discussion of the "extramural" residential quarter and its relationship to a second outer-wall fortification.

[20] Reich and Shukron, "Jerusalem, City of David," 112:82*–83*; idem, "New Excavations on the Eastern Slope," 85–87; and Reich, oral communication (1 January 2003).

"maximalist" proposal regarding the size of Jerusalem has been proven correct by the unambiguous archaeological evidence uncovered in the Jewish Quarter.[21] Today a consensus is emerging regarding both the archaeological evidence for Jerusalem of the Iron IIC and its close correspondence to the biblical account's view of the centrality of Jerusalem during the period following the Assyrian destruction of Samaria and the northern kingdom of Israel.

A second reliable indicator of Jerusalem's importance and impressive size is observable in the late eighth- and seventh-century cemeteries and cave deposits. Many of the burials are rock-cut tombs remarkable for their monumental size and impressive decorative features. These cemeteries again indicate the increased prosperity and wealth of Jerusalem during the late Iron II period. Gabriel Barkay has suggested that the numerous cemeteries as well as their location can be used as indicators of Jerusalem's boundaries and the existence of extramural settlements during the Iron IIC period.[22] This view, termed by Barkay as the "super-maximalist" theory, posits that Jerusalem's eighth- and seventh-century boundaries extended to the north and west, beyond the City of David, Ophel, and western hill.[23] Recently published surveys in the vicinity surrounding Jerusalem confirm the dense population of late Iron II Jerusalem and the existence of numerous small settlements that include tells, fortified sites, villages, structures, agricultural installations, towers, and concentrations of sherds.[24] This provides further evidence for the centrality and significance of Jerusalem during the Iron IIC period.

In summary, archaeological discoveries of the last four decades have transformed our understanding of Jerusalem and clearly supported maximalist views regarding its size and significance during the eighth–early sixth centuries B.C.E. The undeniable physical remains provide proof that

---

[21] See Hillel Geva's detailed discussion of the Jewish Quarter excavations in this volume and the first final report of Avigad's excavations, Geva, *Jewish Quarter Excavations I.* For a summary of the "maximalist" and "minimalist" views of eighth- and seventh-century B.C.E. Jerusalem, see Andrew G. Vaughn, *Theology, History, and Archaeology in the Chronicler's Account of Hezekiah* (SBLABS 4; Atlanta: Scholars Press), 59–71.

[22] For a summary of the various Iron II cemeteries, see Barkay, "Necropoli of Jerusalem," 233–70. For Iron II cave deposits excavated by Kenyon, see also Kay Prag, "Summary of the Report on Caves I, II and III and Deposit IV," in Eshel and Prag, *Excavations in Jerusalem IV,* 209–20.

[23] Vaughn, *Theology, History, and Archaeology,* 69–70.

[24] For a recent summary of the results of these surveys, see, e.g., Nurit Feig, "The Environs of Jerusalem in the Iron II" [Hebrew], in Ahituv and Mazar, *History of Jerusalem,* 387–410.

Jerusalem served as a large administrative, political, and residential center with a well-developed environs. Further, it may well have been the most important and impressive center in Judah. Based on excavations conducted to date, the Ophel (and perhaps the unexcavated Mount Moriah/ Temple Mount) functioned as the administrative-religious-public area of the city, with the City of David and the western hill serving as the residential quarters of the city. The entire city was enclosed by impressive city fortification systems (walls, towers, gates). This royal city of Hezekiah and Josiah, the capital of the kingdom of Judah, does indeed match in glory the earthly Jerusalem described in the biblical accounts. However, the archaeological remains undeniably reveal that the correspondence of earthly Jerusalem to the biblical description of Jerusalem does not occur until the late eighth century.

Archaeological Controversy: Late Bronze–Iron IIB (ca. 1550–720 b.c.e.)—A Fortified Urban City or Modest Regional Center?

Unlike the impressive and unambiguous archaeological evidence for Jerusalem in the Middle Bronze IIB and Iron IIC periods, the excavated record for Jerusalem during the Late Bronze through Iron IIB periods is scant and fraught with controversy. Our most important source of information regarding Jerusalem during the Late Bronze II period are several Amarna letters documenting correspondence between the Egyptian pharaoh and Abdi-heba, the local ruler of Jerusalem.[25] Although Steiner has suggested that there was no settlement on the southeastern hill (i.e., City of David) during the Late Bronze Age,[26] Cahill has argued convincingly that Jerusalem was indeed inhabited, based on numerous Late Bronze II sherds found in the terracing system of the City of David's eastern slope that she dates to the fourteenth and thirteenth centuries b.c.e. as well as on fragmentary architectural remains uncovered by the Shiloh expedition.[27]

---

[25] William L. Moran, *The Amarna Letters* (Baltimore: Johns Hopkins University Press, 1992), 325–34 (EA 285–290).

[26] Steiner, *Excavations in Jerusalem III,* 24. Steiner dates the Late Bronze Age sherds to the very end of the thirteenth century b.c.e., concluding that there is no evidence for settlement during the fourteenth and through most of the thirteenth centuries b.c.e. Regarding Jerusalem's mention in the Amarna letters, she suggests that either Urusalim should not be identified with Jerusalem or that Jerusalem was a royal estate and Abdi-heba was the manager of this small stronghold, perhaps located near the Gihon Spring (ibid., 40–41; however, see below and note 29 regarding the absence of evidence near the spring).

[27] See Cahill's detailed description in this volume.

Although much ink has been spilled regarding the reference to Jerusalem in the fourteenth-century Amarna letters, there is little doubt that Jerusalem was occupied during the Late Bronze Age, though on a significantly smaller scale than its Middle Bronze II predecessor. As discussed above, and contrary to the opinion of Kenyon, Shiloh, and Cahill,[28] I would challenge the hypothesis that the Middle Bronze Age city wall remained in use during the Late Bronze Age and early Iron Age. This highly speculative view that early second-millennium fortifications were reused is unsupported archaeologically, a fact that is admitted by all. Reich has even gone so far as to suggest that the water systems of the Gihon Spring were not in use during the Late Bronze and Iron I–IIA periods due to the lack of any evidence, even sherds, in this area.[29]

The physical evidence of fragmentary walls found on the upper slopes of the City of David excavations and the numerous Late Bronze Age sherds recovered mainly from the fills of the terracing system below the mantle of the stepped stone structure point to the existence of a small, unfortified settlement during the fourteenth–thirteenth centuries B.C.E. This interpretation fits well into the general pattern of Late Bronze Age Canaan under Egyptian domination, when the central hill country region was underdeveloped, sparsely populated, and subject to Apiru raids.[30]

The controversies swirling around Jerusalem intensify as we examine the contested evidence attributed to the twelfth–ninth centuries B.C.E. Due to the lack of contemporary textual evidence for any site in the region until the ninth century B.C.E., Jerusalem is not alone in the chronological crisis facing archaeologists during the past decade.[31] The key element to our

---

[28] See Cahill in this volume regarding the hypothesis that the Middle Bronze Age city wall remained in use through the Iron IIB period.

[29] Reich, oral communication (1 January 2003).

[30] Most of the letters from Abdi-heba mention the threat of the Apiru; see, e.g., Moran, *Amarna Letters,* EA 286–290.

[31] Regarding the lower chronology, see, e.g., Israel Finkelstein, "The Archaeology of the United Monarchy: An Alternative View," *Levant* 28 (1996): 177–87; idem, "Bible Archaeology or Archaeology of Palestine in the Iron Age? A Rejoinder," *Levant* 30 (1998): 167–74; Israel Finkelstein and Neil A. Silberman, *The Bible Unearthed: Archaeology's New Vision of Ancient Israel and the Origin of Its Sacred Texts* (New York: Free Press, 2001), 123–48; and Finkelstein's essay in this volume. Regarding the conventional chronology and replies to Finkelstein, see, e.g., Amihai Mazar, "Iron Age Chronology: A Reply to I. Finkelstein," *Levant* 29 (1997): 157–67; William G. Dever, "Save Us from Postmodern Malarkey," *BAR* 26/2 (2000): 28–35; idem, *What Did the Biblical Writers Know and When Did They Know It? What Archaeology Can Tell Us about the Reality of Ancient Israel* (Grand Rapids: Eerdmans, 2001), 124–57.

understanding of Iron I–IIA Jerusalem is the interpretation and dating of the stepped stone structure. For the purposes of my discussion and to avoid confusion, I will use the conventional chronology for the twelfth to ninth centuries B.C.E., though I recognize the serious and valid chronological challenge to the traditional interpretation and dating of Iron I–Iron IIA layers at sites throughout the Levant.[32]

Interpretations of Jerusalem during the tenth/ninth centuries B.C.E. based on archaeological evidence can be divided into two approaches: (1) Jerusalem was a fortified urban center and could have served as the capital of the united monarchy under David and Solomon, consisting of (a) mainly public structures (Kenyon and Shiloh) or (b) both domestic and as yet undiscovered public structures (Cahill);[33] (2) Jerusalem was a more modest fortified citadel or unfortified center that might have served as a regional administrative and commercial hub (Steiner, Lehmann, Finkelstein, and Ussishkin, either in the tenth or ninth centuries B.C.E.).[34]

The centerpiece of the tenth-century discussion rests on the dating and interpretation of the stepped stone structure. The majority of excavators of the City of David have dated the stepped stone structure to the tenth (or tenth/ninth centuries) B.C.E. These include Kenyon, Shiloh, and Steiner. Recent reinterpretations by archaeologists who have not personally excavated in Jerusalem (Lehmann and Finkelstein) have suggested a ninth-century B.C.E. date.[35]

The only detailed documentation and publication of primary data that presents evidence for a tenth-century B.C.E. date for the stepped stone rampart appears in Steiner's recent final report of Kenyon's excavations.[36] She provides convincing evidence for Kenyon's initial dating of the stepped stone structure as well as for the claim that the stepped stone structure is later in date and structurally distinct from the twelfth-century terracing system below the large boulders of the rampart. Steiner concludes that the terraces were built during the twelfth century[37] and

---

[32] Preliminary radiocarbon C-14 dates tend to support the lower chronology (see, e.g., Ayelet Gilboa and Ilan Sharon, "Early Iron Age Radiometric Dates from Tel Dor: Preliminary Implications for Phoenicia, and Beyond," *Radiocardon* 43 [2000]: 1343–51); however, the jury is still out regarding which chronological scenario is correct.

[33] See Cahill's detailed description and discussion in this volume.

[34] See Steiner, *Excavations in Jerusalem III*, 42–53 and 113–16; see Lehmann's, Finkelstein's, and Ussishkin's articles in this volume.

[35] See note 34 for references.

[36] Steiner, *Excavations in Jerusalem III*, 42–53.

[37] Ibid., 36–37.

suggests a tenth/ninth century or later date for the construction of the rampart's mantle.[38]

The dating of this monumental rampart to the tenth century still forms the centerpiece of nearly every discussion of Solomon's Jerusalem. Views diverge regarding the existence of city fortifications. Kenyon and Shiloh propose that the Middle Bronze IIB city wall remained in use through the ninth century, making Jerusalem a fortified city. Steiner's analysis of Kenyon's excavations reaches somewhat different conclusions. She accepts Kenyon's dating of the stepped stone structure to the tenth/ninth century, but she also recognizes that there is no proof of a larger fortified Jerusalem. In her view, the city was apparently confined mainly to the ridge of the City of David and consisted mainly of a fortified citadel and presumably several public structures that have yet to be found. In Steiner's view, no evidence has yet been uncovered for domestic structures in tenth-century Jerusalem. She concludes that Jerusalem was little more than a regional administrative center.[39] However, I would point out that, when compared to archaeological evidence at other so-called "royal cities" built by Solomon (Gezer, Megiddo, and Hazor) traditionally dated to the tenth century, the excavated physical reality of Jerusalem is modest.

In contrast, several scholars, most recently Cahill, have dated the stepped stone structure to the twelfth century B.C.E., or the "Jebusite" period. The archaeological evidence for this theory is presented for the first time in Cahill's essay in this volume. The stepped stone structure would be roughly contemporary with the site of Giloh, located southwest of Jerusalem not far from the City of David. In Cahill's well-documented presentation of several key loci, she argues that the stepped stone structure and the terracing system below the stone mantle were constructed simultaneously in the twelfth century, with the terracing system providing the necessary structural support for the mantle. It is noteworthy that Shiloh, in his preliminary report, clearly states that in one area it appears that the mantle and terracing system were bonded together while in another section the two elements appear to have been constructed separately,[40] thus also supporting Steiner's stratigraphic interpretation of the stepped stone structure. Contra Shiloh and Steiner, Cahill claims that this rampart went out of use in the tenth century with the construction of four-room houses that cut into its mantle. The earliest floors of these houses contained tenth-century pottery.[41] Other fragmentary remains of domestic structures were found during the Shiloh

---

[38] Ibid., 51–53.

[39] Ibid., 42–53.

[40] Shiloh, *Excavations at the City of David I,* 17.

[41] See Cahill's article in this volume.

expedition, evidence that Cahill uses to propose a larger settlement, though one remarkable for its lack of public structures that would be necessary for Jerusalem's function as the center—administrative or otherwise—for the united monarchy under David and/or Solomon.[42]

Less convincing and lacking any archaeological support are suggestions proposed by Cahill and several scholars (as noted above) for the reuse of the Middle Bronze Age fortification system in the Late Bronze Age through the Iron Ages, including the tenth century. Though an attractive suggestion because it would lend support to the biblical description of Solomon's Jerusalem, it is purely speculative and lacks any archaeological evidence, such as structures or floors that can be demonstrated to relate stratigraphically to this wall's use past the Middle Bronze Age.

If one accepts Cahill's evidence that the stepped stone structure was constructed in the twelfth century, Iron I Jerusalem appears to have consisted of a small, fortified citadel that may have served as a tribal center for the immediate region. However, as pointed out by Lehmann,[43] lack of any evidence of settlement or even the appearance of any architectural remains beyond the City of David rules out any suggestion that Jerusalem was a major urban center. Cahill's comparisons to the very large, highly urbanized, and socially stratified cities, complete with industrial areas and public buildings, of the Philistine and coastal plain are untenable. Following Cahill's description of the actual archaeological evidence for the traditional tenth century, we are left with remnants of domestic structures—with no evidence for any public or monumental buildings thus far discovered. Apologetics for what may have existed, or what has not been found even after over a century of intense archaeological exploration, is inadequate to explain the obvious contradiction between the idealized biblical descriptions of Solomonic Jerusalem and what actually existed. Although some of the most significant structures theoretically could have existed on the archaeologically inaccessible Temple Mount/Haram esh-Sharif compound, the missing strata dating to periods predating the late eighth–seventh centuries B.C.E. in the area north of the City of David (the Southern Wall or "Ophel" excavations) seem to reinforce the existing picture that Jerusalem was a relatively minor settlement in the tenth/ninth centuries B.C.E., confined to the crest of the City of David.[44]

---

[42] Ibid.

[43] See Lehmann's essay in this volume.

[44] The lack of evidence for any fortification system, with the exception of two fragmentary walls at the crest of the City of David that Kenyon postulated may belong to a casemate city wall (a possible proposal that needs to be investigated further), together with an out-of-situ fragmentary Proto-Aeolic capital and a few

Summarizing the available archaeological evidence and its possible interpretations (if one accepts the attribution of the stepped stone structure to the tenth century, as proposed by Kenyon, Shiloh, and Steiner), we are still left with a modest tenth- (or ninth-)century Jerusalem whose size was limited and consisted mainly of a fortified citadel that likely served as a rather limited regional center. If we accept Cahill's interpretation and the actual archaeological evidence, we are left with an even less impressive settlement or village, consisting of domestic structures and no remnants of any public or monumental buildings or fortifications. Could such a modest Jerusalem have served as a capital for the entire kingdom?[45] Moving the dates approximately a century later, as suggested by Finkelstein and others, still does not change the general conclusions regarding Jerusalem during the twelfth–ninth centuries B.C.E.; that is, the settlement was modest in size, thus far lacking in any monumental structures, with the exception of the chronologically contested stepped stone structure, rivaling those in other Iron IIA centers.[46] Additional support for the regional role of Jerusalem within the framework of a relatively underdeveloped hinterland during this period is evident from recent archaeological surveys conducted in the vicinity of Jerusalem.[47]

CONCLUSIONS

In spite of our inabilities to free ourselves of modern preconceptions, the archaeological evidence—or the lack of evidence—does provide us with a physical reality and starting point for our reconstruction of a material preexilic Jerusalem that needs to be fully acknowledged. During

---

scattered ashlar blocks, only further reinforces the view that Jerusalem was neither a large urban capital of a united monarchy nor a village but rather an administrative center that served the immediate region. See Steiner, *Excavations in Jerusalem III*, 48–50, 113.

[45] See Andrew G. Vaughn's essay in this volume for a positive reply to this question in spite of the paucity of archaeological evidence.

[46] Geva has also recently published similar conclusions in an article that summarizes new discoveries in Jerusalem at the present time; see Hillel Geva, "Innovations in Archaeological Research in Jerusalem during the 1990s" [Hebrew], *Qad* 34/2 (122) (2001): 70–77, esp. 72–73. Please note that Cahill and Steiner (in this volume) do not agree with my conclusions regarding Jerusalem's relatively minor role as a regional administrative/cultic/political center. Steiner proposes that Jerusalem was a principal settlement that served as a major regional center of the "state" of Judah, while Cahill prefers to see Jerusalem as a fortified, urban city that was indeed the capital of the united monarchy of the tenth century B.C.E.

[47] See Lehmann's article in this volume for a detailed discussion of the survey data.

periods when Jerusalem served as a significant urban center in the Middle Bronze and Iron IIC periods, abundant archaeological evidence has been excavated and recovered. The contrary must also be acknowledged that during ebbs in Jerusalem's (or the region's) centrality, the archaeological evidence is scant or nonexistent. The physical remains for the Late Bronze through Iron IIA/B periods do in fact indicate with some certainty a material reality that cannot be ignored. However, we do need to recognize that Jerusalem's significance declined, together with a broader regional contraction, during these periods.

The most emotionally contested segment of Jerusalem's past revolve around the attempts to match the physical record with biblical descriptions of David's and Solomon's kingdoms. Although doubtlessly based on a historical kernel, these accounts were aggrandized over time until finally evolving into their final form as presented in the historical books of the Bible. Our attempts to interpret (and manipulate) the scant archaeological record, in spite of extensive excavations, to fit biblical descriptions of the tenth century are increasingly problematic in light of the lack of evidence for Jerusalem as a city with monumental structures and as the central administrative and cultic hub for all of the twelve tribes under a united leadership as described by biblical authors. This dovetails well with most critical analysis of the dating of the redaction and authorship of the Deuteronomistic History to the eighth or seventh centuries B.C.E. Although most mainstream scholars will admit that the histories of tenth- and ninth-century Israelite kings are based on earlier documents, the compilation of these records into a text that resembles our Bible today first occurred during the reign of Hezekiah or later.[48]

Today there is a consensus by most that David and Solomon are in all probability historical figures and that Jerusalem was settled in the tenth century B.C.E., but the physical reality of Jerusalem (no matter which chronology is followed) is far from the city described by the Bible. Heroic efforts to interpret a grander tenth-century Jerusalem based on missing evidence are methodologically flawed and at best misleading, especially to nonarchaeologists. The highly idealized and romantic notions of a glorious Jerusalem as a historically accurate description of a tenth-century reality

---

[48] For a detailed discussion and bibliography relevant to these points, see William Schniedewind's essay in this volume. For alternative solutions, see also J. J. M. Roberts's and Richard E. Friedman's essays in this volume.

[49] See Neil A. Silberman's essay in this volume, which questions our ability ever to approach an "objective" interpretation of what existed in the past, and Vaughn's article, which encourages a more positive view of our ability in our attempts to reach a historical reconstruction.

must be carefully examined in light of what remains rather than what might have been.[49]

Whether we accept the traditional chronology or the low chronology, Jerusalem during the tenth century was a modest settlement that probably served as no more than an administrative-cultic-political center for the surrounding villages of the Iron I and IIA. In light of surveys and excavations, it is difficult to conceive that Jerusalem was the major capital city of a unified southern and northern confederation of tribes. There can be no doubt that Jerusalem was inhabited, but it was hardly the glorious city described in the Bible. Based on the actual physical evidence and critical analysis of the Deuteronomistic History, we are left with the unavoidable conclusion that spiritually, politically, and physically Jerusalem became a major urban and cultic center only during the eighth century, most likely in part due to political policies of the Assyrian Empire and the northern kingdom's fate at the hands of the Assyrians. The archaeological evidence is indisputable and complements what many scholars have already proposed regarding Jerusalem's actual role in biblical Israel. This should not detract from biblical and modern concepts of an idealized Jerusalem that symbolically or otherwise served as a religious and spiritual center throughout the ages until our present times. Having said this, we must all leave open the possibility that the future could bring new revelations and exciting discoveries that will only add to the lively debate surrounding the spiritual and material worlds of Jerusalem. In the meantime, during our cross-disciplinary discussions we need to keep in mind what exists and is probable rather than what has not been discovered and is desirable based on our modern conceptions of what biblical Jerusalem should be.

The Evidence from Kenyon's Excavations in Jerusalem: A Response Essay

Margreet Steiner
Leiden, The Netherlands

Although I did not take part in the Society of Biblical Literature Consultation "Jerusalem in Bible and Archaeology," the editors have kindly invited me to reply to Ann E. Killebrew's overview and assessment of the archaeological evidence in this volume. As so many authors point out, views on the position, status, and role of Jerusalem in the biblical period can only be based on the archaeological evidence: the humble walls and pots found in excavations. From 1961–67 Dame Kathleen M. Kenyon excavated a sizable part of the southeastern hill (City of David) in Jerusalem as well as several trenches in and around the Old City. As my latest report of Kenyon's excavations[1] has been published only recently and seems not to have been available to all authors contributing to this book,[2] I am grateful for the opportunity to recapitulate some of the evidence here.

As Killebrew points out, there is consensus between scholars on many points and controversy over some aspects. The primary controversies concern the following topics:

1. the situation in Jerusalem in the Amarna period (fourteenth century B.C.E.);
2. the large stepped stone structure and earth-filled terraces underneath; and
3. the position of Jerusalem in the beginning of Iron II.

This essay will address these three topics of controversy and present my interpretations based on Kenyon's excavations.

---

[1] Margreet L. Steiner, *Excavations by Kathleen M. Kenyon in Jerusalem, 1961–1967, vol. III, The Settlement in the Bronze and Iron Ages* (Copenhagen International Series 9; London: Sheffield Academic Press, 2001).

[2] [Editors' note: most of the authors submitted their essays for the volume before Steiner's report of Kenyon's excavations was published].

JERUSALEM DURING THE AMARNA PERIOD (FOURTEENTH CENTURY B.C.E.)

Based on the content of the Amarna correspondence, several scholars have concluded that the Urusalim from which Abdi-heba sent his
letters to the pharaoh was an important and large city. It is assumed to
be the center of a city state,[3] the seat of the ruler of a dimorphic chiefdom,[4] or the commercial center for the immediate region.[5] This function
is then supposed to be a continuation from the site's position during the
Middle Bronze Age. However, hardly any archaeological finds from the
fourteenth century B.C.E. have turned up during the many excavations
that have been carried out in and around Jerusalem. No trace has ever
been found of a fortified town—no city wall, no gates, no palaces, no
houses. Moreover, almost no stray sherds dating from the fourteenth
century B.C.E. have been found in the many later fills and debris layers.
In my opinion, the only logical conclusion that can be drawn is that no
fortified town existed in Jerusalem during the period of the Amarna letters. Archaeologically speaking, Jerusalem was simply not occupied
during this period of the Late Bronze Age. This whole situation seems
to be one of the many instances when texts and archaeology contradict
each other.

When Kenyon discovered part of a large earth-filled terrace system
located above the Gihon Spring, she was so thrilled that she attributed it
to the Amarna age without further checking her pottery notebooks. She
should have checked them because in these notebooks she herself had
dated the sherds found in these layers as "LB/EI, " meaning the transition
of the Late Bronze to the Early Iron Age, or the beginning of Iron Age I
(twelfth century B.C.E.). Yigal Shiloh excavated another part of the same
system and followed Kenyon's interpretation, although with some caution. Study of the pottery stored in both Leiden and Jerusalem has now
clearly shown that the terraces did not originate in the Amarna period. In
the terrace fills Kenyon recovered only fifteen pottery sherds from the
fourteenth or thirteenth centuries B.C.E., against several hundred dating to

---

[3] Shlomo Bunimovitz, "On the Edge of Empires—Late Bronze Age (1500–1200
BCE)," in *The Archaeology of Society in the Holy Land* (ed. T. E. Levy; New York:
Facts on File, 1995), 320–29.

[4] Israel Finkelstein, "The Sociopolitical Organization of the Central Hill Country
in the Second Millenium B.C.E.," in *Biblical Archaeology Today, 1990, Precongress
Symposium: Population, Production and Power* (ed. A. Biran and J. Aviram;
Jerusalem: Israel Exploration Society, 1993), 119–31.

[5] Thomas L. Thompson, *Early History of the Israelite People: From Written and
Archaeological Sources* (Leiden: Brill, 1992), 332.

Iron Age I. Hardly any fourteenth-century B.C.E. pottery was found in any of the other terrace fills excavated in the city.

There are three ways to explain the absence of fourteenth-century remains in the discoveries from Jerusalem. Each theory has its advocates:

1. not enough area was excavated;
2. all the remains from the fourteenth century have been eroded away or were or were removed in antiquity; or
3. there were no significant remains to begin with because Jerusalem was not a city during this time period.

NOT ENOUGH AREA WAS EXCAVATED

As the truism goes, "absence of evidence is no evidence of absence." This may be so, but the investigator should remember that neither is it "evidence of presence." Sometimes evidence is not found during an excavation because not enough of the site was excavated or the excavation concentrated on certain areas. In the case of Jerusalem, this argument does not hold water. Since the beginning of the twentieth century, four large trenches have been excavated down to bedrock on the slope of the southeastern hill or City of David:[6] the large trench made by Weill,[7] Crowfoot's trench on the western slope,[8] Kenyon's Trench A,[9] and Shiloh's Areas D and E.[10] None of these excavations produced any fourteenth-century B.C.E. architecture, and these excavations yielded almost no fourteenth-century pottery. In addition to these large-scale excavations, several deep trenches were excavated in and around the Old City; these trenches also failed to yield evidence of occupation during the fourteenth century. They include Kenyon's site C

---

[6] See the map showing excavations in the City of David on page 132 of *Jerusalem Revealed: Archaeology in the Holy City, 1968–1974* (ed. Y. Yadin; New Haven: Yale University Press, 1976).

[7] Raymond Weill, *La Cité de David: Compte-rendu des Fouilles à Jérusalem sur la Site de la Ville Primitive* (2 vols.; Paris: Geuthner, 1920–47).

[8] John W. Crowfoot and Gerald M. Fitzgerald, *Excavations in the Tyropoeon Valley, Jerusalem, 1927* (Palestine Exploration Fund Annual 5; London: Palestine Exploration Fund, 1929).

[9] Hendricus Jacobus Franken and Margreet L. Steiner, *Excavations by Kathleen M. Kenyon in Jerusalem 1961–1967, vol. II, The Iron Age Extramural Quarter on the South-East Hill* (British Academy Monographs: Oxford: Oxford University Press, 1990); Steiner, *Excavations in Jerusalem III.*

[10] Yigal Shiloh, *Excavations at the City of David, vol. I, 1978–1982: Interim Report of the First Five Seasons* (Qedem 19; Jerusalem: Institute of Archaeology, Hebrew University of Jerusalem, 1984).

in Muristan,[11] Avigad's exposures in the Jewish Quarter,[12] Ute Lux's work in the Erlöscherkirche in Muristan,[13] and the excavations by Benjamin Mazar and Eilat Mazar in the Ophel.[14] In my opinion, the vast number of excavations that have been conducted have exposed more than enough of ancient Jerusalem to permit a firm conclusion as to whether or not there was a fourteenth-century B.C.E. fortified town in Jerusalem.

EROSION OR REMOVAL BY LATER BUILDING ACTIVITY

The hypothesis of heavy erosion is well-known from Jericho. The problem is that even if architectural remains from a city or large town were all eroded or removed by later building activity, pottery sherds should have been found in many of the large fills excavated in present-day Jerusalem (contra Na'aman).[15] However, significant amounts of pottery dateable to the fourteenth century have not been found, while vast amounts of material from the Middle Bronze Age and from Iron Age II have been found. In my mind, it is difficult to postulate that not only architecture but also pottery and other small finds have disappeared. Once again, I find that the archaeological data forces the investigator to conclude that Jerusalem was not a significant town during the Amarna period.

JERUSALEM WAS NOT A CITY OR IMPORTANT TOWN DURING THE AMARNA PERIOD

Since extensive excavations have not revealed any trace of the city of Urusalim, maybe it is time to accept the conclusion that no city existed at that time. In my mind, this is the most logical and most probable conclusion.

Nevertheless, six letters were found written by the ruler of Urusalim.[16] Even though no architectural remains have been found of this settlement,

---

[11] See Kathleen M. Kenyon, *Digging Up Jerusalem* (London: Benn, 1974), 227–31, especially fig. 137. Prof. H. J. Franken has analyzed the pottery and confirmed Kenyon's dating (personal communication).

[12] Nahman Avigad, *Discovering Jerusalem* (Nashville: Nelson, 1983).

[13] Karel J. H. Vriezen, *Die Ausgrabungen unter der Erlöscherkirche im Muristan, Jerusalem (1970–1974)* (Abhandlungen der Deutschen Palästina-vereins 19; Wiesbaden: Harrassowitz, 1995).

[14] Eilat Mazar and Benjamin Mazar, *Excavations in the South of the Temple Mount: The Ophel of Biblical Jerusalem* (Qedem 29; Jerusalem: Institute of Archaeology, Hebrew University of Jerusalem, 1989).

[15] See Nadav Na'aman, "The Contribution of the Amarna Letters to the Debate on Jerusalem's Political Position in the Tenth Century B.C.E.," *BASOR* 304 (1996): 17–27; and idem, "Cow Town or Royal Capital? Evidence for Iron Age Jerusalem," *BAR* 23/4 (1997): 43–47, 67.

[16] William L. Moran, *The Amarna Letters* (Baltimore: Johns Hopkins University Press, 1992).

the letters do exist and must be interpreted and explained. When I first realized that Kenyon had not found the Amarna settlement in Jerusalem, I assumed that Urusalim was not ancient Jerusalem but a city located else-where in Palestine;[17] geographical references in the letters, however, make this a very slight possibility.

Realizing that Urusalim from the Amarna letters must be associated with Jerusalem, I began to read the Urusalim letters carefully and discov-ered another possibility that might account for the lack of archaeological evidence from the fourteenth century. There is no reference in any of these letters to the city itself, nor to its walls or its strong gates. Maybe Urusalim of the Amarna period was not a city or large town at all. Maybe we should interpret the "lands of Urusalim" as a royal dominion of the pharaoh, with Abdi-heba as his steward, who lived in a fortified house somewhere near the spring, on top of the hill, or on the Mount of Olives. This does not (as far as I am able to judge) contradict the content of Abdi-heba's letters.

DO THE LARGE STEPPED STONE STRUCTURE AND THE EARTH-FILLED TERRACES CONSTITUTE ONE ARCHITECTURAL SYSTEM OR TWO SEPARATE STRUCTURES, AND WHAT IS THE EVIDENCE FOR THEIR DATING?

Both Kenyon and Shiloh discovered parts of a large stepped stone structure, built over an earth-filled terrace system, hugging the eastern slope of the southeastern hill (City of David). Jane Cahill and David Tar-ler have argued that the terraces have been built as a substructure for the stepped stone structure and that both structures have to be considered as one construction, built at the same time. In other words, the stepped stone structure was a mantle only.[18] They base this idea on a small probe that was made in one of the squares excavated in Shiloh's Area G.[19] Their probe revealed that the lower terraces were capped with stone rubble on top of which the stone mantle was laid.

---

[17] Hendricus J. Franken and Margreet L. Steiner, "Jebus and Urusalim," *ZAW* 104 (1992): 110–11.

[18] Jane M. Cahill and David Tarler, "Response to Margreet Steiner—The Jebusite Ramp of Jerusalem: The Evidence from the Macalister, Kenyon and Shiloh Excavations," in *Biblical Archaeology Today, 1990: Proceedings of the Second International Congress on Biblical Archaeology, Jerusalem, June–July 1990* (ed. A. Biran and J. Aviram; Jerusalem: Israel Exploration Society, 1993), 625–26.

[19] [Editors' note: see pp. 42–54 and figs. 1.4–10 in this volume for a description and photographs of Cahill and Tarler's probe.]

My counterargument is that there may seem to be evidence for simultaneous construction of the terraces and the mantle in Shiloh's Area G, but the situation was completely different to the south and east of Shiloh's Area G.[20] Whereas Cahill and Tarler's probe was very limited in terms of exposure, Kenyon exposed large parts of the stepped stone structure in square A/XXIII and Trench I (see fig. 16.1). In the areas excavated by Kenyon, the stepped stone structure consisted of massive constructions made of enormous boulders, and not of a mantle only. Why not? Because the earth-filled terrace system did not exist here. Kenyon traced the extent of the terrace system at its southern and eastern sides, and it turned out that it occupied a more limited area than the stepped stone structure. At the south side the terraces were bounded by a substantial wall (W70) in Kenyon's square A/I (see figs. 16.2 and 16.3). In Square A/XXIII, to the south of square A/I, no earth-filled terrace system existed, and the stepped stone structure had to be built up from bedrock. Eleven layers of very massive stones were removed before the work had to stop approximately 1.40 m above bedrock because of the dangerous situation (see fig. 16.4). In Trench I, several small earth-filled terraces were found, but the stepped stone structure here consisted of a large tower, at least 8 m high and 5 m wide, which was added to the east side of the terrace system. Here again the stepped stone structure had to be built up from bedrock (see fig. 16.5).

In summary, we see from Kenyon's excavations that the stepped stone structure was quite different both in extension and in construction method from the terrace system. The terraces consisted of small stone walls with a filling of earth, rubble, and stones, while the stepped stone structure was built of massive stones. Moreover, the stone structure formed an extension of these smaller terraces, covering parts of the slope where the terraces did not exist. In light of all of these considerations, I conclude that the stepped stone structure is a separate and later addition. Where the earlier terraces did exist, as in Area G, the architects laid only a mantle of stones, sometimes on a filling of rubble. Where no terraces existed, they had to build up their structure from bedrock.

The dating of the pottery Kenyon recovered from inside the terraces confirms the theory of different construction dates for the terrace and its mantle. Kenyon used a very exact and rigid stratigraphical system, whereby each layer was excavated separately and the pottery from a particular layer was registered and stored separately. In that way it is possible to study the

---

[20] Yigal Shiloh exposed ca. 475 m² in his area G, while Kenyon excavated ca. 1,500 m² to the north, south, and east of area G, thereby touching areas outside the terrace system and the stepped stone structure.

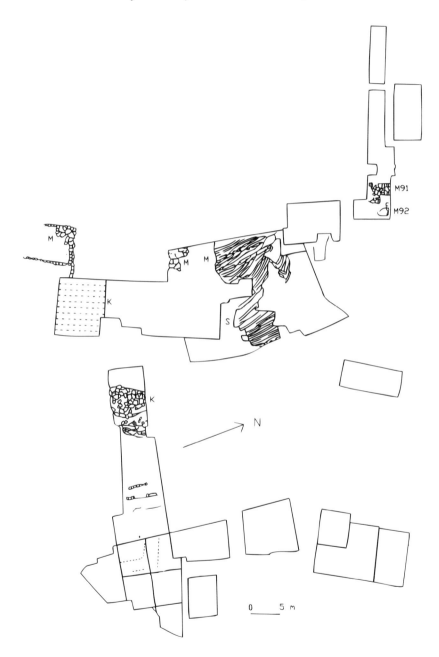

Fig. 16.1. Parts of the stepped stone structure as recovered by Macalister (M), Kenyon (K), and Shiloh (S). Wall M91/92 is a casemate wall.

Fig. 16.2. View of Kenyon's squares A/XXIII (in foreground) and A/I-III, facing north. In the deep hole the walls of an earlier house built on bedrock are visible. Behind it is the stone fill of the twelfth-century B.C.E. terraces, bound by wall 70, running east–west. The stone mass in the lower left corner of the photograph consists of the stones of the (later) stepped stone addition. The person in the background stands on a seventh-century B.C.E. floor.

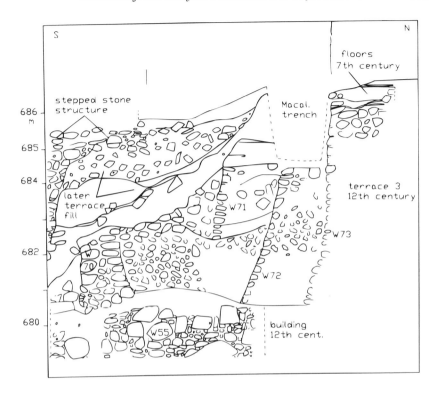

Fig. 16.3. Section through the twelfth-century B.C.E. terraces in square A/I. The terrace system was built over an earlier house (W55), which could be dated to the twelfth century B.C.E. as well, because an almost complete collared rim jar was found on its floor. The stone and earth-filled terraces are bounded at the south side by a sturdy wall W70. South of this wall no terraces have been found.

pottery from the earlier terrace system and that of the stepped stone structure on their own merits. The pottery from the fill of the earth-filled terraces was clearly Iron I in date, with no later material mixed in.

A survey of the pottery found in the fill of these terraces is found in my report.[21] A total of 251 rim sherds was found, as well as several jar handles and some bases and decorated sherds. This repertoire can generally be dated to the transition of Late Bronze Age to the Iron I Period (end of thirteenth/beginning of twelfth century B.C.E.). Several collared rim jars have been found, but the dark red slip, typical of later periods of Iron I, was not encountered. A large number of the bowls and jars (75 percent)

---

[21] Steiner, *Excavations in Jerusalem III,* 29–36.

Fig. 16.4. Square A/XXIII, showing part of the stepped structure made of very large boulders laid in courses

were made of dolomite clay. This clay was used predominantly during the Middle Bronze Age but hardly at all during the Late Iron Age.[22] Pottery from the fourteenth century B.C.E. is missing in the repertoire. According to

---

[22] Hendricus J. Franken, *A History of Pottery and Potters in Ancient Jerusalem* (Sheffield: Sheffield Academic Press, forthcoming), ch. 4.

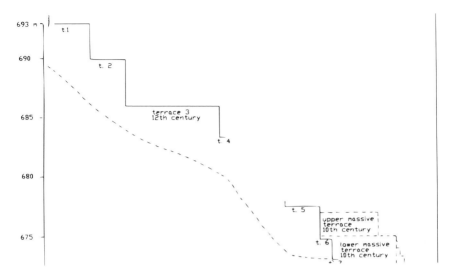

Fig. 16.5. The situation in Trench I. Schematic section through the twelfth-century B.C.E. terraces (t.1–7) on the slope of the hill. At the base of the system a stepped tower made of massive boulders was added in the tenth/ninth century B.C.E.

Kenyon, "a few sherds of Mycenaean ware and White Slip II milk bowls were found."[23] When analyzing this material, Franken counted only a dozen or so LB painted sherds in the pottery repertoire of the terraces, all of which were possibly post–fourteenth century B.C.E.[24]

According to Kenyon the pottery found inside the later massive stepped stone structure could be dated to the tenth century B.C.E.[25] However, very little pottery was found; only thirty-five rim sherds came from between the stones of the tower in Trench I, while hardly any pottery came from square A/XXIII (see fig. 16.6). This material is later than the pottery from the terraces. Collared rim jars are missing, and the bowls are all Iron II in shape. There is, however, a clear difference with the later pottery of phase 2, described in *Excavations in Jerusalem II*, which dates from the (second half of the) ninth century.[26] Bowls with folded rims (class 4) are hardly present in the stepped stone structure, and large storage bowls (class 11) are absent, while most cooking pot sherds were still made in the

23 Kathleen M. Kenyon, "Excavations in Jerusalem, 1962," *PEQ* 95 (1963): 7–21.

24 Franken, *History of Pottery*, ch. 4.

25 Kenyon, "Excavations in Jerusalem, 1962," 14.

26 Franken and Steiner, *Excavations in Jerusalem II*, 10–26.

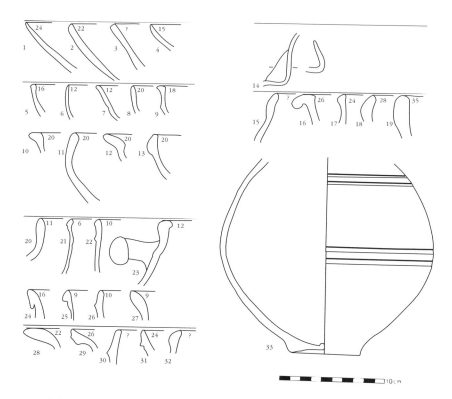

Fig. 16.6. Pottery found between the stones of the stepped tower in Trench I. 1–4: thin-walled bowls and platters; 5–13: thick-walled bowls; 14: lamp; 15–19: large bowls; 20–27: jars; 28–32: cooking pots; 33: decorated jug.

Late Bronze/Iron I tradition. Many bowls have a crisscross burnishing on their inside, but almost none bear the dark red slip layers traditionally ascribed to the tenth century B.C.E. According to Hendricus Franken, this could be a sign that Jerusalem's potters have been quite isolated from the twelfth century B.C.E. onwards,[27] or it may simply mean that this pottery has to be dated somewhat later than the tenth century B.C.E. Based on these criteria, I date the stepped stone structure to the tenth or early ninth centuries B.C.E., according to the conventional chronology.[28]

In conclusion, the two architectural phenomena (the terrace system and the stepped stone structure) do not have similar boundaries, do not

[27] Franken, *History of Pottery,* ch. 5.

[28] The new chronology would push the building of the stepped stone structure forward at least half a century.

contain identical pottery, and were not built utilizing the same construction techniques. I therefore find it safe to conclude that the terrace and the mantle were two different constructions: one was an earth-filled terrace system built in the beginning of Iron I; the other was a massive stone structure built in the beginning of Iron II.

Assuming that the stepped stone structure was built in the tenth century B.C.E., what was its function and when did it go out of use? So far, excavations have revealed that the construction was 27 m high and at least 40 m wide at the top of the hill.[29] The surface of the stones might once have been covered with mud plaster, but no remains of this have survived. One of its functions must have been to contain the debris of earlier occupation levels on the slope of the hill, but its most important function was defensive. It protected a vulnerable part of the settlement, with the Gihon Spring and the entrance to Warren's Shaft further down the slope.

One would logically assume that the stepped stone structure went out of use when this area no longer functioned as a fortification. This was only the case when a city wall was built further down the slope at the end of the eighth century B.C.E. Following the construction of this wall, the area on top of the stepped stone structure and at the foot of it became available for the building of houses, and a residential quarter sprung up there, including several houses Shiloh has extensively excavated, such as Ahiel's House and the Burnt Room. Therefore one would expect the pottery on the earliest floors of these houses to date to the late eighth or early seventh century B.C.E. However, Jane Cahill asserts that the earliest floors of these four-room houses contained tenth-century B.C.E. pottery. Because of this she states that the mantle had already gone out of use during the tenth century B.C.E., which would strengthen her thesis that the stepped stone structure was built in the twelfth century B.C.E.[30]

Kenyon also excavated sections of several houses built on top of the stepped stone structure and the terrace system. To accommodate these houses, terraces were cut into these structures and sometimes a new terrace wall was built (e.g., Shiloh's Wall 753). In Kenyon's Building II in square A/I, some tenth/ninth-century sherds were found in connection with the earliest floor of a room (which I interpreted in my report as the result of the cutting of a terrace there into the stepped stone structure). In two other rooms of the same house, the earliest floors yielded only post–

---

[29] Part of the structure had already been exposed by Robert A. S. Macalister; see Margreet L. Steiner, "The Jebusite Ramp of Jerusalem: The Evidence of the Macalister, Kenyon and Shiloh Excavations," in Biran and Aviram, *Biblical Archaeology Today, 1990,* 585–88 and also illustration 1.

[30] Cahill and Tarler, "Response to Margreet Steiner," 625.

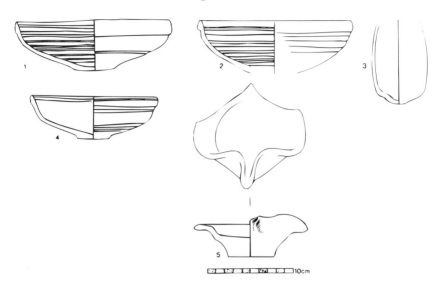

Fig. 16.7. Registered objects found on floor A/103.31

No.	Reg.nr.	Description
1	457	Bowl, burnished inside and over rim. Broken and mended, incomplete.
2	460	Bowl, part only. Burnished inside and over rim.
3	450	Juglet, top half only. Traces of longitudinal burnish.
4	458	Bowl, ring burnish inside and around rim. Broken and mended, section only.
5	427	Lamp.
–	305	Juglet, burnished. Complete.
–	456	Bowl, ring burnished inside and over rim. Broken and mended, incomplete. Similar to reg.nr. 457.
–	462	Platter, pink burnished surface. Broken and mended, incompete.

Iron Age pottery fragments, which was probably due to the many water gullies running down the slope and transporting later (and possibly earlier) material. Later floors in the same building only yielded seventh-century B.C.E. material.

Remains of houses were also found on top of the tower in Trench I. A floor laid directly on top of its massive stones (floor A/103.31 in Building V) yielded only very late Iron II material (see fig. 16.7). The same situation applies to a large house (Building VI) built at the foot of this tower, using the tower as its back wall. Here a complete late Iron II lamp was found on the earliest floor, as well as 110 sherds clearly dating to the seventh century B.C.E. (see fig. 16.8). Based on Kenyon's excavations, there is enough archaeological evidence to conclude that the stepped stone

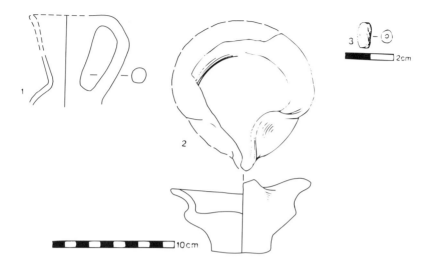

Fig. 16.8. Registered objects found on the earliest floor of Building VI

No. Reg.nr. Description
1   740   Jug, fragment of neck with handle. Dark red slip.
2   698   Lamp, part of rim missing.
3   703   Bead, clay, software, painted light blue, incised, diagonal, linear decoration.

structure went out of use in the late eighth or early seventh century B.C.E., when a new city wall took over its defensive function.

Jerusalem at the Beginning of Iron Age II

Elsewhere in this volume David Ussishkin and Ann E. Killebrew have summarized the archaeological evidence and the various scholarly opinions very clearly, including the controversy surrounding the new chronology. There is no need to recapitulate my position here. I just want to add a few remarks.

First of all, the layout of Jerusalem in the beginning of Iron Age II is completely different from that of the town in earlier and later periods. In the MB II period and the eighth/seventh centuries B.C.E., town walls were built low down on the slope of the southeastern hill. Both Kenyon and Shiloh have excavated large stretches of these fortifications. These walls were built to protect large residential areas built *on* the eastern slope. Apparently, in those periods the top of the hill did not offer enough space for the many inhabitants of the town and they had to use the slope. This was not the case, however, in the intervening periods. In the twelfth century B.C.E. an impressive terrace system was built on the slope, most terraces of which were too small to build houses on. The system probably served to provide enough building space on top of the hill for a citadel there and to protect the access to the Gihon Spring.[31]

In the tenth/ninth century B.C.E. the slope was partly covered by the stepped stone structure. Houses from that period have not been found there; the earliest buildings on bedrock, excavated by Kenyon, dated to the seventh century B.C.E. The building area seems to have been restricted to the top of the hill. Here a fragment of a casemate wall was discovered. Whether the stepped stone structure and the casemate wall protected a modest town with some public buildings and a small residential area, as I asserted in my report, or just a fortified citadel that served as an administrative and probable religious center, as Killebrew suggests, is difficult to decide. I assumed that the casemate wall ran to the north because it is located *outside* an ancient fortification from the Middle Bronze Age that protected the north side of the town. Kenyon and Macalister have excavated parts of a large wall system in Kenyon's Area H and just south of it. This wall was also used during the twelfth century B.C.E. It is remarkable that, apparently, this north wall was not in use anymore in the beginning of Iron II, as the casemate wall was found north of it, outside the protected area. This is why I interpret it as a fortification wall, running north to surround a town quarter there. Maybe it connected up with the large fortifications Charles Warren and Benjamin and Eilat Mazar have discovered on Ophel, although the dating of these buildings is still debated.

Based on the archaeological evidence, the settlement of Jerusalem in the tenth or ninth century B.C.E. can be described as a small fortified town, located on top of the hill, with several public buildings and very little room for residential areas. Thus, it can be described as an administrative center rather than as a residential city.

Secondly, I want to stress that this small administrative center was a *new* settlement. As no *town* from the preceding centuries has ever been excavated in Jerusalem, we have to conclude that in the tenth or ninth century B.C.E. a new town was founded, a town with impressive fortifications and several public buildings on top of the hill but without large residential quarters. In antiquity a new town, especially a new administrative center, was often established by a new political organization. Presumably Jerusalem functioned as the regional administrative center of a new political unity, maybe as the capital of a small newly established state. According to David Jamieson-Drake (and many scholars have followed his

---

[31] See Steiner, *Excavations in Jerusalem III*, 39–40, for a detailed explanation of the function of the terrace system.

ideas) Jerusalem became a "real" city with large public works, a bureau-cracy, and eventually a temple only in the eighth century B.C.E.[32] This would then also be the time when Judah became a state for the first time. However, his analysis is flawed, and his ideas are too simplistic. Even in the tenth or ninth century B.C.E., large fortifications were constructed in Jerusalem, implying at least a concentration of power in the hands of an emerging elite and a growing supremacy of the settlement in the region. Surveys in the hill country of Judah have confirmed this picture of Jerusalem as the center of an hierarchical settlement system in the begin-ning of Iron II.[33]

Although Jerusalem can thus be interpreted as a regional center, established by a new political unity, it seems unlikely that it was the cen-ter of a large state, the capital of the united monarchy of the biblical texts. It was too small and too unimpressive to conform to biblical descriptions of the city under David and Solomon. In a recent article I have argued that both Judah and Israel were "early states" in the beginning of Iron II and that the towns and centers of Judah (Jerusalem, Lachish, Beer-sheba, and Beth-shemesh) were not poorer or more backwards than the famous sites of Megiddo and Hazor.[34] Interpretations of Jerusalem in the begin-ning of Iron II range from a large splendid city to an unimpressive administrative center and even a small village. I propose that the archae-ological remains reveal a more complicated story, the story of a new settlement that established itself firmly on a mostly barren hilltop as the center of an emerging state, competing with the northern cities in power and beauty, only to outshine them completely in the centuries to come.

---

[32] David W. Jamieson-Drake, *Scribes and Schools in Monarchic Judah: A Socio-Archaeological Approach* (SWBA 9; JSOTSup 109; Sheffield: Sheffield Academic Press, 1991).

[33] In a survey conducted by Avi Ofer in the vicinity of Jerusalem he found a growth of 90 percent in the number of settlements during Iron Age IIA, while a sta-tistical analysis of his data (Rank Size Index) showed that (for the first time) the surveyed area was located in the periphery of a hierarchical settlement system. The center of this system lay outside the surveyed area and could only have been Jerusalem. Avi Ofer, "'All the Hill Country of Judah': From Settlement Fringe to a Prosperous Monarchy," in *From Nomadism to Monarchy: Archaeological and His-torical Aspects of Early Israel* (ed. I. Finkelstein and N. Naʾaman; Jerusalem: Yad Izhak Ben-Zvi, 1994), 92–121.

[34] Margreet L. Steiner, "Propaganda in Jerusalem: The Beginning of State Forma-tion in Iron Age Judah," in *"I Will Tell Secret Things from Long Ago" (Abiah Chidot Minei-kedem—Ps 78:2b): Archaeological and Historical Studies in Honor of Amihai Mazar on the Occasion of His Sixtieth Birthday* (ed. A. Maeir and P. de Miroschedji; in press).

When Did Jerusalem Become a Subject of Polemic?[1]

Yairah Amit

Tel Aviv University

Jerusalem is mentioned in the Hebrew Bible—in its Hebrew and Aramaic parts—nearly seven hundred times, without counting its other names or epithets, such as Jebus or the city of the Jebusite (Judg 19:10–11),[2] City of David (Isa 22:9), Zion (Mic 3:10), Salem (Ps 76:3),[3] or its metaphorical epithets, such as Daughter of Zion (Isa 1:8), the faithful city (Isa 1:26), the city of righteousness (Isa 1:26), the sought out (Isa 62:12), the not forsaken (Isa 62:12), and the like.[4] All these are eloquent testimonies to the centrality of Jerusalem in the biblical world and in the minds of authors in biblical times.

But when did Jerusalem first acquire this prominent and central position? To state the question differently, What do we mean when we speak of "biblical times"? Does this date back to the period beginning with the conquest of Jerusalem by David and its construction by Solomon in the tenth century B.C.E. during the united monarchy?[5] Or are we speaking of a later period, beginning in the eighth century B.C.E.?

---

[1] Many of the participants in this volume come from the bride's side—namely, archaeology—while I represent the groom's side—namely, the Bible. But since this is a marriage of cousins, I intend to make reference to other family members and still hope for healthy offspring from this match.

[2] It seems that this name is the creation of a biblical author who was convinced that Jerusalem had a different name through its Jebusite period. However, on the basis of testimonies from the second millennium B.C.E., Benjamin Mazar, "Jerusalem in the Biblical Period," in *Jerusalem Revealed: Archaeology in the Holy City, 1968–1974* (ed. Y. Yadin; Jerusalem: Israel Exploration Society, 1975), 1, states: "The name of the city, Jerusalem, seems to stem from its earliest days."

[3] On the problematic character of this name, see Yairah Amit, *Hidden Polemics in Biblical Narrative* (Leiden: Brill, 2000), 150–58.

[4] I give one reference for each example; no doubt there are more examples and more epithets.

[5] I make no reference to biblical mentions of Jerusalem in the time before David's conquest, because of their anachronistic character. For an attempt to reconstruct this

365

History and archaeology help address these questions and also help create a fuller picture of biblical Jerusalem. The evidence from the late eighth and seventh centuries shows that the city was expanding at that time. According to a cautious phrasing: "Jerusalem developed into a thriving capital with extramural settlements by at least the late 8th century BCE."[6] Its land area quadrupled, and its population increased considerably.[7] Some researchers associate this enlargement with the exiling of the northern kingdom of Israel and the resulting waves of migration.[8] According to others, the ceramic evidence of late ninth- and early eighth-century life proves that the enlargement of the city began gradually by at least the beginning of the eighth century.[9] Actually, the Chronicler reports building activities that are linked with Jerusalem and its surroundings in the days of Uzziah and his son Jotham (2 Chr 26:9–15; 27:3–4); even if this report is greatly exaggerated, it contains—according to Miller and Hayes—"a kernel of truth."[10] It also seems reasonable to consider that the interest in strengthening and building up the city, in preparation for future wars, intensified as a reaction to increased Assyrian involvement in the Levant beginning around 734 B.C.E.[11] Jerusalem's standing in the region had been strengthened by the policies of Ahaz, who submitted to Assyrian rule in the face of the threat by the kingdom of Israel and King Rezin of Damascus. This growth in status continued during the reign of Hezekiah, who, on the one hand, invested much effort in preparing the city and the country for a future revolt and, on the other hand, contributed to the city's development as a spiritual center in

period, see Mazar, "Jerusalem in the Biblical Period," *Jerusalem Revealed,* 1–8. For the new approach that minimizes the significance of Jerusalem during the time of David and Solomon, see Israel Finkelstein and Neil A. Silberman, *The Bible Unearthed: Archaeology's New Vision of Ancient Israel and the Origin of Its Sacred Texts* (New York: Free Press, 2001), 132–34.

[6] Andrew G. Vaughn, *Theology, History and Archaeology in the Chronicler's Account of Hezekiah* (SBLABS 4; Atlanta: Scholars Press, 1999), 69.

[7] See Gabriel Barkay, "Northern and Western Jerusalem in the End of the Iron Age" (Ph.D. diss., Tel Aviv University, 1985), 163–65, 207, 485–500.

[8] Magen Broshi, "The Expansion of Jerusalem in the Reigns of Hezekiah and Manasseh," *IEJ* 24 (1974): 21–26; Eckart Otto, *Jerusalem—Die Geschichte der Heiligen Stadt: Von den Anfängen bis zur Kreuzfahrerzeit* (Stuttgart: Kohlhammer, 1980), 74–75.

[9] See Vaughn, *Theology, History and Archaeology,* 65–70, who follows Barkay. See also the essay by Finkelstein in this volume.

[10] J. Maxwell Miller and John H. Hayes, *A History of Ancient Israel and Judah* (Philadelphia: Westminster, 1986), 311.

[11] See the essay by Younger in this volume for details on the beginning of Assyrian influence and its importance for understanding Judah and Jerusalem.

response to the new conditions in the region after the fall of Samaria. This situation endured until Sennacherib's invasion in 701 B.C.E.[12]

There can be no doubt that for Judah the most traumatic event of this period was the campaign by Sennacherib, who devastated the land and undermined the city's economy and political power.[13] Yet for Jerusalem, Sennacherib's campaign, though greatly damaging, also served as a transforming event.[14] The fact that the city was not destroyed was viewed as a miracle of divine intervention and laid the groundwork for its conversion from a capital and administrative center, the seat of a royal temple and throne of a small kingdom on the edge of the desert, into a divinely chosen place. We might define this unexpected development as the Archimedean fulcrum in the history of Jerusalem, from which it became a city continually charged with symbolic meanings. In other words, the lifting of the menace of Sennacherib in 701 B.C.E. became the establishing event of Jerusalem as a divinely chosen city and eternal capital.[15] Moreover, thanks to this unexpected relief, Hezekiah—who had almost brought his country, his people, and his city to the edge of destruction—was saved from going down in history as an irresponsible megalomaniac. Hezekiah instead won the status of a righteous ruler in whose reign God intervened once more for the sake of his people and his city. This point in history may well have been the start of the tradition about the special relationship between God and his Jerusalem shrine, a tradition that gained strength through the ages, and at the same time the start of a polemic on the status and the character of the city.

The wish to endow the disappearance of Sennacherib's troops with a quality of the miraculous is already noticeable in the Deuteronomistic editing of the book of Kings, which, besides a chronistic record on Sennacherib's campaign (2 Kgs 18:13–16), includes a detailed prophetic description (2 Kgs 18:17–19:37).[16] The prophet Isaiah has a central role,

---

[12] Miller and Hayes, *History of Ancient Israel,* 340–58. See also the essay by Younger in this volume.

[13] According to Nadav Na'aman, "The Kingdom of Judah under Josiah," *TA* 18 (1991): 58, "The destructive results of Sennacherib's campaign remained evident even in the last years of Josiah's reign, almost a century after the campaign."

[14] See the essay by Vaughn on "Hezekiah's success" against Sennacherib in this volume.

[15] See the essay by Roberts in the volume for arguments that would date the beginning of this tradition and divine appointment to the period of the united monarchy.

[16] See Mordechai Cogan and Hayim Tadmor, *II Kings: A New Translation with Introduction and Commentary* (AB 11; Garden City, N.Y.: Doubleday, 1988), 240–44 and the bibliography there.

Rabshakeh with his speech plays the role of an antihero,[17] and God's angel arrives in time to decimate the Assyrian camp.[18] The writer, through this editing, was thus able to present Hezekiah as if "there was none like him among all the kings of Judah after him, nor among those before him" (2 Kgs 18:5).[19] The later book of Chronicles went further and lauded Hezekiah's reforms (2 Chr 29:3–31:20) to the point that they overshadow those of Josiah (2 Chr 34:3–35:19).[20] Likewise, in Ben Sira's "Praise of Israel's Great Ancestors" (48:17–23) and various sayings of the sages,[21] Hezekiah is praised to high heaven.

It is also possible to see how this establishing event became linked with the establishing tradition of the exodus from Egypt. In the Babylonian Talmud it is written:

> A Tanna taught in the name of R. Joshua b. Karha: Pharaoh, who personally blasphemed, was punished by the Holy One, blessed be He, in Person; Sennacherib, who blasphemed through an agent, was punished by the Holy One, blessed be He, through an agent … as it is said, And the angel of the Lord went out…. " (*b. Sanh.* 94a–b)[22]

One might also mention Bar-Kappara of Sepphoris, who commented, "The Holy One, blessed be He, wished to appoint Hezekiah as the Messiah, and Sennacherib as Gog and Magog" (*b. Sanh.* 94a–b). We see that the literature of the sages includes some Tannaitic traditions that compare Hezekiah to Moses and David, giving him an almost messianic status. In other words, they treat the event of the relief of Jerusalem as an establishing tradition, following which Jerusalem became God's chosen dwelling and, in time, the center of the world.

---

[17] See Ehud Ben Zvi, "Who Wrote the Speech of Rabshakeh and When?" *JBL* 109 (1990): 79–92.

[18] Cogan and Tadmor, *II Kings,* 239, emphasize that "the appearance of the angel rather than YHWH himself, looks like a purposeful device of the storyteller; YHWH's *messenger* seeks redress from Sennacherib's *messengers,* who came to 'taunt the living God.'"

[19] Ibid, 217: "It is generally agreed that the last clause ["nor among those before him"] is a 'clumsy' addition." However, it seems to me that the purpose of this latter addition was to prefer Hezekiah over Josiah.

[20] See Sara Japhet, *I and II Chronicles: A Commentary* (OTL; Louisville: Westminster John Knox, 1993), 912.

[21] For example, *b. Pesaḥ.* 119a; *b. Ber.* 28b.

[22] The translation is taken from Isidore Epstein, *The Babylonian Talmud, Seder Nezikin,* vol. 3 (London: Soncino, 1935).

It is common knowledge that significant historical events, painful or otherwise, may give rise to new spiritual movements and to social or cultural revolutions, and it seems that this is what happened in Jerusalem in the latter half of the eighth century B.C.E. With the defeat of Samaria by Sargon II in 720 B.C.E. and the subsequent subjugation of Judah to Assyria, the spiritual face of Jerusalem changed and new ideological directions started.[23] The teaching of the classical prophets fell on some receptive minds;[24] northern traditions and materials that had been told or written in the kingdom of Ephraim before the exile were adopted and studied in depth. In addition to the prophecy of Hosea, one calls to mind the brief, esoteric statement in Prov 25:1 about Hezekiah's copyists. This verse hints at an enterprise initiated by Hezekiah to collect writings. Apparently these materials also awakened new ideologies and spiritual movements. It seems that toward the end of the eighth and the beginning of the seventh century B.C.E. Jerusalem saw the beginning of the growth of a new school, which led to the writing of the book of Deuteronomy in its primary form. These ideologies had practical consequences that were manifested in religious reforms (2 Kgs 22–23).[25]

The book of Kings is informative about the centralization of the cult in Hezekiah's reign, albeit very briefly in two verses (2 Kgs 18:4, 22). Moreover, the information is given mainly in Deuteronomistic formulations.[26] It is therefore legitimate to doubt that such a reform took place in Hezekiah's reign.[27] It is likely that the author of the book of Kings wanted to show why Hezekiah deserved the miraculous deliverance that took place in his reign. The Chronicler must have been aware of the strange contrast between the innovation and boldness required to carry out such a reform

---

[23] See Yairah Amit, *History and Ideology: Introduction to Historiography in the Hebrew Bible* (Sheffield: Sheffield Academic Press, 1999), 28–33.

[24] It is no accident that there are descriptions of the positive relationships between Hezekiah and Isaiah (2 Kgs 19–20), Huldah and Josiah (2 Kgs 22:11–20), Jeremiah and the Shaphan family (Jer 26:24; 29:3; 36:9–13; and more).

[25] Moshe Weinfeld, "The Emergence of the Deuteronomic Movement: The Historical Antecedents," in *Das Deuteronomium: Entstehung, Gestalt und Botschaft* (ed. N. Lohfink; Leuven: Leuven University Press, 1985), 89–95.

[26] Compare the phrases "He abolished the shrines and smashed the pillars and cut down the sacred post" (2 Kgs 18:4) and "whose shrines and altars Hezekiah did away with" (2 Kgs 18:22) to the laws in Deut 7:5; 12:3. On the historical value of Rabshakeh's speech, see Ben Zvi, "Who Wrote the Speech," 79–92.

[27] See Nadav Na'aman, "The Debated Historicity of Hezekiah's Reform in the Light of Historical and Archaeological Research," *ZAW* 107 (1995): 179–95 and nn. 1–2, in which he names scholars who accept the historicity of this reform and those who doubt it.

and the scant references to it. He therefore proceeded to complete the picture by devoting three chapters to a vivid description of Hezekiah's reform and the related events.[28]

Curiously, the Deuteronomistic formulations contain another significant piece of information in addition to the descriptions found in 2 Kgs 18:4: the smashing of the bronze serpent.[29] This report seems to hint at the kind of information that the Deuteronomistic editor neither wanted to suppress nor wished to expand on because of what it implied about the temple from the days of David and Solomon until Hezekiah's reign, namely, the presence of an idol in the midst of the worship of God. Indeed, the prophets of the eighth century (Isa 10:10–11; Hos 11:2; Mic 1:7; 5:12) provide evidence of the cult of idols in the worship of God as well as their protests against it. I would therefore argue that Hezekiah's reform had to do with the removal of images, meaning the iconic cults, from the temple or from temples in general[30] but not with the centralization of the cult. In Becking's opinion, "after the images of the gods in whom the Samarians had vainly trusted were carried away to Assyria, former Israelites living in Judah went on to develop a new view of God."[31] Hezekiah's reform may have been the result of this new view, and his reform was not a reform of centralization but an aniconic reform.

The encounter with Assyrian imperialism focused Judahite intellects on the concept of divinity and God's rule on earth, on God's relations with

---

[28] On the history of the view that doubts the historical reliability of the book of Chronicles, see Japhet, *I and II Chronicles*. On the nonhistoricity of the description of Hezekiah's period in 2 Chr 29–31, see Na²aman, "The Debated Historicity," 180–81.

[29] According to Karen R. Joines, "The Bronze Serpent in the Israelite Cult," *JBL* 87 (1968): 245–56. She states, "Nehushtan was adopted from the Canaanites to affirm the agricultural powers of Yahweh." Or even more: "The southern kingdom regarded Nehushtan as a symbol of Yahweh, just as the northern kingdom so considered the bulls" (256).

[30] See John Gray, *I and II Kings: A Commentary* (2d ed.; OTL; Philadelphia: Westminster, 1970), 670: "but, since there is no mention in the account of Josiah's reformation of the abolition of the brazen serpent, this at least might stand to the credit of Hezekiah." George B. Gray, *A Critical and Exegetical Commentary on Numbers* (ICC; Edinburgh: T&T Clark, 1973), 274, emphasizes: "It was therefore destroyed by Hezekiah, who acted, as we may suppose, under the influence of Isaiah's iconoclastic teaching (Isa 2:8, 17:8, 30:22, 31:7)."

[31] Bob Becking, "Assyrian Evidence for Iconic Polytheism in Ancient Israel?" in *The Image and the Book: Iconic Cults, Aniconism, and the Rise of Book Religion in Israel and the Ancient Near East* (ed. K. van der Toorn; Leuven: Peeters, 1997), 171.

other nations and their gods, and on God's place in the large-scale formations created by the Assyrian expansion. These ideas influenced the religious ritual, which meant primarily a growing distance from concrete objects, as indicated by the example of the brazen serpent. This development led Judah into a second stage: the centralization of the cult and the view of the temple as the dwelling of God's name rather than of the deity in person.[32]

Most critical biblical scholars agree that the book of Deuteronomy was written prior to the reform of Josiah, that is to say, in the seventh century B.C.E. We may therefore describe the end of the eighth century and the seventh century in Jerusalem as a time of spiritual creativity for thinkers, writers, and prophets, who tackled social and cultic issues with political (domestic and external) as well as theological themes.

All this led to a view of history in light of prophetic thought and to the writing of history in the spirit of the pre-Deuteronomistic and Deuteronomistic approaches.[33] While the eighth-century Isaiah showed what must be done in Jerusalem for it to be worthy of the title "city of righteousness, the faithful city" (Isa 1:26), the Deuteronomic legislation set out to ensure the centrality of the chosen place, the nature of its cult, and its social character, which were all interconnected.

The view of Jerusalem as the one and only city chosen for the name of God to dwell in its temple was a radical revolution that may well have changed certain customs, from the secular slaughter of animals for food (Deut 12:15–28) to the domination of the individual's spontaneous religious experience. It seems that the city's deliverance from Sennacherib's siege played a major part in the development of this revolution, since it was seen as proof of God's choice and preference. Many began to believe in the eternal nature of Jerusalem, based on the divine promise of deliverance. Yet some, such as the prophets and their followers, saw things differently, treating this question of the city's eternal nature as a subject of polemic and linking the fate of the city with the conduct of its inhabitants.

The polemic is found mainly in the prophetic writings, but it is also echoed in the book of Deuteronomy and, as we shall see, in the entire Pentateuch.[34]

---

[32] It is possible that the attempt in the reign of Manasseh to undo the results of Hezekiah's aniconic reform led, in the reign of Josiah, to the reform of centralization as a means of control.

[33] On the difference between Deuteronomistic and pre-Deuteronomistic writing, see Amit, *History and Ideology,* 34–72.

[34] See Amit, *Hidden Polemics,* 130–68.

While many believed that the city enjoyed eternal merit and would never fall, the prophets—for example, Micah (3:11)—thought that the city would be destroyed because of the sins of its inhabitants.[35] Micah did not hesitate to compare the lot of Jerusalem to that of Samaria. These views were again voiced in Judah on the eve of the destruction, as may be seen in the prophecy of Jeremiah. Jeremiah warned the people: "Go now to my place that was in Shiloh, where I made my name dwell at first, and see what I did to it for the wickedness of my people Israel" (Jer 7:3–5; see also 26:4–9).[36] The priests and prophets objected to Jeremiah's call and wanted to have him executed, but he was saved thanks to the personal intervention of Ahikam, son of Shaphan. The position of Jeremiah and his supporters is also expressed in the Deuteronomistic exegesis of the book of Kings, which set outs to explain the destruction of the city: "I will stretch over Jerusalem the measuring line of Samaria and the plummet of the house of Ahab, and I will wipe Jerusalem as one wipes a dish, wiping it and turning it upside down" (2 Kgs 21:13). Echoes of this controversy are to be heard in the attempts of the Second Temple prophets Haggai, Zechariah, and especially Second Isaiah (Isa 40–66) to persuade the people that Jerusalem would continue to be the chosen city: "Sing and rejoice, O Daughter of Zion, for lo, I come and I will dwell in the midst of you … and will again choose Jerusalem" (Zech 2:14–16).

The continuing polemic on the eternal nature of Jerusalem, with its currents of anxiety and hope, found expression in the materials worked by the Deuteronomistic school. The historiographic literature expresses the hope that the city's chosen nature would persist despite the destruction, and the book of Kings categorically describes Jerusalem, and only Jerusalem, as the chosen place (1 Kgs 11:32, 36; 2 Kgs 8:16–21; 14:21; 21:7). On the other hand, the legislative literature expresses a fear of the

---

[35] Most scholars link this tradition with the ancient history of the city. John Hayes, for example, thinks that this tradition originated in the pre-Israelite stage and continued to be cultivated in the days of David and Isaiah ("The Tradition of Zion's Inviolability," *JBL* 82 [1963]: 419–26). J. J. M. Roberts, on the other hand, is strongly opposed to this view and connects the glorification of Jerusalem with the days of David and Solomon ("The Davidic Origin of the Zion Tradition," *JBL* 92 [1973]: 329–44).

[36] On the relation between Jer 7 and 26, see Douglas R. Jones, *Jeremiah: Based on the Revised Standard Version* (NCB; Grand Rapids: Eerdmans, 1992), 339–41. Robert P. Carroll, *Jeremiah: A Commentary* (OTL; Philadelphia: Westminster: 1986), 514–22, denies the story's historicity and insists on the social function that it served. For us, even if the story is only a fiction, it still reflects positions and moods that were widespread or that it is reasonable to assume were held during the period described.

explicit, unequivocal attachment to a city, whose destiny was in the balance, whose political and economic situation was unstable, and who was being harshly criticized. This fear was especially marked in the genre of law, whose task it is to shape reality and thus also to decide what is more important: the principle of centralization of the cult or that of concentration specifically in Jerusalem. The legislator in the book of Deuteronomy made it plain that he was concerned above all to stress the centralization of the cult, as part of his overall doctrine, and to leave Jerusalem as a possibility only. He thus made use of the very generalized formula "the place that he will choose," which could refer to any site. It seems reasonable to assume that this expression was understood by him and by his readers and listeners as referring to Jerusalem. However, it also leaves many exegetical possibilities open, subject to changing historical tendencies and data. The law of Deuteronomy did not so much as allude to Jerusalem in order not to place limitations on future historical reality. By using this technique, the legislator declared his main theological principle—the centralization of the cult—and left it to history, with all its vagaries, to determine and to decide what is the chosen place. We find a similar tendency later, in the editing of the Torah literature as a whole, where Jerusalem is not mentioned by name even once, despite the innumerable opportunities to do so.[37] This systematic avoidance of the name of Jerusalem is not accidental; the avoidance is part of the polemic that expresses the doubts that were felt about the city following its changing historical fate.

We see that Jerusalem of the eighth and seventh centuries B.C.E. became a source of polemic and is therefore depicted in biblical literature both as a city redeemed by God's deliverance (2 Kgs 19:34) and as a city whose destiny and status were unclear. As a city redeemed by God, Jerusalem is portrayed in the historiography and in the prophets of the Second Temple as God's dwelling place. As a city with an unclear destiny, Jerusalem could not be discussed in terms of choice and preference. That is the case, explicitly, in the words of the prophets of the time (First Isaiah, Jeremiah, and others), and implicitly in the avoidance of all reference to Jerusalem by name in the book of Deuteronomy and the whole of the Pentateuch, which was edited after the destruction of the First Temple. In other words, the polemic about the status of Jerusalem, which intensified when it lay in ruins, continued in the early Persian period.

---

[37] Note the explicit references to Shechem, Bethel, and Hebron with the avoidance of the name of Jerusalem in the scene of the meeting between Abram and Melchizedek (Gen 14:18–20) and in the story of the binding of Isaac (Gen 22:1–19).

While this polemic was in progress, traditions that attributed an ancient sanctity to the city sprang up. For example, we can find them in Chronicles, which most researchers date to "somewhere in the 4th century BCE"[38] and which is the first source to link Jerusalem and its temple implicitly, by means of allusions, to some of the Torah stories.[39] Yet it should be noted that in the story of the binding of Isaac in the book of Genesis, as in the rest of the Pentateuch—including Deuteronomy—not only is there no mention of Jerusalem, but there seems to be a deliberate avoidance of it. Assuming that through the seventh century B.C.E. the Torah literature was in its inception, this avoidance of the name of Jerusalem is significant, especially in view of the ideological changes that took place in the city from the late eighth century on.

To sum up, it seems to me that it was the historical reality of the latter half of the eighth century and the seventh century that fixed the place of Jerusalem in the minds of future generations. It was not a single event but the start of a process that went on for several centuries while polemic raged over the city's status. The process was supported and ultimately decided by the Deuteronomistic school, by the prophets, and by the political realities of the early days of the Persian occupation, which made possible the rebuilding of the temple of Jerusalem.

Finally, the polemic did not remain unresolved. History decided that Jerusalem was God's chosen dwelling place, and to this day modern political figures declaim, "If I forget thee, O Jerusalem, let my right hand forget her cunning!" (Ps 137:5). Similarly, the Passover Haggadah, the holiday's central ritual, which is linked to the people's establishing tradition, concludes with a reference to the city's defining tradition: "Next year in Jerusalem!"

---

[38] Vaughn, *Theology, History and Archaeology,* 16. According to Japhet, *I and II Chronicles,* 27–28, "at the end of the Persian or, more probably, the beginning of the Hellenistic period, at the end of the fourth century BCE."

[39] See, e.g., the story of the binding of Isaac (Gen 22:1–19) in comparison with 2 Chr 3:1 and 1 Chr 21:16–22:1 and its parallel in 2 Sam. 24:18–25; the purchase of the cave of Machpelah (Gen 23) in comparison with 1 Chr 21:23–25 and its parallel in 2 Sam 24:21–25; and the tabernacle of the Lord, which Moses made in the wilderness, and the altar of burnt offerings (Exod 40:34–35; Lev 9:24) in comparison with 1 Chr 21:29 and 2 Chr 7. For more comparisons, see, e.g., the commentaries of Hugh G. M. Williamson, *1 and 2 Chronicles* (NCB; Grand Rapids: Eerdmans, 1987), 142–51, 203–5; Japhet, *I and II Chronicles,* 383–90, 550–52.

Jerusalem, the Late Judahite Monarchy, and the Composition of the Biblical Texts[1]

William M. Schniedewind
University of California, Los Angeles

When was the Bible written? Where was the Bible written? The answers to these questions are becoming increasingly clearer. Recent archaeological data point to dramatic social changes during the late Judahite monarchy. The late Judahite monarchy saw the emergence of a world economy under the *pax Assyriaca,* the urbanization of Judah, the growth of Jerusalem into an urban political center, and a growing Judahite administrative bureaucracy. All these things provided fertile ground for the composition of biblical literature. As it turns out, archaeological data suggest that Jerusalem in the eighth and seventh centuries was more conducive to the flourishing of biblical literature than Jerusalem of the fifth and fourth centuries B.C.E. In the present paper, I explore some of the changes that took place place in the eighth and seventh centuries in Jerusalem and Judah that made it ripe for the flourishing of biblical literature. I conclude by relating this social context with some prophetic traditions that would have been composed, written down, and edited during the late Judahite monarchy in Jerusalem.

THE CONTEXT FOR WRITING THE BIBLE

The framework for the composition of much of the Bible is quite circumscribed only at the end. That is, while it is difficult to fix the earliest possible date for the composition of many texts, we can set the latest possible date. Manuscripts of the Dead Sea Scrolls fix the latest possible date of several manuscripts, most notably the book of Samuel, in the third century B.C.E. To be sure, we hardly believe that these manuscripts are autographs, so it is conceivable that the initial composition was several

---

[1] A version of this paper was presented in the "Jerusalem in Bible and Archaeology Consultation" at the Society of Biblical Literature meetings during November 1998. The author thanks those who offered criticism and encouragement.

centuries earlier. The tradition of translation into Greek also suggests that the Torah was essentially complete by the end of the third century B.C.E. We must acknowledge, of course, that the transmission and editing process continued long after the composition of these books. For example, the Great Isaiah Scroll from Qumran dates to the first century B.C.E. and demonstrates numerous editorial and scribal innovations.[2] However, no one would reasonably claim that the Great Isaiah Scroll was composed in the first century. Likewise, it is clear that the number, divisions, and order of the Psalter was still in flux as late as the first century C.E.; however, this is not to concede that the individual psalms were composed at such a late date. Thus, the final editorial shaping of the Bible probably continued until the first century C.E., even though the individual books had been composed centuries earlier. The question is, how many centuries earlier?

This issue has been hotly debated in recent years. For example, Philip Davies in his widely cited recent book, *Scribes and Schools: The Canonization of the Hebrew Scriptures,* points to the importance of scribal schools for understanding the origins of the canon. Davies argues that the entire canonical process needs to be set in the late Persian, Hellenistic, and Roman periods. He contends that there was no large scribal class in ancient Palestine during the Iron Age, even though Davies admits that the late Judahite kingdom represented a complex urban state that would have had a scribal infrastructure. Davies gives two reasons why he regards literacy unlikely in monarchic Judah. First, an agrarian society such as Judah "did not have any use for widespread literacy."[3] Second, the monarchy and scribal schools would have been unwilling to relinquish their monopoly on writing. However, it is clear the late Judahite monarchy was increasingly an urbanized society, as I point out below. Further, Davies furnishes no evidence that there was a monopoly on writing or that such a monopoly was closely guarded. Ironically, his reservations might more appropriately be applied to the Persian period.

Charles Carter's book, *The Emergence of Yehud in the Persian Period,* briefly touches on the "Literary Genius in the Post-Exilic Period."[4] The larger part of the book, however, is devoted to a comprehensive analysis of the settlement patterns and population distribution of Yehud. His study

---

[2] See Edward Y. Kutscher, *The Language and Linguistic Background of the Isaiah Scroll (I Q Isa)* (Leiden: Brill, 1974).

[3] Philip R. Davies, *Scribes and Schools: The Canonization of the Hebrew Scriptures* (Louisville: Westminister John Knox, 1998), 82.

[4] Charles Carter, *The Emergence of Yehud in the Persian Period: A Social And Demographic Study* (JSOTSup 294; Sheffield: Sheffield Academic Press, 1999), 286–88.

paints a "general picture of a province based on a subsistence level rural or village economy."[5] This naturally begs the question: How could a subsistence-level rural and village economy be responsible for the prolific literary achievements that are accorded to the Persian period? Carter himself poses the question: "But could a small Jerusalem support this level of literary production?"[6] He reasons that it could because it is essentially a question of the size and nature of urban elites. He suggests that the size of Jerusalem was between 1,250 and 1,500 during this period and that a large percentage of these were literate urban elites (e.g., priests, temple servants, gatekeepers, and a scribal class). However, could these urban elites account for the complexity of the Hebrew Bible? Carter points to historical and sociological parallels in fourteenth-century Paris or Russia of the seventeenth to eighteenth centuries and concludes that this level of literary creativity need not be questioned.

These historical and sociological parallels for literary production are quite suspect, however. While fourteenth-century Paris or seventeenth-century Russia may be analogous in size, the technology of writing had changed dramatically. The use of paper, for example, had become widespread. Invented in China, paper was adopted by the Arabs in the eighth century, and its use spread throughout the Mediterranean world between the ninth and eleventh centuries.[7] The thirteenth century in particular saw dramatic technological innovations in paper production. Moreover, Champagne, not far from Paris, became a center of papermaking in the fourteenth century. As Henri-Jean Martin points out in his *History and Power of Writing:*

> The importance of this movement can hardly be exaggerated. Before paper became available, the hides of a veritable herd of young animals were required to make a single in-folio volume. After the fourteenth century, when the West had access to a writing material in seemingly unlimited quantities, the way was open for printing.[8]

Given these technological changes, Carter's much later sociological and historical analogies to Persian Yehud fall flat. The parallels also fail in another important way. That is, the literary activity of fourteenth-century Paris and eighteenth-century Russia were centered in the classical written

---

[5] Ibid., 248.

[6] Ibid., 287.

[7] See Henri-Jean Martin, *The History and Power of Writing* (trans. L. G. Cochrane; Chicago: University of Chicago Press, 1994), 207.

[8] Ibid., 210.

languages of the day, not in an otherwise dead language such as Hebrew. The language of the Persian Empire was Aramaic, and the scribal training of the literary elites was in Aramaic. That Hebrew should even have been widely known, let alone that its classical form could have been widely written, in the Persian period seems quite unlikely.

The proposed Persian-Hellenistic origins of the Bible have also created the linguistic problem of a Hebrew canonical literature written in a world dominated by an Aramaic and later Greek administrative *lingua franca*. Aside from the few books attributed to the stratum of Late Biblical Hebrew, there is little to suggest that biblical literature was influenced by Aramaic or Greek. Philip Davies, recognizing the problem, proposes that a few scribes preserved the tradition of written Hebrew through the Babylonian and into the Persian periods. However, it seems implausible that such leftover scribes should account for the entire Hebrew Bible and be free from the pervasive influence of the Aramaic language. The books traditionally ascribed to the Persian and Hellenistic periods (e.g., Chronicles, Ezra-Nehemiah, Esther, Daniel) show clear Aramaic influence, in contrast to texts traditionally ascribed to the Iron Age (e.g., Genesis, Joshua, Kings, Hosea). Thus, the preservation of the biblical Hebrew language (with all its diachronic nuances) presents a difficult problem.[9]

The problem of the literary flourishing in Persian Yehud is even worse when one looks at the shape of biblical literature. The great amount of scribal activity is clearly inconsistent with the portrait of the Persian province of Yehud that archaeologists, historians, and biblical scholars have generally agreed on. Indeed, the diversity of biblical literature and the numerous redactional and editorial stages that traditional scholarship has posed are difficult to set within an impoverished Yehud. Apparently aware of this problem, Davies remarks that "the later we move in date, the easier it is to conclude that the temple could sustain a number of scribal schools with a vigorous scribal activity."[10] Not just *one* scribal school but *a number* of them (as Davies recognizes) would be necessary to generate the quantity and variety we find in biblical literature. This does not preclude that some biblical literature was composed and edited during the Persian period, yet the social setting of the Persian period makes a great eruption of Hebrew literature quite implausible. A more suitable setting for the composition of biblical literature from the evidence of archaeology and social history would be the late Judahite monarchy in the city of Jerusalem.

---

[9] See Avi Hurvitz, "The Historical Quest for 'Ancient Israel' and the Linguistic Evidence of the Hebrew Bible: Some Methodological Observations," *VT* 47 (1997): 310–15.

[10] Davies, *Scribes and Schools,* 79.

LATE MONARCHIC JERUSALEM

Archaeological research of the last several decades has made it abundantly clear that dramatic changes in the social life of Judah were ushered in by the Assyrian Empire in the late eighth century. The urbanization of Judah, for example, resulted in a much more complex society where writing was a regular part of burgeoning government bureaucracy. The use of writing by new social classes (military, merchants, craftsmen) is indicated by inscriptional evidence relating to government bureaucracy, economic globalization, and religious ideology (e.g., private seals, royal seal impressions, letters, receipts, graffiti, amulets). Jerusalem would emerge as a large metropolis and a powerful political center in the late eighth century. From the perspective of social anthropology, the changes must have had profound implications for society and ultimately for the composition of biblical texts during this period. These changes would be the primary catalysts for the formation of biblical literature.

The exile of the northern kingdom and the subsequent urbanization of the rural south—particularly Jerusalem—is the *Sitz im Leben* for an eruption of literary activity that resulted in the composition of extended portions of the Hebrew Bible. It produced the prophetic works of Amos, Hosea, Micah, Isaiah of Jerusalem, and a pre-Deuteronomic historical work. The late Judahite monarchy was the ideal social and political context for the flourishing of biblical literature. To begin, the urbanization and accompanying administrative bureaucracy made writing widely accessible. There is a remarkable increase in the epigraphic evidence specifically in the late Iron II period. In contrast, none of the conditions conducive to a literary flourishing existed in the Babylonian or Persian periods. Indeed, these were periods of retrenchment that were best suited to the collection, preservation, and editing of literature, not to its creation. The impoverished economic conditions did not lend themselves to vigorous scribal activity. Moreover, the circumscribed city of Jerusalem and its small temple complex were hardly conducive to the wide-scale scribal activity sometimes ascribed to it. To be sure, literature may be created at any time, but the conditions for a flourishing of literary activity are to be found in the late Judahite monarchy, not the Babylonian or Persian periods.

Since Jerusalem would be a focal point for the production of biblical literature, any analysis must begin there. Up until the last twenty years, there was considerable debate about the size and extent of Jerusalem during the period of the monarchy.[11] After Avigad's excavations in the Jewish

---

[11] Nahman Avigad summarizes the early debate about the size of Jerusalem during the biblical period in *Discovering Jerusalem* (Nashville: Nelson, 1983), 26–31.

Quarter uncovered a city wall more that 7 m wide (i.e., "the broad wall"), it became clear that Jerusalem became quite large during the late monarchy. One remaining question is how to account for this expansion.

The classic explanation for Jerusalem's growth was given by Magen Broshi two decades ago: "the main reasons behind this expansion was the immigration of Israelites who came to Judah from the Northern Kingdom after the fall of Samaria in 721 B.C.E., and the influx of dispossessed refugees from the territories that Sennacherib took from Judah and gave to the Philistine cities."[12] Indeed, these two events must have played a critical role in the changing demographics of Palestine in the late Iron Age. With the aid of recent archaeological evidence we can refine Broshi's explanation and draw out some of its implications.

There is ample evidence that Hezekiah attempted to integrate northern refugees into his kingdom. The tradition that Manasseh followed in the sins of King Ahab of Israel also suggests that the northern émigrés left their mark on religious practice in Jerusalem (2 Kgs 21:3; see also Mic 3:9–10).[13] Perhaps more to the point, Hezekiah named his son Manasseh, a name well known as one of the leading tribes of the northern kingdom. He also arranged a marriage between his son and a family from Jotbah in Galilee (see 2 Kgs 21:19). This can only have been an attempt by Hezekiah to control influx of northern refugees into his capital.[14] Given this evidence, the account in 2 Chr 30:1—"Hezekiah sent word to all Israel and Judah, and wrote letters also to Ephraim and Manasseh, that they should come to the house of YHWH at Jerusalem, to keep the Passover to YHWH the God of Israel"—aptly fits the political situation. Archaeological support for Hezekiah's attempt to integrate the north into his

---

Andrew G. Vaughn brings this debate up to the present in *Theology, History, and Archaeology in the Chronicler's Account of Hezekiah* (SBLABS 4; Atlanta: Scholars Press, 1999), 19–80. My own understanding of Jerusalem's archaeology owes much to graduate courses and conversations with Gabriel Barkay.

[12] Magen Broshi, "Expansion of Jerusalem in the Reigns of Hezekiah and Manasseh," *IEJ* 24 (1974): 21. Although the growth of Jerusalem began already in the ninth century (see Vaughn, *Theology, History, and Archaeology,* 59–70), the late eighth and seventh centuries witnessed a more rapid growth of the city and urbanization of the Judahite state.

[13] See William Schniedewind, "History and Interpretation: The Religion of Ahab and Manasseh in the Book of Kings," *CBQ* 55 (1993): 657–60.

[14] For a similar interpretation, see Hugh G. M. Williamson, *1 and 2 Chronicles* (NCB; Grand Rapids: Eerdmans, 1982), 361; also note Shemaryahu Talmon's interpretation of Hezekiah in his essay, "The Cult and Calendar Reform of Jeroboam I," in *King, Cult, and Calendar in Ancient Israel: Collected Studies* (Jerusalem: Magnes, 1986), 123–30.

kingdom also comes from *lmlk* seals found at northern sites.[15] These *lmlk* seals originate in the late eighth century and most likely were developed by Hezekiah's administration; they reflect an increasingly sophisticated governmental control by Jerusalem.

A second phase of expansion followed Sennacherib's invasion in 701 B.C.E. Sennacherib's invasion devastated the Judean Shephelah. According to the calculations of Israel Finkelstein, "about 85 percent of the settlements of the Shephelah in the eighth century had not been reoccupied in the last phase of the Iron II. The total built-up area decreased by about 70 percent."[16] The decrease was primarily in small agricultural settlements and not in the larger cities and towns. The devastation of the Judean foothills along with the growth of Jerusalem resulted in a corresponding increase in smaller settlements around Jerusalem established in the late eighth or seventh century. New agricultural villages and farmsteads were founded forming an agricultural and industrial hinterland for Jerusalem.[17] Additionally, Gibeon (7 km north) emerges as an industrial center in the late monarchy.[18] The royal administrative center at Ramat Rahel (3 km south of Jerusalem), probably the enigmatic *mmšt* of the *lmlk* seals, was

---

[15] This was first pointed out to me by Gabriel Barkay. See also Hanan Eshel, "A *lmlk* Stamp from Beth-El," *IEJ* 39 (1989): 60–62; Ora Yogev, "Tel Yizre'el—October 1987–January 1988," *ESI* 7–8 (1988–89): 192–93; Nadav Na'aman, "Hezekiah's Fortified Cities and the LMLK Stamps," *BASOR* 261 (1989): 5–21.

[16] Israel Finkelstein, "The Archaeology of the Days of Manasseh," in *Scripture and Other Artifacts: Essays on the Bible and Archaeology in Honor of Philip J. King* (ed. M. Coogan et al.; Louisville: Westminister John Knox, 1994), 173.

[17] Recent surveys of the Jerusalem area have uncovered a number of settlements from the eighth–sixth centuries; see Gershon Edelstein and Ianir Milevski, "The Rural Settlement of Jerusalem Re-evaluated: Surveys and Excavations in the Reph'aim Valley and the Mevasseret Yerushalayim," *PEQ* 126 (1994): 2–11; Zvi Ron, "Agricultural Terraces in the Judean Mountains," *IEJ* 16 (1966): 111–22; Shimon Gibson and Gershon Edelstein, "Investigating Jerusalem's Rural Landscape," *Levant* 17 (1985): 139–55; A. Zahavi, "Malha Hill" [Hebrew], *Hadashot Arkheologiyot* 99 (1993): 59–60; Ruth Ovadiah, "Jerusalem, Giv'at Massu'a," *ESI* 12 (1994): 71–76; and most recently, Nurit Feig, "New Discoveries in the Rephaim Valley, Jerusalem," *PEQ* 128 (1996): 3–7. The material is summarized by Vaughn, *Theology, History, and Archaeology,* 32–45.

[18] See James B. Pritchard, "Industry and Trade at Biblical Gibeon," *BA* 23 (1960): 23–29. The discovery of eighty-six *lmlk* stamps suggests that Gibeon was an important agricultural center in Hezekiah's administration. Gitin also explains the rapid growth of the city of Ekron by relating it to northern refugees; see Seymour Gitin, "Incense Altars from Ekron, Israel and Judah: Context and Typology," *ErIsr* 20 (1989): 52*–67*.

established in the late eighth century and flourished in the seventh century; apparently, the site served as a secondary capital and administrative center alleviating overcrowding in Jerusalem.[19] The City of David itself was apparently expanded by Manasseh: "he built an outer wall for the City of David west of Gihon, in the valley, reaching the entrance at the Fish Gate; he carried it around Ophel, and raised it to a very great height" (2 Chr 33:14).[20] This further growth may be accounted for as the aftermath of Sennacherib's campaign wherein he claimed to have "laid siege to forty-six of [Hezekiah's] strong cities, walled forts and to the countless small villages in their vicinity" (*ANET,* 288; see also 2 Kgs 18:13). Jerusalem's growing hinterland corresponds to (1) the demographic shift from the Shephelah to the hill country, (2) the need for agricultural production to supply Jerusalem and Hezekiah's administration, and (3) the need to replace the devastated agricultural infrastructure of the Shephelah.[21]

One problem this growth must have presented to Jerusalem is water. In fact, Dan Bahat cites this problem as a limiting factor for the size of Jerusalem.[22] While this is quite true, it should not be surprising that the water problem began to be addressed specifically in the late eighth century. Bahat himself points out that the upper pool of Bethesda "provided an additional [water] supply for the growing city" and appears "to belong to the later centuries of the First Temple Period."[23] Josephus mentions the "Pool of the Towers" (*War* 5.468; known today as "Hezekiah's Pool") on the northwest side of the western hill that he associates with the "First

---

[19] Ramat Rahel has been a problem for historical geography. It is often identified by Beth-haccherem (Jer 6:1; Neh 3:14; Josh 15:59a [LXX]). Gabriel Barkay makes a cogent case for its identification with the enigmatic *mmšt* mentioned in the numerous *lmlk* stamps at the site; see Gabriel Barkay, "Ramat Rahel," *NEAEHL* 4:1261–67.

[20] Kenyon excavated a wall on the eastern slope of the City of David and attributed it to Hezekiah ("Wall NA"), but it seems more likely that it should be attributed to Manasseh; see Dan Bahat, "The Wall of Manasseh in Jerusalem," *IEJ* 31 (1981): 235–36.

[21] There was also a sudden expansion of settlement in the more arid regions of the Beer-sheba valley and the Judean Desert; see further Finkelstein, "Archaeology of the Days of Manasseh," 175–76. The Beer-sheba region largely replaced the Shephelah as the "breadbasket" of the small Judahite state.

[22] Dan Bahat, "Was Jerusalem Really That Large?" in *Biblical Archaeology Today, 1990: Proceedings of the Second International Congress on Biblical Archaeology* (ed. A. Biran and J. Aviram; Jerusalem: Israel Exploration Society, 1993), 583; for a summary of Jerusalem's water systems, see Shiloh's contribution on "Water Systems" in "Jerusalem," *NEAEHL* 2:709–12.

[23] Bahat, "Was Jerusalem Really That Large?" 583.

Wall"; this pool dates at least as far back as the Roman period but has never been adequately investigated and could also originate in the late Iron II period. Hezekiah's water projects are also mentioned in three independent biblical accounts (2 Kgs 20:20; 2 Chr 32:2–4, 30; Isa 22:10–11). Water projects point to the ongoing urbanization and centralization of Jerusalem. Karl August Wittfogel's classic study, *Oriental Despotism,* relates the organization of society to the economics of regimes in Mesopotamia.[24] Wittfogel's basic thesis was that centralization of state control arose through the maintenance of water rights and canal systems. The scale of these projects necessitated a centralization of administrative control. Likewise, the problem of water supply in Jerusalem probably also encouraged centralization of state control, even though there were a number of other forces at work. Certainly, the need to prepare and coordinate military defenses in the face of the rising Assyrian Empire also contributed to political centralization.

Such centralization of state control tended to provoke harsh reactions from the countryside. The informal political structures of the rural Judahite state, such as the "elders" or the "people of the land," were marginalized as power shifted to the urban center in Jerusalem. Along these lines, we should probably understand the negative portrait of Manasseh as resulting from the societal dynamics of centralization and urbanization. At the same time, the revolution that followed the assassination of King Amon and placed the eight-year-old king Josiah on the throne was surely tied to the social tensions generated by urbanization and centralization.

In sum, during the late eighth through early seventh century Judah underwent a process of rapid centralization and urbanization. Israel Finkelstein describes it as follows: "in the later days of Hezekiah and in the reign of Manasseh, Judah went through a painful transformation from a relatively large state with a varied economic system to a small community, in fact not much more than a city-state, with a large capital and a small but densely settled countryside."[25] More to the point, though, Judah moved from a large rural state to a smaller but more centralized and urbanized state. The centrality of Jerusalem was the de facto result of the exponential increase in its population. Jerusalem, which had represented about 6 percent of Judah's total population in the mid-eighth century, suddenly became about 29 percent in scarcely two generations.[26] Tumultuous events and the

---

[24] Karl August Wittfogel, *Oriental Despotism* (New Haven: Yale University Press, 1957).

[25] Finkelstein, "Archaeology of the Days of Manasseh," 181.

[26] The exact numbers depend on the exact size of Jerusalem post-701 B.C.E. Finkelstein takes a conservative estimate of 60 ha. This would still translate into an

accompanying demographic revolution must have had a profound impact on ideology and literature that arose during this period.

Dramatic changes in Judah's society between the eighth and seventh century B.C.E. can also be illustrated by a comparison of the ceramic repertoire in the Judahite city of Lachish. Orna Zimhoni emphasizes an almost surprising uniformity among the pottery of the late eighth century at Lachish, especially when compared with the variety of influences represented by the late seventh century; she writes, "The ceramic uniformity of Lachish Level III [= destroyed by Sennacherib in 701 B.C.E.], and its orientation towards the Shephelah-hill country, are replaced in Level II [= destroyed by Nebuchadnezzar in 588 B.C.E.] by a more diverse, coastal plain-oriented assemblage."[27] A similar picture is also reflected at the sites of Timnah (Tel Batash) and Ekron (Tel Miqne). She concludes that the pottery reflects the changing sociopolitical situation of Lachish in the eighth to seventh centuries:

> The Lachish ceramic assemblage reflects the environment of *Pax Assyriaca,* an open political and economic system under the aegis of the Assyrian Empire, conditions which continued to prevail later under Egyptian occupation. The diverse character of the ceramic assemblage complements the historical picture and can be understood in view of the political changes that took place during that period.[28]

In other words, the ceramic assemblage during the period of Hezekiah reflects a highly isolated economy with little significant outside cultural influences reflected in the pottery repertoire. On the other hand, the period of Josiah, or the late monarchy in general, is marked by an open economy in which the pottery reflects a wide variety of cultural influences. Along similar lines, Baruch Halpern addresses changes in attitudes about individual moral responsibility during the late monarchy by adducing a wealth and variety of archaeological evidence pointing to the breakdown of the

---

almost fourfold increase in Jerusalem's size and make Jerusalem's population 23 percent of Judah's total population. Gabriel Barkay argues cogently for a much larger Jerusalem of 100 ha that translates into about 34 percent (Gabriel Barkay, "Northern and Western Jerusalem in the End of the Iron Age" [Ph.D. diss., Tel Aviv University, 1985]). I follow a mediating position, estimating a total built-up area of 80 ha. Of course, this does not include the small agricultural villages that sprang up around Jerusalem.

[27] Orna Zimhoni, "Two Ceramic Assemblages from Lachish Levels III and II," *TA* 17 (1990): 48.

[28] Ibid., 49; also see Nadav Naʾaman "The Kingdom of Judah under Josiah," *TA* 18 (1991): 3–71.

family structure occasioned by urbanization.[29] The architecture of the classic four-room house, for example, becomes smaller, reflecting an increasing urban and mobile society. Even the size of cooking pots shrinks as society moves toward smaller, nuclear families.[30] Implicit in these differences is a momentous shift in Judahite society, away from the isolated, rural nation that characterized its first few centuries into a more urbanized, cosmopolitan state.

The social influences in Jerusalem were twofold. First, there were the numerous northern émigrés. These people came from a more urban and cosmopolitan culture. From the perspective of historical geography, the north was also much more open to contacts, both political and commercial. Although Judah had been a relatively poor, sparsely populated state (especially compared to Samaria), this situation began to change in the late eighth century as wealthier, more cosmopolitan northerners were thrust back into Judahite society. The acceptance of these new settlers— particularly in Jerusalem, as opposed to the rural communities—was probably eased by the lineal ties with the northern dynasty of Ahab through Athaliah.[31] The second social influence came through contact with Assyrian culture and religion.[32] In the late eighth through seventh centuries the rural Judahite state had two foreign cultures, Samaria and Assyria, thrust upon them. The Josianic reforms were a reaction against these cultural incursions.

The urbanization and concomitant centralization of Jerusalem naturally resulted in some resentment among the more rural towns and villages. This is reflected, for example, in the rural prophet Micah from the countryside town of Moresheth-gath:[33]

---

[29] Baruch Halpern, "Jerusalem and the Lineages in the Seventh Century BCE: Kinship and the Rise of Individual Moral Liability," in *Law and Ideology in Monarchic Israel* (ed. B. Halpern and D. Hobson; JSOTSup 124; Sheffield: Sheffield Academic Press, 1991), 11–107.

[30] On family structure in ancient Israel, see Lawrence E. Stager, "The Archaeology of the Family in Ancient Israel," *BASOR* 260 (1985): 1–35.

[31] E.g., 2 Kgs 8:26–27. See Halpern, "Jerusalem and the Lineages in the Seventh Century BCE," 11–107.

[32] There has been extensive discussion concerning the degree of Assyrian imposition of religion; see Morton [Mordechai] Cogan, *Imperialism and Religion: Assyria, Judah and Israel in the Eighth and Seventh Centuries B.C.E.* (SBLMS 19; Missoula, Mont.: Scholars Press, 1974); and John McKay, *Religion in Judah under the Assyrians* (SBT 26; Naperville, Ill.: Allenson, 1973).

[33] Moresheth-gath should probably be identified with Tell ej-Judeideh (aka Tel Goded), a small 6-acre site excavated at the turn of the century; see Felix M. Abel,

> Hear this, you *heads of the house of Jacob and chiefs of the house of Israel,*
> who abhor justice and pervert all equity, who *build* Zion with blood and
> Jerusalem with wrong! Its rulers give judgment for a bribe, its priests teach
> for a price, its prophets give oracles for money; yet they lean upon YHWH
> and say, "Surely YHWH is with us! No harm shall come upon us." There-
> fore because of you Zion shall be plowed as a field; Jerusalem shall
> become a heap of ruins, and the mountain of the house a wooded height.
> (Mic 3:9–12)

The "heads" and "chiefs" are related to the house of "Jacob" and "Israel,"
that is, the north. These are the ones who "build Jerusalem." In the context of the enormous growth in Jerusalem's size at this time, the use of the
verb בנה "to build" should be understood as having a concrete referent.
The new inhabitants of Jerusalem—apparently, many of them from the
north—are accused of bringing perverted social values. Notably absent in
Micah's diatribe is anything reminiscent of the later Deuteronomic religious
critique. Rather, the critique compares with the prophetic critiques in Amos
and Hosea, a hint that these books also received their final form from
Judahite editors around 700 B.C.E.

The critique of these new cultural influences climaxed in the assassination of Hezekiah's grandson, Amon. It is probable that the attempted
coup d'état by the "servants of Amon" was related to the non-Yahwistic (at
least by name) queen mother who was of *northern* descent (see 2 Kgs
21:19). At this point, the *ʿam hāʾāreṣ* ("people of the land" עם הארץ)
moved in to ensure the proper succession. More importantly, this left the
government in the hands of an eight-year-old king whose family came
from Bozkath, a rural town in the Judean foothills.[34] Power apparently
had shifted from the aristocratic urbanites with ties to northern Israel back
to the rural patricians. The role of the enigmatic *ʿam hāʾāreṣ* in the
Josianic coup suggests that they represented the old rural aristocracy.[35]
The tension between the *ʿam hāʾāreṣ* and the urban elite is also quite
explicit in the account of Josiah's overthrow of the Israelian queen
Athaliah, which concludes, "So all *ʿam hāʾāreṣ* rejoiced, but the city was
quiet after Athaliah had been killed with the sword at the king's house"
(2 Kgs 11:20). It is hardly surprising that drastic changes in the politics and
religion were forthcoming.

Géographie politique (vol. 2 of *Géographie de la Palestine;* Paris: Gabalda, 1938),
392; Magen Broshi, "Judeideh, Tell," *NEAEHL* 3:837–38.

[34] There is no consensus on the exact identification of Bozkath, although it was
apparently located in the Judean foothills near Lachish (see Josh. 15:39).

[35] For a good summary of the literature, see John Healy, "Am Haʾarez," *ABD*
1:168–69.

ASPECTS OF THE BIBLICAL LITERARY TRADITION

Rapid growth and change in Jerusalem naturally attracted social, political, and religious interpreters. These conditions invited and even necessitated the creation of literature. There is good reason to believe that the collection and editing of traditions as well as the composition of literature began in earnest with the men of Hezekiah in the late eighth century, as is suggested by Prov 25:1, and continued into the days of Josiah. The time has now come briefly to assess how the sociopolitical context might have shaped the composition of biblical texts. A complete discussion of these texts will require a separate monograph, so I will offer some observations on the Prophets.

ISAIAH OF JERUSALEM

The so-called messianic prophecies in Isa 7–11 were intended initially to address the sociopolitical situation of the late eighth century. These chapters are part of the larger literary unit, Isa 5–12, that focuses on the punishment of the northern kingdom by Assyria and the associated restoration of the Davidic Empire.[36] The dating of these prophecies is naturally critical. There is some consensus that the so-called *Denkschrift* or "Isaianic Memoir" (Isa 6:1–9:6 [Eng. 6:1–9:7]) dates to the eighth-century prophet, even while many parts are assigned to later editors.[37] Its literary envelope (Isa 5:1–30; 9:7–12:6), on the other hand, has been the subject of more debate. First of all, it is difficult to empathize with those few scholars who wish to dissect these chapters on little or no redactional grounds. Usually these analyses are based on the critics' feelings about what could or could not be written in the particular historical context. Yet, as this study shows, all the so-called messianic prophecies in Isa 7–11 are entirely appropriate to the sociopolitical context of the late eighth century.

The "Immanuel prophecy" in Isa 7 is set within the context of the Syro-Ephraimite war, the war that precipitated the Assyrian incursions against Damascus and Israel in 734–732. The alliance between Rezin and Pekah against Judah threatened to overthrow the Davidic dynasty, and "when the house of David [בית דוד] heard that Aram had allied itself with Ephraim" they were afraid and turned to the prophet Isaiah (Isa 7:2–3). The narrative's choice of the expression "house of David" (also in 7:13)

---

36 For a discussion of the literary unit, see Marvin A. Sweeney, *Isaiah 1–39, with an Introduction to Prophetic Literature* (FOTL 16; Grand Rapids: Eerdmans, 1996), 114–15.

37 See recently Hugh G. M. Williamson, *The Book Called Isaiah: Deutero-Isaiah's Role in Composition and Redaction* (Oxford: Clarendon, 1994), 116–55.

here quite intentionally recalls the promise of an eternal house to David's sons (see 2 Sam 7:11–16). The prophet's words conclude by highlighting the rebellion of the northern kingdom from Judah: "YHWH will bring on you and on your people and on your ancestral house such days as have not come *since the day that Ephraim departed from Judah*—the king of Assyria" (Isa 7:17).

The well-known prophecy in Isa 8:23–9:6 [Eng. 9:1–7] begins with the "gloom that is in Galilee," no doubt a reflection of current events. The reversal of this devastating conquest of Samaria by the Assyrians—that is, the light that has shined upon them (9:1)—is found with the chosen son who sits on the throne of David (9:5–6). Likewise, in Isa 11 the Davidide root of Jesse ultimately "will assemble the outcasts of Israel and gather the dispersed of Judah" (11:12). It is easy to see how these prophecies immediately addressed the social setting of the late eighth century in Jerusalem. On the one hand, these prophecies resonated with the recent destruction of the north that vindicated the Davidic monarchy, a monarchy that itself had been threatened by the now-dismantled northern kingdom. On the other hand, these narratives envisioned the ingathering of the northern remnant by the promised Davidic line, which was something that Hezekiah was eager to do in order to strengthen his rule.

THE HEZEKIAN EDITION OF THE DEUTERONOMISTIC HISTORY

The book of Kings preserves two similar assessments of the division of the kingdom that must have originated within the Hezekian period among palace scribes in Jerusalem.[38] The first summarizes the narrative of the division in which Rehoboam foolishly follows his young counselors: "So Israel has been in rebellion against the house of David [בית דוד] until this day" (1 Kgs 12:19). It is noteworthy that there is no prophetic justification in the summary (see 1 Kgs 11:9–13) and that the transgression implied by the verb פשע "to transgress, rebel" is against the *house of David*. The highly edited narrative about the fall of Samaria in 2 Kgs 17 also preserves a fragment from this perspective. In 2 Kgs 17:20–21a we read:

> YHWH rejected all the seed of Israel; he punished them and gave them
> into the hand of plunderers until he had banished them from his pres-

---

[38] The present study cannot discuss this hypothesis in detail. The foundation of the approach has been the study of the regnal and judgment formulae, and I agree with Vanderhooft and Halpern that "the most obvious barometer of editorial shifts within Kings is fluctuation in its skeletal formulary" (David S. Vanderhooft and Baruch Halpern, "The Editions of Kings in the 7th–6th Centuries B.C.E.," *HUCA* 62 [1991]: 183); see my review of literature: "The Problem with Kings: Recent Study of the Deuteronomistic History," *RelSRev* 22 (1995): 22–27.

ence because Israel had torn away from the house of David
[כִּי־קָרַע יִשְׂרָאֵל מֵעַל בֵּית דָּוִד]. Then they made Jeroboam, son of Nebat, king.

Here the exile of the northern kingdom results from Israel breaking away
from Judah. Although the Hebrew syntax is clear, commentators sometimes
miss the point, interpreting the action as passive. For example, the NRSV
translates כִּי־קָרַע יִשְׂרָאֵל מֵעַל בֵּית דָּוִד as a clause dependent on the following statement, "When he had torn Israel from the house of David, they
made Jeroboam son of Nebat king." This translation violates rules of
Hebrew grammar. The verb קָרַע is active, not passive; the noun יִשְׂרָאֵל
is the subject, not the object.[39] The main reason for translating this clause
as a passive would seem to be preconceived notions about how the exile
of Samaria was interpreted in ancient Judah. It should be clear that
Jerusalem interpreted the fall of Samaria as a vindication of the Davidic
dynasty, especially in the immediate aftermath. This perspective was fun-
damentally political, though there were obvious religious aspects as well.
I would suggest that these two passages reflect the perspective of a longer
Hezekian historical work that vindicated the Davidic line as the legitimate
heirs to a united kingdom. Both parts of the kingdom were presented
because Hezekiah reunited the divided kingdom. The early division of the
kingdom after Saul was critical because David reunited the kingdom, and
Hezekiah followed in his steps. Hezekiah reestablished the Davidic kingdom. Here I agree with Ian Provan and others who argue that Hezekiah is
presented in the book of Kings as the "new David."[40] However, this is
more than a literary viewpoint; it reflected a political policy conditioned by
the situation in the late eighth century.

This view must have had far-reaching ramifications for the Josianic
author of the Deuteronomistic History.[41] The Josianic themes are focused
around religious rather than political issues. Whereas Hezekiah tried to
integrate the north, Josiah only *castigated*. Where Josiah's centralization

---

[39] This point is argued cogently by Marc Z. Brettler, "Ideology, History and Theology in 2 Kings XVII 7–23," *VT* 39 (1989): 268–82. However, it is difficult to
understand Brettler's dating of this fragment to the postexilic period, when it would
have little relevance.

[40] Ian W. Provan, *Hezekiah in the Book of Kings* (BZAW, 172; Berlin: de Gruyter,
1988), 116–17. Also see Richard Elliott Friedman, "From Egypt to Egypt in Dtr 1 and
Dtr 2," in *Traditions in Transformations: Turning Points in Biblical Faith* (Winona
Lake, Ind.: Eisenbrauns, 1981), 171–73; Erik Eynikel, *The Reform of King Josiah and
the Composition of the Deuteronomistic History* (Leiden: Brill, 1996), 107–11.

[41] There is considerable debate concerning the composition of the Deuteronomistic History that cannot be taken up in detail here. For a complete survey of
literature, see Eynikel, *Reform of King Josiah,* 7–31.

was unabashedly religious, centralization under Hezekiah was first of all civil and governmental, precipitated by the growth in size and importance of Jerusalem. Positing a major Hezekian history more satisfactorily answers some lingering questions about the Deuteronomistic History. How relevant was an extinct northern kingdom a century later? Two centuries? The book of Chronicles should inform us of the role of the north in later literature, yet the northern kingdom is omitted. The fate of the northern kingdom would have weighed most heavily in the life and literature of Judah in the years immediately following Samaria's destruction and exile.

THE BOOK OF AMOS

The days of Hezekiah evidently saw not only the influx of northern refugees but also the collection of northern prophetic literature such as Amos and Hosea. There is ample reason to believe that the book of Amos also received its final form in the Hezekian period. The composition of Amos has been a matter of considerable debate. The most recent commentaries by David Noel Freedman and Shalom Paul argue that the book essentially dates to the days of the prophet with little subsequent editing.[42] In order to arrive at this conclusion, one must dance around rather unequivocal references pointing to the late eighth century. Certainly the clearest of these is the reference to the disappearance of Philistine Gath in Amos 6:2, which was known to have been destroyed by Sargon's invasion in 712 B.C.E.[43] Undoubtedly Amos was preserved in the south because the prophet was understood to have correctly foreseen the exile of Samaria, and this was interpreted as further legitimizing the Davidic dynasty.

Amos 9:11—"On that day I will raise up the booth of David [סכת דויד] that is fallen, and repair its breaches, and raise up its ruins, and rebuild it as in the days of old"—has been widely analyzed as a late addition to the book.[44] Usually this redactor was situated in the postexilic period, though there is much less agreement on this. The arguments may be summarized as follows: (1) the expectation of the restoration of the Davidic kingdom reflects such a period; (2) the promise of restoration contradicts the threat of destruction throughout the book; (3) the promise of restoration without

---

[42] David Noel Freedman, *Amos: A New Translation with Notes and Commentary* (AB 24A; New York: Doubleday, 1989); Shalom Paul, *Amos: A Commentary on the Book of Amos* (Hermeneia; Philadephia: Fortress, 1991).

[43] It is also noteworthy that Gath is missing from the list of Philistine cities mentioned in Amos 1:6–8. Its fate is apparently summed up in the words of the prophet Micah: "Tell it not in Gath" (Mic 1:10).

[44] E.g., William R. Harper, *A Critical and Exegetical Commentary on Amos and Hosea* (ICC; Edinburgh: T&T Clark, 1904), 195–96.

ethical demands contradicts Amos's message elsewhere; (4) the historical background presupposes exile; and (5) the language is Late Biblical Hebrew. Given the social background described in this essay, the first four arguments may be disregarded. The last linguistic argument has never been properly developed and does not bear up to scrutiny. A critical plank in this argument is the plene spelling of the name David, admittedly a late tendency. However, as James Barr has shown, spelling is not a reliable means of dating, since it often reflects scribal transmission more than authorship.[45] There is then no reason to see this passage as a very late addition when we now have a more plausible context in the late eighth century.

The conclusion of Amos draws from two sources: Amos 5:26–27 and 2 Sam 7. The enigmatic prophecy in Amos 5:26–27 is preserved in the MT as follows:

ונשאתם את סכות מלככם ואת כיון צלמיכם כוכב אלהיכם אשר עשיתם לכם
והגליתי אתכם מהלאה לדמשק אמר יהוה אלהי־צבאות שמו

> You shall take up Sakkuth your king, and Kaiwan your star-god, your images, which you made for yourselves; therefore I will take you into exile beyond Damascus, says the LORD, whose name is the God of hosts. (NRSV)

This text has generated endless debates over its meaning. This debate need not concern us here. What is relevant is not what it meant to the prophet Amos but rather how it was interpreted by the redactor of Amos 9:11.[46] In this enigmatic prophecy the redactor sees a correctly predicted exile of the northern kingdom. More than this, the redactor apparently asks the questions: (1) "Who is your legitimate king [מלככם]?" and "What is the סכות?" The legitimate king must be David, and the fallen "hut" of David (סכת דויד הנופלת) is the division of the kingdom that now will be mended (גדר "to repair"; בנה "to build"; קום "to raise up"). The verbs in 5:26 and 9:11—נשא "to lift up" and קום "to rise up"—should be understood as intentionally parallel. As in Isa 7:17, the book of Amos recalls the former times: the kingdom will be restored "like the days of old" (כימי עולם), namely, the golden age of David and Solomon (see Prov 25:1).

THE BOOK OF HOSEA

The critique of kingship in the book of Hosea probably also received its final shape in the aftermath of Samaria's fall and Jerusalem's survival. In

---

[45] James Barr, *The Variable Spelling of the Hebrew Bible* (Oxford: Oxford University Press, 1989), 201.

[46] The association between Amos 5:26–27 and 9:11 is recognized by the author of the *Damascus Document* (see CD vii, 14–21).

that context, Hosea's prophecies were understood to give divine sanction to the Davidic kings who remained in Jerusalem. Hosea's superscription describes the prophet's activity as continuing into the Hezekian period, and the prophet actually prophesies the miraculous deliverance of Jerusalem: "But I will have pity on the house of Judah, and I will save them by the LORD their God; I will not save them by bow, or by sword, or by war, or by horses, or by horsemen" (Hos 1:7 NRSV). Ronald E. Clements ascribes this verse to a late seventh-century editor.[47] It seems more likely, however, that the verse was part of an editorial framework given the book when it was brought down from the north in the aftermath of the destruction of Samaria. The late seventh century was characterized by a fierce polemic against Jeroboam's religious practices and as such hardly makes an appropriate context for the integration of northern prophetic traditions. If there was to be an integration of northern literary traditions in Jerusalem, it makes more sense to see them in the immediate aftermath of the fall of Samaria with its concomitant influx of refugees to the south than to place it a century later in the context of religious reforms aimed at eradicating northern cultural influences!

Many commentators have pointed out the largely negative portrait of monarchy in the book of Hosea. Perhaps the most oft-quoted example is Hos 8:4, "They made kings, but not through me; they set up princes, but without my knowledge." Ultimately, however, the meaning of this critique within the book as a whole must be read through the lens of Hos 3:4–5:

> For the Israelites shall live [יֵשְׁבוּ] many days without king or prince, without sacrifice or pillar, without ephod or teraphim. Afterward [אַחַר] the Israelites shall return [יָשֻׁבוּ] and seek YHWH their God, and David their king; they shall come in awe to YHWH and to his goodness in the latter days.

The temporal relationship between 3:4 and 5 is marked by the preposition אַחַר "afterward." For a period the northern kingdom did not have a king, but then they were drawn into the fold under the Davidic dynasty. It is natural to assume that this refers to the period following the fall of Samaria until the time of the author. The author argues that David is "*their* king" (מַלְכָּם), implying that the former northern kingdom and its kings were illegitimate. The idea that the Israelites would be incorporated *again* into the kingdom fits into the context we know in the late eighth century and early seventh century, but it is difficult to place within any later exilic

---

[47] See Ronald E. Clements, *Isaiah and the Deliverance of Jerusalem: A Study of the Interpretation of Prophecy in the Old Testament* (JSOTSup 13; Sheffield: JSOT Press, 1980), 60.

or postexilic context. Northern prophetic texts would have been given a Jerusalemite redaction soon after they arrived in the south—that is, if they were to be preserved at all.

In sum, the dramatic social and political changes that accompanied rapid growth and urbanization in Jerusalem during the late eighth and early seventh centuries attracted the composition of literature. Moreover, the more precisely we understand the sociopolitical context, the better we may understand why the literature might have been written and how it was *read* by those for whom it was written.[48]

---

[48] By focusing on the audience as opposed to author, we bypass the intentional fallacy. Yet the onus to understand the context of the audience—that is, what Jauss has termed the readers' "horizon of expectations"—becomes greater; see Hans Robert Jauss, "Literary History As a Challenge to Literary Theory," *New Literary History* 2 (1970): 7–37. For a survey of audience-oriented criticism, see Susan R. Suleiman and Inge Crosman, eds., *The Reader in the Text: Essays on Audience and Interpretation* (Princeton, N.J.: Princeton University Press, 1980).

Archaeology, Ideology, and the Search for David and Solomon

Neil Asher Silberman
Ename Center for Public Archaeology and Heritage Presentation

Way back—once upon a time in the 1950s—when the ideological battle lines were fewer and drawn less sharply, Professor Yigael Yadin was a dominating figure in the world of biblical archaeology. The connection between past and present in Yadin's work, between the Bible and the modern State of Israel, between ancient Israelites and modern Israelis, was something he was never ashamed of expressing. Indeed, he relished and celebrated his composite vision of past and present both to his colleagues and to general audiences. Yadin's name is often evoked in the current scholarly debate about the historicity of the united monarchy, with good reason. His stratigraphic assumptions, historical theories, and archaeological analyses of the main sites of Hazor, Megiddo, and Gezer remain the central props for all who still argue that the biblical descriptions of the Solomonic kingdom are, at least in their main outlines, historically reliable.[1] Yet it may be worthwhile, in the midst of ongoing debates about stratigraphy, biblical texts, and architectural typology, to examine some of the social and political ideologies that underlie the logic of the discipline of biblical archaeology—on which the rival archaeological narratives about the united monarchy of Israel are epistemologically based.

In that respect, Yadin is an obvious subject. Even in his earliest archaeological studies of ancient Israelite warfare, battle customs, and of David's conquest of Jerusalem—all begun during his graduate studies at

---

[1] For example, John S. Holladay, "The Kingdoms of Israel and Judah: Political and Economic Centralization in the Iron IIA–B," in *The Archaeology of Society in the Holy Land* (ed. T. E. Levy; London: Leicester University Press, 1995), 368–98; William G Dever, "Archaeology and the 'Age of Solomon': A Case Study in Archaeology and Historiography," in *The Age of Solomon* (ed. L. K. Handy; Leiden: Brill, 1997), 217–51; Amihai Mazar, "Iron Age Chronology: A Reply to I. Finkelstein," *Levant* 29 (1997): 157–67.

Hebrew University while he also served as one of the Haganah's highest-ranking officers—Yadin offered a new reading of biblical history in which the *realia* of military strategy and battlefield ingenuity, not divine intervention, were the milestones of Israel's national history.[2] It was a subtext (or supertext?) that in the 1950s and early 1960s meshed particularly well with the *Weltanschauung* of Ben-Gurion–era Israel and, for that matter, with the technological modernism of much of the post–World War II West. For during the heyday of his digging career from the beginning of the Hazor excavations in 1955 to the end of the Masada dig a decade later, few scholars and even fewer social commentators voiced doubts about the larger modern *meaning*—historical, much less political or ideological implications—of his purported archaeological confirmation of biblical personalities and events.

In today's discussions of the tenth century, one of the most bitterly debated issues is, of course, Yadin's identification of the "Solomonic" gates at Hazor, Megiddo, and Gezer.[3] Generations of archaeology and Bible students have grown up learning that this is the single most compelling archaeological proof of the historical reality of the united monarchy. Yet what is the logic on which this "proof" is implicitly based? Yadin, clearly attracted to the technological evolutionism of much of early twentieth-century British archaeology, implicitly assumed that the construction of almost identical six-chambered gates in the three cities reported by 1 Kgs 9:15 to have been refortified by Solomon represented a high degree of central planning and thus of advanced political organization. While other explanations for the uniformity of the gates might have been put forward—such as diffusion of architectural styles, employment of similarly trained architects, or regional technological developments—Yadin preferred to see the "Solomonic" gates as a unique and ethnically specific manifestation of unified Israelite rule.

I have been criticized in the past for concentrating too much on Yadin the "showman" rather than Yadin the scholar,[4] yet I must admit that I have always had difficulty separating the two. For example, in one of his most

[2] Yigael Yadin, "On the Types of Weapons Used in Israel's Wars" [Hebrew], *Maarakhot Israel* 1 (1945): 209; idem, "Let the Young Men, I Pray Thee, Arise and Play Before Us," *JPOS* 21 (1948): 110–16; idem, "The Blind and the Lame and David's Conquest of Jerusalem" [Hebrew], in *Proceedings of the First World Congress of Jewish Studies* (Jerusalem: Magnes, 1952), 222. See further Neil Asher Silberman, *A Prophet from amongst You: The Life of Yigael Yadin* (Reading, Mass.: Addison-Wesley, 1993).

[3] Yigael Yadin, "Solomon's City Wall and Gate of Gezer," *IEJ* 8 (1959): 8–18.

[4] William G. Dever, "Taking the Measure of Yigael Yadin," *Arch* 47/2 (1994): 59–61.

famous descriptions of the link between 1 Kgs 9:15 and the "Solomonic" city gates at Hazor, Megiddo, and Gezer, Yadin declared in almost Churchill-like hyperbole (rather than dispassionate scientific description), "Hardly ever in the history of archaeological digging has such a short verse in the Bible helped so much in identifying and dating actual remains found by the spade."[5]

What was the meaning of that scholarly statement? Why, in fact, is it necessary to dwell at such length on the work and words of a scholar who has been dead for many years? I would argue that Yadin and the basic historicist approach to the archaeology of the united monarchy has become such an attractive target precisely because it was so openly and self-consciously tied in its logic and political and ideological assumptions to a particularly vivid—if now bygone—era of modern Jewish history and historiography.[6] For Yadin, brought up from his youth as an activist in the Zionist movement, Solomon was not just another ancient monarch, but the embodiment of self-assured and regal self-determination that had been yearned for by politically powerless Jews all over the world for hundreds of years. Unlike William F. Albright,[7] Yadin was not motivated by a religiously based battle against the higher criticism. Quite beyond his alternative personae of "showman" and/or "scholar," Yadin was fully committed from his late teens to the military objective of establishing a Jewish State. And his identification (retrospectively justified or unjustified) of the ancient apparatus of tenth-century B.C.E. state planning resonated powerfully in the early years of the establishment of the State of Israel. It seemed to bolster the Zionist contention that statelessness and powerlessness was not an inevitable condition of Jewish existence. There *had* been Jewish kingdoms and commonwealths in the past, and so there would be once again.

That implicit nationalist vision underlying the identification of the archaeological remains of the united monarchy has been recently highlighted by Whitelam in his book *The Invention of Ancient Israel*.[8] However,

---

[5] Yigael Yadin, *Hazor: The Rediscovery of a Great Citadel from the Bible* (London: Weidenfeld & Nicholson, 1975), 205.

[6] For two important studies, see Amos Elon, *The Israelis, Fathers and Sons* (New York: Holt, Rinehart & Winston, 1971); and Yael Zerubavel, *Recovered Roots: Collective Memory and the Making of Israeli National Tradition* (Chicago: University of Chicago Press, 1995).

[7] William F. Albright, *From the Stone Age to Christianity* (Baltimore: Johns Hopkins University Press, 1940); idem, *History, Archaeology, and Christian Humanism* (New York: McGraw-Hill, 1964).

[8] Keith W. Whitelam, *The Invention of Ancient Israel: The Silencing of Palestinian History* (London: Routledge, 1996).

in his patronizing espousal of what he has learned to call "subaltern studies," Whitelam and others fail to recognize that there were other stories *no
less important*—and perhaps even unknowingly shared by them—embedded in Yadin's archaeological narrative. It must be remembered that barely
two and a half years before beginning the Hazor excavations, Yadin had
resigned as the chief of staff of the Israel Defense Forces, which like other
armies of the Cold War era was in the midst of a dramatic effort to stan-
dardize and streamline its weapons systems, fortifications, and chain of
command.[9] Thus, the pervasive logic of 1950s corporate standardization—
not even dreamed of or hinted at in the Bible—may have led Yadin to
conclude (in those days before the puzzling discovery of a "Solomonic"
gate at Ashdod) that a single controlling intelligence lay behind the structural similarity of the gates.

The superiority of modern rational planning also found its expression
in Yadin's vision of the role of archaeologist as civilizer, a cultural tamer of
the primitive mind. As the employer at Hazor of large numbers of recent
North African immigrants to Israel, he made no secret of his amusement at
some of their quaint customs and beliefs, yet he was, at the same time,
something of a missionary in the clash of modern archaeology with other,
more traditional approaches to the past. For example, Yadin recalled of the
Hazor excavations:

> I even remember vividly the gimmick we used to impress our laborers,
> even before the contours and plan of the gate became clear. We traced
> the plan of the Megiddo gate on the ground, marking it with pegs to
> denote corners and walls, and then instructed our laborers to dig accord
> ing to the marking, promising: "here you will find a wall," or "there you
> will find a chamber." When our "prophecies" proved correct, our prestige
> went up tremendously.[10]

Suffice it to say that Yadin's archaeological interpretation of the
Solomonic gates is based on far more than crude nationalism. Its complex
web of logic, inference, and emotion did not draw its power from the
intentional falsification of data but from the contemporary resonance of the
rhetorical statements it made. Many archaeologists have and still do assid-
uously assemble data, publish impeccable site reports, and write
meticulous monographs, but few add anything to modern public discourse

---

[9] Yitzhak Greenberg, "The Defense Budget in Ben-Gurion's Policy on National
Security 1949–1952" [Hebrew], *Studies in Zionism* 12 (1991): 43–53; Yoav Gelber,
The Emergence of a Jewish Army: The Veterans of the British Army in the IDF
[Hebrew] (Jerusalem: Yad Izhak Ben-Zvi, 1986).

[10] Yadin, *Hazor,* 193, 195.

about the meaning of the past. Here, I would argue, the archaeologist as showman is important, even though the most powerful or popular shows themselves have only a limited run. The Ben-Gurion era in the history of modern Israel is long past, and it is inevitable that later critics with different backgrounds and agendas would arise to contest Yadin's rhetorical logic. However, in the case of the now-vanishing David and Solomon—or any other historical narrative based on archaeological findings—is there any alternative to utilizing contemporary concepts and ideologies?

I always return to the important and enlightening work of the anthropologist Misia Landau, for in her analysis of competing turn-of-the-century narratives of human evolution, she has shown just how inescapably literary all archaeological narratives are.[11] From her perspective, "literary" is not a characterization that is combatively juxtaposed with "objective" or "scientific." It is rather a recognition that beyond the most local phenomena or rawest of statistical data, archaeologists, and for that matter all historians, must express their generalizations in the form of stories. In addition, each of the stories, like each of the storytellers, is interested not only in the "facts" of the costumes and stage settings but also in the moral of the tale. Thus in her analysis of the evolutionary theories of Darwin, Huxley, Haeckel, Keith, and Elliott Smith, Landau shows that all these scholars' explanations take on the form of the classical folktale in which the primate ancestor of humankind is always the hero, the sequence of evolutionary stages is the adventure, and the transformation of the primate ancestor into a fully modern human is always the end. Yet in each of the competing theories, based on precisely the same fossil record, the basic causation, instrumentalities, and evolutionary processes are different. These are of course drawn from *assumptions* about the underlying data rather than from the data itself. Landau therefore suggests that narrative analysis—setting the stories side by side and noting their different components—offers an effective means of comparing rival historical hypotheses.

Landau's insight on the importance of narratives of human evolution as the primary idiom of historical explanation has far-reaching implications even for the various species and subspecies populating the world of biblical archaeology. Just as *homo habilis,* the Neanderthals, or the Cro-Magnons can be seen as the "heroes" of scholarly folktales, so can the Canaanites, Philistines, Judahites, and Israelites. Indeed, it would perhaps not be too great a leap to recognize that the alternative archaeological reconstructions of the Israelite settlement—invasion, infiltration, insurrection, or cyclic

---

[11] Misia Landau, *Narratives of Human Evolution* (New Haven: Yale University Press, 1991).

adaptation—are each, at their core, the epic adventure of a "chosen people" in search of a promised land. That brings me to the issue of the
vanishing David and Solomon. I would suggest that what we have in the
present debate is not merely a conflict of competing hypotheses but a
cacophony of storytellers, each impatient with the plot lines of the others
and each intent on putting a new ending on the tale.

We might like to be persuaded that archaeology is, at its best, a hard-
headed historical science, hermetically sealed off from the weaving of fairy
tales. However, it is uncanny how all the conflicting reconstructions of
ancient Israelite state-building precisely mirror the major twentieth-century
philosophical traditions (or should I say stories) about the character of the
modern state. Let's talk for a moment about plot lines. The political soci-
ologist John A. Hall has recently suggested that, since the collapse of state
communism and the ongoing privatization of state socialism, there are
basically three.[12] The first, often termed "classical realism" or *Realpolitik,*
envisions the state as the natural and inevitable form into which any people must organize itself in order to survive. It is the ideology of emerging
nations and liberation movements. It has also been, on occasion, the battle banner of ethnic cleansing and racial intolerance. As such the state is
seen as an expression of self-interest and solidarity of a people determined
to survive in the jungle of competing tribes and hostile natural forces.
According to this view, the state is not a sociological condition or a mythic
self-deception. It is the ultimate and only true expression of nationhood.

A second major perspective is the "liberalism" of John Locke and the
British constitutionalists, maintained today by most center and center-
right parties in the West. It acknowledges the necessity and perhaps
inevitability of state-level organization but is deeply suspicious of state
power, arguing that the most important natural rights reside with the
individual. In this view, the operation of the "free market" or other
embedded economic and social relations are generally far more effective
in bringing about the public good than government fiat. In fact, the social
anthropologists' evolutionary progression from band to chiefdom to state
is impeccably "liberal" in the sense that it recognizes qualitative changes
in economic interactions between individuals as the motive force in
human history.

The third perspective is the academic Marxist critique of the state, pro-
pounded most forcefully by Jürgen Habermas and the followers of the

---

[12] For a concise summary of Hall's analysis of state forms and statist (and anti-
statist) ideologies, with basic bibliography, see John A. Hall, "State," in *The Oxford
Companion to the Politics of the World* (ed. J. Krieger; Oxford: Oxford University
Press, 1993), 878–83.

Frankfurt School. This perspective sees the bourgeois nation-state as an instrument of economic and physical subjugation, whose power is maintained by a variety of ideological apparatuses, including social norms, institutionalized religions, and official histories. Needless to say, in this perspective, veneration of ancestors and ancient rulers (real or imagined) represents nothing more or less than a "false consciousness" imposed from above to instill respect and obedience among the subjugated classes for the ruling clique of a given society.

Now what does all this caricatured Poli Sci 101 have to do with David and Solomon? I would argue—and I have argued—that when archaeologists leave the specifics of highly localized phenomena such as the thickness of a fortification wall or the dimensions of a domestic complex, they are forced to rely on contemporary logic, concepts, and philosophies to construct more general statements about the nature of their finds. So it has been with the conflicting identifications of the archaeological remains of the united monarchy for more than a hundred years. It began long before Yadin, of course, perhaps as early as Petrie at Tell el-Hesy in 1890, when Petrie's discovery of a single carved architectural element sparked visions of the greatness of Solomon in his mind.[13]

The real foundation for "Solomonic" archaeology was laid by the Oriental Institute expedition to Megiddo in the interwar years. It is important to remember that the Megiddo dig—and for that matter the work of the Oriental Institute throughout the Fertile Crescent—was just a facet of a much larger whole. Without in any way denigrating the quality of the excavation or the earnestness of the scholars, we must look beyond the confines of the discipline to see Megiddo as just one of several simultaneous projects selected, funded, and watched over by the great American activist, philanthropist, and industrialist John D. Rockefeller in the 1920s and 1930s. All of the Rockefeller projects had an unmistakable unifying theme.[14] Whether it was the restoration of Versailles, the construction of the futuristic Rockefeller Center in Manhattan, the removal and transport of medieval structures to New York's cloisters, the fabrication of colonial Williamsburg, or the excavation of the mound of Armageddon, the message was one of celebration of strikingly modern concepts of stable government, steady technological advancement, institutionalized religion,

---

[13] William M. F. Petrie, *Tell el-Hesy (Lachish)* (London: Palestine Exploration Fund, 1891).

[14] Peter Dobkin Hall, "The Empty Tomb: The Making of Dynastic Identity," in *Lives in Trust: The Fortunes of Dynastic Families in Late Twentieth Century America* (ed. G. Marcus; Boulder, Colo.: Westview, 1992), 255–348; John E. Harr and Peter J. Johnson, *The Rockefeller Conscience* (New York: Scribner's, 1991).

and standardized bureaucracy. Thus, as one of a number of didactic examples of state organization, the "Solomonic" Megiddo evoked by the Oriental Institute can be seen as just another modernist parable of "classical realism" dressed in period costume.

Moreover, it really had little to do with genuine biblical fundamentalism; indeed, Albright bitterly condemned Breasted, the Oriental Institute, and perhaps implicitly even Rockefeller as being little more than secular humanists.[15] It was all about modernization, and in the 1950s Yadin's interpretations of the rise of the united monarchy closely followed that earlier modernist libretto—though of course he sang it in a distinctively Israeli key. The idea that archaeology "proved" the historical accuracy of the Bible was really a statement directed *to society at large* that the Bible and modern statism were completely compatible. Nothing in the archaeological reconstruction of the united monarchy had anything to do with the focus of the traditional religious veneration of Solomon by Jews, Christians, and Muslims, namely, his wisdom, poetry, piety, and the beauty of his wives. The relevant biblical passages were selectively mined by archaeologists and historians to find illustrations of the principles on which modern nation-states were founded: centralized bureaucracy, centralized planning, institutionalized religion, and—in an age of General Electric, Standard Oil, and ARAMCO—even a Solomonic entrepôt on the Gulf of Aqabah for international trade.

While there has been in recent years a serious critique of the dating of the "Solomonic" gates and monumental structures—or their necessary ascription to the building program of a single political center—I would argue that the ideological heart of the matter, modern assumptions about the state retrojected into the Iron Age, have merely shifted paradigms. For those who would prefer, on the basis of comparative stratigraphy or particular readings of paleodemographics, to place the rise of state structures in the ninth or possibly eighth centuries B.C.E., the loss of a historical Solomon has in no way undermined faith in inevitable evolution of ancient Israel toward a centralized state.[16] Jamieson-Drake's oft-quoted study merely specifies the criteria by which one can know when the evolutionary stage of statehood is finally reached.[17] Moreover, if any political nuance

---

[15] Albright, *History, Archaeology, and Christian Humanism.*

[16] Israel Finkelstein, "The Archaeology of the United Monarchy: An Alternative View," *Levant* 28 (1996): 177–87; Israel Finkelstein and Neil Asher Silberman, *The Bible Unearthed* (New York: Free Press, 2001).

[17] David W. Jamieson-Drake, *Scribes and Schools in Monarchic Judah: A Socio-Archaeological Approach* (SWBA 9; JSOTSup 109; Sheffield: Sheffield Academic Press, 1991).

can be identified in the implications of the new "low chronology" and the extended period of dispersed settlement, it is that, in the tradition of liberalism, intensifying economic and political processes, not a preexisting religion or national consciousness, were the underlying basis of the ancient Israelite state.

I will now move on to a different perspective. To identify the school of critical historians who deny any historical basis for the united monarchy—or for that matter any substantial historical basis for the divided monarchy—as "revisionists" or "minimalists" is to misunderstand completely what they are talking about. Their story is no more minimal than any other. It simply has, in Misia Landau's terms, a different cast of characters, a different sequence of events, and a different chain of causality. When we recognize that works such as Thompson's *Early History of the Israelite People* and *The Mythic Past,* Lemche's *The Israelites in History and Tradition,* Davies's *In Search of "Ancient Israel,"* and Whitelam's *The Invention of Ancient Israel* are no less literary than the narratives of Breasted, Albright, or Yadin, we may be able to see what they are *really saying.*[18] In addition, we may finally be able to go beyond their critics' tiresomely empty polemics about "postmodernism" and "anti-Zionism," for the tales told by these scholars depict state structures—or, more precisely, the fabrication of a corpus of narratives about traditional state structures—obviously unreliable as history but effective as ideological tools of imperial control.

The stage setting of this alternative story is the vast Persian Empire and later Hellenistic kingdoms where willing local elites were everywhere anxious to please their imperial overlords and, at the same time, to control the peasantry. In locating the "intellectual matrix" of biblical tradition in the political maneuvering of the Judean exiles in Babylonia, Thompson, for one, identifies it as a distinctive imperial mentality. Analyzing the world of the late Iron Age as one in which most authentic peoples had been shattered by military campaigns and mass deportations, he sees biblical literary creativity as cynically functional: the invention of a Janus-like national ideology, with one face paying homage to the universalism of Babylonia and Persia and the other empowering a returned priesthood and aristocracy as the legitimate heirs of fictional Israelite patriarchs and

---

[18] Thomas L. Thompson, *Early History of the Israelite People: From Written and Archaeological Sources* (Leiden: Brill, 1992); idem, *The Mythic Past* (New York: Basic, 1999); Niels Peter Lemche, *The Israelites in History and Tradition* (Louisville: Westminster John Knox, 1998); Philip R. Davies, *In Search of "Ancient Israel"* (JSOT Sup 148; Sheffield: JSOT Press, 1992); Whitelam, *Invention of Ancient Israel.*

kings. In this version, there was never any inevitable movement toward unified statehood among the peoples of Palestine, just a network of autonomous regions and polities whose independence was suddenly destroyed by the rise of brutal foreign empires.

For all the talk of science versus faith and credulity, what are these alternative reconstructions based on? In its use of archaeological data for the purposes of deconstruction, it is based on an equally innocent reliance on what David Noble has termed the "Religion of Technology"[19] or more specifically the kind of archaeological reductionism that Thomas Patterson has described in his works on the social history of archaeology as a hand-maiden not of history but of transnational economic development.[20] It is, consciously or unwittingly, an archaeology that has become reticent toward all nonfunctionalist, noneconomic considerations and, at the same time, is naively accepting of modern concepts of territorial carrying capacity and economic advantage. That the calculations of ancient population in a given area in a given period may reflect modern preconceptions—and should not be uncritically used as the absolute precondition for a particular form of political or economic organization—is something that has been argued by Michael Fotiadis in his recent examination of the methodology of regional surveys in Greece.[21] It is at least worth consideration, for the twenty-first-century ideology of modernization, sweeping aggressively across the world and paving over ancient tribes, cultures, and traditions, is, I would argue, no less potent or insistent an ideology than nationalism or biblical fundamentalism.

Thus I return to the beginning. Where Yadin proudly trumpeted his modern political position about Israelite statehood from a thousand lecture podiums and Albright's biblical archaeology became a clarion call for American religious renewal, today's scholars are propounding similar visions of the past with enormous political and ideological implications— on every side of the current tenth-century debate. However, because few understand how thoroughly modern beliefs, logic, and perceptions are involved in the construction of all historical and archaeological theories, a certain intellectual blindness prevails. Only *opponents'* political agendas and ideological preconceptions are clearly seen. The wider nature of the

---

[19] David F. Noble, *The Religion of Technology: The Divinity of Man and the Spirit of Invention* (New York: Knopf, 1997).

[20] Thomas C. Patterson, "Some Postwar Trends in U.S. Archaeology," *Culture* 4 (1986): 43–54; idem, "Development, Ecology, and Marginal Utility in Anthropology," *Dialectical Anthropology* 15 (1987): 15–31.

[21] Michael Fotiadis, "Modernity and the Past-Still-Present: Politics of Time in the Birth of Regional Archaeological Projects in Greece," *AJA* 99 (1995): 59–78.

debate as one of interpretation and philosophical difference is often lost in the dispute over data. The denial of historicity to an ancient tradition of Israelite nationhood (justified or unjustified by the data) is a statement with far-reaching modern political and religious implications. Likewise, those who make angry, irresponsible accusations of anti-Semitism, post-Zionism, or "revisionism" (this, with its provocatively suggestive parallel to Holocaust revisionism) against those who might challenge the conventional archaeological wisdom—and do not reveal the political or ideological basis for their anger and do not admit their own religious or political agendas—are disingenuous.[22] If one makes a political assertion, one should be prepared to accept the consequences and debate. Likewise, no one should be allowed to fire inflammatory potshots at colleagues and then scurry back behind the cover of "scholarly objectivity."

There is a memorable line of dialogue from Fellini's *Satyricon* in which an educated Roman youth suddenly finds himself—as the result of his own thoughtless actions—standing in a public arena forced to fight for his life. Looking up toward the emperor in panic, he begs to be excused from the life-and-death combat, pleading through his tears, "But I'm a student, not a gladiator!"

So it is today when scholars enter the brutal arena of debate over issues of statehood, state building, biblical ideology, and national traditions at a time when the stakes in the modern Middle East—as we read almost every day in the newspaper—are dreadfully high. To the extent that an archaeological controversy like this one has implications for the present, those implications must be openly admitted and discussed. Yadin once wrote, "as an archaeologist I cannot imagine a greater thrill than working with the Bible in one hand and a spade in the other. That was the true secret of our discoveries of the Solomonic period."[23] *Every* archaeologist, I maintain, digs with a bible in one hand and a spade in the other. The only open question at the end of the day—and at the end of this phase of the scholarly debate about David and Solomon—is *which* modern bible will seem most persuasive in light of contemporary events. Whether the "realist," "liberal," or "critical" archaeological reading of the history of ancient Israel will prevail in the coming decades, only time will tell.

---

[22] For a summary and prime example of the mean-spirited public polemic that swirls around the tenth-century debate, see William G. Dever, *What Did the Biblical Writers Know and When Did They Know It? What Archaeology Can Tell Us about the Reality of Ancient Israel* (Grand Rapids: Eerdmans, 2001).

[23] Yadin, *Hazor,* 187.

Is Biblical Archaeology Theologically Useful Today? Yes, A Programmatic Proposal

Andrew G. Vaughn
Gustavus Adolphus College

The editors of this volume invited the contributors to present papers and later to write essays with the goal of finding a common ground that might facilitate a broader and more productive conversation between biblical scholars and archaeologists. The essays reveal that, while there is some common ground, there is no consensus. There is more agreement in the later periods than in the earlier periods, but there are differences of interpretation in each of the time periods. Moreover, the essay by Neil A. Silberman emphasizes that the lack of agreement by both archaeologists and biblical scholars is often motivated by political and philosophical presuppositions.

This lack of consensus and the presence of philosophical and political presuppositions force biblical scholars who have theological concerns to ask what they should do when the archaeologists cannot agree. Does one need to wait around until enough data are known to allow agreement? Does our postmodern setting prohibit consensus and the use of history and archaeology anyway? Will enough data ever be available to allow for firm theological conclusions?

These questions illustrate that one of the biggest challenges for Old Testament theology[1] is to articulate how the Bible can be "true" in a postmodern setting. In order to illustrate this challenge, I like to begin my

---

[1] This essay is written from the perspective of a Christian biblical theologian, but my conclusions (especially the definitions of "background" and "critical" history) will also be useful for Jewish interpretations of the Hebrew Bible. On the interaction of Old Testament theology with "Tanakh theology," see Werner E. Lemche, "Is Old Testament Theology an Essentially Christian Theological Discipline?" *HBT* 11/1 (1989): 59–71. This essay is in memory of Donald H. Juel, who passed away while this essay was in press. Don and I had numerous conversations on the relationship of history and theology during a consultation at the Wabash Center that met over three summers. I am indebeted to him and wish that we could continue our conversations.

introduction to the Bible[2] course by assigning an article by William Placher entitled, "Is the Bible True?"[3] I have several reasons for selecting this article. First, it is a well-written and persuasive articulation of what I label the mainstream argument by Protestants and Catholics for the truthfulness of the Bible. The second, more important reason for choosing this article is that it allows students to see how this popular argument leads us into a postmodern quandary from which the church has yet to emerge.

The example is helpful in the context of this volume of collected essays on the archaeology of Jerusalem because biblical theologians face a problem when they are confronted with data like those presented in this book: How can these data be theologically useful in the absence of consensus? If we are unable even to determine with some degree of probability what actually happened, or if scholars disagree on what happened, then interpreters will ask how these data can possibly be used to understand the Bible as "true." Placher's approach is popular. However, as I argue below, it is an approach that we must move beyond.

The present essay moves beyond Placher's approach with an illustration of how the concept that I have defined as "historical imagination" might be used in a programmatic way to allow archaeological data to be theologically useful even in the absence of consensus. Since I have just recently published a detailed description of what I am calling "historical imagination,"[4] the present essay only summarizes the earlier discussion. The focus of the present essay is to present a detailed explanation of how this proposal of historical imagination might be utilized with the archaeological data on Jerusalem. In the process, this review essay summarizes the papers presented in this volume, critiques their conclusions, and puts the different views presented in this volume in conversation with each other by using my programmatic proposal for historical imagination.

PLACHER'S APPROACH (= THE "MEANING" APPROACH)

Placher's argument that we must move beyond can be summarized succinctly. He begins with the acknowledgement that historical-critical research in the nineteenth and twentieth centuries has shown that many

---

[2] REL 110 "The Bible" is an introductory, undergraduate course that I teach at Gustavus Adolphus College. The goals and method are somewhat different from an introductory seminary course.

[3] William Placher, "Is the Bible True?" *ChrCent* 112 (11 October 1995): 924–28.

[4] See Andrew G. Vaughn, "How Can a History of Israel Be Theologically Relevant in a Post-Modern World?" in *The Future of Biblical Archaeology* (ed. J. K. Hoffmeier and A. Millard; Grand Rapids: Eerdmans, forthcoming).

parts of the Bible are not factual. We thus question how the Bible can be "true" if it is not factual. The reader of this volume will notice that many of the articles presented here also conclude that the Bible cannot be considered factual, at least in every detail. Placher responds to this situation by stating that the Bible is true because (1) what it means is true, and (2) his faith experience has shown him that the Bible can be trusted when it is read as a whole and with the guidance of the Holy Spirit.

Students in my classes like this proposal because it makes sense on the surface and is attractive from a faith perspective. Yet one probing question reveals a weakness. I like to ask students, "How could you disprove Placher's second reason, that his faith experience has shown him that the Bible can be trusted?" A few skeptical students inevitably try to argue that Placher has misunderstood his faith experience, but we all quickly realize that Placher has played what I like to call "the faith card." A person's faith experience is neither rational nor irrational. Thus, if the premise can neither be proved nor disproved, it hardly serves as a firm foundation upon which to build a larger argument.

Another problem with Placher's position is that he posits truth to lie in "meaning" and not factual accuracy. Again, on the face of things this is an attractive (and popular) alternative. Even if the Bible is not completely factual, surely the meaning found in the Bible is true. The problem with this position has been thoroughly explored by Hans Frei in *The Eclipse of Biblical Narrative*.[5]

Frei convincingly demonstrates that the historical question of the factualness of the text has become the primary question in our critical method of investigating the Bible. Modern interpreters, including Placher, first ask if the events described in the narrative actually happened. If the event happened, then the narrative is true because there is a factual continuity. If the events are found not to have occurred, interpreters such as Placher argue that the Bible is true for some other deeper reason apart from its factualness. Placher and others argue that the text is true because what it means is true. At this point Frei rightly points out that, by associating *truth* with *meaning,* one must necessarily presuppose the meaning of the text *before* the narrative can be read. The end result is that the narrative itself becomes static—it stops serving as a dynamic guide for and witness to contemporary Christian faith.

Returning to Placher's "meaning" method, we see that the meaning of the text must be determined before the narrative can be read and experienced as true. Yet how is this meaning determined? Placher's faith stance

---

[5] Hans Frei, *The Eclipse of the Biblical Narrative: A Study in Eighteenth and Nineteenth Century Hermeneutics* (New Haven: Yale University Press, 1974).

has determined ahead of time that the Bible makes sense of his life, and this understanding dictates how he will determine meaning. The problem here is that Placher runs the risk of superdogmatism. His preconceived ideas about how God acts in the world control how he finds meaning in the text. Thus, not only does this "meaning" method eclipse the narrative and leave it static, but Placher also runs the risk of creating his own idea of truth when he reads the Bible. Silberman's essay eloquently describes the danger that Placher's system confronts with such a hermeneutic move: Placher runs the risk of letting his philosophical and religious ideology control his interpretation. Whereas Silberman indicates that such a bias is inevitable, I argue that there are ways out of this trap. The present essay is thus a programmatic proposal to assist biblical theologians (and archaeologists) in finding a way out of this philosophical trap.

Background to the Problem[6]

At this point it is enlightening to go back to the end of the eighteenth century to see how the Enlightenment has contributed to the problem articulated above. The Enlightenment philosophers argued that humanity was trapped or bound by anything around us that could not be explained or understood. Thus, there was an intense scientific and philosophical effort to explain the world in which we live. In this middle of this situation, David Hume posed a real problem: he showed that it is impossible to prove a relationship between cause and effect. In a modernist sense Hume's work posed a true conundrum. If he were correct, nothing in the world could be understood, so humans were doomed to be trapped by their ignorance.

Immanuel Kant made a significant contribution by utilizing the idea of postulating instead of proving certain conclusions. Kant used the idea of imagination to show that humans must postulate the relationship between cause and effect, because the world would not make sense otherwise. In a similar manner, Kant postulated the existence of God because the world is not completely evil and there must be some force behind the good in the world that prevents evil from dominating. As we will see, Kant's way of understanding reality is common for many interpreters who use archaeological data to understand the Bible and runs the risk of essentialism: everything must be explained, or there must at least be some essential continuity between what is described in the Bible and what happened. The continuity might not be proved, but it can reasonably be postulated.

---

[6] The following section is a summary of my views published elsewhere. See Vaughn, "How Can a History of Israel Be Theologically Relevant."

The problem with Kant's proof of God is that not all ways of knowing and thinking can be separated into rational and irrational categories. Humans instinctively or intuitively make certain conclusions, and these ways of thinking are central for understanding the concept of God. In other words, it is difficult to classify faith or religious belief as either rational or irrational ways of thinking. Friedrich Scleiermacher raised these problems and presented an alternative solution. For Schleiermacher, an intuitive awareness or feeling is more important for faith and a comprehension of God than is rational thinking. Schleiermacher did not mean that God does not exist outside of our psychological minds; however, that is the only way we as humans can have access to God. Schleiermacher thus concluded that God must be taken to be the "whence" or the object of the feeling (or awareness) of absolute dependence. In this way, Schleiermacher was able to show how the existence of God can be assumed or postulated based on the feeling of absolute dependence.[7]

In summary, we see that by the middle of the nineteenth century, the responses to the Enlightenment presented humanity with a very hopeful situation. God could be understood either rationally or intuitively. As always seems to happen, the hopeful situation did not last long. The problem came to light with the skeptical humanism of Ludwig Feuerbach, who took arguments like those presented by Kant and Schleiermacher further and revealed that these philosophers had created a God who is a human construct. Kant (and, as we will see, archaeologists such as Dever and Cahill) ran the risk of essentialism and of creating a God who is a rational construct. On the other hand, Schleiermacher (and, as we will see, Placher) ran the risk of superdogmaticism. That is, Schleiermacher's concept of what God should be might be controlled by his intuition or his dogma. Feuerbach concluded that in either case God is a concept created by the collective mind of humanity.[8]

---

[7] Friedrich Schleiermacher, *The Christian Faith* (trans. and ed. H. R. Mackintosh and J. S. Stewart; Edinburgh: T&T Clark, 1963), §4.4, p. 16. He says, "As regards the identification of the absolute dependence with 'relation to God' in our proposition: this is to be understood in the sense that the *Whence* of our receptive and active existence, as implied in this self-consciousness, is to be designated by the word 'God,' and that this is for us the really original signification of that word." It is important to note here that for Schleiermacher the idea of "feeling" is not an emotion. It includes the idea of "awareness" or "self-consciousness" (ibid., §3.3, p. 6).

[8] It is interesting to note that the essay by Silberman in this volume draws a similar conclusion. Silberman finds that one's ideology will control any interpretation. The logical result is that, like Feuerbach, Silbermann concludes that all interpretations are human constructs and controlled either by one's dogma or one's concept of essentialism.

Returning to Placher's proposal, we see that this "meaning" solution leads us in Feuerbach's fiery brook. Not only is the narrative eclipsed, as Frei so aptly describes, but we run the risk of superdogmaticism and creating a God who is a human construct. Such a possibility is especially dangerous when we realize that church dogma is guarded and controlled by the dominant and colonizing groups in our society. Silberman reminds us that the same is true for archaeological theories. If the Bible (or a particular archaeological position) is true because its meaning is true, and this meaning is controlled by the dominant groups, then we run the risk of creating an interpretation of God that is dangerous for women, minorities, the poor, and other disenfranchised groups.

So, is there a way to move forward when the historical data cannot be pinned down? Can we move forward when archaeologists do not agree? Are we hopelessly stuck? Clearly, I find that we must and can move forward, or I would not have chosen this topic. Yet before I present my programmatic proposal (and I intentionally choose the term *proposal* rather than *solution*), it is helpful to outline two common yet faulty ways that scholars have attempted to move beyond this impasse. The attempts to move beyond the impasse are especially relevant for the endeavor of using archaeological and historical data such as those presented in the present volume on the archaeology of Jerusalem.

The Essential Continuity Approach

One way to find that the Bible is true is to argue that, even if some of the details in the Bible are found to be in error, there is an essential continuity between what is described in the Bible and the external facts. This approach characterizes the Biblical Theology movement that was promoted by William F. Albright and G. Ernest Wright. Today this approach is especially popular with conservative or fundamentalist Christian and Jewish faith communities. If one is able to find this type of essential continuity, then one is able to rely on an external, rational proof for understanding the concept of God that is described in the Bible. God is not a human construct because there is proof in the Bible that God really exists and acts in history in a particular manner. The problem here is that continued archaeological and historical research has shown that it is impossible to substantiate an essential continuity between the "facts" found in the Bible and external historical facts. Surely our investigation of Jerusalem emphasizes this "fact."

A more recent, albeit somewhat disguised, presentation of this method can be found in a book by archaeologist William Dever. His recent book *What Did the Biblical Writers Know and When Did They*

Know It? is a prime example of an attempt to integrate humanism with essential continuity.[9] Dever's book presents an excellent rebuttal of the simplistic views set forward by the minimalists, but in doing so he limits the parts of the Bible that are relevant for doing history to the books of the Deuteronomistic History.[10] Is one supposed to assume that history is not relevant for the rest of the Hebrew Bible, including all of the Prophets, Chronicles, and the Pentateuch? If one concludes that there must be an essential continuity present in the text for them to be valid, then this is the only logical conclusion that can be drawn.[11]

We therefore see that, even if one attempts to select parts of the Bible that are essentially factual, the results are not satisfactory for biblical theologians. Moreover, the way in which Dever has framed the question places him right back into Frei's eclipse. If one were to use Dever's method for doing Old Testament theology, the texts would either be valuable because there is some degree of historicity in them[12] or because they were true apart from the question of factuality. In either case, the historical question comes first and the meaning of the text second. The dynamic character of the narrative through contemporary interaction comes third, and so it is essentially lost.

RHETORICAL AND LITERARY APPROACHES

The problems with the essential-continuity approach and the presence of a lack of consensus such as exhibited in the archaeology of Jerusalem has led more and more biblical theologians to jettison history and archaeology and to turn to other approaches. Many of these scholars turn to rhetorical or literary readings as the primary means to uncover the theological meat of the Bible. Whereas the essential-continuity method went too far in an attempt to use history as a means to salvage the truth of the

---

[9] William G. Dever, *What Did the Biblical Writers Know and When Did They Know It? What Archaeology Can Tell Us about the Reality of Ancient Israel* (Grand Rapids: Eerdmans, 2001).

[10] Ibid., 97–101.

[11] Another way this problem surfaces is for some faith communities to conclude that some biblical "events" can be sacrificed (e.g., the conquest), while other biblical events must be retained (e.g., the resurrection).

[12] It is interesting that Dever argues for the importance and validity of some part of the historical books because he finds a certain degree of essential continuity between the historical narratives and the verifiable historical "facts." Yet one notes that this very approach of locating an essential continuity between the biblical narratives and the historical "facts" is one of Dever's chief criticisms of G. Ernest Wright (see among many studies William G. Dever, *Recent Archaeological Discoveries and Biblical Research* [Seattle: University of Washington Press, 1990], esp. 17–22, 50).

Bible, scholars who rely solely on literary or rhetorical approaches have gone too far in their rejection of history as an alternative. In the following, I use the example of Jerusalem to illustrate how history (and archaeology) is a necessary corrective of literary and rhetorical readings as the biblical scholar attempts to make theologically relevant conclusions.

The extreme importance placed on knowing God solely through the literary or rhetorical interaction of the text leads to another drawback. If God can be known only through a literary or rhetorical interaction of the text, then one must ask if God is a literary or rhetorical construct. If so, then who creates this construct? Proponents of these approaches typically claim that they assume that there is an external reality of God, but the only way that contemporary faith communities can know God is through rhetorical or literary interactions with the text.[13] In this sense, such approaches are very similar to Friedrich Schleiermacher's argument about how we can know God as the object of the feeling (or awareness) of absolute dependence. Schleiermacher assumes that there is an external reality of God, but this is the only way we can know God. The problem for both Schleiermacher and proponents of literary and rhetorical approaches is that such a philosophical move runs the risk of reducing God to a psychological or rhetorical concept.

HISTORICAL IMAGINATION AS A MEANS TO CORRECT THESE PROBLEMATIC ALTERNATIVES

In the essay cited above, I built upon the work of Leo Perdue and developed the philosophical concept of "imagination" as a helpful means to salvage the role of history in the theological enterprise.[14] The concept of imagination allows us to *take* fragmentary parts *as* representing the whole. The important words in the philosophy of imagination are *take* and *as*.[15] Various types of imagination come into play as we interact with a narrative: common imagination, creative imagination, religious imagination, and even

---

[13] This section is developed more completely in Vaughn, "How Can a History of Israel Be Theologically Relevant."

[14] Leo G. Perdue, *The Collapse of History: Reconstructing Old Testament Theology* (OBT; Minneapolis: Fortress, 1994), 264–65.

[15] It is important to emphasize that the fragmentary parts can be "known" and can be considered "facts." Again, imagination is not make-believe or necessarily hypothetical. Rather, imagination allows a person to consider all the pieces of information that are known and to look at them and evaluate them at the same time. Such a distinction will be important for us to keep in mind so that we realize that the different types of imagination described below presuppose an external reality that is already known. Therefore, in every instance the study of history and what is known is important even when using imagination to interpret texts.

ethical imagination. All of these allow us to *take* the narrative *as* representing reality.

Imagination allows us to organize varied perceptions, experiences, and even feelings into a coherent whole, but the danger is that limits or boundaries might disappear. We run the risk of entering into an "anything goes" type of mentality. If one does not recognize that all types of imagination are based upon a reality that is already established or events that are already known, one runs the risk of running into the problem of superdogmatism. If imagination is purely subjective, then one's theological and philosophical presuppositions will dictate what conclusions one may draw.

This is where the "history" part of what I am defining as "historical imagination" comes into play. The inclusion of history into the equation allows the interpreter to set necessary limits or boundaries around his or her possible interpretations. History defined in this way is what I define as negative or critical history. Critical (or negative) history asks "yes/no" questions and has a corrective function that helps us avoid misunderstandings in the text. As Perdue so aptly puts it, "the distance between text and reader, largely due to historical separation and culture shock, does and should continue.... Historical criticism makes readers in the contemporary world aware of the tremendous gulf that separates them from the narrative world constructed by biblical texts."[16]

This critical (or negative)[17] use of archaeology and history is consistent with what is probably a consensus view among scholars. Roland de Vaux presented a classic articulation of this negative or corrective use of archaeology about thirty years ago. In his essay, "On the Right and Wrong Uses of Archaeology," he rightly affirmed that archaeology cannot prove the Bible.[18] The Scriptures are *true* apart from historical data. Even if an account is found not to be factual, the account is still true in that it explains a religious truth. Thus, de Vaux (like Perdue) holds that the "right" way to use archaeology is to disprove or to support previously constructed interpretations of the biblical texts. I am pointing out that this corrective use of archaeology and history is what I am labeling "critical history" or "negative history." Archaeology can clarify our interpretations, but the actual narrative is true regardless of what archaeology might turn up.

---

[16] Perdue, *Collapse of History,* 259.

[17] Once again, it should be emphasized that critical history can produce positive results. The term *negative* or *critical* is used because the goal is to ask questions that can have a yes or no answer.

[18] Roland de Vaux, "On the Right and Wrong Uses of Archaeology," in *Near Eastern Archaeology in the Twentieth Century* (ed. J. A. Sanders; Garden City, N.Y.: Doubleday, 1970), 70–76.

We need to move beyond these proposals by Perdue and de Vaux, because history as they define it does not adequately allow for positive statements that do not seek to ask yes/no questions. Such positive statements that illuminate the background and setting of the narratives enlighten our interactions with the narratives that are "taken as" reality whether the narratives happened or not. Background history thus can make positive statements about the past without attempting to ask if an event happened or not, and these positive (background) statements serve to increase our imaginative capacity as we enter into these narrative worlds. For example, archaeology and history can help us understand the size of Jerusalem and how people lived in Jerusalem. These data play a role apart from asking critical (yes/no) questions; these data can enlighten and illuminate the narratives and the narrative world. This latter use of history that does not seek to ask yes/no questions is what I call "positive history" or "background history."

I am defining *historical imagination* in such a way as to include both critical history (negative history that asks yes/no questions) and background history (positive history that illuminates the setting of the period without asking yes/no questions). This concept of historical imagination allows a contemporary interpreter of the Bible to be in conversation with the Bible and to avoid the essentialist or superdogmatist pitfalls outlined above. This concept of historical imagination is also useful for the archaeologist. Silberman has shown that Ussishkin is naïve in his essay to think that he is able simply to report on the objective facts; his ideology and philosophical presuppositions influence his conclusions just as much as the biblical scholar. Both the biblical scholar and the archaeologist need to find the middle ground that avoids the traps of superdogmatism and essentialism.[19]

In what follows, I review the archaeological data on Jerusalem in order to increase our historical imagination. There is no consensus, but we will see that many conclusions can be made with some degree of certainty. These conclusions can be separated into positive history (background history) and negative history (critical history). Both background history and

---

[19] The proposal that I am presenting here is similar to the concept of post-positivist objectivity. The term *postpositivist* is used by literary critics to describe the concept that objective knowledge about the world exists even if all knowledge is theory mediated. In this way, postpositivists "refuse the definition of terms such as 'objectivity' and 'knowledge' as postmodernists have conceptualized them" (Paula M. L. Moya, "Introduction—Reclaiming Identity," in *Reclaiming Idenity: Realist Theory and the Predicament of Postmodernism* [ed. P. M. L. Moya and M. R. Hames-García; Berkeley and Los Angeles: University of California Press, 2000], 1–26, here p. 12).

critical history will be seen to have positive ramifications. From a critical-history standpoint, there is much background history that can influence how we read and become involved in the biblical narratives. From a critical-history standpoint, there are many yes/no questions that can be answered. These answers can limit the range of possible interpretations (both from an archaeological and a biblical standpoint). The limits may not be as precise as we might like, but at least they present us with some control and thus can serve as a starting point.

JERUSALEM DURING THE REIGNS OF DAVID AND SOLOMON

The four archaeological essays in this volume that discuss the tenth century B.C.E. (essays by Cahill, Finkelstein, Lehmann, and Ussishkin) present very different opinions about the nature of Jerusalem during the tenth century B.C.E. One the one hand, one might draw a reasonable conclusion that there is no consensus. Archaeologists cannot agree about the *facts* on the ground. Jane M. Cahill argues that the facts on the ground point to the existence of a city (not just a settlement) during the united monarchy. On the other hand, Israel Finkelstein and David Ussishkin use similar approaches to argue that Jerusalem during the tenth century was a small village and could not have been a major capital city. Gunnar Lehmann also concludes that Jerusalem during the tenth century was most likely a small village, and he relies on broader evidence from surveys that have been conducted throughout Judah.

Should the biblical scholar who wishes to speak about Jerusalem during David and Solomon's reign take this three-to-one majority to mean that Jerusalem was not an important city? Certainly not! Yet the same biblical scholar must be careful before speaking about a "united monarchy" in light of these archaeological studies. The one common denominator of all of the studies is that Jerusalem of David and Solomon was not the type of city that previous interpreters such as Yigael Yadin and William F. Albright envisioned. While there is no consensus, one can draw positive and negative conclusions from the data surrounding Jerusalem. The remainder of this section separates these conclusions into the areas of background (positive) history and critical history by using the definitions given above.

The archaeologists disagree on many details and theories, but they are unanimous in their assessment that Jerusalem existed during the reigns of David and Solomon. The archaeologists not only point to the existence of the Tel Dan Stela as evidence that the Davidic dynasty existed,[20] but they

---

[20] See Avraham Biran and Joseph Naveh, "An Aramaic Stele Fragment from Tel Dan," *IEJ* 43 (1993): 93.

also point to the continued settlement of Jerusalem from the Middle Bronze Age until the end of the Iron Age. It is thus reasonable to conclude that both David and Solomon occupied Jerusalem, and the question is about the nature of occupation during their reigns and not about the existence of occupation. This observation may seem trivial, but it is important nevertheless. Just like Merneptah's Stela, which mentions the existence of Israel at the end of the thirteenth century, the occupation of Jerusalem during the tenth century gives us a starting point to begin our investigation of the biblical narratives. Using the labels that I defined above, we can call this conclusion an example of background history or positive history.

The little piece of background history necessitates that we ask questions concerning the nature of Jerusalem during the tenth century. These questions can be labeled yes/no questions or questions involving critical history. These yes/no questions are quite helpful in assisting the historian to choose between previous theories about Jerusalem. During the early and middle decades of the twentieth century, scholars such as Albright and Yadin presented arguments for understanding Jerusalem as a major capital city during the reigns of David and Solomon.[21] On the other hand, Albrecht Alt and his followers understood Jerusalem as an administrative center for the kingdom of Israel. Whereas Albright and Yadin envisioned Jerusalem as a large city, Alt posited that the settlement of Jerusalem would have been limited to the king, the royal guard, and his administration, because the city was to be neutral. Alt read the biblical narratives to suggest that the general populous would have remained in the lands of their inheritance throughout the First Temple period. Therefore, Alt concluded that the size of Jerusalem was more modest in nature through the entire First Temple Period and definitely during the reigns of David and Solomon. Alt did not deny the existence of a palace or temple during Solomon's day, but he emphasized the need for Jerusalem to be neutral while at the same time not growing into a large city.[22]

As we attempt to ask a yes/no question that will clarify the possibilities presented by Yadin and Alt, we once again see that there is some consensus among the archaeologists even in the middle of disagreements. All of the archaeologists agree that the more significant periods of expansion in Jerusalem were during the Middle Bronze Age and the end of the

---

[21] See the essay by Silberman in this volume for a representative bibliography.

[22] Albrecht Alt, "Das Taltor von Jerusalem," *PJ* 24 (1928): 83–84; idem, "The Formation of the Israelite State in Palestine," in *Essays on Old Testament History and Religion* (trans. R. A. Wilson; New York: Doubleday, 1967), 285. See also the similar conclusion of one of Alt's students, Martin Noth, *The History of Israel* (New York: Harper & Row, 1958), 207.

Iron Age (the eighth and seventh centuries). Everyone agrees that during the tenth century the size of Jerusalem was more limited than in the eighth century. Whereas Ussishkin prefers the existence of a small temple and palace on the Temple Mount, Cahill prefers to posit the existence of a more grandiose palace and significant administrative center. Even though Cahill finds that Jerusalem was rather substantial because of extramural settlements outside the city wall, the fact remains that Jerusalem of the tenth century (no matter which chronology is used) was not a very large city. Even if Cahill is correct about the stepped stone structure and its mantle dating to the same time period, the data are more consistent with Lehmann's study that focuses on the population of Jerusalem but not its administrative significance. To be sure, if we were able to date the stepped stone structure and its mantle more convincingly, then we would be able to draw even more precise historical conclusions. At the same time, the little consensus that does emerge allows us to draw some important conclusions. Our yes/no questions reveal that, no, Jerusalem should not be understood as envisioned by Yadin and Albright. Rather, yes, it should be understood more in terms of what was envisioned by Alt. If it turns out that the City of David consisted of houses and not a citadel, then one will need to clarify Alt's administrative-center proposal even further.

In summary, we see that an important positive conclusion can be drawn from this critical (or negative investigation) that seeks to ask a yes/no question. A biblical scholar should prefer the interpretations of Alt concerning Jerusalem rather than the interpretations of Yadin and Albright. Of course, this analysis does not *prove* that Alt was correct, but it does lend credence to his theories. Again, as noted above, this is the very type of critical refinement that was previously advocated by de Vaux: archaeology can either support or disprove a theory about the Bible but not prove or disprove the Bible itself.

It must be emphasized that this critical investigation results in a positive conclusion: Jerusalem must be understood as a smaller town or city. This may or may not prove that Jerusalem functioned as Alt argued, but it does suggest that we should return to his theories once again.[23] It is at this point in our investigation that our conclusions allow us positive statements about the background of Jerusalem. Not only do we see that Jerusalem

---

[23] These historical arguments should been as consistent with the conclusions of Nadav Na'aman, "The Contribution of the Amarna Letters to the Debate on Jerusalem's Political Position in the Tenth Century B.C.E.," *BASOR* 304 (1996): 17–27. Na'aman draws upon the Amarna material from the Late Bronze Age to show that Jerusalem could function as an administrative center without extensive archaeological remains being discovered.

existed during the reigns of David and Solomon, but we have a better idea of what that city was like. Both these positive and negative conclusions are very helpful for modern interpreters of the biblical narratives as they seek to be involved with the text.

Turning now to the theological ramifications of the above analysis, we perceive that these data can be divided into positive and negative categories, as suggested in the definition of historical imagination given above. As our imagination is increased, certain *positive* statements can be made about the background of Jerusalem that illuminates these narratives:

1. David and Solomon existed, as evidenced by the biblical narratives, the occupation of Judah and Israel, and the Tel Dan inscription.
2. Jerusalem was occupied during the tenth century.
3. The archaeological evidence neither confirms nor denies the existence of a temple or palace, but the nature of the temple and palace described in the Bible (if it existed) must be taken to have been more modest than argued by scholars such as Albright and Yadin.

These positive statements are few but nevertheless significant, for they give us a better understanding of the biblical portrait of Jerusalem. As we interact with the biblical narratives concerning Jerusalem, these positive statements allow us to increase our imaginary worlds of what Jerusalem would have looked like. The positive statements facilitate our interaction with the text as narrative.

The hermeneutical shift that I am advocating is similar to and indebted to the method employed by theologian David Tracy when he talks about being "involved with" a classic text. Tracy points out that a classic text "resists definitive interpretation" but continues to help "found or form a particular culture" in a dynamic manner.[24] Tracy points out that the goal of the Christian theologian is to be in "conversation" with our classic text par excellence, the Bible. As one engages in this conversation, the process of imagination is employed, and the above positive historical conclusions serve to illuminate the narratives that the theologian can interact with as narrative.

It should be emphasized at this point in our discussion that this interaction made possible by the heuristic concept of imagination does not mean that we leave the realm of reality.[25] Even while living in an era of

---

[24] David Tracy, *Plurality and Ambiguity: Hermeneutics, Religion, Hope* (San Francisco: Harper & Row, 1987), 12.

[25] I am thankful to Neil A. Silberman for pointing out this truism, though Silberman does not necessarily concur with the way I use his observation.

so-called postmodernism, our ways of thinking and imagining reality are rooted in realistic assumptions and conclusions. This is where what I have defined as critical history (the asking of yes/no questions) comes into play as we undertake to be in conversation with our classic text, the Bible. These critical conclusions help keep us from going too close to the dangers of superdogmatism or essentialism.[26]

In a similar way that we were able to make positive statements about Jerusalem, we can draw certain negative conclusions (answers to yes/no questions) about Jerusalem. The answers may be the result of a negative investigation, but they too will have positive ramifications.

1. Jerusalem was not a large, capital city during the tenth century.
2. Jerusalem did not undergo extensive expansion under Judahite kings until the eighth century. As will be seen below, the expansion may have begun in the ninth century, but the expansion reached a fulcrum in the eighth century.
3. Jerusalem may have had a temple during Solomon's time, but the absence of tenth-century pottery surrounding the Temple Mount suggests that the temple was more modest in size; here I find that David Ussishkin's arguments in his essay in this volume are convincing, whether or not he is correct about the low chronology.
4. As Lehmann shows, Jerusalem did not play a dominant, exclusive role in the administration of Judah during the tenth century. As Alt suggested, it might have served as an administrative center, but it was not the most largest or most populous city in Judah or Israel.
5. The movement of the ark of the covenant to Jerusalem by David can neither be supported nor disproved from the current archaeological data.

These negative conclusions help keep our imaginations in a realm of modernity and away from the dangers of an "anything goes" mentality. The negative conclusions place boundaries around our interactions with the text that we interact with as a literary narrative. For example, historical imagination necessitates that we redefine what is meant by the term *united monarchy*. We also see that the description of the buildup of Jerusalem may very well be rooted in the eighth or seventh centuries. These conclusions do not mean that David and Solomon did not unite a confederation of tribal groups. Rather, these conclusions mean that we must reevaluate

---

[26] In this regard, the proposal I am presenting is similar to the "middle ground" of postpositivism advocated by some literary critics. See the article cited above by Moya, "Introduction—Reclaiming Identity," esp. 6–8.

the factuality of these biblical descriptions. These conclusions help us as modern readers see that the biblical writer(s) had an agenda other than simply reporting the "facts" of the past. From a theological standpoint, surely these conclusions help place some boundaries around our literary and rhetorical interactions with the narratives.

Finally, I should add that the proposal that I am advocating leaves room for future research and refinements of our knowledge. For example, if Cahill's assessment is found to be correct, then one would reasonably conclude that Jerusalem played a more significant role in David and Solomon's reigns than might be the case if Ussishkin and Finkelstein are found to be correct. This conclusion would impact the positive and nega-tive summaries presented above. The important thing is that we be able to begin the discussion without having to wait for all of the questions to be solved. The above example shows that some positive conclusions can be drawn even from the limited data that we have and that the limited data that we have available can also enable us to limit the possible range of interpretations.

Jerusalem during the reigns of Hezekiah and Josiah

Much more can be said about Jerusalem from a historical and an archaeological standpoint during the eighth and seventh centuries B.C.E. than during the tenth century B.C.E. There are several practical reasons for this situation. At some point during the late ninth or early eighth century, Jerusalem began to expand outside the confines of the City of David. Although there was subsequent development in the areas of expansion, the intensity of rebuilding and renovation was not nearly as great in these areas as was found in the City of David from the Middle Bronze Age through the Iron Age. This simple fact means that there is more evidence that can be investigated. Another important reason for the increase in data from the eighth and seventh centuries is the pres-ence of extrabiblical texts from Assyria and Egypt that mention affairs in Israel and Judah. The presence of these texts provide a vast improvement over the situation of the tenth century and the reigns of David and Solomon.

Background (Positive) History from the Eighth Century

The additional data from the eighth century allow us to make a num-ber of positive conclusions about the status of Jerusalem during Hezekiah's reign and beyond. As pointed out above, positive conclusions need not ask yes/no questions to be vital to the task of increasing our background history of the period. The fact that the data before us does not necessitate a response to such yes/no questions does not signify that this information is unimportant, for the background of an event provides valuable insight into the nature of the narrative.

The great expansion of Jerusalem during the eighth century is one of the first things that one notices from the essays included in this volume and a study of the archaeology of Jerusalem. In particular, Hillel Geva's essay on Avigad's excavations in the Jewish Quarter emphasizes that Jerusalem experienced growth in the area of the western hill from the late ninth or early eighth century throughout the eighth century. The presence of domestic architecture (Avigad's Stratum 9 in Area A) under the Broad Wall (Avigad's Stratum 8 in Area A) indicates that this expansion began earlier than the end of the eighth century with Hezekiah's preparations for Sennacherib's campaign. Avigad's Stratum 9 from Area A contains some pottery that is comparable with Lachish IV, but Geva finds that the vast majority of the pottery from Stratum 9 of Area A is very close to forms found at Lachish III.[27] Thus, it seems reasonable to conclude that the expansion on the western hill began toward the beginning of the eighth century or possibly as early as the latter part of the ninth century. In either case, the expansion began well in advance of Sennacherib's campaign at the end of the eighth century.

The conclusions from Avigad's excavations are supplemented by Gabriel Barkay's study of burial in the vicinity of Jerusalem. Barkay has shown that Iron II burial sites were found much farther to the north than the area of the western hill that was explored in Avigad's excavations. Since the custom was to situate burials just outside the city limits, Barkay draws the logical conclusion that Jerusalem would have expanded much farther past the confines of the western hill. The extent of this expansion also suggests that this phase began in either the late ninth century or early eighth century.[28]

Ronny Reich and Eli Shukron's essay in this volume demonstrates that the expansion of Jerusalem in the eighth century was not limited to the west and the north. Reich and Shukron provide evidence from their excavations to show that Jerusalem also expanded to the east of the City of David during the late eighth century. While I find their hypothesis about the precise time frame in the late eighth century difficult to prove, it is clear

---

[27] See the essay in this volume by Hillel Geva. See also the thorough excavation report by Nahman Avigad and Hillel Geva, "Iron Age II, Strata 9–7," in *Jewish Quarter Excavations in the Old City of Jerusalem Conducted by Nahman Avigad, 1969–1982, vol. I, Architecture and Stratigraphy: Areas A, W and X–2, Final Report* (ed. H. Geva; Jerusalem: Israel Exploration Society, 2000), 44–82, esp. 81–82.

[28] Gabriel Barkay, "Northern and Western Jerusalem in the End of the Iron Age" [Hebrew] (Ph.D. diss., Tel Aviv University, 1985), 451–58, fig. 167.

that the expansion toward the end of the eighth century (presumably during Hezekiah's reign) is consistent with the data summarized in the preceding paragraph. Therefore, Reich and Shukron's excavations provide further background history as the archeologists confirm that Jerusalem expanded into a significant city during the eighth century.

Whereas it is still debated whether David and Solomon really existed as anything other than legendary figures, the Assyrian and Egyptian texts from the late eighth century make it clear that Hezekiah and Jerusalem were important players in the world scene. The essays by Younger, Hoffmeier, and Roberts reveal that it is still difficult to interpret the significance of these extrabiblical texts precisely for the illumination of particular biblical narratives, but all of the essays reveal that Jerusalem and its kings played at least a relatively important role in world affairs. These extrabiblical texts thus validate the archaeological picture summarized above: Jerusalem was an important capital city by the end of the eighth century.

In addition to the general picture of Jerusalem at the end of the eighth century, one is able to draw some specific conclusions about the status of the city and its administrative importance during the reign of Hezekiah at the end of the eighth century. First, one cannot help but notice the massive Broad Wall and Israelite Tower found in Avigad's excavations of the Jewish Quarter. These features are associated with Avigad's Stratum 8 from Area A and Stratum 6 from Area W respectively. These strata from Areas A and W are contemporary and date to the late eighth century, or the period of Hezekiah. The Broad Wall and the Israelite Tower seem to have been constructed during the reign of this king in order to strengthen the city against an attack (presumably against the expected campaign of Sennacherib).[29]

To this general image of Jerusalem during Hezekiah's reign, one may add a picture of an extensive central administrative infrastructure. An examination of the *lmlk* jar phenomenon reveals that Hezekiah had a kingdom-wide infrastructure for the distribution of royal goods and that he had significant storage centers throughout the kingdom. The data from the royal jars indicate that the centralized government controlled the distribution of royal commodities. This conclusion is important for our study of Jerusalem because it reinforces Jerusalem as a significant capital city that was central in running the affairs of the Judahite kingdom. These data indicate that not only had the population of Jerusalem grown since the tenth century but that its significance had grown as well.

---

[29] Avigad and Geva, "Iron Age II, Strata 9–7," 45–61; plan 2.1; photos 2.6–2.37. For details on the Israelite Tower, see Hillel Geva and Nahman Avigad, "Area W—Stratigraphy and Architecture," in *Architecture and Stratigraphy,* 131–97, esp. 148–58; plan 3.1.

All of these data illuminate the setting in which Hezekiah, Jerusalem, and Sennacherib interacted at the end of the eighth century. Although Sennacherib referred to Hezekiah as a bird in a cage, one should question the depiction of Hezekiah being completely unsuccessful in his rebellion against Sennacherib. The massive fortifications alluded to in the preceding paragraph appear to have allowed Hezekiah to escape Sennacherib's campaign with his life. In this sense, Hezekiah is the only king that we know of who did not pay for his rebellion against the Assyrian Empire with his life. It may be that the life of the governor at Lachish was sacrificed in order to drain the Assyrian resources, thus enabling Jerusalem and Hezekiah to survive even if they no longer were prosperous.[30] To this picture we should add that there is no evidence of destruction of any cities or villages north of Jerusalem during the late eighth century.[31] Thus, from an examination of the background history leading up Sennacherib's siege of Jerusalem, one can ascertain many positive conclusions regarding the continued existence of Jerusalem during Hezekiah's reign at the end of the eighth century.

CRITICAL (NEGATIVE) HISTORY FROM THE EIGHTH CENTURY

Just as was the case for the study of tenth-century Jerusalem, these positive statements about Jerusalem during the end of the eighth century that were summarized in the preceding paragraphs allow the investigator to ask a number of yes/no questions with regard to previous interpretations of biblical Jerusalem. These yes/no questions (what I am defining as critical [negative] history) allow us to place parameters around the possible interpretations that might arise out of studying biblical texts that mention Jerusalem. Since there is much more data available from the late eighth century, I will only highlight one example of yes/no questions that bring clarity to our understanding of biblical Jerusalem. Other questions are certainly possible and viable, but the question explored in this essay is representative of how my programmatic proposal might be used with regard to the theological use of the archaeology of Jerusalem.

If one common denominator were available from the material of the late eighth century, that common denominator would be that Jerusalem grew into a significant capital city at least by the reign of Hezekiah. Given this conclusion, a question naturally follows: Did this expansion have its genesis during the reigns of David and Solomon or sometime later? In an

---

[30] I am grateful to Jeff Blakely for pointing this possibility out to me and for discussing the general picture of Judah at the end of the eighth century with me.

[31] Andrew G. Vaughn, *Theology, History, and Archaeology in the Chronicler's Account of Hezekiah* (SBLABS 4; Atlanta: Scholars Press, 1999), 44–45.

earlier study of this topic, I argued that the expansion must have logically extended back to the united monarchy. My logic was that the so-called minimalist position about the development of Jerusalem during the eighth century was based upon the biblical interpretation of Albrecht Alt and his student Martin Noth.[32] Alt and Noth argued that Jerusalem was only an administrative center during David and Solomon's reign, so they concluded that Jerusalem during Hezekiah's day would have been an administrative center as well. My earlier conclusion was based on the logic that if one were able to prove that Jerusalem during Hezekiah's reign was an important capital city, then Alt's earlier conclusion about David's Jerusalem could also be disproved.

Clearly, my logic was faulty. Archaeological studies that have been published in just the past five years make it clear that Jerusalem was not a large, thriving city during the tenth century. Jerusalem definitely existed, and there very well may have been a temple, but it does not seem to have been a very large city. Something happened between the end of the tenth century and the end of the eighth century for that situation to change, so there must have been a historical reason for this change.

In his essay in this volume, Israel Finkelstein suggests that the cause of the development of Jerusalem was the influence of the Omrides during the ninth century. He argues that Jerusalem was a small city before the ninth century that was unable to grow because the Judahite monarchy was not powerful enough. However, he posits that the Omrides could have helped Jerusalem grow several decades after the split between the northern and southern kingdoms. Finkelstein presents his theory as a new way of understanding the settlement and expansion of Jerusalem; in reality, his observations are not new at all—they are Alt.

Like Alt and Noth, Finkelstein highlights the limited size of Jerusalem, and he also concludes that there must have been some reason for Jerusalem to change. What Finkelstein fails to recognize is that a small Jerusalem is just what one would expect from the biblical material.

Much of Finkelstein's research that has developed (or evolved) from his important surveys of Judah and Israel builds on Alt and his theory of territorial divisions. In a very important article in *From Nomadism to Monarchy*,[33] Finkelstein updates the theories presented in his dissertation and shows how there is a cyclical pattern of development in the area

---

[32] Ibid., 70–71.

[33] Israel Finkelstein, "The Emergence of Israel: A Phase in the Cyclic History of Canaan in the Third and Second Millennia BCE," in *From Nomadism to Monarchy: Archaeological and Historical Aspects of Early Israel* (ed. I. Finkelstein and N. Na'aman; Jerusalem: Israel Exploration Society, 1994), 150–78.

later identified as Israel from the Early Bronze Age through the Iron Age I. Without going into the reasons for the changes, one sees that from the Early Bronze Age through the Iron Age I there was a pattern of increased settlement followed by decreased settlement. This pattern continued until the Iron Age II, when settlement continued to climb rather than go back down. Finkelstein rightly points out that, in light of this cyclical pattern, what is surprising is not the increased settlement during Iron Age I but the fact that settlement continued to increase during the Iron Age II. Finkelstein previously argued that the reason for this paradigm shift was the united monarchy. In other words, Finkelstein earlier concluded that the united monarchy provided the political reason for settlement to continue to expand instead of cycling downward. Because Finkelstein has redated the archaeological layers from his surveys to the ninth century, he now needs to find the political motivation for this paradigm shift in the ninth century. He may be successful in the north with the Omrides, but his arguments seem stretched when it pertains to the south and Judah.

First, much of the argument is based on evidence that is *not* found in Jerusalem. Even if Finkelstein is correct on his dating of the stepped stone structure in the City of David—and we must emphasize that his opinion is only as likely as other possibilities and not necessarily more probable— the silence of archaeological artifacts found to date does not mean that David and Solomon only ran a fiefdom. In fact, as is pointed out below, one should interpret these data as reflecting an administrative center that served to unite southern and northern groups. This is exactly what one would expect to find during David and Solomon's reigns. True, we may need to redefine what is meant by *united monarchy,* but Jerusalem could have served as a neutral city that was a part neither of the northern nor of the southern tribal allotments.

Second, Finkelstein uses biblical evidence selectively. Fortunately, we have moved away from an era in which biblical scholars scan archaeological finds in order to support a given biblical interpretation that they have already determined. However, one might argue that this is precisely what Finkelstein is doing, except that he is an archaeologist who scans the Bible for data that might support his interpretation without critically examining the biblical evidence. He assumes that the material concerning David's reign is no more reliable for reconstructing history than the material from Saul's reign. However, it is accepted that the character of the texts that describe the two monarchs is very different in form, content, and even number of chapters devoted to each king. Moreover, he assumes that, since the Deuteronomistic History underwent a major redaction during Josiah's reign, none of the material is historically reliable. This assumption does not demonstrate historical sensitivity to the variety of texts concerning both the premonarchical and the monarchical periods. In other words, not all of these stories can be explained as the theological invention of the seventh century and later.

My third type of objection is that if Finkelstein is correct, his solution raises as many problems as it solves. As noted above, it is important to return to Alt's theory that popularized the view that David's Jerusalem was limited and functioned only as an administrative center for the king and his royal troops. Alt reasoned that if Jerusalem functioned as a compromise capital that did not belong to the tribes of the north or to Judah, then Jerusalem must have remained a royal seat and not a city of Judah. Thus, Alt concluded that the City of David must have continued solely as an administrative center. If Finkelstein's interpretation is correct, one must ask why the northern nation of Israel helped support the Judahite buildup of the former capital city, which was supposed to be neutral. Indeed, the stated reason for the establishment of Yahwistic worship in Bethel and Dan was to avoid the very type of influence and interaction that Finkelstein suggests was initiated by the northern rulers.

In conclusion, I find Finkelstein's proposal that Jerusalem began to grow in the ninth century due to the influence of the northern kingdom of Israel a stretch. Again, a return to Alt can make sense of the limited archaeological finds from the Solomonic period in Jerusalem. Alt's arguments do provide the political motivation for breaking the territorial divisions of the north and the south and a change in the character of the monarchy in Israel with the reign of David. By establishing Jerusalem as a neutral capital, David would have had an incentive to settle the City of David only with his troops and to establish an administrative and citadel city.

As noted earlier, the problem with Alt and Noth's theory is that they were wrong about the nature of Jerusalem throughout the end of the Judahite monarchy. We see that just because Alt and Noth were wrong about the nature of eighth-century Jerusalem does not mean that they were wrong about tenth-century Jerusalem. The problem was that they did not explain how and why Jerusalem moved from a more limited administrative center in the tenth century into a thriving capital city in the eighth century. The archaeological data show us that such a development happened; our next step must be to ask why it happened.

With that question is mind, it seems that Alt and Noth were right about Jerusalem during the period of the united monarchy. There would have been a motivation to keep Jerusalem neutral as long as there was a united monarchy, so Jerusalem would likely not have experienced dramatic domestic expansion during Solomon's reign. However, once there was a split between Israel and Judah, the motivation for neutrality would have been lost. Thus, Finkelstein's proposal for an expansion of Jerusalem that began in the ninth century explains the biblical and archaeological data well. As Lehmann has shown in his essay, in the tenth century there was a developed infrastructure in Judah outside of Jerusalem. It seems likely that this infrastructure would have continued to function after the split between the north and the south but that the royal city of Jerusalem that served as a small administrative center also would have begun to grow shortly after this split.

The archaeological data illustrate that the development did not reach an apex until the end of the eighth century. This is also what one would expect. The earlier Judahite kings were not as strong as Hezekiah, so Jerusalem did not reach its zenith of power until the end of the eighth century. At the same time, it is unlikely that Hezekiah's Jerusalem grew out of a vacuum. It seems most likely that the processes for development and growth started shortly after the split between the north and the south and that the crisis of Sennacherib's invasion provided the catalyst for the culmination in the growth.[34]

In summary, all of these yes/no questions allow the modern interpreter to clarify a number of interpretations. We see that Hezekiah was one of the major builders (and probably the most important builder) of Jerusalem. Further, we see that the growth of Jerusalem did not happen overnight; the genesis went back at least a century and maybe even several decades after the split between the north and the south. In light of these observations, one can see just how important Hezekiah was in reforms of Judah and the writing of its history.

As one encounters the history of Judah in the Deuteronomistic History, one is constantly faced with the problem of whether a description is factual or not. As we discussed above with the biblical narratives on David and Solomon, the description of Jerusalem seems to be exaggerated in order to make an ideological point. Drawing upon the comments made by William Schniedewind in his essay, which attributed the genesis of the Deuteronomistic History to Hezekiah's reign, we are able to understand better why Hezekiah's ancestors (David and Solomon) were portrayed in such great terms. Hezekiah was a king who was portrayed as a second David, a king who had plans of expanding the kingdom and reuniting the northern areas with the kingdom of Judah.

Our study of Jerusalem reveals that, while there are factual kernels in these descriptions in the Deuteronomistic History, many of the descriptions are exaggerated. It seems that Jerusalem under David and Solomon was a

---

[34] In this regard, it is interesting to compare Jerusalem with Washington, D.C. The capital city of the United States did not begin to grow into a thriving city until after the Civil War. The parallel is definitely not exact, but the crisis of the Civil War, combined with an increased emphasis on the federal government after the war, certainly played a role in the city's expansion.

more limited administrative center, but this conclusion does not mean that David and Solomon did not succeed in uniting the north and south. Rather, it means that David and Solomon did not utilize Jerusalem in the same manner as Hezekiah would later use Jerusalem. This conclusion also places parameters around our interpretations of Hezekiah's reforms and his attribution as a second David. It seems that this attribution occurred during his reign and that Judahite history was rewritten or reinterpreted in order to emphasize the events of his day.

CONCLUSION

I began this essay by alluding to classes that I teach, and it is helpful to return to how this idea of historical imagination is instructive for my teaching. As students explore the wealth of narratives contained in the Bible, they discover that the biblical writers were constantly reinterpreting past promises in order to have the old promises make sense in a new day and in a new social location. In this way they learn how the biblical writers were doing the very thing that I advocate in this essay. Even when the biblical writers presented new interpretations that might have been considered radical, they were guided and informed by their past traditions and history. They took liberty to be in conversation with those traditions, just as Tracy suggests. In some cases, they even entered into arguments with those traditions.

While I am confident that there are still holes in my proposal and the analyses found in this essay, I humbly and yet passionately suggest that we as students of the Bible must see ourselves as continuing this conversation with our classic text par excellence, the Bible. I also suggest that the archaeologist should find the language to reach out to the biblical scholar who is primarily concerned with theological interpretation. If the archaeologist does not make the effort to reach out to biblical scholars and the larger public who are primarily concerned with understanding the Bible, then public support for the archaeology of the Levant will surely decrease. The proposal that I have presented encourages this conversation, and it is also attractive for our postmodern world, in which readers in different social locations will necessarily experience different texts in differing ways.

In the final analysis, I am confident that the reader will be able to locate my approach as either too essentialist or as falling into the trap of superdogmatism. In a sense, this may be the trap with which contemporary people of faith are doomed to wrestle—yet we must continue to wrestle. What I have presented in this essay is intended as the beginning of the conversation and not the conclusion. I look forward to continuing the conversation even if we can only achieve incomplete conclusions.

Bibliography

Abel, Felix M. *Géographie politique.* Vol. 2 of *Géographie de la Palestine.* Paris: Gabalda, 1938.

Ackroyd, Peter R. *Exile and Restoration.* OTL. Philadelphia: Westminster, 1968.

————. *Israel under Babylon and Persia.* New Clarendon Bible. Oxford: Oxford University Press, 1970.

Adams, John W., and Alice B. Kasakoff. "Factors Underlying Endogamous Group Size." Pages 149–73 in *Regional Analysis 2: Social Systems.* Edited by Carol A. Smith. New York: Academic Press, 1976.

Adler, Ron, et al., eds. *Atlas of Israel.* Jerusalem: Survey of Israel, 1970.

Aharoni, Miriam. "The Pottery of Strata 12–11 of the Iron Age Citadel at Arad" [Hebrew]. *ErIsr* 15 (1981): 181–204. (English summary, 82*)

Aharoni, Yohanan. "Excavations at Ramat Rahel 1954: Preliminary Report." *IEJ* 6 (1956): 137–57.

————. *Excavations at Ramat Rahel: Seasons 1959 and 1960.* Rome: Centro di studi semitia, 1962.

————. *Excavations at Ramat Rahel: Seasons 1961 and 1962.* Rome: Centro di studi semitia, 1964.

————. *Investigations at Lachish: The Sanctuary and the Residency (Lachish V).* Publications of the Institute of Archaeology. Tel Aviv: Gateway, 1975.

————. *The Land of the Bible: A Historical Geography.* 2d ed. Translated by A. F. Rainey. Philadelphia: Westminster, 1979.

————, ed. *Beer-sheba I: Excavations at Tel Beer-Sheba 1969–1971 Seasons.* Tel Aviv: Tel Aviv University Institute of Archaeology, 1973.

Ahituv, Shmuel. "Egypt That Isaiah Knew." Pages 3–7 in *Jerusalem Studies in Egyptology.* Edited by Irene Shirun-Grumach. ÄAT 40. Weisbaden: Harrassowitz, 1998.

Ahituv, Shmuel, and Amihai Mazar, eds. *The History of Jerusalem: The Biblical Period* [Hebrew]. Jerusalem: Yad Izhak Ben-Zvi, 2000.

Ahlström, Gosta W. *The History of Ancient Palestine from the Paleolithic Period to Alexander's Conquest.* Minneapolis: Fortress, 1993.

Albright, William F. "The Date of the Kapara Period at Gozan (Tell Halaf)." *AnSt* 6 (1956): 75–85.

———. *The Excavation of Tell Beit Mirsim, Vol. III, The Iron Age.* AASOR 21–22. New Haven, CT: ASOR, 1943.

———. *From the Stone Age to Christianity.* Baltimore: Johns Hopkins University Press, 1940.

———. *From the Stone Age to Christianity.* 2d ed. Garden City, N.Y.: Doubleday, 1957.

———. "Further Light on Synchronisms between Egypt and Asia in the Period 935–685 B.C." *BASOR* 141 (1956): 23–27.

———. *History, Archaeology, and Christian Humanism.* New York: McGraw-Hill, 1964.

Alt, Albrecht. "The Formation of the Israelite State in Palestine." Pages 223–309 in *Essays of Old Testament History and Religion.* Translated by Robert A. Wilson. New York: Doubleday, 1967.

———. "Das Taltor von Jerusalem." *PJ* 24 (1928): 74–98.

Amiran, Ruth. "The First and the Second Walls of Jerusalem Reconsidered in the Light of the New Wall." *IEJ* 21 (1971): 166–67.

———. "The Necropolis of Jerusalem in the Time of the Monarchy" [Hebrew]. Pages 65–72 in *Judah and Jerusalem: The Twelfth Archaeological Convention.* Jerusalem: Israel Exploration Society, 1957.

Amiran, Ruth, and Avraham Eitan. "Excavations in the Courtyard of the Citadel, Jerusalem, 1968-1969. Preliminary Report." *IEJ* 20 (1970): 9–17.

Amit, Yairah. *Hidden Polemics in Biblical Narrative.* Leiden: Brill, 2000.

———. *History and Ideology: Introduction to Historiography in the Hebrew Bible.* Sheffield: Sheffield Academic Press, 1999.

André-Salvini, Beatrice. "Remarques sur les inscriptions des reliefs du palais du Khorsabad." Pages 15–45 in *Khorsabad, le palais de Sargon II, roi d'Assyrie: Actes du colloque organisé au musée du Louvre par le Service culturel les 21 et 22 janvier 1994.* Edited by A. Caubet. Louvre conférences et colloques. Paris: La documentation Française, 1995.

Ariel, Donald T. *Excavations at the City of David 1978–1985 Directed by Yigal Shiloh, Vol. II, Imported Stamped Amphora Handles, Coins, Worked Bone and Ivory, and Glass.* Qedem 30. Jerusalem: Institute of Archaeology, Hebrew University of Jerusalem, 1990.

———. "Worked Bone and Ivory." Pages 119–48 in *Excavations at the City of David 1978–1985 Directed by Yigal Shiloh, Vol. II, Imported Stamped Amphora Handles, Coins, Worked Bone and Ivory, and Glass.* Qedem 30. Jerusalem: Institute of Archaeology, Hebrew University of Jerusalem, 1990.

———, ed. *Excavations at the City of David 1978–1985 Directed by Yigal Shiloh, Vol. V, Extramural Areas.* Qedem, 40. Jerusalem: Institute of Archaeology, Hebrew University of Jerusalem, 2000.

Ariel, Donald T., Baruch Brandl, Jane M. Cahill, Joseph Naveh, and Yair Shoham. *Excavations at the City of David 1978–1985 Directed by Yigal Shiloh, Vol. VI, Inscriptions.* Edited by Donald T. Ariel. Qedem 41. Jerusalem: Institute of Archaeology, Hebrew University of Jerusalem, 2000.

Ariel, Donald T., and Alon De Groot, "The Iron Age Extramural Occupation at the City of David and Additional Observations on the Siloam Tunnel." Pages 155–69 in *Excavations at the City of David 1978–1985 Directed by Yigal Shiloh, Vol. V, Extramural Areas.* Qedem 40. Edited by Donald T. Ariel. Jerusalem: Institute of Archaeology, Hebrew University of Jerusalem, 2000.

———. "The Israelite Settlement Outside the Walls of City of David." Pages 9–12 in *New Studies on Jerusalem: Proceedings of the Third Conference.* Edited by Araham Faust and Eyal Baruch. Ramat Gan: Bar-Ilan University, 1997.

———, eds. *Excavations at the City of David 1978–1985 Directed by Yigal Shiloh, Vol. IV, Various Reports.* Qedem 35. Jerusalem: Institute of Archaeology, Hebrew University of Jerusalem, 1994.

Ariel, Donald T., Hannah Hirschfeld, and Neta Savir. "Area D1: Stratigraphic Report." Pages 33–89 in *Excavations at the City of David 1978–1985 Directed by Yigal Shiloh, Vol V, Extramural Areas.* Qedem 40. Edited by Donald T. Ariel. Jerusalem: Institute of Archaeology, Hebrew University of Jerusalem, 2000.

Ariel, Donald T., and Yeshayahu Lender. "Area B Stratigraphic Report." Pages 1–32 in *Excavations at the City of David 1978–1985 Directed by Yigal Shiloh, Vol. V, Extramural Areas.* Edited by Donald T. Ariel. Qedem 40. Jerusalem: Institute of Archaeology, Hebrew University of Jerusalem, 2000.

Artzy, Michal. "Incense, Camels and Collard Rim Jars: Desert Trade Routes and Maritime Outlets in the Second Millennium." *OJA* 13/2 (1994): 121–47.

Ash, Paul. *David, Solomon and Egypt: A Reassessment.* JSOTSup 297. Sheffield: Sheffield Academic Press, 1999.

Auld, Graeme, and Margreet Steiner. *Jerusalem I: From the Bronze Age to the Maccabees.* Cities of the Biblical World. Cambridge: Lutterworth, 1996.

Avigad, Nahman. "Archaeology" [Hebrew]. Pages 145–55 in vol. 1 of *Sefer Yerushalayim (The Book of Jerusalem).* Edited by Michael Avi-Yonah. 2 vols. Jerusalem: Bialik Institute and Dvir, 1956–87.

———. *Discovering Jerusalem.* Nashville: Nelson, 1983.

———. "Excavations in the Jewish Quarter of the Old City of Jerusalem, 1970 (Second Preliminary Report)." *IEJ* 20 (1970): 129–40.

———. "Excavations in the Jewish Quarter of the Old City of Jerusalem, 1971 (Third Preliminary Report)." *IEJ* 22 (1972): 194–200.

Avigad, Nahman, and Hillel Geva, "Iron Age II, Strata 9–7." Pages 44–82 in *Jewish Quarter Excavations in the Old City of Jerusalem Conducted by Nahman Avigad, 1969–1982, Vol. I, Architecture and Stratigraphy: Areas A, W and X–2, Final Report.* Edited by Hillel Geva. Jerusalem: Israel Exploration Society, 2000.

Avi-Yonah, Michael. "Topography" [Hebrew]. Pages 156–58 in vol. 1 of *Sefer Yerushalayim (The Book of Jerusalem).* Edited by Michael Avi-Yonah. 2 vols. Jerusalem: Bialik Institute and Dvir, 1956–87.

———. "The Walls of Nehemiah—A Minimalist View." *IEJ* 4 (1954): 239–48.

Avnimelech, Moshe A. "Influence of the Geological Conditions on the Development of Jerusalem." *BASOR* 181 (1966): 24–31.

Ayalon, Eitan "The Iron Age II Pottery Assemblage from Horvat Teiman (Kuntillet 'Ajrud)." *TA* 22 (1995): 141–205.

Bahat, Dan. "City of David Excavations 1998" [Hebrew]. Pages 23–24 in *New Studies on Jerusalem: Proceedings of the Fourth Conference.* Edited by Avraham Faust and Eyal Baruch. Ramat Gan: Bar-Ilan University, 1998.

———. "The Wall of Manasseh in Jerusalem." *IEJ* 31 (1981): 235–36.

———. "Was Jerusalem Really That Large?" Pages 581–84 in *Biblical Archaeology Today, 1990: Proceedings of the Second International Congress on Biblical Archaeology.* Edited by Avraham Biran and Joseph Aviram. Jerusalem: Israel Exploration Society, 1993.

Bahat, Dan, and Magen Broshi. "Excavations in the Armenian Garden." Pages 55–56 in *Jerusalem Revealed: Archaeology in the Holy City 1968–1974.* Edited by Yigael Yadin. New Haven: Yale University Press, 1976.

Bahat, Dan, with Chaim T. Rubinstein. *The Illustrated Atlas of Jerusalem.* Translated by S. Ketko. New York: Simon & Schuster, 1990.

Bailey, Nicholas A. "Nehemiah 3:1–32: An Intersection of the Text and the Topography." *PEQ* 122 (1990): 34–40.

Baly, Denis. *The Geography of the Bible: A Study in Historical Geography.* 2d ed. New York: Harper & Row, 1974.

Barkay, Gabriel. "Excavations at Ketef Hinnom in Jerusalem." Pages 85–106 in *Ancient Jerusalem Revealed.* Edited by Hillel Geva. Jerusalem: Israel Exploration Society, 1994.

———. "The Iron Age II–III." Pages 302–73 in *The Archaeology of Ancient Israel.* Edited by Amnon Ben-Tor. Tel Aviv: Open University of Israel, 1992.

———. "Jerusalem of the Old Testament Times: New Discoveries and New Approaches." *BAIAS* (1985–86): 32–43.

———. "The Necropoli of Jerusalem in the First Temple Period" [Hebrew]. Pages 233–70 in *The History of Jerusalem: The Biblical Period.* Edited by Shmuel Ahituv and Amihai Mazar. Jerusalem: Yad Izhak Ben-Zvi, 2000.

———. "Northern and Western Jerusalem in the End of the Iron Age." Unpublished Ph.D. dissertation. Tel-Aviv University, 1985.

———. "Ramat Rahel." *NEAEHL* 4:1261–67.

Barnett, Richard D. "Layard's Nimrud Bronzes and their Inscriptions." *ErIsr* 8 (1967): 1*–7*.

Barnett, Richard D., Erika Bleibtreu, and G. Turner, *Sculptures from the Southwest Palace of Sennacherib at Nineveh.* 2 vols. London: British Museum Press, 1998.

Barr, James. *The Variable Spelling of the Hebrew Bible.* Oxford: Oxford University Press, 1989.

Barron, John Bernard, comp. *Report and General Abstracts of the Census of 1922 Taken on 23rd of October, 1922.* Britain: Government of Palestine, 1922.

Beck, Pirhiya. "The Cult-Stands from Taᶜanach: Aspects of the Iconographic Tradition of Early Iron Age Cult Objects in Palestine." Pages 352–81 in *From Nomadism to Monarchy: Archaeological and Historical Aspects of Early Israel.* Edited by Israel Finkelstein and Nadav Naᵓaman. Jerusalem: Israel Exploration Society, 1994.

———. "The Drawings from Horvat Teiman (Kuntillet 'Ajrud)." *TA* 9 (1982): 3–68.

———. "On the Identification of the Figure on the Cultic Stand from the City of David" [Hebrew]. *ErIsr* 20 (1989): 147–48.

Beck, Pirhiya, and Moshe Kochavi. "A Dated Assemblage of the Late 13th Century B.C.E. from the Egyptian Residency at Aphek." *TA* 12 (1985): 29–42.

Beckerath, Jurgen von. "Ägypten und der Felzug Sanheribs im Jahre 701 v. Chr." *UF* 24 (1992): 3–8.

———. "Über chronologische Berührungspunkte der altägyptischen und der israelitischen Geschichte." Pages 91–99 in *"Und Mose schrieb dieses Lied auf": Studien zum Alten Testament und zum Alten Orient. Festschrift für Oswald Loretz zur Vollendung seines 70. Lebensjahres mit Beiträgen von Freunden, Schülern und Kollegen.* AOAT 250. Edited by M. Dietrich and I. Kottsieper. Münster: Ugarit-Verlag, 1998.

Becking, Bob. "Assyrian Evidence for Iconic Polytheism in Ancient Israel?" Pages 157–71 in *The Image and the Book: Iconic Cults, Aniconism, and the Rise of Book Religion in Israel and the Ancient Near East.* Edited by Karel van der Toorn. Leuven: Peeters, 1997.

———. *The Fall of Samaria: An Historical and Archaeological Study.* SHANE 2. Leiden: Brill, 1992.

Bedford, Peter R. *Temple Restoration in Early Achaemenid Judah.* JSJSup 65. Leiden: Brill, 2000.

Beentjes, Pancratius C. "Jerusalem in the Book of Chronicles." Pages 15–28 in *The Centrality of Jerusalem.* Edited by Marcel Poorthuis and Chana Safrai. Kampen: Kok Pharos, 1996.

Ben-Dov, Meir. "Excavations and Architectural Survey of the Archaeological Remains Along the Southern Wall of Jerusalem." Pages 311–20 in *Ancient Jerusalem Revealed*. Edited by Hillel Geva. Jerusalem: Israel Exploration Society, 1994.

———. *In the Shadow of the Temple: The Discovery of Ancient Jerusalem*. San Francisco: Harper & Row, 1985.

Ben-Tor, Amnon, and Dror Ben-Ami. "Hazor and the Archaeology of the Tenth Century B.C.E." *IEJ* 48 (1998): 1–37.

Ben Zvi, Ehud. "When the Foreign Monarch Speaks." Pages 109–28 in *The Chronicler As Author: Studies in Text and Texture*. Edited by M. Patrick Graham and Steven L. McKenzie. JSOTSup 263. Sheffield: Sheffield Academic Press, 1999.

———. "Who Wrote the Speech of Rabshakeh and When?" *JBL* 109 (1990): 79–92.

Benoit, Pierre. "Recension de: Hᶜyr Hᶜlywnh šl Yrwšlym." *RB* 88 (1981): 250–56.

Benvenisti, Meron, and Shlomo Khayat. *The West Bank and Gaza Atlas*. Jerusalem: West Bank Data Base Project, 1988.

Bernbeck, Reinhard. *Die Auflösung der häuslichen Produktionsweise*. BBVO 14. Berlin: Reimer, 1994.

Betancourt, Phillip P. *The Aeolic Style in Architecture*. Princeton, N.J.: Princeton University Press, 1977.

Bieberstein, Klaus, and Hanswulf Bloedhorn. *Jerusalem: Grundzüge der Baugeschichte vom Chalkolithikum bis zur Früzeit der osmanischen Herrschaft I–III*. Wiesbaden: Reichert, 1994.

Bienkowski, Piotr. "The Beginning of the Iron Age in Edom." *Levant* 24 (1992): 167–69.

Biger, Gideon, and David Grossman. "Village and Town Population in Palestine during the 1930s–1940s and their Relevance to Ethnoarchaeology." Pages 19–30 in *Biblical Archaeology Today, 1990: The Second International Congress on Biblical Archaeology, Jerusalem, June–July 1990, Supplement*. Edited by Avraham Biran and Joseph Aviram. Jerusalem: Israel Exploration Society, 1993.

Bintliff, John, and Kostas Sbonias, eds. *Reconstructing Past Population Trends in Mediterranean Europe (3000 BC–AD 1800)*. Vol. 1 of *The Archaeology of Mediterranean Landscapes*. Oxford: Oxbow, 1999.

Biran, Avraham, and Joseph Naveh. "An Aramaic Stele Fragment from Tel Dan." *IEJ* 43 (1993): 81–98.

———. "The Tel Dan Inscription: A New Fragment." *IEJ* 45 (1995): 1–18.

Birch, Bruce C. *The Rise of the Israelite Monarchy: The Growth and Development of 1 Samuel 7–15*. SBLDS 27. Missoula, Mont.: Scholars Press, 1976.

Blackman, Aylward M. *Middle Egyptian Stories and the Shipwrecked Sailor*. Bibliotheca Aegyptiaca 2. Leiden: Brill, 1932.

Blakely, Jeff A., and Fred L. Horton. "On Site Identifications Old and New: The Example of Tell el-Hesi." *NEA* 64 (2001): 24–36.

Blenkinsopp, Joseph. "Bethel in the Neo-Babylonian Period." In *Judah and the Judeans in the Neo-Babylonian Period*. Edited by Oded Lipschits and Joseph Blenkinsopp. Winona Lake, Ind.: Eisenbrauns, forthcoming.

——. *Gibeon and Israel: The Role of Gibeon and the Gibeonites in the Political and Religious History of Early Israel*. SOTSMS 2. Cambridge: Cambridge University Press, 1972.

——. "The Judaean Priesthood during the Neo-Babylonian and Achaemenid Periods: A Hypothetical Reconstruction." *CBQ* 60 (1998): 25–43.

——. *The Pentateuch: An Introduction to the First Five Books of the Bible*. ABRL. Garden City, N.Y.: Doubleday, 1992.

——. "Theme and Motif in the Succession History (2 Sam xi 2ff.) and the Yahwist Corpus." Pages 44–57 in *Volume du Congrès: Genève 1965*. VTSup15. Leiden: Brill, 1966.

Bliss, Frederick J., and Archibald C. Dickie. *Excavations at Jerusalem 1894–1897*. London: Palestine Exploration Fund, 1898.

Blum, Erhard. *Die Komposition der Vatergeschichte*. WMANT 57. Neukirchen-Vluyn: Neukirchener Verglag, 1984.

——. *Studien zur Komposition des Pentateuch*. Berlin: de Gruyter, 1990.

Bohak, Gideon. *Joseph and Aseneth and the Jewish Temple in Heliopolis*. SBLEJL 10. Atlanta: Scholars Press, 1996.

Boardman, John. "The Olive in the Mediterranean: Its Culture and Use." Pages 187–96 in *The Early History of Agriculture: A Joint Symposium of the Royal Society and the British Academy*. Oxford: Oxford University Press, 1977.

Boissevain, Jeremy. *Hal-Farrug: A Village in Malta*. New York: Holt, Rinehart, & Winston, 1969.

Bolin, Thomas M. "The Temple of יהו at Elephantine and Persian Religious Policy." Pages 127–42 in *The Triumph of Elohim: From Yahwisms to Judaisms*. Edited by Diana V. Edelman. CBET 13. Kampen: Kok Pharos, 1995.

Borger, Riekele. *Die Inschriften Asarhaddons Königs von Assyrien*. AfO 9. Graz: self-published, 1956.

Borowski, Oded. *Agriculture in Iron Age Israel*. Winona Lake, Ind.: Eisenbrauns, 1987.

Braudel, Fernand. *The Mediterranean and the Mediterranean World in the Age of Philip II*. London: Fontana, 1972.

Braun, Roddy L. "A Reconsideration of the Chronicler's Attitude toward the North." *JBL* 96 (1977) 59–62.

——. *1 Chronicles*. WBC 14. Waco, Tex.: Word, 1986.

Brawer, Moshe. "Frontier Villages in Western Samaria" [Hebrew]. Pages 411–12 in *Judaea and Samaria*. Edited by Avshalom Shmueli, David Grossman, and Rehaveam Zeevy. Jerusalem: Bet hotsaah Kenaan, ha-hafatsah ha-Hotsaah le-or Misrad ha-bitahon, 737/1977.

———. "Transformation in Pattern, Dispersion, and Population Density in Israel's Arab Villages" [Hebrew]. *ErIsr* 17 (1984): 8–15.

Brettler, Marc Z. "Ideology, History and Theology in 2 Kings XVII 7–23." *VT* 39 (1989): 268–82.

Breuer, Stefan. *Der Staat: Entstehung, Typen, Organisationsstadien.* Hamburg: Rowohlt, 1998.

Bright, John. *A History of Israel.* 2d. ed. Philadelphia: Westminster, 1972.

Broshi, Magen. "Excavations on Mount Zion, 1971–1972." *IEJ* 26 (1976): 81–88.

———. "The Expansion of Jerusalem in the Reigns of Hezekiah and Manasseh." *IEJ* 24 (1974): 21–26.

———. "Iron Age Remains in the Chapel of St. Vartan in the Church of the Holy Sepulcher." Pages 82–84 in *Ancient Jerusalem Revealed.* Edited by Hillel Geva. Jerusalem: Israel Exploration Society, 1994.

———. "Judeideh, Tell." *NEAEHL* 3:837–38.

———. "Methodology of Population Estimates: The Roman-Byzantine Period as a Case Study." Pages 420–25 in *Biblical Archaeology Today, 1990: Proceedings of the Second International Congress on Biblical Archaeology.* Edited by Avraham Biran and Joseph Aviram. Jerusalem: Israel Exploration Society, 1993.

———. "La population de l'ancienne Jérusalem." *RB* 82 (1975): 5–14. English translation: "Estimating the Population of Ancient Jerusalem." Pages 110–20 in *Bread, Wine, and Scrolls.* By Magen Broshi. JSPSup 36. London: Sheffield Academic Press, 2001.

Broshi, Magen, and Gabriel Barkay. "Excavations in the Chapel of St. Varten in the Holy Sepulchre," *IEJ* 35 (1985): 108-19.

Broshi, Magen, Gabriel Barkay, and Shimon Gibson. "Two Iron Age Tombs Below the Western City Wall" [Hebrew]. *Cathedra* 28 (1983): 17–32.

Broshi, Magen, and Israel Finkelstein. "The Population of Palestine in 734 BCE" [Hebrew]. *Cathedra* 58 (1990): 3–24.

Broshi, Magen, and Shimon Gibson. "Excavations along the Western and Southern Walls of the Old City of Jerusalem." Pages 147–55 in *Ancient Jerusalem Revealed.* Edited by Hillel Geva. Jerusalem: Israel Exploration Society, 1994.

Broshi, Magen, and Ram Gophna. "The Settlements and Population of Palestine during the Early Bronze Age." *BASOR* 253 (1984): 41–53.

Browne, Laurence E. "A Jewish Sanctuary in Babylonia." *JTS* 17 (1916): 400–401.

Bunimovitz, Shlomo. "The Land of Israel in the Late Bronze Age: A Case Study of Socio Cultural Change in a Complex Society" [Hebrew]. Unpublished Ph.D. dissertation. Tel Aviv University. 1989.

———. "Problems in the 'Ethnic' Identification of the Philistine Material Culture." *TA* 17 (1990): 210–22.

———. "The Study of Complex Societies: The Material Culture of Late Bronze Age Canaan As a Case Study." Pages 443–51 in *Biblical Archaeology Today, 1990: Proceedings of the Second International Congress on Biblical Archaeology.* Edited by Avraham Biran and Joseph Aviram. Jerusalem: Israel Exploration Society, 1993.

Bunimovitz, Shlomo, and Zvi Lederman. "Beth-shemesh: Culture Conflict on Judah's Frontier." *BAR* 23/1 (1997): 42–49, 75–77.

———. "The Iron Age Fortifications of Tel Beth Shemesh: A 1990–2000 Perspective." *IEJ* 51 (2001): 121–47.

Cahill, Jane M. "David's Jerusalem: Fiction or Reality? It is There: The Archaeological Evidence Proves It." *BAR* 24/4 (1998): 34–41, 63.

———. *Excavations at the City of David 1978–1985 Directed by Yigal Shiloh, Vol. VII, Area G.* Forthcoming.

———. "Jerusalem at the Time of the United Monarchy: The Archaeological Evidence" [Hebrew]. Pages 21–28 in *New Studies on Jerusalem: Proceedings of the Seventh Conference, December 2001.* Edited by Avraham Faust and Eyal Baruch. Ramat Gan: Bar-Ilan University, 2001.

———. "Rosette Stamp Seal Impression." In *Jewish Quarter Excavations in the Old City of Jerusalem Conducted by Nahman Avigad, 1969–1982, Vol. II, The Finds from Areas A, W and X-2, Final Report.* Edited by Hillel Geva. Jerusalem: Israel Exploration Society and Institute of Archaeology, 2003.

———. "Who Is Responsible for Publishing the Work of Deceased Archaeologists?" Pages 47–57 in vol. 2 of *Archaeology's Publication Problem.* Edited by Hershel Shanks. Washington, D.C.: Biblical Archaeology Society, 1999.

Cahill, Jane, Karl Reinhard, David Tarler, and Peter Warnock. "It Had to Happen: Scientists Examine Remains of Ancient Bathroom." *BAR* 17/3 (1991): 64–69.

Cahill, Jane M., and David Tarler. "Response to Margreet Steiner—The Jebusite Ramp of Jerusalem: The Evidence from the Macalister, Kenyon and Shiloh Excavations." Pages 625–26 in *Biblical Archaeology Today, 1990: Proceedings of the Second International Congress on Biblical Archaeology.* Edited by Avraham Biran and Joseph Aviram. Jerusalem: Israel Exploration Society, 1993.

Campbell, Antony F. *Of Prophets and Kings: A Ninth Century Document (1 Samuel 1–2 Kings 10).* CBQMS 17. Washington, D.C.: Catholic Biblical Association of America, 1986.

Carmi, Irina, and Dror Segal, "14C Dating of an Israelite Biblical Site at Kuntillet 'Ajrud (Horvat Teiman): Correction, Extension, and Improved Age Estimate." *Radiocarbon* 38 (1996): 385–86.

Carr, David M. "Controversy and Convergence in Recent Studies of the Formation of the Pentateuch." *RelSRev* 23 (1997): 22–31.

Carroll, Robert P. *Jeremiah: A Commentary.* OTL. Philadelphia: Westminster: 1986.

Carter, Charles. *The Emergence of Yehud in the Persian Period: A Social and Demographic Study.* JSOTSup 294. Sheffield: Sheffield Academic Press, 1999.

Cazelles, H. "Bethlehem." *ABD* 1:712–15.

Chen, Doron, Shlomo Margalit, and Bargil Pixner. "Mount Zion: Discovery of the Iron Age Fortifications below the Gate of the Essenes." Pages 76–81 in *Ancient Jerusalem Revealed.* Edited by Hillel Geva. Jerusalem: Israel Exploration Society, 1994.

Childs, Brevard S. *Isaiah.* OTL. Louisville: Westminster John Knox, 2001.

———. *Isaiah and the Assyrian Crisis.* London: SCM, 1967.

Chong, Julia H. "Were There Yahwistic Sanctuaries in Babylon?" *AJT* 10 (1996): 198–217.

Claessen, Henri J. M., and Peter Skalnik, eds. *The Early State.* The Hague: Mouton, 1978.

———. *The Study of the State.* The Hague: Mouton, 1981

Clements, Ronald Ernest. *Isaiah and the Deliverance of Jerusalem: A Study of the Interpretation of Prophecy in the Old Testament.* JSOTSup 13. Sheffield: Sheffield Academic Press, 1980.

Cogan, Mordechai. *Imperialism and Religion: Assyria, Judah and Israel in the Eighth and Seventh Centuries B.C.E.* SBLMS 19. Missoula, Mont.: Scholars Press, 1974.

Cogan, Mordechai, and Hayim Tadmor. *II Kings: A New Translation with Introduction and Commentary.* AB 11. Garden City, N.Y.: Doubleday, 1988.

Cohen, Chaim "Neo-Assyrian Elements in the First Speech of the Biblical Rab-Shaqeh." *IOS* 9 (1979): 32–48.

Cross, Frank Moore. *Canaanite Myth and Hebrew Epic: Essays in the History of the Religion of Israel.* Cambridge: Harvard University Press, 1973.

———. "The Cave Inscriptions from Khirbet Beit Lei." Pages 299–306 in *Near Eastern Archaeology in the Twentieth Century.* Edited by James A. Sanders. Garden City, N.Y.: Doubleday, 1970.

———. "A Reconstruction of the Judean Restoration." *JBL* 94 (1975): 4–18. Rev. in *From Epic to Canon: History and Literature in Ancient Israel.* Baltimore: Johns Hopkins University Press, 1998.

Crowfoot, John W., and Gerald M. Fitzgerald. *Excavations in the Tyropoeon Valley, Jerusalem, 1927.* Palestine Exploration Fund Annual 5. London: Palestine Exploration Fund, 1929.

Crowfoot, John W., Kathleen M. Kenyon, and Eleazar L. Sukenik. *The Buildings at Samaria (Samaria Sebaste I)*. London: Palestine Exploration Fund, 1942.

Dagan, Yehudah. "Cities of the Judean Shephelah and their Divison into Districts Based on Joshua 16" [Hebrew]. *ErIsr* 25 (1996): 136–46.

———. *Map of Lakhish (98)*. Archaeological Survey of Israel. Jerusalem: Israel Antiquities Authority, 1992.

———. "The Shephela during the Period of the Monarchy in Light of Archaeological Excavations and Survey" [Hebrew]. M.A. thesis. Tel Aviv University, 1992.

———. *The Shephelah of Judah: A Collection of Articles* [Hebrew]. Tel Aviv: Tel Aviv University, 1982.

Dalley, Stephanie, and John Nicholas Postgate. *The Tablets from Fort Shalmaneser*. Cuneiform Texts from Nimrud 3. Oxford: Oxford University Press, 1984.

Dalman, Gustaf. *Jerusalem und sein Gelände*. Gutersloh: Bertelsmann, 1930.

Dandamaev, Muhammad A., and Vladimir Lukonin. *The Culture and Social Institutions of Ancient Iran*. Cambridge: Cambridge University Press, 1989.

Dar, Shimon. "Samaria (Archaeology of the Region)." *ABD* 5:926–31.

———. "The Survey of Western Samaria." *NEAEHL* 4:1314–16.

Davies, Philip R. *In Search of "Ancient Israel."* JSOTSup 148. Sheffield: Sheffield Academic Press, 1992.

———. *Scribes and Schools: The Canonization of the Hebrew Scriptures*. Louisville: Westminister John Knox, 1998.

———. "What Separates a Minimalist from a Maximalist? Not Much." *BAR* 26/2 (2000): 24–27, 72.

De Groot, Alon. "City of David Excavations" [Hebrew]. Pages 40–50 in *Jerusalem during the First Temple Period*. Edited by David Amit and Rivka Gonen. Jerusalem: Yad Izhak Ben-Zvi, 1990.

———. "The 'Invisible City' of the Tenth Century B.C.E." [Hebrew]. Pages 29–34 in *New Studies on Jerusalem: Proceedings of the Seventh Conference, December 2001*. Edited by Avraham Faust and Eyal Baruch. Ramat Gan: Bar-Ilan University, 2001.

———. "Jerusalem's First Temple Period Water Systems" [Hebrew]. Pages 124–34 in *Jerusalem during the First Temple Period*. Edited by David Amit and Rivka Gonen. Jerusalem: Yad Itzhak Ben Zvi, 1990.

De Groot, Alon, and Donald T. Ariel. "Ceramic Report." Pages 91–154 in *Excavations at the City of David 1978–1985 Directed by Yigal Shiloh, Vol V, Extramural Areas*. Qedem 40. Edited by Donald T. Ariel. Jerusalem: Institute of Archaeology, Hebrew University of Jerusalem, 2000.

————, eds. *Excavations at the City of David 1978–1985 Directed by Yigal Shiloh, Vol. III, Stratigraphical, Environmental, and Other Reports.* Qedem 33. Jerusalem: Institute of Archaeology, Hebrew University of Jerusalem, 1992.

De Groot, Alon, David Cohen, and Arza Caspi. "Area A1." Pages 1–29 in *Excavations at the City of David 1978–1985 Directed by Yigal Shiloh, Vol. III, Stratigraphical, Environmental, and Other Reports.* Edited by Alon De Groot and Donald T. Ariel. Qedem 33. Jerusalem: Institute of Archaeology, Hebrew University of Jerusalem, 1992.

De Groot, Alon, Hillel Geva, and I. Yezerski. "Iron Age II Pottery." Pages 1–49 in *Jewish Quarter Excavations in the Old City of Jerusalem Conducted by Nahman Avigad, 1969–1982, Vol. II.* Edited by Hillel Geva. Jerusalem: Israel Exploration Society, 2003.

De Groot, Alon, and Dan Michaeli. "Area H: Stratigraphic Report." Pages 35–53 in *Excavations at the City of David 1978–1985 Directed by Yigal Shiloh, Vol. III, Stratigraphcal, Environmental and Other Reports.* Edited by Alon De Groot and Donald T. Ariel. Jerusalem: Institute of Archaeology, Hebrew University of Jerusalem, 1992.

De Roche, C. D. "Population Estimates from Settlement Area and Number of Residences." *Journal of Field Archaeology* 10 (1983): 187–92.

Delcor, Mathias. "Le Temple d'Onias en Égypte." *RB* 75 (1968): 189–203.

Demsky, Aaron "The Clans of Ephrath: Their Territory and History." *TA* 13–14 (1986–87): 46–59.

Dennerlein, Norbert. *Die Bedeutung Jerusalems in den Chronikbüchern.* BEATAJ 46. New York: Lang, 1999.

Depuydt, Leo. "The Date of Piye's Egyptian Campaign and the Chronology of the Twenty-fifth Dynasty." *JEA* 79 (1993): 269–74.

Dever, William G. "Archaeology and the 'Age of Solomon': A Case Study in Archaeology and Historiography." Pages 217–51 in *The Age of Solomon.* Edited by Lowell K. Handy. Leiden: Brill, 1997.

————. "Bethel." *OEANE* 1:300–301.

————. "Book Review—Tushingham, 1985." *AJA* 93 (1989): 610–12.

————. "Ceramics, Ethnicity, and the Questions of Israel's Origins." *BA* 58 (1995): 200–13.

————. "Hyksos, Egyptian Destructions, and the End of the Palestinian Middle Bronze Age." *Levant* 22 (1990): 75–81.

————. "Israelite Origins and the 'Nomadic Ideal:' Can Archaeology Separate Fact from Fiction?" Pages 220–37 in *Mediterranean Peoples in Transition: Thirteenth to Early Tenth Centuries BCE.* Edited by Seymour Gitin, Amihai Mazar, and Ephraim Stern. Jerusalem: Israel Exploration Society, 1998.

————. "Late Bronze Age and Solomonic Defenses at Gezer: New Evidence." *BASOR* 262 (1986): 9–34.

————. *Recent Archaeological Discoveries and Biblical Research*. Seattle: University of Washington Press, 1990.

————. "Save Us from Postmodern Malarkey." *BAR* 26/2 (2000): 28–35, 68.

————. "Taking the Measure of Yigael Yadin." *Archaeology* 47/2 (1994): 59–61.

————. *What Did the Biblical Writers Know and When Did They Know It? What Archaeology Can Tell Us about the Reality of Ancient Israel*. Grand Rapids: Eerdmans, 2001.

Dewar, Robert. "Incorporating Variation in Occupation Span into Settlement-Pattern." *American Antiquity* 56 (1991): 604–20.

Díez, Florentino. "Jerusalem, Church of St. Peter in Gallicantu— 1998–1999." *Hadashot Arkheologiyot* 112 (2000): 84*–85*.

Dillard, Raymond B. "The Chronicler's Solomon." *WTJ* 43 (1980): 289–300.

————. "The Literary Structure of the Chronicler's Solomon Narrative." *JSOT* 30 (1984): 85–93.

————. *2 Chronicles*. WBC 15. Waco, Tex.: Word, 1987.

Dinur, Uri, and Nurit Feig. "Eastern Part of the Map of Jerusalem (Sheet 17–13: Sites 429–544)" [Hebrew]. Pages 414–15 in *Archaeological Survey of the Hill Country of Benjamin*. Edited by Israel Finkelstein and Yizhak Magen. Jerusalem: Israel Antiquities Authority, 1993. (English summary, 70*)

Dion, Paul-Eugène "Sennacherib's Expedition to Palestine." *EgT* 20 (1989): 12–18.

Donner, Herbert. "The Interdependence of Internal Affairs and Foreign Policy during the Davidic-Solomonic Period (with Special Regard to the Phoenician Coast)." Pages 205–14 in *Studies in the Period of David and Solomon and Other Essays*. Edited by Tomoo Ishida. Winona Lake, Ind.: Eisenbrauns, 1982.

————. *Israel unter den Volkern: Die Stellung der klassischen Propheten des 8. Jahrhunderts v. Chr. zur Aussenpolitik der Konige von Israel und Juda*. VTSup 11. Leiden: Brill, 1964.

————. "The Separate States of Israel and Judah." Pages 381–434 in *Israelite and Judaean History*. Edited by John H. Hayes and J. Maxwell Miller. Philadelphia: Westminster, 1977.

Dorsey, David Alden. *The Roads and Highways of Ancient Israel*. Baltimore: Johns Hopkins University Press, 1991.

Dothan, Moshe. "Ashdod." *NEAEHL* 1:93–102.

————. *Ashdod II–III: The Second and Third Seasons of Excavations 1963, 1965, Soundings in 1967*. ʿAtiqot English Series 9–10. Jerusalem: Department of Antiquities and Musuems in the Ministry of Education and Culture; Department of Archaeology, Hebrew University; Israel Exploration Society, 1971.

Dothan, Trude. "The Arrival of the Sea Peoples: Cultural Diversity in Early Iron Age Canaan." Pages 1–22 in *Recent Excavations in Israel: Studies in Iron Age Archaeology*. Edited by Seymour Gitin and William G. Dever. AASOR 49. Winona Lake, Ind.: Eisenbrauns, 1989.

———. "Tel Miqne-Ekron: An Iron Age I Philistine Settlement in Canaan." Pages 96–106 in *The Archaeology of Israel: Constructing the Past, Interpreting the Present*. Edited by Neil Asher Silberman and David Small. JSOTSup 237. Sheffield: Sheffield Academic Press, 1997.

Dothan, Trude, and Moshe Dothan. *People of the Sea: The Search for the Philistines*. New York: Macmillan, 1992.

Dothan, Trude, and Seymour Gitin. "Miqne, Tel (Ekron)." *NEAEHL* 3:1051–59.

Dozeman, Thomas B. "The Institutional Setting of the Late Formation of the Pentateuch in the Work of John Van Seters." Pages 253–64 in *Society of Biblical Literature: 1991 Seminar Papers*. Edited by E. H. Lovering. SBLSP 1991. Missoula, Mont.: Society of Biblical Literature, 1991.

Earle, Timothy K. *How Chiefs Come to Power: The Political Economy in Prehistory*. Stanford, Calif.: Stanford University Press, 1997.

Edelstein, Gershon, and Ianir Milevski. "The Rural Settlement of Jerusalem Re-evaluated: Surveys and Excavations in the Reph'aim Valley and the Meveasseret Yerushalayim." *PEQ* 126 (1994): 2–11.

Edelstein, Gershon, Ianir Milevski, and Sara Aurant. *Villages, Terraces and Stone Mounds: Excavations at Manaht, Jerusalem, 1987–1989*. IAA Reports 3. Jerusalem: Israel Antiquities Authority, 1998.

Eide, Tormod, Tomas Hägg, Richard H. Pierce, and László Török. *Fontes Historiae Nubiorum: Textual Sources for the History of the Middle Nile Region between the Eighth Century BC and the Sixth Century AD*. Vol. 1. Bergen: Univeristy of Bergen, Classics Department, 1994.

Eisenberg, Emanuel, and Alon De Groot. "Jerusalem and Its Environs in the Middle Bronze II Period" [Hebrew]. Pages 7–12 in *New Studies on Jerusalem: Proceedings of the Seventh Conference*. Edited by Avraham Faust and Eyal Baruch. Ramat Gan: Bar-Ilan University, 2001. (English summary, 5*)

Elliott, Jack D. "Lahav Research Project Regional Survey, 1993." *Lahav Research Project, 1993 Season: Report Part II*. Unpublished.

———. "Preliminary Report on the Lahav Regional Survey, 1992 Field Season." Pages 292–323 in *Lahav Research Project, 1992 Season: Report Part II*.

Elon, Amos. *The Israelis, Fathers and Sons*. New York: Holt, Rinehart, & Winston, 1971.

Eph'al, Israel. "Changes in Palestine during the Persian Period in Light of Epigraphic Sources." *IEJ* 48 (1998): 106–19.

———. "Syria-Palestine under Achaemenid Rule." Pages 139–64 in *Persia, Greece and the Western Mediterranean c. 525 to 479 B.C.* Edited by

J. Boardman et al. 2d ed. CAH 4. Cambridge: Cambridge University Press, 1988.

———. "Ways and Means to Conquer a City, Based on Assyrian Queries to the Sungod." Pages 49–53 in *Assyria 1995: Proceedings of the Tenth Anniversary Synoposium of the Neo-Assyrian Text Corpus Project Helsinki, September 7–11, 1995*. Edited by Simo Parpola and Robert M. Whiting. Helsinki: Neo-Assyrian Text Corpus Project, 1997.

Epstein, Isidore. *The Babylonian Talmud, Seder Nezikin*. Vol. 3. London: Soncino, 1935.

Eshel, Hanan. "A *lmlk* Stamp from Beth-El." *IEJ* 39 (1989): 60–62.

Eshel, Itzhak, and Kay Prag, eds. *Excavations by Kathleen M. Kenyon in Jerusalem 1961–1967, Vol. IV, The Iron Age Cave Deposits on the South-east Hill and Isolated Burials and Cemeteries Elsewhere*. Oxford: Oxford University Press, 1995.

Esse, Douglas L. "The Collard Pithos at Megiddo: Ceramic Distribution and Ethnicity." *JNES* 51 (1992): 81–103.

———. "The Collared Store Jars: Scholarly Ideology and Ceramic Typology." *SJOT* 2 (1991): 99–115.

Eynikel, Erik. *The Reform of King Josiah and the Composition of the Deuteronomistic History*. Leiden: Brill, 1996.

Falconer, Steven E., and Stephen H. Savage. "Heartlands and Hinterlands: Alternative Trajectories of Early Urbanization in Mesopotamia and the Southern Levant." *American Antiquity* 60 (1995): 37–58.

Fales, Frederick M., and G. B. Lanfranchi. "The Impact of Oracular Material on the Political Utterances and Political Action in the Royal Inscriptions of the Sargonid Dynasty." Pages 99–114 in *Oracles et prophéties dans l'antiquité: actes du colloque de Strasbourg 15–17 juin 1995*. Edited by Jean-Georges Heintz. Travaux du Centre de Recherche sur le Proche-Orient et la Grèce Antiques 15. Paris: de Boccard, 1997.

Fales, Frederick M., and J. Nicholas Postgate. *Provincial and Military Administration*. Part 2 of *Imperial Administrative Records*. SAA 11. Helsinki: Helsinki University Press, 1995.

Faulkner, Raymond O. *A Concise Dictionary of Middle Egyptian*. Oxford: Oxford University Press, 1962.

Faust, Avraham. "From Hamlets to Monarchy: A View from the Countryside on the Formation of the Israelite Monarchy" [Hebrew]. *Cathedra* 94 (1997): 7–32.

———. "The Impact of Jerusalem's Expansion in the Late Iron Age on the Farms of Rural Settlement in Its Vicinity" [Hebrew]. *Cathedra* 84 (1997): 53–62.

———. "The Social Structure of the Israelite Society during the 8th–7th Centuries BCE according to the Archaeological Evidence" [Hebrew]. Ph.D dissertation. Bar-Ilan University, 1999.

Feig, Nurit. "The Environs of Jerusalem in the Iron Age II" [Hebrew]. Pages 387–410 in *The History of Jerusalem: The Biblical Period*. Edited by Shmuel Ahituv and Amihai Mazar. Jerusalem: Yad Izhak Ben-Zvi, 2000.

———. "New Discoveries in the Rephaim Valley, Jerusalem." *PEQ* 128 (1996): 3–7.

Finkelstein, Israel. "The Archaeology of the Days of Manasseh." Pages 169–87 in *Scripture and Other Artifacts: Essays on the Bible and Archaeology in Honor of Philip J. King*. Edited by Michael D. Coogan, J. Cheryl Exum, and Lawrence Stager. Louisville: Westminister John Knox, 1994.

———. *The Archaeology of the Israelite Settlement*. Jerusalem: Israel Exploration Society, 1988.

———. "The Archaeology of the United Monarchy: An Alternative View." *Levant* 28 (1996): 177–87.

———. "Bible Archaeology or Archaeology of Palestine in the Iron Age? A Rejoinder." *Levant* 30 (1998): 167–74.

———. "City States and States: Polity Dynamics in the 10th–9th Centuries BCE." In *Symbiosis, Symbolism and the Power of the Past: Ancient Israel and Its Neighbors from the Late Bronze Age through Roman Palestine, Proceedings of the W. F. Albright Institute of Archaeological Research and the American Schools of Oriental Research Centennial Symposium*. Forthcoming.

———. "The Emergence of Israel: A Phase in the Cyclic History of Canaan in the Third and Second Millennia BCE." Pages 150–78 in *From Nomadism to Monarchy: Archaeological and Historical Aspects of Early Israel*. Edited by Israel Finkelstein and Nadav Na'aman. Jerusalem: Israel Exploration Society, 1994.

———. "Ethno-Historical Background: Land Use and Demography in Recent Generations." Pages 109–30 in *Highlands of Many Cultures: The Southern Samaria Survey: The Sites*. Edited by Israel Finkelstein, Zvi Lederman, and Shlomo Bunimovitz. Monographs of the Sonia and Mario Nadler Institute of Archaeology 14. Tel Aviv: Institute of Archaeology, Tel Aviv University, 1997.

———. "Hazor and the North in the Iron Age: A Low Chronology Perspective." *BASOR* 314 (1999): 55–70.

———. *Living on the Fringe: The Archaeology and History of the Negev Sinai and Neighbouring Regions in the Bronze and Iron Ages*. Monographs in Mediterranean Archaeology 6. Sheffield: Sheffield Academic Press, 1995.

———. "Omride Architecture." *ZDPV* 116 (2000): 114–38.

———. "Philistine Chronology: High, Middle, or Low?" Pages 140–47 in *Mediterranean Peoples in Transition: Thirteenth to Early Tenth Centuries BCE*. Edited by Seymour Gitin, Amihai Mazar, and Ephraim Stern. Jerusalem: Israel Exploration Society, 1998.

————. "The Philistine Countryside." *IEJ* 46 (1996): 225–42.

————. "The Rise of Jerusalem and Judah: The Missing Link." *Levant* 33 (2001): 105–15.

————. "The Sociopolitical Organization of the Central Hill Country in the Second Millennium B.C.E." Pages 119–31 in *Biblical Archaeology Today, 1990, Precongress Symposium: Population, Production and Power.* Edited by Avrahm Biran and Joseph Aviram. Jerusalem: Israel Exploration Society, 1993.

————. "Southern Samarian Hills Survey." *NEAEHL* 4:1313–14.

————. "State Formation in Israel and Judah: A Contrast in Context, A Contrast in Trajectory." *NEA* 62 (1999): 35–52.

————. "The Stratigraphy and the Chronology of Megiddo and Beth-Shan in the 12th–11th Centuries BCE." *TA* 23 (1996): 170–84.

————. "Stratigraphy, Pottery, and Parallels: A Reply to Bienkowski." *Levant* 24 (1992): 171–72.

————. "The Territorial-Political System of Canaan in the Late Bronze Age." *UF* 28 (1996): 221–55.

Finkelstein, Israel, Zvi Lederman, and Shlomo Bunimovitz. *Highlands of Many Cultures: The Southern Samaria Survey, the Sites.* Monographs of the Sonia and Mario Nadler Institute of Archaeology 14. Tel Aviv: Institute of Archaeology, Tel Aviv University, 1997.

Finkelstein, Israel, and Izchak Magen, eds. *Archaeological Survey of the Hill Country of Benjamin.* Jerusalem: Israel Antiquities Authority, 1993.

Finkelstein, Israel, and Neil Asher Silberman. *The Bible Unearthed: Archaeology's New Vision of Ancient Israel and the Origin of Its Sacred Texts.* New York: Free Press, 2001.

Finley, Moses I. *The Ancient Economy.* London: Hogarth, 1985.

Fotiadis, Michael. "Modernity and the Past-Still-Present: Politics of Time in the Birth of Regional Archaeological Projects in Greece." *AJA* 99 (1995): 59–78.

Fouts, David M. "Another Look at Large Numbers in Assyrian Royal Inscriptions." *JNES* 53 (1994): 205–11.

Frahm, Eckart. *Einleitung in die Sanherib-Inschriften.* AfOB 26. Vienna: Institut für Orientalistik der Universität, 1997.

Frame, Grant. "The Inscription of Sargon II at Tang-i Var." *Or* 68 (1999): 31–57.

Francovich, Riccardo, and Helen Patterson, eds. *Extracting Meaning from Ploughsoil Assemblages.* Vol. 5 of *The Archaeology of Mediterranean Landscapes.* Oxford: Oxbow, 1999.

Franken, Hendricus Jacobus. "The Excavations of the British School of Archaeology in Jerusalem on the South-East Hill in the Light of Subsequent Research." *Levant* 19 (1987): 129–35.

————. *A History of Pottery and Potters in Ancient Jerusalem.* Sheffield: Sheffield Academic Press, forthcoming.

Franken, Hendricus J., and Margreet L. Steiner. *Excavations in Jerusalem 1961–1967, Vol. II, The Iron Age Extramural Quarter on the South-East Hill.* Oxford: Oxford University, 1990.

————. "Urusalim and Jebus." *ZAW* 104 (1992): 110–11.

Frankfort, Henri. "The Origin of the Bit Hilani." *Iraq* 14 (1952): 120–31.

Freeden, Michael. "Ideology." Pages 681–85 in vol. 4 of *Routledge Encyclopedia of Philosophy.* Edited by Edward Craig. 10 vols. London: Routledge, 1998.

Freedman, David Noel. *Amos: A New Translation with Introduction and Commentary.* AB 24A. New York: Doubleday, 1989.

————. "The Chronicler's Purpose." *CBQ* 23 (1961): 432–42.

Frei, Hans. *Eclipse of the Biblical Narrative: A Study in Eighteenth and Nineteenth Century Hermeneutics.* New Haven: Yale University Press, 1974.

Frey, Jorg. "Temple and Rival Temple—The Cases of Elephantine, Mt. Gerizim, and Leontopolis." Pages 183–86 in *Gemeinde ohne Tempel: Zur Substituierung und Transformation des Jerusalemer Tempels und seines Kults im Alten Testament, antiken Judentums und frühen Christentum.* Edited by Beate Ego, Armin Lange, and Peter Pilhofer. WUNT 118. Tübingen: Mohr Siebeck, 1999.

Frick, Frank S. "Palestine, Climate of." *ABD* 5:119–26.

Friedman, Richard Elliott. "The Deuteronomistic School." Pages 70–80 in *Fortunate the Eyes That See: Essays in Honor of David Noel Freedman in Celebration of His Seventieth Birthday.* Edited by Astrid B. Beck, Andrew H. Bartelt, Paul R. Raube, and Chris A. Franke. Grand Rapids: Eerdmans, 1995.

————. *The Exile and Biblical Narrative.* HSM 22. Atlanta: Scholars Press, 1981.

————. "The First Great Writer." Paper presented at the Biblical Colloquium (1986) and in colloquia at Cambridge (1988), Yale (1991), Hebrew University of Jerusalem (1997), University of California, Berkeley (1998), and University of California, San Diego (1998).

————. "From Egypt to Egypt: Dtr^1 and Dtr^2." Pages 167–81 in *Traditions in Transformation: Turning Points in Biblical Faith.* Edited by Baruch Halpern and Jon D. Levenson. Winona Lake, Ind.: Eisenbrauns, 1981.

————. *The Hidden Book in the Bible.* San Francisco: Harper, 1998.

————. *Who Wrote the Bible?* 2d ed. San Francisco: Harper San Francisco, 1997.

Friedman, Richard Elliott, and Sawana D. Overton. "Death and Afterlife: The Biblical Silence." Pages 35–59 in *Judaism in Late Antiquity Part 4: Death, Life-after-Death, Resurrection and the World-to-Come in the*

Judaisms of Antiquity. Edited by Alan J. Avery-Peck and Jacob Neusner. Leiden: Brill, 2000.

Fritz, Volkmar, and Philip R. Davies, eds. *The Origins of the Ancient Israelite States.* JSOTSup 228. Sheffield: Sheffield Academic Press, 1996.

Fuchs, Andreas. "Aḫi-Mīti," PNA 1:65.

———. *Die Annalen des Jahres 711 v. Chr. nach Prismenfragmenten aus Ninive und Assur.* SAAS 8. Helsinki: Neo-Assyrian Text Corpus Project, 1998.

———. "The Ashdod Stele of Sargon II," *FO* 17 (1976): 87–99

———. *Die Inschriften Sargons II. aus Khorsabad.* Göttingen: Cuvillier, 1994.

———. "The Oldest Account of Sargon II's Campaign against Ashdod," *FO* 24 (1987): 29–39.

Gal, Zvi, and Yardenna Alexandre. *Horbat Rosh Zayit: An Iron Age Storage Fort and Village.* Israel Antiquities Reports 8. Jerusalem: Israel Antiquities Authority, 2000.

Galil, Gershon. *The Chronology of the Kings of Israel and Judah.* Leiden: Brill, 1996.

———. "Conflicts between Assyrian Vassals." *SAAB* 6 (1992): 55–63.

———. "Judah and Assyria in the Sargonid Period" [Hebrew]. *Zion* 57 (1992): 111–33.

———. "A New Look at the 'Azekah Inscription.'" RB 102 (1995): 321–29.

———. "Sennacherib versus Hezekiah: A New Look at the Assyrian Campaign to the West in 701 BCE" [Hebrew]. *Zion* 53 (1988): 1–12.

Gallagher, William R. "Assyrian Deportation Propaganda." *SAAB* 8 (1994): 57–65.

———. "On the Identity of Hêlēl Ben Šāḥar of Isa. 14:12–15." *UF* 26 (1994): 131–46.

———. *Sennacherib's Campaign to Judah: New Studies.* SHCANE 18. Leiden: Brill, 1999.

Gauthier, Henri. *Le Livre des Rois d'Égypte IV.* Cairo: Institut français d'archéologie orientale, 1916.

Gelber, Yoav. *The Emergence of a Jewish Army: The Veterans of the British Army in the IDF* [Hebrew]. Jerusalem: Yad Izhak Ben-Zvi, 1986.

Geva, Hillel. "Excavations in the Citadel of Jerusalem, 1979–1980, Preliminary Report." *IEJ* 33 (1983): 55–71.

———. "History of Archaeological Research in Jerusalem." *NEAEHL* 2:801–4.

———. "Innovations in Archaeological Research in Jerusalem during the 1990s" [Hebrew]. *Qad* 34/2 (2001): 70-71.

———. "List of Major Archaeological Excavations in Jerusalem, 1967–1992." Pages 325–30 in *Ancient Jerusalem Revealed.* Edited by Hillel Geva. Jerusalem: Israel Exploration Society, 1994.

———. "Respondent." Pages 620–24 in *Biblical Archaeology Today, 1990: Proceedings of the Second International Congress on Biblical Archaeology*. Edited by Avraham Biran and Joseph Aviram. Jerusalem: Israel Exploration Society, 1993.

———. "The Western Boundary of Jerusalem at the End of the Monarchy." *IEJ* 29 (1979): 84–91.

———, ed. *Jewish Quarter Excavations in the Old City of Jerusalem Conducted by Nahman Avigad, 1969–1982, Vol. I, Architecture and Stratigraphy: Areas A, W and X-2, Final Report*. Jerusalem: Israel Exploration Society, 2000.

Geva, Hillel, and Nahman Avigad. "Area W—Stratigraphy and Architecture." Pages 131–59 in *Jewish Quarter Excavations in the Old City of Jerusalem Conducted by Nahman Avigad, 1969–1982, Vol. I, Architecture and Stratigraphy: Areas A, W and X-2, Final Report*. Jerusalem: Israel Exploration Society, 2000.

Geva, Hillel, and Ronny Reich. "Area A—Stratigraphy and Architecture, IIa. Introduction." Pages 37–43 in *Jewish Quarter Excavations in the Old City of Jerusalem Conducted by Nahman Avigad, 1969–1982, Vol. I, Architecture and Stratigraphy: Areas A, W and X-2, Final Report*. Jerusalem: Israel Exploration Society, 2000.

Gibson, Shimon. "Agricultural Terraces and Settlement Expansion in the Highlands of Early Iron Age Palestine: Is There Any Correlation between the Two?" Pages 113–46 in *Studies in the Archaeology of the Iron Age in Israel and Jordan*. Edited by Amihai Mazar. JSOTSup 331. Sheffield: Sheffield Academic Press, 2001.

———. "The 1961–67 Excavations in the Armenian Garden." *PEQ* 119 (1987): 81–96.

Gibson, Shimon, and Gershon Edelstein. "Investigating Jerusalem's Rural Landscape." *Levant* 17 (1985): 139–55.

Gibson, Shimon, Bridget Ibbs, and Amos Kloner. "The Sataf Project of Landscape Archaeology in the Judaean Hills: A Preliminary Report on Four Seasons of Survey and Excavation (1987–1989)." *Levant* 23 (1991): 29–54.

Gilboa, Ayelet. "The Dynamics of Phoenician Bichrome Pottery: A View from Tel Dor." *BASOR* 316 (1999): 1–22.

———. "Iron I–IIA Pottery Evolution at Dor—Regional Contexts and the Cypriot Connection." Pages 413–25 in *Mediterranean Peoples in Transition Thirteenth to Early Tenth Centuries BCE*. Edited by Seymour Gitin, Amihai Mazar, and Ephriam Stern. Jerusalem: Israel Exploration Society, 1998.

———. "New Finds at Tel Dor and the Beginning of Cypro-Geometric Pottery Import to Palestine." *IEJ* 39 (1989): 204–18.

Gilboa, Ayelet, and Ilan Sharon. "Early Iron Age Radiometric Dates from Tel Dor: Preliminary Implications for Phoenicia, and Beyond." *Radiocarbon* 43/3 (2001): 1343–52.

Gill, Dan. "The Geology of the City of David and Its Ancient Subterranean Waterworks." Pages 1–28 in *Excavations at the City of David 1978–1985 Directed by Yigal Shiloh, Vol. IV, Various Reports.* Edited by Donald T. Ariel and Alon De Groot. Qedem 35. Jerusalem: Institute of Archaeology, Hebrew University of Jerusalem, 1996.

Gillings, Mark, Dan Mattingly, and Jan van Dalen, eds. *Geographical Information and Systems and Landscape Archaeology.* Vol. 3 of *The Archaeology of the Mediterranean Landscapes.* Oxford: Oxbow, 1999.

Ginsberg, Harold Louis. "Reflexes of Sargon in Isaiah after 715 B.C.E." Pages 47–53 in *Essays in Memory of E. A. Speiser.* Edited by William W. Hallo. New Haven: American Oriental Society, 1968.

Gitin, Seymour. "Incense Altars from Ekron, Israel and Judah: Context and Typology." *ErIsr* 20 (1989): 52*–67*.

———. "The Neo-Assyrian Empire and Its Western Periphery: The Levant, with Focus on Philistine Ekron." Pages 77–103 in *Assyria 1995: Proceedings of the Tenth Anniversary Synoposium of the Neo-Assyrian Text Corpus Project Helsinki, September 7–11, 1995.* Edited by Simo Parpola and Robert M. Whiting. Helsinki: Neo-Assyrian Text Corpus Project, 1997.

Gitin, Seymour, and Mordechi Cogan "A New Type of Dedicatory Inscription from Ekron." *IEJ* 49 (1999): 193–202.

Glatt, David A. *Chronological Displacement in Biblical and Related Literatures.* SBLDS 139. Atlanta: Scholars Press, 1993.

Gnuse, Robert K. "Redefinig the Elohist?" *JBL* 119 (2000): 201–20.

Gonçalves, Francolino J. *L'expédition de Sennachérib en Palestine dans la littérature hébraïque ancienne.* Ebib 7. Paris: Gabalda; Leuven: Peeters, 1986.

———. "2 Rois 18,13–20,19 Par. Isaïe 36–39. Encore une fois, lequel des deux livres fut le premier?" Pages 27–55 in *Lectures et relectures de la Bible: Festschrift P.-M. Bogaert.* Edited by Jean-Marie Auwers and André Wénin. BETL 144. Leuven: Leuven University Press, 1999.

Gonen, Rivka. *Burial Patterns and Cultural Diversity in Late Bronze Age Canaan.* ASOR Dissertations 7. Winona Lake, Ind.: Eisenbrauns, 1992.

———. "Urban Canaan in the Late Bronze Age Period." *BASOR* 253 (1984): 61–73.

Goren, Avner. "The Gihon and the Installations Built by It" [Hebrew]. *Teva Vaaretz* 11 (1968–69): 22–26.

Government of Palestine, Office of Statistics. "Survey of Social and Economic Conditions in Arab Villages, 1944." *General Monthly Bulletin of Current Statistics* (1945): 426–47, 509–17, 559–67, 745–64; (1946): 46–56, 554–73.

Grafman, Rafi. "Nehemiah's 'Broad Wall.'" *IEJ* 24 (1974): 50–51.

Granquist, Hilma Natalia. *Marriage Conditions in a Palestinian Village* [Artas]. 2 vols. Helsingsfors: Societas Scientiarum Fennica. 1931–35.

Gray, George B. *A Critical and Exegetical Commentary on Numbers.* ICC. Edinburgh: T&T Clark, 1973.

Gray, John. *I and II Kings: A Commentary.* 2d ed. OTL. Philadelphia: Westminster, 1970.

Grayson, Albert Kirk. "Assyria: Tiglath-Pileser III to Sargon II (744–705 B.C.)." Pages 71–102 in *The Assyrian and Babylonian Empires and Other States of the Near East, from the Eighth to the Sixth Centuries B.C.* Edited by John Boardman et al. 2d ed. CAH 3/2. Cambridge: Cambridge University Press, 1991.

———. "Assyrian Rule of Conquered Territory in Ancient Western Asia." *CANE* 2:959–68.

Greenberg. Raphael. "New Light on the Early Iron Age at Tell Beit Mirsim." *BASOR* 265 (1987): 55–80.

Greenberg, Yitzhak. "The Defense Budget in Ben-Gurion's Policy on National Security 1949–1952" [Hebrew]. *Studies in Zionism* 12 (1991): 43–53.

Greenhut, Zvi. "The Periphery of Jerusalem in the Bronze and Iron Ages— New Discoveries" [Hebrew]. Pages 3–8 in *New Studies on Jerusalem: Proceedings of the Seventh Conference.* Edited by Avraham Faust. Ramat Gan: Bar-Ilan University, 1996.

Grimal, Nicolas C. "Bibliothèques et propagande royale à l'époque éthiopienne." Pages 37–48 in *Livre du centenaire, 1880–1980.* Edited by Jean Vercoutter. Cairo: Institut français d'archéologie orientale. 1980.

———. *A History of Ancient Egypt.* Oxford: Blackwell, 1992.

———. *La Stèle Triomphale Pi(ankh)y au Musée du Caire.* Cairo: Institut français d'archéologie orientale du Caire, 1981.

Grossman, David "The Expansion of the Settlement Frontier on Hebron's Western and Southern Fringes." *Geographical Research Forum* 5 (1982): 57–73.

———. "Population Growth in Reference to Land Quality: The Case of Samaria, 1922–1975." *Geographical Journal* 147/2 (1981): 188–200.

———. "The Relationship between Settlement Pattern and Resource Utilization: The Case of the North-Eastern Samaria." *Transactions of the Institute of British Geographers* 6/1 (1981): 19–38.

Gulick, John. *Social Structure and Culture Change in a Lebanese Village* [al-Munsif]. New York: Viking Fund Publications, 1955.

Haas, Jonathan. *The Evolution of the Prehistoric State.* New York: Columbia University Press, 1982.

Haggett, Peter. *Locational Analysis in Human Geography.* London: Arnold, 1965.

Hall, John A. "State." Pages 878–83 in *The Oxford Companion to the Politics of the World*. Edited by Joel Krieger. Oxford: Oxford University Press, 1993.

Hall, Peter Dobkin. "The Empty Tomb: The Making of Dynastic Identity." Pages 255–348 in *Lives in Trust: The Fortunes of Dynastic Families in Late Twentieth Century America*. Edited by George Marcus. Boulder, Colo.: Westview, 1992.

Hallo, William W. "Jerusalem under Hezekiah: An Assyriological Perspective." Pages 36–50 in *Jerusalem: Its Sanctity and Centrality to Judaism, Christianity, and Islam*. Edited by Lee I. Levine. New York: Continuum, 1999.

Hallo, William W., and W. Simpson. *The Ancient Near East: A History*. 2d ed. Fort Worth: Harcourt Brace College Publishers, 1998.

Halpern, Baruch. *The Constitution of the Monarchy in Israel*. HSM 25. Atlanta: Scholars Press, 1981.

———. *David's Secret Demons: Messiah, Murderer, Traitor, King*. Grand Rapids: Eerdmans, 2001.

———. *The First Historians*. San Francisco: Harper & Row, 1988.

———. "Jerusalem and the Lineages in the Seventh Century BCE: Kinship and the Rise of Individual Moral Liability." Pages 11–107 in *Law and Ideology in Monarchic Israel*. JSOTSup 124. Edited by Baruch Halpern and Deborah W. Hobson. Sheffield: Sheffield Academic Press, 1991.

———. "Sacred History and Ideology: Chronicles' Thematic Structure—Indications of an Earlier Source." Pages 35–54 in *The Creation of Sacred Literature: Composition and Redaction of the Biblical Text*. Edited by Richard E. Friedman. University of California Publications Near Eastern Studies 22. Berkeley and Los Angeles: University of California Press, 1981.

Hamilton, Richard W. "Note on Excavations at Bishop Gobat School." *PEFQS* (1935): 141–43.

Hanson, Paul D. *The Dawn of Apocalyptic: The Historical and Social Roots of Jewish Apocalyptic Eschatology*. Philadelphia: Fortress, 1979.

Harmon, George E. "Floor Area and Population Determination." Unpublished Ph.D. dissertation. Southern Baptist Theological Seminar, 1983.

Harper, William Rainey. *A Critical and Exegetical Commentary on Amos and Hosea*. Edinburgh: T&T Clark, 1953.

Harr, John E., and Peter J. Johnson. *The Rockefeller Conscience*. New York: Scribner's, 1991.

Hassan, Fekri A. *Demographic Archaeology*. New York: Academic, 1981.

———. "Demographic Archaeology." *Advances in Archaeological Method and Theory* 1 (1978): 49–103.

———. "Demography and Archaeology." *Annual Review of Anthropology* 8 (1979): 137–60.

Hayes, John J. "The Tradition of Zion's Inviolability." *JBL* 82 (1963): 419–26.

Hayes, John, and Stuart Irvine. *Isaiah the Eighth-Century Prophet: His Times and His Preaching*. Nashville: Abingdon, 1987.

Healy, John. "Am Haʾarez." *ABD* 1:168–69.

Hecker, Mordechai. "Water Supply of Jerusalem in Ancient Times" [Hebrew]. Pages 191–218 in vol. 1 of in *Sefer Yerushalayim (The Book of Jerusalem)*. Edited by Michael Avi-Yonah. 2 vols. Jerusalem: Bialik Institute and Dvir, 1956–87.

Heidel, Alexander. "The Octogonal Sennacherib Prism in the Iraq Museum." *Sumer* 9 (1953): 117–88.

Heidorn, L. A. "The Horses of Kush." *JNES* 56 (1997): 105–14.

Herbert, Arthur S. *The Book of the Prophet Isaiah, Chapters 1–39*. Cambridge: Cambridge University Press, 1973.

Herr, Larry G. "The History of the Collared Pithos at Tell el-ʿUmeiri, Jordan." Pages 237–50 in *Studies in the Archaeology of Israel and Neighboring Lands in Memory of Douglas L. Esse*. Edited by Samuel R. Wolff. Chicago: Oriental Institute of the University of Chicago; Atlanta: American Schools of Oriental Research, 2001.

———. "The Iron Age II Period: Emerging Nations." *BA* 60 (1997): 114–83.

———. "Tell al-ʿUmayri and the Reubenite Hypothesis." *ErIsr* 26 (1999): 64*–77*.

———. "Tell el-ʿUmayri and the Madaba Plains Region during the Late Bronze-Iron Age I Transition." Pages 251–64 in *Mediterranean Peoples in Transition: Thirteenth to Early Tenth Centuries BCE*. Edited by Seymour Gitin, Amihai Mazar, and Ephraim Stern. Jerusalem: Israel Exploration Society, 1998.

Herzog, Zeʾev. *Archaeology of the City: Urban Planning in Ancient Israel and Its Social Implications*. Sonia and Marco Nadler Institute of Archaeology Monograph Series 13. Tel Aviv: Emery and Claire Yass Archaeology Press of the Institute of Archaeology, Tel Aviv University, 1997.

———. "The Temple of Solomon: Its Plan and Archaeological Background" [Hebrew]. Pages 155–74 in *The History of Jerusalem: The Biblical Period*. Edited by Shmuel Ahituv and Amihai Mazar. Jerusalem: Yad Izhak Ben-Zvi, 2000.

Herzog, Zeʾev, Miriam Aharoni, Anson F. Rainey, and Shmuel Moshkovitz. "The Israelite Fortress at Arad." *BASOR* 254 (1984): 1–34.

Hess, Richard S. "The Bible and Alalakh." Pages 208–20 in *Mesopotamia and the Bible*. Edited by Mark W. Chavalas and K. Lawson Younger Jr. JSOTSup 341. Sheffield: Sheffield Academic Press, 2002.

———. "Hezekiah and Sennacherib in 2 Kings 18–20." Pages 23–41 in *Zion, City of Our God*. Edited by Richard S. Hess and Gordon J. Wenham. Grand Rapids: Eerdmans, 1999.

Hodder, Ian, and Clive Orton. *Spatial Analysis in Archaeology*. Cambridge: Cambridge University Press, 1976.

Hoffmeier, James K. "Egypt As an Arm of Flesh: A Prophetic Response." Pages 79–97 in *Israel's Apostasy and Restoration: Essays in Honor of Roland K. Harrison*. Edited by A. Gileadi. Grand Rapids: Baker, 1988.

———. "Egypt's Foreign Policy in the 18th Dynasty." In *Egypt, Israel, and the Ancient Mediterranean World: Essays in Honor of Donald B. Redford*. Edited by Gary Knoppers. Forthcoming.

———. "Reconsidering Egypt's Part in the Termination of the Middle Bronze Age in Palestine." *Levant* 21 (1989): 181–93.

Holladay, John S. "The Kingdoms of Israel and Judah: Political and Economic Centralization in the Iron IIA–B." Pages 368–98 in *The Archaeology of Society in the Holy Land*. Edited by Thomas E. Levy. London: Leicester University Press, 1995.

Holm-Nielsen, Svend "Did Joab Climb 'Warren's Shaft?'" Pages 38–49 in *History and Tranditions of Early Israel*. Edited by André Lemaire and Benedikt Otzen. Leiden: Brill, 1993.

Hopkins, David Charles. *The Highlands of Canaan: Agricultural Life in the Early Iron Age*. SWBA 3. Sheffield: JSOT Press, 1985.

Horovitz, Avigdor. "The Temple of Solomon" [Hebrew]. Pages 131–54 in *The History of Jerusalem: The Biblical Period*. Edited by Shmuel Ahituv and Amihai Mazar. Jerusalem: Yad Izhak Ben-Zvi, 2000.

Hubbard, R. Pearce S. "The Topography of Ancient Jerusalem." *PEQ* 98 (1966): 130–54.

Hurvitz, Avi. "Continuity and Innovation in Biblical Hebrew—The Case of 'Semantic Change' in Post-Exilic Writings." Pages 1–10 in *Studies in Ancient Hebrew Semantics*. Edited by T. Muraoka. AbrNSup 4. Leuven: Peeters, 1995.

———. "The Evidence of Language in Dating the Priestly Code." *RB* 81 (1974): 24–56.

———. "The Historical Quest for 'Ancient Israel' and the Linguistic Evidence of the Hebrew Bible: Some Methodological Observations." *VT* 47 (1997): 310–15.

———. *A Linguistic Study of the Relationship between the Priestly Source and the Book of Ezekiel*. CahRB. Paris: Gabalda, 1982.

———. ללשון בין לשון. Jerusalem: Bialik Institute, 1972.

———. "The Relevance of Biblical Hebrew Linguistics for the Historical Study of Ancient Israel." Pages 21-33 in *Proceedings of the Twelfth World Congress of Jewish Studies*. Jerusalem, 1999.

———. "The Usage of שש and בוץ in the Bible and Its Implication for the Date of P." *HTR* 60 (1967): 117–21.

James, Francis W., and Patrick E. McGovern. *The Late Bronze Egyptian Garrison at Beth-Shan: A Study of Levels VII and VIII*. Philadelphia: University Museum, 1993.

Jamieson-Drake, David W. *Scribes and Schools in Monarchic Judah: A Socio-Archaeological Approach.* SWBA 9. JSOTSup 109. Sheffield: Sheffield Acadeic Press, 1991.

Japhet, Sara. *I and II Chronicles: A Commentary.* OTL. Louisville: Westminster John Knox, 1993.

———. *The Ideology of the Book of Chronicles and Its Place in Biblical Thought.* BEATAJ 9. Frankfurt am Main: Lang, 1989.

———. "The Temple in the Restoration Period: Reality and Ideology." *USQR* 44 (1991): 195–251.

Jauss, Hans Robert. "Literary History As a Challenge to Literary Theory." *New Literary History* 2 (1970): 7–37.

Johns, Cedric N. "The Citadel, Jerusalem. A Summary of Work Since 1934." *QDAP* 14 (1950): 121–90.

———. "Excavations at the Citadel, Jerusalem, 1934–9." *PEQ* 72 (1940): 1–23.

Joines, Karen R. "The Bronze Serpent in the Israelite Cult." *JBL* 87 (1968): 245–56.

Jones, Douglas Rawlinson. *Jeremiah: Based on the Revised Standard Version.* NCB. Grand Rapids: Eerdmans, 1992.

Kahn, Dan'el. "The Inscription of Sargon II at Tang-i Var and the Chronology of Dynasty 25." *Or* 70 (2001):1-18.

Kaiser, Otto. *Isaiah 13–39.* OTL. Philadelphia: Westminster, 1978.

Kallai, Zecharia. *Historical Geography of the Bible: The Tribal Territories of Israel.* Leiden: Brill; Jerusalem: Magnes, 1986.

———. "The Land of Benjamin and Mt. Ephraim" [Hebrew]. Pages 153-93 in *Judaea, Samaria and the Golan.* Edited by Moshe Kochavi. Jerusalem: Archaeological Surveys of Israel, 1972.

Kapera, Zdzislaw Jan. "The Ashdod Stele of Sargon II." *FO* 17 (1976): 87–99.

———. "The Oldest Account of Sargon II's Campaign Against Ashdod." *FO* 24 (1987): 29–39.

———. "Was Ya-ma-ni a Cypriot?" *FO* 14 (1972): 207–18.

Kaplan, Jacob "Ashdod-Yam." NEAEHL 1:102–3.

Keel, Othmar. *Jahwe-Visionen und Siegelkunst: Eine neue Deutung der Majestätsschilderungen in Jes 6, Ez 1 und 10 und Sach 4.* SBS 84/85. Stuttgart: Verlag Katholisches Bibelwerk, 1977.

Keel, Othmar, and Max Küchler. *Geographisch-geschichtliche Landeskunde.* Vol. 1 of *Orte und Landschaften der Bibel.* Zürich: Benziger; Göttingen: Vandenhoeck & Ruprecht, 1982–84.

Kempinski, Aharon. "Middle and Late Bronze Age Fortifications." Pages 127–42 in *The Architecture of Ancient Israel.* Edited by Aharon Kempinski and Ronny Reich. Jerusalem: Israel Exploration Society, 1992.

Kenyon, Kathleen M. *Digging Up Jerusalem.* London: Benn, 1974.

———. "Excavations in Jerusalem, 1961." *PEQ* 94 (1962): 72–89.

———. "Excavations in Jerusalem, 1962." *PEQ* 95 (1963): 7–21.

———. "Excavations in Jerusalem, 1963." *PEQ* 96 (1964): 7–18.

———. "Excavations in Jerusalem, 1964." *PEQ* 97(1965): 9–20.

———. "Excavations in Jerusalem, 1965." *PEQ* 98 (1966): 73–88.

———. "Excavations in Jerusalem, 1967." *PEQ* 100 (1968): 97–111.

———. *Jerusalem: Excavating 3000 Years of History*. London: Thames & Hudson, 1967.

Killebrew, Ann E. "The Collared Pithos in Context: A Typological, Technological, and Functional Reassessment." Pages 377–98 in *Studies in the Archaeology of Israel and Neighboring Lands in Memory of Douglas L. Esse*. Edited by Samuel R. Wolff. Chicago: Oriental Institute of the University of Chicago; Atlanta: American Schools of Oriental Research, 2001.

King, Leonard W. *Cuneiform Texts 26*. London: British Museum, 1909.

King, Philip. "Jerusalem." *ABD* 3:747–66.

Kinnier Wilson, J. V. *The Legend of Etana*. Warminster: Aris & Phillips, 1985.

Kitchen, Kenneth A. "Ancient Israel, from Abraham to the Roman Destruction of the Temple—A Review Article," *Them* (2000): 93–94.

———. *Ancient Orient and the Old Testament*. Downers Grove, Ill.: InterVarsity, 1966.

———. "Egypt, the Levant and Assyria in 701 B.C." Pages 243–53 in *Fontes atque Pontes: Eine Festgabe für Hellmut Brunner*. ÄAT 5. Edited by Manfred Görg. Wiesbaden: Harrassowitz, 1983.

———. "Hanes." *NBD*[2] 452–53.

———. "The Historical Chronology of Ancient Egypt: A Current Assessment." Page 1–13 in *Absolute Chronology: Archaeological Europe 2500–500 BC*. Edited by Klavs Randsborg. Acta Archaeologica 67. Copenhagen: Munksgaard, 1996.

———. "Late Egyptian Chronology and the Hebrew Monarchy." *JANESCU* 5 (1973): 225–33.

———. *Pharaoh Triumphant: The Life and Times of Ramesses II*. Warminster: Aris & Phillips, 1982.

———. "Regnal and Genealogical Data of Ancient Egypt (Absolute Chronology I). The Historical Chronology of Ancient Egypt, A Current Assessment." Pages 29–42 in *The Synchronisation of Civilisations in the Eastern Mediterranean in the Second Millennium B.C.: Proceedings of an International Symposium at Schloss Haindorf, 15th–17th of November 1996 and at the Austrian Academy, Vienna, 11th–12th of May 1998*. Edited by Manfred Bietak. Vienna: Verlag der Österreichischen Akademie der Wissenschaften, 2000.

———. Review of Bernd Ulrich Schipper, *Israel und Ägypten in der Königszeit, BO* 58 (2001): 376–85.

————. "The Sheshonqs of Egypt and Palestine." *JSOT* 93 (2001): 3–12.

————. *The Third Intermediate Period in Egypt (1100–650 BC)*. 3d ed. Warminster: Aris & Phillips, 1996

Kloner, Amos. "Rehov Hagay." *ESI* 3 (1984): 57–59.

————. *Survey of Jerusalem: The Southern Sector.* Archaeological Survey of Israel. Jerusalem: Israel Antiquities Authority, 2000.

Kloner, Amos, and Dave Davis. "A Burial Cave of the Late First Temple Period on the Slope of Mount Zion." Pages 107–10 in *Ancient Jerusalem Revealed*. Edited by Hillel Geva. Jerusalem: Israel Exploration Society, 1994.

Knauf, Ernst Axel. "Jerusalem in the Late Bronze and Early Iron Ages: A Proposal." TA 27 (2000): 75–90.

————. "King Solomon's Copper Supply." Pages 167–86 in *Phoenicia and the Bible: Proceedings of the Conference Held at the University of Leuven on the 15th and 16th of March 1990*. Edited by Edward Lipiński. Leuven: Departement Oriëntalistiek; Peeters, 1991.

————. "The 'Low Chronology' and How Not to Deal with It." *BN* 101 (2000): 56–63.

Knoppers, Gary N. "'Battling against Yahweh': Israel's War against Judah in 2 Chr 13:2–20." *RB* 100 (1993): 511–32.

————. *I Chronicles*. AB 12. New York: Doubleday, forthcoming.

————. "Jerusalem at War in Chronicles." Pages 57–76 in *Zion, City of Our God*. Edited by Richard S. Hess and Gordon J. Wenham; Grand Rapids: Eerdmans, 1999.

————. "Prayer and Propaganda: The Dedication of Solomon's Temple and the Deuteronomist's Program." *CBQ* 57 (1995): 229–54. Repr., pages 370–96 in *Reconsidering Israel and Judah: The Deuteronomistic History in Recent Thought*. Edited by Gary N. Knoppers and J. Gordon McConville. SBTS 8. Winona Lake, Ind.: Eisenbrauns, 2000.

————. "Rehoboam in Chronicles: Villain or Victim?" *JBL* 109 (1990): 423–40.

————. "Sources, Revisions, and Editions: The Lists of Jerusalem's Residents in MT and LXX Nehemiah 11 and 1 Chronicles 9." *Textus* 20 (2000): 141–68.

————. "'There Was None Like Him': Incomparability in the Books of Kings." *CBQ* 54 (1992): 411–31.

————. *Two Nations Under God: The Deuteronomistic History of Solomon and the Dual Monarchies*. 2 vols. HSM 52–53. Atlanta: Scholars Press, 1993–94.

————. "The Vanishing Solomon: The Disappearance of the United Monarchy from Recent Histories of Ancient Israel." *JBL* 116 (1997): 19–44.

Koch, Klaus. *The Assyrian Period*. Vol. 1 of *The Prophets*. Translated by M. Kohl. Philadelphia: Fortress, 1978.

Kochavi, Moshe. "Khirbet Rabûd = Debir." *TA* 1 (1974): 2–33.

———, ed. *Judaea, Saniaria and the Golan: Archaeological Survey 1967–1968* [Hebrew]. Jerusalem: Archaeological Survey of Israel, 1972.

Kolb, Frank. *Die Stadt im Altertum.* Munich: Beck, 1984.

Kramer, Carol. "Estimating Prehistoric Populations: An Ethnoarchaeological Approach." Pages 315–24 in *L'Archeologie de l'Iraq du début de l'époque néolithique a 333 avant notre ère: Perspectives et limites de l'interprétation anthropologique des documents, Colloque Internationaux, Paris, 1978.* Paris: Centre National de la Recherche Scientifique, 1980.

Kraus, Roff. "Ein wahrscheinlicher Terminus post quem für das Ende von Lachish VI." *MDOG* 126 (1994): 123–30.

Kuhrt, Amelie. *The Ancient Near East, c. 3000–330 BC.* 2 vols. London: Routledge, 1997.

Kutscher, Edward Y. *The Language and Linguistic Background of the Isaiah Scroll (I Q Isa).* Leiden: Brill, 1974.

Laato, Antti. "Assyrian Propaganda and the Falsification of History in the Royal Inscriptions of Sennacherb." *VT* 45 (1995): 198–223.

———. "Hezekiah and the Assyrian Crisis in 701 B.C." *SJOT* 1 (1987): 49–68.

LaBianca, Oystein Sakala, and Randall W. Younker. "The Kingdoms of Ammon, Moab and Edom: The Archaeology of Society in Late Bronze/Iron Age Transjordan (Ca. 1400–500 BCE)." Pages 399–415 in *Archaeology of Society in the Holy Land.* Edited by Thomas E. Levy. London: Leicester University Press, 1995.

Lambert, Wilfred G. "Göttergenealogie." Pages 469–71 in vol 3. of *Reallexikon der Assyriologie.* Edited by Erich Ebeling and Bruno Meissner. Berlin: de Gruyte, 1932.

Landau, Misia. *Narratives of Human Evolution.* New Haven: Yale University Press, 1991.

Laperrousaz, Ernest-Marie. "Jérusalem la Grande." *ErIsr* 24 (1993): 138*–47*.

Layard, Austen Henry. *Discoveries among the Ruins of Nineveh and Babylon; with Travels in Armenia, Kurdistan, and the Desert: Being the Result of a Second Expedition Undertaken for the Trustees of the British Museum.* New York: Harper & Brothers, 1853.

———. *A Second Series of the Monuments of Nineveh Including Bas-Reliefs from the Palace of Sennacherib and Bronzes from the Ruins of Nimroud from Drawings Made on the Spot, during a Second Expedition to Assyria.* London: Murray, 1853.

Leach, Edmund Ronald. *Pul Eliya: A Village in Ceylon: A Study of Land Tenure and Kinship.* Cambridge: Cambridge University Press, 1961.

Lehmann, Gunnar. "Phoenicians in Western Galilee: First Results of an Archaeological Survey in the Hinterland of Akko." Pages 65–112 in *Studies in the Archaeology of the Iron Age in Israel and Jordan*. Edited by Amihai Mazar. JSOTSup 331. Sheffield: Sheffield Academic Press, 2001.

———. "Reconstructing the Social Landscape of Early Israel: Marriage Alliances in a Rural Context." Forthcoming.

Lehmann, Gunnar, Herman M. Niemann, and Wolfgang Zwickel. "Zora und Eschtaol: Ein archäologischer Oberflächensurvey im Gebiet nördlich von Bet Schemesch." *UF* 28 (1996): 343–442.

Lemaire, André. "Date et origine des inscriptions paléo-hébraîque et phéniciennes de Kuntillet ‘Ajrud." *SEL* 1 (1984): 131–43.

———. "Histoire et administration de la Palestine à l'époque perse." Pages 11–53 in *La Palestine à l'époque perse*. Edited by Ernest-Marie Laperrousaz and André Lemaire. Études annexes de la Bible de Jearusalem. Paris: Cerf, 1994.

———. "Un nouveau roi arabe de Qedar dans l'inscription de l'autel à encens de Lakish (Planche I)." *RB* 81 (1974): 63–72.

Lemche, Niels Peter. *The Israelites in History and Tradition*. Louisville: Westminster John Knox, 1998.

Lemche, Werner E. "Is Old Testament Theology an Essentially Christian Theological Discipline?" *HBT* 11/1 (1989): 59–71.

Leuthäusser, Werner. *Die Entwicklung staatlich organisierter Herrschaft in frühen Hochkulturen am Beispiel des Vorderen Orients*. Frankfurt am Main: Lang, 1998.

Leveau, Philippe, Frederic Trément, K. Walsh, and Graeme Barker, eds. *Environmental Reconstruction in Mediterranean Landscape Archaeology*. Vol. 2 of *The Archaeology of Mediterranean Landscapes*. Oxford: Oxbow, 1999.

Levine, Louis D. "Preliminary Remarks on the Historical Inscriptions of Sennacherib." Pages 58–75 in *History, Historiography and Interpretation: Studies in Biblical and Cuneiform Literatures*. Edited by Hayim Tadmor and Moshe Weinfeld. Jerusalem: Magnes, 1983.

Levinson, Bernard M. *Deuteronomy and the Hermeneutics of Legal Innovation*. New York: Oxford University Press, 1997.

Ling-Israel, Pnina "The Sennacherib Prism in the Israel Museum—Jerusalem." Pages 213–48 in *Bar Ilan Studies in Assyriology Dedicated to Pinhas Artzi*. Edited by Jacob Klein and Aaron J. Skaist. Ramat Gan: Bar-Ilan University, 1990.

Lipiński, Edward. *Studies in Aramaic Inscriptions and Onomastics I*. OLA 1. Leuven: Leuven University Press, 1975.

Liverani, Mario. "Critique of Variants and the Titulary of Sennacherib." Pages 225–57 in *Assyrian Royal Inscriptions: New Horizons in Literary,*

Ideological and Historical Analysis. Edited by Frederick M. Fales. Orientis Antiqui Collectio 17. Rome: Istituto per l'oriente, 1981.

———. "L'histoire de Joas." *VT* 24 (1974) 438–45.

———. "*Kitru, Katāru.*" *Mesopotamia* 17 (1982): 43–66.

Livingstone, Alasdair. *Court Poetry and Literary Miscellanea.* SAA 3. Helsinki: Helsinki University Press, 1989.

Long, Burke O. *2 Kings.* FOTL 10. Grand Rapids: Eerdmans, 1991.

Long, V. Phillips, ed. *Israel's Past in Present Research: Essays on Ancient Israelite Historiography.* Winona Lake, Ind.: Eisenbrauns, 1999.

Lubetski, Meir, and Claire Gottlieb. "Isaiah 18: The Egyptian Nexus." Pages 264–303 in *Boundaries of the Ancient Near Eastern World: A Tribute to Cyrus H. Gordon.* Edited by Meir Lubetski, Claire Gottlieb, and Sharon R. Keller. JSOT Sup 273. Sheffield: Sheffield Academic Press, 1998.

Macadam, M. F. Laming. *The Temples of Kawa: The Inscriptions.* London: Oxford University Press, 1941.

Macalister, Robert Alexander Stewart, and J. Garrow Duncan. *Excavations on the Hill of Ophel, Jerusalem, 1923–1925.* Palestine Exploration Fund Annual 4. London: Palestine Exploration Fund, 1926.

Machinist, Peter. "Assyria and Its Image in First Isaiah." *JAOS* 103 (1983): 719–37.

———. "The Assyrians and Their Babylonian Problem: Some Reflections." *Wissenschaftskolleg zu Berlin, Jahrbuch* (1984): 353–64.

———. "The *Rab šāqēh* at the Wall of Jerusalem: Israelite Identity in the Face of the Assyrian 'Other.'" *HS* 41 (2000): 151–68.

MacLean, Samuel. "Jehoiakim." *IDB* 2:814.

Maeir, Aren. "Jerusalem Before King David: An Archaeological Survey from Protohistoric Times to the End of the Iron Age I" [Hebrew]. Pages 33–65 in *The History of Jerusalem: The Biblical Period.* Edited by Shmuel Ahituv and Amihai Mazar. Jerusalem: Yad Izhak Ben-Zvi, 2000.

Magen, Yitzhak. "Mount Gerizim." *NEAEHL* 2:484–92.

———. "Mount Gerizim and the Samaritans." Pages 91–148 in *Early Christianity in Context.* Edited by F. Manns and E. Alliata. Studium Biblicum Franciscanum Collectio Maior 38. Jerusalem: Franciscan Printing, 1993.

———. "Mount Gerizim—A Temple City" [Hebrew]. *Qad* 23/3–4 (1990): 70–96.

———. "Mount Gerizim—A Temple City" [Hebrew]. *Qad* 33/2 (2000): 74–118.

Magen, Yitzhak, L. Tsefania, and Haggai Misgav. "The Hebrew and Aramaic Inscriptions from Mt. Gerizim" [Hebrew]. *Qad* 33/2 (2000): 125–32.

Maisels, Charles Keith. *The Emergence of Civilization: From Hunting and Gathering to Agriculture, Cities, and the State in the Near East.* London: Routledge, 1990.

Marfoe, Leon. "Review of Early Arad I, by Ruth Amiran." *JNES* 31 (1980): 315–22.

Martin, Henri-Jean. *The History and Power of Writing*. Translated by Lydia G. Cochrane. Chicago: University of Chicago Press, 1994.

Marx, Emanuel. *The Bedouin of the Negev*. New York: Praeger, 1967.

Mattingly, Gerald L. "An Archaeological Analysis of Sargon's 712 Campaign Against Ashdod." *NEASB* 17 (1981): 47–64.

Mayer, Walter. *Politik und Kriegskunst der Assyrer*. ALASP 9. Münster: Ugarit-Verlag, 1995.

Mayes, Andrew D. H. *The Story of Israel between Settlement and Exile*. London: SCM, 1983.

Mazar, Amihai. *Archaeology of the Land of the Bible, 10,000–586 B.C.E.* ABRL. New York: Doubleday, 1990.

———. "Iron Age Chronology: A Reply to I. Finkelstein." *Levant* 29 (1997): 157–67.

———. "The Iron Age I." Pages 258–301 in *The Archaeology of Ancient Israel*. Edited by Amnon Ben-Tor. New Haven : Yale University Press, 1992.

———. "The 1997–1998 Excavations at Tel Rehov: Preliminary Report." *IEJ* 49 (1999): 1–42.

———. "On the Appearance of Red Slip in the Iron Age I Period in Israel." Pages 368–78 in *Mediterranean Peoples in Transition: Thirteenth to Early Tenth Centuries BCE*. Edited by Seymour Gitin, Amihai Mazar, and Ephraim Stern. Jerusalem: Israel Exploration Society, 1998.

Mazar, Amihai, and John Camp. "Will Tel Rehov Save the United Monarchy?" *BAR* 26/2 (2000): 38–51, 75.

Mazar, Benjamin. "The Campaign of Pharaoh Shishak to Palestine." Pages 57–66 in *Volume du congrès: Strasbourg, 1956*. VTSup 4. Leiden: Brill, 1957.

———. "The Cities of the Territory of Dan." *IEJ* 10 (1960): 65–77.

———."The Excavations in the Old City of Jerusalem Near the Temple Mount: Second Preliminary Report, 1969-1970 Seasons" [Hebrew]. *ErIsr* 10 (1971): 1–34.

———. "Gath and Gittaim." *IEJ* 4 (1954): 227–35.

———. "Jerusalem in the Biblical Period." Pages 11–44 in *Cities and Districts in Eretz-Israel* [Hebrew]. Edited by Benjamin Mazar. Jerusalem: Hotsaat Mosad Byalik, 1975.

———. "Jerusalem in the Biblical Period." Pages 1–8 in *Jerusalem Revealed: Archaeology in the Holy City 1968–1974*. Edited by Yigael Yadin. New Haven: Yale University Press, 1976.

Mazar, Eilat. "Excavate King David's Palace!" *BAR* 23/1 (1997): 50–57, 74.

———. "Jerusalem, The Ophel—1986." *ESI* 5 (1986): 56–58.

————. "The Undiscovered Palace of King David in Jerusalem—A Study in Biblical Archaeology" [Hebrew]. Pages 9–20 in *New Studies on Jerusalem: Proceedings of the Second Conference*. Edited by Avraham Faust. Ramat Gan: Bar-Ilan University, 1996.

Mazar, Eilat, and Benjamin Mazar. *Excavations in the South of the Temple Mount: The Ophel of Biblical Jerusalem*. Qedem 29. Jerusalem: Institute of Archaeology, Hebrew University of Jerusalem, 1989.

McCarter, P. Kyle, Jr. *1 Samuel*. AB 8. New York: Doubleday, 1980.

————. *II Samuel*. AB 9. Garden City, N.Y.: Doubleday, 1984.

McKay, John. *Religion in Judah under the Assyrians*. SBT 26; Naperville, Ill.: Allenson, 1973.

McKenzie, Steven L. *The Chronicler's Use of the Deuteronomistic History*. HSM 33. Atlanta: Scholars Press, 1985.

————. *The Trouble with Kings: The Composition of the Book of Kings in the Deuteronomistic History*. Leiden: Brill, 1991.

Mercer, Samuel. "A Scarab of Shabaka, First King of the 25th or Ethiopic Dynasty of Egypt." *Bulletin of the Royal Ontario Museum of Archaeology* 10 (May, 1931): 2–5.

Meshorer, Yaakov, and Shraga Qedar. *The Coinage of Samaria in the Fourth Century B.C.E.* Beverly Hills: Numismatics Fine Arts International, 1991.

Metzger, Martin. *Königsthron und Gottesthron: Tronformen und Throndarstellungen in Ägypten und in Vorderen Orient im dritten und zweiten Jahrtausend vor Christus und deren Bedeutung für das Verständnis von Aussagen über den Thron im Alten Testament*. AOAT 15/1–2. Neukirchen-Vluyn: Neukirchener Verlag, 1985.

Meyers, Carol, and Eric Meyers. *Haggai, Zechariah 1–8*. AB 25B. Garden City, N.Y.: Doubleday, 1987.

Michaeli, Frank. *Les Livres des Chroniques, d'Esdras et de Neahéamie*. CAT 16. Neuchactel: Delachaux & Nestlea, 1967.

Millard, Alan Ralph. "Assyrian Involvement in Edom." Pages 35–39 in *Early Edom and Moab: The Beginning of the Iron Age in Southern Jordan*. Sheffield Archaeological Monographs 7. Edited by Piotr Bienkowski. Sheffield: J. R. Collis, 1992.

————. *The Eponyms of the Assyrian Empire 910–612 BC*. SAAS 2. Helinski: Neo-Assyrian Text Corpus Project, 1994.

————. "Large Numbers in the Assyrian Royal Inscriptions." Pages 213–22 in *Ah, Assyria. . . : Studies in Assyrian History and Ancient Near Eastern Historiography Presented to Hayim Tadmor*. Edited by Mordechai Cogan and Israel Eph'al. ScrHier 33. Jerusalem: Magnes, 1991.

————. "Sennacherib's Attack on Hezekiah." *TynBul* 36 (1985): 61–77.

Miller, J. Maxwell. "Separating the Solomon of History from the Solomon of Legend." Pages 1–24 in *The Age of Solomon: Scholarship at the*

Turn of the Millennium. Edited by Lowell K. Handy. Leiden: Brill, 1997.

Miller, J. Maxwell, and John H. Hayes. *A History of Ancient Israel and Judah*. Philadelphia: Westminster, 1986.

Mills, E., ed. *Census of Palestine, 1931*. Alexandria: Government of Palestine, 1933.

Mittmann, Siegfried. "Eine prophetische Totenklage des Jahres 701 v. Chr. (Micha 1:3–5a.8–13a.14–16)." *JNSL* 25 (1999): 31–60.

Monson, John. "The New ʿAin Dārā Temple, Closest Solomonic Parallel." *BAR* 26/3 (2000): 20–35, 67.

Moran, William L. *The Amarna Letters*. Baltimore: Johns Hopkins University Press, 1992.

Mori, Cesare *The Last Struggle with the Mafia*. London: Putnam, 1933.

Mosis, Rudolf. *Untersuchungen zur Theologie des chronistischen Geschichtswerkes*. Freiburg: Herder, 1973.

Moya, Paula M. L., "Introduction—Reclaiming Identity," Pages 1–26 in *Reclaiming Identity: Realist Theory and the Predicament of Postmodernism*. Edited by Paula M. L. Moya and Michael R. Hames-García. Berkeley and Los Angeles: University of California Press, 2000.

Murnane, William. *Ancient Egyptian Coregencies*. Chicago: Oriental Institute, 1977.

Naʾaman, Nadav. "Ahaz's and Hezekiah's Policy toward Assyria in the Days of Sargon II and Sennacherib's Early Years" [Hebrew]. *Zion* 59 (1994): 5–30.

———. "Amarna Letters." *ABD* 1:174–81.

———. *Borders and Districts in Biblical Historiography*. Jerusalem Biblical Studies 4. Jerusalem: Simor, 1986.

———. "The Brook of Egypt and Assyrian Policy on the Border of Egypt." *TA* 6 (1979): 68–90

———. "Canaanite Jerusalem and its Central Hill Country Neighbours in the Second Millennium B.C.E." *UF* 24 (1992): 275–91.

———. "The 'Conquest of Canaan' in the Book of Joshua and in History." Pages 218–81 in *From Nomadism to Monarchy: Archaeological and Historical Aspects of Early Israel*. Edited by Israel Finkelstein and Nadav Naʾaman. Jerusalem: Israel Exploration Society, 1994.

———. "The Contribution of the Amarna Letters to the Debate on Jerusalem's Political Position in the Tenth Century B.C.E." *BASOR* 304 (1996): 17–27.

———. "Cow Town or Royal Capital? Evidence for Iron Age Jerusalem." *BAR* 23/4 (1997): 43–47, 67.

———. "The Debated Historicity of Hezekiah's Reform in the Light of Historical and Archaeological Research." *ZAW* 107 (1995): 179–95.

———. "Hezekiah and the Kings of Assyria." *TA* 21 (1994): 235–54.

———. "Hezekiah's Fortified Cities and the *LMLK* Stamps." *BASOR* 261 (1989): 5–21.

———. "The Historical Portion of Sargon II's Nimrud Inscription." *SAAB* 8 (1994): 17–20.

———. "The Kingdom of Judah under Josiah." *TA* 18 (1991): 3–71.

———. "Sennacherib's Campaign in Judah and the Date of the *lmlk* Stamps." *VT* 29 (1979): 61–81.

———. "Sennacherib's 'Letter to God' on his Campaign to Judah." *BASOR* 214 (1974): 25–39.

———. "Shishak's Campaign to Palestine As Reflected by the Epigraphic, Biblical and Archaeological Evidence" [Hebrew]. *Zion* 63 (1998): 247–76.

Nadelman, Yonatan "Hebrew Inscriptions, Seal Impressions, and Markings of the Iron Age II." Pages 128–137 in *Excavations in the South of the Temple Mount: The Ophel of Biblical Jerusalem*. Edited by Eilat Mazar and Benjamin Mazar. Qedem 29. Jerusalem: Institute of Archaeology, Hebrew University of Jerusalem, 1989.

Naveh, Joseph, and Yitzhak Magen. "Aramaic and Hebrew Inscriptions of the Second-Century BCE at Mount Gerizim." *'Atiqot* 32 (1997): 9*–17*.

Nelson, Richard D. *The Double Redaction of the Deuteronomistic History*. JSOTSup 18. Sheffield: Sheffield Academic Press, 1981.

Nicholson, Ernest W. "The Pentateuch in Recent Research: A Time for Caution." Pages 10–21 in *Congress Volume: Leuven, 1989*. VTSup 43. Leiden: Brill, 1991.

Niditch, Susan. *Ancient Israelite Religion*. New York: Oxford University Press, 1997.

Niemann, Hermann M. *Herrschaft, Königtum und Staat: Skizzen zur soziokulturelle Entwicklung im monarchischen Israel*. FAT 6. Tübingen: Mohr Siebeck, 1993.

———. "Megiddo and Solomon—A Biblical Investigation in Relation to Archaeology." *TA* 27 (2000): 59–72.

———. "The Socio-Political Shadow Cast by Biblical Solomon." Pages 252–95 in *The Age of Solomon: Scholarship at the Turn of the Millennium*. Edited by Lowell K. Handy. Leiden: Brill, 1997.

———. "Stadt, Land und Herrschaft: Skizzen und Materialien zur Sozialgeschichte im monarchischen Israel." Unpublished D.S.T. dissertation. Universität Rostock, 1990.

Noble, David F. *The Religion of Technology: The Divinity of Man and the Spirit of Invention*. New York: Knopf, 1997.

Noth, Martin. *The History of Israel*. New York: Harper & Row, 1958.

———. *Überlieferungsgeschichtliche Studien*. Tübingen: Niemeyer, 1943.

O'Connor, David. *Anceint Nubia: Egypt's Rival in Africa*. Philadelphia: University Museum, 1993.

Oded, Bustenay. "History vis-à-vis Propaganda in the Assyrian Royal Inscriptions." *VT* 48 (1998): 423–25.

Odorico, Marco de. *The Use of Numbers and Quantifications in the Assyrian Royal Inscriptions.* SAAS 3. Helinski: Neo-Assyrian Text Corpus Project, 1995.

Oeming, Manfred. "Die Eroberung Jerusalems durch David in deuteronomisticher und chronistischer Darstellung (II Sam 5,6 und 1 Chr 11,4–8): Ein Beitrag zur narrativen Theologie de beiden Geschichtswerke." *ZAW* 106 (1994): 404–20.

———. *Das wahre Israel: die "genealogische Vorhalle" 1 Chronik 1–9.* BWANT 128. Stuttgart: Kohlhammer, 1990.

Ofer, Avi. "'All the Hill Country of Judah': From a Settlement Fringe to a Prosperous Monarchy." Pages 92–121 in *From Nomadism to Monarchy: Archaeological and Historical Aspects of Early Israel.* Edited by Israel Finkelstein and Nadav Na'aman. Jerusalem: Israel Exploration Society, 1994.

———. "The Highland of Judah during the Biblical Period" [Hebrew]. Unpublished Ph.D. dissertation. Tel Aviv University, 1993.

———. "Judah." *OEANE* 3:253–57.

———. "The Judean Hills in the Biblical Period" [Hebrew]. *Qad* 115 (1998): 40–52.

———. "The Monarchic Period in the Judean Highland: A Spatial Overview." Pages 14–37 in *Studies in the Archaeology of the Iron Age in Israel and Jordan.* Edited by Amihai Mazar. JSOTSup 331. Sheffield: Sheffield Academic Press, 2001.

Ofer, Avi, and Amihai Mazar. "Discussion." Pages 628–30 in *Biblical Archaeology Today, 1990: Proceedings of the Second International Congress on Biblical Archaeology.* Edited by Avraham Biran and Joseph Aviram. Jerusalem: Israel Exploration Society, 1993.

Office of Statistics. *Village Statistics, Jerusalem 1938.* Jerusalem: Government of Palestine, 1938.

———. *Village Statistics, Jerusalem, 1945.* Jerusalem: Government of Palestine, 1945.

Olley, John W. "'Trust in the Lord': Hezekiah, Kings and Isaiah." *TynBul* 50 (1999): 59–77.

Osborne, Robin. *Greece in the Making, 1220–479 B.C.* Routledge History of the Ancient World. London: Routledge, 1996.

Otto, Eckart. *Jerusalem—Die Geschichte der Heiligen Stadt: Von den Anfängen bis zur Kreuzfahrerzeit.* Stuttgart: Kohlhammer, 1980.

Ovadiah, Ruth. "Jerusalem, Giv'at Massu'a." *ESI* 12 (1994): 71–76.

Parpola, Simo. *Letters from Assyria and the West.* Part 1 of *The Correspondence of Sargon II.* SAA 1. Helsinki: Helsinki University Press, 1987.

Pasquinucci, Marinella, and Frederic Trément, eds. *Non-Destructive Techniques Applied to Landscape Archaeology*. Vol. 4 of *The Archaeology of Mediterranean Landscapes*. Oxford: Oxbow, 1999.

Patterson, Thomas C. "Development, Ecology, and Marginal Utility in Anthropology." *Dialectical Anthropology* 15 (1987): 15–31.

———. "Some Postwar Trends in U.S. Archaeology." *Culture* 4 (1986): 43–54.

Paul, Shalom. Amos: *A Commentary on the Book of Amos*. Hermenia. Philadephia: Fortress, 1991.

Perdue, Leo G. *The Collapse of History: Reconstructing Old Testament Theology*. OBT. Minneapolis: Fortress, 1994.

Person, Raymond F., Jr. "II Kings 18–20 and Isaiah 36–39: A Text Critical Case Study in the Redaction History of the Book of Isaiah." *ZAW* 111 (1999): 373–79.

Petrie, William M. F. *Tell el-Hesy (Lachish)*. London: Palestine Exploration Fund, 1891.

Pečírková, Jana. "Assyria under Sennacherib." *ArOr* 61 (1993): 1–10.

Placher, William. "Is the Bible True?" *ChrCent* 112 (11 October 1995): 924–28.

Polignac, François de. *Cults, Territory, and the Origins of the Greek City-State*. Chicago: Chicago University Press, 1995.

Polzin, Robert. *Late Biblical Hebrew: Toward an Historical Typology of Biblical Hebrew Prose*. Atlanta: Scholars Press, 1976.

Pongratz-Leisten, Beate. *Herrschaftswissen in Mesopotamien*. SAAS 10. Helsinki: Neo-Assyrian Text Corpus Project, 1999.

———. "The Interplay of Military Strategy and Cultic Practice in Assyrian Politics." Pages 245–52 in *Assyria 1995: Proceedings of the Tenth Anniversary Synoposium of the Neo-Assyrian Text Corpus Project Helsinki, September 7–11, 1995*. Edited by Simo Parpola and Robert M. Whiting. Helsinki: Neo-Assyrian Text Corpus Project, 1997.

Porten, Bezalel. *Archives From Elephantine*. Berkeley and Los Angeles: University of California Press, 1968.

Porten, Bezalel, and Ada Yardeni. *Letters*. Vol. 1 of *Textbook of Aramaic Documents from Ancient Egypt: Newly Copied, Edited and Translated into Hebrew and English*. Jerusalem: Hebrew University of Jerusalem, Department of the History of the Jewish People, 1986.

Posener, Georges. *Princes et pays d'Asie et de Nubie*. Brussels: Fondation Egyptologique Reine Elisabeth, 1940.

Postgate, John Nicholas. "How Many Sumerians Per Hectare? Probing the Anatomy of an Early City [Tell Abu Salabikh]." *Cambridge Archaeological Journal* 4 (1994): 47–65.

———. *Taxation and Conscription in the Assyrian Empire*. Studia Pohl: Series Maior. Rome: Biblical Institute Press, 1974.

Prag, Kay. "Decorative Architecture in Ammon, Moab, and Judah." *Levant* 19 (1987): 121–27.

———. "Summary of the Report on Caves I, II and III and Deposit IV." Pages 209–20 in *Excavations by Kathleen M. Kenyon in Jerusalem 1961–1967, Vol. IV, The Iron Age Cave Deposits on the South-east Hill and Isolated Burials and Cemeteries Elsewhere*. Edited by Itzhak Eshel and Kay Prag. Oxford: Oxford University Press, 1995.

Pratico, Gary D. *Nelson Glueck's 1938–1940 Excavations at Tell el-Kheleifeh: A Reappraisal*. Atlanta: Scholar's Press, 1993.

Pritchard, James B. "Industry and Trade at Biblical Gibeon." *BA* 23 (1960): 23–29.

Proksch, Otto. "Das Jerusalem Jesajas." *PJ* 26 (1930): 12–40.

Provan, Iain William. *Hezekiah in the Book of Kings*. BZAW 172. Berlin: de Gruyter, 1988.

———. "In the Stable with Dwarves: Testimony, Interpretation, Faith and the History of Israel." Pages 281–319 in *Congress Volume: Oslo, 1998*. Edited by André Lemaire and Maqne Sæbø. VTSup 80. Leiden: Brill, 2000.

Purvis, James D. "Exile and Return." Pages 151–75 in *Ancient Israel: A Short History from Abraham to the Roman Destruction of the Temple*. Edited by Hershel Shanks. Englewood Cliffs, N.J.: Prentice-Hall, 1988.

Pury, Albert de. "Yahwist ('J') Source." *ABD* 6:1016–20.

Raban, Avner. "Standardized Collared-Rim Pithoi and Short-Lived Settlements." Pages 493–518 in *Studies in the Archaeology of Israel and Neighboring Lands in Memory of Douglas L. Esse*. Edited by Samuel R. Wolff. Chicago: Oriental Institute of the University of Chicago; Atlanta: American Schools of Oriental Research, 2001.

Rad, Gerhard von. *The Theology of Israel's Prophetic Traditions*. Vol. 2 of *Old Testament Theology*. 2 vols. New York: Harper & Row, 1965.

Rainey, Anson F. "The Biblical Shephelah of Judah." *BASOR* 251 (1983): 1–22.

———. "The Chronicler and His Sources—Historical and Geographical." Pages 30–72 in *The Chronicler As Historian*. Edited by M. Patrick Graham, Kenneth G. Hoglund, and Steven L. McKenzie. JSOTSup 238. Sheffield: Sheffield Academic Press, 1997.

———. "The Identification of Philistine Gath—A Problem in Source Analysis for Historical Geography." *ErIsr* 12 (1975): 63*–76*.

———. "Taharqa and Syntax." *TA* 3 (1976): 38–41.

Redford, Donald B. *Egypt, Canaan, and Israel in Ancient Times*. Princeton: Princeton University Press, 1992.

———. "A Note on the Chronology of Dynasty 25 and the Inscription of Sargon II at Tang-i Var." *Or* 68 (1999): 58–60.

———. "Sais and the Kushite Invasions." *JARCE* 22 (1985): 5-15.

Reich, Ronny. "The Ancient Burial Ground in the Mamilla Neighbourhood, Jerusalem." Pages 111–18 in: *Ancient Jerusalem Revealed*. Edited by Hillel Geva. Jerusalem: Israel Exploration Society, 1994.

———. "The Ancient Burial Ground in the Mamilla Neighbourhood, Jerusalem." Pages 111–18 in *Ancient Jerusalem Revealed: Expanded Edition 2000*. Edited by Hillel Geva. Jerusalem: Israel Exploration Society, 2000.

———. "Four Notes on Jerusalem." IEJ 37 (1987): 158–67.

———. "The Topography and Archaeology of Jerusalem in the First Temple Period" [Hebrew]. Pages 93–130 in *The History of Jerusalem: The Biblical Period*. Edited by Shmuel Ahituv and Amihai Mazar. Jerusalem: Yad Izhak Ben-Zvi, 2000.

Reich, Ronny, and Eli Shukron. "Channel II in the City of David, Jerusalem, Some Technical Features and Their Chronology" [Hebrew]. Page 3 in *Eleventh International Conference on Water in Antiquity*. Jerusalem: Israel Nature and Parks Authority, 2001.

———. "The Excavations at the Gihon Spring and Warren's Shaft System in the City of David." Pages 327–39 in *Ancient Jerusalem Revealed: Expanded Edition 2000*. Edited by Hillel Geva. Jerusalem: Israel Exploration Society, 2000.

———. "Four Notes on Jerusalem." *IEJ* 37 (1987): 158-167.

———. "Jerusalem, City of David." *ESI* 18 (1998): 91–92.

———. "Jerusalem, City of David." *Hadashot Arkheologiyot* 112 (2000): 82*–83*.

———. "Jerusalem, City of David." *Hadashot Arkheologiyot* 114 (2002): 77*–78*.

———. "Jerusalem, Gihon Spring." *ESI* 20 (2000): 99*–100*.

———. "Light at the End of the Tunnel." *BAR* 25/1 (1999): 22–33.

———. "New Excavations in the City of David" [Hebrew]. Pages 3–8 in *New Studies on Jerusalem: Proceedings of the Third Conference*. Edited by Avraham Faust and Eyal Baruch. Ramat Gan: Bar-Ilan University, 1997.

———. "New Excavations on the Eastern Slope of the City of David" [Hebrew]. *Qad* 34/2 (2001): 78–87.

———. "The System of Rock-Cut Tunnels near Gihon in Jerusalem Reconsidered." *RB* 107 (2000): 5–17.

———. "A Wall from the End of the First Temple Period in the Eastern Part of the City of David" [Hebrew]. Pages 14–16 in *New Studies on Jerusalem: Proceedings of the Fourth Conference*. Edited by Avraham Faust and Eyal Baruch. Ramat Gan: Bar-Ilan University, 1998.

Reiner, Erica *Šurpu: A Collection of Sumerian and Akkadian Incantations*. AfOB 11. Graz: n.p., 1958.

Rendsburg, Gary. "Late Biblical Hebrew and the Date of P." *JANESCU* 12 (1980): 65–80.

Rendtorff, Rolf. *The Problem of the Process of Transmission in the Pentateuch.* Translated by J. Scullion. JSOTSup 89. Sheffield: Sheffield Academic Press, 1990.

———. *Das Überlieferungsgeschichtliche Problem des Pentateuch.* Berlin: de Gruyter, 1977.

Renfrew, Colin. "Systems Collapse As Social Transformation: Catastrophe and Anastrophe in Early State Societies." Pages 481–505 in *Transformations: Mathematical Approaches to Culture Change.* Edited by Colin Renfrew and Kenneth L. Cooke. New York: Academic, 1979.

———. "Transformations." Pages 3–44 in *Transformations: Mathematical Approaches to Culture Change.* Edited by Colin Renfrew and Kenneth L. Cooke. New York: Academic, 1979.

Renger, Johannes. "Neuassyrische Königsinschriften als Genre der Keilschriftliteratur—Zum Stil und zur Kompositionstechnik der Inschriften Sargons II von Assyrien." Pages 109–28 in *Keilschriftliche Literaturen.* Edited by Karl Hecker and Walter Sommerfeld. RAI 32. BBVO 6. Berlin: Reimar, 1986.

Richter, Werner. *Israel und seine Nachbarräume: Ländliche Siedlungen und Landnutzung seit dem 19. Jahrhundert.* Erdwissenschaftliche Forschung 14. Wiesbaden: Steiner, 1979.

Ritmeyer, Leen "Locating the Original Temple Mount." *BAR* 18/2 (1992): 24–45.

Roberts, J. J. M. "Blindfolding the Prophet: Political Resistance to First Isaiah's Oracles in the Light of Ancient Near Eastern Attitudes toward Oracles." Pages 135-46 in *Oracles et Prophéties dans l'Antiquité: Actes du Colloque de Strasbourg 15–17 juin 1995.* Edited by Jean-Georges Heintz. Université des Sciences Humaines de Strasbourg, Travaux du Centre de Recherche sur le Proche-Orient et la Grèce Antiques 15. Strasbourg: de Boccard, 1997.

———. "The Davidic Origin of the Zion Tradition." *JBL* 92 (1973): 329–44.

———. "The Divine King and the Human Community in Isaiah's Vision of the Future." Pages 127–36 in *The Quest for the Kingdom of God: Studies in Honor of George E. Mendenhall.* Edited by Herbert B. Huffmon, Frank A. Spina, and Alberto R. W. Green. Winona Lake, Ind.: Eisenbrauns, 1983.

———. "In Defense of the Monarchy: The Contribution of Israelite Kingship to Biblical Theology." Pages 377–96 in *Ancient Israelite Religion: Essays in Honor of Frank Moore Cross.* Edited by Patrick D. Miller, Paul D. Hanson, and S. Dean McBride. Philadelphia: Fortress , 1987.

———. "Isaiah 2 and the Prophet's Message to the North." *JQR* 75 (1985): 290–308.

———. "Isaiah 33: An Isaianic Elaboration of the Zion Tradition." Pages 15–25 in *The Word of the Lord Shall Go Forth.* Edited by Carol L. Meyers and Michael O'Connor. Winona Lake, Ind.: Eisenbrauns, 1983.

————. "Isaiah and His Children." Pages 193–203 in *Biblical and Related Studies Presented to Samuel Iwry*. Edited by Ann Kort and Scott Morschauser. Winona Lake, Ind.: Eisenbrauns, 1985.

————. "Isaiah in Old Testament Theology." *Int* 36 (April 1982): 130–43.

————. "The King of Glory." *PSB* NS 3/1 (1980): 5–10.

————. "The Meaning of *ṣemaḥ h'* in Isaiah 4:2." Pages 110–18 in Haim M. I. Gevaryahu Memorial Volume. Edited by Joshua J. Adler. Jerusalem: World Jewish Bible Center, 1990.

————. "A Note on Isaiah 28:12." *HTR* (1981): 49–51.

————. "The Old Testament's Contribution to Messianic Expectation." Pages 39–51 in *The Messiah: Developments in Earliest Judaism and Christianity*. Edited by James H. Charlesworth. Minneapolis: Fortress, 1992.

————. "The Religio-Political Setting of Psalm 47." *BASOR* 221 (1976): 129–32.

————. "Yahweh's Foundation in Zion (Isa 28:16)." *JBL* 106 (1987): 27–45.

————. "Zion in the Theology of the Davidic-Solomonic Empire." Pages 93–108 in *Studies in the Period of David and Solomon and Other Essays*. Edited by Tomoo Ishida. Tokyo: Yamakawa-Shuppansha, 1982.

————. "Zion Tradition." *IDBSup*, 985–87.

Robinson, Edward. *Biblical Researches in Palestine, Mount Sinai and Arabia Petraea: A Journal of Travels in the Year 1838 Undertaken in the Reference to Biblical Geography*. Vol. 1. London: Murray, 1841.

Rofé, Alexander "Ephraimite versus Deuteronomistic History." Pages 221–35 in *Storia e tradizioni di Israele*. Brescia: Paideia, 1991.

————. *The Prophetic Stories: The Narratives about the Prophets in the Hebrew Bible, Their Literary Types, and History*. Jerusalem: Magnes, 1988.

Rogers, Jeffrey S. "Synchronism and Structure in 1–2 Kings and Mesopotamian Chronographic Literature." Unpublished Ph.D. dissertation. Princeton Theological Seminary, 1992.

Rohland, Edzard. "Die Bedeutung der Erwählungstraditionen Israels für die Eschatologie der alttestamentlichen Propheten." Ph.D. dissertation. Heidelberg, 1956.

Ron, Zvi. "Agricultural Terraces in the Judean Mountains." *IEJ* 16 (1966): 111–22.

Rose, Martin. *Deuteronomist und Yahwist: Beruhrungspunkte beider Literaturwerke*. Zurich: Theologischer Verlag, 1982.

Rubin, Rehav. "Jerusalem and Its Environs: The Impact of Geographical and Physical Conditions on the Development of Jerusalem" [Hebrew.] Pages 1–12 in *The History of Jerusalem: The Biblical Period*. Edited by Shmuel Ahituv and Amihai Mazar. Jerusalem: Yad Izhak Ben-Zvi, 2000.

Rupprecht, Konrad. *Der Tempel von Jerusalem: Gründung Salomos oder jebusitisches Erbe?* BZAW 144. Berlin: de Gruyter, 1977.

Russell, John Malcolm. *The Writing on the Wall: Studies in the Architectural Context of Late Assyrian Palace Inscriptions.* Winona Lake, Ind.: Eisenbrauns, 1999.

Saggs, Henry William Frederick. "The Nimrud Letters, 1952—Part I, The Mukin-zer Rebellion and Related Texts." *Iraq* 17 (1955): 21–56.

———. "The Nimrud Letters, 1952—Part II." *Iraq* 17 (1955): 126–54.

Saller, Sylvester John. *Excavations at Bethany (1949–1953).* Jerusalem: Franciscan Press, 1957.

———. *The Excavations at Dominus Flevit (Mount Olivet, Jerusalem) Part II: The Jebusite Burial Place.* Publications of the Studium Biblicum Franciscanum 13. Jerusalem: Franciscan Press, 1964.

———. "Jerusalem and Its Surroundings in the Bronze Age." *LA* 12 (1962): 147–76.

Saulcy, Félicien J. C. de. *A Narrative of a Journey Round the Dead Sea and in the Bible Lands: In 1850 and 1851.* Vol 2. London: Bentley, 1854.

Schipper, Bernd Ulrich. *Israel und Ägypten in der Königszeit: Die kulturellen Kontakte von Salomo bis zum Fall Jerusalems.* OBO 170. Fribourg: Universitätsverlag; Göttingen: Vandenhoeck & Ruprecht, 1999.

Schleiermacher, Frederick. *The Christian Faith.* Translated and edited by H. R. Mackintosh and J. S. Stewart. Edinburgh: T&T Clark, 1963.

Schmid, Hans Heinrich. *Der sogenannte Jahwist.* Zurich: Theologischer Verlag, 1976.

Schniedewind, William. "The Geopolitical History of Philistine Gath." *BASOR* 309 (1998): 69–77.

———. "History and Interpretation: The Religion of Ahab and Manasseh in the Book of Kings." *CBQ* 55 (1993): 649–61.

———. "The Problem with Kings: Recent Study of the Deuteronomistic History." *RelSRev* 22 (1995): 22–27.

Scurlock, JoAnn. "Neo-Assyrian Battle Tactics." Pages 491–517 in *Crossing Boundaries and Linking Horizons: Studies in Honor of Michael C. Astour on His Eightieth Birthday.* Edited by Gordon D. Young, Mark W. Chavalas, and Richard E. Averbeck. Bethesda, Md.: CDL, 1997.

Selman, Martin. "Jerusalem in Chronicles." Pages 43–56 in *Zion, City of Our God.* Edited by Richard S. Hess and Gordon J. Wenham. Grand Rapids: Eerdmans, 1999.

Sethe, Kurt. *Die Ächtung feindlicher Fürsten Völker und Dinge auf altägyptischen Tongefässscherben des Mittleren Reiches.* Berlin: Akademie der Wissenschaften, 1926.

Shadmon, Asher. *Stone in Israel.* Jerusalem: Ministry of Development, 1972.

Shanks, Hershel. "Everything You Ever Knew about Jerusalem Is Wrong (Well, Almost)." *BAR* 25/6 (1999): 20–29.

———. *Jerusalem: An Archaeological Biography.* New York: Random House, 1995.

Shavit, Alon. "The Ayalon Valley and Its Vicinity during the Bronze and Iron Ages" [Hebrew]. Unpublished M.A. thesis. Tel Aviv University, 1992.

———. "Settlement Patterns in the Ayalon Valley in the Bronze and Iron Ages." *TA* 27 (2000): 189–230.

Shea, William H. "Jerusalem under Siege. Did Sennacherib Attack Twice?" *BAR* 25/6 (1999): 36–64.

———. "Sennacherib's Second Palestinian Campaign." *JBL* 104 (1985): 401–18.

Shiloh, Yigal. *Excavations at the City of David I, 1978–1982: Interim Report of the First Five Seasons*. Qedem 19. Jerusalem: Institute of Archaeology, Hebrew University of Jerusalem, 1984.

———. "Excavating Jerusalem: The City of David." *Arch* 33/6 (1980): 8–17.

———. "Jerusalem, City of David, 1982." *IEJ* 33 (1983): 129–31.

———. "Jerusalem, City of David, 1984." *IEJ* 35 (1985): 65–67.

———. "Jerusalem, City of David, 1985." *IEJ* 35 (1985): 301–3.

———. "Jerusalem: The Early Periods and the First Temple Period." *NEAEHL* 2:698–712.

———. "The Material Culture of Judah and Jerusalem in Iron Age II: Origins and Influences." Pages 113–46 in *The Land of Israel: Crossroads of Civilizations*. Edited by Edward Lipiński. Leuven: Peeters, 1985.

———. "The Population of Iron Age Palestine in the Light of a Sample Analysis of Urban Plans, Areas and Population Density." *BASOR* 239 (1980): 25–35.

———. *The Proto-Aeolic Capital and Israelite Ashlar Masonry*. Qedem 11. Jerusalem: Institute of Archaeology, Hebrew Univeristy of Jerusalem, 1979.

———. "Water Systems." *NEAEHL* 2:709–12.

Shiloh, Yigal, and Aharon Horowitz. "Ashlar Quarries of the Iron Age in the Hill Country of Israel." *BASOR* 217 (1975): 37–48.

Shukron, Eli. "A New Look at the Overflow Channel (IVA) and the Siloam Channel (II) in the Light of the New Excavations in the City of David— 1995" [Hebrew]. Page 5 in *Twenty-Second Archaeological Conference in Israel: Synopses of Lectures*. Jerusalem: Israel Exploration Society and Israel Antiquities Authority, 1996.

Sigrest, Christian. *Regulierte Anarchie: Untersuchungen zum Fehlen und zur Entstehung politischer Herrschaft in segmentären Gesellschaften Afrikas*. Olten-Frieburg: Walter, 1967.

Silberman, Neil Asher. *A Prophet from amongst You: The Life of Yigael Yadin*. Reading, Mass.: Addison-Wesley, 1993.

Simons, Jan. *Jerusalem in the Old Testament: Researches and Theories*. Leiden: Brill, 1952.

Sivan, Renee, and Giora Solar. "Excavations in the Jerusalem Citadel, 1980–1988." Pages 168–76 in *Ancient Jerusalem Revealed*. Edited by Hillel Geva. Jerusalem: Israel Exploration Society, 1994.

Snodgrass, Anthony M. *Archaic Greece: The Age of Experiment.* London: Dent & Sons, 1980.

Solar, Giora, and Renee Sivan. "Citadel Moat." *ESI* 3 (1984): 47–48.

Spalinger, Anthony J. "Esarhaddon and Egypt: An Analysis of the First Invasion of Egypt." *Or* 43 (1974): 295–326.

———. "The Foreign Policy of Egypt Preceding the Assyrian Conquest." *Chronique d'Égypte* 53 (1978): 22–47.

———. "Notes on the Military in Egypt during the XXVth Dynasty." *SSEAJ* 11 (1981): 37–58.

———. "The Year 712 BC and Its Implication for Egyptian History." *JARCE* 10 (1973): 95–101.

Spiegelberg, Wilhelm. *Aegyptologische Randglossen zum Alten Testamentum.* Strassburg: Schlesier & Schweikhardt, 1904.

Stager, Lawrence E. "The Archaeology of the Family in Ancient Israel." *BASOR* 260 (1985): 1–35.

———. "Jerusalem and the Garden of Eden." *ErIsr* 26 (1999) 183*–94*.

———. "Jerusalem As Eden." *BAR* 26/3 (2000): 36–47.

Starr, Ivan. *Queries to the Sungod: Divination and Politics in Sargonid Assyria.* SAA 4. Helsinki: Helsinki University Press, 1990.

Steiner, Margreet L. "The Archaeology of Ancient Jerusalem." *CurBS* 6 (1998): 143–68.

———. "David's Jerusalem: Fiction or Reality? It's Not There: Archaeology Proves a Negative." *BAR* 24/4 (1998): 26–33, 62–63.

———. *Excavations by Kathleen M. Kenyon in Jerusalem 1961–1967, Vol. III, The Settlement in the Bronze and Iron Ages.* Copenhagen International Series, 9. New York: Sheffield Academic Press, 2001.

———. "The Jebusite Ramp of Jerusalem: The Evidence from the Macalister, Kenyon and Shiloh Excavations." Pages 585–88 in *Biblical Archaeology Today, 1990: Proceedings of the Second International Congress on Biblical Archaeology.* Edited by Avraham Biran and Joseph Aviram. Jerusalem: Israel Exploration Society, 1993.

———. "Jerusalem in the Late Bronze and Early Iron Ages: Archaeological Versus Literary Sources?" Pages 3*–8* in *New Studies on Jerusalem: Proceedings of the Second Conference.* Edited by Avraham Faust. Ramat Gan: Bar-Ilan University, 1996.

———. "Jerusalem in the Tenth and Seventh Centuries BCE: From Administrative Town to Commercial City." Pages 280–88 in *Studies in the Archaeology of the Iron Age in Israel and Jordan.* Edited by Amihai Mazar. JSOTSup 331. Sheffield: Sheffield Academic Press, 2001.

———. "Letter to the Editor." *IEJ* 38 (1988): 203–4.

———. "Propaganda in Jerusalem: The Beginning of State Formation in Iron Age Judah." In *"I Will Tell Secret Things from Long Ago" (Abiah Chidot Minei-Kedem—Ps. 78:2b): Archaeological and Historical Stud-*

ies in Honor of Amihai Mazar on the Occasion of His Sixtieth Birthday. Edited by Aren Maeir and Pierre de Miroschedji. In press.

———. "Re-dating the Terraces of Jerusalem." *IEJ* 44 (1994): 13–20.

Steins, Georg. *Die Chronik als kanonisches AbscluOuphaunomen: Studien zur Enstehung und Theologie von 1/2 Chronik.* BBB 93. Weinheim: Athenauum, 1995.

Stern, Ephraim. "The Archaeology of Persian Palestine." Pages 88–114 in *Introduction; The Persian Period.* Edited by William D. Davies and Louis Finkelstein. CHJ 1. Cambridge: Cambridge University Press, 1984.

———. *The Assyrian, Babylonian, and Persian Periods 732–332 BCE.* Vol. 2 of *Archaeology of the Land of the Bible.* ABRL. New York: Doubleday, 2001

———. "The Persian Empire and the Political and Social History of Palestine in the Persian Period." Pages 70–87 in *Introduction; The Persian Period.* Edited by William D. Davies and Louis Finkelstein. CHJ 1. Cambridge: Cambridge University Press, 1984.

———. "What Happened to the Cult Figurines?" *BAR* 15/4 (1989): 22–29, 53–54.

Stern, Ephraim, and Yitzhak Magen. "The First Phase of the Samaritan Temple on Mount Gerizim—New Archaeological Evidence" [Hebrew]. *Qad* 33/2 (2000): 119–24.

Suleiman, Susan R., and Inge Crosman, eds. *The Reader in the Text: Essays on Audience and Interpretation.* Princeton: Princeton University Press, 1980.

Sweeney, Marvin A. *Isaiah 1–39, with an Introduction to Prophetic Literature.* FOTL 16. Grand Rapids: Eerdmans, 1996.

———. "Sargon's Threat against Jerusalem in Isaiah 10,27–32." *Bib* 75 (1994): 457–70.

Sweet, Louise Elizabeth. *Tell Tooqan: A Syrian Village.* Anthropological Papers of the Museum of Anthropology of the University of Michigan 14. Ann Arbor: University of Michigan Press, 1960.

Tadmor, Hayim. "The Campaigns of Sargon II of Assur: A Chronological-Historical Study." *JCS* 12 (1958): 22–100.

———. *The Inscriptions of Tiglath-Pileser III, King of Assyria.* Jerusalem: Israel Academy of Sciences, 1994.

———. "Judah." Pages 261–96 in *The Fourth Century B.C.* Edited by David M. Lewis et al. 2d ed. CAH 6. Cambridge: Cambridge University Press, 1994.

———. "On the Use of Aramaic in the Assyrian Empire: Three Observations on a Relief of Sargon II" [Hebrew]. *ErIsr* 20 (1989): 249-52.

———. "Philistia under Assyrian Rule." *BA* 39 (1966): 86–90.

———. "Sennacherib's Campaign to Judah: Historical and Historiographical Considerations" [Hebrew]. *Zion* 50 (1985): 65–80.

———. "World Dominion: The Expanding Horizon of the Assyrian Empire." Pages 55–62 in *Landscapes: Territories, Frontiers and Horizons in the Ancient Near East*. Edited by Lucio Milano, Stefano de Martino, Frederick M. Fales, and Giovanni B. Lanfranchi. RAI 44. HANEM 3/1. Padova: Sargon, 1999.

Tadmor, Hayim, Benno Landsberger, and Simo Parpola, "The Sin of Sargon and Sennacherib's Last Will." *SAAB* 3 (1989): 3–51.

Talmon, Shemaryahu. *King, Cult, and Calendar in Ancient Israel: Collected Studies*. Jerusalem: Magnes, 1986.

Tarler, David, and Jane M. Cahill. "David, City of." *ABD* 2:52–67.

Tatum, Lynn. "From Text to Tell: King Manasseh in the Biblical and Archaeological Record." Unpublished Ph.D. dissertation. Duke University, 1988.

———. "King Manasseh and the Royal Fortress at Horvat 'Uza." *BA* 54 (1991): 136–45.

Thom, Rene. *Structural Stability and Morphogenesis*. Translated by D. H. Fowler. Reading, Mass.: Benjamin, 1975.

Thompson, Henry O. "Hanes." *ABD* 3:49–50.

Thompson, Thomas L. *Early History of the Israelite People: From Written and Archaeological Sources*. Leiden: Brill, 1992.

———. *The Mythic Past: Biblical Archaeology and the Myth of Israel*. New York: Basic Books, 1999.

Throntveit, Mark A. "Hezekiah in the Books of Chronicles." Pages 302–11 in *Society of Biblical Literature 1988 Seminar Papers*. Edited by David J. Lull. SBLSP 27. Atlanta: Scholars Press, 1988.

———. *When Kings Speak: Royal Speech and Royal Prayer in Chronicles*. SBLDS 93. Atlanta: Scholars Press, 1987.

Timm, Stefan. *Die Dynastie Omri: Quellen und Untersuchungen zur Geschichte Israels im 9. Jahrhundert vor Christus*. FRLANT 124 Göttingen: Vandenhoeck & Ruprecht, 1982.

Török, Laszlo. *The Kingdom of Kush: Handbook of the Napatan-Merotic Civilization*. HO 31. Leiden: Brill, 1997.

Tracy, David. *Plurality and Ambiguity: Hermeneutics, Religion, Hope*. San Francisco: Harper & Row, 1987.

Trigger, Bruce G., et al. *Ancient Egypt: A Social History*. Cambridge: Cambridge University Press, 1983.

Tsafrir, Yoram, Leah Di Segni, and Judith Green. *Tabula Imperii Romani Iudaea Palestina*. Jerusalem: The Israel Academy of Sciences and Humanities, 1994.

Tufnell, Olga. *Lachish (Tell ed-Duweir), Vol. III, The Iron Age*. London: Oxford University Press, 1953.

Tushingham, A. Douglas. *Excavations by Kathleen M. Kenyon in Jerusalem, 1961–1967, Vol. I*. Toronto: Royal Ontario Museum, 1985.

————. "The 1961–67 Excavations in the Armenian Garden, Jerusalem: A Response." *PEQ* 120 (1988): 142–45.

————. "The Western Hill of Jerusalem: A Critique of the 'Maximalist Position.'" *Levant* 19 (1987): 137–43.

————. "The Western Hill under the Monarchy." *ZDPV* 95 (1979): 39–55.

Ussishkin, David. "The 'Camp of the Assyrians' in Jerusalem." *IEJ* 29 (1979): 137–42.

————. "The Destruction of Lachish by Sennacherib and the Dating of the Royal Judean Storage Jars." *TA* 4 (1977): 28–60.

————. "Excavations and Restoration Work at Tel Lachish 1985–1994: Third Preliminary Report." *TA* 23 (1996): 3–60.

————. "Excavations at Lachish—1973–1977, Preliminary Report." *TA* 5 (1978): 1–97.

————. "Excavations at Tel Lachish 1978–1983: Second Preliminary Report." *TA* 10 (1983): 97–175.

————. "Jerusalem during the Period of David and Solomon—The Archaeological Evidence" [Hebrew]. Pages 57–58 in *New Studies on Jerusalem: Proceedings of the Third Conference*. Edited by Avraham Faust and Eyal Baruch. Ramat Gan: Bar-Ilan University, 1997.

————. "Jezreel, Samaria, and Megiddo: Royal Centers of Omri and Ahab." Pages 351–64 in *Congress Volume: Cambridge, 1995*. Edited by John A. Emerton. VTSup 66. Leiden: Brill, 1997.

————. "King Solomon's Palace and Building 1723 in Megiddo." *IEJ* 16 (1966): 174–86.

————. "King Solomon's Palaces." *BA* 36 (1973): 78–105.

————. "Levels VII and VI at Tel Lachish and the End of the Late Bronze Age in Canaan." Pages 213–30 in *Palestine in the Bronze and Iron Ages: Papers in Honour of Olga Tufnell*. Edited by Jonathan N. Tubb. London: Institute of Archaeology, 1985.

————. "Solomon's Jerusalem: The Text and the Facts on the Ground." *TA*. Forthcoming.

————. *The Village of Silwan: The Necropolis from the Period of the Judean Kingdom*. Jerusalem: Israel Exploration Society, 1993.

————. "The Water Systems of Jerusalem during Hezekiah's Reign." Pages 289–307 in *Meilsteinen: Festgabe für Herbert Donner*. Edited by Manfred Weippert and Stefan Timm. Wiesbaden: Harrassowitz, 1995.

Ussishkin, David, and Woodhead, John. "Excavations at Tel Jezreel 1994–1996: Third Preliminary Report." *TA* 24 (1997): 6–72.

Van Seters, John. *Abraham in History and Tradition*. New Haven: Yale University Press, 1975.

————. *In Search of History: Historiography in the Ancient World and the Origins of Biblical History*. New Haven: Yale University Press, 1983.

———. *The Life of Moses: The Yahwist As Historian in Exodus-Numbers.* Louisville: Westminster John Knox, 1994.

———. "The Pentateuch." Pages 3–49 in *The Hebrew Bible Today.* Edited by Steven McKenzie and M. Patrick Graham. Louisville: Westminster John Knox, 1998.

———. *Prologue to History: The Yahwist As Historian in Genesis.* Louisville: Westminster John Knox, 1992.

Vanderhooft, David S., and Baruch Halpern. "The Editions of Kings in the 7th–6th Centuries B.C.E." *HUCA* 62 (1991): 179–244.

Vaughn, Andrew G. "How Can a History of Israel Be Theologically Relevant in a Post-Modern World?" In *The Future of Biblical Archaeology.* Edited by James Hoffmeier and Alan Millard. Grand Rapids: Eerdmans, forthcoming.

———. *Theology, History and Archaeology in the Chronicler's Account of Hezekiah.* SBLABS 4. Atlanta: Scholars Press, 1999.

Vaux, Roland de. "On the Right and Wrong Uses of Archaeology." Pages 70–76 in *Near Eastern Archaeology in the Twentieth Century.* Edited by James A. Sanders. Garden City, N.Y.: Doubleday, 1970.

Vercoutter, Jean. "The Napatan Kings and Apis Worship" (Serapeum Burials of the Napatan Period). *KUSH* 8 (1960): 62–76.

Vincent, Albert. *La Religion des Judéo-Araméens d'Éléphantine.* Paris: Geuthner, 1937.

Vincent, Louis-Hugues. *Underground Jerusalem: Discoveries on the Hill of Ophel (1909–1911).* London: Cox, 1911.

Vincent, Louis-Hugues, and P. M.-A. Stève. *Jérusalem de L'ancien testament: recherches d'archéologie et d'histoire.* 3 vols. Paris: Gabalda, 1954–56.

Vriezen, Karel J. H. *Die Ausgrabungen unter der Erlöscherkirche im Muristan, Jerusalem (1970–1974).* Abhandlungen der Deutschen Palästina-vereins 19. Wiesbaden: Harrassowitz, 1995.

Wagstaff, John Malcolm. *The Evolution of Middle Eastern Landscapes: An Outline to A.D. 1840.* London: Croom Helm, 1985.

Wanke, Gunther. *Die Zionstheologie der Korachiten in ihrem traditions-geschichtlichen Zusammenhang.* BZAW 97. Berlin: Töpelmann, 1966.

Watzman, Haim. "Biblical Iconoclast: Israel Finkelstein Tilts with Colleagues over the History of Early Iron Age Palestine." *Arch* 54/4 (2001): 30–33.

Weidner, E. F. "Šilkan(ḫe)ni, König von Muṣri, ein Zeitgenosse Sargons II. Nach einem neuen Bruchstück der Prisma-Inschrift des assyrischen Königs." *AfO* (1941–44): 40–56.

Weill, Raymond. *La Cité de David: Compte-rendu des Fouilles à Jérusalem sur la Site de la Ville Primitive.* 2 vols. Paris: Geuthner, 1920–47.

Weinfeld, Moshe. "The Emergence of the Deuteronomic Movement: The Historical Antecedents." Pages 89–95 in *Das Deuteronomium: Entstehung,*

Gestalt und Botschaft. Edited by N. Lohfink. Leuven: Leuven University Press, 1985.

Weinstein, James M. "Egypt and the Middle Bronze IIC/Late Bronze IA Transition in Palestine." *Levant* 23 (1991): 105–15.

———. "The Egyptian Empire in Palestine: A Reassessment." *BASOR* 241 (1981): 1–28.

Weissert, Elhanan. "Creating a Political Climate: Literary Allusions to *Enūma Eliš* in Sennacherib's Account of the Battle of Halule." Pages 191–202 in *Assyrien im Wandel der Zeiten*. Edited by Harmut Waetzoldt and Harold Hauptmann. RAI 39. Heidelberger Studien zum alten Orient 6. Heidelberg: Heidelberger Orientverlag, 1997.

Welten, Peter. *Geschichte und Geschichtsdarstellung in den Chronikbüchern.* WMANT 42. Neukirchen-Vluyn: Neukirchener Verlag, 1973.

———. "Lade-Tempel-Jerusalem: Zur Theologie der Chronikbücher." Pages 169–83 in *Textgemäss: Aufsätze und Beiträge zur Hermeneutik des alten Testaments: Festschrift für Ernst Würthwein zum 70. Geburtstag.* Edited by Antonius H. J. Gunneweg and Otto Kaiser. Göttingen: Vandenhoeck & Ruprecht, 1979.

Wengrow, David. "Egyptian Taskmasters and Heavy Burdens: Highland Exploitation and the Collard-Rim Pithos of the Bronze/Iron Age Levant." *OJA* 15 (1996): 307–26.

Whitelam, Keith W. *The Invention of Ancient Israel: The Silencing of Palestinian History*. London: Routledge, 1996.

Widengren, Geo. "The Persian Period." Pages 489–538 in *Israelite and Judean History*. Edited by John H. Hayes and J. Maxwell Miller. London: SCM, 1977.

Wightman, Gregory J. *The Walls of Jerusalem from the Canaanites to the Mamluks*. Mediterranean Archaeology Supplement 4. Sydney: University of Sydney, 1993.

Williamson, Hugh G. M. *The Book Called Isaiah: Deutero-Isaiah's Role in Composition and Redaction*. Oxford: Clarendon, 1994.

———. *Ezra, Nehemiah*. WBC 16. Waco, Tex.: Word, 1985.

———. *1 and 2 Chronicles*. NCB. Grand Rapids: Eerdmans, 1982.

———. *Israel in the Books of Chronicles*. Cambridge: Cambridge University Press, 1977.

———. "Nehemiah's Walls Revisited." *PEQ* 116 (1984): 81–88.

———. "Tel Jezreel and the Dynasty of Omri." *PEQ* 128 (1996): 41–51.

———. "The Temple in the Books of Chronicles." Pages 15–31 in *Templum Amicitae: Essays on the Second Temple Presented to Ernst Bammel*. Edited by William Horbury. JSNTSup 48. Sheffield: JSOT Press, 1991.

———. " 'We Are Yours, O David': The Setting and Purpose of 1 Chronicles xii 1–23." *OtSt* 21 (1981): 164–76.

Winckler, Hugo. *Die Keilschrifttexte Sargons*. Leipzig: Pfeiffer, 1889.

Winter, Irene J. "North Syrian Ivories and Tell Halaf Reliefs: The Impact of Luxury Goods upon 'Major' Arts." Pages 321–32 in *Essays in Ancient Civilization Presented to Helene J. Kantor.* Edited by Albert Leonard and Bruce B. Williams. Studies in Ancient Oriental Civilization 47. Chicago: Oriental Institute of the Unversity of Chicago, 1989.

Wittfogel, Karl August. *Oriental Despotism.* New Haven: Yale University Press, 1957.

Wright, John Wesley. "The Legacy of David in Chronicles: The Narrative Function of 1 Chronicles 23–27." *JBL* 110 (1991): 229–42.

Yadin, Yigael. "The Blind and the Lame and David's Conquest of Jerusalem" [Hebrew]. Page 222 in *Proceedings of the First World Congress of Jewish Studies.* Jerusalem: Magnes, 1952.

———. *Hazor: The Rediscovery of a Great Citadel from the Bible.* London: Weidenfeld & Nicholson, 1975.

———. "The 'House of Baal' of Ahab and Jezebel in Samaria, and That of Athalia in Judah." Pages 127–35 in *Archaeology in the Levant: Essays for Kathleen Kenyon.* Edited by Roger Moorey and Peter Parr. Warminster, U.K.: Aris & Phillips, 1978.

———. "Let the Young Men, I Pray Thee, Arise and Play Before Us." *JPOS* 21 (1948): 110–16.

———. "On the Types of Weapons Used in Israel's Wars" [Hebrew]. *Maarakhot Israel* 1 (1945): 209.

———. "A Rejoinder." *BASOR* 239 (1980): 19–23.

———. "Solomon's City Wall and Gate of Gezer." *IEJ* 8 (1959): 8–18.

———, ed. *Jerusalem Revealed: Archaeology in the Holy City, 1968– 1974.* New Haven: Yale University Press, 1976.

Yogev, Ora. "Tel Yizre'el—October 1987–January 1988." *ESI* 7–8 (1988–89): 192–93.

Younger, K. Lawson, Jr. "The Deportations of the Israelites." *JBL* 117 (1998): 201–27.

———. "The Fall of Samaria in Light of Recent Research." *CBQ* 61 (1999): 461–82.

———. "Recent Study on Sargon II, King of Assyria: Implications for Biblical Studies." Pages 288–329 in *Mesopotamia and the Bible.* JSOTSup 341. Edited by Mark W. Chavalas and K. Lawson Younger Jr. Sheffield: Sheffield Academic Press, 2002.

———. "Sargon's Campaign against Jerusalem—A Further Note." *Bib* 77 (1996): 108–10.

Yurco, Frank J. "Sennacherib's Third Campaign and the Coregency of Shabaka and Shebitku." *Serapis* 6 (1980): 221-40.

———. "The Shabaka-Shebitku Coregency and the Supposed Second Campaign of Sennacherib against Judah: A Critical Assessment." *JBL* 110 (1991): 35–45.

Zahavi, A. "Malḥa Hill" [Hebrew]. *Hadashot Arkheologiyot* 99 (1993): 59–60.

Zertal, Adam. "The 'Corridor-Builders' of Central Israel: Evidence for the Settlement of the 'Northern Seas Peoples'?" Pages 215–32 in *Defensive Settlements of the Aegean and the Eastern Mediterranean after c. 1200 B.C.: Proceedings of an International Workshop Held at Trinity College Dublin.* Edited by Vassos Karageorghis and Christine E. Morris. Nicosia: The Anastasios G. Leventis Foundation, 2001.

———. "The Mount Manasseh (Northern Samarian Hills) Survey." *NEAEHL* 3:1311–12.

———. "The Pahwah of Samaria (Northern Israel) during the Persian Period: Types of Settlement, Economy, History and New Discoveries." *Transeu* 3 (1990): 9–30.

———. "The Province of Samaria during the Persian and Hellenistic Periods." Pages 75*–98* in *Michael: Historical, Epigraphical and Biblical Studies in Honor of Professor Michael Heltzer.* Edited by Yitzhak Avishur and Robert Deutsch. Tel Aviv-Jaffa: Archaeological Centre Publications, 1999.

———. "'To the Lands of the Perizzites and the Giants': On the Israelite Settlement in the Hill Country of Manasseh." Pages 47-69 in *From Nomadism to Monarchy: Archaeological and Historical Aspects of Early Israel.* Edited by Israel Finkelstein and Nadav Naʾaman. Jerusalem: Israel Exploration Society, 1994.

Zerubavel, Yael. *Recovered Roots: Collective Memory and the Making of Israeli National Tradition.* Chicago: University of Chicago Press, 1995.

Zevit, Ziony. "Converging Lines of Evidence Bearing on the Date of P." *ZAW* 94 (1982): 502–9.

Zimhoni, Orna. *Studies in the Iron Age Pottery of Israel: Typological, Archaeological and Chronological Aspects.* Tel Aviv Occasional Publications 2. Tel Aviv: Tel Aviv University, Institute of Archaeology, 1997.

———. "Two Ceramic Assemblages from Lachish Levels III and II." *TA* 17 (1990): 3–52.

Zorn, Jeffrey R. "Estimating the Population Size of Ancient Settlements: Methods, Problems, Solutions, and a Case Study." *BASOR* 295 (1994): 31–48.

Index of Primary Sources

483

Ancient Near Eastern Writings

GREEK AND JEWISH NONBIBLICAL WRITINGS

Index of Ancient Names and Places

Geographic Names and Regions

Index of Modern Authorities

Contributors

Yairah Amit is Professor, Department of Bible, Tel Aviv University, Tel Aviv, Israel.

Jane M. Cahill is Co-director of the Tell el-Hammah Excavations, Senior Staff Archaeologist at the City of David Archaeological Project, and an attorney employed by the U.S. District Court for the Southern District of Texas.

Israel Finkelstein is Professor of Archaeology at the Institute of Archaeology, Tel Aviv University, Tel Aviv, Israel.

Richard Elliott Friedman is Professor of Hebrew and Comparative Literature and Katzin Professor of Jewish Civilization, University of California, San Diego, California.

James K. Hoffmeier is Professor of Old Testament and Ancient Near Eastern History and Archaeology at Trinity International University, Divinity School, Deerfield, Illinois.

Ann E. Killebrew is Assistant Professor of Classics and Ancient Mediterranean Studies and Jewish Studies at the Pennsylvania State University, University Park, Pennsylvania.

Gary N. Knoppers is Professor of Classics and Ancient Mediterranean Studies, Religious Studies, and Jewish Studies at the Pennsylvania State University, University Park, Pennsylvania.

Gunnar Lehmann is Senior Lecturer in Archaeology at Ben Gurion University of the Negev, Beersheva, Israel.

Ronny Reich is Professor of Archaeology at the University of Haifa, Haifa, Israel.

J. J. M. Roberts is William Henry Green Professor of Old Testament Literature, Princeton Theological Seminary, Princeton, New Jersey.

William M. Schniedewind is Professor of Biblical Studies and Northwest Semitic Languages at University of California, Los Angeles, California.

Eli Shukron is Senior Field Archaeologist, Israel Antiquities Authority, Jerusalem, Israel.

Neil Asher Silberman is Writer and Heritage Consultant, Ename Center for Public Archaeology and Heritage Presentation, Ename, Belgium.

Margreet Steiner is an independent researcher, Leiden, The Netherlands.

Lynn Tatum is Professor of Religion at Baylor University, Waco, Texas.

David Ussishkin is Professor of Archaeology at the Institute of Archaeology, Tel Aviv University, Tel Aviv, Israel.

Andrew G. Vaughn is Associate Professor of Religion at Gustavus Adolphus College, Saint Peter, Minnesota.

K. Lawson Younger Jr. is Professor of Old Testament, Semitic Languages, and Ancient Near Eastern History at Trinity International University, Divinity School, Deerfield, Illinois.